C000080413

THE
CRICKETERS'
WHO'S WHO
1999

THE FICA WORLD CUP QUIZ

FEDERATION OF INTERNATIONAL
CRICKETERS' ASSOCIATIONS

Throughout the book there are 100 quiz questions referring to the history of the World Cup from the first staging of the event in 1975. The answers can be found on page 736.

THE CRICKETERS' WHO'S WHO 1999

Introduction by
MARTIN SPEIGHT

Edited by
CHRIS MARSHALL

Statistics by
RICHARD LOCKWOOD

Portraits photographed or researched by
BILL SMITH

Queen Anne Press

QUEEN ANNE PRESS
a division of Lennard Associates Limited
Mackerye End, Harpenden, Herts AL5 5DR

Published in association with
The Cricketers' Who's Who Limited

First published in Great Britain 1999

British Library Cataloguing in Publication is available

ISBN 1 85291 605 2

Typeset in Times and Univers Condensed
Editor (for Queen Anne Press): Kirsty Ennever
Quiz compiled by Chris Marshall
Cover design by Paul Cooper

Printed and bound by
Butler and Tanner Limited, Frome and London

PICTURE ACKNOWLEDGEMENTS

Cover photographs by Allsport
(main picture and back cover)
Muttiah Muralitharan, Lancashire & Sri Lanka
(inset, top)
Graeme Swann, Northamptonshire and England A
(inset, bottom)
Chris Read, Nottinghamshire and England A

CONTENTS

When it comes to premier banking we really know the score.

Fleming Premier Banking is delighted to sponsor the Professional Cricketers' Association.

At Fleming Premier Banking we offer a comprehensive range of hig interest current accounts and savings accounts for personal client companies, charities, clubs and other organisations.

We aim to provide all our clients with a modern, efficient and competiti banking service - including telephone banking, 7 days a week, 52 weeks a yea

To find out more about Fleming Premier Banking, please contact yo financial adviser, call us on 0800 092 2265 or visit our website at www.flemings.co.uk/premier

FLEMING
Premier Banking

The Professional Cricketers Association is again pleased to endorse the *The Cricketers'Who's Who* and to congratulate the publication on its 20th anniversary. *The Cricketers' Who's Who* continues to prove a unique acquisition for all cricket followers as it is the only publication that contains the views of the professional cricketers in this country. I know these are of particular interest to the current Chairman of Selectors!

Every year seems to be a watershed for the game but I would suggest that 1999 may be the most important for many a year. The hosting of the World Cup in May and June, the Super Cup, the National League and the race for the Championship, in which positions for divisional cricket will be decided, will prove to be a feast of competitive cricket beyond everybody's expectations.

The work of the PCA and PCA Management Ltd continues to gather pace. Our influence is becoming greater within the game. This is entirely due to the efforts of Richard Bevan and former Derbyshire player Tim O'Gorman. A further addition for 1999 is the appointment of Simon Ecclestone (Oxford University and Somerset) as Communications Officer which will ensure that our membership receive the support that they deserve from their Association.

May I take this opportunity of wishing all cricketers a successful season and I hope that England will be holding aloft the World Cup on 20th June 1999!

David Graveney
Chief Executive

NatWest is delighted to be a Partner to the 1999 Cricket World Cup

The NatWest Trophy, the premier one day competition. NatWest, official partner of Excellence, investing in the future of English cricket. NatWest, more than just a bank more than just a sponsor. The future of English cricket. NatWest U19's, world champions. NatWest Development of the Cricket World Cup-England '99.

NatWest

INTRODUCTION

A WATERSHED FOR CRICKET?

Last year in this publication Angus Fraser, in referring to the counties' decision to kick out the recommendations made in Lord McLaurin's report *Raising the Standard*, wrote: 'In years to come, I wonder how people will reflect on the summer of 1997. For what it is worth, I believe it will be seen as a year of missed opportunities.' The major reservation of the first-class counties to vote for a two-divisional Championship was how the ECB's financial distributions to all teams would be treated. It was felt that the wealth gap between counties that host Test matches and the rest would widen, increasing the problems of the smaller counties surviving.

A guarantee that all counties, whether in the 'Premier' or 'First' division, would be treated equally in terms of financial distribution has removed this obstacle, and as a result this 'opportunity' has not been missed this year. The First-class Forum voted to experiment with a two-divisional County Championship from 2000, following a two-day meeting at Lord's on 2/3 December. As a result, the 110-year-old Championship will split into two divisions of nine teams based on the standings at the end of the 1999 season, with promotion and relegation from the end of the 2000 season. In this new competition counties will play each other both home and away, and the points system will be altered, with the number for a win reduced to 12 from 16, and for a draw increased to 4 from 3. It is hoped that there will now be more incentive to save a game.

The decision to vote for a two-divisional Championship has been described by Lord McLaurin as 'an historic one for cricket in this country'. It is felt that the Championship will be much more competitive, sharpening up both individual and team performances and helping to bridge the gap between county and Test cricket. All teams will have an incentive to improve and fight harder – 'in short there will be more pressure and more at stake, which is bound to elevate standards'. In other words this new structure is designed to provide a tougher breeding ground for professional cricketers and give them the necessary skills to play Test cricket successfully. Moreover, the increased tension and drama, with promotion and relegation at the end of the season, will be more attractive to the public, to broadcasters and sponsors, and even to the professionals themselves.

So is this reform the panacea for all England's problems? By raising the standard of county cricket will we naturally raise the standard of England's Test team? After all, this is the real crux of the matter – the failure of England to be consistently competitive and successful. Recent form is a case in point; success over South Africa last summer only to fall 2-0 behind in Australia and then to show real character to win at Melbourne in the Boxing Day Test.

Our oldest enemy, Australia, is seen as the benchmark by which we measure our ability and quality, and our failure to regain the Ashes during the last six series has heightened the call for change. But it must be remembered that Australia has been the best side in the world throughout the 1990s. As Angus Fraser said: ' ... at the moment Australia have better players than we do'. Is our failure at Test level because of a natural cyclical phenomenon, or is our current system failing to produce the goods?

It is quite easy to hide behind the first of these possibilities, which is that every country has periods of dominance – in the late 1970s and 1980s it was the West Indies; in the 1990s Australia – and England's turn will come. Surely this leaves too much to chance, particularly in a country where other sports, in particular football, have such a strong standing. Even Australia cannot be complacent. The Chief Executive of the Australian Cricket Board, Mal Speed, speaks of a need to market the game against 'increasing rivalry from other sport and leisure pursuits'. An illustration of cricket's standing in English sport was given during the fifth Test at Sydney – Darren Gough's hat-trick in Australia's first innings, the only one in an Ashes series this century by an Englishman, was reported after the FA Cup third round on ITV's *News at Ten*!

Some people have suggested that there is little wrong with the current system of eighteen first-class counties all playing one four-day match against each of the others. Matthew Maynard, captain of Glamorgan, the only county to vote against the two-divisional Championship, felt that the Championship had been getting stronger recently. Glamorgan, for example, went from tenth position to first to twelfth in three seasons, whilst Leicestershire went from first to ninth to first again. Any of the eighteen sides had the opportunity to win the Championship, but now this will not be possible for a side in the lower division. Indeed, the 1998 Championship was possibly the most exciting of recent times, with five teams entering the last match all with a chance of winning the title. The top two sides, Surrey and Leicestershire, met at The Oval, and thanks to some top-class batting in the first innings, backed up by some equally fine seam bowling, Leicestershire won the Championship. Surrey, leaders for most of the summer, faltered at the final hurdle. It was a fine reward for Leicestershire who had earlier in the season lost the last Benson and Hedges final to Essex. Lancashire was the other successful county, winning both the AXA League and the NatWest Trophy, and could lay claim to the title 'the best one-day side in England' in 1998.

So why has England been failing at Test level? Indeed, Bob Woolmer said after last summer's series: 'England showed a lot of guts and proved themselves fine players in their own conditions. I don't know why they struggle away from home.' David Green, writing in January's edition of *The Cricketer*, believes that: 'covering [the pitches] eliminated the essential variety in English pitches ... which gave us quality finger spinners, astute and hostile seam bowlers, and batsmen with sound but flexible techniques'. As a result of covered pitches batsmen have lost the ability to play the moving ball, due to a lack of technique. But is the re-introduction of uncovered pitches really the answer? I do not think so. Australia, for example, has been the best side in world cricket throughout the 1990s, and domestic cricket there is played on some of the best pitches in the world. Michael Slater is a case in point – highly successful this winter, he failed to score a Championship hundred with Derbyshire last summer.

The standard of pitches in England has dropped considerably over the past ten years, and as a result bowlers have often been flattered, while batsmen have been unable to gain the confidence they need to be consistently successful. Australian wickets are far truer and more consistent, so their bowlers have had to learn to bowl on good pitches and batsmen have been able to play knowing that the pitch is predictable. Perhaps this is a key factor in Australia's success in producing a wealth of outstanding batsmen. In addition to their established front five, Australia can call upon the likes of Lehmann, Blewett, Ponting, Elliott, Law and Hodge. At the same time they have produced world-class bowlers such as Glenn McGrath and Shane Warne. I believe that the standard of pitches must improve considerably, and the standard of cricket will improve correspondingly.

The First-class Forum has tried to address this problem. Although a roving team of pitch inspectors has been voted out on account of the expense, the idea of visiting teams having the automatic call to bat or bowl is being looked at as an alternative to reducing poor pitch preparation. Pitch requirement is for 'no undue sideways movement with spin on the third/fourth day'. I hope that this requirement is enforced with more vigour than it has been up until now, with sides preparing poor pitches to suit their own bowlers being consistently punished by having points docked.

Does our current system allow too much 'soft' cricket to be played? Graham Gooch has said that 'our domestic system has to be much stronger and leaner and have only the best players involved. You will get stronger characters who are more resilient.' 'Going through the motions' has often been touted around as an excuse for poor performances come mid-August. By then many players are tired – in particular the quick bowlers – due to a very hectic and intense schedule of playing and travelling. It is not surprising that, with the increased pressures in the game, there are now more injuries. No wonder England does not always produce those bowlers with that extra 'something' – it is impossible to run in and bowl quickly for twenty-five overs a day, six or seven days a week, twenty weeks on the trot. Is it any surprise that players picked for England can look jaded? More rest and recovery periods are required between games, with time for the body to mend and time to work on those aspects of the game that need attention. Has the new system done anything to improve this?

On the surface it would seem not, for each side will play only one game fewer than before, with the intention to play more one-day cricket in the future. However the ECB intends to contract a squad of players to the England team to ensure their best preparation for Test duty. This raises two problems: firstly, how will the counties that may lose three or four players for the summer react, especially if they are particularly close to the relegation zone; and secondly, once the original squad of players is selected, how does anyone else break into this squad? However, it should ensure that the England team is prepared for every game both mentally and physically. Bob Woolmer has introduced this system in South Africa with success, producing excellent results, such as their success over the West Indies in the winter Test series.

Inevitably there are going to be some problems with the new two-divisional Championship and there are no guarantees of success, but hopefully it will help to bring England up to world class at Test match level consistently. If the England team is successful the game in this country will grow. Hopefully it will encourage more children to play the game, and with the new structures in both club and county cricket the potential winners will be spotted early, nurtured both mentally and physically, and brought on slowly through competitive cricket at all levels.

Perhaps the easiest way to attract more widespread support for cricket is through the one-day game. Sunday matches are the best supported, and the First-class Forum has tried to create extra excitement for these spectators by the introduction of a 'free hit' following a no-ball in the National League, the batsman being immune to dismissal. This new 45-over competition will also include the first-15-overs fielding restriction as used in One-Day Internationals. Not only will this add more excitement, but it will also bring our domestic one-day cricket into closer alignment with the international game. In one-day cricket, spectators want to see high-scoring games with the ball disappearing to all parts of the ground. Last season's two cup finals were typical of many – one-sided and not much of a spectacle for the 30,000 or so paying spectators. One of the most exciting finals was that of the 1993 NatWest Trophy between Sussex and Warwickshire in which over 600 runs were scored. That is what the public and the game itself needs – lots of runs and a tight, exciting finish.

These are the reforms of the historic forum. Let us hope that they will have the desired effect in the long term. In the short term, all followers of cricket will watch with interest the Cricket World Cup in England this summer. Winning the World Cup would secure years of cricketing enthusiasm and guarantee the health of cricket in England for years to come. Have we got a chance? The Carlton and United series this winter has given an indication of our chances – pitting us against two of the strongest sides, Sri Lanka and Australia. One other very fancied side should be South Africa, arguably the most consistent one-day side of last year. Playing in England should be a large advantage for England, particularly if England's performance in recent Texaco series is taken into account. Nick Knight and Alec Stewart should be an effective opening pair, while Graeme Hick and Neil Fairbrother will hopefully be key middle-order batsmen. Bowlers Darren Gough, Alan Mullally and Robert Croft, supported by several all-rounders, should help us to be both miserly and penetrative. Individual skills make up a cricket eleven, but it is the side that plays as a team that will succeed. England have good individuals, but they also need to be brilliant in the field. Mark Ramprakash's one-handed catch to dismiss Justin Langer in the Melbourne Test seemed to be the catalyst for a sensational victory. Let's hope that England's fielding in the World Cup is in this vein. During the Ashes series England dropped 22 chances, compared with 9 by Australia. If these figures had been reversed, the outcome of the Ashes series may well have been different.

If we play up to our abilities and with the passion and belief that we have shown at times during the Ashes series, then we have as good a chance as anyone. Wouldn't it be nice for everyone to support the team and stop doing what we English all do so well, 'knocking' people. For if there was a World Cup for this, we would win every time. Only during last summer's NatWest final I heard Bob Willis say on Sky, the Lancashire bowlers have made the Derbyshire batsmen look exactly what they are – club cricketers'. Need I say more?

P.S. By the way, a bit of luck wouldn't go amiss either.

Martin Speight
February 1999

13

THE PLAYERS

Ben **Hollioake**
Surrey C.C.C. & England

PCA Young Player of
the Year 1997

Andrew **Flintoff**
Lancashire C.C.C. & England

PCA Young Player of
the Year 1998

Editor's Notes

The cricketers listed in this volume include all those who played for a first-class county at least once last season, in any form of cricket, and all those registered (at the time of going to press) to play for the 18 first-class counties in 1999, even those who have yet to make a first-team appearance. All statistics are complete to the end of the last English season. Figures about 1000 runs and 50 wickets in a season refer to matches in England only. All first-class figures include figures for Test matches which are also extracted and listed separately. One-Day 100s and One-Day five wickets in an innings are for the English domestic competitions and all One-Day Internationals, home and abroad. Career records include 'rebel' tours to South Africa.

The following abbreviations apply: * means not out; All First – all first-class matches; 1-day Int –One-Day Internationals; Sunday – Sunday League; Nat-West – NatWest Trophy; B&H – Benson and Hedges Cup. The figures for batting and bowling averages refer to the full first-class English list for 1998, followed in brackets by the 1997 figures. Inclusion in the batting averages depends on a minimum of six completed innings, and an average of at least 10 runs; a bowler has to have taken at least 10 wickets. A bowler's strike rate refers to balls bowled per wicket taken. A new category – Stop press – has been included for 1999 as a home for highlights of closeseason tours. These highlights are not reflected in the statistics in this edition.

Readers will notice occasional differences in the way the same kind of information is presented. This is because it has been decided to follow the way in which the cricketers themselves have provided the relevant information.

Each year in *The Cricketers' Who's Who,* in addition to those cricketers who are playing during the current season, we also include the biographical and career details of those who played in the previous season but retired at the end of it. The purpose of this is to have, on the record, the full and final cricketing achievements of every player when his career has ended.

A book of this complexity and detail has to be prepared several months in advance of the cricket season, and occasionally there are recent changes in a player's circumstances or the structure of the game which cannot be included in time. Many examples of facts, statistics and even opinions which can quickly become outdated in the period between the actual compilation of the book and its publication, months later, will spring to the reader's mind, and I ask him or her to make the necessary commonsense allowance and adjustments.

Chris Marshall, March 1999

ADAMS, C. J.   Sussex

Name: Christopher John Adams
Role: Right-hand bat, right-arm medium
bowler, slip fielder, county captain
Born: 6 May 1970, Whitwell,
nr Worksop, Notts
Height: 6ft **Weight:** 13st 7lbs
Nickname: Grizzly
County debut: 1988 (Derbyshire),
1998 (Sussex)
County cap: 1992 (Derbyshire),
1998 (Sussex)
One-Day Internationals: 2
1000 runs in season: 4
1st-Class 50s: 43
1st-Class 100s: 23
1st-Class 200s: 2
1st-Class catches: 202
One-Day 100s: 11
One-Day 5 w. in innings: 1
Place in batting averages: 32nd av. 41.92 (1997 116th av. 31.95)
Strike rate: (career 101.27)
Parents: John and Eluned (Lyn)
Wife and date of marriage: Samantha Claire, 26 September 1992
Children: Georgia Louise, 4 October 1993; Sophie Victoria, 'due 7 October 1998'
Family links with cricket: Brother David played 2nd XI cricket for Derbyshire and
Gloucestershire. Father played for Yorkshire Schools and uncle played for Essex 2nd XI
Education: Tapton House School; Chesterfield Boys Grammar School; Repton School
Qualifications: 6 O-levels, NCA coaching awards
Off-season: 'Playing in Canberra, Australia, or at home house-hunting with the family
and getting fit'
Overseas tours: Repton School to Barbados 1987; England NCA North to N Ireland 1987
Overseas teams played for: Takapuna, New Zealand 1987-88; Te Puke, New Zealand
1989-90; Primrose, Cape Town, South Africa 1991-92; Canberra Comets 1998-99
Cricketers particularly admired: Ian Botham, Dean Jones
Young players to look out for: Kevin Dean, Steve Harmison
Other sports played: Football ('mad on it'), golf
Other sports followed: Football (Arsenal FC and Southend United FC)
Relaxations: 'My kids'
Extras: Beat Richard Hutton's 25-year-old record for most runs scored in a season at
Repton. Represented English Schools U15 and U19, MCC Schools U19 and, in 1989,
England YC. Took two catches as 12th man for England v India at Old Trafford in
1990. Holds county records for the fastest century by a Derbyshire batsman (57 mins)

and the highest score in the Sunday League (141*). Whittingdale Young Player Award 1992. Played for an England XI in the Cricket Max tournament in New Zealand in 1997. Was released by Derbyshire at the end of the 1997 season and after much speculation joined Sussex for 1998 as captain. Was selected to represent England in the cancelled World Super Max 8s originally scheduled to take place in Perth in October 1998

Opinions on cricket: 'By far the most rewarding game played. To not only survive but prosper and enjoy the physical and mental tests the game places upon very young players is a testament to the wonderful game of cricket.'

Best batting: 239 Derbyshire v Hampshire, Southampton 1996

Best bowling: 4-29 Derbyshire v Lancashire, Derby 1991

1998 Season

	M	Inns	NO	Runs	HS	Avge	100s	50s	Ct	St	O	M	Runs	Wkts	Avge	Best	5wI	10wM
Test																		
All First	18	29	1	1174	170	41.92	4	4	30	-	30.5	5	109	0	-	-	-	-
1-day Int	2	2	0	28	25	14.00	-	-	2	-								
NatWest	1	1	0	8	8	8.00	-	-	2	-	10.3	0	40	1	40.00	1-40	-	
B & H	3	3	0	164	81	54.66	-	2	3	-								
Sunday	14	14	1	427	100	32.84	1	3	4	-	24.2	0	122	8	15.25	5-16	1	

Career Performances

	M	Inns	NO	Runs	HS	Avge	100s	50s	Ct	St	Balls	Runs	Wkts	Avge	Best	5wI	10wM
Test																	
All First	173	282	21	9605	239	36.80	25	43	202	-	1823	1197	18	66.50	4-29	-	-
1-day Int	2	2	0	28	25	14.00	-	-	2	-							
NatWest	19	18	5	891	129 *	68.53	4	4	9	-	81	55	2	27.50	1-15	-	
B & H	35	32	4	1030	138	36.78	2	7	13	-	24	21	0	-	-	-	
Sunday	134	127	20	3844	141 *	35.92	5	25	69	-	384	388	11	35.27	5-16	1	

AFZAAL, U.   Nottinghamshire

Name: Usman Afzaal
Role: Left-hand bat, slow left-arm bowler
Born: 9 June 1977, Rawalpindi, Pakistan
Height: 6ft **Weight:** 12st 7lbs
Nickname: Usy, Navjot, Ganguly
County debut: 1995
1st-Class 100s: 2
1st-Class 50s: 11
1st-Class catches: 22

Place in batting averages: 139th av. 29.40
(1997 142nd av. 26.66)
Strike rate: 64.85 (career 99.15)
Parents: Mohammed and Firdous
Marital status: Single
Family links with cricket: Brother Kamran
played representative cricket for
Nottinghamshire U15, U17 and U19 and also
played for NAYC. 'Main reason why I started
playing cricket'
Education: Blue Bell Hill; Manvers
Pierrepont Comprehensive; South Notts
College
Qualifications: NCA coaching certificate
plus computer course
Off-season: 'Train harder and harder until I
play England cricket'
Overseas tours: England U19 to West Indies
1994-95, to Zimbabwe 1995-96
Overseas teams played for: Victoria Park, Perth
Cricketers particularly admired: Steve Waugh ('determination to be at the top'),
Mark Ramprakash, Saeed Anwar
Young players to look out for: Matt Whiley, Steve Randall, younger brother Aqib
Other sports played: Squash, indoor football, tennis
Other sports followed: 'A bit of football (Man U)'
Relaxations: 'Spend a lot of time with friends/family. Listen to good music. Relax and
spend time with my missus'
Extras: Played for England U15 against South Africa and, in 1994, for England U17
against India. Broke the U16 bowling record in the Texaco Trophy
Opinions on cricket: 'Play hard and always give 100 per cent.'
Best batting: 109* Nottinghamshire v Derbyshire, Derby 1998
Best bowling: 4-101 Nottinghamshire v Gloucestershire, Trent Bridge 1998

1998 Season

	M	Inns	NO	Runs	HS	Avge	100s	50s	Ct	St	O	M	Runs	Wkts	Avge	Best	5wI	10wM
Test																		
All First	17	30	3	686	109 *	25.40	2	4	7	-	75.4	9	292	7	41.71	4-101	-	-
1-day Int																		
NatWest	1	1	0	13	13	13.00	-	-	-	-								
B & H	2	2	1	132	78	132.00	-	2	-	-								
Sunday	2	2	0	13	12	6.50	-	-	-	-	0.3	0	1	0	-		-	-

Career Performances

	M	Inns	NO	Runs	HS	Avge	100s	50s	Ct	St	Balls	Runs	Wkts	Avge	Best	5wI	10wM
Test																	
All First	48	83	8	1845	109 *	24.60	2	11	22	-	3173	1829	32	57.15	4-101	-	-
1-day Int																	
NatWest	3	2	1	39	26 *	39.00	-	-	1	-	66	57	0	-		-	-
B & H	2	2	1	132	78	132.00	-	2	-	-							
Sunday	10	6	1	44	20	8.80	-	-	3	-	219	187	8	23.37	2-25	-	

ALDRED, P.   Derbyshire

Name: Paul Aldred
Role: Right-hand bat, right-arm medium bowler
Born: 4 February 1969, Chellaston, Derby
Height: 5ft 10in **Weight:** 12st
Nickname: Aldo
County debut: 1995
1st-Class 50s: 1
1st-Class catches: 19
Place in batting averages: 235th av. 15.83 (1997 195th av. 22.16)
Place in bowling averages: 137th av. 46.33 (1997 110th av. 37.83)
Strike rate: 90.83 (career 77.97)
Parents: Harry (deceased) and Lynette
Marital status: Single
Family links with cricket: Father played local cricket
Education: Chellaston and Curbar Primary School; Lady Manners, Bakewell, Derbyshire
Qualifications: 'None to worry about!'
Career outside cricket: Builder
Off-season: 'Keeping the wolf from the door!'
Overseas teams played for: Bentley CC, Melbourne 1994-95
Cricketers particularly admired: Ian Botham, Viv Richards, Phillip DeFreitas
Young players to look out for: Ben Spendlove, Ian Blackwell
Other sports played: Played hockey for Derbyshire U16, U19, U21 and full squad
Other sports followed: Rugby, golf
Injuries: Groin injury, out for nine weeks
Relaxations: Any sports (golf, fishing, rugby), 'having a drink with friends'
Extras: 'Had the great opportunity to play against New Zealand with the England

NCA team in 1994 which was a great day.' Played for Derbyshire U21 hockey team at the age of 15

Opinions on cricket: 'Players should be looked after more in the off-season to enable them to train more intensely. 2nd XI games should be played more like the first-class game – i.e. over four days.'

Best batting: 83 Derbyshire v Hampshire, Chesterfield 1997
Best bowling: 3-28 Derbyshire v Nottinghamshire, Trent Bridge 1997

1998 Season

	M	Inns	NO	Runs	HS	Avge	100s	50s	Ct	St	O	M	Runs	Wkts	Avge	Best	5wI	10wM
Test																		
All First	7	9	3	95	37 *	15.83	-	-	6	-	181.4	38	556	12	46.33	3-30	-	-
1-day Int																		
NatWest																		
B & H	4	1	1	24	24 *	-	-	-	-	-	35	0	161	5	32.20	3-53	-	
Sunday	9	5	2	17	5 *	5.66	-	-	1	-	54.2	2	331	3	110.33	2-38	-	

Career Performances

	M	Inns	NO	Runs	HS	Avge	100s	50s	Ct	St	Balls	Runs	Wkts	Avge	Best	5wI	10wM
Test																	
All First	27	34	7	375	83	13.88	-	1	19	-	3665	1922	47	40.89	3-28	-	-
1-day Int																	
NatWest	3	2	1	4	4	4.00	-	-	1	-	140	99	4	24.75	4-30	-	
B & H	6	2	1	31	24 *	31.00	-	-	-	-	264	214	7	30.57	3-53	-	
Sunday	36	16	6	104	17	10.40	-	-	6	-	1188	1157	26	44.50	4-41	-	

1. Who was the first player to score two
consecutive World Cup centuries?

FIGA

ALLEYNE, D.   Middlesex

Name: David Alleyne
Role: Right-hand bat, wicket-keeper
Born: 17 April 1976, York
Height: 5ft 11in
County debut: No first-team appearance
Marital status: Single
Family links with cricket: Father played for
Northampton Exiles
Education: Enfield Grammar; Hertford
Regional College; City and Islington College;
London Cricket College
Qualifications: Senior cricket coaching
award
Career outside cricket: Within the leisure
sector
Off-season: Working and playing overseas
Overseas teams played for: Stratford,
Inglewood, New Zealand
Young players to look out for: Carl
Greenidge
Other sports played: Golf, football, judo, swimming
Other sports followed: Football (Liverpool FC)
Relaxations: Good restaurants, reading and music
Extras: Has played for Winchmore Hill CC. Represented Middlesex Colts U11 to
U17, Middlesex Schools U14 and U15, Middlesex Cricket Board. Played football for
Middlesex U15 and U16 and for Enfield Borough U16
Opinions on cricket: 'More time on preparation.'

ALLEYNE, M. W.   Gloucestershire

Name: Mark Wayne Alleyne
Role: Right-hand bat, right-arm medium bowler, cover fielder, occasional
wicket-keeper, county captain
Born: 23 May 1968, Tottenham
Height: 5ft 11in **Weight:** 13st 7lbs
Nickname: Boo-Boo
County debut: 1986
County cap: 1990
1000 runs in a season: 6

50 wickets in a season: 1
1st-Class 50s: 60
1st-Class 100s: 15
1st-Class 200s: 1
1st-Class 5 w. in innings: 6
1st-Class catches: 193
1st-Class stumpings: 2
One-Day 100s: 3
One-Day 5 w. in innings: 3
Place in batting averages: 50th av. 38.35
(1997 58th av. 40.73)
Place in bowling averages: 116th av. 34.08
(1997 38th av. 26.09)
Strike rate: 71.04 (career 60.13)
Parents: Euclid Clevis and
Hyacinth Cordeilla
Marital status: Single
Family links with cricket: Brother played

for Gloucestershire 2nd XI and Middlesex YCs. Father played club cricket in Barbados
and England
Education: Harrison College, Barbados; Cardinal Pole School, East London
Qualifications: 6 O-levels, NCA Senior Coaching Award, volleyball coaching
certificate
Off-season: Playing for England in CUB Series in Australia
Overseas tours: England YC to Sri Lanka 1986-87 and Australia 1987-88; England to
Australia (CUB Series) 1998-99
Cricketers particularly admired: Gordon Greenidge, Viv Richards
Other sports followed: Football, volleyball, athletics
Relaxations: Watching films and sport; listening to music
Extras: Youngest player to score a century for Gloucestershire. In 1990 also became
the youngest to score a double hundred for the county. Graduate of Haringey Cricket
College. Cricket Select Sunday League Player of the Year 1992. Highest Sunday
League score for Gloucestershire. Appointed Gloucestershire captain for the 1997
season. Played for an England XI in the Cricket Max tournament in New Zealand in
1997. Was selected to captain England in the cancelled World Super Max 8s originally
scheduled to take place in Perth in October 1998. Awarded a benefit in 1999
Best batting: 256 Gloucestershire v Northamptonshire, Northampton 1990
Best bowling: 6-64 Gloucestershire v Surrey, The Oval 1997
Stop press: Made One-Day International debut for England in CUB Series in
Australia 1998-99

1998 Season

	M	Inns	NO	Runs	HS	Avge	100s	50s	Ct	St	O	M	Runs	Wkts	Avge	Best	5wI	10wM
Test																		
All First	18	33	2	1189	137	38.35	3	6	24	-	284.1	82	818	24	34.08	4-63	-	-
1-day Int																		
NatWest	2	2	0	62	39	31.00	-	-	1	-	24	2	97	3	32.33	2-62	-	
B & H	5	5	1	63	24 *	15.75	-	-	4	-	42	1	170	6	28.33	3-22	-	
Sunday	15	13	0	294	88	22.61	-	2	7	-	83	1	461	18	25.61	3-27	-	

Career Performances

	M	Inns	NO	Runs	HS	Avge	100s	50s	Ct	St	Balls	Runs	Wkts	Avge	Best	5wI	10wM
Test																	
All First	237	392	39	11428	256	32.37	16	60	193	2	16837	8825	280	31.51	6-64	6	-
1-day Int																	
NatWest	29	24	4	478	73	23.90	-	1	10	-	1097	712	25	28.48	5-30	1	
B & H	48	40	8	659	75	20.59	-	1	21	-	1933	1425	43	33.13	5-27	1	
Sunday	190	172	38	4034	134 *	30.10	3	17	72	-	5981	5147	166	31.00	5-28	1	

ALTREE, D. A.   Warwickshire

Name: Darren Anthony Altree
Role: Right-hand bat, left-arm
fast medium bowler
Born: 30 September 1974, Rugby
Height: 5ft 11in **Weight:** 12st 7lbs
Nickname: Bobby, Bobster, Dazzler
County debut: 1996
1st-Class catches: 1
Strike rate: (career 78.75)
Parents: Tony and Margaret
Marital status: Single
Education: Ashlawn School, Rugby
Career outside cricket: Coil operator for
GEC in Rugby
Overseas tours: Warwickshire U19 to Cape
Town 1992-93
Overseas teams played for: Avendale, Cape
Town 1994-95
Cricketers particularly admired: 'Too many to list'
Young players to look out for: 'Too many to list'
Relaxations: Watching television and listening to music
Best batting: 2* Warwickshire v Durham, Edgbaston 1998
Best bowling: 3-41 Warwickshire v Pakistan, Edgbaston 1996

	M	Inns	NO	Runs	HS	Avge	100s	50s	Ct	St	O	M	Runs	Wkts	Avge		Best	5wI	10wM
Test																			
All First	1	2	1	2	2 *	2.00	-	-	-	-	13	4	34	0	-		-	-	-
1-day Int																			
NatWest																			
B & H																			
Sunday																			

Career Performances

	M	Inns	NO	Runs	HS	Avge	100s	50s	Ct	St	Balls	Runs	Wkts	Avge	Best	5wI	10wM
Test																	
All First	5	7	3	2	2 *	0.50	-	-	1	-	630	420	8	52.50	3-41	-	-
1-day Int																	
NatWest																	
B & H																	
Sunday																	

AMIN, R. M.   Surrey

Name: Rupesh Mahesh Amin
Role: Right-hand bat, slow left-arm bowler
Born: 20 August 1977, Clapham
Height: 5ft 11in **Weight:** 10st 7lbs
Nickname: Idi, Plug
County debut: 1997
1st-Class catches: 2
Strike rate: 118.00 (career 105.54)
Parents: Mahesh and Aruna
Marital status: Single
Family links with cricket: Father played
club cricket
Education: Stanford Middle School;
Riddlesdown High School; John Ruskin
Sixth Form; Croydon College
Qualifications: 8 GCSEs, 3 A-levels
Off-season: 'Three months working as
sub-postmaster; three months in India being
coached at Bishen Bedi's academy in Delhi'
Overseas teams played for: Manly Warringah District CC, Sydney 1997-98
Cricketers particularly admired: Saqlain Mushtaq, Sachin Tendulkar
Young players to look out for: Alex Tudor

Other sports played: Snooker
Other sports followed: Football (Liverpool), snooker (Ronnie O'Sullivan), boxing (Prince Naseem Hamed)
Injuries: Out for five weeks with broken right thumb
Relaxations: Going to cinema, eating good food, going out and seeing places
Extras: Played for Croydon District U15 side that won Hobbs Trophy against London Schools
Opinions on cricket: 'Too much cricket is played with little time for players to rest. I think that when a Test match is played there should be no Championship matches played, so teams losing players for international duty can wait for these players to come back.'
Best batting: 12 Surrey v Leicestershire, The Oval 1998
Best bowling: 3-58 Surrey v Durham, The Oval 1997

1998 Season

	M	Inns	NO	Runs	HS	Avge	100s	50s	Ct	St	O	M	Runs	Wkts	Avge	Best	5wI	10wM
Test																		
All First	3	4	2	14	12	7.00	-	-	-	-	59	9	176	3	58.66	2-32	-	-
1-day Int																		
NatWest																		
B & H																		
Sunday	1	0	0	0	0	-	-	-	-	-								

Career Performances

	M	Inns	NO	Runs	HS	Avge	100s	50s	Ct	St	Balls	Runs	Wkts	Avge	Best	5wI	10wM
Test																	
All First	7	10	5	25	12	5.00	-	-	2	-	1161	524	11	47.63	3-58	-	-
1-day Int																	
NatWest																	
B & H																	
Sunday	2	0	0	0	0	-	-	-	1	-	48	43	2	21.50	2-43	-	

ARCHER, G. F.   Nottinghamshire

Name: Graeme Francis Archer
Role: Right-hand bat, right-arm
'very medium'
Born: 26 September 1970, Carlisle, Cumbria
Height: 6ft **Weight:** 13st 7lbs
Nickname: Bunka
County debut: 1992

28

County cap: 1995
1000 runs in season: 1
1st-Class 50s: 25
1st-Class 100s: 9
1st-Class catches: 100
One-Day 100s: 2
Place in batting averages: 117th av. 28.13
(1997 222nd av. 18.75)
Strike rate: (career 75.21)
Parents: Christopher William and
Jean Elizabeth
Marital status: Single
Family links with cricket: Father played for
Carlisle in N Lancashire League; brother Neil
plays in the S Cheshire Alliance League
Education: King Edward VI High School;
Stafford College
Qualifications: 3 O-levels, City & Guilds
and BTEC National Diploma in Leisure Management, NCA Senior Coaching Award
Career outside cricket: 'Still not decided'
Off-season: 'Getting over the 1998 season and training hard'
Overseas teams played for: Hutt District, Wellington, New Zealand 1991-92; Hutt
Valley representative side 1991-92; Old Collegians, Christchurch, New Zealand
1994-96; Lancaster Park, Christchurch 1997-98
Cricketers particularly admired: Graeme Hick, Ian Botham, Derek Randall, Chris
Cairns and Jimmy Adams
Young players to look out for: Chris Read
Other sports played: Golf ('badly'), 'bit of squash', played badminton for
Staffordshire juniors
Other sports followed: Football (Carlisle United and Newcastle United), rugby
(Lutterworth RFC), squash and badminton, ice hockey (Nottingham Panthers)
Relaxations: Music, videos, cinema, spending time with good friends
Extras: Scored 200* in a 15 (8-ball) over match for Walsall U18s. Awarded the
A.A.Thompson Fielding Prize by The Cricket Society in 1990. Made 2nd XI debut for
Notts in 1987 aged 15. Played for Staffordshire in 1990-91. Rapid Cricketline Player
of the Month April/May 1994. Awarded county cap in September 1995. Benson and
Hedges Gold Award against Northants 1998
Opinions on cricket: 'Something must be done about List 1 and List 2. Surely
individuals should have more control over their careers. Cricket is a very special
game!!'
Best batting: 168 Nottinghamshire v Glamorgan, Worksop 1994
Best bowling: 3-18 Nottinghamshire v Hampshire, Southampton 1996

1998 Season

	M	Inns	NO	Runs	HS	Avge	100s	50s	Ct	St	O	M	Runs	Wkts	Avge	Best	5wI	10wM
Test																		
All First	13	23	0	647	107	28.13	1	5	23	-								
1-day Int																		
NatWest	3	3	0	20	12	6.66	-	-	-	-								
B & H	3	3	0	111	70	37.00	-	1	1	-								
Sunday	16	15	2	290	50 *	22.30	-	1	8	-	3	0	18	1	18.00	1-18	-	

Career Performances

	M	Inns	NO	Runs	HS	Avge	100s	50s	Ct	St	Balls	Runs	Wkts	Avge	Best	5wI	10wM
Test																	
All First	85	151	13	4719	168	34.19	9	25	100	-	1053	648	14	46.28	3-18	-	-
1-day Int																	
NatWest	9	7	0	119	39	17.00	-	-	3	-	30	17	1	17.00	1-17	-	
B & H	11	10	1	370	111 *	41.11	1	2	2	-	113	117	1	117.00	1-34	-	
Sunday	66	59	9	1088	104 *	21.76	1	3	24	-	240	234	9	26.00	2-16	-	

ATHERTON, M. A. Lancashire

Name: Michael Andrew Atherton
Role: Right-hand bat, leg-break bowler
Born: 23 March 1968, Manchester
Height: 6ft **Weight:** 12st 7lbs
Nickname: Athers, Dread
County debut: 1987
County cap: 1989
Benefit: 1997 (£307,000)
Test debut: 1989
Tests: 84
One-Day Internationals: 54
1000 runs in a season: 7
1st-Class 50s: 88
1st-Class 100s: 46
1st-Class 5 w. in innings: 3
1st-Class catches: 215
One-Day 100s: 11
Place in batting averages: 42nd av. 39.72
(1997 109th av. 32.80)
Strike rate: (career 83.15)
Parents: Alan and Wendy
Marital status: Single

Family links with cricket: Father and brother both play league cricket
Education: Briscoe Lane Primary; Manchester GS; Downing College, Cambridge
Qualifications: 10 O-levels, 3 A-levels; BA (Hons) (Cantab)
Off-season: Touring Australia with England
Overseas tours: England YC to Sri Lanka 1986-87, to Australia 1987-88; England A to Zimbabwe 1989-90; England to Australia and New Zealand 1990-91, to India and Sri Lanka 1992-93, to West Indies 1993-94, to Australia 1994-95, to South Africa 1995-96, to India and Pakistan (World Cup) 1995-96, to Zimbabwe and New Zealand 1996-97, to West Indies 1997-98, to Australia 1998-99
Cricketers particularly admired: Graham Gooch
Other sports followed: Golf, squash, football
Relaxations: 'Decent novels (Heller, Kundera, etc.), good movies, food and wine, travelling, most sports, music'
Extras: In 1987 was first player to score 1000 runs in his debut season since Paul Parker in 1976. Youngest Lancastrian to score a Test century (151 v NZ at Trent Bridge in 1990); second Lancastrian to score a Test century at Old Trafford (138 v India in 1990). First captained England U19 aged 16. One of *Wisden*'s five Cricketers of the Year 1991. Selected for England tour to New Zealand and also England A tour to Bermuda and West Indies in 1991-92 but ruled out of both through injury. Appointed England captain in 1993. Cornhill England Player of the Year 1994. Voted England's Player of the Series against the West Indies in 1995. Hit 185 not out in the second Test against South Africa in Johannesburg in 1995-96 series. The innings lasted 645 minutes and was the fourth longest by an Englishman in Test matches. Passed Peter May's long-standing record of most Tests as England captain against Australia during the Ashes campaign in 1997. Relinquished England captaincy after 1997-98 Test series v West Indies. Was England's Man of the Series v South Africa 1998. Captained MCC v Rest of the World in the Diana, Princess of Wales Memorial Match at Lord's in July 1998. Run of 62 consecutive Test matches ended when he pulled out of the Test v Sri Lanka at The Oval 1998
Best batting: 199 Lancashire v Durham, Gateshead Fell 1992
Best bowling: 6-78 Lancashire v Nottinghamshire, Trent Bridge 1990

1998 Season

	M	Inns	NO	Runs	HS	Avge	100s	50s	Ct	St	O	M	Runs	Wkts	Avge	Best	5wl	10wM
Test	5	10	1	493	103	54.77	1	3	2	-								
All First	13	24	2	874	152	39.72	2	3	9	-								
1-day Int	1	1	0	64	64	64.00	-	1	-	-								
NatWest	5	5	0	156	76	31.20	-	2	1	-								
B & H	6	6	1	145	93	29.00	-	1	5	-								
Sunday	7	7	0	269	98	38.42	-	2	1	-								

Career Performances

	M	Inns	NO	Runs	HS	Avge	100s	50s	Ct	St	Balls	Runs	Wkts	Avge	Best	5wl	10wM
Test	84	155	6	5935	185 *	39.83	12	37	56	-	408	302	2	151.00	1-20	-	-
All First	271	471	41	17911	199	41.65	46	88	215	-	8981	4733	108	43.82	6-78	3	-
1-day Int	54	54	3	1791	127	35.11	2	12	15	-							
NatWest	27	27	2	946	115	37.84	2	6	9	-	188	154	6	25.66	2-15	-	
B & H	60	59	5	1952	121 *	36.14	3	12	34	-	252	228	7	32.57	4-42	-	
Sunday	90	88	6	2899	111	35.35	4	15	29	-	216	248	7	35.42	3-33	-	

AUSTIN, I. D. Lancashire

Name: Ian David Austin
Role: Left-hand bat, right-arm medium bowler
Born: 30 May 1966, Haslingden, Lancs
Height: 5ft 10in **Weight:** 14st 7lbs
Nickname: Oscar, Bully
County debut: 1986
County cap: 1990
One-Day Internationals: 3
1st-Class 50s: 20
1st-Class 100s: 2
1st-Class 5 w. in innings: 5
1st-Class 10 w. in match: 1
1st-Class catches: 33
One-Day 5 w. in innings: 1
Place in batting averages: 180th av. 21.25
(1997 66th av. 39.28)
Place in bowling averages: 57th av. 26.38
(1997 48th av. 27.06)
Strike rate: 55.94 (career 64.60)
Parents: Jack and Ursula
Wife and date of marriage: Alexandra, 27 February 1993
Children: Victoria, 28 January 1995; Matthew, 26 January 1998
Family links with cricket: Father opened batting for Haslingden CC
Education: Haslingden High School
Qualifications: 4 O-levels, NCA coaching certificate
Off-season: 'Touring with England or being run into the ground by Steve Hampson'
Overseas tours: NAYC to Bermuda 1985; Lancashire to Jamaica 1986-87, 1987-88, to Zimbabwe 1988-89, to Tasmania and Western Australia 1989-90, 1990-91; England to Bangladesh (Wills International Cup) 1998

Overseas teams played for: Maroochydore, Queensland 1987-88, 1991-92; Randwick, Sydney 1990-91

Cricketers particularly admired: Ian Botham, Hartley Alleyne

Young players to look out for: Andrew Flintoff

Other sports followed: Football (Burnley), golf

Relaxations: Golf, and listening to music

Extras: Holds amateur Lancashire League record for highest individual score (147*). Broke Lancashire CCC record for most wickets in the Sunday League in 1991. Scored quickest first-class century in 1991 off authentic bowling (64 balls). Man of the Match in the 1996 Benson and Hedges final and the NatWest semi-final. Lancashire Player of the Year for 1997. Played for an England XI in the Cricket Max tournament in New Zealand in 1997. Man of the Match in the 1998 NatWest final

Opinions on cricket: 'Fitness is now the most important part of the game. It seems that it is even more important than having the ability to play the game and takes over the time that should be spent developing skills.'

Best batting: 115* Lancashire v Derbyshire, Blackpool 1992

Best bowling: 5-23 Lancashire v Middlesex, Old Trafford 1994

1998 Season

	M	Inns	NO	Runs	HS	Avge	100s	50s	Ct	St	O	M	Runs	Wkts	Avge	Best	5wl	10wM
Test																		
All First	13	17	4	304	64	23.38	-	2	7	-	345.4	80	978	36	27.16	4-21	-	-
1-day Int	3	3	1	29	11 *	14.50	-	-	-	-	28.3	1	126	3	42.00	2-37	-	
NatWest	5	3	1	5	2 *	2.50	-	-	1	-	56	19	111	10	11.10	3-14	-	
B & H	6	4	0	36	15	9.00	-	-	-	-	52.1	1	222	7	31.71	2-19	-	
Sunday	14	9	5	64	27 *	16.00	-	-	2	-	83.4	8	277	19	14.57	3-8	-	

Career Performances

	M	Inns	NO	Runs	HS	Avge	100s	50s	Ct	St	Balls	Runs	Wkts	Avge	Best	5wl	10wM
Test																	
All First	118	163	35	3653	115 *	28.53	2	20	33	-	16217	7479	251	29.79	5-23	5	1
1-day Int	3	3	1	29	11 *	14.50	-	-	-	-	171	126	3	42.00	2-37	-	
NatWest	28	20	9	326	97	29.63	-	2	2	-	1839	1031	37	27.86	3-14	-	
B & H	56	36	9	585	80	21.66	-	2	11	-	3238	2089	70	29.84	4-8	-	
Sunday	169	106	43	1133	48	17.98	-	-	33	-	6910	5156	186	27.72	5-56	1	

FIGA

2. Who hosted the World Cup in
a) 1975; b) 1979; c) 1983?

AVERIS, J. M. M.   Gloucestershire

Name: James Maxwell Michael Averis
Role: Right-hand bat, right-arm
medium-fast bowler
Born: 28 May 1974, Bristol
Height: 5ft 11in **Weight:** 13st 4lbs
Nickname: Chess, Fish, Avo, Step, Colgate
County debut: 1994 (one-day),
1997 (first-class)

1st-Class 5 w. in innings: 1
1st-Class catches: 2
Place in batting averages:
(1997 162nd av. 25.09)
Place in bowling averages:
(1997 146th av. 69.00)
Strike rate: 105.00 (career 102.44)
Parents: Michael and Carol
Marital status: Single
Family links with cricket: 'Father
"The Cat" was local club legend. Member of the infamous Frenchay Falcons.
Grandfather played local representative stuff'
Education: Bristol Cathedral School; Portsmouth University; St Cross College,
Oxford University
Qualifications: 10 GCSEs, 3 A-levels, BSc (Hons) Geography, DipSoc (Oxon)
Career outside cricket: 'Not entirely sure yet'
Off-season: Playing rugby for Bristol RFC
Overseas tours: Bristol Schools to Australia 1990-91; Gloucestershire to Zimbabwe
1996; Bristol RFC to South Africa 1995; Oxford University RFC to Japan and
Australia 1996
Cricketers particularly admired: Courtney Walsh, Ian Botham, Gregor Macmillan,
Jamie Whitby Coles
Young players to look out for: Paul Lazenbury, Mark Wagh
Other sports played: Rugby (Bristol RFC – first-team debut 1994)
Other sports followed: Football (Liverpool FC)
Relaxations: Music, watching 'Box of Frogs'. Relaxing with girlfriend
Extras: Double Oxford Blue in 1996-97. Captain of South West U21 rugby in 1995
Opinions on cricket: 'Cricketers generally poorly paid considering time and
dedication needed. Second-team cricket should be as similar to first-team cricket as
possible in terms of set-up and intensity. Cricket can still be the most frustrating and
rewarding game because unlike other sports, results are not directly correlated to
effort.'

Best batting: 42 Oxford University v Sussex, The Parks 1997
Best bowling: 5-98 Oxford University v Hampshire, The Parks 1997

1998 Season

	M	Inns	NO	Runs	HS	Avge	100s	50s	Ct	St	O	M	Runs	Wkts	Avge	Best	5wI	10wM
Test																		
All First	1	2	1	6	6 *	6.00	-	-	-	-	35	10	127	2	63.50	2-40	-	-
1-day Int																		
NatWest																		
B & H																		
Sunday	2	1	0	0	0	0.00	-	-	-	-	13	1	62	2	31.00	2-33	-	

Career Performances

	M	Inns	NO	Runs	HS	Avge	100s	50s	Ct	St	Balls	Runs	Wkts	Avge	Best	5wI	10wM
Test																	
All First	11	17	5	282	42	23.50	-	-	2	-	1844	1231	18	68.38	5-98	1	-
1-day Int																	
NatWest																	
B & H																	
Sunday	7	3	2	3	2 *	3.00	-	-	1	-	252	237	8	29.62	2-33	-	

AYMES, A. N. Hampshire

Name: Adrian Nigel Aymes
Role: Right-hand bat, wicket-keeper
Born: 4 June 1964, Southampton
Height: 6ft **Weight:** 12st 7lbs
Nickname: Aymeser, Adi
County debut: 1987
County cap: 1991
1st-Class 50s: 26
1st-Class 100s: 5
1st-Class catches: 374
1st-Class stumpings: 33
Place in batting averages: 59th av. 35.90
(1997 185th av. 23.26)
Strike rate: 33.00 (career 54.00)
Parents: Michael and Barbara
Wife and date of marriage:
Marie, 14 November 1993
Children: Lucie, 9 November 1994

Family links with cricket: 'Father once walked into a Holt and Haskell Sports Shop'
Education: Shirley Middle; Bellemoor Secondary; Hill College
Qualifications: 4 O-levels, 1 A-level, NCA coaching award
Career outside cricket: 'Working on my fitness/coaching'
Overseas tours: Hampshire CCC to Isle of Wight 1992, to Portugal 1993, to Guernsey 1994
Cricketers particularly admired: Malcolm Marshall, Cardigan Connor, Jimmy Cook and 'wicket-keepers past and present'
Young players to look out for: Ashley Cowan, Andrew Flintoff
Other sports followed: Boxing and non-sport martial arts
Relaxations: Watching videos, exercising
Extras: Half century on debut v Surrey; equalled club record of 6 catches in an innings and 10 in a match. Hampshire Exiles Young Player of the Year 1990. Quickest wicket-keeper to 100 dismissals and 1000 runs in the Sunday League. Promoted to bat at number 5 in 1998, made 450 runs in first four Championship games, including two 100s and two 50s
Opinions on cricket: 'Great game.'
Best batting: 133 Hampshire v Leicestershire, Leicester 1998
Best bowling: 2-135 Hampshire v Northamptonshire, Southampton 1998

1998 Season

	M	Inns	NO	Runs	HS	Avge	100s	50s	Ct	St	O	M	Runs	Wkts	Avge	Best	5wI	10wM
Test																		
All First	18	27	6	754	133	35.90	2	3	53	2	11	0	166	2	83.00	2-135	-	-
1-day Int																		
NatWest	4	4	1	167	73 *	55.66	-	2	8	-								
B & H	5	5	2	78	46 *	26.00	-	-	6	-								
Sunday	17	15	5	219	60 *	21.90	-	2	14	5								

Career Performances

	M	Inns	NO	Runs	HS	Avge	100s	50s	Ct	St	Balls	Runs	Wkts	Avge	Best	5wI	10wM
Test																	
All First	163	239	62	5525	133	31.21	5	26	374	33	162	317	3	105.66	2-135	-	-
1-day Int																	
NatWest	19	9	2	242	73 *	34.57	-	2	30	2							
B & H	36	22	7	304	46 *	20.26	-	-	37	9							
Sunday	126	91	38	1346	60 *	25.39	-	3	117	32							

BAILEY, R. J.

Name: Robert John Bailey
Role: Right-hand bat, off-spin bowler
Born: 28 October 1963, Biddulph,
Stoke-on-Trent
Height: 6ft 3in **Weight:** 14st 7lbs
Nickname: Biff, Nose Bag
County debut: 1982
County cap: 1985
Benefit: 1993
Test debut: 1988
Tests: 4
One-Day Internationals: 4
1000 runs in a season: 13
1st-Class 50s: 101
1st-Class 100s: 39
1st-Class 200s: 4
1st-Class 5 w. in innings: 2
1st-Class catches: 251
One-Day 100s: 9
Place in batting averages: 66th av. 34.50 (1997 46th av. 43.12)
Place in bowling averages: (1997 107th av. 36.70)
Strike rate: 66.00 (career 79.85)
Parents: Marie, father deceased
Wife and date of marriage: Rachel, 11 April 1987
Children: Harry John, 7 March 1991; Alexandra Joy, 13 November 1993
Family links with cricket: Brother plays for Betley in the North Staffs and South
Cheshire League
Education: Biddulph High School
Qualifications: 6 CSEs, 1 O-level, NCA advanced cricket coach
Career outside cricket: Managing Director of Rob Bailey Ceramics, promotional
ceramics business. 'Also sales rep, delivery and packaging for the company!'
Off-season: 'As above!'
Overseas tours: England to Sharjah 1984-85 and 1986-87, to West Indies 1989-90;
Northants to Durban 1991-92, to Cape Town 1992-93, to Zimbabwe 1994-95;
Singapore Sixes October 1994
Overseas teams played for: Rhodes University, South Africa 1982-83; Uitenhage,
Melbourne 1983-84, 1984-85; Fitzroy, Melbourne, 1985-86; Gosnells, Perth 1987-88
Young players to look out for: David Roberts
Other sports followed: Football (Stoke City)
Injuries: 'Bad back'
Relaxations: Walking and drinking at the local village pub

Extras: Played for Young England v Young Australia 1983. Selected for cancelled tour of India 1988-89. Youngest Northamptonshire player to score 10,000 runs. Won three consecutive NatWest Man of the Match Awards 1995. Took over the Northamptonshire captaincy in 1996 season and held post until the end of the 1997 season
Best batting: 224* Northamptonshire v Glamorgan, Swansea 1986
Best bowling: 5-54 Northamptonshire v Nottinghamshire, Northampton 1993

1998 Season

	M	Inns	NO	Runs	HS	Avge	100s	50s	Ct	St	O	M	Runs	Wkts	Avge	Best	5wI	10wM
Test																		
All First	16	24	2	759	188	34.50	1	2	10	-	66	14	178	6	29.66	2-20	-	-
1-day Int																		
NatWest	1	1	0	13	13	13.00	-	-	1	-								
B & H	5	5	0	88	35	17.60	-	-	1	-								
Sunday	13	11	3	253	48 *	31.62	-	-	5	-	8	0	62	1	62.00	1-22	-	

Career Performances

	M	Inns	NO	Runs	HS	Avge	100s	50s	Ct	St	Balls	Runs	Wkts	Avge	Best	5wI	10wM
Test	4	8	0	119	43	14.87	-	-	-	-							
All First	333	561	82	19858	224 *	41.45	43	101	251	-	8864	4739	111	42.69	5-54	2	-
1-day Int	4	4	2	137	43 *	68.50	-	-	1	-	36	25	0	-	-	-	-
NatWest	47	47	12	1575	145	45.00	1	10	18	-	654	407	16	25.43	3-47	-	
B & H	69	66	10	2626	134	46.89	4	19	19	-	390	260	3	86.66	1-1	-	
Sunday	223	209	34	6269	125 *	35.82	4	41	59	-	1342	1291	39	33.10	3-23	-	

BAILEY, T. M. B.   Northamptonshire

Name: Tobin Michael Barnaby Bailey
Role: Right-hand bat, wicket-keeper
Born: 28 August 1976, Kettering
Height: 5ft 10in **Weight:** 12st 6lbs
Nickname: Bill, Mad Dog, Scruff
County debut: 1996
1st-Class catches: 6
Parents: Terry and Penny
Marital status: Single
Family links with cricket: 'Step-dad watches a lot'
Education: Bedford School; Loughborough University
Qualifications: 3 A-levels
Overseas tours: Bedford to South Africa 1994
Cricketers particularly admired: Jack Russell, Mike Atherton, Alan Knott

Young players to look out for:
Michael Davies
Other sports followed: 'Played county
hockey and tennis at youth level for
Bedfordshire.' Rugby (Bedford RFC) and
football (Leicester City FC)
Relaxations: 'Sleeping in the winter,
drinking and spending time with friends'
Extras: Bedfordshire Young Player of the
Year in 1995. Northants County League
Young Player of the Year in 1995.
Holmwoods Schools Cricketer of the Year.
Played for England Schools U19 and was a
reserve for the England U19 tour to
Zimbabwe. Won the BUSA cricket cup with
Loughborough in 1996
Best batting: 31* Northamptonshire v
Lancashire, Northampton 1996

1998 Season

	M	Inns	NO	Runs	HS	Avge	100s	50s	Ct	St	O	M	Runs	Wkts	Avge	Best	5wI	10wM
Test																		
All First	2	2	0	15	12	7.50	-	-	2	-								
1-day Int																		
NatWest																		
B & H	5	4	1	23	12*	7.66	-	-	2	4								
Sunday																		

Career Performances

	M	Inns	NO	Runs	HS	Avge	100s	50s	Ct	St	Balls	Runs	Wkts	Avge	Best	5wI	10wM
Test																	
All First	4	4	1	48	31*	16.00	-	-	6	-							
1-day Int																	
NatWest																	
B & H	10	8	1	97	52	13.85	-	1	5	7							
Sunday	3	0	0	0	0	-	-	-	4	1							

BALL, M. C. J.   Gloucestershire

Name: Martyn Charles John Ball
Role: Right-hand bat, off-spin bowler,
slip fielder
Born: 26 April 1970, Bristol
Height: 5ft 9in **Weight:** 12st 6lbs
Nickname: Benny, Barfo
County debut: 1988
1st-Class 50s: 7
1st-Class 5 w. in innings: 8
1st-Class 10 w. in match: 1
1st-Class catches: 144
Place in batting averages: 157th av. 23.68
(1997 169th av. 24.25)
Place in bowling averages: 119th av. 34.50
(1997 129th av. 43.82)
Strike rate: 76.41 (career 78.17)
Parents: Kenneth Charles and Pamela Wendy
Wife and date of marriage:
Mona, 28 September 1991
Children: Kristina, 9 May 1990; Alexandra, 2 August 1993; Harrison, 5 June 1997
Education: Stanshawes Court; King Edmund Secondary School, Yate; Bath College
of Further Education
Qualifications: 6 O-levels, 2 A-levels
Career outside cricket: Working in Gloucestershire CCC marketing department
Off-season: Marketing. MCC tour to New Zealand
Overseas tours: Gloucestershire to Namibia 1991, to Kenya 1992, to Sri Lanka 1993,
to Zimbabwe 1996, 1997; MCC to New Zealand 1998-99
Overseas teams played for: North Melbourne, Australia 1988-89; Old Hararians,
Zimbabwe 1990-91
Cricketers most admired: Ian Botham, Vic Marks, David Graveney
Young players to look out for: Steve Harmison, Dom Hewson
Other sports played: Football (Horton FC)
Other sports followed: All sports except show-jumping
Relaxations: Music, watching sport, stamp collecting, mountaineering
Extras: Played for Young England against Young New Zealand in 1989. Produced
best bowling figures in a match for the Britannic County Championship 1993 season –
14-169 against Somerset
Opinions on cricket: 'Heading in right direction. Commentators who used to play the
game should stop slagging the England team off and show a bit more patriotism.'
Best batting: 71 Gloucestershire v Nottinghamshire, Bristol 1993
Best bowling: 8-46 Gloucestershire v Somerset, Taunton 1993

1998 Season

	M	Inns	NO	Runs	HS	Avge	100s	50s	Ct	St	O	M	Runs	Wkts	Avge	Best	5wI	10wM
Test																		
All First	18	30	5	592	67 *	23.68	-	3	22	-	433	108	1173	34	34.50	4-26	-	-
1-day Int																		
NatWest	2	2	0	12	12	6.00	-	-	-	-	18	1	89	1	89.00	1-46	-	
B & H	4	3	0	11	6	3.66	-	-	1	-	34	1	161	3	53.66	1-46	-	
Sunday	15	13	8	176	36 *	35.20	-	-	6	-	80	1	381	12	31.75	2-22	-	

Career Performances

	M	Inns	NO	Runs	HS	Avge	100s	50s	Ct	St	Balls	Runs	Wkts	Avge	Best	5wI	10wM
Test																	
All First	121	188	33	2823	71	18.21	-	7	144	-	17902	8510	229	37.16	8-46	8	1
1-day Int																	
NatWest	12	7	2	84	31	16.80	-	-	6	-	666	436	11	39.63	3-42	-	
B & H	26	16	1	149	28	9.93	-	-	11	-	1344	899	23	39.08	4-23	-	
Sunday	98	70	26	559	36 *	12.70	-	-	29	-	3266	2770	70	39.57	4-26	-	

BANES, M. J.   Kent

Name: Matthew John Banes
Role: Right-hand bat (top three), right-arm medium/off-spin bowler
Born: 10 December 1979, Pembury
Height: 5ft 9in **Weight:** 12st
Nickname: Banesy, Bano
County debut: No first-team appearance
Parents: Christopher and Jane Ann
Marital status: Single
Education: Holmewood House Prep School; Tonbridge School; 'in process of applying to Cambridge'
Qualifications: 10 GCSEs, 4 A-levels
Off-season: Travelling
Overseas tours: Tonbridge School to Australia 1996-97
Cricketers most admired: Mike Atherton, Viv Richards
Other sports played: Hockey (Tunbridge Wells 1st XI), rugby, golf
Other sports followed: Football
Relaxations: Good films, good books
Extras: Most centuries (11 in career) for Tonbridge School 1st XI. Highest run

aggregate ever (approx 3100 in career) for Tonbridge School 1st XI
Opinions on cricket: 'More time needed devoted to training and technical enhancement (ie, less matches) so as to be able to compete consistently with the better international teams due to improved county standard.'

BARNETT, K. J. Gloucestershire

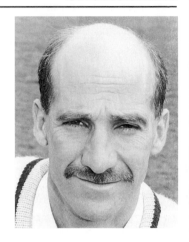

Name: Kim John Barnett
Role: Right-hand bat, leg-break and slow medium bowler
Born: 17 July 1960, Stoke-on-Trent
Height: 6ft **Weight:** 13st 7lbs
Nickname: Barn
County debut: 1979
County cap: 1982
Benefit: 1993 (£37,056)
Test debut: 1988
Tests: 4
One-Day Internationals: 1
1000 runs in a season: 15
1st-Class 50s: 138
1st-Class 100s: 49
1st-Class 200s: 4
1st-Class 5 w. in innings: 3
1st-Class catches: 250
One-Day 100s: 12
One-Day 5 w. in innings: 2
Place in batting averages: 18th av. 47.26 (1997 19th av. 50.23)
Strike rate: 81.00 (career 74.70)
Parents: Derek and Doreen
Wife: Janet
Children: Michael Nicholas, 24 April 1990; Christina, 11 June 1996
Family links with cricket: 'Father local sportsman, mainly football'
Education: Ipstones C of E; Leek High School, Staffs
Qualifications: 7 O-levels
Career outside cricket: Bank clerk
Off-season: Training
Overseas tours: English Schools to India 1977-78; England YC to Australia 1978-79; England B to Sri Lanka 1985-86 (vice-captain); unofficial English XI to South Africa 1989-90
Overseas teams played for: Boland 1980-81, 1982-83
Cricketers particularly admired: Eddie Barlow, Gordon Greenidge

Young players to look out for: Kevin Dean
Other sports followed: Football (Stoke City FC), golf, horse racing
Relaxations: Golf and horse racing
Extras: Played for Northamptonshire 2nd XI when aged 15, Staffordshire and Warwickshire 2nd XI. Became youngest captain of a first-class county when appointed in 1983. One of *Wisden*'s Five Cricketers of the Year 1989. Banned from Test cricket after joining tour to South Africa, suspension remitted in 1992. Relinquished Derbyshire captaincy at the end of the 1995 season. Leading century-maker and run-scorer in all competitions in the history of Derbyshire cricket. Left Derbyshire in 1998-99 off-season and has joined Gloucestershire for 1999
Opinions on cricket: 'We will not produce enough bowlers for the Test arena until we produce pitches that encourage the fast bowlers and leg spinners etc., not just for the batsmen.'
Best batting: 239* Derbyshire v Leicestershire, Leicester 1988
Best bowling: 6-28 Derbyshire v Glamorgan, Chesterfield 1991

1998 Season

	M	Inns	NO	Runs	HS	Avge	100s	50s	Ct	St	O	M	Runs	Wkts	Avge	Best	5wI	10wM
Test																		
All First	17	32	6	1229	162	47.26	1	7	8	-	54	10	148	4	37.00	2-30	-	-
1-day Int																		
NatWest	5	5	0	173	60	34.60	-	1	2	-	29	2	115	3	38.33	2-58	-	
B & H	4	4	0	154	56	38.50	-	1	3	-	17	2	62	3	20.66	2-20	-	
Sunday	14	14	4	405	52 *	40.50	-	3	3	-	63	1	279	11	25.36	4-25	-	

Career Performances

	M	Inns	NO	Runs	HS	Avge	100s	50s	Ct	St	Balls	Runs	Wkts	Avge	Best	5wI	10wM
Test	4	7	0	207	80	29.57	-	2	1	-	36	32	0	-	-	-	-
All First	431	702	68	25556	239 *	40.30	53	138	250	-	13746	6865	184	37.30	6-28	3	-
1-day Int	1	1	0	84	84	84.00	-	1	-								
NatWest	44	42	3	1426	113 *	36.56	2	9	17	-	718	484	24	20.16	6-24	2	
B & H	85	76	5	2749	115	38.71	4	19	33	-	540	356	13	27.38	3-52	-	
Sunday	277	265	43	7794	131 *	35.10	6	43	91	-	1567	1385	49	28.26	4-25	-	

BARRETT, K. A. O.   Surrey

Name: Kevin Andrew Owen Barrett
Role: Left-hand opening bat
Born: 16 November 1975, Swansea
Height: 5ft 11 1/2in **Weight:** 10st 7lbs
County debut: No first-team appearance
Parents: Derek and Sheila
Marital status: Single
Family links with cricket: Father played
club cricket for Pontarddulais
Education: Millfield School; Durham
University
Qualifications: 4 A-levels, BA (Econ)
Off-season: Working for Barclays and Price
Waterhouse Coopers
Overseas tours: West of England Schools to
Trinidad and Tobago 1990-91; Millfield
School to Sri Lanka 1993-94
Overseas teams played for: Randwick,
Sydney 1997-98
Cricketers particularly admired: Graham Gooch, Mark Waugh
Other sports played: Football
Other sports followed: Football (West Ham United), Canadian ice hockey
Relaxations: Spending time with friends. Overseas travel
Extras: Represented England U14 and U15 and Wales U19. Played for Devon 1997
and 1998, including one NatWest match v Yorkshire 1997. Was in Devon's MCC
Trophy winning side at Lord's 1998.
Opinions on cricket: 'Based on my experience of grade cricket in Australia, we play
too much and spend too little time training and working on our game.'

1998 Season (did not make any first-class or one-day appearances)

Career Performances

	M	Inns	NO	Runs	HS	Avge	100s	50s	Ct	St	Balls	Runs	Wkts	Avge	Best	5wI	10wM
Test																	
All First																	
1-day Int																	
NatWest	1	1	0	3	3	3.00	-	-	-	-							
B & H																	
Sunday																	

BATES, J. J.   Sussex

Name: Justin Jonathan Bates
Role: Right-hand bat, off-spin bowler
Born: 9 April 1976, Farnborough, Hants
Height: 6ft **Weight:** 11st 7lbs
County debut: 1996 (one-day),
1997 (first-class)
1st-Class 5 w. in innings: 3
1st-Class catches: 10
Place in batting averages: 284th av. 7.71
(1997 243rd av. 16.14)
Place in bowling averages: 12th av. 19.50
(1997 52nd av. 27.63)
Strike rate: 44.07 (career 60.03)
Parents: Barry and Sandra
Marital status: Single
Family links with cricket: Father played
club cricket and brother Christian played for
Sussex Young Cricketers. Cousin Alan
Igglesden played for Kent and England

Education: St Mark's Primary School; Warden Park Secondary School; Hurstpierpoint
College
Qualifications: 8 GCSEs, 3 A-levels, senior coaching award
Career outside cricket: Freelance graphic designer
Off-season: Playing cricket in South Africa
Overseas tours: Sussex YC to India 1990-91, to Barbados 1992-93, to Sri Lanka 1994-95
Cricketers particularly admired: Carl Hooper, Saqlain Mushtaq
Other sports followed: Golf and rugby
Relaxations: Reading, computing and music
Opinions on cricket: 'Second XI championship cricket should be played over four
days and not three.'
Best batting: 47 Sussex v Gloucestershire, Hove 1997
Best bowling: 5-67 Sussex v Northamptonshire, Northampton 1998

1998 Season

	M	Inns	NO	Runs	HS	Avge	100s	50s	Ct	St	O	M	Runs	Wkts	Avge	Best	5wI	10wM
Test																		
All First	4	7	0	54	38	7.71	-	-	4	-	102.5	24	273	14	19.50	5-67	2	-
1-day Int																		
NatWest																		
B & H																		
Sunday	1	1	1	2	2*	-	-	-	1	-	6	0	42	2	21.00	2-42	-	

Career Performances

	M	Inns	NO	Runs	HS	Avge	100s	50s	Ct	St	Balls	Runs	Wkts	Avge	Best	5wI	10wM
Test																	
All First	11	16	2	167	47	11.92	-	-	10	-	1981	798	33	24.18	5-67	3	-
1-day Int																	
NatWest																	
B & H																	
Sunday	5	5	2	18	8	6.00	-	-	3	-	114	141	3	47.00	2-42	-	

BATES, R. T. Nottinghamshire

Name: Richard Terry Bates
Role: Right-hand bat, off-spin bowler,
slip fielder
Born: 17 June 1972, Stamford, Lincs
Height: 6ft 1in **Weight:** 13st
Nickname: Blaster, Blast, Batesy, Roland
('James "Tap Head" Hindson prefers
"Horn Head"')
County debut: 1993
1st-Class 5 w. in innings: 1
1st-Class catches: 18
Place in batting averages:
(1997 286th av. 9.85)
Place in bowling averages:
(1997 138th av. 52.36)
Strike rate: (career 96.02)
Parents: Terry and Sue
Wife and date of marriage:
Suzanne, 16 March 1996

Children: 'Expecting first child in November 1998!'
Family links with cricket: Father works for ECB; played club cricket for Bourne CC
Education: Abbey Road Primary School, Bourne; Bourne Grammar School; Stamford
College for Further Education
Qualifications: 8 GCSEs, BTEC in Business and Finance, NCA Advanced Coach
Career outside cricket: Employed by Notts CCC to coach during the winter
Off-season: Keeping fit, relaxing
Overseas tours: Lincolnshire Colts (U19) to Australia 1989-90; Notts CCC to
Johannesburg April 1997 and 1998
Overseas teams played for: Redwood CC, Blenheim, New Zealand 1991-92
Cricketers particularly admired: Ian Botham, Derek Randall, Viv Richards
Young players to look out for: Matt Dowman

Other sports played: Football, squash
Other sports followed: 'Watch all sports on TV. Travel to Anfield to watch Liverpool'
Injuries: Out for two weeks with broken finger; for two to three weeks with lower back trouble
Relaxations: 'Eating out, good films, travelling to Anfield, having a beer with mates, walking my dogs and spending as much time as I can with my wife when not cricketing'
Opinions on cricket: '1. Not enough days off to relax. 2. Too much cricket dampens enthusiasm. 3. First it was the dinosaur; spin bowlers will be next!'
Best batting: 34 Nottinghamshire v Worcestershire, Worcester 1996
Best bowling: 5-88 Nottinghamshire v Durham, Chester-le-Street 1995

1998 Season

	M	Inns	NO	Runs	HS	Avge	100s	50s	Ct	St	O	M	Runs	Wkts	Avge	Best	5wI	10wM
Test																		
All First	2	4	2	17	7	8.50	-	-	-	-	21	2	98	0	-		-	-
1-day Int																		
NatWest	3	2	2	0	0 *	-	-	-	2	-	34.5	2	147	4	36.75	2-32	-	
B & H	2	1	0	8	8	8.00	-	-	-	-	15	0	48	1	48.00	1-18	-	
Sunday	16	8	3	53	28 *	10.60	-	-	6	-	88	0	412	13	31.69	2-21	-	

Career Performances

	M	Inns	NO	Runs	HS	Avge	100s	50s	Ct	St	Balls	Runs	Wkts	Avge	Best	5wI	10wM
Test																	
All First	32	47	12	450	34	12.85	-	-	18	-	4801	2437	50	48.74	5-88	1	-
1-day Int																	
NatWest	6	5	2	17	11	5.66	-	-	4	-	329	241	4	60.25	2-32	-	
B & H	9	6	1	61	27	12.20	-	-	4	-	491	331	10	33.10	3-21	-	
Sunday	54	27	7	161	28 *	8.05	-	-	21	-	1804	1546	49	31.55	3-30	-	

BATSON, N. E.   Worcestershire

Name: Nathan Evan Batson
Role: Right-hand (No. 3) bat, off-spin bowler
Born: 24 July 1978, Basildon
Height: 6ft 2in **Weight:** 13st 4lbs
Nickname: Bats, Curly, Penfold, Bish
County debut: 1998
Parents: Anne and John
Marital status: Single
Family links with cricket: 'Dad plays for,
and is chairman of, Billericay CC in Essex.
Mother runs Billericay CC!'
Education: Sunneymede Junior School;
Billericay Senior School; Mayflower
County High
Qualifications: 9 GCSEs, 1 A-level,
coaching certificates to senior level
Career outside cricket: Coaching
Off-season: Playing in Zimbabwe at their
cricket academy
Cricketers particularly admired: Robin Smith, Desmond Haynes
Young players to look out for: Vikram Solanki
Other sports played: Golf and most racquet sports
Other sports followed: Football (Spurs)
Relaxations: Most sports and all kinds of music
Extras: Scored 194 on debut for Worcestershire 2nd XI
Opinions on cricket: '2nd XI cricket should be played on the same grounds with
same time span and conditions as first-class cricket to prepare young players better
when they step up.'
Best batting: 18 Worcester v Warwickshire, Worcester 1998

1998 Season

	M	Inns	NO	Runs	HS	Avge	100s	50s	Ct	St	O	M	Runs	Wkts	Avge	Best	5wl	10wM
Test																		
All First	3	6	0	50	18	8.33	-	-	-	-								
1-day Int																		
NatWest																		
B & H																		
Sunday																		

	M	Inns	NO	Runs	HS	Avge	100s	50s	Ct	St	Balls	Runs	Wkts	Avge	Best	5wI	10wM
Test																	
All First-Class	3	6	0	50	18	8.33	-	-	-		-						
1-day Int																	
NatWest																	
B & H																	
Sunday																	

BATT, C. J.   Middlesex

Name: Christopher James Batt
Role: Left-hand bat, left-arm fast bowler
Born: 22 September 1976, Maidenhead
Height: 6ft 4in **Weight:** 13st
Nickname: Batman, Batty, Nora, Closet
County debut: 1998
1st-Class catches: 2
Parents: Clive and Julia
Marital status: Single
Education: Wessex County Primary School,
Cox Green, Maidenhead; Cox Green
Comprehensive School, Maidenhead
Qualifications: 9 GCSEs
Career outside cricket: Gym instructor;
personal fitness instructor/trainer
Off-season: Playing cricket in New Zealand
Overseas tours: Berkshire U19 to Australia
1994; Berkshire U23 to Barbados 1996
Overseas teams played for: Motueka,
New Zealand 1998-99

Cricketers particularly admired: Richard Hadlee, Dermot Reeve, Graham Thorpe
Young players to look out for: 'Chris Batt!', Jared Payne, Mason Pillon
Other sports played: Golf (U15 Berkshire Schools champion), football
(Berkshire county U16)
Other sports followed: Football (Everton), golf, rugby
Relaxations: Playing golf, 'socialising with friends and women!'
Extras: Local cricket team is Boyne Hill. Colt of the Year 1992 and 1994. Also
member of Julian Cup winning team (senior) in 1993, 1994, 1995 and 1996
Opinions on cricket: 'Too many 2nd XI players not having enough aspirations to
further their careers. Compared to overseas teams we are not as strong mentally and
competitively.'

Best batting: 43 Middlesex v Warwickshire, Lord's 1998
Best bowling: 6-101 Middlesex v Nottinghamshire, Trent Bridge 1998

1998 Season

	M	Inns	NO	Runs	HS	Avge	100s	50s	Ct	St	O	M	Runs	Wkts	Avge	Best	5wI	10wM
Test																		
All First	9	14	2	150	43	12.50	-	-	1	-	201.5	23	846	27	31.33	6-101	2-	
1-day Int																		
NatWest	1	1	0	0	0	0.00	-	-	-	-	8	0	37	1	37.00	1-37	-	
B & H																		
Sunday	2	0	0	0	0	-	-	-	-	-	9	1	47	3	15.66	3-26	-	

Career Performances

	M	Inns	NO	Runs	HS	Avge	100s	50s	Ct	St	Balls	Runs	Wkts	Avge	Best	5wI	10wM
Test																	
All First	10	14	2	150	43	12.50	-	-	2	-	1451	946	33	28.66	6-101	2	-
1-day Int																	
NatWest	1	1	0	0	0	0.00	-	-	-	-	48	37	1	37.00	1-37	-	
B & H																	
Sunday	2	0	0	0	0	-	-	-	-	-	54	47	3	15.66	3-26	-	

BATTY, G. J. Surrey

Name: Gareth Jon Batty
Role: Right-hand bat, off-spin bowler
Born: 13 October 1977, Yorkshire
Height: 5ft 11in **Weight:** 12st
Nickname: Batts, Ian Dowie, Yorkshire Git
County debut: 1997 (Yorkshire),
1998 (one-day, Surrey)
Parents: David and Rosemary
Marital status: Single
Family links with cricket: 'Dad is Yorkshire coach; brother played for Yorkshire and Somerset'
Education: Cullingworth First; Parkside Middle; Bingley Grammar
Qualifications: 9 GCSEs, BTEC in Art Design
Career outside cricket: 'Batty Independent Traders'

Overseas tours: England U15 to South Africa 1993; England U19 to Zimbabwe 1995-96, to Pakistan 1996-97

Cricketers particularly admired: 'Everyone in my team'

Young players to look out for: Ben Grange, Asa Firth, Sam Cummins

Other sports played: Rugby union (Bradford and Bingley), golf

Other sports followed: Rugby (West Hartlepool RFC)

Relaxations: 'Meditation to be at one with myself'

Extras: National U15 bowling award. Made first-class debut for Yorkshire v Lancashire 1997 in non-Championship match. Joined Surrey for 1998

Opinions on cricket: 'Not old enough to comment on such a controversial question.'

Best batting: 18 Yorkshire v Lancashire, Headingley 1997

Best bowling: 1-11 Yorkshire v Lancashire, Headingley 1997

1998 Season

	M	Inns	NO	Runs	HS	Avge	100s	50s	Ct	St	O	M	Runs	Wkts	Avge	Best	5wI	10wM
Test																		
All First																		
1-day Int																		
NatWest																		
B & H																		
Sunday	3	3	1	53	37	26.50	-	-	1	-	22	1	109	2	54.50	1-32	-	

Career Performances

	M	Inns	NO	Runs	HS	Avge	100s	50s	Ct	St	Balls	Runs	Wkts	Avge	Best	5wI	10wM
Test																	
All First	1	2	0	18	18	9.00	-	-	-	-	66	70	2	35.00	1-11	-	-
1-day Int																	
NatWest																	
B & H																	
Sunday	3	3	1	53	37	26.50	-	-	1	-	132	109	2	54.50	1-32	-	

BATTY, J. N.   Surrey

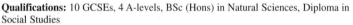

Name: Jonathan Neil Batty
Role: Right-hand bat, wicket-keeper
Born: 18 April 1974, Chesterfield
Height: 5ft 10in **Weight:** 11st 7lbs
Nickname: Batts, Lizard, Nora, Mutant
County debut: 1997
1st-Class 50s: 4
1st-Class catches: 57
1st-Class stumpings: 9
Place in batting averages: 183rd av. 20.64
(1997 158th av. 30.20)
Parents: Roger and Gill
Marital status: Single
Family links with cricket: Father played for
Nottinghamshire Schools and played a good
standard of club cricket
Education: Repton School; Durham
University (St Chad's); Keble College,
Oxford
Qualifications: 10 GCSEs, 4 A-levels, BSc (Hons) in Natural Sciences, Diploma in
Social Studies
Overseas tours: Repton School to Holland 1990; MCC to Bangladesh 1996
Cricketers particularly admired: David Gower, Bruce French, Alec Stewart
Young players to look out for: David Roberts, Stephen Peters, Alex Tudor
Other sports followed: Football (Nottingham Forest), rugby union (Leicester Tigers)
and squash
Relaxations: Going to the cinema, listening to music and reading
Extras: Oxford Blue in 1996. Has also played Minor Counties cricket for Oxfordshire
Opinions on cricket: '2nd XI games should be played on 1st XI wickets.'
Best batting: 63 Surrey v Hampshire, Southampton 1998

1998 Season

	M	Inns	NO	Runs	HS	Avge	100s	50s	Ct	St	O	M	Runs	Wkts	Avge	Best	5wI	10wM
Test																		
All First	16	19	2	351	63	20.64	-	2	39	6	1	0	22	0	-	-	-	-
1-day Int																		
NatWest																		
B & H																		
Sunday	12	11	5	167	40	27.83	-	-	9	5								

Career Performances

	M	Inns	NO	Runs	HS	Avge	100s	50s	Ct	St	Balls	Runs	Wkts	Avge	Best	5wI	10wM
Test																	
All First	31	38	7	747	63	24.09	-	4	57	9	30	31	0	-	-	-	-
1-day Int																	
NatWest	1	1	0	1	1	1.00	-	-	-	-							
B & H	10	8	3	83	26 *	16.60	-	-	9	-							
Sunday	16	14	6	182	40	22.75	-	-	10	5							

BELL, M. A. V. Surrey

Name: Michael Anthony Vincent Bell
Role: Right-hand bat, left-arm
fast-medium bowler
Born: 19 December 1967, Birmingham
Height: 6ft 2in **Weight:** 13st 2lbs
Nickname: Belly, Nelly, Breezer
County debut: 1992 (Warwickshire),
1998 (one-day, Surrey)
1st-Class 5 w. in innings: 3
1st-Class catches: 8
One-Day 5 w. in innings: 2
Strike rate: (career 61.46)
Parents: Vincent and Adelheid
Marital status: Single
Family links with cricket: Father played
cricket mainly for Mitchells & Butler in the
Birmingham League. An uncle played a few
games for Jamaica

Education: Bishop Milner Comprehensive; Dudley Technical College
Qualifications: 5 O-levels, City and Guilds in Recreation and Leisure Parts 1 & 2
Career outside cricket: Casino croupier, worked with the PE staff at Earls High School
and also worked in the corporate hospitality department at EMP plc for two years
Overseas tours: BWIA to Barbados and Trinidad & Tobago 1989; John Morris's
Madcap CC to Australia 1992
Overseas teams played for: Swanbourne, Perth 1986-87; Norwood, Melbourne 1989-
90; Phoenix, Perth 1992-93; Sunshine Heights 1993-94
Cricketers particularly admired: Dennis Lillee, Viv Richards, Michael Holding,
Imran Khan, Wasim Akram, Shane Warne
Other sports followed: Any sport played by the best in that particular field
Relaxations: 'Golf (although I'm no Calvin Peete), good movies and going to a hot
country before winter sets in'

Opinions on cricket: 'When are the batsmen going to be prevented from taking the initiative over the bowlers and get limited to, for instance, one extra-cover drive – on the up – per over ... and when will a cow jump over the moon!'
Best batting: 30 Warwickshire v Nottinghamshire, Trent Bridge 1997
Best bowling: 7-48 Warwickshire v Gloucestershire, Edgbaston 1993

1998 Season

	M	Inns	NO	Runs	HS	Avge	100s	50s	Ct	St	O	M	Runs	Wkts	Avge	Best	5wl	10wM
Test																		
All First																		
1-day Int																		
NatWest																		
B & H	1	0	0	0	0	-	-	-	-	-	4	0	25	0	-	-	-	
Sunday	6	5	2	43	16	14.33	-	-	1	-	39	0	250	6	41.66	3-36	-	

Career Performances

	M	Inns	NO	Runs	HS	Avge	100s	50s	Ct	St	Balls	Runs	Wkts	Avge	Best	5wl	10wM
Test																	
All First	20	23	10	109	30	8.38	-	-	8	-	3012	1565	49	31.93	7-48	3	-
1-day Int																	
NatWest	1	0	0	0	0	-	-	-	-	-	53	41	2	20.50	2-41	-	
B & H	3	0	0	0	0	-	-	-	1	-	90	59	2	29.50	2-34	-	
Sunday	19	10	4	70	16	11.66	-	-	2	-	804	661	28	23.60	5-19	2	

BENJAMIN, J. E.   Surrey

Name: Joseph Emmanuel Benjamin
Role: Right-hand bat, right-arm fast-medium bowler
Born: 2 February 1961, Christchurch, St Kitts, West Indies
Height: 6ft 2in **Weight:** 12st 7lbs
Nickname: Boggy, Moon Man
County debut: 1988 (Warwickshire), 1992 (Surrey)
County cap: 1993 (Surrey)
Test debut: 1994
Tests: 1
One-Day Internationals: 2
50 wickets in a season: 3
1st-Class 5 w. in innings: 17
1st-Class 10 w. in match: 1
1st-Class catches: 24
Place in batting averages: 279th av. 9.50 (1997 238th av. 16.88)

Place in bowling averages: 74th av. 28.45
(1997 144th av. 58.38)
Strike rate: 51.59 (career 58.43)
Parents: Henry and Judith
Marital status: Single
Education: Cayon High School, St Kitts;
Mount Pleasant, Highgate, Birmingham
Qualifications: 4 O-levels
Career outside cricket: Landscape gardener,
store manager
Overseas teams played for: Prahran,
Melbourne 1992-93
Overseas tours: England to Australia
1994-95
Cricketers particularly admired: Imran
Khan, Viv Richards, Malcolm Marshall
Other sports followed: Rugby, squash,
football
Relaxations: Music, going to the cinema, reading
Extras: Released by Warwickshire at the end of the 1991 season and signed up by
Surrey for 1992. Surrey Player of the Year in 1993
Opinions on cricket: 'The four-day game has been very beneficial to county cricket.
It helps batters and bowlers to achieve individual milestones and gives players more
time to recover after the game.'
Best batting: 49 Surrey v Essex, The Oval 1995
Best bowling: 6-19 Surrey v Nottinghamshire, The Oval 1993

1998 Season

	M	Inns	NO	Runs	HS	Avge	100s	50s	Ct	St	O	M	Runs	Wkts	Avge	Best	5wI	10wM
Test																		
All First	8	9	3	57	18 *	9.50	-	-	1	-	189.1	42	626	22	28.45	6-35	1	-
1-day Int																		
NatWest	3	2	2	5	5 *	-	-	-	-	-	21	2	88	1	88.00	1-19	-	
B & H	6	1	1	1	1 *	-	-	-	1	-	53	8	236	3	78.66	2-54	-	
Sunday	16	9	6	16	5	5.33	-	-	2	-	112	11	423	18	23.50	3-16	-	

3. Which Australian batsman scored a century
before lunch v Sri Lanka at The Oval on 11 June 1975?

FIGA

Career Performances

	M	Inns	NO	Runs	HS	Avge	100s	50s	Ct	St	Balls	Runs	Wkts	Avge	Best	5wI	10wM
Test	1	1	0	0	0	0.00	-	-	-	-	168	80	4	20.00	4-42	-	-
All First	124	143	43	1152	49	11.52	-	-	24	-	22556	11510	386	29.81	6-19	17	1
1-day Int	2	1	0	0	0	0.00	-	-	-	-	72	47	1	47.00	1-22	-	
NatWest	21	10	5	69	25	13.80	-	-	3	-	1212	740	22	33.63	4-20	-	
B & H	30	7	5	33	20	16.50	-	-	9	-	1776	1175	34	34.55	4-19	-	
Sunday	107	45	21	206	24	8.58	-	-	18	-	4545	3318	107	31.00	4-44	-	

BETTS, M. M. Durham

Name: Melvyn Morris Betts
Role: Right-hand bat, right-arm
medium-fast bowler
Born: 26 March 1975, Durham
Height: 5ft 11in **Weight:** 12st 2lbs
Nickname: Betsy, Alpha
County debut: 1993
1st-Class 50s: 1
1st-Class 5 w. in innings: 9
1st-Class 10 w. in match: 1
1st-Class catches: 10
Place in batting averages: 263rd av. 12.27
(1997 276th av. 11.50)
Place in bowling averages: 31st av. 22.10
(1997 17th av. 22.14)
Strike rate: 45.37 (career 48.40)
Parents: Melvyn and Shirley
Marital status: Engaged
Family links with cricket: Father and uncle played for local club, Sacriston
Education: Fyndoune Comprehensive
Qualifications: 9 GCSEs, plus qualifications in engineering and sports and
recreational studies
Overseas tours: England U19 to Sri Lanka 1993-94; England A to Zimbabwe and
South Africa 1998-99
Other sports followed: Football (Newcastle United FC)
Relaxations: Football
Extras: Played for England U19 in home series against India in 1994
Opinions on cricket: 'I think that it is getting harder for bowlers due to the reduction
in the seam on the cricket ball and now the one-bouncer-per-over rule.'
Best batting: 57* Durham v Sussex, Hove 1996
Best bowling: 9-64 Durham v Northamptonshire, Northampton 1997

1998 Season

	M	Inns	NO	Runs	HS	Avge	100s	50s	Ct	St	O	M	Runs	Wkts	Avge	Best	5wI	10wM
Test																		
All First	12	18	7	135	29 *	12.27	-	-	3	-	363	81	1061	48	22.10	6-83	4	-
1-day Int																		
NatWest	2	1	0	14	14	14.00	-	-	1	-	24	3	88	2	44.00	2-45	-	
B & H	5	4	2	41	20 *	20.50	-	-	-	-	47.1	9	181	8	22.62	2-26	-	
Sunday	8	6	1	4	1 *	0.80	-	-	2	-	56.3	2	264	13	20.30	3-28	-	

Career Performances

	M	Inns	NO	Runs	HS	Avge	100s	50s	Ct	St	Balls	Runs	Wkts	Avge	Best	5wI	10wM
Test																	
All First	49	75	17	709	57 *	12.22	-	1	10	-	7696	4771	159	30.00	9-64	9	1
1-day Int																	
NatWest	6	5	1	38	14	9.50	-	-	1	-	402	328	9	36.44	3-33	-	
B & H	9	6	3	47	20 *	15.66	-	-	1	-	421	282	11	25.63	2-26	-	
Sunday	31	22	12	100	21	10.00	-	-	5	-	1288	1075	35	30.71	3-22	-	

BEVAN, M. G.   Sussex

Name: Michael Gwyl Bevan
Role: Left-hand bat, slow left-arm bowler
Born: 8 May 1970, Canberra, Australia
County debut: 1995 (Yorkshire),
1998 (Sussex)
County cap: 1995 (Yorkshire),
1998 (Sussex)
Test debut: 1994-95
Tests: 18
One-Day Internationals: 84
1000 runs in a season: 2
1st-Class 50s: 58
1st-Class 100s: 36
1st-Class 200s: 1
1st-Class 5 w. in innings: 1
1st-Class 10 w. in match: 1
1st-Class catches: 91
One-Day 100s: 5
One-Day 5 w. in innings: 1
Place in batting averages: 11th av. 55.00 (1997 89th av. 35.61)
Place in bowling averages: 118th av. 34.36 (1997 140th av. 55.09)
Strike rate: 55.47 (career 71.77)

Wife's name: Tracy
Education: Australian Cricket Academy
Off-season: Playing for New South Wales and Australia
Overseas tours: Australia to Sharjah 1994, to Pakistan 1994-95, to India and Pakistan (World Cup) 1995-96, to Sri Lanka 1996-97, to India 1996-97, to South Africa 1996-97, to England 1997, to New Zealand 1997-98, to India and Sharjah 1997-98, to Pakistan and Bangladesh 1998-99
Overseas teams played for: South Australia 1989-90, New South Wales 1990 –
Extras: In 1990-91 he became the first player to score a century in five successive Sheffield Shield matches. Made 82 on his Test debut against Pakistan in Karachi, 1994-95. Played for Rawtenstall in the Lancashire League in 1993 and 1994. Joined Yorkshire in 1995 and was appointed county vice-captain for the 1996 season. Was part of Australian tour of England in 1997. Joined Sussex for 1998 and was appointed vice-captain. Will not be playing county cricket in 1999
Best batting: 203* New South Wales v Western Australia, Sydney 1993-94
Best bowling: 6-82 Australia v West Indies, Adelaide 1996-97

1998 Season

	M	Inns	NO	Runs	HS	Avge	100s	50s	Ct	St	O	M	Runs	Wkts	Avge	Best	5wl	10wM
Test																		
All First	12	19	2	935	149 *	55.00	3	4	10	-	175.4	27	653	19	34.36	3-36	-	-
1-day Int																		
NatWest	1	1	0	1	1	1.00	-	-	-	-								
B & H	3	3	1	213	95 *	106.50	-	2	-	-	18.5	0	98	0	-		-	-
Sunday	11	11	4	327	78	46.71	-	3	3	-	31	1	158	9	17.55	3-7	-	

Career Performances

	M	Inns	NO	Runs	HS	Avge	100s	50s	Ct	St	Balls	Runs	Wkts	Avge	Best	5wl	10wM
Test	18	30	3	785	91	29.07	-	6	8	-	1285	703	29	24.24	6-82	1	1
All First	155	259	44	11423	203 *	53.13	37	58	91	-	6819	4083	95	42.97	6-82	1	1
1-day Int	84	75	26	2819	108 *	57.53	3	17	33	-	1338	1097	26	42.19	3-36	-	
NatWest	9	9	2	389	91 *	55.57	-	4	-	-	114	89	3	29.66	2-47	-	
B & H	13	12	5	757	95 *	108.14	-	9	1	-	144	123	1	123.00	1-25	-	
Sunday	40	38	9	1435	103 *	49.48	2	10	12	-	631	557	32	17.40	5-29	1	

BICKNELL, D. J. — Surrey

Name: Darren John Bicknell
Role: Left-hand opening bat, slow left-arm
Born: 24 June 1967, Guildford
Height: 6ft 4in **Weight:** 14st 7lb
Nickname: Denz, Herman 'and a few others'
County debut: 1987
County cap: 1990
1000 runs in a season: 6
1st-Class 50s: 59
1st-Class 100s: 28
1st-Class 200s: 2
1st-Class catches: 75
One-Day 100s: 7
Place in batting averages:
(1997 67th av. 39.60)
Strike rate: (career 53.26)
Parents: Vic and Valerie
Wife and date of marriage:
Rebecca, 26 September 1992

Children: Lauren Elizabeth, 1993; Sam, 1995; Emily, 1997
Family links with cricket: Brother plays 'except on Sundays'
Education: Robert Haining County Secondary; Guildford County College
of Technology
Qualifications: 8 O-levels, 2 A-levels, senior coaching award
Career outside cricket: Courage Brewery for last four years
Off-season: 'Supervising my benefit year'
Overseas tours: Surrey to Sharjah 1988, 1989, to Dubai 1990, to Perth 1995; England
A to Zimbabwe and Kenya 1989-90, to Pakistan 1990-91, to Bermuda and West Indies
1991-92
Overseas teams played for: Coburg, Melbourne 1986-87
Cricketers particularly admired: Mark Taylor, Steve Waugh, Saqlain Mushtaq,
Wasim Akram, Waqar Younis
Young players to look out for: Ben Hollioake, Alex Tudor
Other sports played: Football, golf 'and any others that I have time for'
Other sports followed: Football (West Ham United)
Injuries: Out for eight months with stress fracture of the back; played first game of
the season in September 1998
Relaxations: Golf 'and time with the family'
Extras: Shared county record third-wicket stand of 413 with David Ward v Kent at
Canterbury in 1990 – both made career bests. Surrey Batsman of the Year four times.
Hit the fastest hundred of the year in 1990. Awarded a benefit in 1999

Opinions on cricket: 'Two divisions must happen. The standard of pitches is deteriorating rapidly due to pressure on clubs to get results. Pitches should be prepared by independent groundsmen!'

Best batting: 235* Surrey v Nottinghamshire, Trent Bridge 1994

Best bowling: 3-7 Surrey v Sussex, Hove 1996

1998 Season

	M	Inns	NO	Runs	HS	Avge	100s	50s	Ct	St	O	M	Runs	Wkts	Avge	Best	5wI	10wM
Test																		
All First																		
1-day Int																		
NatWest																		
B & H																		
Sunday	1	1	0	23	23	23.00	-	-	-	-								

Career Performances

	M	Inns	NO	Runs	HS	Avge	100s	50s	Ct	St	Balls	Runs	Wkts	Avge	Best	5wI	10wM
Test																	
All First	200	352	34	12696	235 *	39.92	30	59	75	-	1232	789	23	34.30	3-7	-	-
1-day Int																	
NatWest	20	20	4	778	135 *	48.62	1	5	1	-							
B & H	33	32	3	1241	119	42.79	2	9	12	-							
Sunday	97	94	13	2938	125	36.27	4	17	24	-	36	39	2	19.50	1-11	-	

BICKNELL, M. P.   Surrey

Name: Martin Paul Bicknell

Role: Right-hand bat, right-arm fast-medium bowler

Born: 14 January 1969, Guildford

Height: 6ft 4in **Weight:** 14st 7lbs

Nickname: Bickers

County debut: 1986

County cap: 1989

Benefit: 1997

Test debut: 1993

Tests: 2

One-Day Internationals: 7

50 wickets in a season: 7

1st-Class 50s: 11

1st-Class 5 w. in innings: 29

1st-Class 10 w. in match: 2

1st-Class catches: 68
One-Day 5 w. in innings: 1
Place in batting averages: 176th av. 21.65
(1997 207th av. 20.33)
Place in bowling averages: 20th av. 20.61
(1997 45th av. 26.68)
Strike rate: 45.61 (career 53.78)
Parents: Vic and Valerie
Wife and date of marriage:
Loraine, 29 September 1995
Children: Eleanor, 31 March 1995;
Charlotte, 22 July 1996
Family links with cricket: 'Brother plays,
but with no luck'
Education: Robert Haining County
Secondary
Qualifications: 2 O-levels, NCA coach
Career outside cricket: Amateur golfer
Overseas tours: England YC to Sri Lanka 1986-87, to Australia 1987-88; England A to Zimbabwe and Kenya 1989-90, to Bermuda and West Indies 1991-92, to South Africa 1993-94; England to Australia 1990-91
Cricketers particularly admired: Ian Botham, Dennis Lillee, Richard Hadlee, Jason Ratcliffe
Young players to look out for: Ben Hollioake
Other sports followed: Football (Leeds United), golf
Relaxations: Playing golf and spending time with the family
Extras: Youngest player to play for Surrey since David Smith. His figures of 9 for 45 were the best for the county for 30 years. One of four players on stand-by as reserves for England's World Cup squad 1991-92. Supporters' Player of the Year 1993
Opinions on cricket: 'There is still too much cricket. Two divisions are a must.'
Best batting: 88 Surrey v Hampshire, Southampton 1992
Best bowling: 9-45 Surrey v Cambridge University, Fenner's 1988

1998 Season

	M	Inns	NO	Runs	HS	Avge	100s	50s	Ct	St	O	M	Runs	Wkts	Avge	Best	5wI	10wM
Test																		
All First	17	21	1	433	81	21.65	-	1	5	-	494.1	141	1340	65	20.61	5-27	2	-
1-day Int																		
NatWest	3	3	2	69	48 *	69.00	-	-	2	-	30	1	113	5	22.60	3-24	-	
B & H	7	4	4	70	38 *	-	-	-	2	-	63.5	5	270	11	24.54	4-38	-	
Sunday	10	8	5	59	30 *	19.66	-	-	-	-	63	3	263	7	37.57	2-26	-	

Career Performances

	M	Inns	NO	Runs	HS	Avge	100s	50s	Ct	St	Balls	Runs	Wkts	Avge	Best	5wI	10wM
Test	2	4	0	26	14	6.50	-	-	-	-	522	263	4	65.75	3-99	-	-
All First	198	236	59	3412	88	19.27	-	11	68	-	37382	17745	695	25.53	9-45	29	2
1-day Int	7	6	2	96	31 *	24.00	-	-	2	-	413	347	13	26.69	3-55	-	
NatWest	31	17	8	195	66 *	21.66	-	1	15	-	1959	1097	43	25.51	4-35	-	
B & H	51	27	11	278	43	17.37	-	-	10	-	2951	1962	80	24.52	4-38	-	
Sunday	147	68	35	544	57 *	16.48	-	1	33	-	6199	4463	172	25.94	5-12	1	

BISHOP, I. E. Surrey

Name: Ian Emlyn Bishop
Role: Right-hand bat, right-arm fast-medium bowler
Born: 26 August 1977, Taunton
Height: 6ft 2in **Weight:** 11st
Nickname: Bish
County debut: 1996 (Somerset)
1st-Class catches: 1
Parents: Brian and Jane
Marital status: Single
Family links with cricket: Both father and brother play club cricket
Education: Parkfield Primary School, Taunton; Castle Secondary School, Taunton; Scat College of Further Education, Taunton
Qualifications: GCSEs
Cricketers particularly admired: Darren Gough, Chris Lewis, Alec Stewart
Young players to look out for: Andy Harris, Marcus Trescothick
Other sports followed: Football (Liverpool FC)
Relaxations: Sport and socialising with friends
Extras: Played for Devon in 1998. Has joined Surrey for 1999
Best batting: 2 Somerset v Pakistan, Taunton 1996

1998 Season (did not make any first-class or one-day appearances)

Career Performances

	M	Inns	NO	Runs	HS	Avge	100s	50s	Ct	St	Balls	Runs	Wkts	Avge	Best	5wI	10wM
Test																	
All First	1	2	0	4	2	2.00	-	-	1	-	42	29	0	-	-	-	-
1-day Int																	
NatWest	1	1	1	1	1*	-	-	-	-	-	42	27	0	-	-	-	
B & H																		
Sunday																		

BISHOP, J. E. Essex

Name: Justin Edward Bishop
Role: Left-hand middle-order bat, left-arm fast opening bowler
Born: 4 January 1982, Bury St Edmunds
Height: 6ft **Weight:** 12st 2lbs
Nickname: Bish
County debut: No first-team appearance
Parents: Keith and Anne
Marital status: Single
Family links with cricket: Father a member of Bury St Edmunds CC
Education: Ickworth Park School, Bury St Edmunds; Honinger Court Middle School; County Upper School, Bury St Edmunds
Qualifications: '10$^{1}/_{2}$ GCSEs'
Career outside cricket: 'Still studying!'
Off-season: Playing local football and studying
Young players to look out for: Stephen Peters
Other sports played: Football (Suffolk U15; now playing for Bury Town U18)
Other sports followed: Football (Ipswich Town FC)
Injuries: Out for one week with slight back strain
Relaxations: Swimming and playing snooker
Extras: Opening bowler for England U15 1997
Opinions on cricket: 'The game continues to move forward, and the prospect of day/night cricket excites me.'

BLACKWELL, I. D. — Derbyshire

Name: Ian David Blackwell
Role: Left-hand bat, slow left-arm bowler
Born: 10 June 1978, Chesterfield
Height: 6ft 2in **Weight:** 14st 7lbs
Nickname: Blackie, Fupos, Albert, Stewie,
Sidewinder, Purple Pip
County debut: 1997
1st-Class 50s: 2
1st-Class 5 w. in innings: 1
1st-Class catches: 6
Place in batting averages: 250th av. 14.11
Place in bowling averages: 123rd av. 37.42
Strike rate: 67.00 (career 78.12)
Parents: John and Marilyn
Marital status: Single, 'but living in sin'
Family links with cricket: Father plays
for Derbyshire Over 50s
Education: Old Hall Primary School;
Manor Community School; Brookfield Community School
Qualifications: 8 GCSEs, 1 A-level, NCA senior coaching award
Career outside cricket: 'PI'
Off-season: 'Coaching and undercover investigating (honestly)'
Overseas teams played for: Delacombe Park, Victoria, Australia (sub-district cricket)
Cricketers particularly admired: Phillip DeFreitas, Tom Moody, Alec Stewart
Young players to look out for: Andrew Flintoff, Paul Franks, Chris Read
Other sports played: Golf, table tennis, squash, football ('played for Sheffield
Wednesday Young Owls'), tennis, basketball, racquet ball, pool, snooker, badminton,
darts
Other sports followed: Football (Chesterfield FC)
Injuries: Out for two weeks with split webbing of the right hand
Relaxations: Computing, 'ten-mile run every day (Kim Barnett) with the rest of the
F squad (V.P. Clarke, B. Spendlove, T. Tweats, M. May)'
Extras: Played for Derbyshire from the age of eight through to the 2nd XI. Holds
record for number of balls lost (7) in a score of 213 not out at Bolsover, which
included 23 fours and 15 sixes and equalled the Bassetlaw record
Opinions on cricket: 'Players still underpaid, especially the younger ones.'
Best batting: 57 Derbyshire v Durham, Derby 1998
Best bowling: 5-115 Derbyshire v Surrey, The Oval 1998

	M	Inns	NO	Runs	HS	Avge	100s	50s	Ct	St	O	M	Runs	Wkts	Avge	Best	5wI	10wM
Test																		
All First	11	18	0	254	57	14.11	-	2	6	-	156.2	32	524	14	37.42	5-115	1	-
1-day Int																		
NatWest	1	1	0	4	4	4.00	-	-	-	-	6	0	33	0	-		-	-
B & H	4	4	1	46	27	15.33	-	-	2	-								
Sunday	8	6	0	141	89	23.50	-	1	3	-	22	1	129	5	25.80	3-47	-	

Career Performances

	M	Inns	NO	Runs	HS	Avge	100s	50s	Ct	St	Balls	Runs	Wkts	Avge	Best	5wI	10wM
Test																	
All First	15	23	0	305	57	13.26	-	2	6	-	1250	751	16	46.93	5-115	1	-
1-day Int																	
NatWest	1	1	0	4	4	4.00	-	-	-	-	36	33	0	-		-	-
B & H	5	4	1	46	27	15.33	-	-	2	-	30	38	0	-		-	-
Sunday	12	10	0	195	89	19.50	-	1	3	-	132	129	5	25.80	3-47	-	

BLAIN, J. A. R.   Northamptonshire

Name: John Angus Rae Blain
Role: Right-hand bat, right-arm fast-medium bowler
Born: 4 January 1979, Edinburgh
Height: 6ft 2in **Weight:** 12st 10lbs
Nickname: Blainey, Haggis, Chill
County debut: 1997
1st-Class catches: 2
One-Day 5 w. in innings: 1
Strike rate: (career 156.00)
Parents: John and Elma
Marital status: Single
Education: Eastfield Primary School; Penicuik High School; Jewel and Esk Valley College
Qualifications: 8 GCSEs, 2 O-levels, NC Leisure and Recreation, NCA coaching certificate
Off-season: 'Unsure where. Either SA or Ozzie'
Overseas tours: Scotland U19 to Holland for International Youth Tournament 1994-95, to Bermuda 1997, to South Africa (Youth World Cup) 1997; Scotland to Denmark (European Championships) 1996, to Malaysia (ICC Trophy) 1997,

to Malaysia (Commonwealth Games) 1998; Northants CCC to Zimbabwe 1997
Cricketers particularly admired: Allan Donald, Dougie Brown, Steve Waugh, David Ripley
Young players to look out for: Richard Logan, Graeme Swann, Fraser Watts, Dougie Lockhart
Other sports played: Football (schoolboy forms with Hibernian and Falkirk making youth and reserve team appearances)
Other sports followed: Football (Hibernian)
Injuries: Out for ten weeks with torn cartilage in left knee (operation May 1998); for five weeks (August 1998) with pulled intercostal in left side
Relaxations: Playing football and golf, listening to music and going home to see family
Extras: Youngest ever player to play for Scotland national side at 17 years and 114 days. Played for Scotland in the Benson and Hedges and NatWest competitions. Made his first-class debut for Scotland against Ireland in 1996. Captained Scotland U19 at U19 World Cup in South Africa. Took 5 for 24 on Sunday League debut against Derbyshire. Selected for Scotland's 1999 World Cup squad
Opinions on cricket: 'Have a blend of youth and experience in a side, but give youth a chance if good enough because the top level is the only real place to learn. More day/night matches are a must – future of the game.'
Best bowling: 1-18 Northamptonshire v Worcestershire, Northampton 1997

1998 Season

	M	Inns	NO	Runs	HS	Avge	100s	50s	Ct	St	O	M	Runs	Wkts	Avge	Best	5wI	10wM
Test																		
All First	1	0	0	0	0	-	-	-	-	-								
1-day Int																		
NatWest																		
B & H																		
Sunday																		

Career Performances

	M	Inns	NO	Runs	HS	Avge	100s	50s	Ct	St	Balls	Runs	Wkts	Avge	Best	5wI	10wM
Test																	
All First	3	1	0	0	0	0.00	-	-	2	-	312	208	2	104.00	1-18	-	-
1-day Int																	
NatWest	1	0	0	0	0	-	-	-	1	-	66	56	2	28.00	2-56	-	
B & H	3	2	1	14	10*	14.00	-	-	-	-	90	140	3	46.66	2-82	-	
Sunday	3	0	0	0	0	-	-	-	1	-	144	110	7	15.71	5-24	1	

BLAKEY, R. J. — Yorkshire

Name: Richard John Blakey
Role: Right-hand bat, wicket-keeper
Born: 15 January 1967, Huddersfield
Height: 5ft 10in **Weight:** 11st 4lbs
Nickname: Dick
County debut: 1985
County cap: 1987
Benefit: 1998
Test debut: 1992-93
Tests: 2
One-Day Internationals: 3
1000 runs in a season: 4
1st-Class 50s: 70
1st-Class 100s: 8
1st-Class 200s: 2
1st-Class catches: 586
1st-Class stumpings: 48
One-Day 100s: 3

Place in batting averages: 177th av. 21.33 (1997 75th av. 37.77)
Strike rate: (career 63.00)
Parents: Brian and Pauline
Wife and date of marriage: Michelle, 28 September 1991
Children: Harrison Brad, 22 September 1993
Family links with cricket: Father played local cricket
Education: Woodhouse Primary; Rastrick Grammar School
Qualifications: 4 O-levels, Senior NCA Coach
Career outside cricket: Started own leisure company
Overseas tours: England YC to West Indies 1984-85; Yorkshire to Barbados 1986-87, to Cape Town 1990-91; England A to Zimbabwe and Kenya 1989-90, to Pakistan 1990-91; England to India and Sri Lanka 1992-93
Overseas teams played for: Waverley, Sydney 1985-87; Mt Waverley, Sydney 1987-88; Bionics, Zimbabwe 1989-90
Cricketers particularly admired: Martyn Moxon, Dermot Reeve, Ian Botham, Alan Knott
Other sports followed: All
Relaxations: All sports, particularly golf and squash, eating out, drawing, photography
Extras: Established himself in Huddersfield League. Made record 2nd XI score – 273* v Northamptonshire 1986. Yorkshire's Young Player of the Year 1989. Made Test debut in second Test against India at Madras, February 1993. He was awarded a citation by the International Committee for Fair Play in 1995, the only cricketer among the 25 winners worldwide

Opinions on cricket: 'Four-day game is much more enjoyable and the best team wins. National anthem should be played before the start of every international, like football.'

Best batting: 221 England A v Zimbabwe, Bulawayo 1989-90

Best bowling: 1-68 Yorkshire v Nottinghamshire, Sheffield 1986

1998 Season

	M	Inns	NO	Runs	HS	Avge	100s	50s	Ct	St	O	M	Runs	Wkts	Avge	Best	5wI	10wM
Test																		
All First	17	23	2	448	67 *	21.33	-	3	69	2								
1-day Int																		
NatWest	2	1	0	10	10	10.00	-	-	4	-								
B & H	6	5	3	83	43 *	41.50	-	-	7	-								
Sunday	17	14	5	195	29	21.66	-	-	18	2								

Career Performances

	M	Inns	NO	Runs	HS	Avge	100s	50s	Ct	St	Balls	Runs	Wkts	Avge	Best	5wI	10wM
Test	2	4	0	7	6	1.75	-	-	2	-							
All First	275	436	67	11812	221	32.01	10	70	586	48	63	68	1	68.00	1-68	-	-
1-day Int	3	2	0	25	25	12.50	-	-	2	1							
NatWest	29	22	6	398	75	24.87	-	2	34	2							
B & H	52	45	11	997	80 *	29.32	-	6	47	3							
Sunday	167	148	31	4250	130 *	36.32	3	24	140	24							

BLANCHETT, I. N.   Middlesex

Name: Ian Neale Blanchett

Role: Right-hand bat, right-arm fast-medium bowler

Born: 2 October 1975, Melbourne, Australia

Height: 6ft 4in **Weight:** 14st 3lbs

Nickname: Blanchy, Noisy, 'and other descriptive names created by uni housemates based around being very clumsy'

County debut: 1997 (one-day), 1998 (first-class)

1st-Class catches: 1

Strike rate: 100.80 (career 100.80)

Parents: Edward Arthur Blanchett and Susan Anne Billows

Marital status: Single

Family links with cricket: 'Uncle Steve played for Surrey YC when he was younger – a long time ago!'

Education: Feltwell Primary, Norfolk; Methwold High School, Norfolk; Downham Market High School; Luton University

Qualifications: 8 GCSEs, 2 A-levels, 'in process of completing a Health Science/Leisure degree'
Cricketers particularly admired: Ian Botham, Graham Gooch
Young players to look out for: Owais Shah, Aaron Laraman, James Hewitt, Tim Walton, Kevin Innes
Other sports followed: Football (Norwich City), snooker, swimming
Relaxations: 'Enjoy trips to my grandparents in Malaga immensely, where a choice of diving, sailing, and swimming is available. Also enjoy bashing up a nice "spag bol" for myself and Rob Watson, listening to good music. Relaxation often occurs away from my hectic university household'

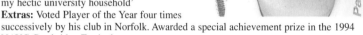

Extras: Voted Player of the Year four times successively by his club in Norfolk. Awarded a special achievement prize in the 1994 NAYC Cambridge Festival
Opinions on cricket: 'It gets better every day. More day/night cricket is a must.'
Best batting: 18 Middlesex v Worcestershire, Uxbridge 1998
Best bowling: 2-38 Middlesex v Glamorgan, Lord's 1998

1998 Season

	M	Inns	NO	Runs	HS	Avge	100s	50s	Ct	St	O	M	Runs	Wkts	Avge	Best	5wI	10wM
Test																		
All First	4	4	0	25	18	6.25	-	-	1	-	84	9	307	5	61.40	2-38	-	-
1-day Int																		
NatWest																			
B & H	1	0	0	0	0	-	-	-	-	-	1	0	12	0	-		-	-
Sunday	4	2	1	16	9 *	16.00	-	-	2	-	21	1	76	1	76.00	1-16	-	

Career Performances

	M	Inns	NO	Runs	HS	Avge	100s	50s	Ct	St	Balls	Runs	Wkts	Avge	Best	5wI	10wM
Test																	
All First	4	4	0	25	18	6.25	-	-	1	-	504	307	5	61.40	2-38	-	-
1-day Int																	
NatWest																		
B & H	2	0	0	0	0	-	-	-	-	-	42	56	1	56.00	1-44	-	
Sunday	9	4	2	18	9 *	9.00	-	-	4	-	288	260	2	130.00	1-16	-	

BLEWETT, G.S. Yorkshire

Name: Gregory Scott Blewett
Role: Right-hand bat, right-arm
medium bowler
Born: 28 October 1971, Adelaide
Height: 6ft **Weight:** 11st
Nickname: Blewy
County debut: No first-team appearance
Test debut: 1994-95
Tests: 31
One-Day Internationals: 26
1st-Class 50s: 42
1st-Class 100s: 16
1st-Class 200s: 3
1st-Class 5 w. in innings: 1
1st-Class catches: 79
Strike rate: (career 86.12)
Parents: Bob and Shirley
Wife and date of marriage:
Jodie, 26 June 1998

Family links with cricket: Father played for South Australia
Education: Angaston Primary School, Adelaide; Prince Alfred College, Adelaide
Overseas tours: Australia U19 to England 1991, to Sri Lanka; Australia to New
Zealand 1994-95, to West Indies 1994-95, to South Africa 1996-97, to England 1997,
to India 1997-98
Overseas teams played for: South Australia 1991-92 –
Cricketers particularly admired: Greg Chappell, Gordon Greenidge, Viv Richards
Other sports played: Golf
Other sports followed: Australian Football League (Adelaide Crows)
Relaxations: Eating and sleeping
Extras: Was due to play for Middlesex in 1997 but was selected for Ashes tour. Was
the only Australian to make 1000 Test runs in 1997 calendar year. Holds the
unenviable record of being the first Australian to be out for 99 twice in Test cricket.
Vice-captain of South Australia. Has joined Yorkshire for the 1999 season
Best batting: 268 South Australia v Victoria, Melbourne 1993-94
Best bowling: 5-29 Australian XI v West Indies, Hobart 1996-97
Stop press: In 1998-99, made 1175 first-class runs (av. 146.86 and including five 100s
and a 200) before Christmas in the Australian season, breaking David Hookes' record
of 1163 set in 1982-83. In the course of achieving this feat he became only the sixth
Australian to score four consecutive first-class 100s; he also scored 143 for South
Australia and 169* and 213* in one match for Australia XI against the England
tourists. Selected for Australia's tour of West Indies 1998-99

Career Performances

	M	Inns	NO	Runs	HS	Avge	100s	50s	Ct	St	Balls	Runs	Wkts	Avge	Best	5wl	10wM
Test	31	53	2	1843	214	36.13	4	10	36	-	1070	520	9	57.77	2-25	-	-
All First	106	183	11	7666	268	44.56	19	42	79	-	5684	2940	66	44.54	5-29	1	-
1-day Int	26	25	3	474	57*	21.54	-	2	7	-	658	551	12	45.91	2-34	-	-
NatWest																	
B & H																	
Sunday																	

BLOOMFIELD, T. F. Middlesex

Name: Timothy Francis Bloomfield
Role: Right-hand bat, right-arm fast-medium bowler
Born: 31 May 1973, Ashford
Height: 6ft 3in **Weight:** 14st
Nickname: Nice, BT, Frank
County debut: 1997
1st-Class 5 w. in innings: 3
1st-Class catches: 2
Place in bowling averages: 85th av. 30.00 (1997 8th av. 19.84)
Strike rate: 46.04 (career 43.51)
Parents: Richard (deceased) and Pauline
Education: Halliford Secondary School
Qualifications: GCSEs
Off-season: Working, training, keeping fit
Overseas tours: Berkshire U25 to Barbados
Cricketers particularly admired:
Ian Botham, Viv Richards, Angus Fraser
Other sports followed: Football (Liverpool)
Relaxations: 'Playing other sports and spending time with Emma'
Extras: Has also played for Sussex 2nd XI and Berkshire
Opinions on cricket: 'We play too much cricket. The powers-that-be need to be more forward thinking.'
Best batting: 20* Middlesex v Sussex, Hove 1998
Best bowling: 5-67 Middlesex v Northamptonshire, Northampton 1998

1998 Season

	M	Inns	NO	Runs	HS	Avge	100s	50s	Ct	St	O	M	Runs	Wkts	Avge	Best	5wl	10wM
Test																		
All First	8	10	5	37	20 *	7.40	-	-	-	-	168.5	34	660	22	30.00	5-67	2	
1-day Int																		
NatWest	2	1	1	0	0 *	-	-	-	-	-	17	2	80	1	80.00	1-35	-	
B & H	2	0	0	0	0	-	-	-	-	-	14	0	90	0	-	-	-	
Sunday	5	1	0	15	15	15.00	-	-	1	-	28	2	127	6	21.16	2-13	-	

Career Performances

	M	Inns	NO	Runs	HS	Avge	100s	50s	Ct	St	Balls	Runs	Wkts	Avge	Best	5wl	10wM
Test																	
All First	12	13	7	41	20 *	6.83	-	-	2	-	1523	918	35	26.22	5-67	3	-
1-day Int																	
NatWest	3	1	1	0	0 *	-	-	-	-	-	150	105	2	52.50	1-25	-	
B & H	2	0	0	0	0	-	-	-	-	-	84	90	0	-	-	-	
Sunday	11	2	0	16	15	8.00	-	-	2	-	402	325	12	27.08	2-8	-	

BOILING, J.   Durham

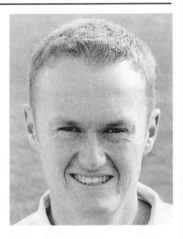

Name: James Boiling
Role: Right-hand bat, right-arm off-spin bowler
Born: 8 April 1968, New Delhi
Height: 6ft 3in **Weight:** 16st 7lbs
Nickname: Hugh, Janus, Norma, Stitz
County debut: 1988 (Surrey), 1995 (Durham)
1st-Class 50s: 2
1st-Class 5 w. in innings: 4
1st-Class 10 w. in match: 1
1st-Class catches: 70
One-Day 5 w. in innings: 2
Place in batting averages: (1997 257th av. 15.18)
Place in bowling averages: (1997 130th av. 44.04)
Strike rate: (career 105.75)
Parents: Graham and Geraldine
Wife and date of marriage: Rachael Anne, 7 October 1995
Family links with cricket: 'Cousin, Gareth, enjoys the music of Buddy Holly and the Crickets. Wife, Rachael, is cricket coordinator at Chilton Junior School. Brother-in-law,

Stuart, used to have a "Fantasy" team, but he's too busy at work now and anyway he likes football better'

Education: Poplar Road Primary School, Merton; Joseph Hood Middle School, Merton; Rutlish School, Merton; Durham University (College of St Hild and Bede); Newcastle University

Qualifications: 'Some O- and A-levels, a history degree, senior NCA coaching award, touch typing (40 wpm), cycling proficiency, Health and Safety at Work (Parts 1 and 2), rhythm guitar (Level 3), HGV licence, juggling and fire-eating (Advanced)'

Career outside cricket: Working with children

Off-season: Studying

Overseas tours: Surrey Schools to Australia 1985-86; England YC to Australia (Youth World Cup) 1987-88; England A to Australia 1992-93; 'Backpackers' to New Zealand 1996

Overseas teams played for: Bionics, Harare 1991-92; St Augustine, Cape Town 1992-93; 'Brits on Tour 1993'; Watsonians, California 1996-97

Cricketers particularly admired: 'I admire any cricketer who has a real "presence" on the field and worries the opposition by the way he behaves. Current English players in this category are: Nathan Wood, Paddy McKeown, Dave Fulton, Martin McCague, Matt Dowman, Nick Trainor, Piran Holloway, Alan Mullally, Dom Williamson'

Young players to look out for: Sam Scott, Kenny Speak, Joe Wood, Ben Cox

Other sports played: 'I have never been much good at other sports, except running'

Other sports followed: 'I really dig "extreme sports" like base jumping'

Injuries: 'Ennui, May to August 1998'

Relaxations: 'Rachael and I are really into "Battleships" at the moment. She leads 26-23 in the series so far'

Extras: 'Voted Durham's "top fielder" in 1997. Could have played Test cricket for India but chose to go on England A tour to Australia instead. Left Surrey at the end of the 1994 season. Has been hit for more sixes than any other Durham bowler in the Sunday League. Described by David Boon as "a genuine eccentric".' Was released by Durham at the end of the 1998 season. 'Currently in talks with seven teams for the 1999 season. Hoping to play for British Universities in 1999. Failing that, it would be nice to help Newcastle University beat Durham in the BUSF competition. Watch out, Foxy!!'

Opinions on cricket: 'Something I was told by an England captain inspired me: "If you take each game as it comes, give 110 per cent, and the luck goes your way, at the end of the day you'll come away with a result." I would like to see Scotland win the World Cup this year.'

Best batting: 69 Durham v West Indies, Chester-le-Street 1995

Best bowling: 6-84 Surrey v Gloucestershire, Bristol 1992

1998 Season

	M	Inns	NO	Runs	HS	Avge	100s	50s	Ct	St	O	M	Runs	Wkts	Avge	Best	5wI	10wM
Test																		
All First																		
1-day Int																		
NatWest																		
B & H	4	4	1	14	9	4.66	-	-	1	-	28	0	114	1	114.00	1-34	-	
Sunday	4	3	1	13	11 *	6.50	-	-	2	-	19.4	0	139	8	17.37	5-23	1	

Career Performances

	M	Inns	NO	Runs	HS	Avge	100s	50s	Ct	St	Balls	Runs	Wkts	Avge	Best	5wI	10wM
Test																	
All First	88	125	38	1160	69	13.33	-	2	70	-	14806	6633	140	47.37	6-84	4	1
1-day Int																	
NatWest	16	7	3	112	46 *	28.00	-	-	8	-	1024	558	13	42.92	4-22	-	
B & H	42	26	14	113	15	9.41	-	-	17	-	2188	1505	34	44.26	3-9	-	
Sunday	103	50	23	318	27	11.77	-	-	41	-	4147	3327	104	31.99	5-23	2	

BOON, D. C. Durham

Name: David Clarence Boon
Role: Right-hand bat, right-arm medium bowler, county captain
Born: 29 December 1960, Launceston, Tasmania
County debut: 1997
Test debut: 1984-85
Tests: 107
One-Day Internationals: 181
1000 runs in a season: 2
1st-Class 50s: 105
1st-Class 100s: 64
1st-Class 200s: 3
1st-Class catches: 267
One-Day 100s: 6
Place in batting averages: 36th av. 40.96 (1997 51st av. 42.37)
Strike rate: 172.00 (career 86.38)
Off-season: Playing for Tasmania
Overseas teams played for: Tasmania, 1978 –
Overseas tours: Young Australia to Zimbabwe 1982-83; Australia to England 1985, 1989 and 1993, to New Zealand 1985-86, 1989-90, 1992-93, to India 1986-87,

to Pakistan 1988-89, 1994-95, to West Indies 1990-91, 1994-95, to Sri Lanka 1992-93, to South Africa 1993-94, to India and Pakistan (World Cup) 1986-87

Extras: With Geoff Marsh, formed Australia's most successful opening pair since Bill Lawry and Bobby Simpson. Dropped from the Test series for poor form against England in 1986-87, he came back to win the International Cricketer of the Year the following season. Was the leading run-scorer in the series against West Indies 1988-89, and followed that with a successful tour of England in 1989. Made his highest Test score against New Zealand at Perth in 1989-90, but had the rest of the season ruined by a knee injury. Recovered to score over 500 runs in successive series against England and India, now batting at No. 3. Returned to opening against the West Indies in 1991-92, scoring 490 runs at an average of over 60. Also one of the world's finest close to the wicket fieldsmen. Retired from Test cricket in 1995-96. Agreed to play for Gloucestershire in the 1995 season, but withdrew through injury and his overseas berth was taken by Javagal Srinath. Joined Durham as captain for the 1997 season

Best batting: 227 Tasmania v Victoria, Melbourne 1983-84

Best bowling: 2-18 Durham v Kent, Darlington 1997

1998 Season

	M	Inns	NO	Runs	HS	Avge	100s	50s	Ct	St	O	M	Runs	Wkts	Avge	Best	5wl	10wM
Test																		
All First	16	29	4	1024	139*	40.96	3	5	12	-	28.4	8	113	1	113.00	1-33	-	-
1-day Int																		
NatWest	2	2	1	109	80*	109.00	-	1	-	-								
B & H	4	4	0	54	31	13.50	-	-	2	-								
Sunday	12	11	0	241	76	21.90	-	1	5	-	8	0	44	2	22.00	2-44	-	

Career Performances

	M	Inns	NO	Runs	HS	Avge	100s	50s	Ct	St	Balls	Runs	Wkts	Avge	Best	5wl	10wM
Test	107	190	20	7422	200	43.65	21	32	99	-	36	14	0	-		-	-
All First	324	543	50	22314	227	45.26	67	105	267	-	1123	682	13	52.46	2-18	-	-
1-day Int	181	177	16	5964	122	37.04	5	37	45	-	82	86	0	-		-	-
NatWest	3	3	1	166	80*	83.00	-	2	1	-							
B & H	8	7	1	225	103	37.50	1	1	3	-							
Sunday	28	27	3	689	76	28.70	-	3	8	-	90	90	2	45.00	2-44	-	

BOSWELL, S. A. J.   Leicestershire

Name: Scott Antony John Boswell
Role: Right-hand bat, right-arm
fast-medium bowler
Born: 11 September 1974, Fulford, York
Height: 6ft 4in **Weight:** 14st 2lbs
Nickname: Bossy, Joey, Grandad
County debut: 1995 (one-day),
1996 (first-class)
1st-Class 5 w. in innings: 1
1st-Class catches: 2
Place in batting averages:
(1997 268th av. 13.55)
Place in bowling averages:
(1997 137th av. 51.26)
Strike rate: (career 70.77)
Parents: Tony and Judy
Marital status: Single
Education: Ebor Prep School; Pocklington
School; Wolverhampton University
('Wolly Poly')
Qualifications: 9 GCSEs, 3 A-levels 'and hopefully BSc (Hons) in Sports Studies'
Career outside cricket: Studying
Off-season: Hopefully playing in Australia or studying Sports Therapy for
four months
Overseas tours: Northamptonshire to Zimbabwe 1998
Overseas teams played for: Hutt Valley, New Zealand 1994-95; Koeburg CC,
South Africa 1997-98
Cricketers particularly admired: Richard Hadlee ('for his dedication')
Young players to look out for: Graeme Swann, Mike Davies
Other sports played: Rugby ('toured Zimbabwe in '92 with school')
Other sports followed: Football (York City), rugby (York)
Relaxations: Watching TV, socialising and spending time with friends
Extras: Attended Dennis Lillee's Pace Foundation in India 1996. Released by
Northamptonshire at end of 1998 season and has joined Leicestershire for 1999
Opinions on cricket: 'Read my dissertation!'
Best batting: 35 Northamptonshire v Leicestershire, Northampton 1997
Best bowling: 5-94 Northamptonshire v Worcestershire, Northampton 1997

1998 Season

	M	Inns	NO	Runs	HS	Avge	100s	50s	Ct	St	O	M	Runs	Wkts	Avge	Best	5wI	10wM
Test																		
All First	1	0	0	0	0	-	-	-	-	-								
1-day Int																		
NatWest																		
B & H																		
Sunday																		

Career Performances

	M	Inns	NO	Runs	HS	Avge	100s	50s	Ct	St	Balls	Runs	Wkts	Avge	Best	5wI	10wM
Test																	
All First	13	16	5	127	35	11.54	-	-	4	-	1557	1012	22	46.00	5-94	1	-
1-day Int																	
NatWest																	
B & H	10	6	1	24	14	4.80	-	-	1	-	536	485	6	80.83	3-39	-	
Sunday	4	1	0	2	2	2.00	-	-	-	-	138	104	3	34.66	1-20	-	

BOWEN, M. N. Nottinghamshire

Name: Mark Nicholas Bowen
Role: Right-hand bat, right-arm
medium bowler
Born: 6 December 1967, Redcar
Height: 6ft 1in **Weight:** 13st
Nickname: Jim
County debut: 1991-92 (Northamptonshire),
1996 (Nottinghamshire)
1st-Class 5 w. in innings: 6
1st-Class 10 w. in match: 1
1st-Class catches: 13
Place in batting averages: 215th av. 17.75
(1997 280th av. 11.15)
Place in bowling averages: 71st av. 28.22
(1997 94th av. 34.00)
Strike rate: 59.83 (career 63.45)
Parents: Keith
Wife and date of marriage:
Lesley, 11 October 1997
Family links with cricket: 'Father always keen player and watcher'
Education: St Mary's, Redcar; Sacred Heart, Redcar; Teesside Polytechnic
Qualifications: 8 O-levels, 3 A-levels, BSc (Hons) in Chemical Engineering

Career outside cricket: Chemical engineer
Off-season: Working at BNFL Sellafield
Overseas tours: Northamptonshire to Durban 1992, to Cape Town 1993; Christians in Sport to Zimbabwe 1994-95; Nottinghamshire CCC to Johannesburg 1997
Cricketers particularly admired: Richard Hadlee, Dennis Lillee, Viv Richards, Graham Gooch, Malcolm Marshall
Young players to look out for: Paul Franks, Andy Oram
Other sports followed: Football (Middlesbrough FC), golf, hockey (played for Durham County)
Relaxations: 'Keeping fit, watching television and a good pint of ale'
Extras: Made debut for Northants first team in Natal on 1991-92 tour to South Africa before playing in the 2nd XI. Released by Northamptonshire at the end of the 1995 season and joined Nottinghamshire for the start of the 1996 season
Best batting: 32 Nottinghamshire v Northamptonshire, Northampton 1997
Best bowling: 7-73 Nottinghamshire v Somerset, Taunton 1998

1998 Season

	M	Inns	NO	Runs	HS	Avge	100s	50s	Ct	St	O	M	Runs	Wkts	Avge	Best	5wl	10wM
Test																		
All First	10	13	5	142	32	17.75	-	-	2	-	309.1	76	875	31	28.22	7-73	1	-
1-day Int																		
NatWest																		
B & H	4	2	1	10	9	10.00	-	-	-	-	34.1	3	155	4	38.75	2-40	-	
Sunday	3	1	1	0	0*	-	-	-	1	-	20	2	95	6	15.83	4-35	-	

Career Performances

	M	Inns	NO	Runs	HS	Avge	100s	50s	Ct	St	Balls	Runs	Wkts	Avge	Best	5wl	10wM
Test																	
All First	52	65	18	604	32	12.85	-	-	13	-	9011	4845	142	34.11	7-73	6	1
1-day Int																	
NatWest	3	2	2	8	8*	-	-	-	1	-	126	97	3	32.33	3-38	-	
B & H	5	3	1	10	9	5.00	-	-	-	-	265	194	5	38.80	2-40	-	
Sunday	48	21	11	182	27*	18.20	-	-	10	-	1850	1643	53	31.00	4-29	-	

BOWLER, P. D.   Somerset

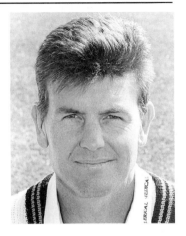

Name: Peter Duncan Bowler
Role: Right-hand opening bat, occasional
off-spin bowler, occasional wicket-keeper
Born: 30 July 1963, Plymouth
Height: 6ft 2in **Weight:** 13st 10lbs
Nickname: Tom
County debut: 1986 (Leicestershire),
1988 (Derbyshire), 1995 (Somerset)
County cap: 1989 (Derbyshire),
1995 (Somerset)
1000 runs in a season: 8
1st-Class 50s: 78
1st-Class 100s: 28
1st-Class 200s: 3
1st-Class catches: 158
1st-Class stumpings: 1
One-Day 100s: 5
Place in batting averages: 132nd av. 26.30
(1997 144th av. 26.64)
Strike rate: 47.75 (career 101.70)
Parents: Peter and Etta
Wife and date of marriage: Joanne, 10 October 1992
Children: Peter Robert, 21 September 1993; Rebekah, 25 August 1995
Education: Scots College, Sydney, Australia; Daramalan College, Canberra, Australia;
Nottingham Trent University
Qualifications: Australian Year 12 certificate, LLB
Cricketers particularly admired: Gus Valence, Rob Jeffery, Bill Carracher,
Phil Russell
Young players to look out for: Matthew Bulbeck, Nick Boulton
Other sports followed: Rugby union
Relaxations: Family and reading
Extras: First Leicestershire player to score a first-class century on debut (100* v
Hampshire 1986). Moved to Derbyshire at end of 1987 season and scored a hundred
on his debut v Cambridge University in 1988. First batsman to 2000 runs in 1992,
finishing equal leading run-scorer (2044) with Mike Roseberry of Middlesex.
Derbyshire Player of the Year 1992. Signed a five-year contract with Somerset starting
in 1995. Took over the Somerset captaincy mid-season 1997 after Andy Hayhurst was
released. Relinquished captaincy after 1998 season
Best batting: 241* Derbyshire v Hampshire, Portsmouth 1992
Best bowling: 3-25 Somerset v Northamptonshire, Taunton 1998

1998 Season

	M	Inns	NO	Runs	HS	Avge	100s	50s	Ct	St	O	M	Runs	Wkts	Avge	Best	5wI	10wM
Test																		
All First	18	32	2	789	104	26.30	2	3	18	-	31.5	7	96	4	24.00	3-25	-	-
1-day Int																		
NatWest	1	1	0	43	43	43.00	-	-	2	-								
B & H	4	4	0	85	41	21.25	-	-	-	-								
Sunday	13	13	2	190	50	17.27	-	1	5	-	4	0	30	0	-		-	-

Career Performances

	M	Inns	NO	Runs	HS	Avge	100s	50s	Ct	St	Balls	Runs	Wkts	Avge	Best	5wI	10wM
Test																	
All First	230	400	35	14227	241 *	38.97	31	78	158	1	3153	1997	31	64.41	3-25	-	-
1-day Int																	
NatWest	19	19	0	553	111	29.10	1	3	10	-	36	26	0	-		-	-
B & H	50	49	1	1449	109	30.18	2	11	21	1	309	182	5	36.40	1-15	-	
Sunday	171	166	19	4890	138 *	33.26	2	39	67	1	308	323	8	40.37	3-31	-	

BRIMSON, M. T.   Leicestershire

Name: Matthew Thomas Brimson
Role: Right-hand bat, slow left-arm bowler
Born: 1 December 1970, Plumstead, London
Height: 6ft **Weight:** 11st 7lbs
Nickname: Brimmo, Doogie
County debut: 1993
County cap: 1998
1st-Class 50s: 1
1st-Class 5 w. in innings: 2
1st-Class catches: 9
Place in batting averages: 248th av. 14.37
Place in bowling averages: 65th av. 27.30
(1997 124th av. 41.00)
Strike rate: 67.24 (career 71.17)
Parents: David and Jennifer
Wife and date of marriage:
Lyn, 29 December 1993
Children: Poppy Lilian, 14 July 1996
Family links with cricket: Brother played a
bit in Kent League and South Thames League
Education: St Joseph's Preparatory School, Blackheath; Chislehurst and Sidcup
Grammar School, Sidcup; Van Mildert College, Durham University

Qualifications: 8 O-levels, 3 A-levels, BA (Hons) Geography, senior cricket coaching award
Career outside cricket: 'Student at the moment'
Off-season: PGCE (teacher training) in Geography at Leicester University
Overseas tours: Kent Schools U17 to Singapore and New Zealand 1987-88; Leicestershire to Bloemfontein 1994 and 1995, to Potchefstroom 1996, to Durban 1997, to Barbados 1998, to Sri Lanka 1999
Cricketers particularly admired: Derek Underwood, Colin Bridge and Chris Bangay
Other sports played: Golf and tennis
Other sports followed: Football (Charlton Athletic)
Injuries: Out for one championship game with 'slight tendon problem in left arm'
Relaxations: 'Family life is great'
Extras: Was on the Kent staff in 1991, Rapidline 2nd XI Player of the Month, July 1995, Leicestershire CCC Player of the Month, June 1998. Awarded county cap 1998
Opinions on cricket: 'There should be two divisions in championship cricket to increase public interest in the four-day game. There should be four-day cricket on good pitches for the 2nd XI games.'
Best batting: 54* Leicestershire v Warwickshire, Edgbaston 1998
Best bowling: 5-12 Leicestershire v Sussex, Leicester 1996

1998 Season

	M	Inns	NO	Runs	HS	Avge	100s	50s	Ct	St	O	M	Runs	Wkts	Avge	Best	5wI	10wM
Test																		
All First	18	14	6	115	54 *	14.37	-	1	3	-	369.5	129	901	33	27.30	4-4	-	-
1-day Int																		
NatWest	3	0	0	0	0	-	-	-	-	-	30	3	87	1	87.00	1-29	-	
B & H	3	1	0	0	0	0.00	-	-	2	-	12	0	56	1	56.00	1-43	-	
Sunday	8	2	2	1	1 *	-	-	-	2	-	52.3	3	216	11	19.63	3-23	-	

Career Performances

	M	Inns	NO	Runs	HS	Avge	100s	50s	Ct	St	Balls	Runs	Wkts	Avge	Best	5wI	10wM
Test																	
All First	52	50	21	332	54 *	11.44	-	1	9	-	7117	3285	100	32.85	5-12	2	-
1-day Int																	
NatWest	5	1	0	9	9	9.00	-	-	-	-	316	137	6	22.83	3-34	-	
B & H	9	2	0	0	0	0.00	-	-	3	-	419	298	8	37.25	2-36	-	
Sunday	20	4	4	17	12 *	-	-	-	4	-	807	599	24	24.95	3-23	-	

BRINKLEY, J. E. — Essex

Name: James Edward Brinkley
Role: Right-hand bat, right-arm fast-medium bowler
Born: 13 March 1974, Helensburgh, Scotland
Height: 6ft 3in **Weight:** 14st
Nickname: JB
County debut: 1993-94 (Worcestershire), 1998 (one-day, Essex)
1st-Class catches: 5
1st-Class 5 w. in innings: 2
Strike rate: (career 65.56)
Parents: Tom and Sharon
Wife and date of marriage:
Kim, 11 October 1997
Family links with cricket: Father played service cricket in the Royal Navy; brother captained Worcester University cricket team

Education: Marist College, Canberra; Trinity College, Perth; Manchester Metropolitan University (currently studying PCA-sponsored Sports Science degree)
Qualifications: Western Australia Tertiary Entrance Examinations, Certificate of Fitness Instruction and Gym Management; Level 1 cricket coach
Career outside cricket: Student and PE teacher
Off-season: Coaching at The Grange and RGS Worcester
Overseas tours: Worcestershire to Zimbabwe 1993-94, to Barbados 1996; Scotland to Kuala Lumpur (Commonwealth Games) 1998, to Sharjah 1999
Overseas teams played for: Scarborough, Perth 1990-93; Western Australian U19 1993; Matabeleland, Zimbabwe 1994-95
Cricketers particularly admired: Michael Holding, Courtney Walsh, Ian Botham, Mark Ramprakash
Other sports played: Rugby union (Worcester RFC; sabbatical for 1998-99 season), golf
Other sports followed: Rugby union (Worcester RFC), golf
Relaxations: Watching videos and movies, golf
Extras: Took a hat-trick in both the 2nd XI Championship and the Bain Clarkson Trophy, against Surrey and Somerset respectively. Made first-class debut on Worcestershire tour of Zimbabwe 1993-94. Took 6-98 (the top six) for Worcestershire v Surrey at The Oval 1994 on County Championship debut. Coached Zimbabwe U19 in South African provincial Coca Cola Cup 1994. Represented Scotland in Commonwealth Games, Kuala Lumpur 1998. Joined Essex for part of 1998 season and was released at end of season. Selected for 1999 Scotland World Cup squad

Opinions on cricket: 'Staff numbers should be reduced to a first-team squad of 16-17 players, thereby increasing the amount of money that can be paid to the players over a 12-month period; the current 2nd XI championship should be scrapped and become regional to close the gap in standard between first-class and 2nd XI cricket.'
Best batting: 29 Matabeleland v Mashonaland U24, Harare 1994-95
Best bowling: 6-35 Matabeleland v Mashonaland Country Districts, Harare South 1994-95

1998 Season

	M	Inns	NO	Runs	HS	Avge	100s	50s	Ct	St	O	M	Runs	Wkts	Avge	Best	5wI	10wM
Test																		
All First																		
1-day Int																		
NatWest																		
B & H	4	4	1	38	30 *	12.66	-	-	-	-	38.3	6	135	4	33.75	1-26	-	
Sunday	1	1	1	0	0 *	-	-	-	-	-	6	0	35	0	-	-	-	

Career Performances

	M	Inns	NO	Runs	HS	Avge	100s	50s	Ct	St	Balls	Runs	Wkts	Avge	Best	5wI	10wM
Test																	
All First	14	16	4	89	29	7.41	-	-	5	-	2229	1115	34	32.79	6-35	2	-
1-day Int																	
NatWest																	
B & H	11	6	3	45	30 *	15.00	-	-	-	-	518	393	11	35.72	2-35	-	
Sunday	5	3	1	7	7	3.50	-	-	-	-	174	141	3	47.00	2-26	-	

4. Who has taken the only World Cup hat-trick?

FICA

BROADHURST, M. — Kent

Name: Mark Broadhurst
Role: Right-hand bat, right-arm medium-fast bowler
Born: 20 June 1974, Barnsley
Height: 6ft **Weight:** 12st
Nickname: Broady
County debut: 1991 (Yorkshire), 1996 (Nottinghamshire)
1st-Class catches: 1
Strike rate: (career 65.28)
Parents: Robert and Pamela
Marital status: Single
Family links with cricket: 'Dad played local league in Barnsley'
Education: Worsborough Common Junior School, Barnsley; Kingstone School, Barnsley
Qualifications: 8 GCSEs, City & Guilds
Career outside cricket: 'Worked in warehouse for Empire Stores for last two years'
Off-season: 'Working in warehouse until season starts. Touring Ibiza, visiting Canada, watching Barnsley FC ("Come on you Reds")'
Overseas tours: England U18 to Canada 1991; England YC to New Zealand 1990-91; England U19 to India 1992-93; Yorkshire to South Africa 1993
Cricketers particularly admired: Allan Donald, Darren Gough, Dennis Lillee
Young players to look out for: Steve Harmison, Usman Afzaal, Guy Welton
Other sports played: Football, snowboarding ('Banff, Canada 1998'), taekwondo
Other sports followed: Football (Barnsley FC; 'season-ticket holder – it's just like watching Brazil')
Injuries: Out for two weeks with inflamed Achilles tendon
Relaxations: Reading, watching snowboard videos, 'as many holidays as possible'
Extras: At age 16 made Yorkshire debut and was picked for England U19. Represented England U19 against Australia in 1991, against Sri Lanka in 1992 and against West Indies in 1993. Has joined Kent for 1999
Opinions on cricket: 'Too many counties discarding young players with no regard for their future.'
Best batting: 6 Yorkshire v Oxford University, The Parks 1994
Best bowling: 3-61 Yorkshire v Oxford University, The Parks 1991

1998 Season (did not make any first-class or one-day appearances)

Career Performances

	M	Inns	NO	Runs	HS	Avge	100s	50s	Ct	St	Balls	Runs	Wkts	Avge	Best	5wI	10wM
Test																	
All First	6	3	0	7	6	2.33	-	-	1	-	457	291	7	41.57	3-61	-	-
1-day Int																	
NatWest																		
B & H																		
Sunday	1	0	0	0	0	-	-	-	-	-	48	27	0	-	-	-	-

BROWN, A. D. Surrey

Name: Alistair Duncan Brown
Role: Right-hand bat, off-spin bowler
Born: 11 February 1970, Beckenham
Height: 5ft 10in **Weight:** 13st
Nickname: Lordy
County debut: 1992
One-Day Internationals: 12
1000 runs in a season: 4
1st-Class 50s: 29
1st-Class 100s: 18
1st-Class catches: 112
One-Day 100s: 9
One-Day 200s: 1
Place in batting averages: 15th av. 49.33
(1997 50th av. 42.40)
Parents: Robert and Ann
Wife and date of marriage:
Sarah, 10 October 1998
Family links with cricket: Father played for
Surrey Young Amateurs in the 1950s
Education: Cumnor House School; Caterham School; 'David Ward's card school for
the technically gifted'
Qualifications: 5 O-levels, NCA Senior Coach
Career outside cricket: 'Actor, thespian and all round good egg'
Off-season: Gardening 'whilst pining for a missed World Cup place'
Overseas tours: England Six-a-side to Singapore 1993, 1994, 1995, to Hong Kong
1997; England to Sharjah 1997-98 (Champions Trophy), to Bangladesh (Wills
International Cup) 1998-99
Overseas teams played for: North Perth, Western Australia 1989-90

Cricketers particularly admired: Ian Botham, Viv Richards

Players to look out for: 'Graeme Thorpe and Darren Bicknell, who I couldn't find anywhere last year'

Other sports played: Golf, football, snooker, 'winner of the Lanzarote Open Pool Championship 1990'

Other sports followed: Football (West Ham United), rugby league (London Broncos)

Injuries: Cracked finger and stress fracture of the shin ('and shoulder injury from propping up AXA all year')

Relaxations: 'Watching Jason Ratcliffe play football and Nadeem Shahid comb his hair'

Extras: Scored three of the eight fastest centuries of the 1992 season (71, 78 & 79 balls). Awarded Man of the Match for 118 against India in the third One-Day International 1996. Played for England in the 1997 Hong Kong Sixes competition in which England finished runners-up to Pakistan. Recorded the highest-ever score in the Sunday League with 203 off 119 balls against Hampshire at Guildford in 1997 and received an individual award at the PCA Dinner for that achievement. Scored 72-ball 100 v Northamptonshire to become joint winner (with Carl Hooper) of the EDS Walter Lawrence Trophy for the fastest first-class 100 of the 1998 season. Scored 31-ball 50 v South Africa in the Texaco Trophy match at Headingley 1998, the fastest 50 in the history of the Texaco Trophy; his score of 59 won him the Man of the Match award

Opinions on cricket: 'Missed a big opportunity for two divisions in Championship last year. Still too much cricket. Floodlights were a success in AXA – Surrey were not!'

Best batting: 187 Surrey v Gloucestershire, The Oval 1995

1998 Season

	M	Inns	NO	Runs	HS	Avge	100s	50s	Ct	St	0	M	Runs	Wkts	Avge	Best	5wl	10wM
Test																		
All First	15	22	1	1036	155	49.33	4	6	20	-	2	1	2	0	-	-	-	-
1-day Int	5	5	0	102	59	20.40	-	1	2	-								
NatWest	3	3	0	29	29	9.66	-	-	-	-								
B & H	7	7	0	256	74	36.57	-	1	1	-								
Sunday	15	14	0	209	30	14.92	-	-	6	-								

Career Performances

	M	Inns	NO	Runs	HS	Avge	100s	50s	Ct	St	Balls	Runs	Wkts	Avge	Best	5wl	10wM
Test																	
All First	108	172	15	6664	187	42.44	18	29	112	-	336	178	0	-	-	-	-
1-day Int	12	12	0	327	118	27.25	1	1	4	-							
NatWest	18	15	1	406	72	29.00	-	2	3	-							
B & H	37	37	6	1243	117 *	40.09	1	6	10	-							
Sunday	122	117	4	3628	203	32.10	8	15	32	-							

BROWN, D. R.   Warwickshire

Name: Douglas Robert Brown
Role: Right-hand bat, right-arm
fast-medium bowler
Born: 29 October 1969, Stirling, Scotland
Height: 6ft 2in **Weight:** 14st 2lbs
Nickname: Bullets, Hoots
County debut: 1992
County cap: 1995
50 wickets in a season: 2
1st-Class 50s: 17
1st-Class 5 w. in innings: 10
1st-Class 10 w. in match: 3
1st-Class catches: 44
One-Day 5 w. in innings: 1
Place in batting averages: 101st av. 30.04
(1997 175th av. 24.00)
Place in bowling averages: 83rd av. 29.78
(1997 6th av. 19.25)
Strike rate: 52.60 (career 47.04)
Parents: Alastair and Janette
Wife and date of marriage: Brenda, 2 October 1993
Children: Lauren, 14 September 1998
Education: St John's Primary, Alloa; Alloa Academy; West London Institute of Higher
Education (Borough Road College)
Qualifications: 9 O-Grades, 5 Higher Grades, BEd (Hons) Physical Education,
NCA Advanced Coach
Career outside cricket: PE teacher
Off-season: England tour to Bangladesh
Overseas tours: Scotland XI to Pakistan 1988-89; England VI to Hong Kong 1997;
England A to Kenya and Sri Lanka 1997-98; England to Sharjah (Champions Trophy)
1997-98, to West Indies 1997-98 (one-day series), to Bangladesh (Wills International
Cup) 1998
Overseas teams played for: Primrose, Cape Town 1992-93; Uredenburg Salohana,
Cape Town 1994; Eastern Suburbs, Wellington 1995-96; Wellington, New Zealand
1995-96
Cricketers particularly admired: 'Everyone who gives 100 per cent for the team's
cause'
Young players to look out for: Tony Frost
Other sports played: Golf
Other sports followed: Football (Alloa Athletic), 'most sports'
Injuries: Out for four weeks with broken finger

Relaxations: Golf, music, 'time with Lauren'
Extras: Played football at Hampden Park for Scotland U18. Played first-class and B & H cricket for Scotland in 1989, and played again for Scotland against Ireland in 1992. Played for England in the 1997 Hong Kong Sixes competition in which England finished runners-up to Pakistan. Played for the victorious England side in Sharjah in 1997 and was called up to the England A tour of Kenya and Sri Lanka after the promotion of Chris Silverwood to England's tour of the West Indies following the withdrawal of Darren Gough through injury
Opinions on cricket: 'Still a great game.'
Best batting: 85 Warwickshire v Essex, Ilford 1995
Best bowling: 8-89 First-Class Counties v Pakistan A, Chelmsford 1997

1998 Season

	M	Inns	NO	Runs	HS	Avge	100s	50s	Ct	St	O	M	Runs	Wkts	Avge	Best	5wI	10wM
Test																		
All First	16	27	4	691	81 *	30.04	-	5	9	-	438.2	93	1489	50	29.78	5-40	2	-
1-day Int																		
NatWest	1	1	0	13	13	13.00	-	-	-	-	5	1	5	1	5.00	1-5	-	
B & H	5	4	0	145	60	36.25	-	2	4	-	43	2	163	3	54.33	1-21	-	
Sunday	13	10	2	175	63	21.87	-	1	8	-	74.3	6	335	14	23.92	3-15	-	

Career Performances

	M	Inns	NO	Runs	HS	Avge	100s	50s	Ct	St	Balls	Runs	Wkts	Avge	Best	5wI	10wM
Test																	
All First	82	127	15	2857	85	25.50	-	17	44	-	12091	6418	257	24.97	8-89	10	3
1-day Int	9	8	4	99	21	24.75	-	-	1	-	324	305	7	43.57	2-28	-	
NatWest	12	11	1	229	67	22.90	-	2	1	-	540	344	7	49.14	2-34	-	
B & H	23	17	1	481	62	30.06	-	4	9	-	1161	772	23	33.56	5-31	1	
Sunday	72	62	9	1104	78 *	20.83	-	5	20	-	2244	1713	62	27.62	4-42	-	

BROWN, J. F.   Northamptonshire

Name: Jason Fred Brown
Role: Right-hand bat, off-spin bowler
Born: 10 October 1974, Stoke-on-Trent
Height: 6ft 1in **Weight:** 12st
Nickname: Macey, Brown Fish
County debut: 1996
1st-Class 5 w. in innings: 4
1st-Class 10 w. in match: 1
1st-Class catches: 4
Place in batting averages: 298th av. 3.00

Place in bowling averages: 30th av. 22.00 (1997 84th av. 32.55)
Strike rate: 50.96 (career 57.28)
Parents: Peter and Cynthia
Marital status: Engaged to Samantha
Education: St Margaret Ward RC School
Qualifications: 9 O-levels
Overseas tours: Kidsgrove League U18 to Australia 1991
Cricketers particularly admired:
John Emburey
Other sports followed: Football, golf, snooker
Relaxations: Watching videos and listening to music. Playing and watching all sports, socialising
Extras: Represented Staffordshire at all junior levels and Staffordshire in Minor Counties. Once took 10 for 16 in a Kidsgrove League game against Haslington Under 18 playing for Sandyford Under 18. Played for Staffordshire in the 1995 NatWest competition
Best batting: 16* Northamptonshire v Durham, Northampton 1997
Best bowling: 6-53 Northamptonshire v Somerset, Taunton 1998

1998 Season

	M	Inns	NO	Runs	HS	Avge	100s	50s	Ct	St	O	M	Runs	Wkts	Avge	Best	5wI	10wM
Test																		
All First	8	11	5	18	6 *	3.00	-	-	1	-	280.2	68	726	33	22.00	6-53	4	1
1-day Int																		
NatWest																		
B & H																		
Sunday																		

Career Performances

	M	Inns	NO	Runs	HS	Avge	100s	50s	Ct	St	Balls	Runs	Wkts	Avge	Best	5wI	10wM
Test																	
All First	15	20	10	43	16*	4.30	-	-	4	-	3036	1441	53	27.18	6-53	4	1
1-day Int																	
NatWest	1	0	0	0	0	-	-	-	-	-	72	72	1	72.00	1-72	-	
B & H																	
Sunday	1	0	0	0	0	-	-	-	-	-	42	26	4	6.50	4-26	-	

BROWN, K. R. Middlesex

Name: Keith Robert Brown
Role: Right-hand bat, wicket-keeper
Born: 18 March 1963, Edmonton
Height: 5ft 11in **Weight:** 13st 7lbs
Nickname: Browny, Scarface, Stally
County debut: 1984
County cap: 1990
Benefit: 1998
1000 runs in a season: 2
1st-Class 50s: 56
1st-Class 100s: 12
1st-Class 200s: 1
1st-Class catches: 465
1st-Class stumpings: 33
One-Day 100s: 4
Place in batting averages: 99th av. 30.31
(1997 123rd av. 30.05)
Strike rate: (career 53.50)
Parents: Kenneth William and Margaret Sonia
Wife and date of marriage: Marie, 3 November 1984
Children: Zachary, 24 February 1987; Rosanna, 18 December 1989;
Alex, 29 December 1992
Family links with cricket: Brother Gary was on Middlesex staff for three years and
then played for Durham. Father is a qualified umpire
Education: Chace Comprehensive School, Enfield
Qualifications: French O-level; NCA Senior Coaching Award; qualified plasterer
Career outside cricket: Plasterer, PE instructor, coach
Overseas tours: NCA Youth tour to Denmark; Middlesex to La Manga 1985, 1986,
to Portugal 1991, 1992, 1993
Overseas teams played for: Sydney University, Australia 1988-89; Motueka Cricket
Association, Nelson, New Zealand 1991-92
Cricketers particularly admired: Clive Radley and Derek Randall
Other sports followed: Most sports apart from motor racing
Relaxations: 'Long country walks with family and pet greyhound, finishing with a
couple of pints in local'
Extras: Had promising boxing career but gave it up in order to concentrate on cricket.
Picked to play rugby for Essex. 1996 Middlesex Player of the Year. Retired at the end
of the 1998 season and teaches in Exeter
Opinions on cricket: 'Over-rate fines should be scrapped. Day/night cricket needs to
be more widely introduced to generate a different type of spectator – i.e. people can
come after work and bring their children etc.'

Best batting: 200* Middlesex v Nottinghamshire, Lord's 1990
Best bowling: 2-7 Middlesex v Gloucestershire, Bristol 1987

1998 Season

	M	Inns	NO	Runs	HS	Avge	100s	50s	Ct	St	O	M	Runs	Wkts	Avge	Best	5wI	10wM
Test																		
All First	17	25	6	576	59 *	30.31	-	2	40	5								
1-day Int																		
NatWest	3	2	0	30	26	15.00	-	-	3	1								
B & H	5	5	0	319	114	63.80	2	-	7	1								
Sunday	10	10	0	133	34	13.30	-	-	5	4								

Career Performances

	M	Inns	NO	Runs	HS	Avge	100s	50s	Ct	St	Balls	Runs	Wkts	Avge	Best	5wI	10wM
Test																	
All First	247	373	75	10487	200 *	35.19	13	56	465	33	321	276	6	46.00	2-7	-	-
1-day Int																	
NatWest	27	23	3	566	103 *	28.30	1	1	26	7	6	8	0	-		-	-
B & H	44	41	7	1045	114	30.73	2	2	35	10	6	0	0	-		-	-
Sunday	172	147	41	2938	102	27.71	1	10	106	32	28	29	0	-		-	-

BROWN, M. J. Middlesex

Name: Michael James Brown
Role: Right-hand bat, right-arm medium or
off-spin bowler, occasional wicket-keeper
Born: 9 February 1980, Burnley
Height: 5ft 11in **Weight:** 10st 12lbs
Nickname: Browny
County debut: No first-team appearance
Parents: Peter and Valerie
Marital status: Single
Family links with cricket: Father played for
Burnley CC (Lancashire League)
1968-75 and 1979-98 and Lancashire 2nd XI
1970-72. Also played for Southgate CC
1976-78, winning National Club Knockout in
1977. Brother David plays for Lancashire
Schools U16
Education: Rosehill Junior School, Burnley;
Queen Elizabeth's Grammar School,

Blackburn; Durham University, studying Economics and Politics from October 1999
Qualifications: 10 GCSEs, 4 A-levels
Career outside cricket: 'Not applicable currently but hope to develop business career'
Overseas teams played for: Western Province CC, Cape Town 1998-99
Cricketers particularly admired: Dale Benkenstein, Ricky Ponting, Michael Atherton
Young players to look out for: Mark Chilton, Graeme Swann
Other sports played: Football ('town team level'), golf
Other sports followed: Football (Burnley FC)
Injuries: Out for four weeks with damaged medial collateral ligament
Relaxations: Playing golf and sleeping
Extras: Opened batting for Burnley CC in Lancashire League 1995-98. Lancashire League Under-25 Batsman of the Season 1997, 1998. Represented Lancashire Schools at U11, U13, U15 and U17 level 1989-97. Represented Lancashire U19 Federation 1997-98. Played for Lancashire 2nd XI 1997-98. Represented ECB U19 A v Pakistan U19 in two one-day games 1998
Opinions on cricket: 'We should have a national development academy. Divisionalise county cricket.'

BROWN, S. J. E. Durham

Name: Simon John Emmerson Brown
Role: Right-hand bat, left-arm medium-fast bowler, gully fielder
Born: 29 June 1969, Cleadon Village, Sunderland
Height: 6ft 3in **Weight:** 13st
Nickname: Chubby
County debut: 1987 (Northamptonshire), 1992 (Durham)
Test debut: 1996
Tests: 1
50 wickets in a season: 5
1st-Class 50s: 2
1st-Class 5 w. in innings: 26
1st-Class 10 w. in match: 2
1st-Class catches: 36
One-Day 5 w. in innings: 2
Place in batting averages:
(1997 301st av. 6.36)

Place in bowling averages: (1997 53rd av. 27.68)
Strike rate: 26.57 (career 54.04)
Parents: Ernest and Doreen

Wife and date of marriage: Sarah, 3 October 1992
Education: Boldon Comprehensive, Tyne & Wear; South Tyneside College
Qualifications: 6 O-levels, qualified electrician
Career outside cricket: Electrician
Overseas tours: England YC to Sri Lanka 1986-87, to Australia for Youth World Cup 1987-88; MCC to Bahrain 1994-95
Overseas teams played for: Marist, Christchurch, New Zealand
Cricketers particularly admired: John Lever, Dennis Lillee
Other sports followed: Basketball and golf
Injuries: Out for whole season with leg injury
Relaxations: Playing basketball and golf
Extras: Offered basketball scholarship in America. Durham Supporters' Player of the Year 1992. Durham Player of the Year 1994. Made his Test debut for England against Pakistan at Lord's in 1996
Best batting: 69 Durham v Leicestershire, Durham University 1994
Best bowling: 7-70 Durham v Australians, Durham University 1993

1998 Season

	M	Inns	NO	Runs	HS	Avge	100s	50s	Ct	St	O	M	Runs	Wkts	Avge	Best	5wI	10wM
Test																		
All First	1	0	0	0	0	-	-	-	-	-	31	12	54	7	7.71	6-17	1	-
1-day Int																		
NatWest																			
B & H	1	0	0	0	0	-	-	-	-	-	10	2	28	1	28.00	1-28	-	
Sunday																			

Career Performances

	M	Inns	NO	Runs	HS	Avge	100s	50s	Ct	St	Balls	Runs	Wkts	Avge	Best	5wI	10wM
Test	1	2	1	11	10 *	11.00	-	-	1	-	198	138	2	69.00	1-60	-	-
All First	125	172	50	1490	69	12.21	-	2	36	-	22429	12746	415	30.71	7-70	26	2
1-day Int																	
NatWest	10	6	3	12	7 *	4.00	-	-	1	-	640	450	18	25.00	5-22	1	
B & H	20	8	4	38	12	9.50	-	-	4	-	1091	654	28	23.35	6-30	1	
Sunday	72	34	12	152	18	6.90	-	-	15	-	3099	2586	79	32.73	4-20	-	

FIGA

5. Which English batsman scored 102 v New Zealand at The Oval on 9 June 1983 on his World Cup debut?

BRYAN, R. B.   Middlesex

Name: Russell Barnaby Bryan
Role: Right-hand bat, right-arm medium-fast
bowler
Born: 14 February 1981, Maidstone
Height: 6ft 1in **Weight:** 11st 6lbs
County debut: No first-team appearance
Parents: Ann and Andrew
Marital status: Single
Family links with cricket: 'Father has
played club cricket for 30-odd years and is
still playing'
Education: Shebbear Primary School;
Shebbear College
Qualifications: 10 GCSEs, 1 A/S-level,
currently studying for 3 A-levels
Career outside cricket: Student
Cricketers particularly admired:
Darren Gough, Allan Donald
Other sports played: Football, rugby, squash
Other sports followed: Football (Tottenham Hotspur FC)
Relaxations: Listening to music (Embrace, Oasis). Playing 'Brian Lara Cricket' on
PlayStation
Extras: Represented Devon at U17 and U19 level in teams that reached both Texaco
finals in 1998
Opinions on cricket: 'Needs to be more aggressive, especially in this country.'

BULBECK, M. P.   Somerset

Name: Matthew Paul Bulbeck
Role: Left-hand bat, left-arm medium-fast bowler
Born: 8 November 1979, Taunton
Height: 6ft 4in **Weight:** 12st 10lbs
Nickname: Bully
County debut: 1998
1st-Class catches: 2
Place in bowling averages: 10th av. 19.03
Strike rate: 29.00 (career 29.00)
Parents: Paul and Carolyn
Marital status: Single

Family links with cricket: Father plays for local club. Sister plays women's cricket for same club
Education: Bishops Hall Primary School; Castle School; Taunton School; Richard Huish College
Qualifications: 8 GCSEs
Off-season: Touring with England U19
Overseas tours: West of England U15 to West Indies; Somerset U16 to South Africa; England U19 to New Zealand 1998-99
Cricketers particularly admired: Wasim Akram, Andy Caddick
Young players to look out for: Matthew Gitsham (Somerset U16)
Other sports played: Football (goalkeeper), golf (12 handicap)
Other sports followed: Football (Manchester United), rugby union (Bath RFC)
Injuries: Out for two weeks with side injury; for two weeks with back injury
Relaxations: 'Going out for a drink with Dougie'
Extras: Went to Madras Pace Foundation and was coached by Dennis Lillee and Jeff Thomson in September 1997. Made Somerset debut in 1998
Opinions on cricket: 'Should get longer for tea.'
Best batting: 25 Somerset v Warwickshire, Taunton 1998
Best bowling: 4-40 Somerset v Derbyshire, Taunton 1998

1998 Season

	M	Inns	NO	Runs	HS	Avge	100s	50s	Ct	St	O	M	Runs	Wkts	Avge	Best	5wI	10wM
Test																		
All First	8	11	6	141	35	28.20	-	-	2	-	154.4	28	609	32	19.03	4-40	-	-
1-day Int																		
NatWest																		
B & H																		
Sunday																		

Career Performances

	M	Inns	NO	Runs	HS	Avge	100s	50s	Ct	St	Balls	Runs	Wkts	Avge	Best	5wI	10wM
Test																	
All First	8	11	6	141	35	28.20	-	-	2	-	928	609	32	19.03	4-40	-	-
1-day Int																	
NatWest																	
B & H																	
Sunday																	

BURNS, M.   Somerset

Name: Michael Burns
Role: Right-hand bat, right-arm medium
bowler, occasional wicket-keeper
Born: 6 February 1969, Barrow-in-Furness
Height: 6ft **Weight:** 13st
Nickname: George
County debut: 1991 (Warwickshire),
1997 (Somerset)
1st-Class 50s: 11
1st-Class catches: 64
1st-Class stumpings: 7
One-Day 100s: 1
Place in batting averages: 129th av. 26.47
(1997 156th av. 25.50)
Strike rate: (career 96.00)
Parents: Robert and Linda, stepfather Stan
Wife and date of marriage:
Carolyn, 9 October 1994
Children: Elizabeth, 12 January 1997
Family links with cricket: 'Grandfather was a great back-garden bowler'
Education: Walney Comprehensive; Barrow College of Further Education
Qualifications: 'Few CSEs, couple of GCEs', qualified fitter at VSEL in Barrow,
coaching award
Career outside cricket: 'Open to offers'
Off-season: Working in club office
Overseas teams played for: Gill College, South Africa 1991-92; Motueka, Nelson,
New Zealand 1992-93; Alex CC, Harare
Cricketers particularly admired: Andy Caddick, Allan Donald
Young players to look out for: Matthew Bulbeck
Other sports played/followed: Rugby league ('had trials for Barrow RLFC and
Carlisle RLFC') and golf
Relaxations: Golf, food. 'Just bought a new house, so a little bit of DIY'
Extras: Played for Cumberland 1989-90. Had a trial with Glamorgan, went to La
Manga with Lancashire junior side 1984. Player of the Tournament at Benson and
Hedges Thailand International Cricket Sixes in 1989. Left Warwickshire and joined
Somerset for the 1997 season
Opinions on cricket: 'I think the national one-day league should be 50-overs per side
to stay in line with one-day internationals.'
Best batting: 96 Somerset v Gloucestershire, Bristol 1998
Best bowling: 2-18 Somerset v Kent, Taunton 1997

1998 Season

	M	Inns	NO	Runs	HS	Avge	100s	50s	Ct	St	O	M	Runs	Wkts	Avge	Best	5wI	10wM
Test																		
All First	10	17	0	450	96	26.47	-	3	15	1	8	1	52	0	-	-	-	-
1-day Int																		
NatWest	2	2	1	113	84 *	113.00	-	1	2	-								
B & H	4	4	0	175	95	43.75	-	2	1	-	3	0	30	2	15.00	1-15	-	
Sunday	16	16	1	309	84 *	20.60	-	2	4	1	26	1	146	4	36.50	1-11	-	

Career Performances

	M	Inns	NO	Runs	HS	Avge	100s	50s	Ct	St	Balls	Runs	Wkts	Avge	Best	5wI	10wM
Test																	
All First	44	72	3	1600	96	23.18	-	11	64	7	480	339	5	67.80	2-18	-	-
1-day Int																	
NatWest	6	6	2	159	84 *	39.75	-	1	2	-	36	27	0	-	-	-	-
B & H	17	15	0	486	95	32.40	-	5	7	2	148	125	7	17.85	3-18	-	
Sunday	62	56	6	1008	115 *	20.16	1	4	37	9	505	470	17	27.64	4-39	-	

BUTCHER, A. R. Surrey

Name: Alan Raymond Butcher
Role: Left-hand bat, slow left-arm or left-arm medium bowler
Born: 7 January 1954, Croydon
Height: 5ft 9in **Weight:** 12st 7lbs
Nickname: Butch, Bouché ('in a flamboyantly French moment from Phil Tufnell')
County debut: 1972 (Surrey), 1987 (Glamorgan)
County cap: 1975 (Surrey), 1987 (Glamorgan)
Benefit: 1985
Test debut: 1979
Tests: 1
One-Day Internationals: 1
1000 runs in a season: 12
1st-Class 50s: 123
1st-Class 100s: 45
1st-Class 200s: 1
1st-Class 5 w. in innings: 1
1st-Class catches: 185

One-Day 100s: 6
Strike rate: (career 71.48)
Parents: Raymond and Jackie
Wife and date of marriage: Madeleine, 29 February 1992
Children: Mark, 23 August 1972; Gary, 11 March 1975; Lisa, 29 July 1979
Family links with cricket: Brother Martin played for MCC Young Professionals.
Brother Ian played for Leicestershire and Gloucestershire. Son Mark plays for Surrey
and England. Son Gary played for Glamorgan and now plays for Surrey
Education: Heath Clark GS
Qualifications: 5 O-levels, 1 A-level
Overseas tours: England Schools to India 1971; Rest of the World (nominally) to
Jamaica; England XI (nominally) to Calcutta
Other sports followed: Football
Relaxations: Reading, writing, music, food, wine, real ale
Extras: Released by Surrey at end of 1986 season. Joined Glamorgan in 1987. First
Englishman to score 1000 runs in both 1989 and 1990. One of *Wisden*'s five
Cricketers of the Year 1991. Appointed captain of Glamorgan during 1989 after Hugh
Morris resigned in mid-season. Believed to be the first father to play against his son
(Mark) in English county cricket – at least this century (Glamorgan v Surrey,
The Oval, August 1991). Joined Essex for the 1993 season as 2nd XI captain/coach. Is
now Surrey coach, but was called up to play one first-class match in 1998
Best batting: 216* Surrey v Cambridge University, Fenner's 1980
Best bowling: 6-48 Surrey v Hampshire, Guildford 1972

1998 Season

	M	Inns	NO	Runs	HS	Avge	100s	50s	Ct	St	O	M	Runs	Wkts	Avge	Best	5wl	10wM
Test																		
All First	1	2	0	34	22	17.00	-	-	-	-								
1-day Int																		
NatWest																		
B & H																		
Sunday																		

Career Performances

	M	Inns	NO	Runs	HS	Avge	100s	50s	Ct	St	Balls	Runs	Wkts	Avge	Best	5wl	10wM
Test	1	2	0	34	20	17.00	-	-	-	-	12	9	0	-	-	-	-
All First	402	684	60	22665	216 *	36.32	46	123	186	-	10056	5454	141	38.68	6-48	1	-
1-day Int	1	1	0	14	14	14.00	-	-	-	-							
NatWest	38	36	4	1083	104 *	33.84	1	5	12	-	404	249	5	49.80	1-27	-	
B & H	79	74	4	1982	127	28.31	1	15	22	-	1125	603	27	22.33	4-36	-	
Sunday	234	223	26	5478	113 *	27.80	4	35	51	-	2073	1556	38	40.94	5-19	1	

BUTCHER, G. P.   Surrey

Name: Gary Paul Butcher
Role: Right-hand bat, right-arm medium
bowler
Born: 11 March 1975, Clapham,
South London
Height: 5ft 9in **Weight:** 12st 7lbs
Nickname: Butch, Billy
County debut: 1994
1st-Class 50s: 8
1st-Class 100s: 1
1st-Class 5 w. in innings: 1
1st-Class catches: 16
Place in batting averages: 135th av. 25.91
(1997 108th av. 32.88)
Place in bowling averages: 78th av. 29.00
(1997 116th av. 38.83)

Strike rate: 48.21 (career 59.22)
Parents: Alan and Elaine
Marital status: Girlfriend (Roz)
Family links with cricket: Brother Mark plays for Surrey and England. Father Alan
played for Surrey, England, and captained Glamorgan. Uncle Ian played for
Gloucestershire and Leicestershire
Education: Cumnor House; Riddlesdown Comprehensive;
Heath Clark College
Qualifications: 4 GCSEs, BTEC 1st Diploma in Leisure Studies
Career outside cricket: Cricket coach
Off-season: Coaching
Overseas tours: England U18 to Denmark 1993; England U19 to Sri Lanka 1993-94;
Glamorgan to Zimbabwe 1995, to Pretoria 1996, to Jersey 1998
Overseas teams played for: Northern Natal, South Africa 1994-95; Hawksbury CC,
Sydney 1996-97
Cricketers particularly admired: Ian Botham, David Gower, Viv Richards, Malcolm
Marshall, Curtly Ambrose, Mark Waugh, Brian Lara
Young players to look out for: Wayne Law, Simon Jones
Other sports played: Football, golf
Other sports followed: Football (Liverpool FC, England)
Injuries: Out for two weeks with a bruised heel
Relaxations: Playing bass guitar, music, going to the gym, socialising, watching 'Alan
Partridge' videos
Extras: Took wicket with first ball on Sunday League debut 1994. Won Glamorgan's
Most Improved Player Award 1996. Nominated for Best Young Player award 1996.

99

Was part of Glamorgan's Championship-winning side 1997. Released by Glamorgan at end of 1998 season and has joined Surrey for 1999
Best batting: 101* Glamorgan v Oxford University, The Parks 1997
Best bowling: 7-77 Glamorgan v Gloucestershire, Bristol 1996

1998 Season

	M	Inns	NO	Runs	HS	Avge	100s	50s	Ct	St	O	M	Runs	Wkts	Avge	Best	5wI	10wM
Test																		
All First	9	14	2	311	85	25.91	-	2	5	-	152.4	24	551	19	29.00	4-14	-	-
1-day Int																		
NatWest																		
B & H	4	4	1	19	13 *	6.33	-	-	1	-	5	0	36	1	36.00	1-36	-	
Sunday	9	9	1	66	27	8.25	-	-	1	-	22.2	0	170	1	170.00	1-37	-	

Career Performances

	M	Inns	NO	Runs	HS	Avge	100s	50s	Ct	St	Balls	Runs	Wkts	Avge	Best	5wI	10wM
Test																	
All First	40	58	10	1357	101 *	28.27	1	8	16	-	3198	2110	54	39.07	7-77	1	-
1-day Int																	
NatWest	4	3	1	77	48	38.50	-	-	-	-	120	122	4	30.50	2-33	-	
B & H	13	10	3	58	17	8.28	-	-	1	-	199	172	4	43.00	2-21	-	
Sunday	34	26	5	317	47	15.09	-	-	3	-	590	683	15	45.53	4-32	-	

BUTCHER, M. A.   Surrey

Name: Mark Alan Butcher
Role: Left-hand bat, right-arm medium bowler
Born: 23 August 1972, Croydon
Height: 5ft 11in **Weight:** 13st
Nickname: Butch, Baz
County debut: 1991
Test debut: 1997
Tests: 14
1000 runs in a season: 4
1st-Class 50s: 44
1st-Class 100s: 10
1st-Class catches: 106
Place in batting averages: 94th av. 30.90 (1997 114th av. 32.36)
Strike rate: 65.27 (career 64.34)
Parents: Alan and Elaine
Wife and date of marriage: Judy, 4 October 1997
Children: 'One on the way, Jan 1999'

Family links with cricket: Father Alan played for Glamorgan, Surrey and England and is now coach with Surrey; brother Gary played for Glamorgan and is now with Surrey; uncle Ian played for Gloucestershire and Leicestershire

Education: Cumnor House School; Trinity School; Archbishop Tenison's, Croydon

Qualifications: 5 O-levels, senior coaching award

Career outside cricket: Singer, guitar player, female impersonator

Off-season: Touring Australia with England

Overseas tours: England YC to New Zealand 1990-91; Surrey to Dubai 1990 and 1993, to Perth 1995; England A to Australia 1996-97; England to West Indies 1997-98, to Australia 1998-99

Overseas teams played for: South Melbourne, Australia 1993-94; North Perth 1994-95

Cricketers particularly admired: Ian Botham, David Gower, Viv Richards, Larry Gomes, Graham Thorpe, Alec Stewart, Michael Holding

Other sports followed: Football (Crystal Palace)

Injuries: Out for one month with broken thumb

Relaxations: Music, playing the guitar, novels, wine

Extras: Played his first game for Surrey against his father's Glamorgan in the Refuge Assurance League at The Oval, the first-ever match of any sort between first-class counties in which a father and son have been in opposition. Made his maiden Test century v South Africa at Headingley in 1998, earning the Man of the Match award

Opinions on cricket: 'I feel that we are still miles behind in our domestic structure, in terms of producing Test cricketers. People have to succeed in spite of our system. Four-day games are constantly over in two and a half days because home teams understandably use their home advantage. Until surfaces are made to some specification that is centrally controlled, the situation will get worse. You can't produce great cricketers on crap surfaces.'

Best batting: 167 Surrey v Durham, The Oval 1995

Best bowling: 4-31 Surrey v Worcestershire, The Oval 1994

FIGA

6. In the 1979 World Cup, one country boasted a Chappell, a Marshall, a Javed and a Patel. Which country?

1998 Season

	M	Inns	NO	Runs	HS	Avge	100s	50s	Ct	St	O	M	Runs	Wkts	Avge	Best	5wl	10wM
Test	4	8	0	363	116	45.37	1	2	1	-	25	7	53	0	-		-	-
All First	16	26	1	1024	116	40.96	3	6	11	-	119.4	29	340	11	30.90	4-41	-	-
1-day Int																		
NatWest	1	1	0	8	8	8.00	-	-	1	-								
B & H	7	7	1	177	67	29.50	-	1	3	-	17.5	1	90	1	90.00	1-30	-	
Sunday	9	8	2	116	85 *	19.33	-	1	4	-	26	1	124	7	17.71	2-34	-	

Career Performances

	M	Inns	NO	Runs	HS	Avge	100s	50s	Ct	St	Balls	Runs	Wkts	Avge	Best	5wl	10wM
Test	14	27	1	742	116	28.53	1	4	13	-	192	83	0	-		-	-
All First	101	177	13	6280	167	38.29	10	44	106	-	5083	2857	79	36.16	4-31	-	-
1-day Int																	
NatWest	11	11	2	378	91	42.00	-	3	7	-	216	127	3	42.33	2-57	-	
B & H	22	18	4	364	67	26.00	-	1	7	-	450	381	7	54.42	3-37	-	
Sunday	61	48	13	798	85 *	22.80	-	3	21	-	1537	1429	35	40.82	3-23	-	

BYAS, D.   Yorkshire

Name: David Byas
Role: Left-hand bat, right-arm medium
bowler, county captain
Born: 26 August 1963, Middledale, Kilham
Height: 6ft 4in **Weight:** 14st 7lbs
Nickname: Bingo, Gadgett
County debut: 1986
County cap: 1991
1000 runs in a season: 5
1st-Class 50s: 67
1st-Class 100s: 23
1st-Class 200s: 1
1st-Class catches: 267
One-Day 100s: 4
Place in batting averages: 91st av. 31.18
(1997 31st av. 45.48)
Strike rate: (career 91.00)
Parents: Richard and Anne
Wife and date of marriage:
Rachael Elizabeth, 27 October 1990
Children: Olivia Rachael, 16 December 1991; Georgia Elizabeth, 30 December 1993;
Benjamin, 1997

Family links with cricket: Father played locally
Education: Kilham Primary School; Lisvane School, Scarborough;
Scarborough College
Qualifications: 1 O-level (Engineering)
Career outside cricket: Partner in family farming business
Off-season: Farming
Overseas teams played for: Papatoetoe, Auckland 1988
Cricketers particularly admired: David Gower, Viv Richards, Ian Botham
Young players to look out for: Matthew Wood, Matthew Hoggard, Ryan Sidebottom,
Ben Hollioake
Other sports played: Hockey
Other sports followed: Most other sports
Relaxations: 'Dining out with my wife. Spending time with my family. Gardening.'
Extras: Became youngest captain (aged 21) of Scarborough CC in 1985. Broke John
Hampshire's Sunday League record with 702 runs in 1994, which had stood since
1976. Runner-up in the Sunday League averages 1994. Played hockey for England
Under 21.
Best batting: 213 Yorkshire v Worcestershire, Scarborough 1995
Best bowling: 3-55 Yorkshire v Derbyshire, Chesterfield 1990

1998 Season

	M	Inns	NO	Runs	HS	Avge	100s	50s	Ct	St	O	M	Runs	Wkts	Avge	Best	5wI	10wM
Test																		
All First	18	28	1	842	116	31.18	4	3	20	-								
1-day Int																		
NatWest	2	2	0	25	14	12.50	-	-	5	-								
B & H	6	6	1	139	52 *	27.80	-	1	3	-								
Sunday	17	16	3	422	86	32.46	-	3	14	-								

Career Performances

	M	Inns	NO	Runs	HS	Avge	100s	50s	Ct	St	Balls	Runs	Wkts	Avge	Best	5wI	10wM
Test																	
All First	218	365	33	12074	213	36.36	24	67	267	-	1092	719	12	59.91	3-55	-	-
1-day Int																	
NatWest	25	23	2	650	73 *	30.95	-	6	17	-	18	23	1	23.00	1-23	-	
B & H	42	39	3	1072	116 *	29.77	1	5	12	-	283	155	5	31.00	2-38	-	
Sunday	173	167	25	4358	111 *	30.69	3	23	58	-	529	463	19	24.36	3-19	-	

CADDICK, A. R.   Somerset

Name: Andrew Richard Caddick
Role: Right-hand bat, right-arm
fast-medium bowler
Born: 21 November 1968, Christchurch,
New Zealand
Height: 6ft 5in **Weight:** 14st 13lbs
Nickname: Des, Shack
County debut: 1991
County cap: 1992
Test debut: 1993
Tests: 21
One-Day Internationals: 9
50 wickets in a season: 5
100 wickets in a season: 1
1st-Class 50s: 5
1st-Class 5 w. in innings: 37
1st-Class 10 w. in match: 11
1st-Class catches: 44
One-Day 5 w. in innings: 3
Place in batting averages: 206th av. 18.94 (1997 229th av. 17.83)
Place in bowling averages: 14th av. 19.82 (1997 44th av. 26.61)
Strike rate: 39.27 (49.21)
Parents: Christopher and Audrey
Wife and date of marriage: Sarah, 27 January 1995
Children: Aston Faye, 24 August 1998
Education: Papanui High School, Christchurch, New Zealand
Qualifications: Qualified plasterer and tiler
Career outside cricket: Plasterer and tiler
Off-season: Building and on standby for Ashes tour
Overseas tours: New Zealand YC to Australia (Youth World Cup) 1987-88, to
England 1988; England A to Australia 1992-93; England to West Indies 1993-94,
to Zimbabwe and New Zealand 1996-97, to West Indies 1997-98
Cricketers particularly admired: Dennis Lillee, Richard Hadlee, Robin Smith,
Jimmy Cook
Young players to look out for: Nasser Hussain, Nick Knight, Marcus Trescothick
Other sports followed: 'Mostly all'
Relaxations: Golf
Extras: Rapid Cricketline Player of the Year 1991. Whyte and Mackay Bowler of the
Year 1997. Took 105 first-class wickets in 1998 season. Has been awarded a benefit
for 1999
Opinions on cricket: 'Batsmen should be warned the same way as bowlers for

running on the wicket. If they continue they should be sent off. It's a batter's game!'
Best batting: 92 Somerset v Worcestershire, Worcester 1995
Best bowling: 9-32 Somerset v Lancashire, Taunton 1993

1998 Season

	M	Inns	NO	Runs	HS	Avge	100s	50s	Ct	St	O	M	Runs	Wkts	Avge	Best	5wI	10wM
Test																		
All First	17	25	8	322	37	18.94	-	-	5	-	687.2	156	2082	105	19.82	8-64	10	3
1-day Int																		
NatWest	2	1	1	2	2 *	-	-	-	-	-	22	6	78	5	15.60	4-63	-	
B & H	4	2	0	10	10	5.00	-	-	1	-	34	2	160	5	32.00	2-25	-	
Sunday	16	6	2	34	16	8.50	-	-	1	-	110	10	507	17	29.82	3-24	-	

Career Performances

	M	Inns	NO	Runs	HS	Avge	100s	50s	Ct	St	Balls	Runs	Wkts	Avge	Best	5wI	10wM
Test	21	33	4	291	29 *	10.03	-	-	8	-	4610	2394	74	32.35	6-65	5	-
All First	128	167	31	2154	92	15.83	-	5	44	-	26725	13959	543	25.70	9-32	37	11
1-day Int	9	5	4	35	20 *	35.00	-	-	2	-	522	398	15	26.53	3-35	-	
NatWest	16	9	3	28	8	4.66	-	-	2	-	980	536	34	15.76	6-30	2	
B & H	21	14	8	124	38	20.66	-	-	4	-	1203	829	30	27.63	5-51	1	
Sunday	74	26	8	226	39	12.55	-	-	13	-	3135	2459	97	25.35	4-18	-	

CAPEL, D. J. Northamptonshire

Name: David John Capel
Role: Right-hand bat, right-arm medium bowler, all-rounder, slip fielder
Born: 6 February 1963, Northampton
Height: 5ft 11in **Weight:** 12st 8lbs
Nickname: Capes, Fiery, Fireball
County debut: 1981
County cap: 1986
Benefit: 1994
Test debut: 1987
Tests: 15
One-Day Internationals: 23
1000 runs in a season: 3
50 wickets in a season: 4
1st-Class 50s: 72
1st-Class 100s: 16
1st-Class 5 w. in innings: 14
1st-Class catches: 156

One-Day 100s: 4
Place in batting averages: (1997 209th av. 20.00)
Strike rate: 78.00 (career 60.56)
Parents: John and Angela
Wife and date of marriage: Deborah Jane, 21 September 1985
Children: Jennifer Anne, 21 October 1987; Jordan David, 18 May 1993
Family links with cricket: Father and brother Andrew both captained
their local league sides. Brother plays for Old Northamptonians
Education: Roade Primary School; Roade Comprehensive School
Qualifications: 3 O-levels, 4 CSEs, NCA advanced coaching certificate
Career outside cricket: About to embark on a new role as full-time Director of
Excellence at Northamptonshire CCC
Overseas tours: England to Sharjah 1986-87, to Pakistan 1987-88, to New Zealand
and Australia 1987-88, to India (Nehru Cup) 1989-90, to West Indies 1989-90;
England A to Australia 1992-93; MCC to Bangladesh 1996
Overseas teams played for: Eastern Province, South Africa 1985-87;
Petersham/Marrickville, Sydney 1991-92
Young players to look out for: Graeme Swann
Other sports followed: Golf and rugby (Northampton RFC)
Injuries: Broken hand and dislocated shoulder, missed a total of 12 weeks
Relaxations: Fishing, listening to music and 'spending time watching family grow up'
Extras: Only second Northampton-born man to play for England. Two centuries in a
match against Sussex 1989. All-Rounder of the Year 'Wetherall Award' 1989. Broke
Northants records for fourth wicket in Sunday League with K.M. Curran and for fifth
wicket in NatWest Trophy with A.J. Lamb. Record Northants CCC benefit of
£192,000. Retired in 1998 and was appointed Northamptonshire's first Director of
Excellence
Best batting: 175 Northamptonshire v Leicestershire, Northampton 1995
Best bowling: 7-44 Northamptonshire v Warwickshire, Edgbaston 1995

1998 Season

	M	Inns	NO	Runs	HS	Avge	100s	50s	Ct	St	O	M	Runs	Wkts	Avge	Best	5wl	10wM
Test																		
All First	2	0	0	0	0	-	-	-	-	-	13	1	66	1	66.00	1-66	-	-
1-day Int																		
NatWest																		
B & H	5	5	0	56	17	11.20	-	-	2	-	15	0	63	2	31.50	1-28	-	
Sunday	6	5	0	43	41	8.60	-	-	1	-	24	0	163	4	40.75	1-28	-	

---

7. Who scored 101 for New Zealand v England
in the opening match of the 1996 World Cup?

FICA

Career Performances

	M	Inns	NO	Runs	HS	Avge	100s	50s	Ct	St	Balls	Runs	Wkts	Avge	Best	5wl	10wM
Test	15	25	1	374	98	15.58	-	2	6	-	2000	1064	21	50.66	3-88	-	-
All First	313	477	66	12202	175	29.68	16	72	156	-	33070	17573	546	32.18	7-44	14	-
1-day Int	23	19	2	327	50 *	19.23	-	1	6	-	1038	805	17	47.35	3-38	-	
NatWest	39	34	8	916	101	35.23	1	4	10	-	1702	1120	33	33.93	3-21	-	
B & H	66	60	5	1237	97	22.49	-	5	17	-	2722	1762	66	26.69	5-51	1	
Sunday	191	172	33	4024	121	28.94	3	16	47	-	5629	4616	137	33.69	4-30	-	

CARPENTER, J. R.   Sussex

Name: James Robert Carpenter
Role: Left-hand bat, slow left-arm bowler
Born: 20 October 1975, Birkenhead
Height: 6ft 1in **Weight:** 13st
Nickname: Carps
County debut: 1997
1st-Class 50s: 2
1st-Class catches: 5
Place in batting averages: 252nd av. 13.87
(1997 157th av. 25.50)
Strike rate: (career 129.00)
Parents: John and Jo
Marital status: Single
Family links with cricket: Father played
Minor Counties cricket for Cheshire
Education: Gayton Primary School;
Birkenhead School
Qualifications: 9 GCSEs and 4 A-levels
Off-season: Playing grade cricket for
Randwick CC in Sydney
Overseas teams played for: Randwick CC, Sydney, Australia 1996-99
Cricketers particularly admired: Ian Botham, Allan Border, Steve Waugh
Young players to look out for: Brett Lee (Mosman CC, New South Wales),
Jamie Keggin (Bootle CC), Adam Warren
Other sports played: Played county schools rugby for Cheshire and schoolboy
football with Liverpool FC. Had schoolboy forms with Everton and trials with Bolton
Wanderers. Played football for Runcorn FC
in Vauxhall Conference
Relaxations: Golf and 'lying on Coogee beach, Sydney, in the off-season'
Extras: Captained MCC Young Professionals at Lord's. *Daily Telegraph* Bowling
Award. Awarded the Wetherall Trophy by the Cricket Society for the year's

outstanding schoolboy cricketer. Leading catcher in AXA League for 1998 season
Opinions on cricket: 'More floodlit cricket.'
Best batting: 65 Sussex v Nottinghamshire, Trent Bridge 1998
Best bowling: 1-50 Sussex v Nottinghamshire, Hove 1997

1998 Season

	M	Inns	NO	Runs	HS	Avge	100s	50s	Ct	St	O	M	Runs	Wkts	Avge	Best	5wI	10wM
Test																		
All First	9	16	0	222	65	13.87	-	1	3	-								
1-day Int																		
NatWest																		
B & H	3	3	1	50	36	25.00	-	-	1	-								
Sunday	16	14	3	201	53	18.27	-	1	15	-								

Career Performances

	M	Inns	NO	Runs	HS	Avge	100s	50s	Ct	St	Balls	Runs	Wkts	Avge	Best	5wI	10wM
Test																	
All First	12	22	0	375	65	17.04	-	2	5	-	129	81	1	81.00	1-50	-	-
1-day Int																	
NatWest																	
B & H	3	3	1	50	36	25.00	-	-	1	-							
Sunday	18	16	4	236	53	19.66	-	1	15	-	6	15	0	-	-	-

CASSAR, M. E. Derbyshire

Name: Matthew Edward Cassar
Role: Right-hand bat, right-arm medium bowler
Born: 16 October 1972, Sydney, Australia
Height: 6ft **Weight:** 13st 7lbs
Nickname: Charchie
County debut: 1994
1st-Class 50s: 8
1st-Class 100s: 1
1st-Class catches: 8
One-Day 100s: 1
Place in batting averages: 121st av. 27.23 (1997 113th av. 32.42)
Place in bowling averages: 143rd av. 61.40
Strike rate: 94.20 (career 60.92)
Parents: Edward and Joan
Wife and date of marriage: Jane, 5 October 1996
Family links with cricket: Wife, Jane, is the England Women's wicket-keeper

Education: Punchbowl Primary School, Sydney; Sir Joseph Banks High School, Sydney; Manchester Metropolitan University
Qualifications: School certificate and senior coaching award
Off-season: Coaching cricket in the schools of Derbyshire. Working hard in the gym
Overseas teams played for: Petersham/Marrickville, Sydney 1988-95
Cricketers particularly admired: Jane
Other sports played: Squash, golf
Other sports followed: Football (Derby County)
Relaxations: Playing social sports, listening to music, going to the cinema
Extras: Played for New South Wales Colts
Opinions on cricket: 'Overseas players are a vital part of the English game. Playing with

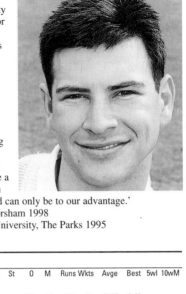

and against the greatest players in the world can only be to our advantage.'
Best batting: 121 Derbyshire v Sussex, Horsham 1998
Best bowling: 4-54 Derbyshire v Oxford University, The Parks 1995

1998 Season

	M	Inns	NO	Runs	HS	Avge	100s	50s	Ct	St	O	M	Runs	Wkts	Avge	Best	5wI	10wM
Test																		
All First	17	31	5	708	121	27.23	1	5	4	-	157	29	614	10	61.40	3-26	-	-
1-day Int																		
NatWest	5	5	1	118	90 *	29.50	-	1	-	-	6	0	32	0	-		-	-
B & H																		
Sunday	11	11	3	347	134	43.37	1	2	4	-	2	0	11	1	11.00	1-11	-	

Career Performances

	M	Inns	NO	Runs	HS	Avge	100s	50s	Ct	St	Balls	Runs	Wkts	Avge	Best	5wI	10wM
Test																	
All First	27	43	6	1069	121	28.89	1	8	8	-	1584	1023	26	39.34	4-54	-	-
1-day Int																	
NatWest	5	5	1	118	90 *	29.50	-	1	-	-	36	32	0	-		-	-
B & H																	
Sunday	15	14	3	383	134	34.81	1	2	6	-	78	96	3	32.00	1-11	-	

CATTERALL, D. N. Worcestershire

Name: Duncan Neil Catterall
Role: Right-hand bat, right-arm
medium-fast bowler
Born: 19 September 1978, Preston
Height: 5ft 11in **Weight:** 12st 2lbs
Nickname: Cats, Coney
County debut: 1998
Parents: David and Christine
Marital status: Single
Family links with cricket: Father and
brother play for Leyland DAF in the
Northern League
Education: Horncliffe School, Blackburn;
Queen Elizabeth's Grammar School,
Blackburn; Loughborough University
Qualifications: 11 GCSEs and 4 A-levels
Off-season: Studying
Overseas tours: Queen Elizabeth's Grammar
School to Australia, December 1996
Cricketers particularly admired: 'I rate Steve Waugh and Allan Donald very highly'
Other sports followed: Football (Blackburn Rovers) and badminton
Relaxations: Pop music
Opinions on cricket: 'I believe that there should be an overseas player allowed to
play in each county second team. However, I have not been in the game long enough
to say any more.'

1998 Season

	M	Inns	NO	Runs	HS	Avge	100s	50s	Ct	St	O	M	Runs	Wkts	Avge	Best	5wI	10wM
Test																		
All First	1	1	0	0	0	0.00	-	-	-	-	13	2	31	0	-		-	-
1-day Int																		
NatWest																			
B & H																			
Sunday	3	2	1	16	11 *	16.00	-	-	1	-	13	1	50	1	50.00	1-28	-	

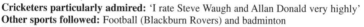

8. Who holds the record for the highest individual
score in the World Cup?

FICA

Career Performances

	M	Inns	NO	Runs	HS	Avge	100s	50s	Ct	St	Balls	Runs	Wkts	Avge	Best	5wI	10wM
Test																	
All First	1	1	0	0	0	0.00	-	-	-	-	78	31	0	-		-	-
1-day Int																	
NatWest																	
B & H																	
Sunday	3	2	1	16	11 *	16.00	-	-	1	-	78	50	1	50.00	1-28	-

CAWDRON, M. J. Gloucestershire

Name: Michael John Cawdron
Role: Left-hand bat, right-arm
medium-fast bowler
Born: 7 October 1974, Luton
Height: 6ft 3in **Weight:** 13st 7lbs
Nickname: Muscles
County debut: 1995 (one-day)
Parents: William and Mandy
Marital status: Single
Family links with cricket: Father and
brother played local village cricket
Education: Cheltenham College
Qualifications: 10 GCSEs, 3 A-Levels,
NCA coaching award
Career outside cricket: 'Vocationally
challenged'
Off-season: 'Getting ready for the '99
season'
Overseas tours: West of England U14 to
Holland; Cheltenham College to Zimbabwe 1992; Gloucestershire YC to Sri Lanka
1993-94; Gloucestershire Gypsies to Zimbabwe 1994-95; Gloucestershire Gypsies to
Cape Town 1997; Christians In Sport to Zimbabwe 1998
Cricketers particularly admired: Ben Gannon – 'the world's best lodger!!'
Young players to look out for: S. Pope
Other sports followed: Rugby, hockey, rackets, clay-pigeon shooting, golf
Injuries: Three weeks out with sore back
Relaxations: Cinema, videos, eating and going out with friends
Extras: Winner of the *Daily Telegraph* Regional Bowling Award 1993. Captain of
MCC Schools and ESCA U19, 1993. 'Made 50 off 32 balls on Sunday League debut
against Essex at my old school' (Cheltenham College)
Opinions on cricket: 'Twelve-month contracts would be of great benefit to those

players who do not wish to winter abroad, as work opportunities are not secure, as other employers are not eager to take on people on such a temporary basis.'

1998 Season

	M	Inns	NO	Runs	HS	Avge	100s	50s	Ct	St	O	M	Runs	Wkts	Avge	Best	5wI	10wM
Test																		
All First																		
1-day Int																		
NatWest																		
B & H	2	1	1	5	5 *	-	-	-	-	-	15	1	55	5	11.00	4-28	-	
Sunday	6	3	2	20	17 *	20.00	-	-	-	-	25	1	145	3	48.33	2-46	-	

Career Performances

	M	Inns	NO	Runs	HS	Avge	100s	50s	Ct	St	Balls	Runs	Wkts	Avge	Best	5wI	10wM
Test																	
All First																	
1-day Int																	
NatWest																	
B & H	3	1	1	5	5 *	-	-	-	-	-	126	103	7	14.71	4-28	-	
Sunday	14	9	3	154	50	25.66	-	1	2	-	438	370	6	61.66	2-46	-	

CHAPMAN, C. A. — Yorkshire

Name: Colin Anthony Chapman
Role: Right-hand bat, wicket-keeper
Born: 8 June 1971, Bradford
Height: 5ft 8in **Weight:** 12st
Nickname: Chappy
County debut: 1990
1st-Class 50s: 1
1st-Class catches: 13
1st-Class stumpings: 3
Parents: Mick and Joyce
Wife and date of marriage:
Amanda, 11 November 1996
Children: Elizabeth Bronte, 6 October 1997
Education: Nabwood Middle; Beckfoot Grammar; Bradford & Ilkley Community College
Qualifications: 5 O-levels, BTEC Diploma in Graphic Design, senior coaching certificate

Off-season: Coaching in the Yorkshire Indoor Cricket School
Overseas teams played for: Waitamata, Auckland 1989-91
Overseas tours: Yorkshire CCC to South Africa 1993, 1995 and 1998, to West Indies 1997
Cricketers particularly admired: Phil Carrick, Alan Knott, Mark Nicklin
Young players to look out for: James Middlebrook, Matthew Hoggard
Other sports followed: Football (Liverpool and Bradford City)
Injuries: Out for two months with epilepsy
Relaxations: Spending time with family
Extras: Retired at end of 1998 season
Opinions on cricket: 'It will be interesting to see if next year's competitions will boost spectators.'
Best batting: 80 Yorkshire v Lancashire, Headingley 1997

1998 Season

	M	Inns	NO	Runs	HS	Avge	100s	50s	Ct	St	O	M	Runs	Wkts	Avge	Best	5wI	10wM
Test																		
All First	2	2	1	27	20	27.00	-	-	5	-								
1-day Int																		
NatWest																		
B & H																		
Sunday																		

Career Performances

	M	Inns	NO	Runs	HS	Avge	100s	50s	Ct	St	Balls	Runs	Wkts	Avge	Best	5wI	10wM
Test																	
All First	8	13	2	238	80	21.63	-	1	13	3							
1-day Int																	
NatWest	1	0	0	0	0	-	-	-	1	-							
B & H																		
Sunday	7	6	3	89	36 *	29.66	-	-	2	-							

CHAPMAN, R. J.   Worcestershire

Name: Robert James Chapman
Role: Right-hand bat, right-arm
fast-medium bowler
Born: 28 July 1972, Nottingham
Height: 6ft 1in **Weight:** 14st
Nickname: Wig, Slapnut, Melon, Bobby, Tree
County debut: 1992 (Nottinghamshire),
1997 (Worcestershire)
1st-Class 5 w. in innings: 1
1st-Class catches: 6
One-Day 5 w. in innings: 1
Place in batting averages: 259th av. 12.75
Place in bowling averages: 76th av. 28.57
(1997 104th av. 36.00)
Strike rate: 44.78 (career 55.32)
Parents: Sam and Hazel
Wife and date of marriage:

Kirsty, 23 January 1999
Family links with cricket: Father Sammy
plays club cricket for Clifton CC and was a pro footballer with Nottingham Forest,
Notts County and Shrewsbury Town
Education: South Wilford Endowed; Farnborough School, Clifton, Nottingham; South
Nottinghamshire College
Qualifications: 7 GCSEs, 2 A-levels, NCA Coaching Award
Career outside cricket: Accounts
Off-season: Haines Watts Accountants
Overseas tours: Worcestershire CCC to Zimbabwe 1997
Overseas teams played for: South Barwon, Melbourne 1995-96
Cricketers particularly admired: Stuart Lampitt, Paul Franks, Damien Fleming,
Martin Bicknell
Young players to look out for: James Pipe
Other sports played: Football, 5-a-side, indoor cricket, 'darts with my Dad in "The Sun"'
Other sports followed: Football (Nottingham Forest)
Relaxations: Listening to music (U2, Oasis, Radiohead, Smashing Pumpkins, Manic
Street Preachers), 'going to "Mr Mann's" with Kirst'.
Extras: Left Nottinghamshire at the end of the 1996 season and joined Worcestershire
for 1997
Best batting: 43* Worcestershire v Durham, Worcester 1998
Best bowling: 6-105 Worcestershire v Nottinghamshire, Kidderminster 1998

1998 Season

	M	Inns	NO	Runs	HS	Avge	100s	50s	Ct	St	O	M	Runs	Wkts	Avge	Best	5wI	10wM
Test																		
All First	11	16	8	102	43 *	12.75	-	-	2	-	246.2	44	943	33	28.57	6-105	1	-
1-day Int																		
NatWest																			
B & H																				
Sunday	10	3	2	2	1 *	2.00	-	-	2	-	49.3	2	234	15	15.60	5-30	1	

Career Performances

	M	Inns	NO	Runs	HS	Avge	100s	50s	Ct	St	Balls	Runs	Wkts	Avge	Best	5wI	10wM
Test																	
All First	32	36	12	226	43 *	9.41	-	-	8	-	3928	2702	71	38.05	6-105	1	-
1-day Int																	
NatWest	2	0	0	0	0	-	-	-	-	-	72	40	0	-	-	-	
B & H	1	1	0	0	0	0.00	-	-	-	-	36	27	0	-	-	-	
Sunday	30	8	4	8	4 *	2.00	-	-	2	-	960	816	29	28.13	5-30	1	

CHAPMAN, S.   Durham

Name: Steven Chapman
Role: Right-hand middle-order bat,
slow left-arm bowler
Born: 2 October 1971, Crook,
County Durham
Height: 6ft 4in **Weight:** 16st 5lbs
Nickname: Chappie, Dr Chaplaw
County debut: 1998
Parents: Elizabeth and Roy
Marital status: Single
Family links with cricket: Parents are keen
spectators. No playing relatives.
Education: Crook Primary; Willington
Parkside Comprehensive
Qualifications: 9 GCSEs, senior cricket
coach
Career outside cricket: Groundsmanship
(cricket/football)
Off-season: Last three winters spent playing
for Hallam CC in Melbourne
Overseas teams played for: Roodepoort, Johannesburg 1993; Riversdale, Trinidad
1994; Hallam, Melbourne 1996-99

Cricketers particularly admired: Jimmy Adams, Clint Yorke (Trinidad), Mark Taylor, Paul Furby (Bishop Auckland)
Young players to look out for: Gary Peatt, Chris Hewison (Durham Academy)
Other sports played: Chung do kwan, taekwondo
Other sports followed: Football (Man Utd, Middlesbrough)
Relaxations: Languages, reading
Extras: Past three years were spent playing as pro at Bishop Auckland CC
Opinions on cricket: 'World Cup every two years.'
Best batting: 11 Durham v Sussex, Eastbourne 1998

1998 Season

	M	Inns	NO	Runs	HS	Avge	100s	50s	Ct	St	O	M	Runs	Wkts	Avge	Best	5wI	10wM
Test																		
All First	1	2	0	13	11	6.50	-	-	-	-	29	6	79	0	-		-	-
1-day Int																		
NatWest																		
B & H																		
Sunday	2	2	0	17	14	8.50	-	-	1	-	14	0	92	2	46.00	2-57	-	

Career Performances

	M	Inns	NO	Runs	HS	Avge	100s	50s	Ct	St	Balls	Runs	Wkts	Avge	Best	5wI	10wM
Test																	
All First	1	2	0	13	11	6.50	-	-	-	-	174	79	0	-		-	-
1-day Int																	
NatWest																	
B & H																	
Sunday	2	2	0	17	14	8.50	-	-	1	-	84	92	2	46.00	2-57	-	

CHAPPLE, G.   Lancashire

Name: Glen Chapple
Role: Right-hand bat, right-arm medium-fast bowler
Born: 23 January 1974, Skipton, Yorkshire
Height: 6ft 2in **Weight:** 12st 7lbs
Nickname: Chappy, Boris, Boomor, Cheeky
County debut: 1992
50 wickets in a season: 2
1st-Class 50s: 4
1st-Class 100s: 1
1st-Class 5 w. in innings: 9
1st-Class catches: 31
One-Day 5 w. in innings: 4

Place in batting averages: 208th av. 18.80
(1997 180th av. 23.70)
Place in bowling averages: 26th av. 21.40
(1997 90th av. 33.33)
Strike rate: 42.68 (career 54.78)
Parents: Eileen and Michael
Marital status: Single
Family links with cricket: Father played in
Lancashire League for Nelson and was a
professional for Darwen and Earby
Education: West Craven High School;
Nelson and Colne College
Qualifications: 8 GCSEs, 2 A-levels
(Geography and Economics)
Overseas tours: England U18 to Canada
1991; England U19 to New Zealand 1990-91,
to Pakistan 1991-92, to India 1992-93;
England A to India 1994-95, to Australia
1996-97

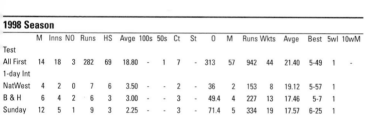

Cricketers particularly admired: Dennis Lillee, Robin Smith
Other sports followed: Football (Liverpool), golf
Relaxations: 'Watching films, cinema, music, socialising'
Extras: Hit fastest century (21 minutes) against Glamorgan at Old Trafford 1993. Man
of the Match in the 1996 NatWest final against Essex after taking 6 for 18
Best batting: 109* Lancashire v Glamorgan, Old Trafford 1993
Best bowling: 6-48 Lancashire v Durham, Stockton 1994

1998 Season

	M	Inns	NO	Runs	HS	Avge	100s	50s	Ct	St	O	M	Runs	Wkts	Avge	Best	5wl	10wM
Test																		
All First	14	18	3	282	69	18.80	-	1	7	-	313	57	942	44	21.40	5-49	1	-
1-day Int																		
NatWest	4	2	0	7	6	3.50	-	-	2	-	36	2	153	8	19.12	5-57	1	
B & H	6	4	2	6	3	3.00	-	-	3	-	49.4	4	227	13	17.46	5-7	1	
Sunday	12	5	1	9	3	2.25	-	-	3	-	71.4	5	334	19	17.57	6-25	1	

9. Which batsman has the all-time highest England
World Cup career batting average?

FICA

Career Performances

	M	Inns	NO	Runs	HS	Avge	100s	50s	Ct	St	Balls	Runs	Wkts	Avge	Best	5wI	10wM
Test																	
All First	88	120	41	1668	109 *	21.11	1	4	31	-	14134	7412	258	28.72	6-48	9	-
1-day Int																	
NatWest	13	7	1	13	6	2.16	-	-	4	-	696	508	20	25.40	6-18	2	
B & H	20	8	5	26	8	8.66	-	-	5	-	1048	811	26	31.19	5-7	1	
Sunday	65	24	11	155	43	11.92	-	-	12	-	2398	1916	69	27.76	6-25	1	

CHERRY, D. D. Glamorgan

Name: Daniel David Cherry
Role: Left-hand bat, right-arm
medium bowler
Born: 7 February 1980, Newport
Height: 5ft 9in **Weight:** 13st
Nickname: Chesney, Rhino, Banners
County debut: 1998
Parents: David and Elizabeth
Marital status: Single
Family links with cricket: Dad is a qualified
coach and played club cricket
Education: Feltonfleet Prep School,
Cobham, Surrey; Tonbridge School, Kent;
University of Wales, Swansea
Qualifications: 10 GCSEs, 3 A-levels
Career outside cricket: Student
Off-season: Starting a History degree at
University of Wales, Swansea
Overseas tours: Tonbridge School to
Australia 1996-97
Cricketers particularly admired: Michael Atherton, Graham Thorpe,
Matthew Maynard
Young players to look out for: Wayne Law, Mark Wallace
Other sports played: Rugby, rackets (Public Schools doubles champion)
Other sports followed: Rugby (Wales), football (Everton)
Relaxations: Listening to music, reading crime books, watching rugby when not
playing
Opinions on cricket: 'More day/night cricket to increase the appeal of the game to the
public'
Best batting: 11 Glamorgan v Derbyshire, Cardiff 1998

1998 Season

	M	Inns	NO	Runs	HS	Avge	100s	50s	Ct	St	O	M	Runs	Wkts	Avge	Best	5wI	10wM
Test																		
All First	1	1	0	11	11	11.00	-	-	-	-								
1-day Int																		
NatWest																		
B & H																		
Sunday																		

Career Performances

	M	Inns	NO	Runs	HS	Avge	100s	50s	Ct	St	Balls	Runs	Wkts	Avge	Best	5wI	10wM
Test																	
All First	1	1	0	11	11	11.00	-	-	-	-							
1-day Int																	
NatWest																	
B & H																	
Sunday																	

CHILTON, M. J.   Lancashire

Name: Mark James Chilton
Role: Right-hand top-order bat, right-arm medium bowler
Born: 2 October 1976, Sheffield
Height: 6ft 3in **Weight:** 12st 8lbs
Nickname: Chill, Chinny, Prof
County debut: 1997
One-Day 5 w. in innings: 1
Place in batting averages: 130th av. 26.33
Parents: Jim and Sue
Marital status: Single
Family links with cricket: Father played local cricket
Education: Brooklands Primary School; Manchester Grammar School; Durham University
Qualifications: 10 GCSEs, 3 A-levels, BA (Hons) Business Economics, senior coaching award
Off-season: 'With the 12-month contracts at Lancashire I will be linked with them throughout'
Overseas tours: Manchester Grammar School to Barbados 1993-94, to South Africa

1995-96; Durham University to Zimbabwe 1997-98
Cricketers particularly admired: Alec Stewart, Michael Atherton
Young players to look out for: Stuart Adamson, Jon Humphreys
Other sports played: Golf, tennis
Other sports followed: Football (Manchester United)
Relaxations: Music ('any type'), eating out, 'a good video'
Extras: Represented England U14, U15, U17. Played for North of England v New Zealand U19 in 1996. Awarded England U15 Batsman of the Year in 1992. Played for British Universities in 1997 Benson and Hedges Cup winning the Gold Award against Sussex. Played for Lancashire in the first day/night game held in Britain. Awarded 2nd XI cap 1998
Opinions on cricket: 'The new 12-month contracts at Lancashire are a good thing. They allow players to consider other options apart from cricket.'
Best batting: 47 Lancashire v Glamorgan, Colwyn Bay 1998

1998 Season

	M	Inns	NO	Runs	HS	Avge	100s	50s	Ct	St	O	M	Runs	Wkts	Avge	Best	5wI	10wM
Test																		
All First	3	6	0	158	47	26.33	-	-	-	-	14	3	48	0	-		-	-
1-day Int																		
NatWest	1	1	0	41	41	41.00	-	-	2	-								
B & H	5	5	1	168	56	42.00	-	2	4	-	33	2	157	6	26.16	4-28	-	
Sunday	3	2	0	20	20	10.00	-	-	1	-	2	0	25	0	-		-	-

Career Performances

	M	Inns	NO	Runs	HS	Avge	100s	50s	Ct	St	Balls	Runs	Wkts	Avge	Best	5wI	10wM
Test																	
All First	4	7	0	167	47	23.85	-	-	-	-	108	71	0	-		-	-
1-day Int																	
NatWest	1	1	0	41	41	41.00	-	-	2	-							
B & H	10	10	1	272	56	30.22	-	2	4	-	369	316	14	22.57	5-26	1	
Sunday	6	5	0	51	22	10.20	-	-	1	-	108	105	3	35.00	2-27	-	

CHURCH, M. J.   Gloucestershire

Name: Matthew John Church
Role: Right-hand bat, right-arm medium bowler
Born: 26 July 1972, Guildford
Height: 6ft 2in **Weight:** 13st
Nickname: Churchy, Larse
County debut: 1994 (Worcestershire), 1997 (Gloucestershire)

1st-Class 50s: 1
1st-Class 100s: 1
1st-Class catches: 13
Place in batting averages: 264th av. 12.14
(1997 195th av. 25.45)
Strike rate: (career 26.77)
Parents: Anthony and Annette
Marital status: Single
Education: Hoebridge School, Woburn Hill;
St George's College, Weybridge; Guildford
Technical College; Stuart Cricket Academy
Qualifications: 4 GCSEs, 1 A-level ('Thanks
Mr Dav and Les')
Career outside cricket: 'Not sure yet'
Off-season: 'In Argentina until Christmas'
Overseas tours: Surrey U19 to Australia
1989-90; St George's College to Zimbabwe;
Troubadours to Argentina 1997
Overseas teams played for: Harmony CC, Orange Free State 1991-92; North Shore,
Geelong 1992-93; Adelaide University 1994-95; St George's College and Hurlingham,
Argentina 1996-97; Bell Post Hill, Geelong 1997-98
Cricketers particularly admired: Basil D'Oliveira, Viv Richards, Albert E. Trott,
Colin Milburn
Young players to look out for: Russ Abbot and 'the Lazerman'
Other sports played: 'All sports at school', hockey (Old Georgians HC – 'Premier
League 2001')
Other sports followed: 'Enjoy boxing, rugby (Bristol RFC), football (Arsenal FC)'
Injuries: Out for three and a half weeks with a broken rib
Relaxations: 'I enjoy reading (now that I am not at school). Would like to visit Inca
ruins in Peru'
Extras: Former MCC Young Cricketer, signed by Worcestershire at the beginning of the
1994 season. Sold scorecards at the 1993 Benson and Hedges Cup final and was 12th
Man for Worcestershire at the NatWest final the following year. Fielded for England as
substitute in 1995 Lord's Test against South Africa. Played for Surrey from U12 to U19.
Released by Worcestershire at the end of the 1996 season and joined Gloucestershire in
1997. Gold Award v Hampshire in B & H Cup 1998
Opinions on cricket: 'Many! It is an incredible rollercoaster of a game. An exciting
sport if allowed to be. The Sri Lankans. Need I say more?!'
Best batting: 152 Worcestershire v Oxford University, The Parks 1996
Best bowling: 4-50 Worcestershire v Oxford University, The Parks 1996

1998 Season

	M	Inns	NO	Runs	HS	Avge	100s	50s	Ct	St	O	M	Runs	Wkts	Avge	Best	5wI	10wM
Test																		
All First	4	7	0	85	30	12.14	-	-	5	-								
1-day Int																		
NatWest																		
B & H	1	1	1	64	64 *	-	-	-	1	-	-							
Sunday	5	5	0	46	25	9.20	-	-	-	-								

Career Performances

	M	Inns	NO	Runs	HS	Avge	100s	50s	Ct	St	Balls	Runs	Wkts	Avge	Best	5wI	10wM
Test																	
All First	20	36	1	629	152	17.97	1	1	13	-	241	163	9	18.11	4-50	-	-
1-day Int																	
NatWest	1	1	0	35	35	35.00	-	-	-	-	30	34	0	-		-	-
B & H	2	1	1	64	64 *	-	-	-	1	-							
Sunday	20	16	0	144	25	9.00	-	-	7	-	6	12	0	-		-	-

CLARKE, V. P. Derbyshire

Name: Vincent Paul Clarke
Role: Right-hand bat, right-arm leg-break and medium bowler
Born: 11 November 1971, Liverpool
Height: 6ft 3in **Weight:** 16st 7lbs
Nickname: FC, Fat Cat, Franky, Jelly, Big Lad, Pommy, Aussie
County debut: 1994 (Somerset), 1995 (Leicestershire), 1997 (Derbyshire)
1st-Class 50s: 5
1st-Class catches: 15
Place in batting averages: 278th av. 9.57 (1997 90th av. 35.29)
Place in bowling averages: (1997 145th av. 64.23)
Strike rate: 123.00 (career 101.54)
Parents: Sandra and Vinnie
Wife and date of marriage: Natasha, 7 November 1998
Family links with cricket: Father played representative schoolboy cricket. Sister played school cricket. Mum played indoor cricket

Education: Craigie Primary School, Perth, Western Australia; Sacred Heart College, Sorrento, Perth; Perth TAFE
Qualifications: Diploma in Social Training, Year 12 TEE Certificate
Career outside cricket: Social trainer
Off-season: 'Go back to Perth, Western Australia, to play and coach for Nollamara Turf Cricket Club. Get married and enjoy some sunshine!!'
Overseas teams played for: Wanneroo Districts CC, Perth 1983-94; Hammersley Carine CC, Perth 1995; Nollamara Turf CC, Perth 1996-99
Cricketers particularly admired: Shane Warne, Ian Botham
Other sports played: Indoor cricket (represented Western Australia in national tournament – winners). Softball (represented Western Australia as pitcher)
Other sports followed: Football (Everton FC), Aussie Rules (West Coast Eagles)
Relaxations: Playing the guitar, music, windsurfing, 'spending lazy free weekends at home with Natasha listening to music, doing some gardening, then having a BBQ'
Extras: Brought up in Australia but has English birth qualification. Was in Western Australian Development Squads from U14 to U19. Represented Western Australia at indoor cricket in 1991. Played for Bridgwater and Somerset 2nd XI in 1993. Joined Leicestershire at the start of the 1995 season but was released at the end of the 1996 season. Joined Derbyshire for the 1997 season. Derby Cricket Lovers' Society Young Cricketer of the Year 1997. Wombwell Cricket Lovers' Society Young Cricketer of the Year 1997. Suburban Turf Player of the Year, Perth 1997 and 1998
Opinions on cricket: 'I love it!!'
Best batting: 99 Derbyshire v Warwickshire, Edgbaston 1997
Best bowling: 3-47 Derbyshire v Cambridge University, Fenner's 1997

1998 Season

	M	Inns	NO	Runs	HS	Avge	100s	50s	Ct	St	O	M	Runs	Wkts	Avge	Best	5wI	10wM
Test																		
All First	4	7	0	67	26	9.57	-	-	4	-	41	4	173	2	86.50	1-50	-	-
1-day Int																		
NatWest	5	2	1	23	13	23.00	-	-	3	-	43.4	3	129	3	43.00	2-29	-	
B & H	4	4	0	64	48	16.00	-	-	1	-	34	2	157	5	31.40	2-22	-	
Sunday	12	10	4	118	27	19.66	-	-	4	-	71.5	2	372	10	37.20	3-47	-	

Career Performances

	M	Inns	NO	Runs	HS	Avge	100s	50s	Ct	St	Balls	Runs	Wkts	Avge	Best	5wI	10wM
Test																	
All First	30	50	7	1058	99	24.60	-	5	15	-	2234	1449	22	65.86	3-47	-	-
1-day Int																	
NatWest	8	4	2	58	24 *	29.00	-	-	5	-	424	221	5	44.20	2-29	-	
B & H	10	10	1	167	52	18.55	-	1	3	-	372	299	12	24.91	4-49	-	
Sunday	35	33	7	422	77 *	16.23	-	2	10	-	883	800	22	36.36	3-47	-	

CLOUGH, G. D. Yorkshire

Name: Gareth David Clough
Role: Right-hand bat, right-arm medium bowler
Born: 23 May 1978, Leeds
Height: 6ft **Weight:** 11st 7lbs
Nickname: Woofit, Banger, Horse
County debut: 1998
1st-Class catches: 1
Parents: David and Gillian
Marital status: Single
Family links with cricket: Brother-in-law plays local league cricket
Education: Pudsey Greenside; Pudsey Grangefield
Qualifications: GCSEs and A-levels
Career outside cricket: Cricket coach. Lifeguard
Off-season: Coaching cricket in local primary schools
Overseas teams played for: Somerset West, Cape Town 1996-97
Cricketers particularly admired: Darren Lehmann, Michael Slater
Young players to look out for: Gary Fellows, Matthew Wood, Paul Hutchison
Other sports played: Football (for Royal Hotel), golf
Other sports followed: Football (Everton FC), rugby league (Leeds Rhinos)
Injuries: Out for six weeks with a hernia
Relaxations: Watching football and socialising with friends
Opinions on cricket: 'I think the game would improve if the Championship was divided into two divisions. Longer contracts as well.'
Best batting: 33 Yorkshire v Glamorgan, Cardiff 1998

1998 Season

	M	Inns	NO	Runs	HS	Avge	100s	50s	Ct	St	O	M	Runs	Wkts	Avge	Best	5wl	10wM
Test																		
All First	1	2	0	34	33	17.00	-	-	1	-	2	0	11	0	-	-	-	-
1-day Int																		
NatWest																		
B & H																		
Sunday																		

Career Performances

	M	Inns	NO	Runs	HS	Avge	100s	50s	Ct	St	Balls	Runs	Wkts	Avge	Best	5wl	10wM
Test																	
All First	1	2	0	34	33	17.00	-	-	1	-	12	11	0	-	-	-	-
1-day Int																	
NatWest																	
B & H																	
Sunday																	

COLLINGWOOD, P. D. Durham

Name: Paul David Collingwood
Role: Right-hand bat, right-arm
medium bowler
Born: 26 May 1976, Shotley Bridge,
Tyneside
Height: 5ft 11in **Weight:** 11st 8lbs
Nickname: Colly, Savage, The Savage, The
Savager 'and many more along them lines!'
County debut: 1995 (one-day),
1996 (first-class)
1st-Class 50s: 8
1st-Class 100s: 2
1st-Class catches: 33
Place in batting averages: 98th av. 30.85
(1997 148th av. 26.63)
Place in bowling averages: 135th av. 44.76
Strike rate: 92.38 (career 82.77)
Parents: David and Janet
Marital status: Single
Family links with cricket: Father and brother play in the Tyneside Senior League for
Shotley Bridge CC
Education: Benfieldside Junior School; Blackfyne Comprehensive School;
Derwentside College
Qualifications: 9 GCSEs and 2 A-levels
Career outside cricket: 'Whatever job I can find'
Off-season: Player/coach for Alberton CC in Johannesburg, 'plenty of golf and
enjoying the sights and sounds of Jo'burg, especially at night!!'
Overseas tours: Durham Cricket Academy to Sri Lanka 1996 (captain)
Overseas teams played for: Bulleen CC, Melbourne 1995-96, 1997 ('won flag on both
occasions'); Cornwall CC, Auckland 1997-98; Alberton CC, Johannesburg 1998-99

Cricketers particularly admired: Graham Gooch, Darren Gough, Michael Atherton, Shaun Pollock, Jonty Rhodes, Allan Donald

Young players to look out for: Matthew Wood, Simon Brown ('the Prince'), Steve Harmison ('Son of'), 'and Bettsy, of course'

Other sports played: 'Cards on a rainy day. A bit of footy'

Other sports followed: Football (Sunderland AFC – 'I'm red and white through and through')

Injuries: 'Burst left eardrum from Badger; damaged joint in shoulder and a lot more niggles. Out for one week only at beginning of May'

Relaxations: 'Watching Sunderland when I'm not away. Reading the *Sports Echo* (SAFC paper) when I am away. Sampling many fine lagers from around the world'

Extras: Took wicket with first ball on first-class debut against Northants, then scored 91. 'A hole-in-one on Durham's golf day'

Opinions on cricket: 'Everyone should have their own room on away trips. Bettsy should pitch the ball further towards the batsmen in the nets. Our slips should be provided with ear muffs. J.J. should work on a new diving technique and grow his legs. Wickets should improve.'

Best batting: 107 Durham v Oxford University, The Parks 1997

Best bowling: 3-46 Durham v Lancashire, Old Trafford 1997

1998 Season

	M	Inns	NO	Runs	HS	Avge	100s	50s	Ct	St	O	M	Runs	Wkts	Avge	Best	5wI	10wM
Test																		
All First	19	33	6	833	105	30.85	1	5	16	-	200.1	53	582	13	44.76	3-89	-	-
1-day Int																		
NatWest	2	1	0	23	23	23.00	-	-	-	-	15	1	36	1	36.00	1-25	-	
B & H	3	3	1	85	39	42.50	-	-	-	-	7	0	51	0	-	-	-	
Sunday	13	12	0	326	62	27.16	-	3	5	-	39.2	0	205	11	18.63	3-20	-	

Career Performances

	M	Inns	NO	Runs	HS	Avge	100s	50s	Ct	St	Balls	Runs	Wkts	Avge	Best	5wI	10wM
Test																	
All First	38	66	7	1613	107	27.33	2	8	33	-	1821	966	22	43.90	3-46	-	-
1-day Int																	
NatWest	5	4	0	92	28	23.00	-	-	-	-	102	56	1	56.00	1-25	-	
B & H	12	11	2	250	49	27.77	-	-	2	-	307	275	7	39.28	3-28	-	
Sunday	37	35	3	694	62	21.68	-	5	16	-	498	415	15	27.66	3-20	-	

CONNOR, C. A. Hampshire

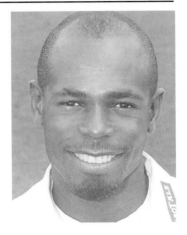

Name: Cardigan Adolphus Connor
Role: Right-hand bat, right-arm
fast-medium bowler
Born: 24 March 1961, West End, Anguilla
Height: 5ft 10in **Weight:** 12st 8lbs
Nickname: Cardy, CC
County debut: 1984
County cap: 1988
Benefit: 1997 (£131,414)
50 wickets in a season: 5
1st-Class 50s: 2
1st-Class 5 w. in innings: 18
1st-Class 10 w. in match: 4
1st-Class catches: 61
Place in bowling averages:
(1997 88th av. 33.07)
Strike rate: 153.00 (career 60.90)
Parents: Ethleen
Wife and date of marriage:
Jacqui, 18 March 1995
Education: The Valley Secondary School, Anguilla; Windsor and Langley College
Qualifications: Engineer, trainer
Career outside cricket: Keep-fit instructor and masseur
Overseas teams played for: Merewether DCC, Newcastle, Australia 1983-93; Valley
Secondary School, Anguilla 1992-98
Cricketers particularly admired: Malcolm Marshall, Viv Richards
Young players to look out for: Andrew Flintoff, Ben Hollioake
Other sports followed: Football (Arsenal)
Relaxations: Keeping fit
Extras: Played for Buckinghamshire in Minor Counties before joining Hampshire.
First Anguillan-born player to appear in the County Championship. Retired from first-
class cricket during the 1998-99 off-season
Best batting: 59 Hampshire v Surrey, The Oval 1993
Best bowling: 9-38 Hampshire v Gloucestershire, Southampton 1996

FIGA

10. In the World Cup match at Trent Bridge on 9 June 1983,
both sides had opening bowlers named Hogg. Who were
the bowlers and who did they play for?

1998 Season

	M	Inns	NO	Runs	HS	Avge	100s	50s	Ct	St	O	M	Runs	Wkts	Avge	Best	5wI	10wM
Test																		
All First	4	1	1	0	0*	-	-	-	-	-	51	11	154	2	77.00	2-23	-	-
1-day Int																		
NatWest	4	1	1	2	2*	-	-	-	-	-	35	8	101	11	9.18	4-13	-	
B & H	1	1	1	1	1*	-	-	-	-	-	10	2	40	1	40.00	1-40	-	
Sunday	14	6	1	17	7*	3.40	-	-	1	-	96.2	11	349	16	21.81	3-27	-	

Career Performances

	M	Inns	NO	Runs	HS	Avge	100s	50s	Ct	St	Balls	Runs	Wkts	Avge	Best	5wI	10wM
Test																	
All First	221	206	54	1814	59	11.93	-	2	61	-	37397	19492	614	31.74	9-38	18	4
1-day Int						*											
NatWest	38	8	5	39	13	13.00	-	-	10	-	2406	1400	80	17.50	4-11	-	
B & H	56	16	8	40	11	5.00	-	-	10	-	3151	2103	81	25.96	4-19	-	
Sunday	201	61	19	256	25	6.09	-	-	34	-	8821	6545	244	26.82	5-25	1	

COOK, S. J.   Middlesex

Name: Simon James Cook
Role: Right-hand bat, right-arm medium-fast bowler
Born: 15 January 1977, Oxford
Height: 6ft 4in **Weight:** 12st
Nickname: Cookie
County debut: 1997 (one-day)
Parents: Phil and Sue
Marital status: Single
Education: Botley Primary School; Matthew Arnold School
Qualifications: GCSEs, NVQ Business Administration II
Career outside cricket: Sales and marketing within the computer industry
Off-season: Working and training
Cricketers particularly admired: Angus Fraser, Allan Donald, Mark Waugh
Young players to look out for: Owais Shah, Neil Martin, David Nash
Other sports followed: Football (Liverpool), 'any other ball sport'
Injuries: Shin splints, missed a total of three weeks during the season

Relaxations: Sleeping, playing any sport, watching television and videos
Opinions on cricket: 'Cut down the number of games that we play and have more short, sharp quality training sessions.'

1998 Season (did not make any first-class or one-day appearances)

Career Performances

	M	Inns	NO	Runs	HS	Avge	100s	50s	Ct	St	Balls	Runs	Wkts	Avge	Best	5wI	10wM
Test																	
All First																	
1-day Int																	
NatWest																	
B & H	1	1	0	6	6	6.00	-	-	-	-	54	71	0	-		-	-
Sunday																	

COOMBES, M. A.   Gloucestershire

Name: Mark Andrew Coombes
Role: Left-hand bat, left-arm medium bowler
Born: 19 April 1978, Bristol
Height: 6ft 2in **Weight:** 14st 3lbs
Nickname: Coomber
County debut: No first-team appearance
Parents: Andrew and Rosemaire
Marital status: Single
Education: Ilminster Av; Hengrove Comprehensive; South Bristol College
Qualifications: NVQ Level 2 in Bricklaying
Career outside cricket: Bricklayer
Off-season: Bricklaying
Cricketers particularly admired:
Ian Botham
Young players to look out for:
Paul Lazenbury, Dominic Hewson, Jon Lewis, Matt Windows
Other sports played: Football
Other sports followed: Football (Man Utd)
Relaxations: Fishing

CORK, D. G.   Derbyshire

Name: Dominic Gerald Cork
Role: Right-hand bat, right-arm,
fast-medium bowler, county captain
Born: 7 August 1971,
Newcastle-under-Lyme, Staffordshire
Height: 6ft 3in **Weight:** 13st
Nickname: Corky
County debut: 1990
County cap: 1993
Test debut: 1995
Tests: 25
One-Day Internationals: 25
50 wickets in a season: 4
1st-Class 50s: 27
1st-Class 100s: 3
1st-Class 5 w. in innings: 15
1st-Class 10 w. in match: 2
1st-Class catches: 97
One-Day 5 w. in innings: 4
Place in batting averages: 171st av. 22.00 (1997 176th av. 24.00)
Place in bowling averages: 77th av. 28.89 (1997 126th 41.54)
Strike rate: 58.39 (career 54.10)
Parents: Gerald and Mary
Children: Gregory Theodore Gerald, 29 September 1994
Family links with cricket: Father and two brothers play for Betley CC in the North
Staffs and South Cheshire League
Education: St Joseph's College, Stoke-on-Trent; Newcastle College of Further
Education
Qualifications: History O-level, leisure and recreation, qualified coach
Career outside cricket: 'None at the moment but I would love to work in the media
or in television'
Overseas tours: England YC to Australia 1989-90; England A to Bermuda and West
Indies 1991-92, to Australia 1992-93, to South Africa 1993-94, to India 1994-95;
England to South Africa 1995-96, to India and Pakistan (World Cup) 1995-96, to New
Zealand 1996-97, to Australia 1998-99
Overseas teams played for: East Shirley, Christchurch, New Zealand 1990-91
Cricketers particularly admired: Ian Botham, Kim Barnett, 'and particularly Shane
Warne'
Young players to look out for: Vikram Solanki, Andrew Harris and Phil DeFreitas
('off-spin')
Other sports followed: Horse racing, football (Stoke), rugby union (England and Bath)

Relaxations: Gardening ('I love weeding'), listening to music

Extras: First played cricket for Betley CC in the North Staffs & South Cheshire League. In 1990 he took a wicket in his first over in first-class cricket v New Zealand at Derby and scored a century as nightwatchman for England U19 v Pakistan at Taunton. Played Minor Counties cricket for Staffordshire in 1989 and 1990. Selected for England A in 1991 – his first full season of first-class cricket. The Professional Cricketers' Association (PCA) Young Player of 1991. Took eight wickets for 53 runs on 20th birthday. Achieved first-class hat-trick against Kent 1994. Took seven wickets for 43 runs on Test debut against West Indies at Lord's. Achieved hat-trick against the West Indies at Old Trafford in the fourth Test – the first by an Englishman in Test cricket for thirty years. Won two Man of the Match awards in three Test matches. Voted Player of the Year by the PCA for 1995. Finished at the top of the Whyte and Mackay ratings for bowling in 1995. One of *Wisden*'s five Cricketers of the Year 1996. Withdrew from the Zimbabwe leg of England's 1996-97 winter tour for personal reasons, but joined up with the team in New Zealand. Appointed Derbyshire captain for the 1998 season

Best batting: 104 Derbyshire v Gloucestershire, Cheltenham 1993

Best bowling: 9-43 Derbyshire v Northamptonshire, Derby 1995

1998 Season

	M	Inns	NO	Runs	HS	Avge	100s	50s	Ct	St	O	M	Runs	Wkts	Avge	Best	5wI	10wM
Test	6	11	1	113	36	11.30	-	-	2	-	212.4	34	704	20	35.20	6-119	2	-
All First	16	27	4	506	102 *	22.00	1	3	11	-	545	111	1618	56	28.89	6-119	3	-
1-day Int																		
NatWest	5	5	4	104	61 *	104.00	-	1	2	-	58.2	13	177	9	19.66	4-46	-	
B & H	4	4	0	79	35	19.75	-	-	3	-	37	2	158	3	52.66	2-42	-	
Sunday	9	8	1	97	38	13.85	-	-	4	-	65	6	268	11	24.36	3-26	-	

Career Performances

	M	Inns	NO	Runs	HS	Avge	100s	50s	Ct	St	Balls	Runs	Wkts	Avge	Best	5wI	10wM
Test	25	38	5	595	59	18.03	-	2	12	-	5621	2953	94	31.41	7-43	5	
All First	153	228	34	4722	104	24.34	3	27	97	-	26243	13086	485	26.98	9-43	15	2
1-day Int	25	15	2	132	31 *	10.15	-	-	6	-	1440	1071	35	30.60	3-27	-	
NatWest	17	15	4	394	62	35.81	-	4	5	-	1107	658	35	18.80	5-18	2	
B & H	22	18	5	360	92 *	27.69	-	2	11	-	1298	870	23	37.82	5-49	1	
Sunday	78	63	7	964	66	17.21	-	2	30	-	3264	2561	90	28.45	6-21	1	

COSKER, D. A. Glamorgan

Name: Dean Andrew Cosker
Role: Right-hand bat, slow left-arm bowler
Born: 7 January 1978, Weymouth, Dorset
Height: 5ft 11in **Weight:** 12st 5lbs
Nickname: 'The Lurker'
County debut: 1996
1st-Class 5 w. in innings: 1
1st-Class catches: 21
Place in batting averages: 288th av. 6.83
Place in bowling averages: 120th av. 35.13
(1997 112th av. 37.93)
Strike rate: 80.63 (career 72.77)
Parents: Des and Carol
Marital status: 'Available'
Family links with cricket: 'Brother Gareth
plays and my grandfather claims to have had
trials with Glamorgan but anyone who knows
him will know that he is mad'
Education: 'Brannigan's, a place for eating
and cavorting'; Millfield School; 'any conversation that involves Tony Cottey's sharp wit'
Qualifications: 10 GCSEs, 4 A-levels, Class 3 soccer referee, 'meeting the required
hygenic attributes to live with Alun Evans'
Career outside cricket: 'A practising hermit'
Off-season: Training, shuttles, weights; socialising, marathons etc. England A to
Zimbabwe and South Africa
Overseas tours: West of England U15 to West Indies 1993-94; Millfield School to Sri
Lanka 1994-95; England U17 to Holland 1995; England U19 to Pakistan 1996-97;
England A to Kenya and Sri Lanka 1997-98; Glamorgan CCC to Jersey 1998; England
A to Zimbabwe and South Africa 1998-99
Overseas teams played for: Gordon, Sydney 1996-97
Cricketers particularly admired: Steve Watkin – 'the bowling machine'; Owen
Parkin 'for his calamari-like features'
Young players to look out for: Wayne 'Alien' Law 'for his defensive approach to the
game'
Other sports played: Ten-pin bowling
Other sports followed: Soccer (Tottenham Hotspur FC)
Injuries: Strained neck in Leicester – 'In a neck brace for two days and one very
eventful night'
Relaxations: 'Listening to the friendly but amusing banter between A.D. Shaw and
Tony Cottey; eating out with a few friends and with a few pints'
Extras: *Daily Telegraph* Regional Bowling Award, England U15 and U17. Played for

U19 TCCB Development of Excellence XI against South Africa U19 in 1995. Played for England U19 against Zimbabwe in 1997
Opinions on cricket: 'Hard, when the wind is blowing'
Best batting: 37 Glamorgan v Essex, Chelmsford 1998
Best bowling: 6-140 Glamorgan v Lancashire, Colwyn Bay 1998

1998 Season

	M	Inns	NO	Runs	HS	Avge	100s	50s	Ct	St	O	M	Runs	Wkts	Avge	Best	5wI	10wM
Test																		
All First	15	21	3	123	37	6.83	-	-	11	-	483.5	127	1265	36	35.13	6-140	1	-
1-day Int																		
NatWest	1	1	1	4	4*	-	-	-	-	-	5.2	0	20	0	-	-	-	-
B & H	4	3	2	2	1*	2.00	-	-	1	-	23	2	90	3	30.00	2-26	-	
Sunday	13	6	3	39	19	13.00	-	-	4	-	80	0	463	17	27.23	3-18	-	

Career Performances

	M	Inns	NO	Runs	HS	Avge	100s	50s	Ct	St	Balls	Runs	Wkts	Avge	Best	5wI	10wM
Test																	
All First	42	42	13	209	37	7.20	-	-	21	-	7277	3509	100	35.09	6-140	1	-
1-day Int																	
NatWest	2	2	2	7	4*	-	-	-	-	-	104	46	3	15.33	3-26	-	
B & H	5	4	2	2	1*	1.00	-	-	1	-	174	128	4	32.00	2-26	-	
Sunday	21	9	3	48	19	8.00	-	-	6	-	840	751	25	30.04	3-18	-	

11. Which former South Africa Test player, at the time
representing Zimbabwe, was the oldest player
in the 1992 World Cup at 44?

FIGA

COTTEY, P. A. Sussex

Name: Phillip Anthony Cottey
Role: Right-hand bat, right-arm off-spin bowler
Born: 2 June 1966, Swansea
Height: 5ft 5in **Weight:** 10st 10lbs
Nickname: Cotts, Baba Oily
County debut: 1986 (Glamorgan)
County cap: 1992 (Glamorgan)
1000 runs in season: 7
1st-Class 50s: 59
1st-Class 100s: 20
1st-Class 200s: 1
1st-Class catches: 142
Place in batting averages: 63rd av. 34.89 (1997 134th av. 27.94)
Strike rate: 80.00 (career 83.75)
Parents: Bernard John and Ruth
Wife and date of marriage:
Gail, 5 October 1992
Children: Lowri Rhiannon, 16 October 1993; Seren Nia, 6 August 1997
Family links with cricket: Father played club cricket for Swansea CC
Education: Bishopston Comprehensive School, Swansea
Qualifications: 9 O-levels, advanced coach
Career outside cricket: Cricket Development Officer for West Wales
Off-season: As above
Overseas tours: Glamorgan to La Manga, Barbados, Trinidad, Zimbabwe and Cape Town 1987-96; Glamorgan CCC to Jersey 1998
Overseas teams played for: Penrith, Sydney 1986-88; Benoni, Johannesburg 1990-93; Eastern Transvaal 1991-92
Cricketers particularly admired: Ian Botham, Wasim Akram, Stuart Law
Young players to look out for: Wayne Law, Dean Cosker, Darren Thomas
Other sports followed: Golf, soccer (Swansea City AFC), rugby union (Dunvant RFC) and marathon running
Relaxations: Videos, golf, marathon running and 'lager tasting'
Extras: Left school at 16 to play for Swansea City FC for three years as a professional. Three Welsh Youth caps (one as captain). Glamorgan Player of the Year in 1994. Ran the New York Marathon in 1995 and the Athens Marathon in 1996. Left Glamorgan at the end of the 1998 season and joined Sussex
Opinions on cricket: 'Day/night cricket is a great innovation to the English game as long as it's played at the right time of year – ie not April, May and September. Too cold!!'

Best batting: 203 Glamorgan v Leicestershire, Swansea 1996
Best bowling: 4-49 Glamorgan v Leicestershire, Swansea 1996

1998 Season

	M	Inns	NO	Runs	HS	Avge	100s	50s	Ct	St	O	M	Runs	Wkts	Avge	Best	5wI	10wM
Test																		
All First	19	32	3	1012	123	34.89	2	5	20	-	40	9	92	3	30.66	1-14	-	-
1-day Int																		
NatWest	2	2	0	76	68	38.00	-	1	-	-								
B & H	4	4	0	162	96	40.50	-	2	3	-	2	1	3	0	-		-	-
Sunday	15	15	1	410	78	29.28	-	4	8	-	9	1	67	2	33.50	2-22	-	

Career Performances

	M	Inns	NO	Runs	HS	Avge	100s	50s	Ct	St	Balls	Runs	Wkts	Avge	Best	5wI	10wM
Test																	
All First	203	329	49	10619	203	37.92	21	59	142	-	1340	859	16	53.68	4-49	-	-
1-day Int																	
NatWest	25	24	6	515	68	28.61	-	4	8	-	150	96	3	32.00	1-9	-	
B & H	33	31	5	624	96	24.00	-	3	11	-	78	53	1	53.00	1-49	-	
Sunday	132	112	20	2367	92 *	25.72	-	14	47	-	509	523	15	34.86	4-56	-	

COUSINS, D. M. Essex

Name: Darren Mark Cousins
Role: Right-hand bat, right-arm fast-medium bowler, outfielder
Born: 24 September 1971, Cambridge
Height: 6ft 1in **Weight:** 13st 7lbs
Nickname: Mad Dog, Cuz, Cuzzi, Skuz
County debut: 1993
1st-Class 5 w. in innings: 1
1st-Class catches: 5
Strike rate: 90.00 (career 73.33)
Parents: Dennis Charles and
Deanna Maureen (deceased)
Marital status: Single
Family links with cricket: Father opened the
bowling and was capped for Cambridgeshire
Education: Milton Primary School;
Impington Village College
Qualifications: 7 GCSEs
Career outside cricket: Coaching and

teaching PE in local secondary school

Overseas teams played for: Gold Coast Dolphins, Queensland 1994-95; Maritzburg Old Boys, Pietermaritzburg, South Africa 1995–96

Cricketers particularly admired: Neil Foster, Geoff Arnold, Alan Butcher, Keith Fletcher and 'anyone else who has given me help, advice and guidance during my career'

Young players to look out for: Robert Rollins, Ashley Cowan, Stephen Peters, Darren Robinson

Other sports followed: Football (Liverpool, Cambridge United), 'I used to be a county swimmer and a county footballer but had to give up all other sports due to glass back syndrome'

Relaxations: 'Socialising. Listening to all types of music from Indie to soul to swing'

Extras: Represented Cambridgeshire at football and swimming and every level at cricket. Played for a Bull Development Squad against Australia in 1991, taking four wickets in each innings. Played 2nd XI cricket for Northants and Worcs. Holds the record for both number of wickets in any single Colts festival (21) and number of wickets taken in the Hilda Overy Festival overall (74). Awarded 2nd XI cap and Essex Young Player of the Year 1994. Essex Cricket Society 2nd XI Player of the Year 1994. Leading Essex wicket-taker in Sunday League and top of the bowling averages in 1994. Underwent three back operations in 22 months and missed three seasons of cricket. Released by Essex at end of 1998 season

Best batting: 18* Essex v Durham, Chelmsford 1995

Best bowling: 6-35 Essex v Cambridge University, Fenner's 1994

1998 Season

	M	Inns	NO	Runs	HS	Avge	100s	50s	Ct	St	O	M	Runs	Wkts	Avge	Best	5wI	10wM
Test																		
All First	1	2	0	14	8	7.00	-	-	-	-	15	5	52	1	52.00	1-52	-	-
1-day Int																		
NatWest																		
B & H																		
Sunday	6	1	0	1	1	1.00	-	-	1	-	41	2	178	10	17.80	3-23	-	

Career Performances

	M	Inns	NO	Runs	HS	Avge	100s	50s	Ct	St	Balls	Runs	Wkts	Avge	Best	5wI	10wM
Test																	
All First	15	25	5	159	18 *	7.95	-	-	5	-	1980	1138	27	42.14	6-35	1	-
1-day Int																	
NatWest	4	2	1	1	1 *	1.00	-	-	-	-	150	145	1	145.00	1-33	-	
B & H	6	2	1	22	12 *	22.00	-	-	1	-	239	171	2	85.50	1-33	-	
Sunday	35	12	4	19	6	2.37	-	-	3	-	1449	1108	48	23.08	3-18	-	

COWAN, A. P.   Essex

Name: Ashley Preston Cowan
Role: Right-hand bat, right-hand
fast-medium bowler
Born: 7 May 1975, Hitchin, Hertfordshire
Height: 6ft 5in **Weight:** 14st
Nickname: Victor, Dic Dic
County debut: 1995
50 w. in a season: 1
1st-Class 50s: 3
1st-Class 5 w. in innings: 4
1st-Class catches: 20
One-Day 5 w. in innings: 1
Place in batting averages: 218th av. 17.53
(1997 194th av. 22.35)
Place in bowling averages: 136th av. 45.21
(1997 34th av. 25.65)
Strike rate: 75.31 (career 61.79)
Parents: Jeff and Pam
Marital status: Single
Family links with cricket: 'Father tried to play in local village team'
Education: Kingshott Prep; Framlingham College
Qualifications: 5 GCSEs, 1 A-level, Business Vocation Degree
Career outside cricket: Family business
Overseas tours: England to West Indies 1997-98
Overseas teams played for: Zingan CC, Pietermaritzburg, South Africa 1995-97
Cricketers particularly admired: Ian Botham, Graham Dilley, Curtly Ambrose
Young players to look out for: Robert Rollins
Other sports followed: Rugby, hockey, golf, football (Newcastle United)
Injuries: Out for three to four months with shoulder injury
Relaxations: Socialising, playing golf, 'having fun'
Extras: Played rugby and hockey for East of England U18. The youngest person to
play for Cambridgeshire. First-class hat-trick at Colchester in 1996. Was the joint
leading scorer in the 1996 NatWest final
Opinions on cricket: 'Looking for a younger and more dedicated cricket crowd who
will inspire the players through their enthusiasm.'
Best batting: 94 Essex v Leicestershire, Leicester 1998
Best bowling: 5-45 Essex v Sussex, Hove 1997

1998 Season

	M	Inns	NO	Runs	HS	Avge	100s	50s	Ct	St	O	M	Runs	Wkts	Avge	Best	5wI	10wM
Test																		
All First	8	13	0	228	94	17.53	-	2	4	-	238.3	54	859	19	45.21	3-18	-	-
1-day Int																		
NatWest	2	1	0	13	13	13.00	-	-	-	-	14.1	2	60	4	15.00	2-16	-	
B & H	7	5	3	38	15 *	19.00	-	-	-	-	63	6	246	9	27.33	5-28	1	
Sunday	10	5	4	51	40 *	51.00	-	-	9	-	70.1	2	323	11	29.36	3-22	-	

Career Performances

	M	Inns	NO	Runs	HS	Avge	100s	50s	Ct	St	Balls		Runs	Wkts	Avge	Best	5wI	10wM
Test																		
All First	44	66	14	936	94	18.00	-	3	20	-	6983		3970	113	35.13	5-45	4	-
1-day Int																		
NatWest	9	5	2	46	17 *	15.33	-	-	4	-	541		357	13	27.46	3-29	-	
B & H	13	7	4	48	15 *	16.00	-	-	1	-	714		508	15	33.86	5-28	1	
Sunday	36	24	11	212	40 *	16.30	-	-	17	-	1385		1120	38	29.47	4-31	-	

COWDREY, G. R.   Kent

Name: Graham Robert Cowdrey
Role: Right-hand bat, right-arm medium
bowler, cover fielder
Born: 27 June 1964, Farnborough, Kent
Height: 5ft 11in **Weight:** 13st 9lbs
Nickname: Van, Cow
County debut: 1984
County cap: 1988
Benefit: 1997 (£303,000)
1000 runs in season: 3
1st-Class 50s: 46
1st-Class 100s: 17
1st-Class catches: 97
One-Day 100s: 3
Place in batting averages:
(1997 127th av. 29.46)
Strike rate: (career 100.50)
Parents: Michael Colin and Penelope Susan
Wife and date of marriage:
Maxine, 20 February 1993
Family links with cricket: Father (M.C.) and brother (C.S.) played for, and captained,
Kent and England

Education: Wellesley House, Broadstairs; Tonbridge School; Durham University
Qualifications: Potter
Overseas tours: Christians in Sport to India 1985-86, 1989-90; MCC to West Indies 1991-92
Overseas teams played for: Avendale, Cape Town 1983-84; Mossman, Sydney 1985-86; Randwick, Sydney 1986-87
Cricketers particularly admired: Aravinda De Silva, Steve Marsh, Mark Waugh
Young players to look out for: Ed Smith
Other sports followed: Horse racing, golf ('I am Frank Nobilo's greatest fan') and rugby league
Relaxations: Music, theatre and carp fishing
Extras: Played for England YC. Made 1000 runs for Kent 2nd XI first season on staff, and broke 2nd XI record with 1300 runs in 26 innings in 1985. Plays in contact lenses. Holds Kent record partnership for any wicket with Aravinda De Silva, 368 runs against Derbyshire 1995. Retired from first-class cricket at the end of the 1998 season and has joined City Index, a sports spread-betting company, as a cricket analyst
Best batting: 147 Kent v Gloucestershire, Bristol 1992
Best bowling: 1-5 Kent v Warwickshire, Edgbaston 1988

1998 Season

	M	Inns	NO	Runs	HS	Avge	100s	50s	Ct	St	O	M	Runs	Wkts	Avge	Best	5wI	10wM
Test																		
All First																		
1-day Int																		
NatWest																		
B & H	5	5	0	28	12	5.60	-	-	-	-								
Sunday	10	6	2	46	17	11.50	-	-	1	-	7	0	45	0	-		-	-

Career Performances

	M	Inns	NO	Runs	HS	Avge	100s	50s	Ct	St	Balls	Runs	Wkts	Avge	Best	5wI	10wM
Test																	
All First	179	284	29	8858	147	34.73	17	46	97	-	1206	872	12	72.66	1-5	-	-
1-day Int																	
NatWest	23	20	4	416	65	26.00	-	1	3	-	303	157	8	19.62	2-4	-	
B & H	60	55	4	1092	77	21.41	-	6	19	-	202	139	2	69.50	1-6	-	
Sunday	175	152	25	3575	105 *	28.14	3	17	57	-	732	589	24	24.54	4-15	-	

COX, J. Somerset

Name: Jamie Cox
Role: Right-hand bat, off-spin bowler, county captain
Born: 15 October 1969, Burnie, Tasmania
Height: 6ft **Weight:** 12st 8lbs
County debut: No first-team appearance
1st-Class 50s: 33
1st-Class 100s: 17
1st-Class 200s: 1
1st-Class catches: 42
Parents: David and Kaye
Marital status: Single
Family links with cricket: Father played state colts and is life member of local club
Education: Wynyard Primary; Wynyard High; Deakin University (current)
Qualifications: School Certificate, Diploma of Management; currently studying for Bachelor of Business degree

Career outside cricket: Banking operations analyst – Trust Bank
Overseas tours: Australia U19 to West Indies 1989; Australia A to Zimbabwe 1990; Australia XI to Zimbabwe 1991-92; Tasmania to Zimbabwe 1995-96
Overseas teams played for: Tasmania 1987 –
Cricketers particularly admired: Kim Hughes, Ian Botham
Young players to look out for: Gerrard Denton (Tasmanian fast bowler)
Other sports played: Australian Rules football, golf
Other sports followed: Australian Rules football (Western Bulldogs)
Relaxations: Music, driving, bushwalking
Extras: Scored 1349 runs in the 1996-97 Australian season, with five 100s, including two in one match v New South Wales. Players' Player of the Year 1996-97. Tasmanian Cricket Player of the Year 1996-97. Vice-captain of Tasmania. Scored an unbeaten 115 in the first innings of the 1997-98 Sheffield Shield final v Western Australia, becoming the first player to carry his bat in a Shield final. Has joined Somerset for 1999 as overseas player and captain
Opinions on cricket: 'It needs to find a balance between preserving tradition whilst adopting innovation to attract new markets and audiences.'
Best batting: 200 Tasmania v Pakistan, Hobart 1996-97

Career Performances

	M	Inns	NO	Runs	HS	Avge	100s	50s	Ct	St	Balls	Runs	Wkts	Avge	Best	5wl	10wM
Test																	
All First	103	188	12	7046	200	40.03	18	33	42	-		78	77	0	-	-	-	-
1-day Int																	
NatWest																	
B & H																	
Sunday																	

CRAWLEY, J. P. Lancashire

Name: John Paul Crawley
Role: Right-hand bat, occasional
wicket-keeper, county captain
Born: 21 September 1971, Maldon, Essex
Height: 6ft 2in **Weight:** 13st 2lbs
Nickname: Creeps, Jonty, JC
County debut: 1990
Test debut: 1994
Tests: 26
One-Day Internationals: 10
1000 runs in a season: 7
1st-Class 50s: 74
1st-Class 100s: 26
1st-Class 200s: 4
1st-Class catches: 134
One-Day 100s: 3
Place in batting averages: 1st av. 74.04
(1997 21st av. 49.60)
Strike rate: (career 84.00)
Parents: Frank and Jean
Marital status: Single
Family links with cricket: Father played in Manchester Association; brother Mark played for Lancashire before moving to Nottinghamshire; other brother Peter plays for Warrington CC and has played for Scottish Universities and Cambridge University; uncle was excellent fast bowler; godfather umpires in Manchester Association
Education: Manchester Grammar School; Trinity College, Cambridge
Qualifications: 10 O-levels, 2 AO-Levels, 3 A-levels, 2 S-levels, BA in History
Off-season: Touring Australia with England
Overseas tours: England YC to Australia 1989-90, to New Zealand 1990-91; England A to South Africa 1993-94; England to Australia 1994-95, to South Africa 1995-96,

to Zimbabwe and New Zealand 1996-97, to West Indies 1997-98, to Australia 1998-99
Overseas teams played for: Midland Guildford, Perth 1990
Cricketers particularly admired: Michael Atherton, Neil Fairbrother, Graham Gooch, Alec Stewart, David Gower, Allan Donald, Ian Salisbury
Other sports followed: Football (Manchester United), golf
Relaxations: 'Playing or trying to play the guitar'
Extras: Captained England YC (U19) to New Zealand 1990-91 and played for England YC in three home series v New Zealand 1989, Pakistan 1990 and Australia (as captain) 1991. Made his maiden first-class century for Cambridge University on the same day that brother Mark made his for Notts. First to score 1000 runs in U19 Tests. Scored 286 for England A against Eastern Province at Port Elizabeth in 1994, the highest score by an Englishman on an England or England A tour for almost 30 years. Finished top of the first-class batting averages on England's tour to South Africa in 1995-96 with 336 runs at 67.20, but had to fly home after suffering a hamstring injury whilst fielding in the third Test at Durban. Scored his maiden Test match hundred (106) in the third Test against Pakistan at The Oval in 1996, followed by 112 in England's next Test against Zimbabwe in Bulawayo in 1996-97. Lancashire vice-captain for the 1998 season. Scored century in each innings v Glamorgan 1998. Topped first-class batting averages for 1998 season. Appointed Lancashire captain for the 1999 season
Best batting: 286 England A v Eastern Province, Port Elizabeth 1993-94
Best bowling: 1-90 Lancashire v Sussex, Hove 1992

1998 Season

	M	Inns	NO	Runs	HS	Avge	100s	50s	Ct	St	O	M	Runs	Wkts	Avge	Best	5wI	10wM
Test	1	2	1	170	156 *	170.00	1	-	1	-								
All First	18	28	3	1851	239	74.04	8	5	7	-	1	0	21	0	-	-	-	-
1-day Int																		
NatWest	5	5	1	194	79	48.50	-	2	4	-								
B & H	6	6	0	305	88	50.83	-	3	1	-								
Sunday	13	13	0	350	100	26.92	1	1	3	-								

Career Performances

	M	Inns	NO	Runs	HS	Avge	100s	50s	Ct	St	Balls	Runs	Wkts	Avge	Best	5wI	10wM
Test	26	41	5	1243	156 *	34.52	3	7	23	-							
All First	178	288	29	13083	286	50.51	30	74	134	-	84	129	1	129.00	1-90	-	-
1-day Int	10	9	0	180	73	20.00	-	2	1	-							
NatWest	16	16	2	556	113 *	39.71	1	4	6	-	6	4	0	-	-	-	-
B & H	36	35	1	1262	114	37.11	1	7	11	-							
Sunday	71	69	2	1718	100	25.64	1	11	20	-							

CROFT, R. D. B.   Glamorgan

Name: Robert Damien Bale Croft
Role: Right-hand bat, off-spinner
Born: 25 May 1970, Swansea
Height: 5ft 11in **Weight:** 11st 5lbs
Nickname: Crofty
County debut: 1989
County cap: 1992
Test debut: 1996
Tests: 14
One-Day Internationals: 29
50 wickets in a season: 5
1st-Class 50s: 25
1st-Class 100s: 2
1st-Class 5 w. in innings: 22
1st-Class 10 w. in match: 3
1st-Class catches: 105
One-Day 5 w. in innings: 1
Place in batting averages: 166th av. 22.86
(1997 151st av. 26.08)
Place in bowling averages: 142nd av. 57.20 (1997 51st av. 27.38)
Strike rate: 136.15 (career 80.26)
Parents: Malcolm and Susan
Family links with cricket: Father and grandfather played local cricket
Education: St John Lloyd Catholic School; Neath Trinity College; West Glamorgan
Institute of Higher Education
Qualifications: 6 O-levels; OND Business Studies; HND Business Studies; NCA
senior coaching certificate
Career outside cricket: Personnel management ('not as yet!')
Off-season: Touring Australia with England
Overseas tours: England A to Bermuda and West Indies 1991-92, to South Africa
1993-94; England to Zimbabwe and New Zealand 1996-97, to West Indies 1997-98, to
Australia 1998-99
Cricketers particularly admired: Alan Jones, Tom Cartwright, Don Shepherd,
John Steele, John Emburey
Other sports followed: Rugby, soccer
Relaxations: Shooting, fishing, driving, music, golf
Extras: Captained England South to victory in International Youth Tournament 1989
and was voted Player of the Tournament. Glamorgan Young Player of the Year 1992.
Opinions on cricket: 'Enjoyment is of the utmost importance.'
Best batting: 143 Glamorgan v Somerset, Taunton 1995
Best bowling: 8-66 Glamorgan v Warwickshire, Swansea 1992

1998 Season

	M	Inns	NO	Runs	HS	Avge	100s	50s	Ct	St	O	M	Runs	Wkts	Avge	Best	5wI	10wM
Test	3	6	4	90	37 *	45.00	-	-	1	-	87	20	211	0	-	-	-	-
All First	13	22	7	343	63 *	22.86	-	1	9	-	453.5	117	1144	20	57.20	4-76	-	-
1-day Int	6	5	1	42	17	10.50	-	-	-	-	57	0	265	9	29.44	3-51	-	
NatWest	2	2	0	19	19	9.50	-	-	-	-	24	3	96	3	32.00	3-62	-	
B & H	4	4	0	253	77	63.25	-	4	1	-	30	4	104	3	34.66	2-16	-	
Sunday	9	9	2	144	50	20.57	-	1	2	-	64	1	289	6	48.16	2-21	-	

Career Performances

	M	Inns	NO	Runs	HS	Avge	100s	50s	Ct	St	Balls	Runs	Wkts	Avge	Best	5wI	10wM
Test	14	22	5	268	37 *	15.76	-	-	8	-	3221	1254	34	36.88	5-95	1	-
All First	201	295	56	6054	143	25.33	2	25	105	-	42941	19670	535	36.76	8-66	22	3
1-day Int	29	20	7	179	30 *	13.76	-	-	8	-	1614	1107	31	35.70	3-51	-	
NatWest	24	20	5	358	64	23.86	-	3	4	-	1480	826	23	35.91	3-30	-	
B & H	27	23	7	580	77	36.25	-	5	8	-	1517	945	32	29.53	4-30	-	
Sunday	109	84	24	1299	68	21.65	-	4	27	-	4396	3309	96	34.46	6-20	1	

CROWE, C. D.   Leicestershire

Name: Carl Daniel Crowe
Role: Right-hand bat, off-spin bowler
Born: 25 November 1975, Leicester
Height: 6ft **Weight:** 12st 7lbs
Nickname: Scuby
County debut: 1995
1st-Class catches: 4
Strike rate: 61.66 (career 64.66)
Parents: Edward Patrick and Jeannette
Marital status: Single
Family links with cricket: Brother Craig has
played for Leicestershire 2nd XI
Education: Lutterworth High School;
Lutterworth Grammar School
Qualifications: 11 GCSEs, 2 A-levels,
NCA Senior Coach
Off-season: Playing in Melbourne
Overseas tours: Leicestershire U19 to South
Africa 1993-94; Leicestershire to Holland
1996, 1998; to Barbados 1998
Overseas teams played for: Old Mentonians, Melbourne 1997-98
Cricketers particularly admired: Mark and Steve Waugh, Kumara Dharmasena,
Sven Samild

Young players to look out for: Jimmy Ormond, Kevin Dean, Craig Crowe
Other sports followed: Try all sports, 'had a hole in one'. 'Support Leicester at everything and follow Spurs'
Injuries: 'Fell through neighbour's garage roof. I needed stitches in my leg but missed no cricket'
Relaxations: 'Taking my girlfriend out. Going out for meals with friends'
Extras: Played for Leicestershire U12-U19 and Midlands Schools U14-U19. One of the Cricketers of the Festival at Cambridge U19 Festival 1994. Won Leics 2nd XI batting award 1998
Opinions on cricket: 'The experiment of four-day cricket in 2nd XI cricket seemed to be the best way forward if that level of cricket is going to survive.'
Best batting: 29* Leicestershire v Lancashire, Old Trafford 1998
Best bowling: 3-49 Leicestershire v Durham, Darlington 1998

1998 Season

	M	Inns	NO	Runs	HS	Avge	100s	50s	Ct	St	O	M	Runs	Wkts	Avge	Best	5wI	10wM
Test																		
All First	6	6	1	88	29 *	17.60	-	-	3	-	61.4	10	201	6	33.50	3-49	-	-
1-day Int																		
NatWest																		
B & H																		
Sunday	1	1	1	4	4 *	-	-	-	-	-	-							

Career Performances

	M	Inns	NO	Runs	HS	Avge	100s	50s	Ct	St	Balls	Runs	Wkts	Avge	Best	5wI	10wM
Test																	
All First	7	8	1	98	29 *	14.00	-	-	4	-	388	205	6	34.16	3-49	-	-
1-day Int																	
NatWest																	
B & H																	
Sunday	2	1	1	4	4 *	-	-	-	-	-							

CUNLIFFE, R. J.   Gloucestershire

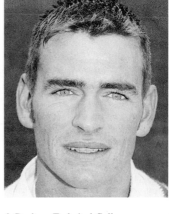

Name: Robert John Cunliffe
Role: Right-hand bat, cover fielder
Born: 8 November 1973, Oxford
Height: 5ft 10in **Weight:** 12st 8lbs
Nickname: 'Forrest Gump for some reason'
County debut: 1993 (one-day),
1994 (first-class)
1st-Class 100s: 2
1st-Class 50s: 7
1st-Class catches: 29
One-Day 100s: 3
Place in batting averages: 239th av. 15.40
(1997 206th av. 21.00)
Parents: Barry and Janet
Marital status: Engaged to Claire
Family links with cricket: 'Dad played in
his younger days for his wife's village team
and was groundsman for nine years at
Banbury Twenty CC'
Education: Grimsbury Primary; Banbury School; Banbury Technical College
Qualifications: Carpentry course, coaching award
Career outside cricket: Coaching
Off-season: Coaching
Overseas tours: England U19 to India 1992-93
Overseas teams played for: Richmond City CC, Melbourne 1995-97
Cricketers particularly admired: Robin Smith
Young players to look out for: Darren Maddy
Other sports played: Football
Relaxations: Walking the dog, watching TV
Extras: Played in England U19 home series against West Indies in 1993
Best batting: 190* Gloucestershire v Oxford University, The Parks 1995

1998 Season

	M	Inns	NO	Runs	HS	Avge	100s	50s	Ct	St	O	M	Runs	Wkts	Avge	Best	5wl	10wM
Test																		
All First	12	22	0	339	53	15.40	-	2	14	-								
1-day Int																		
NatWest																		
B & H	5	5	0	115	58	23.00	-	1	4	-								
Sunday	5	5	3	55	37	27.50	-	-	1	-								

Career Performances

	M	Inns	NO	Runs	HS	Avge	100s	50s	Ct	St	Balls	Runs	Wkts	Avge	Best	5wI	10wM
Test																	
All First	41	68	5	1630	190 *	25.87	2	7	29	-							
1-day Int																	
NatWest	5	4	0	110	40	27.50	-	-	1	-							
B & H	15	15	3	649	137 *	54.08	3	2	7	-							
Sunday	19	19	4	383	56	25.53	-	3	3	-							

CURRAN, K. M. Northamptonshire

Name: Kevin Malcolm Curran
Role: Right-hand bat, right-arm
fast-medium bowler
Born: 7 September 1959, Rusape, Zimbabwe
Height: 6ft 2in **Weight:** 14st
Nickname: KC
County debut: 1985 (Gloucestershire),
1991 (Northamptonshire)
County cap: 1985 (Gloucestershire),
1992 (Northamptonshire)
One-Day Internationals: 11
1000 runs in a season: 7
50 wickets in a season: 5
1st-Class 50s: 83
1st-Class 100s: 25
1st-Class 5 w. in innings: 15
1st-Class 10 w. in match: 4
1st-Class catches: 208
One-Day 100s: 1

One-Day 5 w. in innings: 1
Place in batting averages: 78th av. 32.22 (1997 29th av. 46.90)
Place in bowling averages: (1997 68th av. 29.79)
Strike rate: 234.00 (career 52.92)
Parent: Kevin
Wife and date of marriage: Sarah, 5 June 1992
Children: Thomas Kevin, 12 March 1995; Benjamin Jack, 6 June 1996;
Sam, 3 June 1998
Family links with cricket: Father played for Rhodesia 1947-54. Cousin Patrick
Curran played for Rhodesia 1975
Education: Marandellas High School, Zimbabwe
Qualifications: 6 O-levels, 2 M-levels

Career outside cricket: Tobacco buyer/farmer
Off-season: 'Trying to make ends meet and looking for a job'
Overseas tours: Zimbabwe to Sri Lanka 1982 and 1984, to England 1982 and for World Cup 1983, to Pakistan and India for World Cup 1987
Overseas teams played for: Zimbabwe and Natal 1988-92; Boland 1994-95
Other sports followed: Rugby union
Relaxations: 'Game fishing, especially along the North Natal coast, the Mozambique coast, and Magaruque Island'
Extras: First player to take a Sunday League hat-trick and score 50 in the same match, Gloucestershire v Warwickshire, Edgbaston 1989. Released by Gloucestershire at end of 1990 after he had completed the season's double of 1000 runs and 50 wickets. Chose to join Northamptonshire for the 1991 season after he had been approached by several counties. Northants captain 1998. Granted a benefit in 1999
Best batting: 159 Northamptonshire v Glamorgan, Abergavenny 1997
Best bowling: 7-47 Northamptonshire v Yorkshire, Harrogate 1993

1998 Season

	M	Inns	NO	Runs	HS	Avge	100s	50s	Ct	St	O	M	Runs	Wkts	Avge	Best	5wI	10wM
Test																		
All First	18	26	4	709	90 *	32.22	-	6	23	-	78	20	265	2	132.50	1-25	-	-
1-day Int																		
NatWest	1	1	0	53	53	53.00	-	1	1	-	5	0	27	0	-		-	-
B & H	4	4	0	140	71	35.00	-	1	3	-	17	2	67	1	67.00	1-10	-	
Sunday	15	15	1	437	59	31.21	-	3	7	-	44.3	2	272	8	34.00	2-36	-	

Career Performances

	M	Inns	NO	Runs	HS	Avge	100s	50s	Ct	St	Balls	Runs	Wkts	Avge	Best	5wI	10wM
Test																	
All First	323	508	83	15739	159	37.03	25	83	208	-	31964	16709	604	27.66	7-47	15	4
1-day Int	11	11	0	287	73	26.09	-	2	1	-	506	398	9	44.22	3-65	-	
NatWest	42	36	7	862	78 *	29.72	-	4	13	-	2153	1231	41	30.02	4-34	-	
B & H	57	52	8	1142	71	25.95	-	7	13	-	2550	1768	53	33.35	4-38	-	
Sunday	200	190	38	5006	119 *	32.93	1	29	45	-	5958	4965	177	28.05	5-15	1	

DAGNALL, C. E. Warwickshire

Name: Charles Edward Dagnall
Role: Right-hand bat, right-arm
fast bowler
Born: 10 July 1976, Bury, Lancashire
Height: 6ft 4in **Weight:** 14st 10lbs
Nickname: Colonel, Charlie
County debut: No first-team appearance
Parents: Mike and Jacqueline
Marital status: Single
Family links with cricket: Parents both
umpires
Education: Bolton School; Bridgwater
School, Worsley; UMIST
Qualifications: 10 O-levels, 3 A-levels,
BSc (Hons) Chemistry
Off-season: Playing overseas in Australia
Overseas teams played for: Newtown
1994-95; St Josephs, Melbourne 1998-99

Cricketers particularly admired:
Viv Richards, Ian Botham, David Gower
Young players to look out for: Paddy McKeown
Other sports played: Volleyball (Manchester League), golf (18 handicap)
Other sports followed: Football (Burnley FC)
Relaxations: Music, travel
Opinions on cricket: 'Transitional and potentially exciting future'

1998 Season

	M	Inns	NO	Runs	HS	Avge	100s	50s	Ct	St	O	M	Runs	Wkts	Avge	Best	5wI	10wM
Test																		
All First																		
1-day Int																		
NatWest	1	1	0	4	4	4.00	-	-	-	-	9	0	37	1	37.00	1-37	-	
B & H																		
Sunday																		

---

12. For whom did Salim Raza score 84 v Netherlands
in Lahore, his birthplace, on 1 March 1996?

FICA

149

	M	Inns	NO	Runs	HS	Avge	100s	50s	Ct	St	Balls	Runs	Wkts	Avge	Best	5wI	10wM
Test																	
All First																	
1-day Int																	
NatWest	1	1	0	4	4	4.00	-	-	-	-	54	37	1	37.00	1-37	-	
B & H																	
Sunday																	

DAKIN, J. M.   Leicestershire

Name: Jonathan Michael Dakin
Role: Left-hand bat, right-arm
medium-fast bowler
Born: 28 February 1973, Hitchin, Herts
Height: 6ft 5in **Weight:** 15st 8lbs
Nickname: Babe
County debut: 1993
1st-Class 50s: 3
1st-Class 100s: 3
1st-Class catches: 11
One-Day 100s: 1
Place in batting averages: 178th av. 21.33
Strike rate: 99.00 (career 84.96)
Parents: Fred John and Gloria May
Marital status: Single
Family links with cricket: Brother plays for
Wanderers CC in South Africa
Education: King Edward VII School,
Johannesburg, South Africa

Qualifications: Matriculation
Overseas tours: Rutland Tourists to Jersey 1992; Leicestershire CCC to South Africa
1996 and 1997
Overseas teams played for: Wanderers, South Africa, 1986-92; Alberts, South Africa
1993; Kaponga CC, New Zealand 1995-96
Cricketers particularly admired: Phil Simmons, Vince 'Legend' Wells
Young players to look out for: Darren 'Roasting' Maddy, Gary Outram
Other sports followed: Football (Leicester City and Qwa Qwa Stars FC), rugby union
(Leicester Tigers)
Relaxations: Cinema, television, golf, having *a* drink in a pub
Extras: Won three Bain Hogg trophies in four years. Scored 193 against Middlesex in
the Bain Hogg in 1996. Won the Gold Award against Durham in the 1996 B&H

Opinions on cricket: 'Tea should be 30 minutes.'
Best batting: 190 Leicestershire v Northamptonshire, Northampton 1997
Best bowling: 4-45 Leicestershire v Cambridge University, Fenner's 1993

1998 Season

	M	Inns	NO	Runs	HS	Avge	100s	50s	Ct	St	O	M	Runs	Wkts	Avge	Best	5wI	10wM
Test																		
All First	6	6	0	128	79	21.33	-	1	2	-	132	31	374	8	46.75	4-110	-	-
1-day Int																		
NatWest																		
B & H	4	1	0	44	44	44.00	-	-	-	-	21.3	1	114	3	38.00	3-68	-	
Sunday	15	13	0	126	29	9.69	-	-	2	-	32	6	112	13	8.61	4-14	-	

Career Performances

	M	Inns	NO	Runs	HS	Avge	100s	50s	Ct	St	Balls	Runs	Wkts	Avge	Best	5wI	10wM
Test																	
All First	22	30	3	834	190	30.88	3	3	11	-	2124	1107	25	44.28	4-45	-	-
1-day Int																	
NatWest	4	4	0	63	26	15.75	-	-	-	-	144	100	1	100.00	1-63	-	
B & H	12	9	3	295	108 *	49.16	1	-	5	-	327	317	10	31.70	3-68	-	
Sunday	66	59	6	696	45	13.13	-	-	14	-	1398	1302	52	25.03	4-14	-	

DALE, A.   Glamorgan

Name: Adrian Dale
Role: Right-hand bat, right-arm
medium bowler
Born: 24 October 1968, Johannesburg
Height: 5ft 11in **Weight:** 11st 8lbs
Nickname: Arthur, Arnie
County debut: 1989
County cap: 1992
1000 runs in a season: 3
1st-Class 50s: 43
1st-Class 100s: 13
1st-Class 200s: 1
1st-Class 5 w. in innings: 2
1st-Class catches: 64
One-Day 100s: 2
One-Day 5 w. in innings: 2
Place in batting averages: 79th av. 32.12
(1997 76th av. 3739)

Place in bowling averages: 52nd av. 25.61 (1996 109th av. 39.16)
Strike rate: 48.29 (career 69.90)
Parents: John and Maureen
Wife and date of marriage: Ruth, 9 January 1999
Family links with cricket: Father played for Chepstow CC and the odd game for Glamorgan 2nd XI
Education: Pembroke Primary; Chepstow Comprehensive; Swansea University
Qualifications: 9 O-levels, 3 A-levels, BA (Hons) Economics
Career outside cricket: 'Tried estate agency'
Off-season: 'Going to New Zealand'
Overseas tours: Welsh Schools U16 to Australia 1986-87; Combined Universities to Barbados 1988-89; Glamorgan to Trinidad 1989-90, to Zimbabwe 1990-91, to Trinidad 1991-92, to Cape Town 1992-93; England A to South Africa 1993-94
Overseas teams played for: Bionics, Zimbabwe 1990-91; Cornwall, New Zealand 1991-93, 1995-97
Cricketers particularly admired: Ian Botham, Michael Holding, Mike Gatting
Young players to look out for: Mike Powell, Wayne Law
Other sports followed: Football (Arsenal), athletics, US basketball, rugby league (Auckland Warriors and Wales), rugby union (Wales), ice hockey (Cardiff Devils)
Relaxations: Eating out, following other sports, travelling
Extras: Played in successful Combined Universities sides of 1989 and 1990. Only batsman to score two half-centuries against the West Indies tourists in the same match in 1991. Took a wicket with his first delivery at Lord's. Recorded Glamorgan's best one-day bowling figures, 6-22 against Durham 1993. Recorded Glamorgan's highest ever partnership, 425, with Viv Richards against Middlesex, 1993
Opinions on cricket: 'I think two divisions in the County Championship will not necessarily improve the standard. It may, however, improve the viability for sponsors. A transfer system is sure to follow if two divisions are put in place. No one can say with any confidence the financial effect on the game, and it could lead to the shambles that we now see in rugby.'
Best batting: 214* Glamorgan v Middlesex, Cardiff 1993
Best bowling: 6-18 Glamorgan v Warwickshire, Cardiff 1993

1998 Season

	M	Inns	NO	Runs	HS	Avge	100s	50s	Ct	St	O	M	Runs	Wkts	Avge	Best	5wl	10wM
Test																		
All First	19	33	1	1028	92	32.12	-	9	7	-	249.3	46	794	31	25.61	5-25	1	-
1-day Int																		
NatWest	2	2	0	115	89	57.50	-	1	-	-	5	1	23	0	-		-	
B & H	4	4	0	49	18	12.25	-	-	-	-	8	1	35	3	11.66	2-6	-	
Sunday	15	15	0	427	82	28.46	-	2	3	-	63.3	0	358	11	32.54	4-36	-	

Career Performances

	M	Inns	NO	Runs	HS	Avge	100s	50s	Ct	St	Balls	Runs	Wkts	Avge	Best	5wI	10wM
Test																	
All First	165	273	24	8157	214 *	32.75	14	43	64	-	11394	6152	163	37.74	6-18	2	-
1-day Int																	
NatWest	26	23	2	680	110	32.38	1	3	6	-	1066	753	21	35.85	3-54	-	
B & H	33	32	4	758	100	27.07	1	1	10	-	1268	902	39	23.12	5-41	1	
Sunday	129	114	13	2835	82	28.06	-	16	30	-	3936	3570	110	32.45	6-22	1	

DALEY, J. A. Durham

Name: James Arthur Daley
Role: Right-hand bat
Born: 24 September 1973, Sunderland
Height: 5ft 11in **Weight:** 12st
Nickname: Bebs, Jonty
County debut: 1992
1st-Class 50s: 14
1st-Class 100s: 2
1st-Class catches: 31
Place in batting averages: 86th av. 31.70
(1997 188th av. 26.50)
Strike rate: 6.00 (career 18.00)
Parents: William and Christine
Marital status: Single
Family links with cricket: Brother played
representative cricket for Durham
Education: Hetton Comprehensive
Qualifications: 5 GCSEs
Career outside cricket: Travel agent
Overseas tours: Durham to Zimbabwe 1991-92; England U19 to India 1992-93;
England XI to Holland 1993
Cricketers particularly admired: David Graveney, Wayne Larkins, Jimmy Adams
Other sports followed: Most sports
Relaxations: Socialising, listening to all types of music
Extras: Scored three centuries in 1991 for MCC Young Cricketers at Lord's. Northern
Electric Foundation for Sport award winner 1992
Best batting: 159* Durham v Hampshire, Portsmouth 1994
Best bowling: 1-12 Durham v Cambridge University, Fenner's 1998

1998 Season

	M	Inns	NO	Runs	HS	Avge	100s	50s	Ct	St	O	M	Runs	Wkts	Avge	Best	5wl	10wM
Test																		
All First	12	22	2	634	157	31.70	1	1	5	-	1	0	12	1	12.00	1-12	-	-
1-day Int																		
NatWest																		
B & H	1	1	0	7	7	7.00	-	-	-	-								
Sunday	6	5	2	120	69	40.00	-	1	2	-								

Career Performances

	M	Inns	NO	Runs	HS	Avge	100s	50s	Ct	St	Balls	Runs	Wkts	Avge	Best	5wl	10wM
Test																	
All First	58	101	10	2858	159 *	31.40	2	14	31	-	18	21	1	21.00	1-12	-	-
1-day Int																	
NatWest																	
B & H	7	6	0	79	33	13.16	-	-	-	-	12	19	0	-		-	-
Sunday	26	23	8	581	98 *	38.73	-	4	7	-	1	4	0	-		-	-

DAVIES, A. P.   Glamorgan

Name: Andrew Philip Davies
Role: Left-hand bat, right-arm
medium bowler
Born: 7 November 1976, Neath
Height: 5ft 10in **Weight:** 12st 9lbs
Nickname: Diver
County debut: 1995
1st-Class catches: 1
Place in bowling averages: 69th av. 27.85
Strike rate: 58.21 (career 65.93)
Parents: Phil and Anne
Marital status: Single; girlfriend Samantha
Family links with cricket: 'Dad plays for
local league side'
Education: Coedffranc; Dwr-y-felin
Comprehensive School; Christ College,
Brecon
Qualifications: 6 GCSEs, 1 A-level;
Coaching Certificate
Career outside cricket: Teaching and coaching
Off-season: 'Considering New Zealand'
Overseas tours: Wales MC to Barbados; Glamorgan to South Africa 1995-96

Overseas teams played for: Marist CC, Whangarei, New Zealand 1995-96
Cricketers particularly admired: Steve Watkin, Allan Donald, Steve James, Matthew Maynard
Young players to look out for: Leighton Jones, Philip George, Andrew Phillips, 'Des, pool champion in "The Farmers Arms"'
Other sports played: Golf, football
Other sports followed: Football (Swansea City)
Injuries: Out for four weeks with broken wrist
Relaxations: 'A quiet drink or two down "The Greyhound" in Neath with girlfriend'
Extras: Trials at Birmingham City FC. Rugby trials for Wales U17. Welsh U19 Player of the Year 1995
Opinions on cricket: '2nd XI cricket should either be two-day with one innings per side or four-day cricket.'
Best batting: 34 Glamorgan v Essex, Chelmsford 1998
Best bowling: 2-22 Glamorgan v Sussex, Hove 1998

1998 Season

	M	Inns	NO	Runs	HS	Avge	100s	50s	Ct	St	O	M	Runs	Wkts	Avge	Best	5wI	10wM
Test																		
All First	5	6	1	55	34	11.00	-	-	1	-	135.5	41	390	14	27.85	2-22	-	-
1-day Int																		
NatWest																			
B & H																			
Sunday	6	4	3	23	18	23.00	-	-	1	-	38.4	3	165	8	20.62	2-17	-	

Career Performances

	M	Inns	NO	Runs	HS	Avge	100s	50s	Ct	St	Balls	Runs	Wkts	Avge	Best	5wI	10wM
Test																	
All First	8	8	2	74	34	12.33	-	-	1	-	989	525	15	35.00	2-22	-	-
1-day Int																	
NatWest																	
B & H																	
Sunday	7	5	3	26	18	13.00	-	-	1	-	280	190	10	19.00	2-17	-	

DAVIES, M. K.   Northamptonshire

Name: Michael Kenton Davies
Role: Right-hand bat, slow left-arm bowler
Born: 17 July 1976, Ashby-de-la-Zouch
Height: 6ft **Weight:** 12st
Nickname: Dickie, Spaceman
County debut: 1997
1st-Class 5 w. in innings: 2
1st-Class catches: 2
Place in bowling averages:
(1997 65th av. 29.30)
Strike rate: 70.28 (career 63.26)
Parents: Lyndon and Ann
Marital status: Single
Family links with cricket:
'Mum watches a lot'
Education: Fairfield Primary School,
Loughborough; Loughborough Grammar
School; Loughborough University

Qualifications: 8 GCSEs, 4 A-levels,
BSc PE, Sports Science and Recreation Management
Off-season: Relaxing, training and travelling
Cricketers particularly admired: Phil Tufnell, Allan Donald
Young players to look out for: Scott Boswell, Toby Bailey
Other sports played: Golf, 5-a-side football
Other sports followed: Football (Derby County) 'and Wales at anything, especially rugby'
Relaxations: Listening to music, socialising and travelling
Extras: Leicestershire U19 Player of the Year. Was a member of BUSA's cricket squad in the 1997 Benson and Hedges Cup. Has represented British Universities for the past two seasons
Opinions on cricket: 'We are playing too much cricket, which means less time is available to practise particular skills.'
Best batting: 17 Northamptonshire v Glamorgan, Abergavenny 1997
Best bowling: 5-19 Northamptonshire v Sussex, Northampton 1998

---

13. Who holds the all-time record for the most
World Cup matches umpired?

1998 Season

	M	Inns	NO	Runs	HS	Avge	100s	50s	Ct	St	O	M	Runs	Wkts	Avge	Best	5wI	10wM
Test																		
All First	2	3	1	23	16	11.50	-	-	-	-	82	23	192	7	27.42	5-19	1	-
1-day Int																		
NatWest																		
B & H	5	2	1	3	2 *	3.00	-	-	-	-	38	3	176	4	44.00	3-18	-	
Sunday																		

Career Performances

	M	Inns	NO	Runs	HS	Avge	100s	50s	Ct	St	Balls	Runs	Wkts	Avge	Best	5wI	10wM
Test																	
All First	8	12	5	72	17	10.28	-	-	2	-	1898	866	30	28.86	5-19	2	-
1-day Int																	
NatWest																	
B & H	6	3	2	4	2 *	4.00	-	-	-	-	278	245	5	49.00	3-18	-	
Sunday																	

DAVIS, R. P. Sussex

Name: Richard Peter Davis
Role: Right-hand bat, slow left-arm bowler
Born: 18 March 1966, Westbrook, Margate
Height: 6ft 4in **Weight:** 14st 4lbs
Nickname: Dicky
County debut: 1986 (Kent),
1994 (Warwickshire), 1996 (Gloucestershire),
1998 (one-day, Sussex)
County cap: 1990 (Kent),
1994 (Warwickshire)
50 wickets in a season: 2
1st-Class 50s: 4
1st-Class 5 w. in innings: 16
1st-Class 10 w. in match: 2
1st-Class catches: 155
One-Day 5 w. in innings: 1
Place in batting averages:
(1997 278th av. 11.25)
Place in bowling averages:
(1997 102nd av. 35.70)
Strike rate: (career 74.87)
Parents: Brian and Sylvia

Wife and date of marriage: Samantha Jane, 3 March 1990
Family links with cricket: Father played club cricket and is an NCA coach; father-in-law, Colin Tomlin, helped with England's fitness training for tours from 1990-93; brother-in-law, Raj Sharma, played for Derbyshire
Education: King Ethelbert's School, Birchington; Thanet Technical College
Qualifications: CSEs, NCA Coaching Certificate
Overseas tours: Kent Schools to Canada 1983; Kent to Zimbabwe 1992-93; Warwickshire to Zimbabwe 1993-94, to Cape Town 1994-95
Young players to look out for: Vikram Solanki
Other sports followed: Football (Derby County), rugby, squash, golf, badminton
Relaxations: Eating out with my wife, Sam, television and reading
Extras: Moved to Warwickshire at the end of the 1993 season after nine years with Kent. Released by Warwickshire at the end of the 1995 season and joined Gloucestershire for the 1996 season. Retired from first-class cricket at the end of the 1997 season to become cricket development officer for Greater London. Joined Sussex for 1998 as a one-day player. Released by Sussex at end of 1998 season
Best batting: 67 Kent v Hampshire, Southampton 1989
Best bowling: 7-64 Kent v Durham, Gateshead Fell 1992

1998 Season

	M	Inns	NO	Runs	HS	Avge	100s	50s	Ct	St	O	M	Runs	Wkts	Avge	Best	5wI	10wM
Test																		
All First																		
1-day Int																		
NatWest																		
B & H	2	1	0	16	16	16.00	-	-	-	-	7	0	45	0	-		-	-
Sunday	2	2	0	10	8	5.00	-	-	-	-	13	1	73	1	73.00	1-28	-

Career Performances

	M	Inns	NO	Runs	HS	Avge	100s	50s	Ct	St	Balls	Runs	Wkts	Avge	Best	5wI	10wM
Test																	
All First	169	208	46	2452	67	15.13	-	4	155	-	30998	14543	414	35.12	7-64	16	2
1-day Int																	
NatWest	14	7	2	47	22	9.40	-	-	10	-	801	436	15	29.06	3-19	-
B & H	29	12	5	81	18 *	11.57	-	-	12	-	1508	1063	20	53.15	2-26	-
Sunday	97	49	19	265	40 *	8.83	-	-	31	-	3584	2841	101	28.12	5-52	1

DAWOOD, I.   Glamorgan

Name: Ismail Dawood
Role: Right-hand bat, wicket-keeper
Born: 23 July 1976, Dewsbury
Height: 5ft 8in
Nickname: Hectic
County debut: 1994 (Northamptonshire), 1996 (Worcestershire), 1998 (Glamorgan)
1st-Class catches: 23
1st-Class stumpings: 3
Place in batting averages: 216th av. 17.63
Parents: Saleem and Rashida
Marital status: Single
Family links with cricket: Grandfather and father played local league cricket
Education: Batley Grammar School
Qualifications: 8 GCSEs, NCA Coaching Award
Overseas tours: England U19 to Sri Lanka 1993-94, to West Indies 1994-95
Overseas teams played for: Grafton, Auckland 1992-93
Cricketers particularly admired: Mohammed Azharuddin, Allan Border, Ian Healy 'and many others'
Other sports followed: Local soccer team
Relaxations: 'Spending time with family and friends'
Extras: Left Northamptonshire at the end of 1995 season and joined Worcestershire in 1996. Joined Glamorgan for the 1998 season
Opinions on cricket: 'The game should be played in good spirit and enjoyed at all levels from junior to Test cricket.'
Best batting: 40 Glamorgan v Somerset, Cardiff 1998

1998 Season

	M	Inns	NO	Runs	HS	Avge	100s	50s	Ct	St	O	M	Runs	Wkts	Avge	Best	5wI	10wM
Test																		
All First	7	12	1	194	40	17.63	-	-	19	1								
1-day Int																		
NatWest																		
B & H																		
Sunday	7	7	3	112	57	28.00	-	1	7	3								

	M	Inns	NO	Runs	HS	Avge	100s	50s	Ct	St		Balls		Runs	Wkts	Avge	Best	5wI	10wM
Test																			
All First	10	16	3	207	40	15.92	-	-	23	3									
1-day Int																			
NatWest																			
B & H																			
Sunday	9	9	3	115	57	19.16	-	1	7	3									

DAWSON, R.   Yorkshire

Name: Richard Dawson
Role: Right-hand bat, right-arm
off-spin bowler
Born: 4 August 1980, Doncaster
Height: 6ft 3in
Nickname: Billy Dog
County debut: No first-team appearance
Parents: Kevin and Pat
Marital status: Single
Education: Hill House Preparatory School;
Batley Grammar School; Exeter University
Qualifications: 10 GCSEs, 4 A-levels
Career outside cricket: Student
Off-season: University studies
Overseas tours: England U18 to Bermuda
1997; England U19 to New Zealand 1998-99
Cricketers particularly admired:
Steve Waugh
Young players to look out for:
Graeme Swann, Gary Fellows
Other sports played: 5-a-side football
Other sports followed: Football (Doncaster Rovers FC)
Relaxations: Music, photography
Extras: Sir John Hobbs Jubilee Memorial Prize 1995. Captained England U15
Opinions on cricket: 'Lack of opportunities to develop cricketing skills in schools.'

DAWSON, R. I. — Gloucestershire

Name: Robert Ian Dawson
Role: Right-hand bat, right-arm
leg-spin bowler
Born: 29 March 1970, Exmouth, Devon
Height: 5ft 11in **Weight:** 14st
Nickname: Daws, Giggsy
County debut: 1991 (one-day),
1992 (first-class)
1000 runs in a season: 1
1st-Class 50s: 12
1st-Class 100s: 3
1st-Class catches: 30
Place in batting averages: 255th av. 13.61
(1997 183rd av. 23.50)
Strike rate: 17.40 (career 49.37)
Parents: Barry and Shirley
Marital status: Single
Family links with cricket: Father and
brother both played club cricket
Education: Beacon School, Exmouth; Millfield School; Newcastle Polytechnic
Qualifications: 8 O-levels, 3 A-levels
Off-season: Playing football
Overseas tours: Exeter University to Barbados 1989; Gloucestershire Gypsies to
Zimbabwe 1995, to South Africa 1996, 1998; Gloucestershire CCC to Zimbabwe
1996, 1997
Overseas teams played for: Amamzimtoti, South Africa, 1993-94; Strathfield CC,
Sydney 1996-97; Vaal Tech Uni, Johannesburg 1997-98
Cricketers particularly admired: Ian Botham, David Gower, Sachin Tendulkar
Young players to look out for: Steve Harmison, Matthew Church, James Averis
Other sports played: Football (Man Utd), golf
Other sports followed: 'Most sports bar motor racing'
Injuries: Out for one match with shoulder injury
Relaxations: 'Watching sport and spending time with my mates'
Extras: Played in NatWest for Devon (from 1988), before joining Gloucestershire
Best batting: 127* Gloucestershire v Cambridge University, Bristol 1994
Best bowling: 3-15 Gloucestershire v Lancashire, Old Trafford 1998

FICA

14. Who is the youngest batsman to score
a century in the World Cup?

1998 Season

	M	Inns	NO	Runs	HS	Avge	100s	50s	Ct	St	O	M	Runs	Wkts	Avge	Best	5wl	10wM
Test																		
All First	8	15	2	177	46	13.61	-	-	3	-	14.3	0	67	5	13.40	3-15	-	-
1-day Int																		
NatWest	2	2	0	35	35	17.50	-	-	-	-								
B & H	4	4	0	87	31	21.75	-	-	-	-								
Sunday	14	14	2	555	75	46.25	-	4	7	-								

Career Performances

	M	Inns	NO	Runs	HS	Avge	100s	50s	Ct	St	Balls	Runs	Wkts	Avge	Best	5wl	10wM
Test																	
All First	63	113	9	2552	127 *	24.53	3	12	30	-	395	199	8	24.87	3-15	-	-
1-day Int																	
NatWest	7	6	0	108	60	18.00	-	1	-	-	24	37	1	37.00	1-37	-	
B & H	18	17	0	345	38	20.29	-	-	1	-	18	12	0	-	-	-	
Sunday	82	74	8	1693	85	25.65	-	8	18	-	38	59	1	59.00	1-19	-	

DEAN, K. J. Derbyshire

Name: Kevin James Dean
Role: Left-hand bat, left-arm
medium-fast bowler
Born: 16 October 1975, Derby
Height: 6ft 4in **Weight:** 13st 7lbs
Nickname: Deany, George, The Wall,
Red Face, Mr Dead
County debut: 1996
County cap: 1998
50 wickets in a season: 1
1st-Class 5 w. in innings: 5
1st-Class 10 w. in match: 1
1st-Class catches: 4
One-Day 5 w. in innings: 1
Place in batting averages: 200th av. 19.25
(1997 277th av. 11.28)
Place in bowling averages: 23rd av. 21.24
(1997 64th av. 28.96)
Strike rate: 37.74 (career 42.93)
Parents: Ken and Dorothy
Marital status: Single

Education: Waterhouses First School; Leek High School; Leek College of Further Education
Qualifications: 8 GCSEs, 3 A-levels, 1 AS-level
Career outside cricket: Working for Ladbrokes
Off-season: Managing a branch of Ladbrokes in Derby 'and getting ready for the pre-season running!'
Overseas teams played for: Sturt CC, Adelaide 1996-97
Cricketers particularly admired: Wasim Akram, Courtney Walsh, Dominic Cork
Young players to look out for: Matt Bulbeck, Dimitri Mascarenhas
Other sports played: Football (Blue Circle), golf, tennis, ten-pin bowling
Other sports followed: Football (Derby County), tennis ('Anna Kournikova!!')
Relaxations: 'Trying to tip Krikk the winner of the most difficult horse race of the day!! Going to the races. Playing golf. Trying to do the *Express* crossword with A.J. before Rolly has chance to help us'
Extras: A member of the Staffordshire U16 Texaco winning team. Awarded county cap in 1998. Achieved first-class hat-trick against Kent at Derby
Opinions on cricket: 'The audience is there for day/night cricket, so let there be more of it.'
Best batting: 27* Derbyshire v South Africa, Derby 1998
Best bowling: 6-63 Derbyshire v Somerset, Taunton 1998

1998 Season

	M	Inns	NO	Runs	HS	Avge	100s	50s	Ct	St	O	M	Runs	Wkts	Avge	Best	5wI	10wM
Test																		
All Firsts	15	21	13	154	27 *	19.25	-	-	1	-	465.3	96	1572	74	21.24	6-63	5	1
1-day Int																		
NatWest	5	1	1	0	0 *	-	-	-	2	-	51	8	201	10	20.10	3-13	-	
B & H	1	1	1	14	14 *	-	-	-	-	-	10	0	62	2	31.00	2-62	-	
Sunday	11	6	4	35	16 *	17.50	-	-	1	-	78	5	340	13	26.15	4-26	-	

Career Performances

	M	Inns	NO	Runs	HS	Avge	100s	50s	Ct	St	Balls	Runs	Wkts	Avge	Best	5wI	10wM
Test																	
All First	33	41	19	266	27 *	12.09	-	-	4	-	5066	2854	118	24.18	6-63	5	1
1-day Int																	
NatWest	9	2	2	0	0 *	-	-	-	3	-	528	390	16	24.37	3-13	-	
B & H	6	2	1	20	14 *	20.00	-	-	-	-	240	211	5	42.20	2-62	-	
Sunday	33	10	7	45	16 *	15.00	-	-	8	-	1347	1028	36	28.55	5-32	1	

DEANE, M.   Derbyshire

Name: Michael John Deane
Role: Right-hand bat, right-arm
fast-medium bowler
Born: 9 March 1977, Chesterfield
Height: 6ft 2in **Weight:** 11st 11lbs
Nickname: Deano, Deanie
County debut: No first-team appearance
Parents: John Anthony and Betty Deane
Marital status: Single
Family links with cricket: Father played for
Trinidad plus cricket clubs in Leicestershire
and Derbyshire. Grandmother played cricket
for school

Education: Christ the King, Alfreton; St
Joseph's RC School, Staveley; St Mary's
High School, Chesterfield; Abbotsholme
School, Rocester; Coventry University
('one year; wished to continue with cricket')
Qualifications: 8 GCSEs, 2 A-levels
Career outside cricket: Works for Beechdale Saab when not abroad
Off-season: Playing and coaching cricket abroad
Overseas teams played for: Alma Marist, Cape Town 1997-98; Queen's Park CC,
West Indies (temporary membership) 1998-99
Cricketers particularly admired: Stephen Waugh, Michael Holding
Young players to look out for: 'Myself'
Other sports played: Soccer and other ball games
Other sports followed: Football (Derby County), 'interested in all sports'
Injuries: Out for three weeks with groin strain
Relaxations: Cinema, travel, music
Extras: Cricket bat signed by living England captains for 112 in 56 deliveries v MCC
at Abbotsholme. Represented Derbyshire at every level from age of eight to U21 and
2nd XI. Represented North of England team. Set World Independent Schools 100-
metre record of 10.90 seconds at age 17
Opinions on cricket: 'I am formulating ideas and learning about the game as I go
along. I like being actively involved at all times. I just love the sport'

DEFREITAS, P. A. J.   Derbyshire

Name: Phillip Anthony Jason DeFreitas
Role: Right-hand bat, right-arm
fast-medium bowler
Born: 18 February 1966, Scotts Head,
Dominica
Height: 6ft **Weight:** 13st 7lbs
Nickname: Daffy, Lunchy
County debut: 1985 (Leics),
1989 (Lancs), 1994 (Derbys)
County cap: 1986 (Leics),
1989 (Lancs), 1994 (Derbys)
Test debut: 1986-87
Tests: 44
One-Day Internationals: 103
50 wickets in a season: 11
1st-Class 50s: 40
1st-Class 100s: 6
1st-Class 5 w. in innings: 50
1st-Class 10 w. in match: 5
1st-Class catches: 102
One-Day 5 w. in innings: 6
Place in batting averages: 174th av. 21.75 (1997 205th av. 21.04)
Place in bowling averages: 56th av. 26.21 (1997 47th av. 27.01)
Strike rate: 55.69 (career 57.08)
Parents: Sybil and Martin
Wife and date of marriage: Nicola, 10 December 1990
Children: Alexandra Elizabeth Jane, 5 August 1991
Family links with cricket: Father played in Windward Islands. All six brothers play
Education: Willesden High School
Qualifications: 2 O-levels
Overseas tours: England YC to West Indies 1984-85; England to Australia 1986-87,
to Pakistan, Australia and New Zealand 1987-88, to India and West Indies 1989-90, to
Australia 1990-91, to New Zealand 1991-92, to India and Sri Lanka 1992-93, to
Australia 1994-95, to South Africa 1995-96, to India and Pakistan (World Cup) 1995-96
Overseas teams played for: Port Adelaide, South Australia 1985; Mossman, Sydney
1988; Boland, South Africa 1993-94, 1995-96
Cricketers particularly admired: Ian Botham, Graham Gooch, Geoff Boycott, Mike
Gatting
Other sports followed: Football (Manchester City) and rugby league (Warrington)
Relaxations: 'Golf, gardening, visiting stately homes, spending spare time with wife
and daughter Alexandra'

Extras: Left Leicestershire and joined Lancashire at end of 1988 season. Originally agreed to join unofficial English tour of South Africa 1989-90, but withdrew under pressure. Man of the Match in 1990 NatWest Trophy final. One of *Wisden*'s Five Cricketers of the Year 1992. Man of the Tournament in the Hong Kong Sixes 1993. Left Lancashire at the end of the 1993 season. Player of the Series against New Zealand 1994. Was called up to the England one-day squad in South Africa 1995-96 after spending the winter with Boland and went on to play in the World Cup. Captained Derbyshire for part of 1997 season after the departure of Dean Jones. Played for an England XI in the Cricket Max tournament in New Zealand in 1997
Best batting: 113 Leicestershire v Nottinghamshire, Worksop 1988
Best bowling: 7-21 Lancashire v Middlesex, Lord's 1989

1998 Season

	M	Inns	NO	Runs	HS	Avge	100s	50s	Ct	St	O	M	Runs	Wkts	Avge	Best	5wI	10wM
Test																		
All First	14	23	3	435	87	21.75	-	2	6	-	482.4	114	1363	52	26.21	5-38	3	-
1-day Int																		
NatWest	4	2	0	40	40	20.00	-	-	-	-	43.4	5	176	3	58.66	1-43	-	
B & H	4	4	2	119	51 *	59.50	-	1	1	-	27	0	115	3	38.33	2-28	-	
Sunday	11	10	1	253	69	28.11	-	2	1	-	81.3	2	357	12	29.75	3-12	-	

Career Performances

	M	Inns	NO	Runs	HS	Avge	100s	50s	Ct	St	Balls	Runs	Wkts	Avge	Best	5wI	10wM
Test	44	68	5	934	88	14.82	-	4	14	-	9838	4700	140	33.57	7-70	4	-
All First	287	408	38	8059	113	21.78	6	40	102	-	55254	26979	968	27.87	7-21	50	5
1-day Int	103	66	23	690	67	16.04	-	1	26	-	5712	3775	115	32.82	4-35	-	
NatWest	36	24	4	363	69	18.15	-	1	6	-	2277	1152	51	22.58	5-13	4	
B & H	59	40	9	712	75 *	22.96	-	3	15	-	3307	1882	84	22.40	5-16	1	
Sunday	165	123	23	1945	72 *	19.45	-	5	30	-	6588	4935	184	26.82	5-26	1	

15. Who captained Pakistan in the 1979 World Cup?

FICA

DE LA PENA, J. M.   Kent

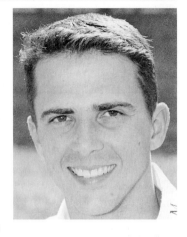

Name: Jason Michael de la Pena
Role: Right-hand bat, right-arm
fast-medium bowler
Born: 16 September 1972, Middlesex
Height: 6ft 6in **Weight:** 14st 7lbs
Nickname: Greasy Wop, Gin, Flying
Spaniard
County debut: 1991 (Gloucestershire),
1994 (Surrey, one-day), 1995 (Surrey,
first-class), 1998 (Kent)
Strike rate: 84.00 (career 54.37)
Parents: Michael and Jacqueline,
Mikki and Loy
Marital status: Single
Education: Lambrook Prep School, Ascot;
Stowe School; Bournside Sixth Form
College, Cheltenham
Qualifications: 8 GCSEs, 3 A-levels
Overseas tours: Gloucestershire to Namibia
1990, to Kenya 1991, to Sri Lanka 1992-93
Overseas teams played for: North Hobart, Tasmania 1991-93; Mossman, Sydney
1994-95
Cricketers particularly admired: David 'Syd' Lawrence, Dennis Lillee, Graham
Dilley, Michael Holding, Allan Donald, Richard Hadlee
Other sports followed: Golf, tennis, surfing, windsurfing, rugby union
Relaxations: Cinema, music
Extras: Represented England U19 v Young Australia. Selected for England U19 tour
to Pakistan 1991-92 but had to pull out two hours before leaving owing to severe
illness and underwent an operation one day later. Joined Surrey from Gloucestershire
in 1994. Left Surrey at end of 1996 season. Is also registered for Hertfordshire
Best batting: 7* Gloucestershire v Yorkshire, Sheffield 1993
Best bowling: 4-77 Gloucestershire v Australians, Bristol 1993

1998 Season

	M	Inns	NO	Runs	HS	Avge	100s	50s	Ct	St	O	M	Runs	Wkts	Avge	Best	5wI	10wM
Test																		
All First	2	1	1	0	0*	-	-	-	-	-	42	6	154	3	51.33	2-54	--	
1-day Int																		
NatWest																		
B & H																		
Sunday																		

Career Performances

	M	Inns	NO	Runs	HS	Avge	100s	50s	Ct	St	Balls	Runs	Wkts	Avge	Best	5wl	10wM
Test																	
All First	8	8	6	10	7 *	5.00	-	-	-	-	870	656	16	41.00	4-77	-	-
1-day Int																	
NatWest																		
B & H																		
Sunday	2	2	2	2	2 *	-	-	-	-	-	42	61	0	-		-	-

DI VENUTO, M. J. Sussex

Name: Michael James Di Venuto
Role: Left-hand bat, right-arm medium/leg-break bowler
Born: 12 December 1973, Hobart, Tasmania
County debut: No first-team appearance
One-Day Internationals: 9
1st-Class 50s: 21
1st-Class 100s: 8
1st-Class catches: 40
Overseas tours: Tasmania to Zimbabwe 1995-96; Australia to South Africa (One-Day series) 1996-97; Australia A to Scotland and Ireland 1998
Overseas teams played for: Kingborough, Tasmania; Tasmania
Extras: Scored career-best 189 v Western Australia in 1997-98 Sheffield Shield final, contributing more than 50 per cent of Tasmania's total in their second innings.
Captained Australia A on tour of Scotland and Ireland 1998. Has joined Sussex as overseas player for 1999, replacing Michael Bevan
Best batting: 189 Tasmania v Western Australia, Perth 1997-98

1998 Season (did not make any first-class or one-day appearances)

Career Performances

	M	Inns	NO	Runs	HS	Avge	100s	50s	Ct	St	Balls	Runs	Wkts	Avge	Best	5wI	10wM
Test																	
All First	55	98	3	3830	189	40.31	8	21	40	-	228	157	0	-	-	-	-
1-day Int	9	9	0	241	89	26.77	-	2	1	-	-	-	-	-	-	-	-
NatWest																	
B & H																	
Sunday																	

DOBSON, M. C.   Northamptonshire

Name: Martyn Colin Dobson
Role: Right-hand top-order bat, off-spin bowler
Born: 28 May 1982, Scunthorpe, N. Lincolnshire
Height: 6ft **Weight:** 13st 10lbs
Nickname: Bonz
County debut: No first-team appearance
Parents: David and Susan
Marital status: Single
Family links with cricket: 'Dad played 2nd XI cricket and was a league pro for many years. Brother Michael was with Northants up until last season'
Education: Bottesford Junior School; Frederick Gough Comp; Oundle School ('studying A-levels')
Qualifications: 9 GCSEs
Career outside cricket: Student
Off-season: Studying for A-levels
Cricketers particularly admired: Carl Hooper, Viv Richards
Young players to look out for: Michael Dobson, John Sadler
Other sports played: Rugby (Oundle 1st XV, Lincs County Schools U15 and U16)
Other sports followed: Football (Liverpool FC, Scunthorpe Utd – 'somebody has to'), rugby union (Scunthorpe RFC), rugby league (Bradford Bulls)
Relaxations: Music, socialising, any sport
Extras: Captain of ESCA U14 and U15. Sir John Hobbs U16 prize from the Cricket Society 1997. Top of both batting and bowling averages for Yorkshire U19 1998
Opinions on cricket: 'Too young to have formed any opinion. Simply looking forward to my first year with Northants.'

DONALD, A. A.   Warwickshire

Name: Allan Anthony Donald
Role: Right-hand bat, right-arm fast bowler
Born: 20 October 1966, Bloemfontein,
South Africa
Height: 6ft 3in **Weight:** 14st
County debut: 1987
County cap: 1989
Test debut: 1991-92
Tests: 47
One-Day Internationals: 107
50 wickets in a season: 5
1st-Class 50s: 1
1st-Class 5 w. in innings: 59
1st-Class 10 w. in match: 8
1st-Class catches: 98
One-Day 5 w. in innings: 10
Place in batting averages:
(1997 210th av. 20.00)
Place in bowling averages: 17th av. 20.12
(1997 2nd av. 15.63)
Strike rate: 46.51 (career 47.01)
Parents: Stuart and Francine
Wife and date of marriage: Tina, 21 September 1991
Family links with cricket: Father and uncle played club cricket
Education: Grey College High School;Technical High School, Bloemfontein
Qualifications: Matriculation
Off-season: Playing for South Africa
Overseas tours: South Africa to India 1991-92, to Australia and New Zealand (World Cup) 1991-92, to West Indies 1991-92, to Sri Lanka 1992-93, to Australia 1992-93, to England 1994, to New Zealand 1994-95, to Zimbabwe 1995-96, to India and Pakistan (World Cup) 1995-96, to India 1996-97, to Kenya 1996-97, to Pakistan 1997-98, to Australia 1997-98, to England 1998
Overseas teams played for: Free State, South Africa 1985 –
Cricketers particularly admired: Richard Hadlee, Malcolm Marshall, Gladstone Small, Andy Lloyd, Eddie Barlow
Other sports followed: Rugby, golf, tennis
Relaxations: 'Listening to music, having a barbecue, playing golf and having a few beers with my friends'
Extras: Played for South African XI v Australian XI in 1986-87 and v English XI in 1989-90. Retained by Warwickshire for 1991 season ahead of Tom Moody. Toured with South Africa on first-ever visit to India and to West Indies in 1991-92. One of

Wisden's Five Cricketers of the Year 1992. Took his 100th Test wicket against England in Johannesburg 1995-96. Voted Man of the Series against England finishing with 19 wickets at an average of 26.15. Returned as overseas player for Warwickshire in 1997 after spending a year as the county's fitness coach. Took his 500th wicket for Warwickshire during the 1997 season. Was awarded his country's highest sporting honour when he was presented with a Gold Medal by Nelson Mandela at an awards ceremony in Pretoria on 15 August 1997. Took his 200th Test wicket (Sanath Jayasuriya) v Sri Lanka in 1998 in his 42nd Test, becoming the first South African to reach this landmark. Was South Africa's Man of the Series v England 1998. Has returned to Warwickshire as overseas player for 1999 and has been granted a benefit in 1999

Best batting: 55* South Africa v Tasmania, Devonport 1997-98
Best bowling: 8-37 Orange Free State v Transvaal, Johannesburg 1986-87

1998 Season

	M	Inns	NO	Runs	HS	Avge	100s	50s	Ct	St	O	M	Runs	Wkts	Avge	Best	5wI	10wM
Test	5	6	3	29	7*	9.66	-	-	1	-	243.2	69	653	33	19.78	6-88	4	-
All First-	7	6	3	29	7*	9.66	-	-	1	-	302.2	89	785	39	20.12	6-56	5	-
1-day Int	5	2	1	19	13	19.00	-	-	-	-	42.4	3	193	11	17.54	3-32	-	
NatWest																		
B & H																		
Sunday																		

Career Performances

	M	Inns	NO	Runs	HS	Avge	100s	50s	Ct	St	Balls	Runs	Wkts	Avge	Best	5wI	10wM
Test	47	63	24	427	33	10.94	-	-	12	-	11005	5233	237	22.08	8-71	15	2
All First	260	301	115	2281	55*	12.26	-	1	98	-	49034	23137	1043	22.18	8-37	59	8
1-day Int	107	26	11	74	13	4.93	-	-	14	-	5706	3864	182	21.23	6-23	2	
NatWest	29	10	6	32	14*	8.00	-	-	4	-	1829	1023	73	14.01	5-12	5	
B & H	26	15	8	87	23*	12.42	-	-	4	-	1489	996	38	26.21	5-25	1	
Sunday	71	24	12	139	18*	11.58	-	-	16	-	3109	2074	102	20.33	6-15	2	

17. What was unusual about the dismissal of New Zealand's Chris Harris by Pakistan's Mushtaq Ahmed at Christchurch on 18 March 1992?

FIGA

DOWMAN, M. P.   Nottinghamshire

Name: Matthew Peter Dowman
Role: Left-hand bat, right-arm
medium bowler
Born: 10 May 1974, Grantham, Lincs
Height: 5ft 11in **Weight:** 12st
Nickname: Doomer, Rid Rod
County debut: 1993 (one-day),
1994 (first-class)
County cap: 1998
1000 runs in a season: 1
1st-Class 50s: 9
1st-Class 100s: 6
1st-Class catches: 29
Place in batting averages: 196th av. 19.60
(1997 100th av. 34.09)
Place in bowling averages: 106th av. 33.08
Strike rate: 69.50 (career 81.90)
Parents: Clive and Jackie
Marital status: Single
Family links with cricket: Dad played for Grantham Town. Three brothers also play for Grantham, two of them representing Lincolnshire Schools and Lincolnshire U19
Education: Earl of Dysart Primary; St Hugh's Comprehensive; Grantham College
Qualifications: Senior coach
Career outside cricket: Undecided
Overseas tours: England U19 to India 1992-93; Lincolnshire U16 to Zimbabwe 1988-89; Nottinghamshire to Cape Town 1992-93, to Johannesburg 1996-97; also to Guernsey for Tim Robinson's benefit 1992
Overseas teams played for: South Burwon, Geelong, Melbourne 1995-96; East Shirley, Christchurch, New Zealand 1997-98
Cricketers particularly admired: Robin Smith, Mike Gatting, Malcolm Marshall, Jimmy Adams
Young players to look out for: Owais Shah, James Ormond, Andy Oram
Other sports followed: Golf, football ('follow Notts Forest and County and Lincoln City')
Relaxations: Watching films, playing golf, listening to music
Extras: Played in winning Midlands team at ESCA Festival 1989. Most runs in a season for Lincolnshire Schools and holds record for most runs in Lincolnshire Schools career. Played for England U19 in home series against West Indies in 1993, scoring 267 in second 'Test'. Winner of the 1997 Uncapped Whyte and Mackay Batting Award. Awarded county cap 1998
Opinions on cricket: 'None of any value.'

Best batting: 149 Nottinghamshire v Leicestershire, Leicester 1997
Best bowling: 3-10 Nottinghamshire v Pakistan A, Trent Bridge 1997

1998 Season

	M	Inns	NO	Runs	HS	Avge	100s	50s	Ct	St	O	M	Runs	Wkts	Avge	Best	5wI	10wM
Test																		
All First	13	24	1	451	63	19.60	-	2	7	-	139	31	397	12	33.08	2-10	-	-
1-day Int																		
NatWest	3	3	0	90	47	30.00	-	-	2	-	18	3	63	2	31.50	1-23	-	
B & H	4	3	0	139	82	46.33	-	1	2	-	15	0	47	3	15.66	2-18	-	
Sunday	16	16	0	348	55	21.75	-	1	6	-	31	1	168	2	84.00	1-11	-	

Career Performances

	M	Inns	NO	Runs	HS	Avge	100s	50s	Ct	St	Balls	Runs	Wkts	Avge	Best	5wI	10wM
Test																	
All First	53	94	4	2538	149	28.20	6	9	29	-	1638	854	20	42.70	3-10	-	-
1-day Int																	
NatWest	4	4	0	104	47	26.00	-	-	2	-	108	63	2	31.50	1-23	-	
B & H	14	10	2	329	92	41.12	-	2	5	-	332	248	11	22.54	3-21	-	
Sunday	53	53	2	986	74 *	19.33	-	4	14	-	719	692	13	53.23	2-31	-	

DRIVER, R. K.   Worcestershire

Name: Ryan Craig Driver
Role: Left-hand bat, right-arm medium bowler
Born: 30 April 1979, Truro
Height: 6ft 3in **Weight:** 14st
Nickname: Bambi, Screw
County debut: 1998
Parents: Les and Jan
Marital status: 'Girlfriend'
Family links with cricket: Grandfather and uncle played club cricket. Father was captain of Truro CC for six years and still plays for the club. Mother follows very closely
Education: St Gluvias; Trewirgie Junior School, Redruth; Redruth Community School; Durham University
Qualifications: 9 GCSEs, 3 A-levels, NCA coaching award
Off-season: 'At university working hard'

Overseas tours: ESCA West U14 to West Indies 1993-94; Cornwall U17 to South Africa 1996; Cornwall Colts to South Africa 1997

Cricketers particularly admired: Graeme Hick, Allan Donald

Young players to look out for: Patrick Ellis, Adam Barber

Other sports played: Basketball, squash ('part-time')

Other sports followed: Football (Derby County)

Injuries: Out June to August with slight tear in infraspiatus, affected throwing ability

Relaxations: Socialising, watching TV, enjoying life

Extras: CSCA Batting Award 1993-96. Played for ESCA U19 and MCC Schools in 1997. Has played for Cornwall CCC since 1995. West Region *Daily Telegraph* Batsman of the Year 1995. England Schoolboy Cricketer of the Year 1997. The opening bat for Truro CC (Cornwall Champions in 1996 and 1997). 2nd XI Player of the Month August/September 1998. 'I owe a lot to Malcolm Broad, Peter Bolland and the CSCA'

Opinions on cricket: 'Too much cricket played during domestic season. Second XI games should be played at first-class grounds. More publicity should be placed on one-day game to build crowds up more.'

Best batting: 5 Worcestershire v Durham, Worcester 1998

1998 Season

	M	Inns	NO	Runs	HS	Avge	100s	50s	Ct	St	O	M	Runs	Wkts	Avge	Best	5wI	10wM
Test																		
All First	1	2	0	5	5	2.50	-	-	-	-								
1-day Int																		
NatWest																		
B & H																		
Sunday																		

Career Performances

	M	Inns	NO	Runs	HS	Avge	100s	50s	Ct	St	Balls	Runs	Wkts	Avge	Best	5wI	10wM
Test																	
All First	1	2	0	5	5	2.50	-	-	-	-							
1-day Int																	
NatWest	1	1	0	0	0	0.00	-	-	-	-							
B & H																	
Sunday																	

DUTCH, K. P.   Middlesex

Name: Keith Philip Dutch
Role: Right-hand bat, off-spin bowler
Born: 21 March 1973, Harrow, Middlesex
Height: 5ft 9in **Weight:** 11st 6lbs
Nickname: Dutchy, Double, Zoro
County debut: 1993
1st-Class 50s: 1
1st-Class catches: 11
Place in batting averages:
(1997 216th av. 19.71)
Strike rate: 147.00 (career 76.78)
Parents: Alan and Ann
Marital status: Single
Family links with cricket: Father is a
qualified coach

Education: Nower Hill High School, Pinner;
Weald College, Harrow
Qualifications: 5 GCSEs and 1 AS-level
Off-season: Coaching
Overseas tours: MCC to Central and East Africa 1997
Overseas teams played for: Worcester United, South Africa 1992-93; Geelong City,
Australia, 1994; Rygersdal CC, Cape Town 1997-98
Cricketers particularly admired: Mark Ramprakash, John Emburey
Young players to look out for: Owais Shah, David Nash, Stephen Peters
Other sports followed: Football (Arsenal FC)
Relaxations: Music, TV and shopping for clothes
Extras: On MCC groundstaff for one year before becoming a contracted player. Rapid
Cricketline 2nd XI Player of the Year 1993, Middlesex 2nd XI Player of the Year
1995. In 1996 scored over 1,000 2nd XI Championship runs and took 65 wickets.
During this time he achieved highest-ever batting total and bowling figures by a
Middlesex player in the history of the 2nd XI Championship with 261 against
Somerset and 15 for 157 against Leicestershire – each was the fourth highest in the
championship record books. Named 2nd XI Player of the Year in 1996
Best batting: 79 Middlesex v Gloucestershire, Bristol 1997
Best bowling: 3-25 Middlesex v Somerset, Uxbridge 1996

---

18. Who captained England in the 1983 World Cup?

FIGA

1998 Season

	M	Inns	NO	Runs	HS	Avge	100s	50s	Ct	St	O	M	Runs	Wkts	Avge	Best	5wl	10wM
Test																		
All First	4	5	0	41	16	8.20	-	-	3	-	49	11	131	2	65.50	1-25	-	-
1-day Int																		
NatWest	3	2	1	84	49 *	84.00	-	-	2	-	34	0	135	4	33.75	2-30	-	
B & H	1	1	1	5	5 *	-	-	-	2	-	10	0	34	1	34.00	1-34	-	
Sunday	14	13	5	193	40	24.12	-	-	4	-	97	2	447	22	20.31	4-22	-	

Career Performances

	M	Inns	NO	Runs	HS	Avge	100s	50s	Ct	St	Balls	Runs	Wkts	Avge	Best	5wl	10wM
Test																	
All First	16	18	2	218	79	13.62	-	1	11	-	1075	547	14	39.07	3-25	-	-
1-day Int																	
NatWest	5	4	2	93	49 *	46.50	-	-	3	-	336	213	5	42.60	2-30	-	
B & H	6	6	1	48	20	9.60	-	-	2	-	186	152	7	21.71	4-42	-	
Sunday	40	33	10	374	58	16.26	-	1	10	-	1266	1028	39	26.35	4-22	-	

EALHAM, M. A.   Kent

Name: Mark Alan Ealham
Role: Right-hand bat, right-arm
medium-fast bowler
Born: 27 August 1969, Willesborough, Kent
Height: 5ft 10in **Weight:** 13st 9lbs
Nickname: Ealy, Skater
County debut: 1989
County cap: 1992
Test debut: 1996
Tests: 8
One-Day Internationals: 17
1000 runs in a season: 1
1st-Class 50s: 35
1st-Class 100s: 5
1st-Class 5 w. in innings: 11
1st-Class 10 w. in match: 1
1st-Class catches: 50
One-Day 5 w. in innings: 2
One-Day 100s: 1
Place in batting averages: 151st av. 24.26 (1997 15th av. 52.75)
Place in bowling averages: 53rd av. 25.78 (1997 77th av. 30.95)
Strike rate: 63.30 (career 60.76)

Parents: Alan and Sue
Wife and date of marriage: Kirsty, 24 February 1996
Family links with cricket: Father played county cricket for Kent
Education: Stour Valley Secondary School
Qualifications: 9 CSEs
Off-season: England one-day squad to Bangladesh and Australia
Overseas tours: England A to Australia 1996-97, to Kenya and Sri Lanka 1997-98; England VI to Hong Kong 1997; England to Sharjah 1997-98, to Bangladesh (Wills International Cup) 1998, to Australia (CUB Series) 1998-99
Overseas teams played for: South Perth, Australia 1992-93; University, Perth, Australia 1993-94
Cricketers particularly admired: Ian Botham, Viv Richards, Robin Smith, Paul Blackmore and Albert 'for his F and G'
Other sports followed: Football (Manchester United) and most other sports
Relaxations: Playing golf and snooker, watching films
Extras: Scored fastest Sunday League century off 44 balls. Made his Test debut against India in the third Test at Trent Bridge in 1996. Represented England in the 1997 Hong Kong Sixes tournament in which England finished as runners-up to Pakistan
Best batting: 139 Kent v Leicestershire, Canterbury 1997
Best bowling: 8-36 Kent v Warwickshire, Edgbaston 1996

1998 Season

	M	Inns	NO	Runs	HS	Avge	100s	50s	Ct	St	O	M	Runs	Wkts	Avge	Best	5wI	10wM
Test	2	4	0	24	8	6.00	-	-	-	-	38	10	105	2	52.50	1-50	-	-
All First	12	22	3	461	121	24.26	1	2	2	-	242.4	83	593	23	25.78	5-23	3	-
1-day Int	3	2	0	13	12	6.50	-	-	-	-	30	0	116	5	23.20	3-44	-	
NatWest	2	1	0	6	6	6.00	-	-	2	-	21	1	56	2	28.00	1-22	-	
B & H	5	5	1	163	56	40.75	-	2	-	-	33.2	3	114	8	14.25	3-20	-	
Sunday	11	9	5	180	55	45.00	-	2	5	-	65.3	1	380	10	38.00	3-47	-	

Career Performances

	M	Inns	NO	Runs	HS	Avge	100s	50s	Ct	St	Balls	Runs	Wkts	Avge	Best	5wI	10wM
Test	8	13	3	210	53 *	21.00	-	2	4	-	1060	488	17	28.70	4-21	-	-
All First	124	203	34	5433	139	32.14	5	35	50	-	16164	7853	266	29.52	8-36	11	1
1-day Int	17	12	1	231	45	21.00	-	-	2	-	810	550	18	30.55	3-44	-	
NatWest	16	15	4	304	58 *	27.63	-	2	6	-	893	443	18	24.61	4-10	-	
B & H	39	36	9	781	75	28.92	-	6	14	-	1975	1309	57	22.96	4-29	-	
Sunday	116	94	28	1715	112	25.98	1	9	29	-	4416	3467	108	32.10	6-53	2	

ECCLESTONE, S. C. Somerset

Name: Simon Charles Ecclestone
Role: Left-hand bat
Born: 16 July 1971, Great Dunmow, Essex
Height: 6ft 3in **Weight:** 15st 7lbs
Nickname: Major, Eccles
County debut: 1994
1st-Class 50s: 12
1st-Class 100s: 3
1st-Class catches: 22
One-Day 100s: 3
Place in batting averages: 127th av. 26.57
(1997 33rd av. 45.28)
Strike rate: (career 73.54)
Parents: Jonathan and Pippa
Marital status: Single
Family links with cricket: Brother Giles
played for Essex and Cambridgeshire
Education: Bryanston School; Durham
University; Keble College, Oxford

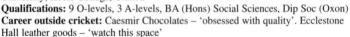

Qualifications: 9 O-levels, 3 A-levels, BA (Hons) Social Sciences, Dip Soc (Oxon)
Career outside cricket: Caesmir Chocolates – 'obsessed with quality'. Ecclestone
Hall leather goods – 'watch this space'
Off-season: Travelling South America. Working as above and for PCA
Overseas tours: Bryanston to West Indies 1989; Durham University to South Africa
1992-93
Cricketers particularly admired: David Gower, Gregor Macmillan 'and any who
play the game their way, undeterred by pressures to comply with the norms'
Young players to look out for: 'M. Trescothick, K. Shine will hit the headlines in one
way or another'
Other sports followed: Football (West Ham FC), rugby (Bath RFC)
Relaxations: Food and wine, theatre, concerts, opera, writing, 'and working at being
as obnoxious and pretentious as possible, thereby keeping a smile on Mr P. Bowler's
face and irritating Mr K. Shine'
Extras: Played for Essex from U11 to U19/2nd XI and for ESCA U19 v New Zealand
1989; captained Durham University, played for Cambridgeshire, Blue for Oxford
University 1994, 'brother of first *Daily Telegraph* Fantasy League winner'. Forced to
retire in 1998 by knee injury. Appointed communications manager of the PCA
Opinions on cricket: 'County cricket is becoming more professional – no doubt about
it. Standards of fitness, fielding and general playing intensity have markedly improved
in the last two to three years. Unfortunately there are things ingrained in the county
"system" both on and off the field that inhibit the game. The situation stems largely

from the gap that exists between the three main bodies involved in county cricket – the players, the county clubs and the ECB. They operate as separate and competing bodies. The priorities of the groups are different and contradictory.

– Top of the agenda for the ECB is the state of English cricket generally, the focal point being the national side.

– The individual counties are preoccupied with the economic frailties of running a county club, ensuring they receive their slice of the pie from the ECB and subsidies from major sponsors – all of which is justified under the guise of keeping a handful of members happy, rather than creating an effective infrastructure to produce the best county and, ultimately, national teams.

– The players' priority is self-interest. They commit a significant amount of their working life to making what they can of their cricketing talent at the expense of constructing a long-term, secure career. It is not surprising that their intention is to get what they can from the game for as long as possible.

As a result, the conflict of interests between the players and the county clubs is plain to see. To maintain economic buoyancy, the clubs must dominate the relationship with the players, with only Test and fringe players having any bargaining power around the negotiating table. The rest scrap around for what is left, which is often, especially for young players, not a lot. It is not surprising that negative and defensive attitudes to life and cricket develop. Individual flair and innovation can quickly be drowned by the unwritten rules of survival. County clubs allow these insecurities to exist and exploit them to keep wages down. But this does not get the best out of players, and the cricket suffers.

The authorities in English cricket should invest in the cricketers. In particular there should be investment in facilities and opportunities, such as injury and medical insurance, further education, career training and advice. The benefits would be felt in a number of ways:

– Reducing the players' dependency on the county clubs and the pressure on the summer six months and cricket as their only earning opportunity.

– Giving players greater independence and allowing them to take more responsibility for their careers, cricket included. Expanding their options and experiences will increase self-confidence, a positive attribute for any sportsman.

– Recycling cricketers into the game at the end of their playing careers as qualified personnel, from coaches and physios to marketing and administrative professionals.

– Ultimately such investment will provide opportunities to develop a greater strength of character and mind, attributes so important to cricket.

It sounds very idealistic – a new age of enlightenment for English cricketers. The important thing is for there to be a supporting network of opportunities available; if there was, there would be no justification for cricketers using the county clubs as scapegoats for their bad lot in life. Such a scheme would go a long way to reducing this anxiety and releasing players' energy and enthusiasm back into their cricket.

The dressing-room culture in county cricket is defensive and suspicious. Left as it is, the system will continue to inhibit players on the pitch because they are so preoccupied with matters off the pitch. As it stands the few such provisions there are are coordinated through an underfunded Professional Cricketers' Association (PCA). Used constructively and properly funded, the PCA would be invaluable to English cricket. The PCA would take the responsibilty of the well-being of the players out of the hands of the county clubs and ECB, allowing them to get on with the business end of running English cricket.'

Best batting: 133 Somerset v Oxford University, Taunton 1997
Best bowling: 4-66 Oxford University v Surrey, The Oval 1994

1998 Season

	M	Inns	NO	Runs	HS	Avge	100s	50s	Ct	St	O	M	Runs	Wkts	Avge	Best	5wl	10wM
Test																		
All First	5	7	0	186	94	26.57	-	1	4	-								
1-day Int																		
NatWest																		
B & H	1	1	0	0	0	0.00	-	-	-	-								
Sunday	4	4	0	77	29	19.25	-	-	-	-								

Career Performances

	M	Inns	NO	Runs	HS	Avge	100s	50s	Ct	St	Balls	Runs	Wkts	Avge	Best	5wl	10wM
Test																	
All First	46	74	9	2277	133	35.03	3	12	22	-	2427	1208	33	36.60	4-66	-	-
1-day Int																	
NatWest	7	7	0	295	101	42.14	1	2	-	-	66	53	0	-		-	-
B & H	15	14	2	465	112 *	38.75	1	3	4	-	210	155	3	51.66	2-44	-	-
Sunday	46	45	4	1074	130	26.19	1	3	7	-	590	593	18	32.94	4-31	-	-

EDMOND, M. D.   Warwickshire

Name: Michael Dennis Edmond
Role: Right-hand bat, right-arm medium-fast bowler
Born: 30 July 1969, Barrow-in-Furness
Height: 6ft 1in **Weight:** 14st 7lbs
Nickname: Eddo, Aus
County debut: 1996
1st-Class catches: 2
Strike rate: 99.00 (career 92.42)
Parents: Tom and Carol
Marital status: Single
Children: Ryen

Family links with cricket: 'My brother plays'
Education: Briar Road Public School, Campbelltown, NSW; Airds High School, Campbelltown, NSW
Qualifications: Level 0 coach in Australia
Career outside cricket: Barman
Overseas teams played for: Campbelltown, Sydney 1988-93; Fairfield, Sydney 1994
Cricketers particularly admired: Ian Botham, Viv Richards, Len Pascoe
Young players to look out for: 'All with an ambition to play for England'
Other sports followed: Indoor cricket (played for Australia 1993-96), football (Manchester United), rugby league (Manly-Warringam)
Relaxations: Spending time with friends, going out and listening to music

Best batting: 32 Warwickshire v Durham, Edgbaston 1998
Best bowling: 2-26 Warwickshire v Oxford University, The Parks 1997

1998 Season

	M	Inns	NO	Runs	HS	Avge	100s	50s	Ct	St	O	M	Runs	Wkts	Avge	Best	5wI	10wM
Test																		
All First	3	5	1	64	32	16.00	-	-	1	-	33	8	94	2	47.00	1-13	-	-
1-day Int																		
NatWest																			
B & H																			
Sunday																			

Career Performances

	M	Inns	NO	Runs	HS	Avge	100s	50s	Ct	St	Balls	Runs	Wkts	Avge	Best	5wI	10wM
Test																	
All First	7	9	3	107	32	17.83	-	-	2	-	647	348	7	49.71	2-26	-	-
1-day Int																	
NatWest	1	1	0	0	0	0.00	-	-	-	-	48	24	1	24.00	1-24	-	
B & H																	
Sunday	8	5	2	43	19	14.33	-	-	2	-	311	233	12	19.41	2-4	-	

EDWARDS, A. D.   Sussex

Name: Alexander David Edwards
Role: Right-hand bat, right-arm
fast-medium bowler
Born: 2 August 1975, Cuckfield, Sussex
Height: 6ft **Weight:** 12st 9lbs
Nickname: Al, Steads, Elvis
County debut: 1994 (one-day),
1995 (first-class)
1st-Class 5 w. in innings: 1
1st-Class catches: 10
Place in batting averages: 293rd av. 4.28
(1997 293rd av. 8.25)
Place in bowling averages:
(1997 20th av. 22.88)
Strike rate: 118.00 (career 58.00)
Parents: Richard John and Angela Janet
Marital status: Single
Family links with cricket: 'Parents drove
me everywhere to play or practise cricket and
have been absolutely wonderful'

Education: Felbridge Primary; Imberhorne Comprehensive; Loughborough University
Qualifications: 10 GCSEs, 4 A-levels
Overseas tours: Sussex U18 to India 1990-91; England U18 to South Africa 1992-93,
to Denmark 1993
Cricketers particularly admired: Dennis Lillee, Michael Holding, Viv Richards,
Stan Berry and Pat Cale 'for their tremendous support, belief and encouragement'
Other sports followed: Football (Liverpool FC)
Relaxations: Snooker, swimming, training, listening to a variety of music, watching
sport on television
Extras: Lord's Taverners U15 Young Cricketer of the Year 1991 and a *Cricketer*
magazine Young Cricketer of the Month in the same year. Played for England U19
against India U19 in 1994
Opinions on cricket: 'Second XI cricket should mirror the first-class game, e.g. same
grounds, practice facilities and duration of matches in the championship (four days).
This would help young players to make the transition from 2nd XI to first-class
cricket. Young players should be given ample opportunity to prove themselves in first-
class cricket. They shouldn't be afraid of initial failure.'
Best batting: 22 Sussex v Young Australia, Hove 1995
Best bowling: 5-34 Sussex v Pakistan A, Hove 1997

1998 Season

	M	Inns	NO	Runs	HS	Avge	100s	50s	Ct	St	O	M	Runs	Wkts	Avge	Best	5wI	10wM
Test																		
All First	4	7	0	30	10	4.28	-	-	3	-	59	9	213	3	71.00	2-60	-	-
1-day Int																		
NatWest																		
B & H	3	3	0	71	43	23.66	-	-	-	-	23.3	0	170	3	56.66	2-55	-	
Sunday	13	8	0	56	20	7.00	-	-	1	-	71	7	320	12	26.66	3-34	-	

Career Performances

	M	Inns	NO	Runs	HS	Avge	100s	50s	Ct	St	Balls	Runs	Wkts	Avge	Best	5wI	10wM
Test																	
All First	13	20	2	134	22	7.44	-	-	10	-	1334	912	23	39.65	5-34	1	-
1-day Int																	
NatWest																	
B & H	10	9	2	101	43	14.42	-	-	5	-	585	511	8	63.87	2-51	-	
Sunday	18	12	1	67	20	6.09	-	-	2	-	563	426	15	28.40	3-34	-	

ELLIS, S. W. K.   Worcestershire

Name: Scott William Kenneth Ellis
Role: Right-hand bat, right-arm
fast-medium bowler
Born: 3 October 1975, Newcastle-under-Lyme
Height: 6ft 4in **Weight:** 14st 7lbs
Nickname: Llama, Fleece Head
County debut: 1996
1st-Class catches: 8
1st-Class 5 w. in innings: 1
Strike rate: 126.00 (career 67.80)
Parents: Tony and Valerie Anne
Marital status: Single
Education: Shrewsbury School;
Warwick University
Qualifications: 9 GCSEs, 3 A-levels, 2:1 in
Ancient History and Philosophy
Overseas tours: England U19 to West Indies
1994-95
Cricketers particularly admired: Courtney
Walsh, Alec Stewart
Other sports followed: Football
Relaxations: Listening to music, reading

Extras: Played for England U18 against India U19 in 1994. Made first-class debut for Combined Universities against West Indies in 1995. Released by Worcestershire at end of 1998 season
Best batting: 15 Worcestershire v Middlesex, Lord's 1996
Best bowling: 5-59 Combined Universities v West Indies, The Parks 1995

1998 Season

	M	Inns	NO	Runs	HS	Avge	100s	50s	Ct	St	O	M	Runs	Wkts	Avge	Best	5wI	10wM
Test																		
All First	2	2	1	0	0*	0.00	-	-	1	-	21	7	48	1	48.00	1-15	-	-
1-day Int																		
NatWest																		
B & H																		
Sunday	3	2	1	22	20	22.00	-	-	-	-								

Career Performances

	M	Inns	NO	Runs	HS	Avge	100s	50s	Ct	St	Balls	Runs	Wkts	Avge	Best	5wI	10wM
Test																	
All First	12	13	5	63	15	7.87	-	-	8	-	1356	880	20	44.00	5-59	1	-
1-day Int																	
NatWest	1	1	1	0	0*	-	-	-	-	-	42	34	2	17.00	2-34	-	
B & H	1	1	0	4	4	4.00	-	-	-	-	54	50	1	50.00	1-50	-	
Sunday	9	3	1	23	20	11.50	-	-	2	-	156	141	4	35.25	2-35	-	

ELLISON, C. J.   Yorkshire

Name: Christopher John Ellison
Role: Right-hand bat, slow left-arm orthodox bowler
Born: 12 April 1979, Sheffield, South Yorkshire
Height: 5ft 10in **Weight:** 11st 7lbs
Nickname: Elly
County debut: No first-team appearance
Parents: Graham and Sheila
Marital status: Single
Family links with cricket: 'Two brothers play cricket with me, as does Dad. Mother performs never-ending things such as cleaning grass-stained whites, making teas and supporting us when we are all playing'
Education: St Mewan County Primary School; Penrice School; St Austell College, Exeter University
Qualifications: 10 GCSEs, 3 A-levels, 2 NCF awards in coaching
Career outside cricket: Student
Off-season: Studying for Sports Science degree at Exeter University

Overseas tours: Cornwall U17 to South Africa 1996
Overseas teams played for: Sutherland District CC, Sydney 1997-98
Cricketers particularly admired: Darren Gough, Michael Bevan
Young players to look out for: Ryan Driver, Carl Gazzard, Rupert Wilder, Daniel Jarman
Other sports played: Football, rugby, golf (8 handicap)
Other sports followed: Football (Sheffield Wednesday); rugby (St Austell)
Relaxations: Going out with friends, watching sport on TV
Extras: On debut for Cornwall in the Minor Counties Championship against Cheshire took 9-80, including a hat-trick, in the second innings. Overall match figures 14-154. St Austell CC Player of the Year 1997
Opinions on cricket: 'Too much cricket is played by the very best players. Test players have very little rest in between matches, playing in Championship games as well as national one-day competitions straight after Test matches. All 2nd XI Championship matches to be four days in length. More money should be put into cricket at club level.'

FIGA

19. Who were the losing semi-finalists in the 1987 World Cup?

EVANS, A. W. — Glamorgan

Name: Alun Wyn Evans
Role: Right-hand bat, right-arm medium bowler
Born: 20 August 1975, Glanamman, Dyfed
Height: 5ft 8in **Weight:** 12st 2lbs
Nickname: Troll
County debut: 1996
1st-Class 50s: 3
1st-Class 100s: 1
1st-Class catches: 13
Place in batting averages: 102nd av. 29.69
Parents: Gareth and Lynfa
Marital status: Single
Family links with cricket: Brother played for Welsh Schools at all age groups and also Glamorgan. Father played for Ammanford CC
Education: Glanamman Primary School, Fishguard Primary School; Fishguard County High School; Neath Tertiary College
Qualifications: 11 GCSEs, BTEC National Diploma in Sports Science, Senior Cricket Coaching Award
Career outside cricket: 'Haven't thought about it yet'
Off-season: 'Hoping to play in Perth (Fremantle)'
Overseas tours: Welsh Schools U17 to Sydney, Australia 1992-93
Overseas teams played for: Marist CC, Whangarei, New Zealand 1995-96, 1997
Cricketers particularly admired: Brian Lara, Mark Ramprakash, Wasim Akram
Young players to look out for: Daniel Cherry, Graeme Swann
Other sports played: Rugby, golf, pool, played soccer for Wimbledon U13, U14, U15
Other sports followed: Rugby (Cardiff), football (Tottenham Hotspur FC), tennis (Boris Becker)
Injuries: Out for three months with stress fracture of the shin
Relaxations: 'Getting the odd tip off my mate Ross'; playing for Fishguard RFC in the winter
Extras: Welsh Schools Player of the Year 1994, MCC Young Cricketer 1995. Balconiers 2nd XI Player of the Year 1996. ASW Young Player of the Year
Opinions on cricket: 'Too many overs in a day. Tea intervals should be longer. 2nd teams should play four-dayers every game.'
Best batting: 125 Glamorgan v Cambridge University, Fenner's 1998

1998 Season

	M	Inns	NO	Runs	HS	Avge	100s	50s	Ct	St	O	M	Runs	Wkts	Avge	Best	5wl	10wM
Test																		
All First	8	14	1	386	125	29.69	1	1	7	-								
1-day Int																		
NatWest																		
B & H	2	2	0	24	14	12.00	-	-	-	-								
Sunday	7	6	2	62	26 *	15.50	-	-	1	-								

Career Performances

	M	Inns	NO	Runs	HS	Avge	100s	50s	Ct	St	Balls	Runs	Wkts	Avge	Best	5wl	10wM
Test																	
All First	17	30	4	823	125	31.65	1	3	13	-							
1-day Int																	
NatWest																	
B & H	2	2	0	24	14	12.00	-	-	-	-							
Sunday	20	18	5	231	50 *	17.76	-	1	4	-							

EVANS, K. P. Nottinghamshire

Name: Kevin Paul Evans
Role: Right-hand bat, right-arm
medium bowler
Born: 10 September 1963, Calverton,
Nottingham
Height: 6ft 2in **Weight:** 14st
Nickname: Ghost, Tex
County debut: 1984
County cap: 1990
Benefit: 1998
1st-Class 50s: 21
1st-Class 100s: 3
1st-Class 5 w. in innings: 10
1st-Class catches: 111
One-Day 5 w. in innings: 2
Place in batting averages: 274th av. 9.92
(1997 274th av. 12.23)
Place in bowling averages: 64th av. 27.22
(1997 59th av. 28.37)
Strike rate: 60.66 (career 68.39)
Parents: Eric and Eileen
Wife and date of marriage: Sandra, 19 March 1988

Children: Ryan Matthew, 24 January 1997

Family links with cricket: Brother Russell played for Nottinghamshire and still plays for Minor Counties and Lincolnshire. Father played local cricket

Education: William Lee Primary; Colonel Frank Seely Comprehensive, Calverton

Qualifications: 10 O-levels, 3 A-levels, qualified coach

Off-season: 'Benefit and training'

Overseas teams played for: Wanuiomata, New Zealand 1989-91

Cricketers particularly admired: Richard Hadlee, Clive Rice

Young players to look out for: Guy Welton

Other sports followed: Football (Leeds United), tennis, squash

Injuries: Out for one week with a neck strain

Relaxations: Listening to music, reading, DIY, gardening

Extras: With brother, Russell, first brothers to bat together for Nottinghamshire in first-class cricket for 50 years. Kept wicket for the first time in the Championship match against Essex at Colchester in 1992. Second Notts cricketer to bowl Sunday League hat-trick v Glamorgan at Trent Bridge; Mark Saxelby was the other

Opinions on cricket: 'The two-tier system will eventually take over from the present system, but the logistics of this must be looked at in far more detail. Four-day cricket on covered wickets should remain the norm.'

Best batting: 104 Nottinghamshire v Surrey, Trent Bridge 1992
104 Nottinghamshire v Sussex, Trent Bridge 1994

Best bowling: 6-40 Nottinghamshire v Lancashire, Old Trafford 1997

1998 Season

	M	Inns	NO	Runs	HS	Avge	100s	50s	Ct	St	O	M	Runs	Wkts	Avge	Best	5wI	10wM
Test																		
All First	9	13	0	129	36	9.92	-	-	3	-	273	73	735	27	27.22	5-92	2	-
1-day Int																		
NatWest	3	2	1	17	15	17.00	-	-	1	-	31	3	110	4	27.50	2-51	-	
B & H	1	1	1	2	2 *	-	-	-	-	-	10	0	27	4	6.75	4-27	-	
Sunday	15	10	7	80	23 *	26.66	-	-	1	-	98	6	438	18	24.33	2-10	-	

Career Performances

	M	Inns	NO	Runs	HS	Avge	100s	50s	Ct	St	Balls	Runs	Wkts	Avge	Best	5wI	10wM
Test																	
All First	160	220	44	4198	104	23.85	3	21	111	-	24691	12027	361	33.31	6-40	10	-
1-day Int																	
NatWest	25	17	3	143	21	10.21	-	-	7	-	1532	834	35	23.82	6-10	1	
B & H	34	22	6	245	47	15.31	-	-	10	-	1898	1288	49	26.28	4-19	-	
Sunday	148	91	38	856	30	16.15	-	-	27	-	6044	5051	159	31.76	5-29	1	

FAIRBROTHER, N. H.   Lancashire

Name: Neil Harvey Fairbrother
Role: Left-hand bat, left-arm medium bowler
Born: 9 September 1963, Warrington, Cheshire
Height: 5ft 8in **Weight:** 11st 4lbs
Nickname: Harvey
County debut: 1982
County cap: 1985
Benefit: 1995
Test debut: 1987
Tests: 10
One-Day Internationals: 56
1000 runs in a season: 10
1st-Class 50s: 96
1st-Class 100s: 36
1st-Class 200s: 3
1st-Class 300s: 1
1st-Class catches: 231
One-Day 100s: 6

Place in batting averages: 13th av. 50.60
(1997 61st av. 40.31)
Strike rate: (career 134.60)
Parents: Les and Barbara
Wife and date of marriage: Audrey, 23 September 1988
Children: Rachael Elizabeth, 4 April 1991; Sam, 3 April 1994
Family links with cricket: Father and two uncles played local league cricket
Education: St Margaret's Church of England School, Oxford; Lymm Grammar School
Qualifications: 5 O-levels
Overseas tours: England to Sharjah 1986-87, to India and Pakistan (World Cup)
1987-88, to Australia and New Zealand 1987-88; England A to Pakistan 1990-91;
England to New Zealand 1991-92, to India 1992-93, to Australia 1994-95, to South
Africa 1995-96, to India and Pakistan (World Cup) 1995-96, to Bangladesh (Wills
International Cup) 1998-99, to Australia (CUB Series) 1998-99
Cricketers particularly admired: Clive Lloyd, Allan Border, David Gower
Other sports followed: Football, rugby union, rugby league
Relaxations: Music and playing sport
Extras: 'I was named after the Australian cricketer Neil Harvey, who was my mum's
favourite cricketer.' Played for England YC v Australia 1983. His innings of 366 in
1990 was the third highest score ever made in the County Championship, the second
highest first-class score by a Lancashire batsman and the best at The Oval. Appointed
Lancashire captain for 1992 but resigned in 1993. Called up to join England tour party
as a replacement in Australia 1994-95 but was immediately injured in a collision with

Steven Rhodes while fielding and forced to return home. Played in the one-day series between England and South Africa and represented England in the World Cup in 1995-96
Opinions on cricket: 'There is too much cricket. The game has to be made more entertaining.'
Best batting: 366 Lancashire v Surrey, The Oval 1990
Best bowling: 2-91 Lancashire v Nottinghamshire, Old Trafford 1987

1998 Season

	M	Inns	NO	Runs	HS	Avge	100s	50s	Ct	St	O	M	Runs	Wkts	Avge	Best	5wl	10wM
Test																		
All First	12	17	2	759	138	50.60	3	3	11	-								
1-day Int																		
NatWest	4	4	2	179	76 *	89.50	-	2	1	-								
B & H	5	5	0	109	68	21.80	-	1	-	-								
Sunday	10	9	3	387	82 *	64.50	-	4	3	-								

Career Performances

	M	Inns	NO	Runs	HS	Avge	100s	50s	Ct	St	Balls	Runs	Wkts	Avge	Best	5wl	10wM
Test	10	15	1	219	83	15.64	-	1	4	-	12	9	0	-	-	-	-
All First	315	500	70	17941	366	41.72	40	96	231	-	673	440	5	88.00	2-91	-	-
1-day Int	56	54	13	1539	113	37.53	1	11	24	-	6	9	0	-	-	-	
NatWest	38	37	7	1433	93 *	47.76	-	11	19	-	48	44	1	44.00	1-28	-	
B & H	74	71	21	2580	116 *	51.60	1	21	34	-	54	67	1	67.00	1-17	-	
Sunday	210	195	48	5939	116 *	40.40	4	40	63	-	48	48	1	48.00	1-33	-	

FELLOWS, G. M.   Yorkshire

Name: Gary Fellows
Role: Right-hand bat, right-arm
medium bowler
Born: 30 July 1978, Halifax, West Yorkshire
Height: 5ft 9in **Weight:** 11st
Nickname: Mouse, Micky
County debut: 1998
1st-Class 50s: 1
Parents: Eric and Tina
Marital status: Single
Family links with cricket: Dad and two brothers play league cricket
Education: Whitehill Primary School, Illingworth, Halifax; North Halifax Grammar School, Illingworth, Halifax
Qualifications: 10 GCSEs, 1 A-level, first coaching badge
Off-season: Playing club cricket in Australia

Overseas teams played for: Bulawayo Athletic Club, Bulawayo, Matabeleland, Zimbabwe 1996-97
Cricketers particularly admired: Craig White, Mark Waugh
Young players to look out for: Gareth Clough, John Inglis
Other sports played: Football ('on Bradford City one season')
Other sports followed: Football (Halifax Town)
Relaxations: Most sports 'and a laugh with the lads after the game'. Golf
Extras: Most catches by a fielder in a season (11) for Yorkshire Schools U15 1993. Awarded Yorkshire 2nd XI cap 1998
Opinions on cricket: 'General four-day cricket does not provide enough entertainment to bring in new spectators.'
Best batting: 50 Matabeleland v Mashonaland, Bulawayo 1996-97

1998 Season

	M	Inns	NO	Runs	HS	Avge	100s	50s	Ct	St	O	M	Runs	Wkts	Avge	Best	5wI	10wM
Test																		
All First	1	2	0	21	18	10.50	-	-	-	-	3	0	21	0	-	-	-	-
1-day Int																		
NatWest																		
B & H																		
Sunday	1	1	0	1	1	1.00	-	-	-	-	5.3	0	36	0	-	-	-	

Career Performances

	M	Inns	NO	Runs	HS	Avge	100s	50s	Ct	St	Balls	Runs	Wkts	Avge	Best	5wI	10wM
Test																	
All First	3	5	0	87	50	17.40	-	1	-	-	24	26	0	-	-	-	-
1-day Int																	
NatWest																	
B & H																	
Sunday	1	1	0	1	1	1.00	-	-	-	-	33	36	0	-	-	-	

FISHER, I. D.   Yorkshire

Name: Ian Douglas Fisher
Role: Left-hand bat, slow left-arm bowler
Born: 31 March 1976, Bradford
Height: 5ft 11in **Weight:** 13st 10lbs
Nickname: Fish, Gramps, Yoda
County debut: 1996
1st-Class 5 w. in innings: 1
Strike rate: (career 53.50)
Parents: Geoff and Linda
Marital status: Single
Family links with cricket: Father played
club cricket
Education: Denholme First School; Parkside
Middle School; Beckfoot Grammar School
Qualifications: 8 GCSEs, NCA coaching
award, Sports Leaders Award
Career outside cricket: Lumberjack
Off-season: 'Working until Christmas.
Practising and training after'
Overseas tours: Yorkshire to Zimbabwe 1996, to South Africa 1998
Overseas teams played for: Somerset West, South Africa 1994-95; Petone Riverside,
Wellington, New Zealand 1997-98
Cricketers particularly admired: Shane Warne, Steve Waugh
Young players to look out for: Gary Fellows, James Middlebrook
Other sports played: Football (Wibsey AFC)
Other sports followed: Football (Leeds United)
Injuries: Out for two weeks with broken finger
Relaxations: Music, watching TV and movies, socialising with friends
Extras: Played England U17 and Yorkshire Schools U15, U16 and Yorkshire U19
Opinions on cricket: '2nd XI cricket should be four days on first-class grounds.
Should have gone for the two-league system.'
Best batting: 37 Yorkshire v Derbyshire, Derby 1997
Best bowling: 5-35 Yorkshire v Lancashire, Old Trafford 1996

20. Who topped the bowling averages in the 1996 World Cup?

FIGA

1998 Season

	M	Inns	NO	Runs	HS	Avge	100s	50s	Ct	St	O	M	Runs	Wkts	Avge	Best	5wl	10wM
Test																		
All First	1	0	0	0	0	-	-	-	-	-	3	1	3	0	-	-	-	-
1-day Int																		
NatWest																		
B & H	1	0	0	0	0	-	-	-	1	-	8	1	26	1	26.00	1-26	-	
Sunday	6	3	2	9	4 *	9.00	-	-	1	-	29	0	118	7	16.85	3-25	-	

Career Performances

	M	Inns	NO	Runs	HS	Avge	100s	50s	Ct	St	Balls	Runs	Wkts	Avge	Best	5wl	10wM
Test																	
All First	6	5	1	75	37	18.75	-	-	-	-	642	288	12	24.00	5-35	1	-
1-day Int																	
NatWest																	
B & H	1	0	0	0	0	-	-	-	1	-	48	26	1	26.00	1-26	-	
Sunday	8	3	2	9	4 *	9.00	-	-	1	-	270	165	11	15.00	3-25	-	

FLANAGAN, I. N. Essex

Name: Ian Nicholas Flanagan
Role: Left-hand bat, off-spin bowler
Born: 5 June 1980, Colchester
Height: 6ft **Weight:** 12st 5lbs
Nickname: Bud
County debut: 1997
1st-Class 50s: 2
1st-Class catches: 9
Place in batting averages: 162nd av. 23.09
Parents: Roy and Anita
Marital status: Single
Family links with cricket: Father played
league cricket for Colchester and Carlisle.
Mother makes teas
Education: Millfield County Primary School;
The Colne Community School; The Sixth
Form College, Colchester

Qualifications: 10 GCSEs
Off-season: Touring with England U19
Overseas tours: England U19 to Pakistan 1996-97, to South Africa (including Youth
World Cup) 1997-98, to New Zealand 1998-99
Cricketers particularly admired: Keith Fletcher, Carl Hooper, Nasser Hussain

Young players to look out for: Graeme Swann
Other sports followed: Rugby, football (Tottenham Hotspur and Colchester United)
Injuries: Out for a week with strained medial knee ligament
Relaxations: Sleeping, watching films, spending time with friends 'and playing on my PlayStation'
Extras: Also played for England U17 and U18
Opinions on cricket: 'There is a need for greater wickets around the country, as some games struggle to get past the second day. Also there need to be improvements in the structure of county cricket so there are bigger crowds and money generated.'
Best batting: 61 Essex v Warwickshire, Edgbaston 1998

1998 Season

	M	Inns	NO	Runs	HS	Avge	100s	50s	Ct	St	O	M	Runs	Wkts	Avge	Best	5wl	10wM
Test																		
All First	6	11	0	254	61	23.09	-	2	9	-	1	0	1	0	-	-	-	-
1-day Int																		
NatWest																		
B & H																		
Sunday																		

Career Performances

	M	Inns	NO	Runs	HS	Avge	100s	50s	Ct	St	Balls	Runs	Wkts	Avge	Best	5wl	10wM
Test																	
All First	8	14	1	326	61	25.07	-	2	9	-	6		1	0	-	-	-
1-day Int																	
NatWest																	
B & H																	
Sunday																	

FLEMING, M. V.   Kent

Name: Matthew Valentine Fleming
Role: Right-hand bat, right-arm medium bowler, county captain
Born: 12 December 1964, Macclesfield
Height: 5ft 11ins **Weight:** 12st 8lbs
Nickname: Jazzer, Swan Vesta etc
County debut: 1988
County cap: 1990
One-Day Internationals: 11
1st-Class 50s: 37
1st-Class 100s: 9

1st-Class catches: 69
1st-Class 5 w. in innings: 2
One-Day 100s: 2
Place in batting averages: 158th av. 23.53
(1997 128th av. 29.95)
Place in bowling averages: 59th av. 26.52
(1997 76th av. 30.94)
Strike rate: 63.89 (career 78.65)
Parents: Valentine and Elizabeth
Wife and date of marriage:
Caroline, 23 September 1989
Children: Hannah, 9 October 1992;
Victoria, 16 June 1994; Matilda
Family links with cricket: Great-grandfather
C.F.H. Leslie played for England in 1882 –
hit an all-run seven at Lord's; father played
for Eton 2nd XI; mother opened the bowling
for Heathfield School
Education: Chiddingstone; St Aubyns School, Rottingdean; Eton College
Qualifications: 8 O-levels, 3 A-levels, granted short-service commission in Royal
Green Jackets 1985
Career outside cricket: 'Desperately trying to delay the day it's applicable'
Off-season: Intend to spend it 'with my fingers crossed'
Overseas tours: England VI to Hong Kong 1997; England to Sharjah 1997-98, to
West Indies 1997-98 (one-day series); to Bangladesh (Wills International Cup) 1998
Overseas teams played for: Avendale, Cape Town 1983-84
Cricketers particularly admired: 'James Whitaker and the Leicester team most
recently.' Lord Cowdrey, Ian Botham, Sachin Tendulkar, Courtney Walsh, Aravinda De
Silva
Young players to look out for: Rob Key
Other sports played: Golf, squash
Other sports followed: Football (Arsenal)
Injuries: Out for a day after treading on three-inch nail
Relaxations: Field sports, cappuccino, bonfiring
Extras: Ex-army officer in the Royal Green Jackets. First two scoring shots in
Championship cricket were sixes. Chairman of the Professional Cricketers'
Association. Out twice before lunch batting at number three for Kent against West
Indies in 1995. Played for England in the 1997 Hong Kong Sixes tournament in which
England finished runners-up to Pakistan and was named Player of the Tournament.
Called up to the England squad for the one-day competition in Sharjah 1997 after the
withdrawal of Darren Gough. Appointed captain of Kent for the 1999 season
Opinions on cricket: 'There are too many opinions and not enough action'
Best batting: 138 Kent v Essex, Canterbury 1997
Best bowling: 5-51 Kent v Nottinghamshire, Trent Bridge 1997

1998 Season

	M	Inns	NO	Runs	HS	Avge	100s	50s	Ct	St	O	M	Runs	Wkts	Avge	Best	5wI	10wM
Test																		
All First	17	30	4	612	51	23.53	-	1	9	-	404.4	115	1008	38	26.52	4-24	-	-
1-day Int	2	2	0	23	18	11.50	-	-	-	-	18	1	92	1	92.00	1-41	-	
NatWest	2	1	0	5	5	5.00	-				17	1	76	2	38.00	1-16	-	
B & H	5	5	1	141	105 *	35.25	1	-	2	-	30.4	0	135	7	19.28	2-19	-	
Sunday	16	7	1	103	28	17.16	-	-	1	-	74.4	2	418	21	19.90	3-18	-	

Career Performances

	M	Inns	NO	Runs	HS	Avge	100s	50s	Ct	St	Balls	Runs	Wkts	Avge	Best	5wI	10wM
Test																	
All First	166	274	31	7301	138	30.04	9	37	69	-	16597	7734	211	36.65	5-51	2	-
1-day Int	11	10	1	139	33	15.44	-	-	1	-	523	434	17	25.52	4-45	-	
NatWest	20	19	1	331	53	18.38	-	1	10	-	795	504	20	25.20	3-28	-	
B & H	47	44	3	1063	105 *	25.92	1	5	14	-	2230	1584	65	24.36	5-27	2	
Sunday	156	136	16	2809	112	23.40	1	12	37	-	5629	4985	195	25.56	4-13	-	

FLINTOFF, A. Lancashire

Name: Andrew Flintoff
Role: Right-hand bat, right-arm
medium bowler
Born: 6 December 1977, Preston
Height: 6ft 4in **Weight:** 13st 10lb
County debut: 1995
County cap: 1998
Test debut: 1998
Tests: 2
1st-Class 50s: 5
1st-Class 100s: 5
1st-Class catches: 35
Place in batting averages: 150th av. 24.32
(1997 121st av. 30.37)
Strike rate: 119.14 (career 120.00)
Parents: Colin and Susan
Family links with cricket: Brother Chris and
father both play local league cricket
Education: Greenlands County Primary;
Ribbleton Hall High School
Qualifications: 9 GCSEs
Off-season: Touring with England A

Overseas tours: England Schools U15 to South Africa 1993; England U19 to West Indies 1994-95, to Zimbabwe 1995-96, to Pakistan 1996-97; England A to Kenya and Sri Lanka 1997-98, to Zimbabwe and South Africa 1998-99

Cricketers particularly admired: Jason Gallian, John Crawley, Stephen Titchard, Warren Hegg

Other sports followed: Football (Preston North End and Liverpool FC)

Relaxations: Listening to music and sleeping

Extras: Won a *Daily Telegraph* regional award for batting. Represented England U14 to U19 and played for U17 against India in 1994. Captained the England U19 tour to Pakistan in 1996-97 and was again captain in the series against Zimbabwe in 1997. Scored 61 off 24 balls in Championship match v Surrey at Old Trafford in June 1998, including 34 from one over by Alex Tudor. Awarded county cap 1998. Became the 50th recipient of the Cricket Writers' Club Young Player of the Year award in September 1998. Professional Cricketers' Association's Young Player of the Year 1998. Was selected to represent England in the cancelled World Super Max 8s originally scheduled to take place in Perth in October 1998

Opinions on cricket: 'Cricket should be promoted more in state schools.'

Best batting: 124 Lancashire v Northamptonshire, Northampton 1998

Best bowling: 3-51 Lancashire v Worcestershire, Lytham 1998

1998 Season

	M	Inns	NO	Runs	HS	Avge	100s	50s	Ct	St	O	M	Runs	Wkts	Avge	Best	5wI	10wM
Test	2	3	0	17	17	5.66	-	-	1	-	35	4	112	1	112.00	1-52	-	-
All First	17	25	0	608	124	24.32	1	3	23	-	139	30	429	7	61.28	3-51	-	-
1-day Int																		
NatWest	5	4	0	82	35	20.50	-	-	3	-	15	2	42	2	21.00	1-4	-	
B & H	6	6	0	173	92	28.83	-	1	3	-	5	0	31	1	31.00	1-12	-	
Sunday	14	14	1	365	93 *	28.07	-	3	2	-	25	0	124	4	31.00	1-9	-	

Career Performances

	M	Inns	NO	Runs	HS	Avge	100s	50s	Ct	St	Balls	Runs	Wkts	Avge	Best	5wI	10wM
Test	2	3	0	17	17	5.66	-	-	1	-	210	112	1	112.00	1-52	-	-
All First	27	41	3	959	124	25.23	2	5	35	-	960	479	8	59.87	3-51	-	-
1-day Int																	
NatWest	6	5	0	84	35	16.80	-	-	3	-	125	63	2	31.50	1-4	-	
B & H	8	7	0	173	92	24.71	-	1	3	-	90	58	2	29.00	1-10	-	
Sunday	21	21	1	484	93 *	24.20	-	3	4	-	150	124	4	31.00	1-9	-	

FOLLETT, D.

Name: David Follett
Role: Right-hand bowler, right-arm
fast bowler
Born: 14 October 1968, Hanley,
Stoke-on-Trent
Height: 6ft 2in **Weight:** 12st 10lbs
Nickname: Foll
County debut: 1995 (Middlesex),
1997 (Northamptonshire)
1st-Class 5 w. in innings: 3
1st-Class 10 w. in match: 1
1st-Class catches: 5
Place in batting averages: 299th av. 2.16
Place in bowling averages: 100th av. 32.50
Strike rate: 61.80 (career 50.80)
Parents: Gordon and Sandra
Marital status: 'Engaged to Jo'
Family links with cricket: 'Dad played for
Burslem CC in Stoke-on-Trent in the NSSC
League'

Education: Clarence Street Middle School, Hanley, Stoke-on-Trent; Moorland Road
High School, Burslem, Vale-on-Trent; Stoke-on-Trent Technical College
Qualifications: 2 O-levels
Career outside cricket: Engineer
Off-season: Touring South Africa with my fiancée and playing some cricket
Overseas teams played for: Australian Capital Territory 1994-95; Queenbeyan,
Canberra, 1994-95
Cricketers particularly admired: Imran Khan, Allan Donald, Derek Randall
Young players to look out for: Tony Naylor, Gareth Ainsworthy
Other sports followed: Football (Port Vale)
Injuries: Missed last two weeks of season with broken finger
Relaxations: Watching football
Extras: Played for Staffordshire in the Minor Counties before joining Middlesex. Was
first team Player of the Month for April and May in 1996. Took 8 for 22 in the
Championship game against Durham. Moved to Northamptonshire for the 1996 season
Best batting: 17 Middlesex v Yorkshire, Lord's 1996
Best bowling: 8-22 Middlesex v Durham, Chester-le-Street 1996

1998 Season

	M	Inns	NO	Runs	HS	Avge	100s	50s	Ct	St	O	M	Runs	Wkts	Avge	Best	5wI	10wM
Test																		
All First	5	7	1	13	7	2.16	-	-	2	-	103	17	325	10	32.50	3-48	-	-
1-day Int																		
NatWest																		
B & H																		
Sunday	8	2	2	3	3 *	-	-	-	2	-	59.3	3	266	12	22.16	3-26	-	

Career Performances

	M	Inns	NO	Runs	HS	Avge	100s	50s	Ct	St	Balls	Runs	Wkts	Avge	Best	5wI	10wM
Test																	
All First	13	17	7	43	17	4.30	-	-	5	-	1829	1132	36	31.44	8-22	3	1
1-day Int																	
NatWest																	
B & H	9	3	0	8	4	2.66	-	-	-	-	408	302	12	25.16	4-39	-	
Sunday	15	4	3	5	3 *	5.00	-	-	6	-	651	526	22	23.90	3-26	-	

FORD, J. A. Kent

Name: James Anthony Ford
Role: Right-hand bat, slow left-arm bowler
Born: 30 March 1976, Pembury, Kent
Height: 5ft 9in **Weight:** 12st
Nickname: Fordy, Didge
County debut: 1996
1st-Class catches: 1
Parents: Anthony and Linda
Marital status: Single
Family links with cricket: Father is a keen follower
Education: Sevenoaks Prep School; Tonbridge School; University of Durham
Qualifications: 11 GCSEs, 3 A-levels, BA(Hons) Combined Social Sciences
Career outside cricket: Works for Colonial Financial Services
Overseas tours: Tonbridge School to South Africa 1992-93
Cricketers particularly admired: Viv Richards, Malcolm Marshall, Steve Waugh
Young players to look out for: Robin Martin-Jenkins
Other sports played: Golf

Other sports followed: Football (Tottenham Hotspur), rugby union (London Irish),
'all sports'
Injuries: Out for two weeks with dislocated and broken finger; also suffered from a
back problem
Relaxations: Reading
Extras: Played hockey for Durham University and England Students. Played cricket
for HMC Schools. Represented British Universities in the B&H Cup in 1997. Durham
University Sportsman of the Year 1997
Opinions on cricket: 'We play too much cricket. Unfortunately opportunities for
youngsters are not as easy to come by as they could be. If cricket was encouraged
throughout the school system, it would go a long way towards improving the standard
of the English game.'

1998 Season (did not make any first-class or one-day appearances)

Career Performances

	M	Inns	NO	Runs	HS	Avge	100s	50s	Ct	St	Balls	Runs	Wkts	Avge	Best	5wI	10wM
Test																	
All First	1	0	0	0	0	-	-	-	1	-	67	54	0	-	-	-	-
1-day Int																	
NatWest																	
B & H	4	4	0	63	38	15.75	-	-	2	-	30	27	0	-	-	-	
Sunday																	

FOSTER, M. J.   Durham

Name: Michael James Foster
Role: Right-hand bat, right arm
medium-fast bowler
Born: 17 September 1972, Leeds
Height: 6ft 2in **Weight:** 15st
Nickname: Foz, Bear
County debut: 1993 (Yorkshire), 1995 (Northamptonshire, one-day), 1996 (Durham)
1st-Class 50s: 6
1st-Class 100s: 1
1st-Class catches: 10
One-Day 100s: 1
Place in batting averages: 125th av. 26.75 (1997 177th av. 23.95)
Place in bowling averages: 21st av. 20.64 (1997 96th av. 34.23)
Strike rate: 39.88 (career 52.81)
Parents: Paul and Margaret
Wife and date of marriage: Lynne, 7 March 1998

Family links with cricket: 'Sister played for Yorkshire. Grandfather played in the Forces and for Great Preston. Father played for Great Preston'
Education: 'Las Vegas College'
Qualifications: 7 GCSEs, 2 A-levels
Overseas tours: England U19 to Pakistan 1991-92; Yorkshire to West Indies
Overseas teams played for: Fremantle, Perth, Western Australia; Queenstown, New Zealand; Ringwood, Melbourne, Australia
Cricketers particularly admired: Jeff Thomson, Ian Botham, Steve Waugh, Richie Richardson
Other sports followed: Rugby league (Castleford Tigers), football (Huddersfield Town), squash, 'various drinking games'
Relaxations: Socialising, sleeping, eating and keeping fit
Extras: 'Captained all the junior sides I played in up to and including Yorkshire Academy.' Off the mark with a six in first first-class game
Opinions on cricket: 'One-day cricket is a pain in the arse.'
Best batting: 129 Durham v Glamorgan, Cardiff 1997
Best bowling: 4-21 Durham v Middlesex, Lord's 1996

1998 Season

	M	Inns	NO	Runs	HS	Avge	100s	50s	Ct	St	O	M	Runs	Wkts	Avge	Best	5wI	10wM
Test																		
All First	8	13	1	321	76 *	26.75	-	2	2	-	113	23	351	17	20.64	4-41	-	-
1-day Int																		
NatWest																			
B & H	5	5	0	118	54	23.60	-	1	-	-	41	3	160	4	40.00	3-26	-	
Sunday	10	10	2	229	70	28.62	-	2	1	-	62	3	333	9	37.00	3-34	-	

Career Performances

	M	Inns	NO	Runs	HS	Avge	100s	50s	Ct	St	Balls	Runs	Wkts	Avge	Best	5wI	10wM
Test																	
All First	30	50	2	1128	129	23.50	1	6	10	-	3222	1839	61	30.14	4-21	-	-
1-day Int																	
NatWest	1	1	1	56	56 *	-	-	1	-	-	48	37	2	18.50	2-37	-	
B & H	12	12	3	297	73 *	33.00	-	3	-	-	578	434	9	48.22	3-26	-	
Sunday	48	39	4	604	118	17.25	1	2	9	-	1362	1288	29	44.41	3-34	-	

FRANCIS, S. R. G. Hampshire

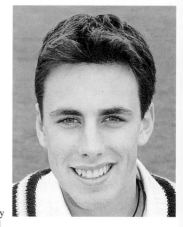

Name: Simon Richard George Francis
Role: Right-hand lower-order bat, right-arm fast-medium bowler
Born: 15 August 1978, Bromley
Height: 6ft 2in **Weight:** 14st
Nickname: Frankie, Mr Arrogance
County debut: 1997
Strike rate: 64.50 (career 93.00)
Parents: Daniel and Linda
Marital status: Single
Family links with cricket: 'Brother was the leading run-scorer in the 1996 U15 World Cup for England U15. Also played England U17 and is at Hampshire Academy. Grandfather played club cricket and for the Navy. Father plays club cricket'
Education: Yardley Court, Tonbridge; King Edward VI, Southampton; Durham University
Qualifications: 10 GCSEs, 3 A-levels, Level 1 coaching in cricket and hockey
Career outside cricket: Student
Off-season: 'Working towards finals and enjoying my final year at uni'
Overseas tours: England U17 to Holland for International Youth Tournament 1995; England U19 to Pakistan 1996-97; Durham University to Zimbabwe 1997-98
Cricketers particularly admired: Malcolm Marshall, Allan Donald, Kevan James
Young players to look out for: Lee Savident, Elliot Wilson
Other sports played: Hockey (England U18 1995 and Durham University 1st XI), golf
Other sports followed: Football ('follow Southampton FC's demise')
Injuries: Out for two weeks with shin splints
Relaxations: Socialising, working out, reading
Extras: *Daily Telegraph* West Region Bowling Award U15
Opinions on cricket: 'Haven't experienced first-class cricket enough to comment on that. Find the game hypocritical when there are all new ideas about nutrition, diet etc and yet lunch and tea are still no more than 40 minutes. Complete contradiction to nutritional guidance for players.'
Best batting: 6* British Universities v South Africa, Fenner's 1998
Best bowling: 2-21 Hampshire v Sri Lanka, Southampton 1998

1998 Season

	M	Inns	NO	Runs	HS	Avge	100s	50s	Ct	St	O	M	Runs	Wkts	Avge	Best	5wI	10wM
Test																		
All First	2	1	1	6	6 *	-	-	-	-	-	43	8	141	4	35.25	2-21	-	-
1-day Int																		
NatWest																			
B & H																			
Sunday																			

Career Performances

	M	Inns	NO	Runs	HS	Avge	100s	50s	Ct	St	Balls	Runs	Wkts	Avge	Best	5wI	10wM
Test																	
All First	3	3	1	14	6 *	7.00	-	-	-	-	372	238	4	59.50	2-21	-	-
1-day Int																	
NatWest																		
B & H																		
Sunday	1	0	0	0	0	-	-	-	-	-	48	31	2	15.50	2-31	-

FRANKS, P. J.   Nottinghamshire

Name: Paul John Franks
Role: Left-hand bat, right-arm fast-medium bowler
Born: 3 February 1979, Sutton-in-Ashfield
Height: 6ft 1in **Weight:** 13st
Nickname: Franksie, Pike, Franno
County debut: 1996
50 wickets in a season: 1
1st-Class 50s: 3
1st-Class 5 w. in innings: 4
1st-Class catches: 13
Place in batting averages: 175th av. 21.66 (1997 200th av. 21.53)
Place in bowling averages: 58th av. 26.44 (1997 114th av. 38.60)
Strike rate: 46.65 (career 57.74)
Parents: John and Patricia
Marital status: Single
Family links with cricket: Father played league cricket for 30 years
Education: Walter D'Ayncourt Primary School; Minster, Southwell; West Notts College

Qualifications: 9 GCSEs, Advanced GNVQ Leisure and Tourism, NCA coaching award
Off-season: 'Working in coaching in community scheme'
Overseas tours: England U19 to Pakistan 1996-97, to South Africa (including Youth World Cup) 1997-98; Notts CCC to Johannesburg 1998; Kevin Evans' Benefit Tour to Guernsey
Cricketers particularly admired: Dennis Lillee, Allan Donald, Glenn McGrath, Matt 'Nobby' Dowman
Young players to look out for: Mark Wallace, Stephen Randall, Matthew Whiley, Chris Schofield, Owais Shah
Other sports played: Golf ('when Doomer can find his ball')
Other sports followed: Football (Manchester United), golf (Tiger Woods), Eric Cantona
Injuries: Out for three weeks with a broken nose; for ten days with a broken finger
Relaxations: Socialising, training, playing golf
Extras: Youngest ever Notts player (and third-youngest player ever, aged 18 years 163 days) to take a hat-trick, v Warwickshire in July 1997. Won Youth World Cup winner's medal in Johannesburg 1998. Attended Dennis Lillee coaching school, Madras, February 1997 and March 1998. Was selected to represent England in the cancelled World Super Max 8s originally scheduled to take place in Perth in October 1998
Opinions on cricket: 'Too many overs in a day – 94 is a more realistic number, then both lunch and tea could be extended by five minutes.'
Best batting: 66* Nottinghamshire v Kent, Canterbury 1998
Best bowling: 6-63 Nottinghamshire v Worcestershire, Kidderminster 1998
Stop press: Called up for England A tour of Zimbabwe and South Africa as pace-bowling cover after early return of Paul Hutchison with back injury

1998 Season

	M	Inns	NO	Runs	HS	Avge	100s	50s	Ct	St	O	M	Runs	Wkts	Avge	Best	5wI	10wM
Test																		
All First	12	20	2	390	66 *	21.66	-	2	6	-	404.2	87	1375	52	26.44	6-63	4	-
1-day Int																		
NatWest	3	3	1	58	26 *	29.00	-	-	-	-	25	1	111	3	37.00	3-40	-	
B & H																		
Sunday	12	9	1	72	17 *	9.00	-	-	2	-	83.4	5	357	22	16.22	4-21	-	

Career Performances

	M	Inns	NO	Runs	HS	Avge	100s	50s	Ct	St	Balls	Runs	Wkts	Avge	Best	5wI	10wM
Test																	
All First	27	39	8	670	66 *	21.61	-	3	13	-	4908	2635	85	31.00	6-63	4	-
1-day Int																	
NatWest	6	4	1	62	26 *	20.66	-	-	2	-	312	226	8	28.25	3-40	-	
B & H																	
Sunday	16	11	2	87	17 *	9.66	-	-	2	-	664	520	26	20.00	4-21	-	

FRASER, A. G. J. Middlesex

Name: Alastair Gregory James Fraser
Role: Right-hand bat, right-arm fast-medium
bowler
Born: 17 October 1967, Edgware, Middlesex
Height: 6ft 1in **Weight:** 13st 7lbs
County debut: 1986 (Middlesex),
1991 (Essex)
1st-Class 50s: 1
1st-Class catches: 1
Strike rate: (career 62.08)
Parents: Don and Irene
Marital status: Single

Family links with cricket: Brother Angus –
Middlesex and England. 'Dad played for
Stanmore CC many moons ago!'
Education: Weald First School; Gayton High
School, Harrow; John Lyon School; Harrow
Weald Sixth Form College
Qualifications: 5 O-levels, cricket coaching
award, sports injuries course award
Career outside cricket: 'Work full-time for Amtrak Express Parcels'
Off-season: 'Continue work for Amtrak'
Overseas tours: NCA U19 to Bermuda 1985; England YC to Sri Lanka 1986-87;
OKS to India and Dubai 1994, to Malaysia 1997; four tours to Jersey with
Buckingham Cavaliers
Overseas teams played for: Plimmerton, Wellington 1986-88; Greenpoint, Cape
Town 1988-89; Western Suburbs, Sydney 1989-90; Northerns-Goodwood, Cape Town
1992; Queen's Park, Trinidad 1993
Cricketers particularly admired: Allan Donald, Ian Botham, Jeff Hurrell
Young players to look out for: Aaron Laraman, Dave Mawson
Other sports played: Football (Old Lyonians in Southern Amateur League)
Other sports followed: Rugby union, rugby league, football (Liverpool FC)
Injuries: Out for four weeks with a shoulder injury; for three weeks with a groin
injury
Relaxations: 'Having a pint and putting the world to rights with the lads from
Stanmore CC'
Extras: Returned to county cricket in 1998 after six years. Benson and Hedges Gold
Award against Essex ('one up on big brother!')
Opinions on cricket: 'The English game will never go forward with the tail wagging
the dog! ECB should give contracts and take control of the top 25 players. The way I
have been employed by Middlesex this year could be a way forward for other clubs.'

Best batting: 52* Essex v Sussex, Horsham 1991
Best bowling: 3-46 Middlesex v New Zealand, Lord's 1986

1998 Season

	M	Inns	NO	Runs	HS	Avge	100s	50s	Ct	St	O	M	Runs	Wkts	Avge	Best	5wl	10wM
Test																		
All First																		
1-day Int																		
NatWest	1	1	0	18	18	18.00	-	-	-	-	12	2	39	1	39.00	1-39	-	
B & H	3	0	0	0	0	-	-	-	1	-	22	1	107	6	17.83	4-45	-	
Sunday	7	5	0	34	14	6.80	-	-	1	-	43	3	192	8	24.00	4-19	-	

Career Performances

	M	Inns	NO	Runs	HS	Avge	100s	50s	Ct	St	Balls	Runs	Wkts	Avge	Best	5wl	10wM
Test																	
All First	10	10	5	137	52 *	27.40	-	1	1	-	745	386	12	32.16	3-46	-	-
1-day Int																	
NatWest	1	1	0	18	18	18.00	-	-	-	-	72	39	1	39.00	1-39	-	
B & H	4	1	0	6	6	6.00	-	-	1	-	163	138	7	19.71	4-45	-	
Sunday	20	10	2	61	14	7.62	-	-	2	-	762	560	20	28.00	4-19	-	

FRASER, A. R. C. Middlesex

Name: Angus Robert Charles Fraser
Role: Right-hand late-order bat, right-arm
fast-medium bowler, outfielder 'specialist'
Born: 8 August 1965, Billinge, Lancashire
Height: 6ft 6in **Weight:** 'Should be under
16st'
Nickname: Gus, Lard, Wiggy, Recall
County debut: 1984
County cap: 1988
Benefit: 1997
Test debut: 1989
Tests: 44
One-Day Internationals: 37
50 wickets in a season: 7
1st-Class 50s: 1
1st-Class 5 w. in innings: 31
1st-Class 10 w. in match: 4
1st-Class catches: 44
One-Day 5 w. in innings: 1

Place in batting averages: 277th av. 9.57 (1997 260th av. 14.35)

Place in bowling averages: 16th av. 20.06 (1997 78th av. 31.06)

Strike rate: 47.26 (career 661.63)

Parents: Don and Irene

Wife and date of marriage: Denise, March 1996

Children: Alexander Charles Mitchell, May 1993; Bethan Louise, July 1995

Family links with cricket: 'Mum and dad keen followers. Brother Alastair has played for Middlesex, Essex, then Middlesex again'

Education: Weald First School; Gayton High School, Harrow; Orange Hill Senior High School, Edgware

Qualifications: 7 O-levels, qualified cricket coach

Career outside cricket: 'Worked for Whittingdale Holding Ltd. while injured in 1991-92. Write for *Sunday Telegraph* and commentate for Sky Sports currently on days off'

Off-season: 'In Australia playing for England, then resting'

Overseas tours: Thames Valley Gentlemen to Barbados 1985; Middlesex to La Manga 1985 and 1986, to Portugal 1991-93; England to India (Nehru Cup) 1989-90, to West Indies 1989-90, to Australia 1990-91, to West Indies 1993-94, to Australia 1994-95, to South Africa 1995-96, to West Indies 1997-98, to Australia 1998-99

Overseas teams played for: Plimmerton, Wellington 1985-86 and 1987-88; Western Suburbs, Sydney 1988-89 and 1994-95

Cricketers particularly admired: Graham Gooch, Allan Border, Curtly Ambrose, Courtney Walsh

Young players to look out for: Stephen Peters, Andrew Flintoff

Other sports played: 'Golf with a sombrero on'

Other sports followed: 'Follow Liverpool FC keenly. Enjoy watching rugby internationals at my local rugby club, Harrow'

Injuries: Out for one week with sore back

Relaxations: Spending time with family, golf, Liverpool FC, drinking good red wine

Extras: Middlesex Player of the Year 1988 and 1989. Took a hat-trick in the Benson and Hedges Cup in 1989. Selected for England tour to New Zealand 1991-92 but ruled out by injury. Originally left out of England tour party to Australia 1994-95 but called up when Martin McCague was injured. Took his 100th Test wicket (Brian Lara) against West Indies in 1995. Finished 2nd in the Whyte and Mackay bowling ratings for 1995. One of *Wisden*'s five Cricketers of the Year 1996. His 8-53 v West Indies at Trinidad in 1998 are the best figures by an English bowler in the West Indies. Is the only bowler to have taken eight wickets twice in Tests in the West Indies. Has taken more Test wickets in the West Indies than any other touring bowler. Peter Smith Award 1998. Winner of the KUMALA Cape Wines 'Century of Bottles' award for the best individual performance against the 1998 South Africans. Awarded MBE in New Year honours list 1999

Opinions on cricket: 'I'd say you'd have had enough of them by now.'

Best batting: 92 Middlesex v Surrey, The Oval 1990

Best bowling: 8-53 England v West Indies, Port of Spain 1997-98

1998 Season

	M	Inns	NO	Runs	HS	Avge	100s	50s	Ct	St	O	M	Runs	Wkts	Avge	Best	5wI	10wM
Test	6	10	3	71	32	10.14	-	-	-	-	228.3	58	606	27	22.44	5-42	3	1
All First	14	19	5	134	32	9.57	-	-	1	-	480.3	122	1224	61	20.06	6-23	4	1
1-day Int	1	0	0	0	0	-	-	-	-	-	10	1	23	2	11.50	2-23	-	
NatWest	3	1	0	3	3	3.00	-	-	1	-	34	6	89	4	22.25	2-39	-	
B & H	5	1	1	14	14 *	-	-	-	2	-	50	2	221	5	44.20	2-40	-	
Sunday	8	4	2	0	0 *	0.00	-	-	-	-	60	5	215	8	26.87	2-17	-	

Career Performances

	M	Inns	NO	Runs	HS	Avge	100s	50s	Ct	St	Balls	Runs	Wkts	Avge	Best	5wI	10wM
Test	44	64	13	380	32	7.45	-	-	8	-	10462	4607	173	26.63	8-53	11	1
All First	242	286	69	2362	92	10.88	-	1	44	-	46409	20049	753	26.62	8-53	31	4
1-day Int	37	16	7	122	38 *	13.55	-	-	2	-	2092	1245	42	29.64	4-22	-	
NatWest	31	11	8	68	19	22.66	-	-	5	-	2037	1016	45	22.57	4-34	-	
B & H	44	23	12	114	30 *	10.36	-	-	9	-	2595	1534	54	28.40	4-49	-	
Sunday	153	60	26	366	33	10.76	-	-	21	-	6752	4492	159	28.25	5-32	1	

FROST, T.   Warwickshire

Name: Tony Frost
Role: Right-hand bat, wicket-keeper
Born: 17 November 1975, Stoke-on-Trent
Height: 5ft 10in **Weight:** 10st 6lbs
County debut: 1997
1st-Class 50s: 2
1st-Class 100s: 1
1st-Class catches: 47
1st-Class stumpings: 2
Place in batting averages: 76th av. 32.41
(1997 232nd av. 17.55)
Parents: Ivan and Christine
Marital status: Single
Family links with cricket: Father played for
Staffordshire
Education: James Brinkley High School;
Stoke-on-Trent College
Qualifications: 5 GCSEs
Overseas tours: Kidsgrove U18 to Australia
1990-91

Cricketers particularly admired: Ashley Giles 'could be described as a legend',
'Pop' Welch and George Burns 'in the JT bracket'

Other sports followed: Football, golf

Relaxations: Listening to music, watching films, reading aircraft magazines

Extras: Represented Staffordshire at all levels from U11 to U19. Won Texaco U16 competition with Staffordshire in 1992. Played for Development of Excellence XI U17 v South Africa and U18 v West Indies and U19 v India

Opinions on cricket: 'A lot of people are too critical. If they spent more time building up the players' confidence instead of putting the player down then they may get better results. '

Best batting: 111* Warwickshire v Oxford University, The Parks 1998

1998 Season

	M	Inns	NO	Runs	HS	Avge	100s	50s	Ct	St	O	M	Runs	Wkts	Avge	Best	5wI	10wM
Test																		
All First	8	14	2	389	111*	32.41	1	1	21	-	1	0	6	0	-		-	-
1-day Int																		
NatWest																		
B & H																		
Sunday	3	1	1	1	1*	-	-	-	2	1								

Career Performances

	M	Inns	NO	Runs	HS	Avge	100s	50s	Ct	St	Balls	Runs	Wkts	Avge	Best	5wI	10wM
Test																	
All First	17	25	4	547	111*	26.04	1	2	47	2	6	6	0	-		-	-
1-day Int																	
NatWest	1	1	0	0	0	0.00	-	-	2	1							
B & H	2	2	1	11	10*	11.00	-	-	1	-							
Sunday	10	3	2	3	2*	3.00	-	-	9	1							

21. What is the significance of Joel Garner's 37 for West Indies v India at Old Trafford in the 1983 World Cup?

FIGA

FULTON, D. P.   Kent

Name: David Paul Fulton
Role: Right-hand opening/top-order bat,
occasional wicket-keeper
Born: 15 November 1971, Lewisham
Height: 6ft 2in **Weight:** 12st 7lbs
Nickname: Raver, Tav
County debut: 1992
County cap: 1998
1st-Class 50s: 23
1st-Class 100s: 4
1st-Class 200s: 1
1st-Class catches: 111
Place in batting averages: 84th av. 31.80
(1997 80th av. 36.65)
Strike rate: (career 67.00)
Parents: John and Ann
Marital status: Single
Family links with cricket: Father used to
play for village side. 'When they blocked the
mid-wicket area he was forced to retire'
Education: Otford County Primary; The Judd School, Tonbridge; University of Kent
at Canterbury
Qualifications: 10 GCSEs, 3 A-levels, BA (Hons) Politics and International Relations,
advanced cricket coach, rugby coach, gym instructor qualification
Career outside cricket: 'Part-time journalist/politician/entrepreneur'
Off-season: Petersham-Marrickville CC, Sydney
Overseas tours: Kent Schools U17 to Singapore and New Zealand 1986-87; Kent to
France 1998
Overseas teams played for: Avendale CC, Cape Town 1993-94; Victoria CC, Cape
Town 1994-95, University of WA, Perth 1995-96; Petersham-Marrickville CC, Sydney
1998-99
Cricketers particularly admired: Graham Gooch, Gordon Greenidge, Courtney Walsh
Young players to look out for: Rob Key, 'Me'
Other sports played: Chess (England junior), table tennis ('top 10 in UK as a junior';
played for South England juniors); rugby, football, tennis ('useful'); golf, swimming
('lousy')
Other sports followed: Rugby (Harlequins), football (Nottingham Forest and
Canterbury City)
Injuries: 'Repeated blows to the body at bat-pad'
Relaxations: Politics, 'Churchill's Wine Bar and socialising with the boys and my
girlfriend Holly'

Extras: Helped Dean Headley's hat-trick against Derbyshire by catching Kim Barnett and Chris Adams. Was the last person to catch Viv Richards in a first-class match. Opened the batting and the bowling against South Africa in their first county game. His 207 against Yorkshire at Maidstone in 1998 is the longest innings ever played by a Kent batsman. 'Once scored 2000 runs without being dismissed against my little sister in the back garden.' Awarded county cap 1998

Opinions on cricket: 'It's important we keep pace with rugby, football etc. Marketing is the key. We need heroes in our game, which itself must be conducive to the watching public. Day/night cricket is a good start, but we must continue to embrace change. Groundsmen should be employed by ECB and be neutral.'

Best batting: 207 Kent v Yorkshire, Maidstone 1998
Best bowling: 1-37 Kent v Oxford University, Canterbury 1996

1998 Season

	M	Inns	NO	Runs	HS	Avge	100s	50s	Ct	St	O	M	Runs	Wkts	Avge	Best	5wI	10wM
Test																		
All First	17	31	1	954	207	31.80	1	7	21	-								
1-day Int																		
NatWest	2	2	0	15	13	7.50	-	-	-	-								
B & H																		
Sunday	1	1	0	4	4	4.00	-	-	1	-								

Career Performances

	M	Inns	NO	Runs	HS	Avge	100s	50s	Ct	St	Balls	Runs	Wkts	Avge	Best	5wI	10wM
Test																	
All First	76	137	9	4059	207	31.71	5	23	111	-	67	65	1	65.00	1-37	-	-
1-day Int																	
NatWest	6	6	0	65	19	10.83	-	-	-	-	6	9	0	-	-	-	
B & H	2	2	0	42	25	21.00	-	-	3	-							
Sunday	13	13	0	100	29	7.69	-	-	5	-							

GALLIAN, J. E. R.   Nottinghamshire

Name: Jason Edward Riche Gallian
Role: Right-hand bat, right-arm
medium bowler, county captain
Born: 25 June 1971, Manly, NSW, Australia
Height: 6ft **Weight:** 13st
Nickname: Gally
County debut: 1990 (Lancashire),
1998 (Nottinghamshire)
County cap: 1994 (Lancashire),
1998 (Nottinghamshire)
Test debut: 1995
Tests: 3
1000 runs in a season: 2
1st-Class 50s: 31
1st-Class 100s: 12
1st-Class 300s: 1
1st-Class 5 w. in innings: 1
1st-Class catches: 70
One-Day 100s: 5
One-Day 5 w. in innings: 1
Place in batting averages: 122nd av. 26.90 (1997 124th av. 29.76)
Strike rate: 141.50 (career 70.71)
Parents: Ray and Marilyn
Marital status: Single
Family links with cricket: Father played for Stockport
Education: The Pittwater House Schools, Australia; Oxford University
Qualifications: Higher School Certificate, Diploma in Social Studies
(Keble College, Oxford)
Overseas tours: Australia U20 to West Indies 1989-90; England A to India 1994-95,
to Pakistan 1995-96, to Australia 1996-97; England to South Africa 1995-96
Overseas teams played for: NSW and Australia U19 1988-89; NSW Colts and NSW
2nd XI 1990-91; Australia U20 and U21 1991-92; Manly 1993-94
Cricketers particularly admired: Desmond Haynes, Mike Gatting
Other sports followed: Rugby league and union, football
Relaxations: Listening to music, playing golf
Extras: Captained Australia YC v England YC 1989-90. Took wicket of D. A. Hagan
of Oxford University with his first ball for Lancashire in first-class cricket. Played for
Oxford University in 1992 and for Combined Universities in the B&H Cup. Captained
Oxford University 1993. Was called up to the England squad in South Africa in 1995-
96 as a replacement for the injured John Crawley and played in the fourth Test at Port
Elizabeth. He was dogged by finger injuries throughout the England A tour to

Australia in 1996-97. Left Lancashire during the 1997-98 off-season and joined
Nottinghamshire for 1998, being appointed captain after resignation of Paul Johnson
Best batting: 312 Lancashire v Derbyshire, Old Trafford 1996
Best bowling: 6-115 Lancashire v Surrey, Southport 1996

1998 Season

	M	Inns	NO	Runs	HS	Avge	100s	50s	Ct	St	O	M	Runs	Wkts	Avge	Best	5wI	10wM
Test																		
All First	14	25	3	592	113 *	26.90	1	3	8	-	47.1	13	103	2	51.50	1-14	-	-
1-day Int																		
NatWest	3	3	0	196	83	65.33	-	3	3	-								
B & H	5	5	1	147	74 *	36.75	-	1	1	-	31	0	165	2	82.50	1-49	-	
Sunday	13	13	1	324	74	27.00	-	2	6	-	8	0	47	2	23.50	1-23	-	

Career Performances

	M	Inns	NO	Runs	HS	Avge	100s	50s	Ct	St	Balls	Runs	Wkts	Avge	Best	5wI	10wM
Test	3	6	0	74	28	12.33	-	-	1	-	84	62	0	-	-	-	-
All First	105	184	16	6320	312	37.61	13	31	70	-	5940	3435	84	40.89	6-115	1	-
1-day Int																	
NatWest	11	11	1	408	101 *	40.80	1	3	6	-	120	88	1	88.00	1-11	-	
B & H	30	29	2	910	134	33.70	2	6	5	-	665	548	15	36.53	5-15	1	
Sunday	59	58	8	1726	104	34.52	2	11	24	-	742	700	28	25.00	2-10	-	

22. Who is the all-time leading wicket-keeper in the
World Cup in terms of dismissals?

FICA

GARAWAY, M.   Hampshire

Name: Mark Garaway
Role: Right-hand bat, wicket-keeper
Born: 20 July 1973, Swindon, Wilts
Height: 5ft 7in **Weight:** 12st
Nickname: Wolf, Garas, Scenariohead
County debut: 1996
1st-Class catches: 9
1st-Class stumpings: 1
Parents: Sam and Val
Marital status: Single ('hugely')
Family links with cricket: 'Sam still whacks
it for Ventnor CC. Grandfather was a steady
player'
Education: Carhampton Primary, Somerset;
Ventnor Middle and Sandown High School,
Isle of Wight; 'Ventnor CC, the Astoria
(Hermanus, SA)'
Qualifications: 10 O-levels, 3 A-levels, NCA
cricket coach
Overseas tours: Isle of Wight U14 and U17 to Jersey and Guernsey 1988-91; Ventnor
to Winchester 1994; Hampshire to Val de Lobo 1994
Overseas teams played for: Worcester, Boland, South Africa 1991-93; Hermanus,
South Africa 1993, 1995-97; 'Ventnor, Isle of Wight 1982-94'
Cricketers particularly admired: Ian Botham, Robin Smith, Mark Brumer, Simon
Rodney, Jeff Hose, Kevan James
Young players to look out for: Dimitri Mascarenhas, Simon Francis
Other sports followed: Football (Swindon Town), squash
Relaxations: Music, art
Extras: Represented England at U15, U17 and U19 level. Played for Isle of Wight at
U16, U17, U21 and senior level in the same season. Spent two years (1991 and 1992)
as MCC Young Professional. Hampshire Schools Wicketkeepers Award 1988. Andrew
Swallow Memorial Cup 1987. Wight Waters Sports Award 1989-91. 2nd XI Player of
the Month June 1997
Opinions on cricket: 'Apparently first-class cricket is a good game.'
Best batting: 44 Hampshire v Cambridge University, Fenner's 1996

---

23. Whose 82-ball century helped set up victory for West Indies v
Australia in the 1975 World Cup final?

FIGA

1998 Season

	M	Inns	NO	Runs	HS	Avge	100s	50s	Ct	St	O	M	Runs	Wkts	Avge	Best	5wI	10wM
Test																		
All First	1	1	0	19	19	19.00	-	-	-	-								
1-day Int																		
NatWest																		
B & H																		
Sunday																		

Career Performances

	M	Inns	NO	Runs	HS	Avge	100s	50s	Ct	St	Balls	Runs	Wkts	Avge	Best	5wI	10wM
Test																	
All First	3	3	0	68	44	22.66	-	-	9	1							
1-day Int																	
NatWest																	
B & H																	
Sunday																	

GATTING, M. W.   Middlesex

Name: Michael William Gatting
Role: Right-hand bat, right-arm medium
bowler, slip fielder
Born: 6 June 1957, Kingsbury, Middlesex
Height: 5ft 10in **Weight:** 15st 7lbs
Nickname: Gatt, Jabba
County debut: 1975
County cap: 1977
Benefit: 1988 (£205,000)
Test debut: 1977-78
Tests: 79
One-Day Internationals: 92
1000 runs in a season: 18
1st-Class 50s: 181
1st-Class 100s: 84
1st-Class 200s: 10
1st-Class 5 w. in innings: 2
1st-Class catches: 493
One-Day 100s: 12
Place in batting averages: 23rd av. 43.80 (1997 71st av. 39.00)
Strike rate: 30.00 (career 63.63)
Parents: Bill and Vera

Wife and date of marriage: Elaine, 9 September 1980
Children: Andrew, 21 January 1983; James, 11 July 1986
Family links with cricket: Father used to play club cricket. Brother Steve played for Middlesex 2nd XI
Education: Wykeham Primary School; John Kelly Boys' High School
Qualifications: 4 O-levels
Off-season: Travelling with the England A side as coach
Overseas tours: England to New Zealand and Pakistan 1977-78, to West Indies 1980-81, to India and Sri Lanka 1981-82, to New Zealand and Pakistan 1983-84, to India 1984-85, to West Indies 1985-86, to Australia 1986-87, to India and Pakistan (World Cup), Australia and New Zealand 1987-88; unofficial English XI to South Africa 1989-90; England to India and Sri Lanka 1992-93, to Australia 1994-95; England U19 to New Zealand 1998-99 (manager)
Cricketers particularly admired: Gary Sobers, Len Hutton
Young players to look out for: David Nash, Owais Shah
Other sports followed: Football, golf, tennis, swimming, indoor cricket, rugby
Relaxations: Golf, swimming, reading, music
Extras: Awarded OBE in Queen's Birthday Honours 1987 for services to cricket. Captain of Middlesex from 1983 until relinquished captaincy during 1997 season. Captain of England from 1986 to 1988. Published autobiography *Leading From the Front* in 1988. Won a bronze medal for ballroom dancing at the Neasden Ritz. Played football for Edgware Town as a teenager. Started as a goalkeeper, but also played centre-half for Middlesex Schools. Was recommended to West Ham, had a trial with QPR and offered an apprenticeship by Watford. His brother Steve has had a successful football career with Arsenal and Brighton. Mike started his cricket career as wicket-keeper for his school team. He toured West Indies with England Young Cricketers in 1976 and 'to my immense pleasure (and to most other people's total disbelief) I was given the job of opening the bowling in the "Test" matches.' One of *Wisden*'s Five Cricketers of the Year 1984. His finest achievement was as captain of England on victorious tour of Australia, 1986-87, when they won the Ashes, the Perth Challenge Cup and World Series Cup. Was relieved of England captaincy after the First Test against West Indies in 1988. Captain of unofficial English team in South Africa in 1989-90 and was banned from Test cricket for five years; suspension remitted in 1992. Captained Middlesex to Championship title in 1990 and 1993. Retired from Test cricket after the final Test of the 1994-95 series against Australia. With Justin Langer, put on 372 v Essex at Southgate in 1998, setting a new Middlesex record for the first wicket; during his innings of 241, he became the second-highest run-scorer in Middlesex history behind Patsy Hendren. His record of 14 county trophy wins as a player is unequalled. Retired from county cricket at the end of the 1998 season and was appointed Middlesex director of coaching. Is now a Test selector. Is president of the Professional Cricketers' Association
Best batting: 258 Middlesex v Somerset, Bath 1984
Best bowling: 5-34 Middlesex v Glamorgan, Swansea 1982

1998 Season

	M	Inns	NO	Runs	HS	Avge	100s	50s	Ct	St	O	M	Runs	Wkts	Avge	Best	5wl	10wM
Test																		
All First	17	29	3	1139	241	43.80	2	7	19	-	5	1	9	1	9.00	1-9	-	-
1-day Int																		
NatWest	3	3	0	35	17	11.66	-	-	1	-								
B & H																			
Sunday	2	2	0	2	2	1.00	-	-	1	-								

Career Performances

	M	Inns	NO	Runs	HS	Avge	100s	50s	Ct	St	Balls	Runs	Wkts	Avge	Best	5wl	10wM
Test	79	138	14	4409	207	35.55	10	21	59	-	752	317	4	79.25	1-14	-	-
All First	551	861	123	36549	258	49.52	94	181	493	-	10055	4703	158	29.76	5-34	2	-
1-day Int	92	88	17	2095	115 *	29.50	1	9	22	-	392	336	10	33.60	3-32	-	
NatWest	67	65	13	2148	132 *	41.30	2	15	26	-	1004	643	19	33.84	2-14	-	
B & H	96	90	18	2921	143 *	40.56	3	18	30	-	1382	940	41	22.92	4-49	-	
Sunday	270	243	30	6673	124 *	31.32	6	40	91	-	3196	2730	90	30.33	4-30	-	

GIDDINS, E. S. H. — Warwickshire

Name: Edward Simon Hunter Giddins
Role: Right-hand bat, right-arm
medium-fast bowler
Born: 20 July 1971, Eastbourne
Height: 6ft 4in **Weight:** 13st 7lbs
Nickname: Geezer
County debut: 1991 (Sussex),
1998 (Warwickshire)
County cap: 1994 (Sussex)
50 wickets in a season: 3
1st-Class 5 w. in innings: 18
1st-Class 10 w. in match: 2
1st-Class catches: 16
Place in batting averages: 296th av. 3.35
Place in bowling averages: 38th av. 23.88
Strike rate: 47.73 (career 52.01)
Parents: Simon and Pauline
Marital status: Single
Family links with cricket: None
Education: St Bede's Prep School; Eastbourne College
Qualifications: 'Various O- and A-levels, national coaching certificate, recorder
(grade 2), shorthand and typing 100/60'

Career outside cricket: None
Overseas tours: England A to Pakistan 1995-96
Overseas teams played for: Mossman, Sydney 1994-95
Cricketers particularly admired: Derek Randall
Other sports followed: Football (Brighton & Hove Albion FC – 'fingers crossed')
Relaxations: Gym, fitness and mountain biking
Extras: Joined Warwickshire for the 1998 season
Best batting: 34 Sussex v Essex, Hove 1995
Best bowling: 6-47 Sussex v Yorkshire, Eastbourne 1996

1998 Season

	M	Inns	NO	Runs	HS	Avge	100s	50s	Ct	St	O	M	Runs	Wkts	Avge	Best	5wl	10wM
Test																		
All First	18	23	9	47	11 *	3.35	-	-	4	-	668.2	161	2006	84	23.88	6-79	5	1
1-day Int																		
NatWest	2	1	1	0	0 *	-	-	-	1	-	19	5	42	4	10.50	2-19	-	
B & H	5	2	2	5	4 *	-	-	-	2	-	45	7	154	8	19.25	3-35	-	
Sunday	13	4	2	6	6 *	3.00	-	-	1	-	86.2	4	355	17	20.88	2-20	-	

Career Performances

	M	Inns	NO	Runs	HS	Avge	100s	50s	Ct	St	Balls	Runs	Wkts	Avge	Best	5wl	10wM
Test																	
All First	98	119	48	368	34	5.18	-	-	16	-	17269	9433	332	28.41	6-47	18	2
1-day Int																	
NatWest	12	5	3	25	13	12.50	-	-	1	-	779	435	15	29.00	3-24	-	
B & H	17	5	4	5	4 *	5.00	-	-	5	-	974	622	19	32.73	3-28	-	
Sunday	75	32	13	31	9 *	1.63	-	-	9	-	3122	2610	87	30.00	4-23	-	

GIE, N. A.   Nottinghamshire

Name: Noel Addison Gie
Role: Right-hand bat, right-arm
medium bowler
Born: 12 April 1977, Pretoria, South Africa
Height: 6ft **Weight:** 12st 8lbs
County debut: 1995
1st-Class 50s: 2
1st-Class catches: 7
Place in batting averages: 232nd av. 16.00 (1997 262nd av. 14.16)
Parents: Clive and Lindy
Marital status: Single
Family links with cricket: Father played first-class cricket in South Africa for

Western Province, Northern Transvaal and Natal
Education: Fornwood School, Nottingham; Trent College, Nottingham; Nottingham Trent University
Qualifications: Studying for degree in Business Studies from October 1996, NCA coaching award
Overseas tours: Trent College to Australia 1993-94; England U19 to Zimbabwe 1995-96
Overseas teams played for: Berea Rovers, Durban, South Africa 1995
Cricketers particularly admired: Robin Smith
Other sports followed: Squash, tennis, rugby league
Relaxations: Reading and cycling
Extras: Scored 3153 runs for the 1st XI during his time at Trent College
Best batting: 50 Nottinghamshire v Oxford University, The Parks 1997
50 Nottinghamshire v Gloucestershire, Trent Bridge 1998

1998 Season

	M	Inns	NO	Runs	HS	Avge	100s	50s	Ct	St	O	M	Runs	Wkts	Avge	Best	5wI	10wM
Test																		
All First	4	8	0	128	50	16.00	-	1	3	-								
1-day Int																		
NatWest																		
B & H	1	1	0	70	70	70.00	-	1	-	-								
Sunday	7	7	1	104	57	17.33	-	1	2	-								

Career Performances

	M	Inns	NO	Runs	HS	Avge	100s	50s	Ct	St	Balls	Runs	Wkts	Avge	Best	5wI	10wM
Test																		
All First	11	20	0	311	50	15.55	-	2	7	-								
1-day Int																		
NatWest																		
B & H	4	4	0	131	70	32.75	-	1	-	-								
Sunday	15	13	2	253	75 *	23.00	-	2	5	-								

GILES, A. F. Warwickshire

Name: Ashley Fraser Giles
Role: Right-hand bat, slow left-arm bowler
Born: 19 March 1973, Chertsey, Surrey
Height: 6ft 4in **Weight:** 15st 7lbs
Nickname: Skinny, Splash, Melink
County debut: 1993
Test debut: 1998
Tests: 1
One-Day Internationals: 2
50 wickets in a season: 1
1st-Class 50s: 12
1st-Class 100s: 1
1st-Class 5 w. in innings: 6
1st-Class catches: 27
One-Day 5 w. in innings: 2
Place in batting averages: 114th av. 28.52
(1997 72nd av. 39.00)
Place in bowling averages: 75th av. 28.47
(1997 83rd av. 32.23)

Strike rate: 76.58 (career 68.01)
Parents: Michael and Paula
Marital status: 'Girlfriend Stine'
Family links with cricket: 'Dad used to play. Brother Andrew still plays at Ripley, Surrey. Used to play with sisters Tracy and Carrie in the Colts at Ripley. Mum did the teas.'
Education: Kingfield Primary School, Old Woking; George Abbott County Secondary, Burpham, Guildford
Qualifications: 9 GCSEs, 2 A-levels, qualified cricket coach
Career outside cricket: 'Good question!'
Off-season: 'Bangladesh with England for the one-dayers, then hopefully Australia after Christmas'
Overseas tours: Surrey U19 to Barbados 1990-91; England A to Australia 1996-97, to Kenya and Sri Lanka 1997-98; England to Sharjah 1997-98 (Champions Trophy), to Bangladesh (Wills International Cup) 1998, to Australia (CUB Series) 1998-99; Warwickshire to Cape Town 1996 and 1997, to Bloemfontein 1998
Overseas teams played for: Vredenburg/Saldanha, Cape Town 1992-95; Avendale CC, Cape Town 1995-96
Cricketers particularly admired: Dougie Brown, Allan Donald, Mark Ealham, Tim Munton, Dermot Reeve
Young players to look out for: Mark Wagh, Ian Bell (Warwicks)
Other sports played: Golf, football

Other sports followed: Football (QPR), golf, basketball
Injuries: Out for six weeks with Achilles tendon injury
Relaxations: Music, cinema, *FHM* and *Maxim*, 'having a pint with the Bears down "The Swan"', 'spending time with girlfriend Stine'
Extras: Surrey Young Cricketer of the Year 1991, NBC Denis Compton Award for Warwickshire in 1996, Warwickshire Player of the Year in 1996, Warwickshire Most Improved Player 1996, Cricket Society Young Allrounder of the year 1996. Made Test debut v South Africa at Old Trafford in 1998
Opinions on cricket: 'Change to the divisional system. Play the game hard and always to win. Don't worry too much, enjoy it.'
Best batting: 106* Warwickshire v Lancashire, Edgbaston 1996
Best bowling: 6-45 Warwickshire v Durham, Edgbaston 1996

1998 Season

	M	Inns	NO	Runs	HS	Avge	100s	50s	Ct	St	O	M	Runs	Wkts	Avge	Best	5wl	10wM
Test	1	2	1	17	16 *	17.00	-	-	-	-	36	7	106	1	106.00	1-106	-	-
All First	14	21	4	485	83	28.52	-	3	8	-	459.3	154	1025	36	28.47	5-48	1	-
1-day Int	1	1	0	2	2	2.00	-	-	-	-	9	0	37	2	18.50	2-37	-	
NatWest	3	3	1	10	5	5.00	-	-	-	-	22.2	2	66	6	11.00	4-29	-	
B & H	5	5	0	51	37	10.20	-	-	2	-	35.2	3	178	11	16.18	3-22	-	
Sunday	14	10	2	127	38 *	15.87	-	-	3	-	70.4	6	269	18	14.94	4-17	-	

Career Performances

	M	Inns	NO	Runs	HS	Avge	100s	50s	Ct	St	Balls	Runs	Wkts	Avge	Best	5wl	10wM
Test	1	2	1	17	16 *	17.00	-	-	-	-	216	106	1	106.00	1-106	-	-
All First	64	87	19	2067	106 *	30.39	1	12	27	-	12787	5016	188	26.68	6-45	6	-
1-day Int	2	1	0	2	2	2.00	-	-	-	-	108	85	2	42.50	2-37	-	
NatWest	11	8	2	137	69	22.83	-	1	-	-	563	344	20	17.20	5-21	1	
B & H	15	12	2	161	37	16.10	-	-	8	-	634	494	19	26.00	3-22	-	
Sunday	48	27	7	396	57	19.80	-	1	14	-	1355	1020	58	17.58	5-36	1	

GOODCHILD, D. J.   Middlesex

Name: David John Goodchild
Role: Right-hand opening bat, right-arm
medium bowler
Born: 17 September 1976, Harrow
Height: 6ft 2in **Weight:** 15st 7lbs
Nickname: G, Golden, Gee Man
County debut: 1996
1st-Class 50s: 2
1st-Class 100s: 1
1st-Class catches: 1
Place in batting averages: 143rd av. 24.92
Parents: John and Brenda
Marital status: Single
Family links with cricket:
'Dad played club cricket'
Education: Vaughan First and Middle
School; Whitmore High School; Weald
College; North London University
Qualifications: 9 GCSEs, 3 A-levels, degree
in Sports Management, NCA coaching award
Off-season: Training, coaching, practising
Cricketers particularly admired: Mark Ramprakash, Mike Gatting, Brian Lara
Young players to look out for: Steffan and Rodri James
Other sports played: All sports – football, squash, basketball
Other sports followed: Football (Arsenal), American football (Miami Dolphins)
Injuries: Out for three days with shoulder injury
Relaxations: Fishing, cinema, socialising
Extras: Holds the top score for Middlesex U11 side (153) and the top total aggregate
for that age group (563); youngest player to be awarded junior county cap (U11).
Awarded 2nd XI county cap at the end of the 1996 season. First-ever game for
Middlesex was for the 1st XI against Gloucestershire at Lord's in 1996. Scored maiden
first-class century (105) v Sri Lanka at Lord's in 1998
Opinions on cricket: 'The demands of the modern game result in less and less time to
practise and remedy faults. I feel the format of the season must change to enable better
quality not quantity.'
Best batting: 105 Middlesex v Sri Lanka, Lord's 1998

---

24. Which two England batsmen put on 129 for the first wicket
v West Indies in the 1979 World Cup final?

FICA

1998 Season

	M	Inns	NO	Runs	HS	Avge	100s	50s	Ct	St	O	M	Runs	Wkts	Avge	Best	5wI	10wM
Test																		
All First	7	14	1	324	105	24.92	1	2	1	-	17	1	62	0	-	-	-	-
1-day Int																		
NatWest																		
B & H																		
Sunday	6	5	2	84	38 *	28.00	-	-	5	-								

Career Performances

	M	Inns	NO	Runs	HS	Avge	100s	50s	Ct	St	Balls	Runs	Wkts	Avge	Best	5wI	10wM
Test																	
All First	8	16	1	328	105	21.86	1	2	1	-	131	88	0	-	-	-	-
1-day Int																	
NatWest																	
B & H																	
Sunday	6	5	2	84	38 *	28.00	-	-	5	-							

GOUGH, D. Yorkshire

Name: Darren Gough
Role: Right-hand bat, right-arm fast bowler
Born: 18 September 1970, Barnsley
Height: 5ft 11in **Weight:** 13st 5lbs
Nickname: Dazzler, Rhino
County debut: 1989
County cap: 1993
Test debut: 1994
Tests: 26
One-Day Internationals: 44
50 wickets in a season: 3
1st-Class 50s: 11
1st-Class 100s: 1
1st-Class 5 w. in innings: 21
1st-Class 10 w. in innings: 3
1st-Class catches: 35
One-Day 5 w. in innings: 5
Place in batting averages: 202nd av. 19.21
(1997 269th av. 13.06)
Place in bowling averages: 50th av. 25.40 (1997 46th av. 26.72)
Strike rate: 48.64 (career 51.61)
Parents: Trevor and Christine

Wife and date of marriage: Anna Marie, 16 October 1993
Children: Liam James, 24 November 1994; Brennan Kyle, 9 December 1997
Education: St Helens Junior; Priory Comprehensive; Airedale and Wharfdale College (part-time)
Qualifications: 2 O-levels, 5 CSEs, BTEC Leisure, NCA coaching award
Off-season: England tours to Australia and Sharjah
Overseas tours: England YC to Australia 1989-90; Yorkshire to Barbados 1989-90, to South Africa 1991-92 and 1992-93; England A to South Africa 1993-94; England to Australia 1994-95, to South Africa 1995-96, to India and Pakistan (World Cup) 1995-96, to Zimbabwe and New Zealand 1996-97, to Australia 1998-99
Overseas teams played for: East Shirley, Christchurch, New Zealand 1991-92
Cricketers particularly admired: Ian Botham, Steve Waugh, Shane Warne, Michael Atherton ('mental strength')
Young players to look out for: Paul Hutchison, Andrew Flintoff, Gareth Batty, Ryan Sidebottom, Liam James Gough (aged $4^1/2$)
Other sports played: Golf
Other sports followed: Football (Tottenham Hotspur and Barnsley)
Injuries: Out for four weeks after breaking finger in the first Test against South Africa
Relaxations: Cinema, 'spending time with family'
Extras: England Cornhill Player of the Year 1994. Yorkshire Sports Personality of the Year 1994. Voted Man of the Match in England's third Test match against Australia at Sydney in 1994-95. Took a hat-trick against Kent in 1995. Named Player of the Year by Cornhill Insurance for 1995 season. Whyte and Mackay Bowler of the Year in 1996. Had to withdraw from the England tour to West Indies 1997-98 due to a persistent hamstring injury which required surgery. England Player of the Series in the Texaco one-day rubber v South Africa 1998
Opinions on cricket: 'Read my book – *My Guide to your Success.*'
Best batting: 121 Yorkshire v Warwickshire, Headingley 1996
Best bowling: 7-28 Yorkshire v Lancashire, Headingley 1995
Stop press: Took Test hat-trick v Australia at Sydney in January 1999, the first Ashes hat-trick by an England bowler since J. Hearne's at Leeds in 1899

1998 Season

	M	Inns	NO	Runs	HS	Avge	100s	50s	Ct	St	O	M	Runs	Wkts	Avge	Best	5wI	10wM
Test	5	8	1	62	16*	8.85	-	-	-	-	160.5	31	490	19	25.78	6-42	1	-
All First	11	15	1	269	89	19.21	-	2	1	-	340.3	65	1067	42	25.40	6-42	2	-
1-day Int	6	5	2	18	15	6.00	-	-	-	-	60	4	274	13	21.07	4-35	-	
NatWest	1	1	0	42	42	42.00	-	-	-	-	12	1	50	4	12.50	4-50	-	
B & H	5	2	0	30	30	15.00	-	-	4	-	46.2	5	178	8	22.25	3-27	-	
Sunday	7	6	2	22	9	5.50	-	-	-	-	46	3	189	17	11.11	5-25	1	

Career Performances

	M	Inns	NO	Runs	HS	Avge	100s	50s	Ct	St	Balls	Runs	Wkts	Avge	Best	5wI	10wM
Test	26	38	5	425	65	12.87	-	2	8	-	5487	2891	104	27.79	6-42	4	-
All First	147	197	32	2744	121	16.63	1	11	35	-	26066	13692	505	27.11	7-28	21	3
1-day Int	44	29	9	221	45	11.05	-	-	4	-	2480	1712	71	24.11	5-44	2	
NatWest	22	12	0	225	46	18.75	-	-	3	-	1410	785	45	17.44	7-27	1	
B & H	29	16	5	160	48 *	14.54	-	-	11	-	1538	964	34	28.35	3-27	-	
Sunday	95	63	16	593	72 *	12.61	-	1	18	-	4046	3022	122	24.77	5-13	2	

GOUGH, M. A. Durham

Name: Michael Andrew Gough
Role: Right-hand bat, off-spin bowler
Born: 18 December 1979, Hartlepool
Height: 6ft 5in **Weight:** 13st 7lbs
Nickname: Goughy
County debut: 1998
1st-Class 50s: 2
1st-Class 100s: 1
1st-Class catches: 12
Place in batting averages: 116th av. 28.22
Strike rate: 97.00 (career 97.00)
Parents: Michael and Jean
Marital status: Single

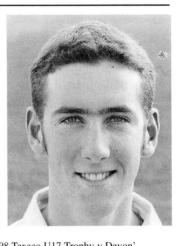

Family links with cricket: 'Dad has played cricket for nearly 30 years and also represented Durham as an opening batsman in the Minor Counties. Mam is an avid follower and supporter – washes and irons endless cricket kit. Cousin Paul Gough was a part of the Durham U17 team that won the 1998 Texaco U17 Trophy v Devon'
Education: Sacred Heart RC Primary School, Hartlepool; English Martyrs School and Sixth Form College, Hartlepool
Qualifications: 10 GCSEs, basic coaching award. 'Studied English, Sociology and Business Studies at A-level but dropped out after first year because of selection to tour South Africa with England U19'
Career outside cricket: 'Not decided'
Off-season: 'Plenty of work in the gym. Running and swimming. Lots of cricket practice. Watching England on the TV in Australia. Hopefully touring'
Overseas tours: Durham U21 to Sri Lanka November 1996; England U17 to Bermuda (International Youth Tournament) June 1997; England U19 to South Africa (inc Youth World Cup) 1997-98, to New Zealand 1998-99 (captain)

Cricketers particularly admired: Shane Warne, Mike Atherton, Alec Stewart, David Boon, Michael Gough Senior
Young players to look out for: Mark Symington, Steve Harmison, Mark Wallace
Other sports played: Football (had trials with Arsenal and Sheffield United and attended Middlesbrough FC School of Excellence)
Other sports followed: Football (Hartlepool United season-ticket holder)
Relaxations: Listening to all types of music. Spending time with friends and family. Reading the papers. Eating out. Cinema. Football and cricket. 'Generally keeping busy'
Extras: Captained North of England and England U15. Part of winning England U17 team at the International Youth Tournament in Bermuda 1997. Durham CCC Young Player of the Year 1997. Part of winning England U19 team at the Youth World Cup in South Africa 1998. Scored 62 on first-class debut, against Essex 1998. Youngest player to score a century for Durham, against Cambridge University 1998
Best batting: 123 Durham v Cambridge University, Fenner's 1998
Best bowling: 1-4 Durham v Cambridge University, Fenner's 1998

1998 Season

	M	Inns	NO	Runs	HS	Avge	100s	50s	Ct	St	O	M	Runs	Wkts	Avge	Best	5wl	10wM
Test																		
All First	10	18	0	508	123	28.22	1	2	12	-	32.2	8	119	2	59.50	1-4	-	-
1-day Int																		
NatWest																		
B & H																		
Sunday																		

Career Performances

	M	Inns	NO	Runs	HS	Avge	100s	50s	Ct	St	Balls	Runs	Wkts	Avge	Best	5wl	10wM
Test																	
All First	10	18	0	508	123	28.22	1	2	12	-	194	119	2	59.50	1-4	-	-
1-day Int																	
NatWest																	
B & H																	
Sunday																	

GRAYSON, A. P.   Essex

Name: Adrian Paul Grayson
Role: Right-hand bat, slow left-arm
bowler
Born: 31 March 1971, Ripon
Height: 6ft 1in **Weight:** 12st
Nickname: Larry
County debut: 1990 (Yorkshire),
1996 (Essex)
County cap: 1996 (Essex)
1000 runs in a season: 2
1st-Class 50s: 25
1st-Class 100s: 4
1st-Class catches: 84
Place in batting averages: 230th av. 16.41
(1997 57th av. 40.88)
Place in bowling averages: 125th av. 38.63
(1997 105th av. 36.03)
Strike rate: 78.42 (career 92.93)
Parents: Adrian and Carol
Wife and date of marriage: Alison, 30 September 1994
Children: Oliver, 30 January 1997
Family links with cricket: 'Father played good standard of league cricket and is an
excellent [NCA staff] coach; brother plays when free from football commitments'
Education: Bedale Comprehensive School
Qualifications: 8 CSEs, BTEC in Leisure Studies, Advanced cricket coach
Off-season: 'Working for Essex's sponsors, Ridley's Brewery, selling beer in the north
of England'
Overseas tours: England YC to Australia 1989-90; Yorkshire to Barbados 1989-90, to
Cape Town 1991-92, 1992-93, 1994-95, to Leeward Islands 1993-94
Overseas teams played for: Petone, Wellington 1992-93 and 1995-96
Cricketers particularly admired: Martyn Moxon, Graham Gooch, Darren Gough
Young players to look out for: Dean Cosker, Graeme Swann
Other sports played: Golf (16 handicap), football ('was offered apprentice forms with
Middlesbrough FC at 16 but signed for Yorkshire')
Other sports followed: 'Follow any team my brother Simon is playing for. At the
moment he plays for Aston Villa FC. Blood is thicker than water'
Relaxations: Golf, 'spending time with the family and having the odd pint in my local
pub "The King William"'
Extras: Played for England YC v New Zealand 1989 and Pakistan 1990. Brother plays
football for Aston Villa. Scored 1000 runs for first time in 1994. Yorkshire Player of
the Year 1994. Released by Yorkshire at end of 1995 but joined Essex for 1996 season.

Awarded county cap 1996. Essex Player of the Year 1997

Opinions on cricket: 'Better pitches provided for four-day cricket. Too many games finish on the second and third day. This will not produce top-class Test cricketers. For example, if home teams produce a green and damp pitch, the opposing captain should have the option of batting or fielding.'

Best batting: 140 Essex v Middlesex, Lord's 1996

Best bowling: 4-53 Essex v Northamptonshire, Northampton 1997

1998 Season

	M	Inns	NO	Runs	HS	Avge	100s	50s	Ct	St	O	M	Runs	Wkts	Avge	Best	5wI	10wM
Test																		
All First	17	31	0	509	59	16.41	-	4	9	-	248.2	62	734	19	38.63	3-13	-	-
1-day Int																		
NatWest	2	1	0	9	9	9.00	-	-	-	-								
B & H	7	6	2	103	25	25.75	-	-	1	-	45.3	2	192	9	21.33	3-32	-	
Sunday	14	9	1	138	59	17.25	-	1	2	-	90.4	1	476	13	36.61	4-28	-	

Career Performances

	M	Inns	NO	Runs	HS	Avge	100s	50s	Ct	St	Balls	Runs	Wkts	Avge	Best	5wI	10wM
Test																	
All First	105	169	16	4428	140	28.94	4	25	84	-	7249	3348	78	42.92	4-53	-	-
1-day Int																	
NatWest	19	15	1	310	82 *	22.14	-	2	7	-	809	629	20	31.45	3-24	-	
B & H	25	20	6	325	49 *	23.21	-	-	7	-	903	632	24	26.33	3-30	-	
Sunday	96	74	11	1016	69 *	16.12	-	3	27	-	2964	2700	82	32.92	4-25	-	

GREEN, R. J.   Lancashire

Name: Richard James Green

Role: Right-hand bat, right-arm medium-fast bowler

Born: 13 March 1976, Grappenhall, Warrington

Height: 6ft **Weight:** 12st 12lbs

Nickname: Slimey, Greendog, Spotty, Captain Darling

County debut: 1995

1st-Class 50s: 1

1st-Class 5 w. in innings: 1

1st-Class catches: 4

Strike rate: 157.50 (career 76.79)

Parents: Jim and Christina

Marital status: Single

Family links with cricket: 'Father Manchester Association League legend'

Education: Bridgewater County High School, Warrington; Hartford College

Qualifications: 5 GCSEs, BTEC National Business and Finance

Career outside cricket: 'One day will own a wine bar'

Overseas tours: Lancashire to Jamaica 1996, to Cape Town 1997

Overseas teams played for: Waratah-Mayfield CC, Newcastle, NSW 1994-95; Prahran CC, Melbourne, Australia 1996-97

Cricketers particularly admired: Warren Hegg

Young players to look out for: David Sales

Other sports followed: Football (Manchester United)

Relaxations: Music, fast Rover cars, the occasional night out

Extras: Cheshire County League's youngest century-maker. Played for England U17 and England U19. Denis Compton Award winner in 1996

Opinions on cricket: 'Staffs of 16 players and pay them more money. Should be a two-division league system and more day/night cricket.'

Best batting: 51 Lancashire v Essex, Old Trafford 1997

Best bowling: 6-41 Lancashire v Yorkshire, Old Trafford 1996

1998 Season

	M	Inns	NO	Runs	HS	Avge	100s	50s	Ct	St	O	M	Runs	Wkts	Avge	Best	5wl	10wM
Test																		
All First	6	3	1	14	14	7.00	-	-	1	-	126	28	424	4	106.00	1-32	-	-
1-day Int																		
NatWest	1	1	0	0	0	0.00	-	-	-	-	11	2	35	1	35.00	1-35	-	
B & H																		
Sunday	6	0	0	0	0	-	-	-	-	-	42	0	230	7	32.85	3-37	-	

Career Performances

	M	Inns	NO	Runs	HS	Avge	100s	50s	Ct	St	Balls	Runs	Wkts	Avge	Best	5wl	10wM
Test																	
All First	18	19	6	199	51	15.30	-	1	4	-	2611	1425	34	41.91	6-41	1	-
1-day Int																	
NatWest	1	1	0	0	0	0.00	-	-	-	-	66	35	1	35.00	1-35	-	
B & H	5	3	1	13	7	6.50	-	-	1	-	249	231	6	38.50	2-33	-	
Sunday	18	1	1	0	0 *	-	-	-	1	-	714	635	24	26.45	3-18	-	

GREENFIELD, K.   Sussex

Name: Keith Greenfield
Role: Right-hand bat, right-arm
off-spin bowler, emergency wicket-keeper
Born: 6 December 1968, Brighton
Height: 6ft **Weight:** 13st 2lbs
Nickname: Grubby, G-Man
County debut: 1987
1st-Class 50s: 13
1st-Class 100s: 9
1st-Class catches: 65
One-Day 100s: 2
Place in batting averages:
(1997 230th av. 17.71)
Strike rate: (career 162.80)
Parents: Leslie Ernest and Sheila
Wife and date of marriage:
Caroline Susannah, 22 February 1992
Family links with cricket: Father keen
spectator; father-in-law played club cricket
for 20 years and now umpires and spectates
Education: Coldean First and Middle Schools; Falmer High School
Qualifications: 3 O-levels, BTEC National Diploma in Leisure and Management,
junior, senior and advanced coaching certificates
Off-season: Coaching at Sussex CCC
Overseas tours: Sussex U16 to Guernsey 1985; Select XI to Malaga 1994, 1995;
MCC Tour to SE Asia and Far East 1994-95, to Bangladesh 1996; Sussex U19 to
Barbados 1997 (as coach)
Overseas teams played for: Cornwall Districts, Auckland 1988-90
Cricketers particularly admired: Ian Botham, Paul Parker, Derek Randall,
Mike Atherton
Young players to look out for: Grant Morrish, Matthew Prior, Dominic Clapp,
Michael Yardy, Krashma Singh
Other sports played: Golf
Other sports followed: Golf, football (Liverpool FC)
Injuries: Out for three weeks with a fractured foot
Relaxations: 'Going out with friends for a drink. Eating out, Chinese and Italian food;
concerts and listening to music. Doing up house'
Extras: First person taken on Youth Training Scheme to become a professional
cricketer at Sussex. Only uncapped player to have captained Sussex in first-class
match, at Hove (v Cambridge U); scored century in this game. Captained 2nd XI to
Championship title in 1990. Sussex Young Player of the Year 1990. Sussex Team Man

of the Year 1990, 1993. Joined Bill Athey on a trip to Belarus to take aid to the cancer hospital near Chernobyl. Sussex 2nd XI captain/coach 1998

Opinions on cricket: 'Day/night cricket should become a must for every county. Groundsmen should become employees of ECB, not each particular county, so the best possible pitch gets prepared, not one to suit own bowlers.'

Best batting: 154* Sussex v India, Hove 1996

Best bowling: 2-40 Sussex v Essex, Hove 1993

1998 Season

	M	Inns	NO	Runs	HS	Avge	100s	50s	Ct	St	O	M	Runs	Wkts	Avge	Best	5wl	10wM
Test																		
All First																		
1-day Int																		
NatWest																		
B & H	2	2	1	93	93*	93.00	-	1	-	-								
Sunday	5	5	0	101	48	20.20	-	-	-	-	5	0	24	1	24.00	1-24	-	

Career Performances

	M	Inns	NO	Runs	HS	Avge	100s	50s	Ct	St	Balls	Runs	Wkts	Avge	Best	5wl	10wM
Test																	
All First	78	135	15	3550	154*	29.58	9	13	65	-	814	524	5	104.80	2-40	-	-
1-day Int																	
NatWest	15	14	3	431	129	39.18	1	2	7	-	402	303	3	101.00	2-35	-	
B & H	25	24	3	611	93*	29.09	-	4	8	-	432	354	2	177.00	1-17	-	
Sunday	116	114	10	2735	102	26.29	1	16	34	-	994	978	22	44.45	3-34	-	

25. At which ground did Kapil Dev score his 175* for India v Zimbabwe on 18 June 1983?

FICA

GREENIDGE, C. G. Surrey

Name: Carl Gary Greenidge
Role: Right-hand bat, right-arm
fast-medium bowler
Born: 20 April 1978, Basingstoke
Height: 5ft 11in **Weight:** 12st 6lbs
County debut: 1998 (one-day)
Family links with cricket: Father Gordon
played for Hampshire and West Indies
Extras: Spent a year on Lord's groundstaff.
Made Surrey debut in Sunday League 1998

1998 Season

	M	Inns	NO	Runs	HS	Avge	100s	50s	Ct	St	O	M	Runs	Wkts	Avge	Best	5wI	10wM
Test																		
All First																		
1-day Int																		
NatWest																		
B & H																		
Sunday	1	0	0	0	0	-	-	-	-	-	7	0	35	0	-		-	-

Career Performances

	M	Inns	NO	Runs	HS	Avge	100s	50s	Ct	St	Balls	Runs	Wkts	Avge	Best	5wI	10wM
Test																	
All First																	
1-day Int																	
NatWest																	
B & H																	
Sunday	1	0	0	0	0	-	-	-	-	-	42	35	0	-		-	-

GRIFFITHS, S. P.   Derbyshire

Name: Steven Paul Griffiths
Role: Right-hand bat, wicket-keeper
Born: 31 May 1973, Hereford
Height: 5ft 11in **Weight:** 12st
Nickname: 'Too many to name'
County debut: 1995
1st-Class catches: 22
Parents: Paul Griffiths and Lesley Simmons
Marital status: 'Partner – Ceri Fenty'
Children: Joel Oliver Thomas Griffiths, 1
May 1998
Family links with cricket: 'Father has
played a good standard of club cricket
for many years'

Education: Bathford Junior School; Beechen
Cliff School, Bath; Brunel College of Art and
Design, Bristol
Qualifications: 7 GCSEs, City and Guilds in
Furniture Restoration, basic coaching award
Career outside cricket: Antique furniture restorer
Off-season: Working in London for a furniture restorer
Overseas tours: Bath Schools to Zimbabwe and Kenya 1989
Overseas teams played for: CBC Old Boys, Bloemfontein, South Africa 1992-93
Cricketers particularly admired: Jack Russell, Carl Hooper, Gregg Brown, Dougie
C. Storey
Young players to look out for: Ben Spendlove, Phil Smith
Other sports played: Rugby ('Not golf!!')
Other sports followed: Rugby (Bath RFC)
Relaxations: 'Spending time with Ceri and Joel. Socialising with friends in Bath.
Listening to music, reading, and discussing the imminent demise of Leek Town
Football Club with Tim Tweats'
Extras: Took six catches on first-class debut against Worcestershire in 1995 (five of
them in the first innings). Played for Somerset 2nd XI before joining Derbyshire.
Member of Bath CC and Buccaneers CC. Captain of Derbyshire CCC 2nd XI 1998.
Reached final of AON Risk Trophy
Opinions on cricket: '2nd XI cricket must be brought into line with the first-class
game. Four-day matches nearly always produce a result in second-class cricket, rather
than a manufactured conclusion. Better grounds and first-class and reserve umpires
would enhance the quality of matches, which can sometimes suffer due to indifferent
local umpires, poor grounds and bad practice facilities.'
Best batting: 20 Derbyshire v Surrey, Derby 1995

1998 Season

	M	Inns	NO	Runs	HS	Avge	100s	50s	Ct	St	O	M	Runs	Wkts	Avge	Best	5wl	10wM
Test																		
All First	1	2	0	15	12	7.50	-	-	5	-								
1-day Int																		
NatWest																		
B & H																		
Sunday																		

Career Performances

	M	Inns	NO	Runs	HS	Avge	100s	50s	Ct	St	Balls	Runs	Wkts	Avge	Best	5wl	10wM
Test																	
All First	7	12	0	91	20	7.58	-	-	22	-							
1-day Int																	
NatWest																	
B & H																	
Sunday	1	0	0	0	0	-	-	-	1	-							

GROVE, J. O. — Essex

Name: Jamie Oliver Grove
Role: Right-hand bat, right-arm
fast-medium bowler
Born: 3 July 1979, Bury St Edmunds
Height: 6ft 3in **Weight:** 12st 1lb
Nickname: Grover, Groover
County debut: 1998
Place in batting averages: 246th av. 14.66
Strike rate: 49.44 (career 49.44)
Parents: Chris John and Patricia Susan
Marital status: Single
Family links with cricket: Father played in
the local leagues for many years
Education: Whepstead Primary School; St
James Middle School, Bury St Edmunds;
County Upper School, Bury St Edmunds
Qualifications: 8 GCSEs, City and Guilds in
Basic Engineering
Career outside cricket: Mechanical engineer
Overseas tours: England U19 to South Africa 1997-98
Cricketers particularly admired: Dennis Lillee

Young players to look out for: Stephen Peters, Paul Franks
Other sports followed: Hockey and football (West Ham United)
Relaxations: Listening to music and going out with friends
Extras: Played for England at U15, U17 and U19 level. Was part of the successful England U19 World Cup-winning squad in South Africa in 1997-98
Opinions on cricket: 'The pitches favour the batsman too much.'
Best batting: 33 Essex v Surrey, Chelmsford 1998
Best bowling: 3-74 Essex v Surrey, Chelmsford 1998

1998 Season

	M	Inns	NO	Runs	HS	Avge	100s	50s	Ct	St	O	M	Runs	Wkts	Avge	Best	5wI	10wM
Test																		
All First	4	7	1	88	33	14.66	-	-	-	-	74.1	8	347	9	38.55	3-74	-	-
1-day Int																		
NatWest																		
B & H																		
Sunday																		

Career Performances

	M	Inns	NO	Runs	HS	Avge	100s	50s	Ct	St	Balls	Runs	Wkts	Avge	Best	5wI	10wM
Test																	
All First	4	7	1	88	33	14.66	-	-	-	-	445	347	9	38.55	3-74	-	-
1-day Int																	
NatWest																	
B & H																	
Sunday																	

GUY, S. Yorkshire

Name: Simon Mark Guy
Role: Right-hand bat, wicket-keeper
Born: 17 November 1978
Height: 5ft 6in **Weight:** 10st
Nickname: Shy Guy, Roland Rat
County debut: No first-team appearance
Parents: Darrell and Denise
Marital status: Single
Family links with cricket: 'Two brothers
and father play cricket. Elder brother played
Yorkshire Senior School U19 (when 17).
Father played for Notts and Worcs 2nd XI
and for Rotherham Town in Yorks League'
Education: Listerdale Junior; Wickersley
Comprehensive
Qualifications: Pass in GNVQ Leisure and
Recreation, qualified cricket coach, 'two
years at the Yorkshire Cricket School under
Ralph Middlebrook'

Off-season: Training, keeping fit, indoor cricket 'and looking for temp employment'
Cricketers particularly admired: Keith Piper, Karl Krikken, Richard Blakey
Young players to look out for: Richard Dawson, John Sadler
Other sports played: 'Interested in all sports', rugby (Rotherham RUFC, South
Yorkshire and Yorkshire)
Other sports followed: Rugby (Rotherham RUFC), football (Liverpool FC)
Relaxations: Playing all sports, socialising, having a good time, watching cartoons
Extras: Holds 5th wicket record in Yorkshire League (199 unbroken). Topped
Yorkshire 2nd XI batting averages 1998 (106.00). Scored first 50 for Yorkshire 2nd XI
in 1998. Followed up with 112 not out in next game
Opinions on cricket: 'The game would be more competitive if the County
Championship was divided into two divisions with promotion and relegation.'

HABIB, A. Leicestershire

Name: Aftab Habib
Role: Right-hand bat, right-arm slow-medium bowler
Born: 7 February 1972, Reading, Berks
Height: 5ft 11in **Weight:** 12st
Nickname: Afie, Tabby, Scabby, Habbiby, Alvin, Inzaman

County debut: 1992 (Middlesex),
1995 (Leicestershire)
County cap: 1998 (Leicestershire)
1st-Class 50s: 6
1st-Class 100s: 5
1st-Class 200s: 1
1st-Class catches: 26
One-Day 100s: 1
Place in batting averages: 9th av. 56.00
(1997 66th av. 39.70)
Parents: Hussain and Tahira
Marital status: Single
Family links with cricket: Cousin of Zahid
Sadiq (ex-Surrey and Derbyshire)
Education: Alfred Sutton Primary School;
Millfield Junior School; Taunton School
Qualifications: 7 GCSEs, NCA coaching
certificate
Overseas tours: England YC to Australia 1989-90, to New Zealand 1990-91;
Berkshire CCC to South Africa 1996
Overseas teams played for: Globe Wakatu, Nelson, New Zealand, 1992-93 and 1996-
97; Riccarton CC, Christchurch, New Zealand 1997-98
Cricketers particularly admired: Vince Wells, Mark Waugh, Steve Waugh, Saeed
Anwar, Paul Nixon, Darren Maddy, Graham Lloyd, Sachin Tendulkar, Phil Simmons
Young players to look out for: Darren Maddy, James Ormond, Chris Schofield
Other sports followed: Football ('follow Reading FC and enjoy watching Liverpool')
Relaxations: Music, cinema, reading, books, playing golf
Extras: 2nd XI Seaxe Player of the Year 1992. Released by Middlesex at end of 1994
season. Leicestershire 2nd XI Player of the Year in 1995. Championship medal with
Leicestershire in 1996 and 1998. Gold Award-winner in the Benson and Hedges Cup with
111 against Durham in 1997. Holds Leicestershire's fifth-wicket partnership record with
James Whitaker of 320 set against Worcestershire at Leicester in 1996. Awarded
Leicestershire cap 1998
Best batting: 215 Leicestershire v Worcestershire, Leicester 1996

1998 Season

	M	Inns	NO	Runs	HS	Avge	100s	50s	Ct	St	O	M	Runs	Wkts	Avge	Best	5wI	10wM
Test																		
All First	19	22	5	952	198	56.00	3	3	12	-	4	0	15	0	-	-	-	-
1-day Int																		
NatWest	4	3	0	124	67	41.33	-	2	-	-								
B & H	6	2	0	11	6	5.50	-	-	3	-								
Sunday	14	12	2	204	71	20.40	-	1	8	-								

Career Performances

	M	Inns	NO	Runs	HS	Avge	100s	50s	Ct	St	Balls	Runs	Wkts	Avge	Best	5wI	10wM
Test																	
All First	48	67	14	2390	215	45.09	6	6	26	-	48	52	0	-	-	-	-
1-day Int																	
NatWest	6	5	0	162	67	32.40	-	2	-	-							
B & H	12	8	1	260	111	37.14	1	1	6	-							
Sunday	32	28	8	542	99 *	27.10	-	3	13	-	1	4	0	-	-	-	

HAFEEZ, A. Worcestershire

Name: Abdul Hafeez
Role: Right-hand bat, right-arm medium bowler
Born: 21 March 1977, Birmingham
Height: 6ft 3in **Weight:** 14st 7lbs
Nickname: King, Yogi
County debut: 1998
1st-Class catches: 6
Place in batting averages: 214th av. 17.82
Parents: Abdul Ghafoor and Khushnooda Parveen
Marital status: Single
Family links with cricket: Younger brother plays for Warwickshire youth team (U12)
Education: Springfield Junior; Handsworth Grammar; Solihull College
Qualifications: GCSEs, A-levels, coaching award
Career outside cricket: Student
Off-season: Studying Law course
Overseas tours: Birmingham Schools to India and Pakistan 1996
Overseas teams played for: Primrose CC, Cape Town 1996-97
Cricketers particularly admired: Graeme Hick, Alec Stewart, Sachin Tendulkar, Wasim Akram, Jacques Kallis
Young players to look out for: Maneer Mirza, Depesh Patel, Duncan Catterall
Other sports played: Football, table tennis
Other sports followed: Rugby
Relaxations: Spending time with friends, travelling
Extras: Part of Warwickshire side that won Oxbridge U19 Festival 1996. Coney Edmunds U19 Player of the Year award 1996 (Warwickshire)
Opinions on cricket: 'Second-team cricket to be four days and also all 2nd XI

Championship matches to be played on first-class grounds. Increase the number of day/night games.'

Best batting: 55 Worcestershire v Gloucestershire, Worcester 1998

1998 Season

	M	Inns	NO	Runs	HS	Avge	100s	50s	Ct	St	O	M	Runs	Wkts	Avge	Best	5wI	10wM
Test																		
All First	10	18	1	303	55	17.82	-	1	6	-								
1-day Int																		
NatWest	1	1	0	33	33	33.00	-	-	-	-								
B & H																			
Sunday	6	3	0	9	7	3.00	-	-	2	-								

Career Performances

	M	Inns	NO	Runs	HS	Avge	100s	50s	Ct	St	Balls	Runs	Wkts	Avge	Best	5wI	10wM
Test																	
All First	10	18	1	303	55	17.82	-	1	6	-							
1-day Int																	
NatWest	1	1	0	33	33	33.00	-	-	-	-							
B & H																		
Sunday	6	3	0	9	7	3.00	-	-	2	-							

HAMBLIN, J. R. C. Hampshire

Name: James Rupert Christopher Hamblin
Role: Right-hand bat, right-arm medium bowler
Born: 16 August 1978, Pembury, Kent
Height: 6ft **Weight:** 13st 7lbs
Nickname: Hambo, Jazzer Junior, Hambles
County debut: No first-team appearance
Parents: Bryan and Amanda
Marital status: Single
Family links with cricket: Father played for Oxford University 1971-73 and Sussex 2nd XI. Brothers are both keen cricketers
Education: Vinehall Preparatory School; Charterhouse School; Bristol University of West of England
Qualifications: 9 GCSEs, 2 A/O-levels, 2 A-levels
Career outside cricket: Student

Off-season: University
Overseas teams played for: Harare Sports Club, Zimbabwe 1996-97
Cricketers particularly admired: James Kirtley, James Williams
Young players to look out for: James Pyemont
Other sports played: Rackets, real tennis, golf
Other sports followed: 'Follow most sports'
Relaxations: 'Watching'
Opinions on cricket: 'I haven't been in the game long enough.'

HAMILTON, G. M. Yorkshire

Name: Gavin Mark Hamilton
Role: Right-hand bat, right-arm fast-medium bowler
Born: 16 September 1974, Broxburn
Height: 6ft 1in **Weight:** 12st 7lbs
Nickname: Hammy, Scotty, 'anything Scottish'
County debut: 1994
County cap: 1998
50 wickets in a season: 1
1st-Class 50s: 7
1st-Class 5 w. in innings: 6
1st-Class 10 w. in match: 2
1st-Class catches: 13
One-Day 5 w. in innings: 1
Place in batting averages: 80th av. 32.11 (1997 235th av. 17.14)
Place in bowling averages: 19th av. 20.54 (1997 91st av. 33.59)
Strike rate: 42.20 (career 51.34)
Parents: Gavin and Wendy
Marital status: Single
Family links with cricket: 'Brother opening bat for Scotland. Father long-term club cricketer with Sidcup (Kent) and West Lothian (Scotland). Mother long-term tea-maker'
Education: Dulverton Primary School, New Eltham; Hurstmere School, Sidcup
Qualifications: 10 GCSEs and 'numerous coaching awards'
Off-season: Playing club cricket in Melbourne
Overseas tours: 'Yorkshire pre-season for four years'
Overseas teams played for: Wellington, Boland; Municipals, Free State; Stellenbosch University, Boland; Spotswood, Melbourne
Cricketers particularly admired: Craig White, Dougie Brown, Mark Robinson
Young players to look out for: Andrew Flintoff, Matthew Wood

Other sports played: Golf, football (Arsenal YTS)
Other sports followed: Football (Falkirk FC)
Injuries: Out for two weeks with sore shins
Relaxations: 'Playing a full day of golf with mates'
Extras: Took 10 wickets and scored 149 runs v Glamorgan at Cardiff in 1998, the second best all-round contribution in Yorkshire history. Has represented Scotland. Was selected to represent England in the cancelled World Super Max 8s originally scheduled to take place in Perth in October 1998. Awarded county cap 1998
Opinions on cricket: 'Over-rates far too high. You end up rushing and not concentrating on the job in hand.'
Best batting: 79 Yorkshire v Glamorgan, Cardiff 1998
Best bowling: 7-50 Yorkshire v Surrey, Headingley 1998

1998 Season

	M	Inns	NO	Runs	HS	Avge	100s	50s	Ct	St	O	M	Runs	Wkts	Avge	Best	5wl	10wM
Test																		
All First	15	19	1	578	79	32.11	-	6	3	-	415	100	1212	59	20.54	7-50	4	2
1-day Int																		
NatWest	2	1	0	39	39	39.00	-	-	1	-	14	2	41	3	13.66	3-27	-	
B & H	6	3	2	37	20	37.00	-	-	1	-	47	5	188	10	18.80	4-33	-	
Sunday	16	9	2	129	34 *	18.42	-	-	5	-	96.2	6	415	21	19.76	5-16	1	

Career Performances

	M	Inns	NO	Runs	HS	Avge	100s	50s	Ct	St	Balls	Runs	Wkts	Avge	Best	5wl	10wM
Test																	
All First	40	51	8	1054	79	24.51	-	7	13	-	6059	3245	118	27.50	7-50	6	2
1-day Int																	
NatWest	4	2	0	41	39	20.50	-	-	2	-	204	127	7	18.14	3-27	-	
B & H	8	4	3	45	20	45.00	-	-	1	-	360	230	10	23.00	4-33	-	
Sunday	38	21	7	203	34 *	14.50	-	-	7	-	1353	1187	46	25.80	5-16	1	

HANCOCK, T. H. C. Gloucestershire

Name: Timothy Harold Coulter Hancock
Role: Right-hand bat, right-arm medium
bowler, short-leg or cover fielder
Born: 20 April 1972, Reading
Height: 5ft 11in **Weight:** 12st 7lbs
Nickname: Herbie
County debut: 1991
County cap: 1998
1000 runs in a season: 1
1st-Class 50s: 31
1st-Class 100s: 5
1st-Class 200s: 1
1st-Class catches: 74
One-Day 5 w. in innings: 1
Place in batting averages: 51st av. 38.34
(1997 120th av. 30.50)
Place in bowling averages: 5th av. 16.46
Strike rate: 31.38 (career 51.34)
Parents: John and Jennifer

Wife: Rachael
Family links with cricket: 'Dad and brother play'
Education: St Piran's, Maidenhead; St Edward's, Oxford; Henley College
Qualifications: 8 GCSEs, senior coaching award
Off-season: 'Doing a Sports Science degree'
Overseas tours: Gloucestershire to Kenya 1991, to Sri Lanka 1992-93, to Zimbabwe
(two visits)
Overseas teams played for: CBC Old Boys, Bloemfontein 1991-92; Wynnum
Manley, Brisbane 1992-93; Durban Harlequins 1994-95
Cricketers particularly admired: 'Any successful Test player'
Young players to look out for: 'None really stand out, but Ben Hollioake is the best
of the current crop'
Other sports played: Hockey, golf
Other sports followed: 'Love watching rugby union and enjoy watching Bristol'
Relaxations: 'I like golf and generally winding down'
Extras: Played hockey for Oxfordshire U19. Awarded county cap 1998
Best batting: 220* Gloucestershire v Glamorgan, Cardiff 1998
Best bowling: 3-5 Gloucestershire v Essex, Colchester 1998

1998 Season

	M	Inns	NO	Runs	HS	Avge	100s	50s	Ct	St	O	M	Runs	Wkts	Avge	Best	5wI	10wM
Test																		
All First	18	34	2	1227	220 *	38.34	2	7	16	-	68	16	214	13	16.46	3-5	-	-
1-day Int																		
NatWest	2	2	0	70	60	35.00	-	1	1	-	10	0	47	3	15.66	3-30	-	
B & H	5	5	0	103	56	20.60	-	1	1	-	17	0	93	4	23.25	2-23	-	
Sunday	15	12	1	254	73	23.09	-	2	3	-	35	0	221	9	24.55	3-18	-	

Career Performances

	M	Inns	NO	Runs	HS	Avge	100s	50s	Ct	St	Balls	Runs	Wkts	Avge	Best	5wI	10wM
Test																	
All First	112	199	15	5242	220 *	28.48	6	31	74	-	1893	1159	31	37.38	3-5	-	-
1-day Int																	
NatWest	8	7	0	158	60	22.57	-	1	4	-	173	144	11	13.09	6-58	1	
B & H	26	23	3	460	71 *	23.00	-	2	3	-	319	243	10	24.30	3-13	-	
Sunday	83	74	2	1238	73	17.19	-	4	32	-	585	564	18	31.33	3-18	-	

HARDEN, R. J. Yorkshire

Name: Richard John Harden
Role: Right-hand bat, left-arm
medium bowler
Born: 16 August 1965, Bridgwater
Height: 5ft 11in **Weight:** 13st 7lbs
Nickname: Sumo, Curtis
County debut: 1985 (Somerset)
County cap: 1989 (Somerset)
1000 runs in a season: 6
1st-Class 50s: 67
1st-Class 100s: 28
1st-Class catches: 187
One-Day 100s: 4
Place in batting averages: 234th av. 15.84
(1997 42nd av. 43.88)
Strike rate: (career 73.90)
Parents: Chris and Anne
Wife and date of marriage:
Nicki Rae, 25 September 1992
Family links with cricket: Grandfather played club cricket for Bridgwater
Education: King's College, Taunton
Qualifications: 8 O-levels, 2 A-levels, coaching award

Overseas teams played for: Central Districts, New Zealand 1987-88
Cricketers particularly admired: Viv Richards, Jimmy Cook
Other sports followed: Squash, golf, rugby
Relaxations: 'Love my domestic duties (dusting, Hoovering, etc.) rather than golf. Good food and the odd drink.'
Extras: Has joined Yorkshire for the 1999 season on a two-year contract after 13 years with Somerset
Best batting: 187 Somerset v Nottinghamshire, Taunton 1992
Best bowling: 2-7 Central Districts v Canterbury, Blenheim 1987-88

1998 Season

	M	Inns	NO	Runs	HS	Avge	100s	50s	Ct	St	O	M	Runs	Wkts	Avge	Best	5wl	10wM
Test																		
All First	12	21	2	301	63	15.84	-	2	15	-	4	1	12	0	-		-	-
1-day Int																		
NatWest	2	1	0	61	61	61.00	-	1	2	-								
B & H	4	4	0	47	39	11.75	-	-	1	-								
Sunday	8	8	2	122	52	20.33	-	1	-	-								

Career Performances

	M	Inns	NO	Runs	HS	Avge	100s	50s	Ct	St	Balls	Runs	Wkts	Avge	Best	5wl	10wM
Test																	
All First	241	395	60	12897	187	38.49	28	67	187	-	1478	1023	20	51.15	2-7	-	-
1-day Int																	
NatWest	23	20	2	794	108 *	44.11	3	3	14	-	18	23	0	-		-	-
B & H	56	54	4	1083	76	21.66	-	6	15	-							
Sunday	168	162	30	4252	100 *	32.21	1	27	51	-	1	0	0	-		-	-

HARMISON, S. J.   Durham

Name: Stephen James Harmison
Role: Right-hand bat, right-arm fast-medium bowler
Born: 23 October 1978, Ashington, Northumberland
Height: 6ft 3in **Weight:** 12st
County debut: 1996
50 wickets in a season: 1
1st-Class 5 w. in innings: 1
1st-Class catches: 2
Place in batting averages: 261st av. 12.38
Place in bowling averages: 88th av. 30.29
Strike rate: 53.62 (career 54.68)
Marital status: Single

Family links with cricket: Father and younger brother play for Ashington
Education: Bedlington School
Off-season: Touring Zimbabwe and South Africa with England A
Overseas tours: England U19 to Pakistan 1996-97; England A to Zimbabwe and South Africa 1998-99
Other sports followed: Football (Newcastle United)
Relaxations: Snooker
Extras: Represented Northumberland U17. Described as 'seriously fast' by Justin Langer. Played football for Ashington in the Northern League
Best batting: 36 Durham v Worcestershire, Worcester 1998
Best bowling: 5-70 Durham v Gloucestershire, Riverside 1998

1998 Season

	M	Inns	NO	Runs	HS	Avge	100s	50s	Ct	St	O	M	Runs	Wkts	Avge	Best	5wI	10wM
Test																		
All First	14	22	4	223	36	12.38	-	-	2	-	455.5	93	1545	51	30.29	5-70	1-	
1-day Int																		
NatWest																		
B & H	1	0	0	0	0	-	-	-	-	-	6	0	36	0	-		-	-
Sunday	3	1	1	1	1 *	-	-	-	1	-	20	2	104	0	-		-	-

Career Performances

	M	Inns	NO	Runs	HS	Avge	100s	50s	Ct	St	Balls	Runs	Wkts	Avge	Best	5wI	10wM
Test																	
All First	15	24	4	233	36	11.65	-	-	2	-	2789	1622	51	31.80	5-70	1	-
1-day Int																	
NatWest																	
B & H	1	0	0	0	0	-	-	-	-	-	36	36	0	-		-	-
Sunday	3	1	1	1	1 *	-	-	-	1	-	120	104	0	-		-	-

HARRIS, A. J. Derbyshire

Name: Andrew James Harris
Role: Right-hand bat, right-arm fast bowler
Born: 26 June 1973, Ashton-under-Lyne
Height: 6ft **Weight:** 11st 7lbs
Nickname: AJ
County debut: 1994
County cap: 1996
1st-Class 5 w. in innings: 2
1st-Class 10 w. in match: 1
1st-Class catches: 12
Place in batting averages:
(1997 291st av. 8.55)
Place in bowling averages:
(1997 132nd av. 48.50)
Strike rate: 48.00 (career 55.43)
Parents: Norman and Joyce
Marital status: Single
Education: Tintwistle Primary School;
Hadfield Comprehensive School;
Glossopdale Community College
Qualifications: 6 GCSEs, 1 A-level
Off-season: 'At home. A season on the sidelines due to a stress fracture of the lower back means a winter of intense training in the hope of an injury free '99'
Overseas tours: England A to Australia 1996-97
Overseas teams played for: Ginninderra, West Belconnen, Australia 1992-93; Victoria University of Wellington CC, New Zealand 1997-98
Cricketers particularly admired: Kim Barnett, Merv Hughes 'for his effort and determination'
Young players to look out for: Matthew Wood
Other sports followed: 'Soccer, as my brother plays for Altrincham, but I support the True Blues, Manchester City, and every sport I will view with great determination'
Injuries: Stress fracture of lower back and broken thumb. 'My season ended on 15 May, but a stronger and fitter AJ will be back in 1999'
Relaxations: 'Playing any sport, golf in particular. As relaxing goes, watching television, playing on my Sega, and how could I forget having quite a few beers, although I have never been to the Pink Coconut'
Opinions on cricket: 'Looking forward to the new one-day structure in 1999.'
Best batting: 36 Derbyshire v Worcestershire, Worcester 1997
Best bowling: 6-40 Derbyshire v Middlesex, Derby 1996

246

1998 Season

	M	Inns	NO	Runs	HS	Avge	100s	50s	Ct	St	O	M	Runs	Wkts	Avge	Best	5wI	10wM
Test																		
All First	2	3	0	9	5	3.00	-	-	-	-	32	3	136	4	34.00	2-53	-	-
1-day Int																		
NatWest																		
B & H	3	0	0	0	0	-	-	-	-	3	-	25.4	2	113	6	18.83	2-22	-
Sunday	3	0	0	0	0	-	-	-	-	-	22	1	100	5	20.00	3-36	-

Career Performances

	M	Inns	NO	Runs	HS	Avge	100s	50s	Ct	St	Balls	Runs	Wkts	Avge	Best	5wI	10wM
Test																		
All First	39	54	11	344	36	8.00	-	-	12	-	6153	3783	111	34.08	6-40	2	1
1-day Int																		
NatWest	4	2	2	16	11 *	-	-	-	1	-	234	156	6	26.00	3-58	-	
B & H	10	3	1	11	5	5.50	-	-	4	-	549	435	16	27.18	3-41	-	
Sunday	38	12	6	31	10 *	5.16	-	-	9	-	1530	1307	56	23.33	4-22	-	

HART, J. P. Nottinghamshire

Name: Jamie Paul Hart
Role: Right-hand bat, right-arm
medium bowler
Born: 31 December 1975, Blackpool
Height: 6ft 2in **Weight:** 13st 8lbs
Nickname: Harty
County debut: 1995 (one-day),
1996 (first-class)
Parents: Paul and Vicky
Marital status: Single
Education: Grosvenor School, Nottingham;
Millfield School
Qualifications: 8 GCSEs and 1 A-level
Career outside cricket: Sales
Overseas tours: Millfield School
to Sri Lanka 1993
Cricketers particularly admired: Ian
Botham, Dermot Reeve
Other sports followed: Football (Leeds Utd)
Relaxations: Listening to music and reading
Extras: Father played professional football and is now at Leeds United on the
coaching staff

Opinions on cricket: 'The different standards of second-class pitches compared with first-class pitches and grounds often make the step-up harder – i.e. more often than not one can get more out of a 2nd XI pitch than a first-class one (as a bowler).'
Best batting: 18* Nottinghamshire v Yorkshire, Scarborough 1996

1998 Season (did not make any first-class or one-day appearances)

Career Performances

	M	Inns	NO	Runs	HS	Avge	100s	50s	Ct	St	Balls	Runs	Wkts	Avge	Best	5wl	10wM
Test																	
All First	1	2	2	18	18*	-	-	-	-	-	108	51	0	-	-	-	-
1-day Int																	
NatWest																	
B & H																	
Sunday	2	0	0	0	0	-	-	-	-	-	72	87	1	87.00	1-48	-	

HARTLEY, P. J. Hampshire

Name: Peter John Hartley
Role: Right-hand bat, right-arm medium-fast bowler
Born: 18 April 1960, Keighley
Height: 6ft **Weight:** 14st 1lb
Nickname: Jack, PJ
County debut: 1982 (Warwickshire), 1985 (Yorkshire), 1998 (Hampshire)
County cap: 1987 (Yorkshire), 1998 (Hampshire)
Benefit: 1996 (Yorkshire)
50 wickets in a season: 6
1st-Class 50s: 13
1st-Class 100s: 2
1st-Class 5 w. in innings: 21
1st-Class 10 w. in match: 2
1st-Class catches: 65
One-Day 5 w. in innings: 4
Place in batting averages: 262nd av. 12.30 (1997 275th av. 12.10)
Place in bowling averages: 110th av. 33.60 (1997 21st av. 23.13)
Strike rate: 64.33 (career 54.59)
Parents: Thomas and Molly
Wife and date of marriage: Sharon Louise, 12 March 1988

Children: Megan Grace, 25 April 1992; Courtney, 25 July 1995
Family links with cricket: Father played local league cricket
Education: Haworth; Hartington Middle/Greenhead Grammar School; Bradford College
Qualifications: City & Guilds in textile design and management, NCA coaching award
Career outside cricket: Sales rep
Off-season: 'Above job. Playing golf. Spending time with the family'
Overseas tours: Yorkshire pre-season tours to Barbados 1986-87, to South Africa 1991-92, 1992-93
Overseas teams played for: Melville, New Zealand 1983-84; Adelaide, Australia 1985-86; Harmony and Orange Free State, South Africa 1988-89
Cricketers particularly admired: Malcolm Marshall, Richard Hadlee, Ian Botham
Young players to look out for: Lee Westwood, Darren Clarke
Other sports played: Golf (4 handicap)
Other sports followed: Football (Chelsea FC)
Injuries: Out for one match with torn groin, two matches with torn shoulder, one match with torn cartilage
Relaxations: Golf, gardening, walking
Extras: Awarded Hampshire cap 1998
Best batting: 127* Yorkshire v Lancashire, Old Trafford 1988
Best bowling: 9-41 Yorkshire v Derbyshire, Chesterfield 1995

1998 Season

	M	Inns	NO	Runs	HS	Avge	100s	50s	Ct	St	O	M	Runs	Wkts	Avge	Best	5wI	10wM
Test																		
All First	13	16	3	160	29	12.30	-	-	3	-	353.5	66	1109	33	33.60	4-42	-	-
1-day Int																		
NatWest	3	1	0	0	0	0.00	-	-	-	-	25.4	1	86	5	17.20	2-18	-	
B & H	5	4	0	35	20	8.75	-	-	-	-	47	8	171	7	24.42	3-32	-	
Sunday	14	9	5	49	18 *	12.25	-	-	2	-	93.1	4	389	18	21.61	3-24	-	

Career Performances

	M	Inns	NO	Runs	HS	Avge	100s	50s	Ct	St	Balls	Runs	Wkts	Avge	Best	5wI	10wM
Test																	
All First	211	257	55	4035	127 *	19.97	2	13	65	-	33524	18762	614	30.55	9-41	21	2
1-day Int																	
NatWest	31	18	8	250	83	25.00	-	2	2	-	1869	1194	50	23.88	5-46	1	
B & H	48	30	10	230	29 *	11.50	-	-	12	-	2625	1710	68	25.14	5-43	1	
Sunday	160	111	36	1213	52	16.17	-	2	28	-	6760	5186	192	27.01	5-36	2	

HARVEY, I. J.   Gloucestershire

Name: Ian Joseph Harvey
Role: Right-hand bat, right-arm fast-medium bowler
Born: 10 April 1972, Wonthaggi, Victoria
Nickname: Freak
County debut: No first-team appearance
One-Day Internationals: 11
1st-Class 50s: 10
1st-Class 100s: 2
1st-Class 5w. in innings: 3
1st-Class catches: 27
Overseas tours: Australian Academy to New Zealand 1994-95; Australia to Sharjah 1997-98
Overseas teams played for: Dandenong, Victoria; Victoria
Extras: Took a wicket (Jonty Rhodes) with his second ball in One-Day International cricket. Has joined Gloucestershire for 1999 as overseas player

Best batting: 136 Victoria v South Australia, Melbourne 1995-96
Best bowling: 7-44 Victoria v South Australia, Melbourne 1996-97

1998 Season (did not make any first-class or one-day appearances)

Career Performances

	M	Inns	NO	Runs	HS	Avge	100s	50s	Ct	St	Balls	Runs	Wkts	Avge	Best	5wI	10wM
Test																	
All First	34	61	3	1469	136	25.32	2	10	27	-	-	2612	73	35.78	7-44	3	-
1-day Int	11	9	2	101	43	14.42	-	-	6	-		325	7	46.42	3-17	-	-
NatWest																	
B & H																	
Sunday																	

HARVEY, M. E.   Lancashire

Name: Mark Edward Harvey
Role: Right-hand bat, off-spin bowler
Born: 26 June 1974, Burnley, Lancs
Height: 5ft 9in **Weight:** 12st 8lbs

Nickname: Harv, Vadge, Baz, Getiton
County debut: 1994
1st-Class catches: 2
Parents: David and Wendy
Marital status: Single
Family links with cricket: Brother Jonathan
spent four years as MCC young player and
was professional for Greenmount CC in the
Bolton League; is now professional for Earby
CC in the Ribblesdale League. 'Father,
David, is still playing local club cricket'
Education: Worsthorne County Primary;
Habergham High School, Burnley;
Loughborough University
Qualifications: 8 GCSEs, 3 A-levels,
BSc (Hons) PE Sports Management and
Recreational Management
Career outside cricket: 'None yet!'

Off-season: 'Relaxing until December, when we will be back in training at Old
Trafford as part of the new 12-month contracts at Lancashire'
Overseas tours: England U19 to India 1992-93
Overseas teams played for: Queanbeyan CC, Canberra, Australia 1996-97
Cricketers particularly admired: 'David Gower (someone who makes it all look so
easy), Dean Jones (exciting both batting and fielding), Mudassar Nazar (an admired
professional for many years at Burnley), Les "The Whirlwind" Seal'
Young players to look out for: Chris Schofield
Other sports played: Football ('Burnley Town team!'), golf, squash 'and almost anything'
Other sports followed: Football (Manchester United, Burnley and Oxford United)
Injuries: Out for two weeks with strained groin; for two weeks with badly bruised elbow
Relaxations: 'I'd love to say that watching Burnley FC was a relaxation, but
unfortunately it's very frustrating; drinking at the Crooked Billet, Workthorne, with
father and brother'
Extras: Captained England U17, represented England at U17, U18 and U19 levels,
represented Lancashire from U13 to U19. In an attempt to produce a result in a rain-
affected 2nd XI match v Yorkshire at Todmorden, he bowled an over costing 108 runs
from 18 no-balls, all of which went for four without hitting the bat. 'This allowed both
teams to contrive a game in five rather than 50 minutes. A claim to fame which earns me
never-ending stick at the local pub!' Played for Combined Universities in 1995 and 1996
Opinions on cricket: 'The increasing introduction of top-class, ex-Test playing
coaches, and the like, whether foreign or British, can only be a good thing, allowing
young players such as myself to benefit from their vast knowledge and experience.
Different methods and approaches can only serve to widen our horizons of the game.
The introduction of the 12-month contract at Lancs was welcomed by many players
and certainly has many benefits which are vital to the "modern-day" cricketer.'
Best batting: 25 Lancashire v Gloucestershire, Bristol 1997

1998 Season

	M	Inns	NO	Runs	HS	Avge	100s	50s	Ct	St	O	M	Runs	Wkts	Avge	Best	5wI	10wM
Test																		
All First	1	2	1	0	0*	0.00	-	-	-	-	5	0	48	0	-		-	-
1-day Int																		
NatWest																		
B & H																		
Sunday	1	1	0	39	39	39.00	-	-	-	-								

Career Performances

	M	Inns	NO	Runs	HS	Avge	100s	50s	Ct	St	Balls	Runs	Wkts	Avge	Best	5wl	10wM
Test																	
All First	6	10	1	116	25	12.88	-	-	2	-	30	48	0	-		-	-
1-day Int																	
NatWest	1	1	0	86	86	86.00	-	1	1	-							
B & H	4	4	0	9	5	2.25	-	-	3	-							
Sunday	3	2	0	47	39	23.50	-	-	-	-							

HAYDEN, M. L. — Northamptonshire

Name: Matthew Lawrence Hayden
Role: Left-hand bat, right-arm medium bowler, county captain
Born: 29 October 1971, Kingaroy, Australia
County debut: 1997 (Hampshire)
Test debut: 1993-94
Tests: 7
One-Day Internationals: 13
1000 runs in a season: 1
1st-Class 50s: 45
1st-Class 100s: 29
1st-Class 200s: 4
1st-Class catches: 107
One-Day 100s: 3
Place in batting averages:
(1997 14th av. 53.55)
Strike rate: (career 92.75)

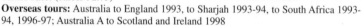

Overseas tours: Australia to England 1993, to Sharjah 1993-94, to South Africa 1993-94, 1996-97; Australia A to Scotland and Ireland 1998
Overseas teams played for: Queensland 1991 –
Extras: Scored 149 on his first-class debut for Queensland against South Australia and went on to become the youngest Australian to score 1000 runs in his first season.
Played in his first Test match in South Africa in 1994 after a sequence of impressive

run-scoring in the Sheffield Shield forced his inclusion in the tour squad, but has failed to hold down a regular place in the Test side. Was given another chance after opener Matthew Elliott was injured and played in the Test series against West Indies in 1996-97 and solid performances warranted his inclusion in the squad to tour South Africa. Has played league cricket for Greenmount in the Bolton League, breaking the club record with an aggregate of 1483 runs. Hampshire's overseas player 1997, scoring 1438 runs av. 57.52. Has joined Northants for 1999 on a two-year contract as overseas player. Appointed county captain for 1999

Best batting: 235* Hampshire v Warwickshire, Southampton 1997
Best bowling: 2-17 Hampshire v Sussex, Southampton 1997

1998 Season (did not make any first-class or one-day appearances)

Career Performances

	M	Inns	NO	Runs	HS	Avge	100s	50s	Ct	St	Balls	Runs	Wkts	Avge	Best	5wl	10wM
Test	7	12	0	261	125	21.75	1	-	8	-							
All First	122	216	23	10455	235 *	54.17	33	45	107	-	371	282	4	70.50	2-17	-	-
1-day Int	13	12	1	286	67	26.00	-	2	4	-							
NatWest	2	2	0	110	90	55.00	-	1	1	-							
B & H	5	5	1	216	120 *	54.00	1	-	3	-	54	45	2	22.50	2-45	-	
Sunday	16	15	0	654	118	43.60	2	3	7	-	81	78	2	39.00	2-38	-	

HAYNES, G. R. Worcestershire

Name: Gavin Richard Haynes
Role: Right-hand bat, right-arm medium bowler
Born: 29 September 1969, Stourbridge
Height: 5ft 10in **Weight:** 12st
Nickname: Splash
County debut: 1991
County cap: 1994
1000 runs in a season: 1
1st-Class 50s: 23
1st-Class 100s: 3
1st-Class 5 w. in innings: 2
1st-Class catches: 39
One-Day 100s: 1
Place in batting averages: 72nd av. 33.25 (1997 85th av. 36.09)
Place in bowling averages: 63rd av. 27.11 (1997 57th av. 28.22)
Strike rate: 52.57 (career 69.62)

Parents: Nicholas and Dorothy

Wife and date of marriage: Joanne, 25 October 1997

Family links with cricket: Father played club cricket and manages Worcester U14 side. Cousin Peter Haynes played very good club cricket

Education: Gigmill Junior School; High Park Comprehensive; King Edward VI College, Stourbridge

Qualifications: 5 O-levels, 1 A-level, NCA advanced coaching award

Overseas tours: Worcestershire to Zimbabwe, to South Africa, to Barbados 1996, to Guernsey 1997

Overseas teams played for: Sunrise Sports Club, Zimbabwe 1989-90

Cricketers particularly admired: Ian Botham, Graham Dilley, Graham Gooch, Malcolm Marshall, Viv Richards, Graeme Hick

Young players to look out for: 'The good ones'

Other sports followed: Football (Aston Villa), golf

Injuries: Out for two months with knee injury

Relaxations: Playing golf, watching television

Extras: Represented England Schools U15. Worcestershire Uncapped Player of the Year 1993. 'In 1998 I managed three games on the trot without taking a Brufen'

Opinions on cricket: 'We should play more cricket, one division playing each other home and away in the Championship, so 34 four-day games. Continue with the two league one-day idea, playing every team in your league twice, plus the other teams in the other league once, so 25 one-day games, plus NatWest. Cut staffs to 14 players, and the ones who are released could become physios and orthopaedic surgeons as there will be plenty of need for them.'

Best batting: 158 Worcestershire v Kent, Worcester 1993

Best bowling: 6-50 Worcestershire v Hampshire, Worcester 1998

1998 Season

	M	Inns	NO	Runs	HS	Avge	100s	50s	Ct	St	O	M	Runs	Wkts	Avge	Best	5wl	10wM
Test																		
All First	12	21	5	532	86	33.25	-	4	2	-	227.5	61	705	26	27.11	6-50	2	-
1-day Int																		
NatWest	1	1	0	74	74	74.00	-	1	-	-	8	2	10	0	-		-	-
B & H	4	4	0	69	35	17.25	-	-	2	-	16	1	63	3	21.00	2-20	-	
Sunday	10	8	1	153	39	21.85	-	-	1	-	44	4	199	4	49.75	1-12	-	

Career Performances

	M	Inns	NO	Runs	HS	Avge	100s	50s	Ct	St	Balls	Runs	Wkts	Avge	Best	5wl	10wM
Test																	
All First	92	143	14	3996	158	30.97	3	23	39	-	6475	3263	93	35.08	6-50	2	-
1-day Int																	
NatWest	10	8	1	383	116*	54.71	1	2	3	-	366	214	5	42.80	1-9	-	
B & H	21	19	3	372	65	23.25	-	1	6	-	815	486	18	27.00	3-17	-	
Sunday	73	60	7	1294	83	24.41	-	3	18	-	2074	1445	49	29.48	4-13	-	

HAYNES, J. J. Lancashire

Name: Jamie Jonathan Haynes
Role: Right-hand bat, wicket-keeper
Born: 5 July 1974, Bristol
Height: 5ft 10in **Weight:** 12st 5lbs
Nickname: Haynesy, JJ, Lead Balloon
County debut: 1996
1st-Class catches: 12
1st-Class stumpings: 1
Parents: Steve Haynes and Moiya Ford
Marital status: Single
Family links with cricket: Father and uncle
both played for Gloucestershire CCC
Education: Garran Primary; St Edmunds
College, Canberra; University of Canberra
Qualifications: Year 12 Certificate,
BA Sports Media, coaching certificate
Career outside cricket: Working for
Manchester Evening News
Off-season: Training with Lancashire as part of 12-month contract
Overseas teams played for: Tuggeranong Valley CC, Australia 1995-96; South
Canberra CC, Australia 1996-97
Cricketers particularly admired: Warren Hegg, Mike Atherton, Ian Austin, Peter Sleep
Young players to look out for: Chris Schofield
Other sports played: Australian Rules Football (Queanbeyan Tigers Football Club)
Other sports followed: Football (Manchester United, Burnley)
Injuries: Out for two weeks with dislocated thumb
Relaxations: Golf, movies, 'eating good food with my girlfriend, Ainsley, in restaurants'
Opinions on cricket: 'The introduction of year-long contracts helps young cricketers
to develop a life outside cricket, which is proving to be extremely beneficial.'
Best batting: 21 Lancashire v Yorkshire, Headingley 1997

1998 Season (did not make any first-class or one-day appearances)

Career Performances

	M	Inns	NO	Runs	HS	Avge	100s	50s	Ct	St	Balls	Runs	Wkts	Avge	Best	5wI	10wM
Test																	
All First	3	5	0	67	21	13.40	-	-	12	1							
1-day Int																		
NatWest																		
B & H																			
Sunday	1	0	0	0	0	-	-	-	1	-							

HAYWOOD, G. R. Sussex

Name: Giles Ronald Haywood
Role: Left-hand bat, right-arm medium bowler
Born: 8 September 1979, Chichester
Height: 6ft 1in **Weight:** 12st 4lbs
Nickname: Porno, Chopper, Lord Lucan
County debut: 1996 (one-day)
Parents: Ron and Shirley
Marital status: Single
Family links with cricket: Father still plays club cricket, as does brother. 'Mother knows more about cricket than I do'
Education: The Prebendal, Chichester; Lancing College; Sussex University
Qualifications: 11 GCSEs, 3 A-levels
Career outside cricket: Student
Off-season: Studying at Sussex University. England U19 tour to New Zealand 1998-99
Overseas tours: Sussex U19 to Sri Lanka

1995; England U17 to Bermuda (International Youth Tournament) 1997; England U19 to South Africa (including Youth World Cup) 1997-98, to New Zealand 1998-99
Cricketers particularly admired: Michael Bevan, Michael Strong
Young players to look out for: Joseph Tucker, Paul Robbins, David Eggington
Other sports played: Football, hockey, golf
Other sports followed: Football (Bognor Regis Town FC)
Relaxations: 'Relaxing with friends and going out for a drink. Follow most sports except rugby'
Extras: Played for ESCA U15, England U16. Made Sunday League debut at age 17
Opinions on cricket: 'More one-day cricket. 2nd XI cricket should be four-day and not three. England players should be contracted by the ECB to ensure they are fit and fresh for international fixtures.'

1998 Season

	M	Inns	NO	Runs	HS	Avge	100s	50s	Ct	St	O	M	Runs	Wkts	Avge	Best	5wI	10wM
Test																		
All First-Class																		
1-day Int																		
NatWest																		
B & H																		
Sunday	1	1	0	14	14	14.00	-	-	-	-	3	0	16	0	-		-	-

Career Performances

	M	Inns	NO	Runs	HS	Avge	100s	50s	Ct	St	Balls	Runs	Wkts	Avge	Best	5wl	10wM
Test																	
All First																	
1-day Int																	
NatWest																	
B & H																	
Sunday	2	2	0	18	14	9.00	-	-	-	-		18	16	0	-	-	-

HEADLEY, D. W. — Kent

Name: Dean Warren Headley
Role: Right-hand bat, right-arm medium-fast bowler
Born: 27 January 1970, Stourbridge
Height: 6ft 5in **Weight:** 13st 10lbs
Nickname: Frog
County debut: 1991 (Middlesex), 1993 (Kent)
County cap: 1993 (Kent)
Test debut: 1997
Tests: 10
One-Day Internationals: 9
50 wickets in a season: 2
1st-Class 50s: 5
1st-Class 5 w. in innings: 23
1st-Class 10 w. in match: 2
1st-Class catches: 47
One-Day 5 w. in innings: 2
Place in batting averages: 228th av. 16.56 (1997 266th av. 13.83)
Place in bowling averages: 27th av. 21.75 (1997 75th av. 30.84)
Strike rate: 45.59 (career 54.43)
Parents: Ronald George Alphonso and Gail
Marital status: Single
Family links with cricket: Grandfather (George) and father (Ron) both played for West Indies
Education: Gigmill Junior School; Oldswinford Hospital School; Royal Grammar School, Worcester
Qualifications: 7 O-levels
Career outside cricket: 'None yet'
Off-season: England tour of Australia

Overseas tours: RGS Worcester to Zimbabwe 1988; Christians in Sport to India 1989-90; England A to Pakistan 1995-96, to Australia 1996-97; England to Sharjah (Champions Trophy) 1997-98, to West Indies 1997-98, to Australia 1998-99
Overseas teams played for: Melbourne, Jamaica 1991-92; Primrose CC, South Africa 1993-95
Cricketers particularly admired: Malcolm Marshall, 'my dad', Ian Botham, Gavin O'Hanlon, Adam Patrick, Min Patel
Young players to look out for: Matthew Walker, Owais Shah, Andrew Harris
Other sports followed: 'Have a go at anything'
Relaxations: Socialising, watching films, playing golf and eating out
Extras: Took five wickets on debut including a wicket with his first ball in Championship cricket. Played for Worcestershire 2nd XI 1988-89. Left Middlesex at the end of 1992 season and signed for Kent. Called up as a replacement for the England A tour to Pakistan 1995-96. Took a record-breaking three hat-tricks during the summer of 1996. The third generation of his family to play Test cricket, both his father and grandfather played Test cricket for West Indies
Best batting: 91 Middlesex v Leicestershire, Leicester 1992
Best bowling: 8-98 Kent v Derbyshire, Derby 1996
Stop press: Received Man of the Match award for his 6-60 in Australia's second innings in the fourth Test at Melbourne 1998-99, which included a burst of 5-9

1998 Season

	M	Inns	NO	Runs	HS	Avge	100s	50s	Ct	St	O	M	Runs	Wkts	Avge	Best	5wI	10wM
Test	1	2	0	3	2	1.50	-	-	-	-	22	2	69	2	34.50	2-69	-	-
All First	14	21	5	265	81	16.56	-	1	5	-	410.2	88	1175	54	21.75	6-71	4	-
1-day Int																		
NatWest	2	1	0	2	2	2.00	-	-	2	-	24	5	71	3	23.66	2-48	-	
B & H	4	2	0	2	1	1.00	-	-	1	-	34	2	148	5	29.60	3-33	-	
Sunday	15	3	2	7	6 *	7.00	-	-	1	-	99.5	7	376	22	17.09	4-36	-	

Career Performances

	M	Inns	NO	Runs	HS	Avge	100s	50s	Ct	St	Balls	Runs	Wkts	Avge	Best	5wI	10wM
Test	10	17	4	111	31	8.53	-	-	5	-	1949	1059	37	28.62	4-72	-	-
All First	119	158	41	2007	91	17.15	-	5	47	-	21774	11186	400	27.96	8-98	23	2
1-day Int	9	4	3	10	6 *	10.00	-	-	2	-	438	385	8	48.12	2-38	-	
NatWest	14	7	4	46	24 *	15.33	-	-	2	-	877	525	24	21.87	5-20	1	
B & H	27	10	3	62	26	8.85	-	-	6	-	1505	1007	30	33.56	4-19	-	
Sunday	89	28	16	136	29 *	11.33	-	-	16	-	3730	2853	114	25.02	6-42	1	

26. Who is England's all-time leading
World Cup wicket-taker?

FICA

HEGG, W. K. Lancashire

Name: Warren Kevin Hegg
Role: Right-hand bat, wicket-keeper
Born: 23 February 1968, Manchester
Height: 5ft 9in **Weight:** 12st 10lbs
Nickname: Chucky, Bertie
County debut: 1986
1st-Class 50s: 37
1st-Class 100s: 4
1st-Class catches: 570
1st-Class stumpings: 66
Place in batting averages: 55th av. 36.94
(1997 159th av. 25.33)
Parents: Glenda and Kevin (deceased)
Wife and date of marriage:
Joanne, 29 October 1994
Children: 'First baby due 5 November (will
miss the birth due to Ashes tour)'
Family links with cricket: Father and
brother Martin play in local leagues

Education: Unsworth High School; Stand College, Whitefield
Qualifications: 5 O-levels, 7 CSEs, qualified coach
Off-season: Ashes tour
Overseas tours: NCA North U19 to Bermuda 1985; England YC to Sri Lanka 1986-87,
to Australia (Youth World Cup) 1987-88; England A to Pakistan and Sri Lanka 1990-91,
to Australia 1996-97; England to Australia 1998-99
Overseas teams played for: Sheffield, Tasmania 1988-90, 1992-93
Cricketers particularly admired: Ian Botham, Alan Knott, Bob Taylor, Gehan
Mendis, Ian Healy
Young players to look out for: Mark Chilton, Chris Schofield, Gordon Howarth
Other sports played: Football (Old Standians)
Other sports followed: Football (Manchester United), rugby league (Salford Reds)
Injuries: Out for two games with bruised thumb
Relaxations: 'Golf, golf, golf'
Extras: Youngest player for 30 years to score a century for Lancashire, 130 v
Northamptonshire in his fourth first-class game. Eleven catches in match v Derbyshire,
equalling world first-class record. Wombwell Cricket Lovers' Society joint Wicket-
keeper of the Year 1993. Awarded a benefit in 1999
Opinions on cricket: 'Enjoy it as long as you can. It doesn't last forever!'
Best batting: 134 Lancashire v Leicestershire, Old Trafford 1996
Stop press: Made Test debut v Australia at Melbourne on 1998-99 tour

1998 Season

	M	Inns	NO	Runs	HS	Avge	100s	50s	Ct	St	O	M	Runs	Wkts	Avge	Best	5wI	10wM
Test																		
All First	15	21	4	628	85	36.94	-	6	34	3								
1-day Int																		
NatWest	4	2	0	43	28	21.50	-	-	7	-								
B & H	6	5	3	113	44 *	56.50	-	-	7	-								
Sunday	14	9	2	119	31	17.00	-	-	19	3								

Career Performances

	M	Inns	NO	Runs	HS	Avge	100s	50s	Ct	St	Balls	Runs	Wkts	Avge	Best	5wI	10wM
Test																	
All First	238	346	67	7373	134	26.42	4	37	570	66	6	7	0	-	-	-	-
1-day Int																	
NatWest	31	18	1	331	37	19.47	-	-	42	2							
B & H	60	29	13	484	81	30.25	-	2	81	5							
Sunday	173	101	44	1239	52	21.73	-	1	179	27							

HEMP, D. L. Warwickshire

Name: David Lloyd Hemp
Role: Left-hand bat, right-arm
medium bowler
Born: 15 November 1970,
Hamilton, Bermuda
Height: 6ft 1in **Weight:** 12st 7lbs
Nickname: Hempy, Jonesy
County debut: 1991 (Glamorgan),
1997 (Warwickshire)
County cap: 1994 (Glamorgan),
1997 (Warwickshire)
1000 runs in a season: 2
1st-Class 50s: 31
1st-Class 100s: 10
1st-Class catches: 74
One-Day 100s: 3
Place in batting averages: 136th av. 25.84
(1997 56th av. 41.00)
Strike rate: 46.50 (career 50.14)
Parents: Clive and Elisabeth
Wife and date of marriage: Angie, 16 March 1996
Family links with cricket: Father plays for Ffynone CC, brother Tim captains

Swansea and plays for Wales Minor Counties, sister Charlotte played for Parklands Junior School

Education: Parklands Junior; Olchfa Comprehensive School; Millfield School; West Glamorgan Institute of Higher Education

Qualifications: 5 O-levels, 2 A-levels, NCA coaching awards

Off-season: Schools coaching at Warwickshire CCC

Overseas tours: Welsh Cricket Association U18 to Barbados 1986; Welsh Schools U19 to Australia 1987-88; Glamorgan to Trinidad 1990; South Wales Cricket Association to New Zealand and Australia 1991-92; England A to India 1994-95

Overseas teams played for: Hirsh Crusaders, Durban, South Africa 1992-98

Cricketers particularly admired: David Gower, Viv Richards

Young players to look out for: Paul Hutchison, Tony Frost, Anurag Singh, Mark Wagh

Other sports followed: Football (West Ham United, Swansea City), golf

Relaxations: Playing golf

Extras: Scored 258* for Wales v MCC 1991. In 1989 scored 104* and 101* for Welsh Schools U19 v Scottish Schools U19 and 120 and 102* v Irish Schools U19. Left Glamorgan at the end of the 1996 season and joined Warwickshire on a three-year contract

Opinions on cricket: 'Reduce amount of cricket played, which would allow for more quality practice in between games. Bowlers would remain fairly fresh all season. Batters should become more disciplined because of less innings, which would hopefully raise standard and competitiveness of cricket played. Away captain should have choice of whether to bat or bowl.'

Best batting: 157 Glamorgan v Gloucestershire, Abergavenny 1995

Best bowling: 3-23 Glamorgan v South Africa A, Cardiff 1996

1998 Season

	M	Inns	NO	Runs	HS	Avge	100s	50s	Ct	St	O	M	Runs	Wkts	Avge	Best	5wI	10wM
Test																		
All First	15	26	1	646	102	25.84	1	4	15	-	31	3	140	4	35.00	2-68	-	-
1-day Int																		
NatWest	3	3	0	104	59	34.66	-	1	-	-	8	1	43	1	43.00	1-40	-	
B & H	5	5	0	186	55	37.20	-	2	1	-	8.1	0	32	4	8.00	4-32	-	
Sunday	12	11	1	154	28	15.40	-	-	4	-	6	0	43	2	21.50	2-43	-	

Career Performances

	M	Inns	NO	Runs	HS	Avge	100s	50s	Ct	St	Balls	Runs	Wkts	Avge	Best	5wI	10wM
Test																	
All First	109	190	17	5630	157	32.54	10	31	74	-	702	590	14	42.14	3-23	-	-
1-day Int																	
NatWest	14	13	1	539	112	44.91	2	2	3	-	48	43	1	43.00	1-40	-	
B & H	18	17	0	480	121	28.23	1	3	2	-	49	32	4	8.00	4-32	-	
Sunday	76	64	7	1101	74	19.31	-	5	36	-	74	86	3	28.66	2-43	-	

HEWITT, J. P.   Middlesex

Name: James Peter Hewitt
Role: Left-hand bat, right-arm
medium-fast bowler
Born: 26 February 1976, Southwark, London
Height: 6ft 3in **Weight:** 12st 8lbs
Nickname: Shoes, Hewey, Danny,
Bambi, Dumbo
County debut: 1995 (one-day),
1996 (first-class)
County cap: 1998
50 wickets in a season: 1
1st-Class 50s: 3
1st-Class 5 w. in innings: 4
1st-Class catches: 16
Place in batting averages: 236th av. 15.76
(1997 244th av. 15.52)
Place in bowling averages: 111th av. 33.60
(1997 23rd av. 23.15)
Strike rate: 55.24 (career 47.71)
Parents: Gillian Underhay and Terry Hewitt
Marital status: Single
Family links with cricket: Father played club cricket and had trials with Surrey.
Grandfather 'played a bit'
Education: Buckingham Primary School, Hampton; Teddington Secondary School,
Middlesex; Richmond College; Kingston College; City of Westminster College
Qualifications: GCSEs; City and Guilds Part I, II and III in Recreation and Leisure;
GNVQ Leisure and Tourism; coaching awards in cricket (intermediate and advanced),
squash, basketball, hockey, gymnastics, badminton, football, volleyball, plus referee
qualifications; Community Sports Leadership Award
Off-season: Gym and 'visiting as many night clubs as possible'
Overseas teams played for: Western Australia University 1997-98
Cricketers particularly admired: Richard Hadlee, David Gower, Curtly Ambrose,
Dominic Cork, Richard Johnson, Philip Hudson
Young players to look out for: Stephen Peters, Owais Shah, Paul Franks, Graeme
Swann, Matthew Wood, 'and Angus Fraser'
Other sports played/followed: Athletics ('represented South of England at cross-
country'), football ('played for Chelsea Youth'), badminton, volleyball, rugby
(Harlequins)
Relaxations: Watching and playing a number of sports and sports quiz programmes
Extras: 'I was invited back to my old school, Teddington, to present the sports awards
to the pupils – I consider this to be an honour'. Awarded county cap 1998

Opinions on cricket: 'Teatime should be longer.'
Best batting: 75 Middlesex v Essex, Chelmsford 1997
Best bowling: 6-14 Middlesex v Glamorgan, Cardiff 1997

1998 Season

	M	Inns	NO	Runs	HS	Avge	100s	50s	Ct	St	O	M	Runs	Wkts	Avge	Best	5wl	10wM
Test																		
All First	15	19	2	268	53	15.76	-	1	5	-	377.3	63	1378	41	33.60	6-71	2	-
1-day Int																		
NatWest	1	0	0	0	0	-	-	-	-	-	8	0	31	0	-	-	-	
B & H	4	0	0	0	0	-	-	-	1	-	31	2	166	1	166.00	1-47	-	
Sunday	13	9	5	69	21 *	17.25	-	-	5	-	79	5	316	13	24.30	4-24	-	

Career Performances

	M	Inns	NO	Runs	HS	Avge	100s	50s	Ct	St	Balls	Runs	Wkts	Avge	Best	5wl	10wM
Test																	
All First	43	55	10	844	75	18.75	-	3	16	-	5964	3448	125	27.58	6-14	4	-
1-day Int																	
NatWest	4	2	2	18	14 *	-	-	-	1	-	198	148	2	74.00	1-37	-	
B & H	8	4	0	22	14	5.50	-	-	2	-	396	344	5	68.80	2-49	-	
Sunday	40	22	9	187	32 *	14.38	-	-	13	-	1473	1053	42	25.07	4-24	-	

HEWSON, D. R.   Gloucestershire

Name: Dominic Robert Hewson
Role: Right-hand bat, right-arm
medium bowler
Born: 3 October 1974, Cheltenham
Height: 5ft 10in **Weight:** 13st
Nickname: Chopper
County debut: 1996
1st-Class 50s: 6
1st-Class catches: 9
Place in batting averages: 159th av. 23.52
Strike rate: 18.00 (career 18.00)
Parents: Robert and Julie
Marital status: Single
Children: Peter (aged 8); Debbie (aged 4)
Family links with cricket: Dad played for
Upper Fathergill CC near Chopperton
Education: Cheltenham College; University
of West of England

Qualifications: 10 GCSEs, 3 A-levels
Cricketers particularly admired: Jon Lewis, Jack Russell, Courtney Walsh, Mark Snape
Young players to look out for: Jon Lewis, Dom Hewson, Matt Windows, Rob Cunliffe, Andrew Symonds
Other sports followed: Rugby, ice hockey, Aussie rules, football
Relaxations: Seeing friends
Extras: Made debut for Gloucestershire 2nd XI in July 1993
Best batting: 87 Gloucestershire v Hampshire, Southampton 1996
Best bowling: 1-7 Gloucestershire v Kent, Bristol 1998

1998 Season

	M	Inns	NO	Runs	HS	Avge	100s	50s	Ct	St	O	M	Runs	Wkts	Avge	Best	5wI	10wM
Test																		
All First	12	22	3	447	78 *	23.52	-	3	4	-	3	1	7	1	7.00	1-7	-	-
1-day Int																		
NatWest	2	2	0	57	45	28.50	-	-	1	-								
B & H																			
Sunday	3	1	0	25	25	25.00	-	-	-	-								

Career Performances

	M	Inns	NO	Runs	HS	Avge	100s	50s	Ct	St	Balls	Runs	Wkts	Avge	Best	5wI	10wM
Test																	
All First	21	38	4	764	87	22.47	-	6	9	-	18	7	1	7.00	1-7	-	-
1-day Int																	
NatWest	2	2	0	57	45	28.50	-	-	1	-							
B & H																		
Sunday	5	2	0	28	25	14.00	-	-	-	-							

HIBBERT, A. J. E.   Essex

Name: Andrew James Edward Hibbert
Role: Right-hand bat, right-arm medium bowler
Born: 17 December 1974, Harold Wood, Essex
Height: 6ft **Weight:** 13st 10lbs
Nickname: Buns, Hibby
County debut: 1995
1st-Class 50s: 1
1st-Class catches: 5
Strike rate: 33.00 (career 35.00)
Parents: Tony and Thelma (both deceased)

Marital status: Single
Family links with cricket: 'Dad played club cricket and Mum followed avidly'
Education: St Edward's C of E Comprehensive, Romford
Qualifications: 8 GCSEs, NCA senior coaching award
Career outside cricket: 'In the City'
Off-season: Working for NatWest stockbrokers
Overseas tours: England U18 to Denmark (International Youth Tournament) 1993
Overseas teams played for: University of Newcastle, New South Wales, Australia 1995-96, 1997-98
Cricketers particularly admired: Graham Thorpe, Graham Gooch, Nasser Hussain Mark Waugh
Young players to look out for: Graeme Swann, Stephen Peters
Other sports followed: Golf, football (Tottenham Hotspur), snooker
Relaxations: Music – 'would love to be a DJ'; drinking wine
Extras: Played for Essex from U14 upwards. *Daily Telegraph* (South) Batting Award 1990. Hartwell 2nd XI Player of the Year 1996. Awarded 2nd XI cap in 1996. Scored 607 runs at an average of 101.4 in Bain Hogg Trophy. Essex Cricket Society 2nd XI Player of the Year in 1996. Released by Essex at end of 1998 season
Opinions on cricket: 'Too many overs in a day. Four-day cricket is good if games/wickets last four days. Should use more technology. All hotel rooms should be like the Mount Somerset in Taunton.'
Best batting: 85 Essex v Cambridge University, Fenner's 1996
Best bowling: 3-16 Essex v Hampshire, Portsmouth 1998

1998 Season

	M	Inns	NO	Runs	HS	Avge	100s	50s	Ct	St	O	M	Runs	Wkts	Avge	Best	5wI	10wM
Test																		
All First	3	5	0	85	47	17.00	-	-	2	-	16.3	4	48	3	16.00	3-16	-	-
1-day Int																		
NatWest																		
B & H																		
Sunday																		

Career Performances

	M	Inns	NO	Runs	HS	Avge	100s	50s	Ct	St	Balls	Runs	Wkts	Avge	Best	5wI	10wM
Test																	
All First	7	12	1	236	85	21.45	-	1	5	-	105	49	3	16.33	3-16	-	-
1-day Int																	
NatWest																	
B & H																	
Sunday	6	6	2	45	25	11.25	-	-	1	-							

HICK, G. A.   Worcestershire

Name: Graeme Ashley Hick
Role: Right-hand bat, off-spin bowler,
county vice-captain
Born: 23 May 1966, Harare, Zimbabwe
Height: 6ft 3in **Weight:** 14st 7lbs
Nickname: Hicky, Ash
County debut: 1984
County cap: 1986
Test debut: 1991
Tests: 49
One-Day Internationals: 74
1000 runs in a season: 14
1st-Class 50s: 109
1st-Class 100s: 91
1st-Class 200s: 10
1st-Class 300s: 1
1st-Class 400s: 1
1st-Class 5 w. in innings: 5
1st-Class 10 w. in match: 1
1st-Class catches: 441
One-Day 100s: 22
Place in batting averages: 25th av. 43.46 (1997 1st av. 69.27)
Strike rate: 70.28 (career 88.41)
Parents: John and Eve
Wife and date of marriage: Jackie, 5 October 1991
Children: Lauren Amy, 12 September 1992
Family links with cricket: Father has served on Zimbabwe Cricket Union Board of Control since 1984 and played representative cricket in Zimbabwe
Education: Banket Primary; Prince Edward Boys' High School, Zimbabwe
Qualifications: 4 O-levels, NCA coaching award
Off-season: England to Bangladesh, then to Australia for Ashes tour

Overseas tours: Zimbabwe to England (World Cup) 1983, to Sri Lanka 1983-84, to England 1985; England to New Zealand and Australia (World Cup) 1991-92, to India and Sri Lanka 1992-93, to West Indies 1993-94, to Australia 1994-95, to South Africa 1995-96, to India and Pakistan (World Cup) 1995-96, to Sharjah 1997-98, to West Indies 1997-98 (one-day series), to Bangladesh (Wills International Cup) 1998-99, to Australia 1998-99

Overseas teams played for: Old Hararians, Zimbabwe 1982-90; Northern Districts, New Zealand 1987-89; Queensland, Australia 1990-91; Auckland 1997-98

Cricketers particularly admired: Duncan Fletcher (Zimbabwe captain) for approach and understanding of the game, David Houghton, Basil D'Oliveira

Other sports followed: Football (Liverpool FC), golf, tennis, squash, hockey

Relaxations: 'Leaning against Steve Rhodes at first slip'

Extras: Made first century aged six for school team. Youngest player participating in 1983 Prudential World Cup (aged 17); youngest player to represent Zimbabwe. Scored 1234 runs in Birmingham League and played for Worcestershire 2nd XI in 1984 – hitting six successive centuries. In 1986, at age 20, he became the youngest player to score 2000 runs in an English season. One of *Wisden*'s Five Cricketers of the Year 1987. In 1988 he made 405* v Somerset at Taunton, the highest individual score in England since 1895, and scored 1000 first-class runs by end of May, hitting a record 410 runs in April. In 1990 became youngest batsman ever to make 50 first-class centuries and scored 645 runs without being dismissed – a record for English cricket. Also in 1990 became the fastest to 10,000 runs in county cricket (179 innings). Qualified as an English player in 1991. Scored first Test century v India in Bombay 1992-93 and was England's leading batsman, bowler and fielder. Published *Hick 'n' Dilley Circus* and *A Champion's Diary*. Also played hockey for Zimbabwe. Finished third in the Whyte and Mackay batting ratings in 1995 and top of the first-class batting averages in 1997. Scored hundredth first-class 100 v Sussex at Worcester in 1998 with his second 100 of the match; at the age of 32, he became the second youngest player after Wally Hammond to score one hundred 100s; received an Individual Performance Award from the PCA in recognition of his achievement. Awarded a benefit in 1999

Opinions on cricket: 'What a great game.'

Best batting: 405* Worcestershire v Somerset, Taunton 1988

Best bowling: 5-18 Worcestershire v Leicestershire, Worcester 1995

Stop press: Added late to the 1998-99 Ashes tour party as cover for Michael Atherton, remaining for the rest of the tour

1998 Season

	M	Inns	NO	Runs	HS	Avge	100s	50s	Ct	St	O	M	Runs	Wkts	Avge	Best	5wI	10wM
Test	3	5	0	116	107	23.20	1	-	3	-								
All First	17	30	0	1304	166	43.46	7	2	24	-	82	18	242	7	34.57	3-25	-	-
1-day Int	3	3	0	164	86	54.66	-	2	1	-	0.1	0	4	0	-		-	-
NatWest	1	1	0	29	29	29.00	-	-	-	-								
B & H	4	4	1	128	61*	42.66	-	2	1	-								
Sunday	14	13	1	427	116	35.58	1	2	5	-	11	0	64	4	16.00	4-46	-	

Career Performances

	M	Inns	NO	Runs	HS	Avge	100s	50s	Ct	St	Balls	Runs	Wkts	Avge	Best	5wI	10wM
Test	49	85	6	2788	178	35.29	5	15	65	-	2973	1247	22	56.68	4-126	-	-
All First	363	595	59	29777	405 *	55.55	103	109	441	-	19187	9460	217	43.59	5-18	5	1
1-day Int	74	73	7	2475	105 *	37.50	2	18	34	-	853	713	18	39.61	3-41	-	
NatWest	36	36	6	1561	172 *	52.03	4	8	19	-	1193	716	22	32.54	4-54	-	
B & H	62	61	12	2717	127 *	55.44	7	18	38	-	732	562	12	46.83	3-36	-	
Sunday	182	175	31	6555	130	45.52	9	48	49	-	2469	2114	78	27.10	4-21	-	

HOCKLEY, J. B. Kent

Name: James Bernard Hockley
Role: Right-hand bat, off-spin bowler
Born: 16 April 1979, Stone Park, Beckenham
Height: 6ft 2in **Weight:** 13st
Nickname: Hockers, Ice, Ghost
County debut: 1998
Parents: Bernard and Joan
Marital status: Single
Education: Churchfields Primary School,
Beckenham; Kelsey Park School, Beckenham
Qualifications: 7 GCSEs, NCA coaching
award
Career outside cricket: Working for Legal
Aid Board
Off-season: 'As above'
Cricketers particularly admired:
Ian Botham, Aravinda De Silva
Young players to look out for: Robert Key,
Richard Clinton
Other sports played: Football, tennis, golf, rugby, snooker
Other sports followed: Football (Arsenal)
Relaxations: Playing golf and snooker. Listening to music
Extras: AKCL Player of the Year Award in 1995. Equalled Trevor Ward's Kent U15
batting record with a total of 1,000 runs in the season. Kent Schools Player of the Year
in 1996
Opinions on cricket: 'The 2nd XI Championship should be played over four days, to
give the younger players the experience of playing the longer game.'
Best batting: 21 Kent v Oxford University, Canterbury 1998

1998 Season

	M	Inns	NO	Runs	HS	Avge	100s	50s	Ct	St	O	M	Runs	Wkts	Avge	Best	5wI	10wM
Test																		
All First	1	2	0	30	21	15.00	-	-	-	-								
1-day Int																		
NatWest																		
B & H																		
Sunday																		

Career Performances

	M	Inns	NO	Runs	HS	Avge	100s	50s	Ct	St	Balls	Runs	Wkts	Avge	Best	5wI	10wM
Test																		
All First	1	2	0	30	21	15.00	-	-	-	-								
1-day Int																		
NatWest																		
B & H																		
Sunday																		

HODGSON, T. P.   Essex

Name: Timothy Philip Hodgson
Role: Left-hand bat
Born: 27 March 1975, Guildford
Height: 5ft 10in **Weight:** 12st
Nickname: Jimmy Widges
County debut: 1996 (one-day), 1997 (first-class)
1st-Class 50s: 1
1st-Class catches: 4
One-Day 100s: 1
Place in batting averages: 212th av. 18.15 (1997 239th av. 16.83)
Parents: Simon and Victoria
Marital status: Single
Family links with cricket: 'Dad bowls leg-spin off 24 yards. Brother Jamie played for Cambridge University, Mark for Surrey 2nds and Charlie for England Schools U19'
Education: Milbourne Lodge, Esher; Wellington College, Berkshire; Durham University
Qualifications: GCSEs, A-levels, 2:2 in Sociology
Off-season: Playing for Balmain DCC, Sydney

Overseas tours: Wellington College to South Africa; Durham University to Vienna for European Indoor Cricket Championships
Overseas teams pl;ayed for: Balmain 1997-99
Cricketers particularly admired: Graham Gooch, Stuart Law
Young players to look out for: Graeme Swann
Other sports followed: Football (Southampton FC and Woking FC) and golf
Relaxations: Watching or playing most sports, spending time at home
Extras: Highest first wicket partnership in second team (366). Played Surrey U12 to U19 and several second team games. Member of Wellington Cricketer Cup winning side in 1995. Member of Durham University's UAU winning side in 1995 and 1997. Scored the highest ever score on 'The Turf' (Wellington school ground) with 205 not out. Played for British Universities XI in 1997. Essex 2nd XI Player of the Year 1998
Opinions on cricket: 'Less, more competitive cricket should be played using two divisions, so that each county match becomes more of an event to work and train towards.'
Best batting: 54 Essex v Yorkshire, Scarborough 1998

1998 Season

	M	Inns	NO	Runs	HS	Avge	100s	50s	Ct	St	O	M	Runs	Wkts	Avge	Best	5wI	10wM
Test																		
All First	7	13	0	236	54	18.15	-	1	4	-								
1-day Int																		
NatWest																		
B & H																		
Sunday	1	1	0	8	8	8.00	-	-	-	-								

Career Performances

	M	Inns	NO	Runs	HS	Avge	100s	50s	Ct	St	Balls	Runs	Wkts	Avge	Best	5wI	10wM
Test																	
All First	10	19	0	337	54	17.73	-	1	4	-							
1-day Int																	
NatWest	1	1	0	2	2	2.00	-	-	-	-							
B & H	5	5	0	237	113	47.40	1	1	2	-							
Sunday	6	5	0	47	21	9.40	-	-	-	-							

FICA

27. For which country did D. Pringle make his One-Day International debut v India at Headingley on 11 June 1975?

HOGGARD, M. J. Yorkshire

Name: Matthew James Hoggard
Role: Right-hand bat, right-arm fast-medium bowler
Born: 31 December 1976, Leeds
Height: 6ft 2in **Weight:** 14st 7lbs
Nickname: Karpoff, Ivon Drago
County debut: 1996
1st-Class 5 w. in innings: 1
1st-Class catches: 3
Place in batting averages: 292nd av. 5.00
Place in bowling averages: 28th av. 21.82
Strike rate: 37.75 (career 40.90)
Parents: Margaret and John ('Mum and Dad')
Marital status: Single
Education: Lowtown Junior and Infant; Pudsey Grangefield; Pudsey Grangefield Sixth Form

Qualifications: GCSEs and A-levels
Career outside cricket: 'Beer taster'
Off-season: 'Being the overseas pro for Orange Free State in South Africa'
Overseas tours: England U19 to Zimbabwe 1995-96; Yorkshire CCC to South Africa
Overseas teams played for: Johannesburg Pirates 1995-97
Cricketers particularly admired: Viv Richards, Ian Botham, Allan Donald
Young players to look out for: Matthew Wood
Other sports played: Rugby
Other sports followed: Rugby league (Leeds Rhinos)
Injuries: Out for two weeks with groin strain
Relaxations: 'Walking my dog'
Extras: Joined England U19 tour to Zimbabwe as a replacement in 1995-96
Opinions on cricket: 'Too many four-day games. We need two leagues with promotion and relegation to keep teams fresh and interested for the entire season. More day/night games should be played to gain support from more people, and there should be a 40-over competition for the enjoyment of the spectators.'
Best batting: 13* Yorkshire v Durham, Riverside 1998
Best bowling: 5-57 Yorkshire v Essex, Scarborough 1998

1998 Season

	M	Inns	NO	Runs	HS	Avge	100s	50s	Ct	St	O	M	Runs	Wkts	Avge	Best	5wI	10wM
Test																		
All First	9	10	3	35	13 *	5.00	-	-	3	-	258	51	895	41	21.82	5-57	1	-
1-day Int																		
NatWest																			
B & H																			
Sunday	2	2	0	1	1	0.50	-	-	-	-	9	0	33	2	16.50	2-12	-	

Career Performances

	M	Inns	NO	Runs	HS	Avge	100s	50s	Ct	St	Balls	Runs	Wkts	Avge	Best	5wI	10wM
Test																	
All First	11	13	4	47	13 *	5.22	-	-	3	-	1800	1091	44	24.79	5-57	1	-
1-day Int																	
NatWest																	
B & H																	
Sunday	2	2	0	1	1	0.50	-	-	-	-	54	33	2	16.50	2-12	-	

HOLLIOAKE, A. J.   Surrey

Name: Adam John Hollioake
Role: Right-hand bat, right-arm
medium-fast bowler, county captain
Born: 5 September 1971,
Melbourne, Australia
Height: 5ft 11in **Weight:** 13st 4lbs
Nickname: Smokey, Smokin' Joe, Wolf,
Rock, Rambo, Holly, Strong Dance,
Millionaire, Oaky, The Oak, Hokey Cokey,
Abo, Bong, Stumpy, Raj Maru, Gatt, Judgy
County debut: 1992 (one-day),
1993 (first-class)
County cap: 1995
Test debut: 1997
Tests: 4
One-Day Internationals: 19
1000 runs in a season: 2
1st-Class 50s: 32
1st-Class 100s: 12
1st-Class 5 w. in innings: 1
1st-Class catches: 80
One-Day 5 w. in innings: 3

Place in batting averages: 68th av. 34.20 (1997 78th av. 37.12)
Place in bowling averages: (1997 73rd av. 30.53)
Strike rate: 69.62 (career 73.69)
Parents: John and Daria
Marital status: Single
Family links with cricket: 'Brother Ben tries to play but is far too skinny to really progress any further'
Education: St Joseph's College, Sydney; St Patrick's College, Ballarat, Australia; St George's School, Weybridge; Surrey Tutorial College, Guildford
Qualifications: 'Some GCSEs and A-levels'
Off-season: Captaining England in one-day tournament in Bangladesh then to Australia for CUB Series
Overseas tours: School trip to Zimbabwe; Surrey YC to Australia; England YC to New Zealand 1990-91; England A to Australia 1996-97; England to Sharjah (Champions Trophy) 1997-98, to West Indies 1997-98, to Bangladesh (Wills International Cup) 1998-99, to Australia (CUB Series) 1998-99
Overseas teams played for: Fremantle, Western Australia 1990-91; North Shore, Sydney 1992-93; Geelong, Victoria; North Perth, Western Australia 1995-97
Cricketers particularly admired: Steve Waugh, 'anyone who gives 100 per cent'
Young players to look out for: Alex Tudor
Other sports followed: Rugby, boxing, Aussie rules football, American football, 'chess and mind games'
Extras: Played rugby for London Counties, Middlesex and South of England as well as having a trial for England U18. Scored a century on first-class debut against Derbyshire. Surrey Young Player of the Year 1993. Fastest ever one-day 50 – in 15 balls v Yorkshire. Surrey Supporters' Player of the Year 1996 and Surrey Players' Player of the Year 1996. Captained the England A side on their 1996-97 tour to Australia. His 39 wickets in the Sunday league in 1996 was a record for the competition. Man of the Match in the first One-Day International against Australia at Headingley in 1997. Along with brother Ben became the first brothers to make their England Test debut together this century in the fifth Test against Australia at Trent Bridge. Captained England in the 1997 Hong Kong Sixes tournament in which England finished runners-up to Pakistan. Captained England in Champions Trophy in Sharjah in 1997, in one-day series v West Indies 1997-98, in the Texaco Trophy one-day series v South Africa 1998 and in the Wills International Cup in Bangladesh 1998-99. Is contracted to Surrey until 2003
Opinions on cricket: 'Boundaries are too small and outfields are too short – it is too easy to score runs. How come everyone in England knows we are playing too much quantity and not enough quality cricket, but no one has the balls to do anything about it?'
Best batting: 182 Surrey v Middlesex, Lord's 1997
Best bowling: 5-62 Surrey v Glamorgan, Swansea 1998

1998 Season

	M	Inns	NO	Runs	HS	Avge	100s	50s	Ct	St	O	M	Runs	Wkts	Avge	Best	5wI	10wM
Test																		
All First	15	22	2	684	112	34.20	1	4	15	-	92.5	29	247	8	30.87	5-62	1	-
1-day Int	5	4	0	91	46	22.75	-	-	1	-	10	0	61	1	61.00	1-18	-	
NatWest	3	3	0	131	88	43.66	-	1	2	-	17	0	58	0	-	-	-	
B & H	7	7	2	272	85	54.40	-	2	5	-	50	1	276	7	39.42	2-21	-	
Sunday	16	15	0	220	70	14.66	-	1	6	-	82.3	1	462	22	21.00	4-18	-	

Career Performances

	M	Inns	NO	Runs	HS	Avge	100s	50s	Ct	St	Balls	Runs	Wkts	Avge	Best	5wI	10wM
Test	4	6	0	65	45	10.83	-	-	4	-	144	67	2	33.50	2-31	-	-
All First	97	151	14	5557	182	40.56	12	32	80	-	6706	3655	91	40.16	5-62	1	-
1-day Int	19	18	4	373	66 *	26.64	-	2	8	-	628	537	21	25.57	4-23	-	
NatWest	15	13	2	433	88	39.36	-	3	8	-	602	446	14	31.85	4-53	-	
B & H	28	22	3	590	85	31.05	-	4	10	-	992	878	28	31.35	4-34	-	
Sunday	86	76	10	1730	93	26.21	-	9	19	-	3014	2907	127	22.88	5-38	3	

HOLLIOAKE, B. C.   Surrey

Name: Ben Caine Hollioake
Role: Right-hand bat, right-arm medium-fast bowler
Born: 11 November 1977, Melbourne, Australia
Height: 6ft 2in **Weight:** 14st 7lbs
Nickname: Pely, Big Dog, Bedroom Bully
County debut: 1996
Test debut: 1997
Tests: 2
One-Day Internationals: 6
1st-Class 50s: 6
1st-Class 100s: 2
1st-Class catches: 29
One-Day 5 w. in innings: 1
Place in batting averages: 185th av. 20.39 (1997 145th av. 26.61)
Place in bowling averages: 48th av. 25.22 (1997 95th av. 34.00)
Strike rate: 45.94 (career 50.92)
Parents: John and Daria
Marital status: Single

Family links with cricket: 'Dad played for Victoria, brother for Surrey and England'
Education: Edgarley Hall; Millfield School; Wesley College, Perth, Western Australia; 'Joey Benjamin's house'
Qualifications: 'A couple of GCSEs and NCA coaching award'
Career outside cricket: 'Beach lizard'
Off-season: Ashes tour to Australia
Overseas tours: Millfield to Zimbabwe 1992; West of England to West Indies 1992; England U19 to Pakistan 1996-97; England A to Kenya and Sri Lanka 1997-98; England to Sharjah (Champions Trophy) 1997-98, to West Indies 1997-98 (one-day series), to Australia 1998-99
Overseas teams played for: Mellville, Perth 1992-95; North Perth 1996-97
Cricketers particularly admired: 'Waugh bros, Waqar and Wasim, Mr G. Dilley, Peter Carlstien'
Young players to look out for: Graeme Swann, Robert Key, 'and I'm still only 21'
Other sports played: Golf ('First of three holes-in-one at the Belfry 10th 1996')
Other sports followed: Football (Chelsea), Aussie Rules (West Coast Eagles)
Injuries: No bowling for a month with out-of-line pelvis
Relaxations: Music, playing guitar, socialising
Extras: Played England U14 and U15. Played Western Australia U17 and U19. The youngest player to take five wickets in a Sunday League game (5 for 10). His first two appearances at Lord's both resulted in him winning Man of the Match awards – his 63 off 48 balls in the third One-Day International against Australia in 1997 and his 98 off 113 balls for Surrey against Kent in the Benson and Hedges Cup final in 1997. Became the youngest player (aged 19) to make his Test debut for England since Brian Close in 1949 and he and brother Adam became the first brothers to make their Test debuts together for England this century. Played for England during the 1997 Hong Kong Sixes tournament in which they finished runners-up to Pakistan. Was voted the Young Cricketer of the Year by both the Cricket Writers' Club and the PCA in 1997. Scored 100s (103 and 163) for England A in the second and third 'Tests' v Sri Lanka 1998. Is contracted to Surrey until 2001
Opinions on cricket: 'England is approaching a golden era.'
Best batting: 163 England A v Sri Lanka A, Moratuwa 1997-98
Best bowling: 4-28 Surrey v Nottinghamshire, Trent Bridge 1998

1998 Season

	M	Inns	NO	Runs	HS	Avge	100s	50s	Ct	St	O	M	Runs	Wkts	Avge	Best	5wI	10wM
Test	1	2	0	14	14	7.00	-	-	1	-	27	2	116	2	58.00	2-105	-	-
All First	17	26	3	469	60	20.39	-	2	8	-	275.4	51	908	36	25.22	4-28	-	-
1-day Int																		
NatWest	3	3	0	58	33	19.33	-	-	-	-	26	0	99	5	19.80	2-28	-	
B & H	7	6	1	215	91	43.00	-	2	2	-	55.1	4	316	13	24.30	3-23	-	
Sunday	12	11	0	133	40	12.09	-	-	4	-	59.2	2	343	15	22.86	3-30	-	

Career Performances

	M	Inns	NO	Runs	HS	Avge	100s	50s	Ct	St	Balls	Runs	Wkts	Avge	Best	5wI	10wM
Test	2	4	0	44	28	11.00	-	-	2	-	252	199	4	49.75	2-105	-	-
All First	38	57	4	1502	163	28.33	2	6	29	-	4023	2264	79	28.65	4-28	-	-
1-day Int	6	5	0	118	63	23.60	-	1	-	-	126	97	2	48.50	2-43	-	
NatWest	6	4	0	58	33	14.50	-	-	3	-	276	194	6	32.33	2-28	-	
B & H	16	14	1	474	98	36.46	-	4	2	-	681	612	20	30.60	3-23	-	
Sunday	34	29	3	416	61	16.00	-	1	10	-	1170	1055	41	25.73	5-10	1	

HOLLOWAY, P. C. L. Somerset

Name: Piran Christopher Laity Holloway
Role: Left-hand bat, off-spin bowler,
wicket-keeper
Born: 1 October 1970, Helston, Cornwall
Height: 5ft 8in **Weight:** 11st 5lbs
Nickname: Oggy, Leg, Piras
County debut: 1988 (Warwickshire),
1994 (Somerset)
County cap: 1997 (Somerset)
1st-Class 50s: 18
1st-Class 100s: 6
1st-Class catches: 61
1st-Class stumpings: 1
One-Day 100s: 1
Place in batting averages: 142nd av. 24.96
(1997 122nd av. 30.16)
Parents: Chris and Mary
Marital status: 'Engaged to the lovely Nikki'
Family links with cricket: 'Mum and Dad
are keen'

Education: Nansloe CP School, Helston; Millfield School; Taunton School;
Loughborough University
Qualifications: 7 O-levels, 2 A-levels, BSc (Hons) Sports Science
Career outside cricket: Coaching
Off-season: 'Having a winter off coaching'
Overseas tours: Millfield School to Barbados 1986; England YC to Australia 1989-
90; Warwickshire CCC to Cape Town 1992 and 1993; Somerset CCC to Holland 1994
Overseas teams played for: North Perth, 1993-94; Nedlands, Perth 1994-96;
Claremont Nedlands 1996-98
Cricketers particularly admired: Neil 'Noddy' Holder
Young players to look out for: Matthew Elliott

Other sports followed: Squash, football, rugby, tennis, surfing
Injuries: Out for one week with torn ankle ligaments
Relaxations: Music, surfing, travel
Extras: Won the Jack Hobbs Trophy in 1990, played Young England for three years. Was fourth in the county averages in 1991. Somerset Young Player of the Year 1995. Scored the most runs in A-grade cricket in Perth in 1997-98 season in which Claremont Nedlands won the Bank West Cup
Opinions on cricket: 'We are going back to three-day wickets. Simply impossible to maintain a good standard of competition with the amount of cricket played in this country. Too much one-day cricket in particular. I don't necessarily think that the more one-day cricket you play the better you get at it. I believe a conscious decision has to be made on what way the game is heading in the country. A compromise will be worse than opting for a system acceptable to the counties or the ECB. A first and second division is not a very clever idea. It hasn't worked for soccer, so why will it work for cricket?'
Best batting: 168 Somerset v Middlesex, Uxbridge 1996

1998 Season

	M	Inns	NO	Runs	HS	Avge	100s	50s	Ct	St	O	M	Runs	Wkts	Avge	Best	5wI	10wM
Test																		
All First	16	28	3	624	123	24.96	1	1	7	-								
1-day Int																		
NatWest	2	2	1	50	28 *	50.00	-	-	-	-								
B & H	1	1	0	0	0	0.00	-	-	-	-								
Sunday	10	10	0	251	77	25.10	-	2	1	-								

Career Performances

	M	Inns	NO	Runs	HS	Avge	100s	50s	Ct	St	Balls	Runs	Wkts	Avge	Best	5wI	10wM
Test																	
All First	75	127	21	3545	168	33.44	6	18	61	1	40	46	0	-	-	-	-
1-day Int																	
NatWest	8	7	2	246	90	49.20	-	2	4	1							
B & H	7	7	1	67	27	11.16	-	-	7	-							
Sunday	64	55	11	1020	117	23.18	1	4	29	7							

HOOPER, C. L.   Kent

Name: Carl Llewellyn Hooper
Role: Right-hand bat, off-spin bowler
Born: 15 December 1966, Guyana
Height: 6ft **Weight:** 13st
County debut: 1992
County cap: 1992
Test debut: 1987-88
Tests: 73
One-Day Internationals: 167
1000 runs in a season: 7
1st-Class 50s: 79
1st-Class 100s: 45
1st-Class 200s: 2
1st-Class 5 w. in innings: 14
1st-Class catches: 288
One-Day 100s: 11
One-Day 5 w. in innings: 1
Place in batting averages: 21st av. 45.00
Place in bowling averages: 93rd av. 30.87
Strike rate: 74.77 (career 81.44)
Off-season: Playing for West Indies
Overseas tours: West Indies to India and Pakistan 1987-88, to Australia 1988-89, to Pakistan 1990-91, to England 1991, to Pakistan and Australia (World Cup) 1991-92, to Australia and South Africa 1992-93, to Sharjah, India (Hero Cup) and Sri Lanka 1993-94, to India 1994-95, to England 1995, to Australia 1996-97, to Sharjah 1997-98, to Pakistan 1997-98, to Bangladesh 1998-99, to South Africa 1998-99
Overseas teams played for: Guyana 1984 –
Extras: AXA Equity & Law Award 1993. Withdrew from the West Indies squad for tours to Australia and the World Cup in 1995-96 through illness. Unable to play the 1997 county season due to commitments with the West Indies. His overseas slot was taken by Zimbabwe's Paul Strang, but he returned for 1998. Released by Kent at the end of the 1998 season
Best batting: 236* Kent v Glamorgan, Canterbury 1993
Best bowling: 7-93 Kent v Surrey, The Oval 1998

---

28. Who kept wicket for Australia in the 1979 World Cup?

FICA

1998 Season

	M	Inns	NO	Runs	HS	Avge	100s	50s	Ct	St	O	M	Runs	Wkts	Avge	Best	5wI	10wM
Test																		
All First	15	28	1	1215	203	45.00	6	1	15	-	386.2	104	957	31	30.87	7-93	1	-
1-day Int																		
NatWest	2	1	0	38	38	38.00	-	-	1	-	21	1	89	2	44.50	1-29	-	
B & H	5	5	0	163	69	32.60	-	2	4	-	41	2	144	4	36.00	2-28	-	
Sunday	17	14	3	583	100	53.00	1	4	9	-	90	2	446	11	40.54	2-18	-	

Career Performances

	M	Inns	NO	Runs	HS	Avge	100s	50s	Ct	St	Balls	Runs	Wkts	Avge	Best	5wI	10wM
Test	73	122	13	3826	178 *	35.10	9	17	81	-	9207	3847	80	48.08	5-26	4	-
All First	258	412	41	16898	236 *	45.54	47	79	288	-	34450	14885	423	35.18	7-93	14	-
1-day Int	167	151	35	4174	113 *	35.98	5	23	81	-	6853	4934	148	33.33	4-34	-	
NatWest	13	12	1	461	136 *	41.90	1	1	8	-	777	472	7	67.42	2-12	-	
B & H	17	17	0	617	98	36.29	-	6	8	-	900	529	16	33.06	3-28	-	
Sunday	82	76	10	3065	145	46.43	5	23	43	-	3325	2344	68	34.47	5-41	1	

HOUSE, W. J.   Kent

Name: William John House
Role: Left-hand bat, right-arm medium bowler (all-rounder)
Born: 16 March 1976, Sheffield
Height: 5ft 11in **Weight:** 13st
Nickname: Wendy, Curry, Housey
County debut: 1997
1st-Class 50s: 7
1st-Class 100s: 2
1st-Class catches: 16
One-Day 5 w. in innings: 1
Place in batting averages: 108th av. 29.27 (1997 158th av. 25.46)
Strike rate: 264.00 (career 403.66)
Parents: Bill and Anna
Marital status: Single
Family links with cricket: 'Dad played Yorkshire League'
Education: British School in the Netherlands, The Hague; Sevenoaks School; University of Cambridge (Gonville and Caius College)
Qualifications: 11 GCSEs, International Baccalaureate, NCA coaching award

Career outside cricket: Teaching/business
Off-season: Teaching at Sevenoaks School (History, rugby, football)
Overseas teams played for: Royal Hague CC 1985-89; University CC, Adelaide 1994-95
Cricketers particularly admired: Ian Botham, David Gower
Young players to look out for: Robert Key, Anurag Singh
Other sports played: Rugby (Cambridge University U21 XV 1996-97), football (Cambridge Blue 1998)
Other sports followed: Rugby, football (Sheffield Wednesday), golf
Relaxations: Music, history
Extras: Cricket Society's leading all-rounder in schools cricket in 1993. Kent CCC's Most Improved Player 1996. Cambridge University's Player of the Year 1996 and 1998. Benson and Hedges Gold Awards for British Universities v Surrey 1997 (93 runs), v Gloucestershire 1998 (5-34)
Opinions on cricket: 'Sooner or later the first-class structure must be reformed so that less cricket is played and the best players and teams play against each other more often. A higher-quality and more competitive domestic game must be the feeder for the Test team.'
Best batting: 136 Cambridge University v Derbyshire, Fenner's 1996
Best bowling: 1-34 Cambridge University v Oxford University, Lord's 1998

1998 Season

	M	Inns	NO	Runs	HS	Avge	100s	50s	Ct	St	O	M	Runs	Wkts	Avge	Best	5wl	10wM
Test																		
All First	8	11	0	322	65	29.27	-	3	3	-	44	8	135	1	135.00	1-34	-	-
1-day Int																		
NatWest																		
B & H	5	5	0	137	64	27.40	-	1	2	-	11.5	0	82	5	16.40	5-58	1	
Sunday	6	2	0	45	38	22.50	-	-	-	-	7.3	0	42	1	42.00	1-4	-	

Career Performances

	M	Inns	NO	Runs	HS	Avge	100s	50s	Ct	St	Balls	Runs	Wkts	Avge	Best	5wl	10wM
Test																	
All First	26	40	6	1179	136	34.67	2	7	16	-	1211	831	3	277.00	1-34	-	-
1-day Int																	
NatWest																	
B & H	11	11	0	314	93	28.54	-	2	3	-	89	96	5	19.20	5-58	1	
Sunday	11	7	1	91	38	15.16	-	-	1	-	45	42	1	42.00	1-4	-	

HUMPHRIES, S. Sussex

Name: Shaun Humphries
Role: Right-hand bat, right-arm in-swing bowler, wicket-keeper
Born: 11 January 1973, Horsham, West Sussex
Height: 5ft 11in **Weight:** 10st 7lbs
Nickname: Stan, Gooner
County debut: 1993
1st-Class 50s: 1
1st-Class catches: 34
Place in batting averages: 254th av. 13.61
Parents: Peter John and Marilyn Christine
Marital status: Single
Education: The Weald School, Billingshurst; Kingston College of Further Education
Qualifications: 5 GCSEs, BTEC National Diploma in Leisure Studies
Career outside cricket: Coaching 'and anything to pay the bills'
Off-season: 'Working, DIY, following Arsenal and looking after Kate'
Overseas tours: Sussex U13 to Barbados 1987; Sussex U18 to India 1990-91
Overseas teams played for: Sutherland, Sydney 1994-95
Cricketers particularly admired: Peter Moores, Alec Stewart, John Berry, Geoff Kirkham, Ian Healy, Nick 'the Ledge'
Young players to look out for: Chris Nash, Andrew Hodd
Other sports played: 9-ball pool, golf ('poorly')
Other sports followed: 'Watching the Arsenal', cycling, US football
Injuries: Out for three weeks with a broken finger
Relaxations: 'Music, raves, Kate, and "enjoying the proceedings happening at White Hart Lane!"'
Extras: 'Always keep an eye out for Michael Berry's Trinity Army'
Opinions on cricket: 'Too many people who are deciding the future are so out of touch with the modern game.'
Best batting: 66 Sussex v Kent, Tunbridge Wells 1998

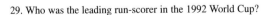

29. Who was the leading run-scorer in the 1992 World Cup?

FICA

1998 Season

	M	Inns	NO	Runs	HS	Avge	100s	50s	Ct	St	O	M	Runs	Wkts	Avge	Best	5wI	10wM
Test																		
All First	14	22	1	286	66	13.61	-	1	25	-								
1-day Int																		
NatWest	1	1	0	10	10	10.00	-	-	2	-								
B & H	1	1	0	16	16	16.00	-	-	1	-								
Sunday	12	7	3	40	13	10.00	-	-	7	5								

Career Performances

	M	Inns	NO	Runs	HS	Avge	100s	50s	Ct	St	Balls	Runs	Wkts	Avge	Best	5wI	10wM
Test																		
All First	18	25	2	338	66	14.69	-	1	34	-								
1-day Int																		
NatWest	1	1	0	10	10	10.00	-	-	2	-								
B & H	1	1	0	16	16	16.00	-	-	1	-								
Sunday	12	7	3	40	13	10.00	-	-	7	5								

HUNT, T. Middlesex

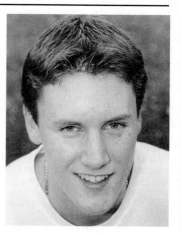

Name: Thomas Aaron Hunt
Role: Left-hand bat, right-arm medium-fast bowler
Born: 19 January 1982, Melbourne, Australia
Height: 6ft 2in **Weight:** 13st 4lbs
Nickname: Thos
County debut: No first-team appearance
Parents: Jennifer Hunt and Tim Woodbridge
Education: Brackenbury, Hammersmith; Acton High; St Clement Danes (A-levels)
Qualifications: 7 GCSEs
Off-season: 'Overseas tour'
Cricketers particularly admired:
Curtly Ambrose, Waqar Younis, Michael Holding, Brian Lara
Other sports played: Football, tennis, golf
Other sports followed: Football (Man Utd)
Injuries: Out for a year with a knee injury
Relaxations: Music

HUSSAIN, N.   Essex

Name: Nasser Hussain
Role: Right-hand bat, county captain
Born: 28 March 1968, Madras, India
Height: 6ft **Weight:** 12st 7lbs
Nickname: Nashwan
County debut: 1987
Test debut: 1989-90
Tests: 34
One-Day Internationals: 18
1000 runs in a season: 5
1st-Class 50s: 66
1st-Class 100s: 37
1st-Class 200s: 1
1st-Class catches: 275
One-Day 100s: 4
Place in batting averages: 94th av. 31.10
(1997 73rd av. 38.60)
Strike rate: (career 138.00)
Parents: Joe and Shireen
Wife and date of marriage: Karen, 24 September 1993
Family links with cricket: Father played zonal cricket in India. Played for Madras in Ranji Trophy 1966-67. Brother Mel played for Hampshire. Brother Abbas played for Essex 2nd XI
Education: Forest School, Snaresbrook; Durham University
Qualifications: 10 O-levels, 3 A-levels; BSc (Hons) in Natural Sciences; NCA cricket coaching award
Off-season: Touring Australia with England
Overseas tours: England YC to Sri Lanka 1986-87, to Australia (Youth World Cup) 1987-88; England A to Pakistan and Sri Lanka 1990-91, to Bermuda and West Indies 1991-92, to Pakistan 1995-96; England to India (Nehru Cup) 1989-90, to West Indies 1989-90, 1993-94 and 1997-98, to Zimbabwe and New Zealand 1996-97, to Australia 1998-99
Overseas teams played for: Madras 1986-87; Petersham, Sydney 1992-93; Adelaide University 1990; Stellenbosch University, South Africa 1994-95; Primrose, Cape Town; Petersham, Sydney
Cricketers particularly admired: Mark Waugh, Graham Gooch, Sachin Tendulkar
Young players to look out for: Stephen Peters, Ian Flanagan
Other sports played: Golf (10 handicap), football
Other sports followed: Football (Leeds United)
Injuries: Out for last four weeks of season with hernia
Relaxations: Listening to music. Listening to Mark Ilott. Watching television

Extras: Played for England Schools U15 for two years (one as captain). Youngest player to play for Essex Schools U11 at the age of eight and U15 at the age of 12. At 15, was considered the best young leg-break bowler in the country. Cricket Writers' Club Young Cricketer of the Year, 1989. Holds record for third, fourth and fifth wicket partnerships for Essex (with Mark Waugh, Salim Malik and Mike Garnham). Essex Player of the Year 1993. Appointed Essex's vice-captain 1996. Captained the England A tour to Pakistan in 1995-96. Finished 2nd in the Whyte and Mackay batting ratings in 1995. Appointed England's vice-captain in 1996-97. Appointed Essex's captain for 1999. Awarded benefit in 1999

Opinions on cricket: 'Too much soft cricket. Quality not quantity. Better one-day wickets, especially in September at Lord's.'

Best batting: 207 England v Australia, Edgbaston 1997

Best bowling: 1-38 Essex v Worcestershire, Kidderminster 1992

1998 Season

	M	Inns	NO	Runs	HS	Avge	100s	50s	Ct	St	O	M	Runs	Wkts	Avge	Best	5wI	10wM
Test	5	10	0	347	105	34.70	1	2	2	-								
All First	10	19	0	591	105	31.10	1	4	9	-								
1-day Int	6	6	1	101	39	20.20	-	-	1	-								
NatWest	2	1	0	0	0	0.00	-	-	3	-								
B & H	7	6	0	416	101	69.33	1	4	3	-								
Sunday	7	7	1	196	73	32.66	-	2	5	-								

Career Performances

	M	Inns	NO	Runs	HS	Avge	100s	50s	Ct	St	Balls	Runs	Wkts	Avge	Best	5wI	10wM
Test	34	61	5	2033	207	36.30	7	6	27	-							
All First	230	367	37	14227	207	43.11	38	66	275	-	276	307	2	153.50	1-38	-	-
1-day Int	18	18	5	256	49 *	19.69	-	-	6	-							
NatWest	25	23	3	857	108	42.85	2	4	17	-							
B & H	47	42	8	1654	118	48.64	2	15	21	-							
Sunday	129	118	18	3033	83	30.33	-	19	53	-							

HUTCHISON, P. M.   Yorkshire

Name: Paul Michael Hutchison
Role: Left-hand bat, left-arm fast-medium swing bowler
Born: 9 June 1977, Leeds
Height: 6ft 4in **Weight:** 12st 4lbs
Nicknames: Hutch, Hooch, Lara, Stonewall, Alcatraz
County debut: 1996
County cap: 1998
50 wickets in a season: 1

1st-Class 5 w. in innings: 6
1st-Class 10 w. in match: 1
1st-Class catches: 6
Place in batting averages: 233rd av. 15.87
Place in bowling averages: 41st av.24.27
(1997 10th av. 20.02)
Strike rate: 48.25 (career 42.58)
Parents: David Hutchison and Rita Laycock
Marital status: Single
Family links with cricket: 'Brother Richard
played a bit for Pudsey St Lawrence in the
Bradford League'
Education: Pudsey Greenside; Pudsey
Crawshaw High; Yorkshire Cricket School
Qualifications: 8 GCSEs, sports leadership
coaching award, GNVQ Leisure and Tourism,
qualified cricket coach
Career outside cricket: 'No thanks!!'
Off-season: 'Holiday, bit of time off relaxing with friends, then training to build up
for England A tour to Zimbabwe and South Africa'
Overseas tours: England U19 to Zimbabwe 1995-96; Yorkshire CCC to Zimbabwe
and Botswana 1996; England A to Kenya and Sri Lanka 1997-98, to Zimbabwe and
South Africa 1998-99; Yorkshire CCC pre-season to South Africa 1999
Cricketers particularly admired: David Gower, Ian Botham, Martyn Moxon, Mark
Ramprakash, Darren Lehmann, Mark Ilott, 'anybody who's been successful and gained
enjoyment for the game'
Young players to look out for: Gary Fellows, Ryan Sidebottom
Other sports played: 'Bit of soccer, bit of golf, most other sports'
Other sports followed: Football (Leeds United), rugby league (Leeds Rhinos)
Injuries: Out for one game/week with broken right thumb
Relaxations: Relaxing with friends, cinema
Extras: Represented England at U17, U18 and U19 levels. Played for Pudsey St
Lawrence in the Bradford League. Had a place at the Yorkshire Academy. Took 7 for
50 on county debut against Hampshire at Portsmouth, only bettered by Wilfred Rhodes
99 years previously. Took 7 for 38 on first first-class appearance in 1997 against
Pakistan A. Voted Wombwell Cricket Lovers' Young Player of the Year for 1997.
Awarded county cap 1998
Opinions on cricket: 'There is too much cricket played in the season, which destroys
quality and increases injury. Contracts should be nine or 12 months instead of the
present six. Better marketing of the game is required if we are to make it more
attractive to youngsters. Two-divisional Championship plus more floodlit games.'
Best batting: 30 Yorkshire v Essex, Scarborough 1998
Best bowling: 7-31 Yorkshire v Sussex, Hove 1998
Stop press: Returned early from England A tour of Zimbabwe and South Africa with a
back injury

1998 Season

	M	Inns	NO	Runs	HS	Avge	100s	50s	Ct	St	O	M	Runs	Wkts	Avge	Best	5wI	10wM
Test																		
All First	17	16	8	127	30	15.87	-	-	4	-	474.3	119	1432	59	24.27	7-31	3	-
1-day Int																		
NatWest	2	1	1	4	4 *	-	-	-	-	-	14	4	24	3	8.00	3-18	-	
B & H	5	1	1	4	4 *	-	-	-	-	-	26.5	4	82	7	11.71	3-14	-	
Sunday	12	5	2	5	2	1.66	-	-	1	-	73.2	2	331	11	30.09	4-34	-	

Career Performances

	M	Inns	NO	Runs	HS	Avge	100s	50s	Ct	St	Balls	Runs	Wkts	Avge	Best	5wI	10wM
Test																	
All First	31	30	17	169	30	13.00	-	-	6	-	5068	2655	119	22.31	7-31	6	1
1-day Int																	
NatWest	2	1	1	4	4 *	-	-	-	-	-	84	24	3	8.00	3-18	-	
B & H	5	1	1	4	4 *	-	-	-	-	-	161	82	7	11.71	3-14	-	
Sunday	12	5	2	5	2	1.66	-	-	1	-	440	331	11	30.09	4-34	-	

HUTTON, B. L.   Middlesex

Name: Benjamin Leonard Hutton
Role: Left-hand opening bat, right-arm
medium bowler
Born: 29 January 1977,
Johannesburg, South Africa
Height: 6ft 2in **Weight:** 12st
Nickname: Gibbs
County debut: No first-team appearance
Parents: Richard and Charmaine
Marital status: Single
Family links with cricket: Son of Richard
and grandson of Sir Leonard
Education: Holmwood House Primary
School; Radley College; Durham University
Qualifications: 10 GCSEs, 3 A-levels, NCA
coaching award, 'hopefully university
degree!'
Career outside cricket: Student
Off-season: 'Touring. Earning a living.
Training and getting fit'
Overseas tours: Durham University to Zimbabwe 1997-98; Middlesex to Portugal
1997

Overseas teams played for: Wanderers CC, Johannesburg 1995-96; Pirates CC, Johannesburg 1995-96
Cricketers particularly admired: Sir Leonard Hutton, Richard Hutton, D. A. Brocklehurst, Michael Atherton, Brian Lara, Mark Ramprakash
Young players to look out for: Oliver Hutton, Robin Martin-Jenkins, Mike Vandrau, James Boyd, Owais Shah, David Nash
Other sports played: Golf (12 handicap), darts
Other sports followed: Football (Chelsea, Ipswich Town)
Injuries: Three months off bowling with lower back pain
Relaxations: 'A quiet drink with my friends!'
Extras: BUSA Halifax medal 1997. Palatinate at Durham University
Opinions on cricket: 'Two divisions will create competitiveness in the game, reduce stalemate games and above all increase the appeal of the game, which at the moment is at an all-time low. The performance of the England team is all-important for the survival of the game, especially for the grass roots.'
Best batting: 10 British Universities v South Africa, Fenner's 1998

1998 Season (did not make any first-class or one-day appearances)

Career Performances

	M	Inns	NO	Runs	HS	Avge	100s	50s	Ct	St	Balls	Runs	Wkts	Avge	Best	5wI	10wM
Test																	
All First	1	1	0	10	10	10.00	-	-	-	-	60	42	0	-		-	-
1-day Int																	
NatWest																	
B & H	4	2	0	4	4	2.00	-	-	1	-	127	101	4	25.25	2-43	-	
Sunday																	

HUTTON, S.

Durham

Name: Stewart Hutton
Role: Left-hand bat, cover fielder
Born: 30 November 1969, Stockton-on-Tees
Height: 6ft **Weight:** 12st
Nickname: Len
County debut: 1992
1st-Class 50s: 13
1st-Class 100s: 4
1st-Class catches: 34
Place in batting averages:
(1997 201st av. 21.50)
Parents: Leonard and Mavis
Marital status: Single
Education: De Brus Comprehensive;
Cleveland Technical College
Qualifications: 6 O-levels (equivalent),
A-level Economics
Overseas tours: Durham to Zimbabwe
1991-92
Cricketers particularly admired: Mike Gatting
Other sports followed: Golf, football
Relaxations: Playing golf
Extras: Scored century for Durham on pre-season tour to Zimbabwe in 1991-92.
Appeared as 12th man for England in the fourth Test against West Indies at Old
Trafford in 1995. Released by Durham at the end of the 1998 season
Best batting: 172* Durham v Oxford University, The Parks 1996

1998 Season

	M	Inns	NO	Runs	HS	Avge	100s	50s	Ct	St	O	M	Runs	Wkts	Avge	Best	5wI	10wM
Test																		
All First	1	1	0	100	100	100.00	1	-	-	-								
1-day Int																		
NatWest																		
B & H	1	1	0	38	38	38.00	-	-	-	-								
Sunday	4	4	1	79	44	26.33	-	-	1	-								

FIGA

30. Which former Warwickshire player dismissed Graeme Hick
by running out his runner, Mike Atherton, in the opening match
of the 1996 World Cup?

Career Performances

	M	Inns	NO	Runs	HS	Avge	100s	50s	Ct	St	Balls	Runs	Wkts	Avge	Best	5wI	10wM
Test																	
All First	66	119	6	3341	172 *	29.56	4	13	34	-	25	18	0	-	-	-	-
1-day Int																	
NatWest	8	8	1	287	125	41.00	1	1	3	-							
B & H	3	3	0	82	38	27.33	-	-	-	-							
Sunday	60	57	6	1298	81	25.45	-	4	17	-							

HYAM, B. J. Essex

Name: Barry James Hyam
Role: Right-hand bat, wicket-keeper
Born: 9 September 1975, Romford, Essex
Height: 5ft 11in **Weight:** 11st 7lbs
Nickname: Bazza
County debut: 1993
1st-Class catches: 52
1st-Class stumpings: 3
Place in batting averages: 203rd av. 19.18
(1997 285th av. 9.87)
Parents: Peter and Gloria
Marital status: Single
Family links with cricket: Brother Matthew
plays for Harold Wood; brother Richard plays
for Gidea Park. 'Matt also has NCA coaching
award. Mum and Dad are keen fans'
Education: Marshalls Park; Havering Sixth
Form College; Westminster College
Qualifications: 9 GCSEs, 1 A-level, NCA
coaching award

Cricketers particularly admired: Graham Gooch, Jack Russell
Young players to look out for: Stephen Peters, Jonathan Powell
Other sports followed: Football (West Ham), hockey and golf
Relaxations: Playing any sport and socialising with friends
Extras: Made first-class debut on his 18th birthday
Opinions on cricket: 'Second XI should play more four-day cricket to prepare them
for first-class cricket. They should also play less friendlies on bad wickets.'
Best batting: 49 Essex v Pakistan, Chelmsford 1996

1998 Season

	M	Inns	NO	Runs	HS	Avge	100s	50s	Ct	St	O	M	Runs	Wkts	Avge	Best	5wI	10wM
Test																		
All First	10	19	3	307	47 *	19.18	-	-	32	2								
1-day Int																		
NatWest																		
B & H																		
Sunday	5	3	0	18	11	6.00	-	-	2	-								

Career Performances

	M	Inns	NO	Runs	HS	Avge	100s	50s	Ct	St	Balls	Runs	Wkts	Avge	Best	5wI	10wM
Test																	
All First	20	35	5	460	49	15.33	-	-	52	3							
1-day Int																	
NatWest																	
B & H																	
Sunday	10	6	1	22	11	4.40	-	-	8	-							

IGGLESDEN, A. P.   Kent

Name: Alan Paul Igglesden
Role: Right-hand bat, right-arm
fast-medium bowler
Born: 8 October 1964, Farnborough, Kent
Height: 6ft 6in **Weight:** 15st 8lbs
Nickname: Iggy, Norm, Silver Spice
County debut: 1986
Test debut: 1989
Tests: 3
One-Day Internationals: 4
50 wickets in a season: 4
1st-Class 5 w. in innings: 23
1st-Class 10 w. in match: 4
1st-Class catches: 40
One-Day 5 w. in innings: 2
Place in bowling averages:
(1997 70th av. 29.88)
Strike rate: 210.00 (career 52.84)
Parents: Alan Trevor and Gillian Catherine
Family links with cricket: 'Brother Kevin due to failing eyesight has been reduced to the ranks of the complete hacker that bowls dibbley dobbleys'
Education: St Mary's Primary School, Westerham; Churchill School, Westerham; 'the Kent dressing-room'

Qualifications: Advanced coaching certificate
Overseas tours: England A to Kenya and Zimbabwe 1989-90; England to West Indies 1993-94; Fred Rumsey's XI to Barbados 1993
Overseas teams played for: Avendale CC, Cape Town 1984-89, Green Point CC, Cape Town 1990-91, Western Province 1986-90; Boland Cricket Union 1991-92
Cricketers particularly admired: Dennis Lillee, Terry Alderman, Carl Hooper, Aravinda De Silva, Paul Strang
Young players to look out for: Robert Key
Other sports followed: Football (Crystal Palace FC), rugby union and golf
Relaxations: 'Walking and cycling with Sara and Jessica'
Extras: 'Lots of runners-up medals.' Testimonial in 1998. Retired at the end of the 1998 season due to back problems
Best batting: 41 Kent v Surrey, Canterbury 1988
Best bowling: 7-28 Boland v Griqualand West, Kimberley 1992-93

1998 Season

	M	Inns	NO	Runs	HS	Avge	100s	50s	Ct	St	O	M	Runs	Wkts	Avge	Best	5wl	10wM
Test																		
All First	3	4	3	8	4 *	8.00	-	-	2	-	70	13	202	2	101.00	2-36	-	-
1-day Int																		
NatWest																		
B & H	4	2	2	0	0 *	-	-	-	-	-	29	2	137	4	34.25	2-34	-	
Sunday	9	2	2	4	3 *	-	-	-	-	-	53	0	240	4	60.00	2-24	-	

Career Performances

	M	Inns	NO	Runs	HS	Avge	100s	50s	Ct	St	Balls	Runs	Wkts	Avge	Best	5wl	10wM
Test	3	5	3	6	3 *	3.00	-	-	1	-	555	329	6	54.83	2-91	-	-
All First	154	170	65	876	41	8.34	-	-	40	-	26579	13488	503	26.81	7-28	23	4
1-day Int	4	3	1	20	18	10.00	-	-	1	-	168	122	2	61.00	2-12	-	
NatWest	14	4	3	23	12 *	23.00	-	-	3	-	728	375	18	20.83	4-29	-	
B & H	29	12	9	43	26 *	14.33	-	-	5	-	1631	1029	39	26.38	3-24	-	
Sunday	96	29	19	97	13 *	9.70	-	-	19	-	4272	2872	117	24.54	5-13	2	

ILLINGWORTH, R. K.   Worcestershire

Name: Richard Keith Illingworth
Role: Right-hand bat, slow left-arm bowler
Born: 23 August 1963, Bradford
Height: 6ft **Weight:** 13st
Nickname: Lucy, Harry
County debut: 1982
County cap: 1986
Benefit: 1997 (£271,275)
Test debut: 1991
Tests: 9
One-Day Internationals: 25
50 wickets in a season: 5
1st-Class 50s: 19
1st-Class 100s: 4
1st-Class 5 w. in innings: 27
1st-Class 10 w. in match: 6
1st-Class catches: 151
One-Day 5 w. in innings: 2
Place in batting averages: 88th av. 31.53
Place in bowling averages: 144th av. 65.61 (1997 30th av. 24.55)
Strike rate: 140.30 (career 77.87)
Parents: Keith and Margaret
Wife and date of marriage: Anne, 20 September 1985
Children: Miles, 28 August 1987; Thomas, 20 April 1989
Family links with cricket: Father played Bradford League cricket
Education: Wrose Brow Middle; Salts Grammar School ('same school as the late Jim Laker')
Qualifications: 6 O-levels, advanced coaching award
Career outside cricket: 'None as yet'
Off-season: Touring Kenya with MCC
Overseas tours: England A to Zimbabwe and Kenya 1989-90, to Pakistan and Sri Lanka 1990-91; England to New Zealand and Australia (World Cup) 1991-92, to South Africa 1995-96, to India and Pakistan (World Cup) 1995-96
Overseas teams played for: Natal 1988-89
Cricketers particularly admired: Ian Botham, Wasim Akram, Derek Underwood
Young players to look out for: Reuben Spiring, Alamgir Sheriyar
Other sports played: Golf
Other sports followed: Football (Leeds United), rugby league (Bradford Bulls), rugby union (Worcester), golf (European PGA)
Injuries: Hamstring problems
Relaxations: 'Watching Miles and Thomas play rugby, football and cricket. DIY. Nice

winter evenings in with Anne watching *Monday Night Live*'

Extras: Took 11 for 108 on South African first-class debut for Natal B v Boland 1988. In 1991, v West Indies, became 11th person in history to take a wicket with first ball in Test cricket. Took a hat-trick in Sunday League v Sussex in 1993, the first Worcestershire player to take hat-trick in one-day cricket. Won 1993 Dick Lygon award for contribution to Worcestershire CCC. Has made three centuries as a nightwatchman

Opinions on cricket: 'I've been very fortunate to play this game for 16 years and enjoyed most of it. I hope everyone gets the same enjoyment as myself.'

Best batting: 120* Worcestershire v Warwickshire, Worcester 1987
Best bowling: 7-50 Worcestershire v Oxford University, The Parks 1985

1998 Season

	M	Inns	NO	Runs	HS	Avge	100s	50s	Ct	St	O	M	Runs	Wkts	Avge	Best	5wl	10wM
Test																		
All First	15	21	6	473	84	31.53	-	3	5	-	304	80	853	13	65.61	3-28	-	-
1-day Int																		
NatWest	1	1	1	0	0*	-	-	-	-	-	12	0	48	0	-		-	-
B & H	4	3	1	46	35*	23.00	-	-	1	-	20.1	3	51	3	17.00	2-21	-	
Sunday	15	9	3	53	15	8.83	-	-	4	-	87.5	1	401	17	23.58	3-27	-	

Career Performances

	M	Inns	NO	Runs	HS	Avge	100s	50s	Ct	St	Balls	Runs	Wkts	Avge	Best	5wl	10wM
Test	9	14	7	128	28	18.28	-	-	5	-	1485	615	19	32.36	4-96	-	-
All First	345	389	114	6291	120*	22.87	4	19	151	-	61751	24647	793	31.08	7-50	27	6
1-day Int	25	11	5	68	14	11.33	-	-	8	-	1501	1059	30	35.30	3-33	-	
NatWest	34	17	7	139	29*	13.90	-	-	10	-	2041	1062	28	37.92	4-20	-	
B & H	58	29	16	260	36*	20.00	-	-	13	-	2915	1670	54	30.92	4-27	-	
Sunday	196	89	45	595	31	13.52	-	-	44	-	7491	5414	228	23.74	5-24	2	

ILOTT, M. C.   Essex

Name: Mark Christopher Ilott
Role: Left-hand bat, left-arm
medium-fast bowler
Born: 27 August 1970, Watford
Height: 6ft 1in **Weight:** 13st 4lbs
Nickname: Ramble, Choock
County debut: 1988
County cap: 1993
Test debut: 1993
Tests: 5
50 wickets in a season: 5
1st-Class 50s: 4
1st-Class 5 w. in innings: 25
1st-Class 10 w. in match: 3
1st-Class catches: 35
One-Day 5 w. in innings: 1
Place in batting averages: 267th av. 11.80
(1997 220th av. 19.33)
Place in bowling averages: 36th av. 23.18 (1997 16th av. 22.00)
Strike rate: 52.43 (career 54.96)
Parents: John and Glenys
Wife and date of marriage: Sandra Jane, 14 October 1994
Children: James, 6 October 1996
Family links with cricket: 'Dad now umpires Minor Counties and continues to test me
about my knowledge of the rules – sorry, Dad – laws. Brother plays in Hertfordshire
premier league and has played for Hertfordshire. Mum's still watching.'
Education: Kingsway Junior; Francis Combe Secondary Modern; '*The Simpsons* and
Linguaphone'
Qualifications: 6 O-levels, 2 AO-levels, 2 A-levels, senior coach, diploma in Fitness
and Nutrition, Securities and Futures Authority (SFA) registered
Career outside cricket: Bond options broker for Gerrard and National Inter-
commodities in London
Off-season: 'Taking over from Peter Such as secretary of the ECCBA, and working
for GNI in London, and trying to decorate '
Overseas tours: England A to Sri Lanka 1990-91, to Australia 1992-93, to South
Africa 1993-94, to India 1994-95; England to South Africa 1995-96
Overseas teams played for: East Torrens District, Adelaide 1989-91
Cricketers particularly admired: Graham Gooch, Nasser Hussain, Ronnie Irani,
Geoff Arnold, Angus Fraser
Young players to look out for: Darren Cousins ('whoops'), Tim Hodgson, Stephen
Peters, Jamie Grove, Ian Flanagan ('DD')

Other sports played: '2nd North Watford Venture Cub Scouts football team ("Quick Feet Marky"), golf ("Never Yip Ilott"), snooker ("Pot the Pink Choock")'
Other sports followed: Golf, football (Watford and Liverpool), snooker; 'in fact, most sports'
Injuries: Out for one game with bad toe
Relaxations: 'Golf, playing my guitar and growing vegetables, especially my Pentland Javelins. You can't beat fresh veg'
Best batting: 60 England A v Warwickshire, Edgbaston 1995
Best bowling: 9-19 Essex v Northamptonshire, Luton 1995

1998 Season

	M	Inns	NO	Runs	HS	Avge	100s	50s	Ct	St	O	M	Runs	Wkts	Avge	Best	5wI	10wM
Test																		
All First	17	30	4	307	38	11.80	-	-	3	-	506.5	138	1345	58	23.18	6-20	2	-
1-day Int																		
NatWest	2	1	0	8	8	8.00	-	-	-	-	20.5	7	43	3	14.33	2-23	-	
B & H	7	2	0	12	8	6.00	-	-	-	-	61.1	6	232	11	21.09	3-10	-	
Sunday	16	6	2	34	12 *	8.50	-	-	3	-	106.1	2	470	21	22.38	3-43	-	

Career Performances

	M	Inns	NO	Runs	HS	Avge	100s	50s	Ct	St	Balls	Runs	Wkts	Avge	Best	5wI	10wM
Test	5	6	2	28	15	7.00	-	-	-	-	1042	542	12	45.16	3-48	-	-
All First	154	198	43	2190	60	14.12	-	4	35	-	28910	14353	526	27.28	9-19	25	3
1-day Int																	
NatWest	20	11	5	119	54 *	19.83	-	1	5	-	1278	771	21	36.71	2-23	-	
B & H	33	11	1	81	21	8.10	-	-	3	-	1776	1045	52	20.09	5-21	1	
Sunday	102	62	20	438	56 *	10.42	-	1	17	-	4317	3227	120	26.89	4-15	-	

31. Which Indian player scored 26 runs and took 3-12 to win the Man of the Match award in the 1983 World Cup final?

INGLIS, J. W. Yorkshire

Name: John William Inglis
Role: Right-hand opening bat
Born: 19 October 1979, Ripon,
North Yorkshire
Height: 6ft 1in **Weight:** 12st 7lbs
Nickname: Jingles
County debut: No first-team appearance
Parents: William and June
Marital status: Single
Education: St Wilfrid's RC, Ripon;
Holy Trinity Juniors; Ripon Grammar School;
St Aidan's Sixth Form, Harrogate
Qualifications: 10 GCSEs
Off-season: Scholarship to Cape Town.
England U19 to New Zealand ('if selected')
Overseas teams played for: Marist Newman
Old Boys, Perth 1997-98
Cricketers particularly admired:
Hasan Raza
Young players to look out for: John Sadler, Chris Taylor
Other sports played: Rugby (captain of Ripon GS; captain of Harrogate U13)
Other sports followed: Rugby league (Hull FC Sharks)
Injuries: Groin strain, also split webbing against Pakistan U19; out for seven weeks
Relaxations: Watching rugby league 'and socialising with my friends'
Extras: Wombwell Neil Lloyd Cricket Association winner (Bunbury Festival) 1995.
Daily Telegraph Batsman of the Year 1995. Yorkshire League Batsman Senior and
Junior winner (youngest ever) 1997. Played for England U19 v Pakistan U19 1998
Opinions on cricket: 'Not enough money in the game today for the grass-roots players.'

INIFF, D. L. Northamptonshire

Name: Dale Lee Iniff
Role: Right-hand bat, left-arm medium/medium-fast bowler
Born: 18 September 1977, Penrith, Cumbria
Height: 6ft 1in **Weight:** 12st 7lbs
Nickname: Emma, Bertie
County debut: No first-team appearance
Parents: John and Yvonne
Marital status: Single

Education: Langwathby CofE School, Cumbria; Queen Elizabeth Grammar School, Penrith, Cumbria; University of Glamorgan, Pontypridd, South Wales

Qualifications: 9 GCSEs, 4 A-levels

Career outside cricket: Cardiac rehabilitation

Off-season: Currently at university. 'Hope to go abroad next winter'

Cricketers particularly admired: Michael Atherton, Wasim Akram, Waqar Younis

Young players to look out for: Mike Powell (Glamorgan)

Other sports played: Volleyball, basketball, tennis, golf

Other sports followed: Football (Carlisle United)

Relaxations: Cars, nightclubbing 'and spending time with my girlfriend'

Extras: North Lancashire League U21 Player of the Year 1994. Became only the second player this century to take nine wickets in an innings for Penrith when he was just 16

Opinions on cricket: 'I think that the standard of international cricket is increasing all the time. I think that professional cricketers are becoming much fitter and players are having to work harder to make the grade, which can only be good for the game. I think that reducing county staffs to 15 or 16 will put off a lot of youngsters who wish to become professional as it will be harder for them to get contracts.'

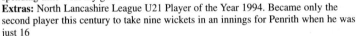

32. Who is West Indies' all-time leading World Cup wicket-taker?

FICA

INNES, K. J.   Northamptonshire

Name: Kevin John Innes
Role: Right-hand bat, right-arm
medium bowler
Born: 24 September 1975, Wellingborough
Height: 5ft 10in **Weight:** 10st 5lbs
Nickname: Ernie, Ken, Milkman, KJ
County debut: 1994
1st-Class 50s: 1
1st-Class catches: 5
Strike rate: (career 66.75)
Parents: Peter and Jane
Education: Boothville Middle School;
Weston Favell Upper School, Northampton
Qualifications: 6 GCSEs, 4 O-levels,
NCA coaching award
Overseas tours: England U18 to South
Africa 1992-93, to Denmark 1993;
England U19 to Sri Lanka 1993-94
Cricketers particularly admired:
Mark Waugh, Carl Hooper, Greg Blewett, Curtly Ambrose
Young players to look out for: Owais Shah, Vikram Solanki, Melvyn Betts
Other sports followed: Snooker, golf, tennis 'and many more'
Relaxations: 'Spending time with my friends, watching and playing most sports,
music, sleeping and reading magazines'
Extras: Played for England U19 in home series against India in 1994. Won the MCC
Lord's Taverners Award U13 and U15
Opinions on cricket: 'It is a shame that employment is not found at the end of the
season for a lot more cricketers.'
Best batting: 63 Northamptonshire v Lancashire, Northampton 1996
Best bowling: 4-61 Northamptonshire v Lancashire, Northampton 1996

1998 Season

	M	Inns	NO	Runs	HS	Avge	100s	50s	Ct	St	O	M	Runs	Wkts	Avge	Best	5wI	10wM
Test																		
All First	1	2	0	37	31	18.50	-	-	2	-								
1-day Int																		
NatWest																		
B & H	1	1	0	1	1	1.00	-	-	-	-	4	0	31	0	-		-	-
Sunday	1	1	1	0	0 *	-	-	-	-	-								

Career Performances

	M	Inns	NO	Runs	HS	Avge	100s	50s	Ct	St	Balls	Runs	Wkts	Avge	Best	5wI	10wM
Test																	
All First	7	10	1	153	63	17.00	-	1	5	-	534	275	8	34.37	4-61	-	-
1-day Int																	
NatWest	1	1	0	25	25	25.00	-	-	-	-							
B & H	2	1	0	1	1	1.00	-	-	-	-	60	56	1	56.00	1-25	-	
Sunday	12	5	3	34	19 *	17.00	-	-	4	-	256	309	3	103.00	1-35	-	

IRANI, R. C. Essex

Name: Ronald Charles Irani
Role: Right-hand bat, right-arm
medium bowler
Born: 26 October 1971, Leigh, Lancashire
Height: 6ft 4in **Weight:** 13st 10lbs
Nickname: Reggie, Ledge
County debut: 1990 (Lancashire),
1994 (Essex)
County cap: 1994 (Essex)
Test debut: 1996
Tests: 2
One-Day Internationals: 10
1000 runs in a season: 3
1st-Class 50s: 31
1st-Class 100s: 9
1st-Class catches: 43
1st-Class 5 w. in innings: 4
One-Day 100s: 2

Place in batting averages: 77th av. 32.29
(1997 97th av. 34.47)
Place in bowling averages: 115th av. 33.95 (1997 115th av. 38.61)
Strike rate: 65.04 (career 63.89)
Parents: Jimmy and Anne
Marital status: Single
Family links with cricket: 'Father played local league cricket in Bolton for 30 years;
mother did teas for many years!'
Education: Church Road Primary School; Smithills Comprehensive School
Qualifications: 9 GCSEs
Overseas tours: England YC to Australia 1989-90; England A to Pakistan 1995-96;
England to Zimbabwe and New Zealand 1996-97
Overseas teams played for: Technicol Natal, Durban 1992-93; Eden-Roskill,
Auckland 1993-94

Cricketers particularly admired: Mark Waugh, Javed Miandad, Wasim Akram, John Crawley, Graham Gooch
Other sports followed: 'Most sports especially football'
Relaxations: Sleeping and watching football
Extras: Played for England U19 in home series v Australia 1991, scoring a century and three 50s in six innings and being named Bull Man of the Series. Made his Test debut in the first Test against India at Edgbaston in 1996. Was selected to represent England in the cancelled World Super Max 8s originally scheduled to take place in Perth in October 1998
Opinions on cricket: 'Too much cricket played by English county cricket professionals.'
Best batting: 127* Essex v Somerset, Bath 1998
Best bowling: 5-19 England A v Board XI, Karachi 1995-96

1998 Season

	M	Inns	NO	Runs	HS	Avge	100s	50s	Ct	St	O	M	Runs	Wkts	Avge	Best	5wI	10wM
Test																		
All First	18	33	2	1001	127 *	32.29	2	2	6	-	444.3	105	1392	41	33.95	5-47	1	-
1-day Int																		
NatWest	2	1	0	5	5	5.00	-	-	2	-	22	6	54	7	7.71	4-41	-	
B & H	7	6	0	214	69	35.66	-	1	2	-	52	5	254	5	50.80	2-21	-	
Sunday	16	15	7	528	95 *	66.00	-	4	5	-	97	2	454	22	20.63	4-26	-	

Career Performances

	M	Inns	NO	Runs	HS	Avge	100s	50s	Ct	St	Balls	Runs	Wkts	Avge	Best	5wI	10wM
Test	2	3	0	76	41	25.33	-	-	-	-	126	74	2	37.00	1-22	-	-
All First	104	172	18	5335	127 *	34.64	9	31	43	-	11245	5939	176	33.74	5-19	4	-
1-day Int	10	10	2	78	45 *	9.75	-	-	2	-	329	246	4	61.50	1-23	-	
NatWest	16	14	2	466	124	38.83	1	4	4	-	986	632	21	30.09	4-41	-	
B & H	23	17	2	605	82 *	40.33	-	3	4	-	1080	836	29	28.82	4-30	-	
Sunday	84	78	13	1834	101 *	28.21	1	10	19	-	2681	2156	90	23.95	4-26	-	

JAMES, K. D.   Hampshire

Name: Kevan David James
Role: Left-hand bat, left-arm medium bowler
Born: 18 March 1961, Lambeth, South London
Height: 6ft 0½in **Weight:** 13st 8lbs
Nickname: Jambo, Jaimo, Jockey
County debut: 1980 (Middlesex), 1985 (Hampshire)
County cap: 1989
1000 runs in a season: 2
1st-Class 50s: 42

1st-Class 100s: 10
1st-Class 5 w. in innings: 11
1st-Class 10 w. in match: 1
1st-Class catches: 76
One-Day 5 w. in innings: 2
Place in batting averages: 69th av. 33.52
(1997 138th av. 27.61)
Place in bowling averages: 114th av. 33.84
(1997 5th av. 18.66)
Strike rate: 63.75 (career 62.61)
Parents: David (deceased) and Helen
Wife and date of marriage:
Debbie, October 1987
Children: Natalie Ann, 8 October 1992;
Naomi Claire, 25 October 1995
Family links with cricket: Late father
played club cricket in North London; brother
Martin plays for Hertfordshire
Education: Edmonton County High School
Qualifications: 5 O-levels, qualified coach, City and Guilds in Electric Theories
Career outside cricket: 'Yes, please'
Off-season: 'I have been very lucky and been awarded a benefit year in 1999 by
Hampshire CCC. I intend to see that the New Year kicks off with good fun events.
Everyone is welcome'
Overseas tours: England YC to Australia 1978-79, to West Indies 1979-80; England
to Hong Kong Sixes 1996
Overseas teams played for: Wellington, New Zealand 1982-83, 1983-84
Cricketers particularly admired: Chris Smith
Young players to look out for: Simon Francis
Other sports followed: 'Football but never achieved anything – about the same as
cricket'
Injuries: 'None that stopped me playing. Just the usual wear and tear on a 37-year-old
body that's been dragged through hell and back'
Relaxations: 'Enjoy my work with local radio. Find it a welcome relaxation during
the summer when I am writing my scripts'
Extras: Left Middlesex at end of 1984 season and joined Hampshire. Achieved a
world record in 1996 when he became the first player in a first-class match to score a
century and take four wickets in four balls in Hampshire's game against India at
Southampton. Awarded a benefit for 1999
Opinions on cricket: 'Losing the 40-over game is the biggest mistake made for years.
Sunday mornings are quality family time, leaving the afternoons for outings such as
cricket. Once our sport crosses that boundary and encroaches into that precious time,
we will lose supporters, just as we did several years ago when we switched to 50 overs
on Sundays and started at 12 o'clock. I can't believe people have such short memories
and have forgotten everything that was wrong then.'

Best batting: 162 Hampshire v Glamorgan, Cardiff 1989
Best bowling: 8-49 Hampshire v Somerset, Basingstoke 1997

1998 Season

	M	Inns	NO	Runs	HS	Avge	100s	50s	Ct	St	O	M	Runs	Wkts	Avge	Best	5wI	10wM
Test																		
All First	18	26	9	570	57	33.52	-	3	6	-	340	70	1083	32	33.84	4-22	-	-
1-day Int																		
NatWest	4	2	0	76	52	38.00	-	1	2	-	19	4	62	1	62.00	1-24	-	
B & H	4	4	1	81	33 *	27.00	-	-	2	-	33	2	133	6	22.16	2-28	-	
Sunday	8	6	2	67	30 *	16.75	-	-	3	-	43.3	4	163	4	40.75	1-13	-	

Career Performances

	M	Inns	NO	Runs	HS	Avge	100s	50s	Ct	St	Balls	Runs	Wkts	Avge	Best	5wI	10wM
Test																	
All First	223	333	57	8498	162	30.78	10	42	76	-	24356	12406	389	31.89	8-49	11	1
1-day Int																	
NatWest	27	16	3	235	52	18.07	-	1	6	-	1540	958	35	27.37	4-42	-	
B & H	46	33	7	511	56	19.65	-	1	12	-	2215	1497	38	39.39	3-31	-	
Sunday	167	113	33	1657	66	20.71	-	5	46	-	6592	4834	161	30.02	6-35	2	

JAMES, S. P. Glamorgan

Name: Stephen Peter James
Role: Right-hand opening bat,
county vice-captain
Born: 7 September 1967, Lydney
Height: 6ft **Weight:** 13st
Nickname: Sid, Jamo
County debut: 1985
County cap: 1992
Test debut: 1998
Tests: 2
1000 runs in a season: 6
1st-Class 50s: 46
1st-Class 100s: 32
1st-Class 200s: 3
1st-Class catches: 146
One-Day 100s: 6
Place in batting averages: 14th av. 49.59
(1997 2nd av. 68.26)
Parents: Peter and Margaret

Wife and date of marriage: Jane Louise, 26 September 1997
Children: Bethan Amy, 28 August 1998 ('during Test match!')
Family links with cricket: Father played for Gloucestershire 2nd XI. Distant relative of Dominic Ostler
Education: Monmouth School; University College, Swansea; Cambridge University
Qualifications: BA (Hons) Wales – Classics; BA (Hons) Cantab – Land Economy
Off-season: 'Coaching /journalism, house husband and watching Cardiff RFC'
Overseas tours: Welsh Schools to Barbados 1984; Monmouth Schools to Sri Lanka 1985; Combined Universities to Barbados 1989; Glamorgan to Trinidad 1989-90, to Zimbabwe 1990-91, Cape Town 1993-94, to Pretoria 1996; England A to Kenya and Sri Lanka 1997-98
Overseas teams played for: Bionics, Zimbabwe 1990-92; Universals Sports Club, Zimbabwe 1992-96
Cricketers particularly admired: Michael Atherton, Graham Burgess
Young players to look out for: Mike Powell, Dean Cosker, Darren Thomas, Alun Evans, Wayne Law
Other sports played/followed: Rugby union (Cardiff RFC and Lydney RFC; 'played for Lydney, Gloucestershire and Cambridge University and was on bench for Varsity Match'), football (West Ham United)
Injuries: Out for two weeks with calf injury, two weeks with finger injury, one week with virus
Relaxations: Reading, *Telegraph* crosswords, videos, weight-training
Extras: Scored maiden century in only second first-class game. Broke Matthew Maynard's club record for number of one-day runs in a season in 1995. Also broke Hugh Morris's club record for number of Sunday League runs in a season. First player to reach 1000 runs in 1997 and was voted the Cricketer of the Year by both the Wombwell Cricket Lovers' Society and the PCA. Appointed vice-captain for the England A tour to Kenya and Sri Lanka 1997-98. Appointed vice-captain of Glamorgan for 1999
Best batting: 235 Glamorgan v Nottinghamshire, Worksop 1996

1998 Season

	M	Inns	NO	Runs	HS	Avge	100s	50s	Ct	St	O	M	Runs	Wkts	Avge	Best	5wI	10wM
Test	2	4	0	71	36	17.75	-	-	-	-								
All First	15	28	1	1339	227	49.59	4	5	9	-								
1-day Int																		
NatWest	2	2	0	79	65	39.50	-	1	-	-								
B & H	4	4	0	134	71	33.50	-	1	-	-								
Sunday	10	10	0	223	78	22.30	-	1	1	-								

Career Performances

	M	Inns	NO	Runs	HS	Avge	100s	50s	Ct	St	Balls	Runs	Wkts	Avge	Best	5wI	10wM
Test	2	4	0	71	36	17.75	-	-	-	-							
All First	188	332	26	12110	235	39.57	35	46	146	-	2	3	0	-		-	-
1-day Int																	
NatWest	21	20	1	787	123	41.42	2	5	5	-							
B & H	33	33	2	1118	135	36.06	2	9	10	-							
Sunday	99	96	11	2986	107	35.12	2	21	23	-							

JARVIS, P. W. Somerset

Name: Paul William Jarvis
Role: Right-hand bat, right-arm
fast-medium bowler
Born: 29 June 1965, Redcar, North Yorkshire
Height: 5ft 11in **Weight:** 12st 7lbs
Nickname: Gnash, Jarv
County debut: 1981 (Yorkshire),
1994 (Sussex)
County cap: 1986 (Yorkshire)
Test debut: 1987-88
Tests: 9
One-Day Internationals: 16
50 wickets in a season: 4
1st-Class 50s: 10
1st-Class 5 w. in innings: 22
1st-Class 10 w. in match: 3
1st-Class catches: 62
One-Day 5 w. in innings: 5
Place in batting averages: 211th av. 18.33

(1997 184th av. 23.37)
Place in bowling averages: (1997 106th av. 36.36)
Strike rate: 92.57 (career 54.28)
Parents: Malcolm and Marjorie
Marital status: Divorced
Children: Alexander Michael, 13 June 1989; Isabella Grace, 21 March 1993
Family links with cricket: Father still plays league cricket for Sudbrooke CC in
Gwent. Brother plays in Yorkshire (Selby Londesborough)
Education: Bydales Comprehensive School, Marske, Cleveland
Qualifications: 4 O-levels, advanced cricket coach
Off-season: Studying for a Sports Science degree
Overseas tours: Yorkshire to St Lucia and Barbados 1987, to South Africa 1991;

England to India/Pakistan (World Cup) and Pakistan 1987-88, to Australia and New Zealand 1987-88, to India and Sri Lanka 1992-93; unofficial English XI to South Africa 1989-90

Overseas teams played for: Mossman Middle Harbour, Sydney 1984-85; Avendale, Cape Town 1985-86; Manly Warringah, Sydney 1987; Onslow, Wellington 1994-95

Cricketers particularly admired: Ian Botham, Malcolm Marshall

Young players to look out for: James Kirtley, Danny Law

Other sports followed: Football

Injuries: Out for three weeks with broken middle finger of right hand

Relaxations: DIY, cooking, golf, fishing, music, eating out, going to the pub

Extras: Youngest player ever to play for Yorkshire in County Championship (16 years, 2 months, 13 days) and youngest player to take hat-trick in Sunday League (1982) and Championship (1985). Played for England YC v West Indies 1982 and Australia 1983. Banned from Test cricket for joining 1989-90 tour of South Africa; suspension remitted in 1992. Released by Sussex at end of 1998 season and has joined Somerset for 1999

Opinions on cricket: 'You could write a book on them, but still too much one-day cricket.'

Best batting: 80 Yorkshire v Northamptonshire, Scarborough 1992

Best bowling: 7-55 Yorkshire v Surrey, Headingley 1986

1998 Season

	M	Inns	NO	Runs	HS	Avge	100s	50s	Ct	St	O	M	Runs	Wkts	Avge	Best	5wI	10wM
Test																		
All First	5	7	1	110	39	18.33	-	-	4	-	108	13	368	7	52.57	3-67	-	-
1-day Int																		
NatWest	1	1	0	33	33	33.00	-	-	1	-	10	0	50	2	25.00	2-50	-	
B & H	2	1	0	16	16	16.00	-	-	-	-	20	0	114	2	57.00	2-63	-	
Sunday	3	2	0	34	24	17.00	-	-	-	-	16	1	73	4	18.25	3-34	-	

Career Performances

	M	Inns	NO	Runs	HS	Avge	100s	50s	Ct	St	Balls	Runs	Wkts	Avge	Best	5wI	10wM
Test	9	15	2	132	29 *	10.15	-	-	2	-	1912	965	21	45.95	4-107	-	-
All First	206	259	67	3299	80	17.18	-	10	62	-	34092	18154	628	28.90	7-55	22	3
1-day Int	16	8	2	31	16 *	5.16	-	-	1	-	879	672	24	28.00	5-35	1	
NatWest	22	14	3	172	34 *	15.63	-	-	5	-	1385	940	24	39.16	4-41	-	
B & H	47	26	9	352	63	20.70	-	1	4	-	2702	1667	76	21.93	4-34	-	
Sunday	141	85	28	626	43	10.98	-	-	30	-	5900	4399	201	21.88	6-27	4	

JEFFERSON, W. I. Essex

Name: William Ingleby Jefferson
Role: Right-hand bat, right-arm
medium bowler
Born: 25 October 1979, Derby
Height: 6ft 8in
Nickname: Big Bird
County debut: No first-team appearance
Parents: Richard and Pauline
Marital status: Single
Family links with cricket: Grandfather
Jefferson played for the Army and Combined
Services in the 1920s. Father, R. I. Jefferson,
played for Cambridge University 1961 and
Surrey 1961-66
Education: Beeston Hall School, Norfolk;
Oundle School, Northants; 'starting at
Durham University autumn 1999'
Qualifications: 3 A-levels, cricket coaching
award 1998
Career outside cricket: Student
Off-season: 'In South Africa in a gap year between school and university'
Overseas tours: Oundle School to South Africa 1995
Overseas teams played for: Young People's Club, Paarl, South Africa 1998-99
Cricketers particularly admired: Graeme Hick
Other sports played: Squash, Rugby fives, golf, tennis
Relaxations: Card games, films, sports videos
Extras: Holmwoods School Cricketer of the Year 1998

JOHNSON, P. Nottinghamshire

Name: Paul Johnson
Role: Right-hand bat, right-arm medium 'occasional' bowler
Born: 24 April 1965, Newark
Height: 'Below average' **Weight:** 'Above average'
Nickname: Johno, Midget, Gus
County debut: 1982
County cap: 1986
Benefit: 1995
1000 runs in a season: 7
1st-Class 50s: 102

1st-Class 100s: 36
1st-Class catches: 202
1st-Class stumpings: 1
One-Day 100s: 13
Place in batting averages: 48th av. 39.04
(1997 49th av. 42.81)
Strike rate: (career 105.66)
Parents: Donald Edward and Joyce
Wife and date of marriage:
Jackie, 24 December 1993
Children: Ruth, 28 September 1994;
Eve, 9 September 1996
Family links with cricket: Father played
local cricket and is a qualified coach
Education: Grove Comprehensive School,
Newark
Qualifications: 9 CSEs, NCA advanced
coach
Overseas tours: England A to Bermuda and West Indies 1991-92
Overseas teams played for: RAU Johannesburg, 1985-86; Hutt District, Wellington,
New Zealand 1988-89
Cricketers particularly admired: Clive Rice and Mike Gatting
Young players to look out for: Usman Afzaal, Noel Gie
Other sports followed: Ice hockey (Nottingham Panthers), football
(Nottingham Forest and Notts County)
Relaxations: 'Listening to music, crosswords and reading autobiographies'
Extras: Played for English Schools in 1980-81 and England YC 1982 and 1983.
Youngest player to join the Nottinghamshire staff. Made 235 for Nottinghamshire 2nd
XI, July 1982, aged 17. Won Man of the Match award in his first NatWest game (101*
v Staffordshire) in 1985, but missed the final owing to appendicitis. Sunday morning
soccer referee in Nottingham. Took over the Nottinghamshire captaincy from Tim
Robinson at the start of the 1996 season. Relinquished captaincy during 1998 season
Opinions on cricket: 'Who would take any notice?'
Best batting: 187 Nottinghamshire v Lancashire, Old Trafford 1993
Best bowling: 1-9 Nottinghamshire v Oxford University, Trent Bridge 1984

1998 Season

	M	Inns	NO	Runs	HS	Avge	100s	50s	Ct	St	O	M	Runs	Wkts	Avge	Best	5wl	10wM
Test																		
All First	15	26	1	976	139	39.04	2	4	14	-								
1-day Int																		
NatWest	3	3	0	68	40	22.66	-	-	2	-	1	0	4	0	-		-	-
B & H	5	4	0	91	69	22.75	-	1	-	-								
Sunday	16	16	3	621	88 *	47.76	-	5	4	-								

Career Performances

	M	Inns	NO	Runs	HS	Avge	100s	50s	Ct	St	Balls	Runs	Wkts	Avge	Best	5wI	10wM
Test																	
All First	316	527	50	17731	187	37.17	36	102	202	1	634	595	6	99.16	1-9	-	-
1-day Int																	
NatWest	34	34	2	947	146	29.59	3	1	12	-	18	20	0	-		-	-
B & H	58	54	11	1455	104 *	33.83	2	10	15	-							
Sunday	218	207	27	6175	167 *	34.30	8	36	74	-	1	1	0	-		-	-

JOHNSON, R. L.   Middlesex

Name: Richard Leonard Johnson
Role: Right-hand bat, right-arm fast-medium
bowler, outfielder
Born: 29 December 1974, Chertsey, Surrey
Height: 6ft 2in **Weight:** 13st 6lbs
Nickname: Jono, Lenny
County debut: 1992
50 wickets in a season: 2
1st-Class 50s: 1
1st-Class 5 w. in innings: 5
1st-Class 10 w. in match: 2
1st-Class catches: 28
One-Day 5 w. in innings: 1
Place in batting averages: 257th av. 13.44
(1997 263rd av. 13.91)
Place in bowling averages: 67th av. 27.38
(1997 61st av. 28.58)
Strike rate: 45.28 (career 51.12)
Parents: Roger and Mary Ann
Marital status: Single

Family links with cricket: Father and grandfather played club cricket
Education: Sunbury Manor School; Spelthorne College
Qualifications: 9 GCSEs, A-level in Physical Education, NCA senior coaching award
Overseas tours: England U18 to South Africa 1992-93; England U19 to Sri Lanka
1993-94; England A to India 1994-95
Cricketers particularly admired: Ian Botham, Richard Hadlee and Angus Fraser 'for
his quality bowling and his dedication to moaning'
Young players to look out for: David Nash, Owais Shah
Other sports followed: Basketball, soccer, snooker and most other sports
Relaxations: Sport and music
Extras: Plays for Sunbury CC, has represented Middlesex at all levels since U11.

Took 10 for 45 v Derbyshire in July 1994, becoming first person to take 10 wickets in an innings since Ian Thomson (Sussex) in 1964; also most economical figures since Hedley Verity's 10 for 10. Had to pull out of England's 1995-96 tour to South Africa due to a persistent back injury

Best batting: 50* Middlesex v Cambridge University, Fenner's 1994
Best bowling: 10-45 Middlesex v Derbyshire, Derby 1994

1998 Season

	M	Inns	NO	Runs	HS	Avge	100s	50s	Ct	St	O	M	Runs	Wkts	Avge	Best	5wl	10wM
Test																		
All First	14	21	3	242	43	13.44	-	-	5	-	377.2	77	1369	50	27.38	7-86	1	-
1-day Int																		
NatWest	3	2	1	49	45 *	49.00	-	-	1	-	30	5	119	4	29.75	2-25	-	
B & H	5	3	0	59	26	19.66	-	-	1	-	50	4	229	13	17.61	3-33	-	
Sunday	13	12	1	121	23	11.00	-	-	2	-	78	1	400	12	33.33	4-45	-	

Career Performances

	M	Inns	NO	Runs	HS	Avge	100s	50s	Ct	St	Balls	Runs	Wkts	Avge	Best	5wl	10wM
Test																	
All First	70	98	11	1247	50 *	14.33	-	1	28	-	10634	5786	208	27.81	10-45	5	2
1-day Int																	
NatWest	14	11	3	155	45 *	19.37	-	-	1	-	780	535	21	25.47	5-50	1	
B & H	14	11	0	117	26	10.63	-	-	2	-	756	609	18	33.83	3-33	-	
Sunday	64	43	13	377	29	12.56	-	-	8	-	2557	2272	62	36.64	4-45	-	

---

33. Which Pakistan great made his One-Day International debut v West Indies at Edgbaston in the 1975 World Cup, scoring 24 and taking 1-46?

FIGA

JONES, P. S. Somerset

Name: Philip Steffan Jones
Role: Right-hand bat, right-arm fast-medium
bowler
Born: 9 February 1974, Llanelli
Height: 6ft 2in **Weight:** 14st 6lbs
Nickname: Jona, Jonesy, Elvis, Cracker,
Delilah
County debut: 1997
1st-Class 5 w. in innings: 1
1st-Class catches: 4
One-Day 5 w. in innings: 1
Place in batting averages:
(1997 261st av. 14.20)
Place in bowling averages:
(1997 81st av. 32.13)
Strike rate: 112.25 (career 62.81)
Parents: Lyndon and Anne
Marital status: Single
Family links with cricket: Father played for
Glamorgan 2nd XI, Welsh junior levels and Hendy
Education: Llangennech Primary School; Ysgol Gyfun y Strade, Llanelli;
Loughborough University; Cambridge University
Qualifications: BSc Sports Science, PGCE in Physical Education
Career outside cricket: Professional rugby player for Moseley
Off-season: Playing rugby for Moseley in the Allied Dunbar Premiership Two
Overseas tours: Wales Minor Counties to Barbados 1993
Cricketers particularly admired: Dermot Reeve, Courtney Walsh
Young players to look out for: Ed Smith, Matthew Bulbeck
Other sports played: Rugby union (Welsh Schools, Youth, U20s, U21s;
Loughborough University, Cambridge University, Swansea, Bristol, Exeter)
Other sports followed: Rugby union (Wellington Hurricanes in Super 12), basketball
(Chicago Bulls)
Relaxations: 'Going to the cinema. Fitness training. Dining out with my darling!!
Spending time with my family in Wales'
Extras: Took nine wickets in the Varsity match at Lord's in 1997. Man of the Match
(5-23) in Sunday League game against Warwickshire 1998
Opinions on cricket: 'Too much emphasis on technique and all that rubbish. Coaches
should leave players alone to develop their own technique and methods. Players
should be encouraged to enjoy and entertain. Flair and individualism should not be
stifled!! Over-coaching leads to your typical boring, technically correct English
cricketer!!! Good coaches listen and guide you in the right way!!'

310

Best batting: 36 Cambridge University v Essex, Fenner's 1997
Best bowling: 6-67 Cambridge University v Oxford University, Lord's 1997

1998 Season

	M	Inns	NO	Runs	HS	Avge	100s	50s	Ct	St	O	M	Runs	Wkts	Avge	Best	5wI	10wM
Test																		
All First	4	5	3	31	22 *	15.50	-	-	-	-	74.5	16	245	4	61.25	2-25	-	-
1-day Int																		
NatWest	1	0	0	0	0	-	-	-	-	-	8	1	36	2	18.00	2-36	-	
B & H																			
Sunday	13	5	3	7	6 *	3.50	-	-	3	-	77.5	6	355	18	19.72	5-23	1	

Career Performances

	M	Inns	NO	Runs	HS	Avge	100s	50s	Ct	St	Balls	Runs	Wkts	Avge	Best	5wI	10wM
Test																	
All First	14	18	6	173	36	14.41	-	-	4	-	1696	984	27	36.44	6-67	1	
1-day Int																	
NatWest	2	1	1	26	26 *	-	-	-	-	-	66	66	2	33.00	2-36	-	
B & H	5	3	2	26	12	26.00	-	-	2	-	258	188	5	37.60	2-51	-	
Sunday	14	5	3	7	6 *	3.50	-	-	4	-	479	374	18	20.77	5-23	1	

JONES, S. P. Glamorgan

Name: Simon Philip Jones
Role: Left-hand bat, right-arm fast bowler
Born: 25 December 1978, Morriston
Hospital, Swansea
Height: 6ft 3in **Weight:** 13st 7lbs
Nickname: Racehorse
County debut: 1998
1st-Class catches: 1
Strike rate: 73.71 (career 73.71)
Parents: Jeff and Irene
Marital status: Single
Family links with cricket: Father (Jeff)
former Glamorgan and England left-arm fast
bowler
Education: Halfway CP School; Coedcae
Comprehensive; Millfield School, Street,
Somerset
Qualifications: 12 GCSEs, 1 A-level
Off-season: Relaxing. Coaching courses

Overseas tours: Dyfed U15 to Zimbabwe
Cricketers particularly admired: Allan Donald
Young players to look out for: Wayne Law, Mike Powell
Other sports followed: Football (Manchester United)
Injuries: Out for last three games of season with stress fracture of left foot
Relaxations: Listening to music, keeping fit, going out with friends
Best batting: 2* Glamorgan v Yorkshire, Cardiff 1998
Best bowling: 3-94 Glamorgan v Yorkshire, Cardiff 1998

1998 Season

	M	Inns	NO	Runs	HS	Avge	100s	50s	Ct	St	O	M	Runs	Wkts	Avge	Best	5wl	10wM
Test																		
All First	3	3	3	2	2 *	-	-	-	1	-	86	11	345	7	49.28	3-94	-	-
1-day Int																		
NatWest																		
B & H																		
Sunday																		

Career Performances

	M	Inns	NO	Runs	HS	Avge	100s	50s	Ct	St	Balls	Runs	Wkts	Avge	Best	5wl	10wM
Test																	
All First	3	3	3	2	2 *	-	-	-	1	-	516	345	7	49.28	3-94	-	-
1-day Int																	
NatWest																	
B & H																	
Sunday																	

KALLIS, J. H.   Glamorgan

Name: Jacques Henry Kallis
Role: Right-hand bat, right-arm medium-fast bowler
Born: 16 October 1975, Pinelands, South Africa
County debut: 1997 (Middlesex)
County cap: 1997 (Middlesex)
Test debut: 1995-96
Tests: 19
One-Day Internationals: 48
1st-Class 50s: 27
1st-Class 100s: 13
1st-Class 5 w. in innings: 2
One-Day 100s: 3
Place in batting averages: 10th av. 55.63 (1997 28th av. 47.00)

Place in bowling averages: 104th av. 33.06 (1997 12th av. 20.46)

Strike rate: 84.81 (career 68.53)

Overseas tours: Western Province to Queensland 1995-96; South Africa U24 to Sri Lanka 1995-96; South Africa A to England 1996; South Africa to India and Pakistan (World Cup) 1995-96, to Sharjah 1995-96, to Pakistan 1997-98, to Australia 1997-98, to England 1998

Overseas teams played for: Western Province 1993-94 –

Extras: Made first-class debut in 1993-94. Signed as overseas player for Middlesex after Greg Blewett, the county's original choice, was selected for the 1997 Ashes series. He was struck down with appendicitis during South Africa's 1997-98 tour of Pakistan. Hit both his maiden Test and One-Day International centuries during South Africa's 1997-98 winter tour of Australia

Best batting: 186* Western Province v Queensland, Brisbane 1995-96

Best bowling: 5-54 Middlesex v Kent, Lord's 1997

Stop press: Scored 113* v Sri Lanka in South Africa's semi-final victory in the Wills International Cup 1998, then followed up with 5-30 as South Africa beat West Indies in the final. Man of the Match in fourth Test v West Indies at Cape Town 1998-99, scoring 110 and 88* and taking 7-124 in the match. Man of the Series, South Africa v West Indies 1998-99 with 485 runs, 16 wickets and seven catches

1998 Season

	M	Inns	NO	Runs	HS	Avge	100s	50s	Ct	St	O	M	Runs	Wkts	Avge	Best	5wl	10wM
Test	5	7	0	294	132	42.00	1	1	7	-	158.1	65	306	11	27.81	4-24	-	-
All First-	10	14	3	612	132	55.63	2	3	9	-	226.1	79	529	16	33.06	4-24	-	-
1-day Int	5	5	0	97	62	19.40	-	1	1	-	17	0	80	2	40.00	1-22	-	
NatWest																		
B & H																		
Sunday																		

Career Performances

	M	Inns	NO	Runs	HS	Avge	100s	50s	Ct	St	Balls	Runs	Wkts	Avge	Best	5wl	10wM
Test	19	30	1	842	132	29.03	2	3	16	-	2187	804	24	33.50	4-24	-	-
All First	80	123	14	4847	186 *	44.46	13	27	56	-	7402	3284	108	30.40	5-54	2	-
1-day Int	48	47	9	1442	111	37.94	2	8	13	-	991	812	19	42.73	3-21	-	
NatWest	3	3	0	116	100	38.66	1	-	1	-	138	107	5	21.40	4-47	-	
B & H	2	2	0	82	72	41.00	-	1	-	-	90	79	2	39.50	2-49	-	
Sunday	11	10	0	140	24	14.00	-	-	4	-	206	124	5	24.80	2-19	-	

KEECH, M.   Hampshire

Name: Matthew Keech
Role: Right-hand bat, right-arm 'military
medium' bowler
Born: 21 October 1970, Hampstead
Height: 6ft **Weight:** 13st 4lbs
County debut: 1991 (Middlesex),
1994 (Hampshire)
1st-Class 50s: 14
1st-Class 100s: 3
1st-Class catches: 48
Place in batting averages: 153rd av. 23.92
(1997 45th av. 43.16)
Strike rate: (career 94.50)
Parents: Ron and Brenda
Marital status: Single
Family links with cricket: 'Mother and
father like to watch a good game'
Education: Northumberland Park School,
Tottenham; 'Middlesex and Hampshire
dressing-rooms'
Qualifications: 5 O-levels, NCA coaching certificate
Career outside cricket: Coaching
Overseas tours: England YC to Australia 1989-90
Overseas teams played for: Mossman, Sydney 1988-89; Lancaster Park,
Christchurch, New Zealand 1990-91
Cricketers particularly admired: Mike Gatting, Robin Smith and Tony Middleton
Young players to look out for: Jason Laney, Owais Shah
Other sports followed: Football, golf, squash
Relaxations: 'Caffrey's, avoiding jobs to be done around the house'
Best batting: 127 Hampshire v Oxford University, The Parks 1997
Best bowling: 2-28 Middlesex v Gloucestershire, Bristol 1993

1998 Season

	M	Inns	NO	Runs	HS	Avge	100s	50s	Ct	St	O	M	Runs	Wkts	Avge	Best	5wI	10wM
Test																		
All First	12	14	0	335	70	23.92	-	3	12	-								
1-day Int																		
NatWest	1	0	0	0	0	-	-	-	-	-								
B & H	5	5	0	122	74	24.40	-	1	1	-								
Sunday	10	10	1	168	49	18.66	-	-	4	-								

314

Career Performances

	M	Inns	NO	Runs	HS	Avge	100s	50s	Ct	St	Balls	Runs	Wkts	Avge	Best	5wI	10wM
Test																	
All First	61	98	11	2471	127	28.40	3	14	48	-	756	383	8	47.87	2-28	-	-
1-day Int																	
NatWest	5	3	0	62	34	20.66	-	-	3	-	66	47	0	-		-	-
B & H	14	13	0	313	74	24.07	-	1	8	-	66	47	1	47.00	1-37	-	
Sunday	76	71	10	1385	98	22.70	-	4	15	-	492	393	9	43.66	2-22	-	

KEEDY, G. Lancashire

Name: Gary Keedy
Role: Left-hand bat, slow left-arm 'with a few revs on it'
Born: 27 November 1974, Wakefield
Height: 6ft **Weight:** 11st 7lbs
Nickname: Bod, Seedy, Linus, Binbag
County debut: 1994 (Yorkshire), 1995 (Lancashire)
1st-Class 5 w. in innings: 2
1st-Class 10 w. in match: 1
1st-Class catches: 12
Place in bowling averages: 96th av. 31.27 (1997 93rd av. 33.96)
Strike rate: 60.83 (career 83.17)
Parents: Roy and Pat
Marital status: Single
Family links with cricket: Twin brother plays for Castleford in the Yorkshire League
Education: Garforth Comprehensive
Qualifications: 4 GCSEs, junior coaching award
Overseas tours: England U18 to South Africa 1992-93, to Denmark 1994; England U19 to Sri Lanka 1993-94
Overseas teams played for: Frankston, Melbourne 1995-96
Cricketers particularly admired: Shane Warne, Graham Gooch
Other sports followed: Rugby league (Leeds), football (Leeds United)
Extras: Player of the Series for England U19 v West Indies U19 in 1993. Graduate of the Yorkshire Cricket Academy. Played for England U19 in the home series against India in 1994
Best batting: 26 Lancashire v Essex, Chelmsford 1996
Best bowling: 6-79 Lancashire v Surrey, The Oval 1997

1998 Season

	M	Inns	NO	Runs	HS	Avge	100s	50s	Ct	St	O	M	Runs	Wkts	Avge	Best	5wI	10wM
Test																		
All First	7	10	5	44	13	8.80	-	-	2	-	182.3	38	563	18	31.27	5-35	1	-
1-day Int																		
NatWest																		
B & H																		
Sunday																		

Career Performances

	M	Inns	NO	Runs	HS	Avge	100s	50s	Ct	St	Balls	Runs	Wkts	Avge	Best	5wI	10wM
Test																	
All First	45	50	32	202	26	11.22	-	-	12	-	8900	4266	107	39.86	6-79	2	1
1-day Int																	
NatWest																	
B & H																	
Sunday	5	0	0	0	0	-	-	-	-	-	175	175	1	175.00	1-40	-	

KENDALL, W. S.   Hampshire

Name: William Salwey Kendall
Role: Right-hand bat, right-arm medium
bowler, occasional wicket-keeper
Born: 18 December 1973, Wimbledon
Height: 5ft 10in **Weight:** 12st 7lbs
Nickname: Villy, Lemon
County debut: 1996
1000 runs in a season: 1
1st-Class 50s: 12
1st-Class 100s: 4
1st-Class catches: 40
Place in batting averages: 30th av. 42.50
(1997 172nd av. 24.29)
Strike rate: (career 65.40)
Parents: Tom and Sue
Marital status: Single
Family links with cricket: Father played
club cricket with East Horsley, Hampshire
Hogs and MCC. Older brother James played
for Durham University
Education: Bradfield College, Berkshire; Keble College, Oxford University
Qualifications: 10 GCSEs, 3 A-levels, 1 AS-level, BA (Hons) Modern History

Overseas tours: Bradfield College to Barbados, 1991; Troubadours to Argentina 1997; Hampshire CCC to Anguilla 1997
Overseas teams played for: Frankston Peninsular CC, Melbourne 1997-98
Cricketers particularly admired: Robin Smith, Graham Thorpe, Mark Ramprakash
Young players to look out for: Simon Francis, Lee Savident, Derek Kenway
Other sports played/followed: Hockey (for Oxford University), football (offered terms by Reading) and golf
Relaxations: Playing or watching sport, socialising with friends, relaxing at home
Extras: Surrey Young Cricketer of the Year 1992. Awarded Gray-Nicolls Trophy for Schoolboy Cricketer of the Year in memory of Len Newbery 1992. Made first-class debut for Oxford University in 1994. Played football for Independent Schools 1992. Offered one-year contract with Reading FC. Hampshire Exiles Player of the Year for 1996
Best batting: 145* Oxford University v Cambridge University, Lord's 1996
Best bowling: 3-37 Oxford University v Derbyshire, The Parks 1995

1998 Season

	M	Inns	NO	Runs	HS	Avge	100s	50s	Ct	St	O	M	Runs	Wkts	Avge	Best	5wI	10wM
Test																		
All First	8	11	3	340	78 *	42.50	-	2	8	-	4	0	16	0	-	-	-	-
1-day Int																		
NatWest																		
B & H	2	2	0	8	5	4.00	-	-	-	-								
Sunday	5	4	0	73	44	18.25	-	-	-	-								

Career Performances

	M	Inns	NO	Runs	HS	Avge	100s	50s	Ct	St	Balls	Runs	Wkts	Avge	Best	5wI	10wM
Test																	
All First	52	79	14	2508	145 *	38.58	4	12	40	-	654	399	10	39.90	3-37	-	-
1-day Int																	
NatWest	2	2	1	16	16	16.00	-	-	-	-							
B & H	9	9	0	129	26	14.33	-	-	-	-							
Sunday	29	25	1	438	55	18.25	-	1	18	-	12	22	0	-	-	-

KENNIS, G. J. Somerset

Name: Gregor John Kennis
Role: Right-hand bat, right-arm
off-spin bowler
Born: 9 March 1974, Yokohama, Japan
Height: 6ft 2in **Weight:** 12st
Nickname: Nesty
County debut: 1994 (Surrey),
1998 (Somerset)
1st-Class catches: 11
Place in batting averages: 266th av. 11.83
Parents: Michael and Sally
Marital status: Single
Family links with cricket: 'Dad played for his
company side and is now a qualified coach'
Education: Tiffin Boys' School; Stewart
Cricket Academy
Qualifications: 9 GCSEs, 1 A-level, NCA
senior coach
Career outside cricket: 'Interior designing'
Overseas tours: Surrey U19 to Barbados 1991
Overseas teams played for: Claremont Nedlands, Perth 1995-96; Marist Newman
Old Boys CC, Perth 1996-97
Cricketers particularly admired: David Boon, James Bond, Alec Stewart,
Neil Stewart, Neil Sargeant
Other sports followed: Horse racing and football (West Ham)
Relaxations: Horse racing, drinking with friends
Extras: 1995 Surrey 2nd XI Batsman of the Year. Scored 258 against Leicestershire in
1995, a record for Surrey 2nd XI. Joined Somerset for 1998 and was released at end of
1998 season
Opinions on cricket: 'We should be grateful. We are getting paid for something we
enjoy doing, although getting paid more would be good.'
Best batting: 49 Somerset v Derbyshire, Taunton 1998

1998 Season

	M	Inns	NO	Runs	HS	Avge	100s	50s	Ct	St	O	M	Runs	Wkts	Avge	Best	5wI	10wM
Test																		
All First	3	6	0	71	49	11.83	-	-	5	-								
1-day Int																		
NatWest																		
B & H																		
Sunday																		

Career Performances

	M	Inns	NO	Runs	HS	Avge	100s	50s	Ct	St	Balls	Runs	Wkts	Avge	Best	5wI	10wM
Test																	
All First	9	17	1	211	49	13.18	-	-	11	-	24	4	0	-	-	-	-
1-day Int																	
NatWest																		
B & H																		
Sunday	1	1	0	5	5	5.00	-	-	-	-							

KENWAY, D. A. Hampshire

Name: Derek Anthony Kenway
Role: Right-hand bat, right-arm medium
bowler, occasional wicket-keeper
Born: 12 June 1978, Fareham
Height: 5ft 10in **Weight:** 12st 10lbs
Nickname: Kenners, Kendog, Bad Boy
County debut: 1997
1st-Class 50s: 1
1st-Class catches: 2
Strike rate: (career 33.00)
Parents: Keith and Geraldine
Marital status: Single
Family links with cricket: Brother captains
Hambledon in the Southern League
Education: Botley Primary School;
St George's, Southampton; Barton Peveril
Qualifications: 6 GCSEs, NCA coaching
award, qualified snowboard instructor
Career outside cricket: 'Winter seasons
abroad'
Off-season: 'Australia or coaching'
Overseas tours: West of England U15 to West Indies 1993
Overseas teams played for: Beaumaris CC, Melbourne 1997-98
Cricketers particularly admired: Mike Gatting, Robin Smith
Young players to look out for: Jon Birdikin, Terry Goss ('talented batsman'),
Simon James ('good all-rounder')
Other sports played: Kickboxing, indoor cricket, golf
Other sports followed: Football (Southampton FC)
Injuries: Out for one month with knee injury
Relaxations: 'Music, tapas bar, walking'
Extras: *Daily Telegraph* Batting Award (West) 1994. Southern League Player of the
Year in 1996. Made 1st XI debut in 1997 against Warwickshire

Opinions on cricket: 'Lunch and tea should be extended.'
Best batting: 57 Hampshire v Lancashire, Old Trafford 1998
Best batting: 1-5 Hampshire v Warwickshire, Southampton 1997

1998 Season

	M	Inns	NO	Runs	HS	Avge	100s	50s	Ct	St	O	M	Runs	Wkts	Avge	Best	5wI	10wM
Test																		
All First	3	5	0	118	57	23.60	-	1	1	-	2	0	17	0	-	-	-	-
1-day Int																		
NatWest																			
B & H																			
Sunday	3	1	0	5	5	5.00	-	-	-	-								

Career Performances

	M	Inns	NO	Runs	HS	Avge	100s	50s	Ct	St	Balls	Runs	Wkts	Avge	Best	5wI	10wM
Test																	
All First	4	7	1	140	57	23.33	-	1	2	-	66	75	2	37.50	1-5	-	-
1-day Int																	
NatWest																	
B & H																	
Sunday	3	1	0	5	5	5.00	-	-	-	-							

KERR, J. I. D. Somerset

Name: Jason Ian Douglas Kerr
Role: Right-hand bat, right-arm
fast-medium bowler, (wicket-keeper 'if required')
Born: 7 April 1974, Bolton, Lancashire
Height: 6ft 3in **Weight:** 12st 6lbs
Nickname: Junior B
County debut: 1993
1st-Class 50s: 3
1st-Class 5 w. in innings: 1
1st-Class catches: 10
Place in bowling averages: (1997 109th av. 37.40)
Strike rate: (career 60.40)
Parents: Len and Janet
Marital status: Single
Family links with cricket: 'Brother Andy is becoming a young legend'
Education: Withins High School; Bolton Met College
Qualifications: 5 GCSEs, BTEC National Diploma in Business Studies, cricket coach
Off-season: 'Rehabilitation of the shoulder'

Overseas tours: England U19 to India 1992-93; Lancashire U19 to Isle of Man
Overseas teams played for: Gordon Districts CC, Sydney, Australia 1994-95; Taita CC, Wellington, New Zealand 1996-97; Subiaco Floriat, Perth
Cricketers particularly admired: A.R. Caddick ('bowling machine')
Young players to look out for: Andy Kerr
Other sports followed: Bolton 'The Great' Wanderers
Injuries: No bowling in 1998 due to torn cartilage and muscle in the shoulder
Relaxations: 'Playing golf, socialising, squash, television, swimming, sleeping, listening to music, spending time with friends and girlfriend Emma'
Opinions on cricket: 'Still the best.'

Best batting: 80 Somerset v West Indies, Taunton 1995
Best bowling: 5-82 Somerset v West Indies, Taunton 1995

1998 Season

	M	Inns	NO	Runs	HS	Avge	100s	50s	Ct	St	O	M	Runs	Wkts	Avge	Best	5wI	10wM
Test																		
All First																		
1-day Int																		
NatWest																		
B & H																		
Sunday	3	2	0	47	29	23.50	-	-	-	-								

Career Performances

	M	Inns	NO	Runs	HS	Avge	100s	50s	Ct	St	Balls	Runs	Wkts	Avge	Best	5wI	10wM
Test																	
All First	32	47	9	730	80	19.21	-	3	10	-	3866	2590	64	40.46	5-82	1	-
1-day Int																	
NatWest	4	3	0	3	3	1.00	-	-	-	-	156	147	7	21.00	3-32	-	
B & H	6	3	0	31	17	10.33	-	-	-	-	234	173	7	24.71	3-34	-	
Sunday	43	26	8	221	33	12.27	-	-	5	-	1597	1477	50	29.54	4-28	-	

KETTLEBOROUGH, R. A. Middlesex

Name: Richard Allan Kettleborough
Role: Left-hand bat, right-arm
medium bowler
Born: 15 March 1973, Sheffield
Height: 5ft 10in **Weight:** 12st
Nickname: Ketts
County debut: 1994 (Yorkshire),
1998 (Middlesex)
1st-Class 50s: 5
1st-Class 100s: 1
1st-Class catches: 16
Place in batting averages: 115th av. 28.44
Strike rate: (career 112.00)
Parents: Allan and Pat
Marital status: Single
Family links with cricket: Father played for
Yorkshire and is now coach at Worksop
College
Education: Laughton All Saints Junior
School; Worksop College; Airedale and Wharfdale College, Leeds
Qualifications: 5 GCSEs, BTEC in Recreational Management, senior coaching award
Career outside cricket: 'Would like to own my own pub'
Overseas tours: Worksop College to Australia 1988-89; England U18 to Canada 1991;
Yorkshire CCC to South Africa 1995
Overseas teams played for: Somerset West, Cape Town 1993-94
Cricketers particularly admired: David Gower and 'all the Yorkshire team'
Young players to look out for: Anthony McGrath
Other sports followed: Football (Sheffield Wednesday FC)
Relaxations: 'Spending time with friends in Sheffield'
Extras: Won the Lord's Taverners U15 award for the Most Promising Young Cricketer
in 1988. 2nd XI cap at Yorkshire. Joined Middlesex for 1998
Opinions on cricket: 'Not enough time to practise during the season.'
Best batting: 108 Yorkshire v Essex, Headingley 1996
Best bowling: 2-26 Yorkshire v Nottinghamshire, Scarborough 1996

---

34. Name the former Somerset all-rounder whose 5-39 v Sri Lanka
at Taunton in the 1983 World Cup remains the
best English World Cup return.

FIGA

1998 Season

	M	Inns	NO	Runs	HS	Avge	100s	50s	Ct	St	O	M	Runs	Wkts	Avge	Best	5wl	10wM
Test																		
All First	12	22	4	512	92 *	28.44	-	3	7	-	23	1	89	0	-		-	-
1-day Int																		
NatWest																		
B & H																		
Sunday	4	4	1	73	48	24.33	-	-	1	-	6	0	29	0	-		-	-

Career Performances

	M	Inns	NO	Runs	HS	Avge	100s	50s	Ct	St	Balls	Runs	Wkts	Avge	Best	5wl	10wM
Test																	
All First	25	41	6	958	108	27.37	1	5	16	-	336	242	3	80.66	2-26	-	-
1-day Int																	
NatWest																	
B & H																	
Sunday	14	10	4	144	48	24.00	-	-	5	-	102	101	3	33.66	2-43	-	

KEY, R. W. T.   Kent

Name: Robert William Trevor Key
Role: Right-hand bat, 'right-arm fast bowler'
Born: 12 May 1979, Dulwich
Height: 6ft 1in **Weight:** 12st 7lbs
Nickname: Keysy
County debut: 1998
1st-Class 50s: 1
1st-Class 100s: 2
1st-Class catches: 11
Place in batting averages: 126th av. 26.60
Parents: Trevor and Lynn
Marital status: Single
Family links with cricket: Mother played for Kent Ladies. Father played club cricket in Derby. Sister Elizabeth played for her junior school side
Education: Worsley Bridge Primary School; Langley Park Boys' School
Qualifications: 10 GCSEs, NCA coaching award, GNVQ Business
Career outside cricket: 'Work in the futures market'
Off-season: England A tour to Zimbabwe

Overseas tours: Kent U13 to Holland; England U17 to Bermuda; England U19 to South Africa (including Youth World Cup) 1997-98; England A to Zimbabwe and South Africa 1998-99

Overseas teams played for: Green Point CC, Cape Town 1996-97

Cricketers particularly admired: Alan Wells, Steve Marsh, Graham Cowdrey, 'and all the Kent staff'

Young players to look out for: Andrew Pickering, Matthew Walker, Darren Thomas, Graeme Swann, Nev Wharton

Other sports played: Hockey, football, snooker

Other sports followed: Football (Chelsea), basketball (Chicago Bulls)

Relaxations: Snooker, socialising with friends

Extras: Played for England U17 and England U19 Development XI. Also played for South England U14 and U19. County tennis player. Played for England U19 against Zimbabwe in 1997 and captained the England U17 side to victory in the international Under 19 tournament in Bermuda in July; played for the victorious England side in the U19 World Cup in South Africa. Shared England U19 Man of the Series award with Graeme Swann v Pakistan U19 1998

Opinions on cricket: 'The game needs to marketed a lot better by highly qualified marketing people.'

Best batting: 115 Kent v Nottinghamshire, Canterbury 1998

1998 Season

	M	Inns	NO	Runs	HS	Avge	100s	50s	Ct	St	O	M	Runs	Wkts	Avge	Best	5wI	10wM
Test																		
All First	13	23	0	612	115	26.60	2	1	11	-	1	0	1	0	-	-	-	-
1-day Int																		
NatWest	2	2	0	24	18	12.00	-	-	-	-								
B & H	1	1	0	4	4	4.00	-	-	-	-								
Sunday	11	8	0	226	62	28.25	-	3	-	-								

Career Performances

	M	Inns	NO	Runs	HS	Avge	100s	50s	Ct	St	Balls	Runs	Wkts	Avge	Best	5wI	10wM
Test																	
All First	13	23	0	612	115	26.60	2	1	11	-	6	1	0	-	-	-	-
1-day Int																	
NatWest	2	2	0	24	18	12.00	-	-	-	-							
B & H	1	1	0	4	4	4.00	-	-	-	-							
Sunday	11	8	0	226	62	28.25	-	3	-	-							

KHAN, A. A. Leicestershire

Name: Amer Ali Khan
Role: Right-hand bat, leg-break bowler
Born: 5 November 1969, Lahore, Pakistan
Height: 5ft 10in **Weight:** 12st
Nickname: Aga
County debut: 1995 (Middlesex),
1997 (Sussex)
1st-Class 50s: 1
1st-Class 5 w. in innings: 1
1st-Class catches: 9
One-Day 5 w. in innings: 1
Place in batting averages:
(1997 256th av. 15.31)
Place in bowling averages:
(1997 127th av. 42.33)
Strike rate: 116.00 (career 81.25)
Parents: M. Hanif Khan and
Shireen Hanif
Family links with cricket: 'Dad played club cricket, and two of my cousins, Sajid
Hussain and Amir Raza, played first-class cricket for Rawalpindi and Islamabad. Sajid
also played for PIA for two years'
Education: 25F Model Town; Muslim Model High School; MAO College (all Lahore)
Qualifications: Coaching
Off-season: Playing overseas
Overseas teams played for: Wakatu CC, Nelson, New Zealand 1995-96; Motueka
Cricket Association, New Zealand 1997-98; Kuils River CC, South Africa 1998-99
Cricketers particularly admired: Mark Ramprakash, Mark Waugh, Mark Robinson
Other sports played: Touch rugby
Relaxations: Listening to music and going to cinema
Extras: Released by Sussex at end of 1998 season and has joined Leics for 1999
Best batting: 52 Sussex v Hampshire, Southampton 1997
Best bowling: 5-137 Sussex v Middlesex, Lord's 1997

1998 Season

	M	Inns	NO	Runs	HS	Avge	100s	50s	Ct	St	O	M	Runs	Wkts	Avge	Best	5wl	10wM
Test																		
All First	4	4	0	41	23	10.25	-	-	4	-	116	26	389	6	64.83	2-24	-	-
1-day Int																		
NatWest																		
B & H																		
Sunday																		

Career Performances

	M	Inns	NO	Runs	HS	Avge	100s	50s	Ct	St	Balls	Runs	Wkts	Avge	Best	5wI	10wM
Test																	
All First	22	28	5	332	52	14.43	-	1	9	-	3819	1928	47	41.02	5-137	1	-
1-day Int																	
NatWest	4	1	0	4	4	4.00	-	-	1	-	240	196	2	98.00	1-13	-	
B & H	5	3	0	15	8	5.00	-	-	2	-	294	217	8	27.12	3-31	-	
Sunday	13	9	3	48	22 *	8.00	-	-	2	-	545	474	15	31.60	5-40	1	

KHAN, W. G. Sussex

Name: Wasim Gulzar Khan
Role: Left-hand bat, leg-break bowler
Born: 26 February 1971, Birmingham
Height: 6ft 1in **Weight:** 11st 5lbs
Nickname: Wazby, Dog
County debut: 1992 (one-day, Warwicks),
1995 (first-class, Warwicks), 1998 (Sussex)
1st-Class 50s: 14
1st-Class 100s: 5
1st-Class catches: 35
Place in batting averages: 110th av. 28.86
(1997 180th av. 27.33)
Parents: Gulzar Khan (deceased)
and Zarina Begum
Marital status: Single
Education: Small Heath Secondary School,
Birmingham; Josiah Mason Sixth Form
College, Birmingham

Qualifications: 6 O-levels, 1 A-level, NCA
coaching award
Overseas tours: Warwickshire to Cape Town 1993, 1995
Overseas teams played for: Western Suburbs, Sydney 1990-91; North Perth 1991-93;
Albion, Melbourne 1993-95; Petone Riverside, Wellington, New Zealand 1996-97
Cricketers particularly admired: Graham Thorpe, Saeed Anwar
Young players to look out for: Anurag Singh, Darren Altree
Other sports followed: Football (Leeds United), golf, tennis, squash
Relaxations: Listening to music, spending time with family and friends
Extras: Most Promising Young Cricketer 1990. Scored four centuries in a row for
Warwickshire U19. Scored 171* v Northants in second trial game for Warwickshire
2nd XI. England Schools U19. Won Oxford/Cambridge U19 Festival 1989, 1990. Left
Warwickshire at the end of the 1997 season to join Sussex
Best batting: 181 Warwickshire v Hampshire, Southampton 1995

1998 Season

	M	Inns	NO	Runs	HS	Avge	100s	50s	Ct	St	O	M	Runs	Wkts	Avge	Best	5wI	10wM
Test																		
All First	18	30	1	837	125	28.86	1	6	5	-	1.5	0	7	0	-	-	-	-
1-day Int																		
NatWest	1	1	0	2	2	2.00	-	-	1	-								
B & H	1	1	0	33	33	33.00	-	-	-	-								
Sunday	7	5	0	78	33	15.60	-	-	1	-								

Career Performances

	M	Inns	NO	Runs	HS	Avge	100s	50s	Ct	St	Balls	Runs	Wkts	Avge	Best	5wI	10wM
Test																	
All First	49	86	8	2524	181	32.35	5	14	35	-	72	31	0	-	-	-	-
1-day Int																	
NatWest	1	1	0	2	2	2.00	-	-	1	-							
B & H	2	2	1	33	33	33.00	-	-	1	-							
Sunday	17	15	0	143	33	9.53	-	-	3	-							

KILLEEN, N. Durham

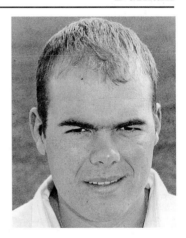

Name: Neil Killeen
Role: Right-hand bat, right-arm
fast-medium bowler
Born: 17 October 1975, Shotley Bridge
Height: 6ft 2in **Weight:** 14st 12lbs
Nickname: Killer, Squeaky, Quinny
County debut: 1995
1st-Class 5 w. in innings: 2
1st-Class catches: 10
One-Day 5 w. in innings: 1
Place in batting averages:
(1997 306th av. 6.66)
Place in bowling averages: 79th av. 29.08
(1997 102nd av. 36.16)
Strike rate: 50.66 (career 59.45)
Parents: Glen and Thora
Marital status: Single
Education: Greencroft Comprehensive
School; Derwentside College, University of
Teesside
Qualifications: 8 GCSEs, 2 A-levels, advanced coaching award
Overseas tours: Durham CCC to Zimbabwe 1992; England U19 to West Indies 1994-95

Cricketers particularly admired: Ian Botham, Curtly Ambrose
Young players to look out for: Melvyn Betts
Other sports followed: Athletics (English Schools javelin) and football
Relaxations: 'Spending time with friends and going out. Listening to music and watching television'
Extras: First Durham bowler to take five wickets in a Sunday League game (5-26 against Northamptonshire in 1995)
Opinions on cricket: 'Too many overs in a day in the first-class game.'
Best batting: 48 Durham v Somerset, Chester-le-Street 1995
Best bowling: 5-49 Durham v Lancashire, Riverside 1998

1998 Season

	M	Inns	NO	Runs	HS	Avge	100s	50s	Ct	St	O	M	Runs	Wkts	Avge	Best	5wI	10wM
Test																		
All First	3	3	1	27	15 *	13.50	-	-	3	-	101.2	25	349	12	29.08	5-49	1	-
1-day Int																		
NatWest	2	1	1	1	1 *	-	-	-	-	-	24	2	109	3	36.33	2-46	-	
B & H	3	3	2	25	24 *	25.00	-	-	-	-	27	3	127	4	31.75	2-28	-	
Sunday	13	10	5	95	28	19.00	-	-	2	-	80.5	2	425	13	32.69	3-33	-	

Career Performances

	M	Inns	NO	Runs	HS	Avge	100s	50s	Ct	St	Balls	Runs	Wkts	Avge	Best	5wI	10wM
Test																	
All First	18	26	7	228	48	12.00	-	-	10	-	2854	1755	48	36.56	5-49	2	-
1-day Int																	
NatWest	3	1	1	1	1 *	-	-	-	1	-	216	155	4	38.75	2-46	-	
B & H	16	10	3	46	24 *	6.57	-	-	2	-	880	653	13	50.23	2-28	-	
Sunday	42	29	9	180	32	9.00	-	-	7	-	1732	1502	52	28.88	5-26	1	

KIRBY, S. P.   Leicestershire

Name: Steven P. Kirby
Role: Right-hand bat, right-arm fast bowler
Born: 4 October 1977, Bury, Lancashire
Height: 6ft 4in **Weight:** 12st
Nickname: Poukaka
County debut: No first-team appearance
Parents: Paul and Alison
Marital status: Single
Education: St Joseph's RC, Heywood, Lancs; Elton High School, Bury; Bury College, Lancs
Qualifications: 9 GCSEs, BTEC GNVQ Advanced Leisure and Tourism

Off-season: 'Undergoing a big rehab programme'
Overseas teams played for: Taranaki, Egmont Plains, New Zealand 1997-98
Young players to look out for: Chris Schofield, Jimmy Ormond
Other sports followed: Football (Manchester United), rugby (Leicester Tigers), basketball, tennis, golf, table tennis, squash, 'anything competitive'
Injuries: Out for last three months of season with sacroiliac instability
Relaxations: Spending time with my girlfriend and friends
Opinions on cricket: 'I believe that we do not play on enough good pitches, therefore not promoting enough good techniques with bat and ball from an early age. Also I do not

believe that we are producing enough world-class bowlers, because we are expecting the pitch to do the work for us, instead of learning to do something with the ball, which in turn goes back to the standard of the pitches.'

KIRTLEY, R. J. Sussex

Name: Robert James Kirtley
Role: Right-hand bat, right-arm fast-medium bowler
Born: 10 January 1975, Eastbourne
Height: 6ft **Weight:** 12st
Nickname: Ambi, Hurtler, Orange, Dufus
County debut: 1995
County cap: 1998
50 wickets in a season: 1
1st-Class 50s: 1
1st-Class 5 w. in innings: 7
1st-Class 10 w. in match: 1
1st-Class catches: 13
One-Day 5 w. in innings: 1
Place in batting averages: 190th av. 20.00 (1997 304th av. 5.44)
Place in bowling averages: 73rd av. 28.37 (1997 101st av. 35.29)
Strike rate: 54.51 (career 50.15)

Parents: Bob and Pip
Marital status: Single
Family links with cricket: Brother plays league cricket
Education: St Andrews School, Eastbourne; Clifton College, Bristol
Qualifications: 9 GCSEs, 2 A-levels, NCA coaching first level
Overseas tours: Sussex YC to Barbados 1993, to Sri Lanka 1995
Overseas teams played for: Mashonaland, Zimbabwe 1996-97
Cricketers particularly admired: Curtly Ambrose, Jim Andrew, Darren Gough
Other sports followed: Hockey, golf, football (Brighton & Hove Albion)
Relaxations: Sleeping
Extras: Played in the Mashonaland side which defeated England on their 1996-97 tour of Zimbabwe, taking seven wickets in the match. Winner of an NBC Denis Compton Award for promising cricketers. Awarded county cap 1998
Opinions on cricket: 'With hard ground and indoor facilities, the workload of bowlers should be lessened in order to prolong careers and keep bowlers fresh.'
Best batting: 59 Sussex v Durham, Eastbourne 1998
Best bowling: 7-29 Sussex v Nottinghamshire, Trent Bridge 1998

1998 Season

	M	Inns	NO	Runs	HS	Avge	100s	50s	Ct	St	O	M	Runs	Wkts	Avge	Best	5wI	10wM
Test																		
All First	18	26	10	320	59	20.00	-	1	2	-	490.4	116	1532	54	28.37	7-29	3	1
1-day Int																		
NatWest	1	1	0	6	6	6.00	-	-	-	-	9	1	38	2	19.00	2-38	-	
B & H	1	1	0	2	2	2.00	-	-	-	-	10	0	57	2	28.50	2-57	-	
Sunday	16	8	4	50	15 *	12.50	-	-	6	-	107	5	494	25	19.76	4-21	-	

Career Performances

	M	Inns	NO	Runs	HS	Avge	100s	50s	Ct	St	Balls	Runs	Wkts	Avge	Best	5wI	10wM
Test																	
All First	41	57	23	397	59	11.67	-	1	13	-	6420	3657	128	28.57	7-29	7	1
1-day Int																	
NatWest	3	1	0	6	6	6.00	-	-	-	-	198	138	9	15.33	5-39	1	
B & H	1	1	0	2	2	2.00	-	-	-	-	60	57	2	28.50	2-57	-	
Sunday	32	15	8	67	15 *	9.57	-	-	8	-	1213	1048	37	28.32	4-21	-	

KNIGHT, N. V.   Warwickshire

Name: Nicholas Verity Knight
Role: Left-hand bat, right-arm medium-fast
bowler, close fielder, county vice-captain
Born: 28 November 1969, Watford
Height: 6ft 1in **Weight:** 13st
Nickname: Stitch, Fungus
County debut: 1991 (Essex),
1995 (Warwickshire)
County cap: 1994 (Essex),
1995 (Warwickshire)
Test debut: 1995
Tests: 12
One-Day Internationals: 27
1000 runs in a season: 2
1st-Class 50s: 38
1st-Class 100s: 20
1st-Class catches: 178
One-Day 100s: 8
Place in batting averages: 22nd av. 44.54
(1997 23rd av. 49.21)
Strike rate: (career 159.00)
Parents: John and Rosemary
Wife and date of marriage: Trudie, 3 October 1998
Family links with cricket: Father played for Cambridgeshire. Brother Andy plays
club cricket in local Cambridge leagues
Education: St John's School, Cambridge; Felsted Prep; Felsted School;
Loughborough University
Qualifications: 9 O-levels, 3 A-levels, BSc (Hons) Sociology, coaching qualification
Off-season: To Bangladesh with England for Wills International Cup, then to Australia
for CUB Series
Overseas tours: Felsted School to Australia 1986-87; England A to India 1994-95, to
Pakistan 1995-96, to Kenya and Sri Lanka 1997-98; England to Zimbabwe and New
Zealand 1996-97, to Sharjah 1997-98 (one-day tournament), to West Indies 1997-98
(one-day series), to Bangladesh (Wills International Cup) 1998, to Australia (CUB
Series) 1998-99
Overseas teams played for: Northern Districts, Sydney 1991-92; East Torrens,
Adelaide 1992-94
Cricketers particularly admired: David Gower, Graham Gooch
Young players to look out for: Mark Wagh, Anurag Singh
Other sports played: Rugby, hockey
Injuries: Out for one week with ankle injury

Relaxations: Eating good food, painting
Extras: Captained English Schools 1987 and 1988, England YC v New Zealand 1989 and Combined Universities 1991. Played hockey for Essex and Young England. Played rugby for Eastern Counties. Won *Daily Telegraph* award 1988; voted Gray-Nicolls Cricketer of the Year 1988, Cricket Society Cricketer of the Year 1989, Essex Young Player of the Year 1991 and Essex U19 Player of the Year. Left Essex at the end of 1994 season to join Warwickshire. Scored successive centuries in the Texaco Trophy against Pakistan in 1996. Won successive one-day Man of the Match awards v West Indies 1997-98
Opinions on cricket: 'Tea break not long enough and too many overs in a day.'
Best batting: 192 Warwickshire v Lancashire, Edgbaston 1998
Best bowling: 1-61 Essex v Middlesex, Uxbridge 1994

1998 Season

	M	Inns	NO	Runs	HS	Avge	100s	50s	Ct	St	O	M	Runs	Wkts	Avge	Best	5wI	10wM
Test	1	2	0	12	11	6.00	-	-	-	-								
All First	15	26	2	1069	192	44.54	4	4	19	-	1.5	0	15	0	-		-	-	-
1-day Int	6	6	0	334	94	55.66	-	4	3	-								
NatWest	3	3	1	156	143 *	78.00	1	-	1	-								
B & H	5	5	0	93	33	18.60	-	-	2	-								
Sunday	14	13	2	378	92 *	34.36	-	1	2	-								

Career Performances

	M	Inns	NO	Runs	HS	Avge	100s	50s	Ct	St	Balls	Runs	Wkts	Avge	Best	5wI	10wM
Test	12	21	0	585	113	27.85	1	4	21	-							
All First	128	216	23	7842	192	40.63	20	38	178	-	159	191	1	191.00	1-61	-	-
1-day Int	27	27	3	1151	125 *	47.95	3	7	10	-							
NatWest	15	15	2	575	151	44.23	2	3	6	-							
B & H	30	27	3	698	104	29.08	1	3	9	-	6	4	0	-		-	-
Sunday	89	79	11	2045	134	30.07	2	6	32	-	84	85	2	42.50	1-14	-

KNOTT, J. A. Surrey

Name: James Alan Knott
Role: Right-hand bat, leg-spin bowler, wicket-keeper
Born: 14 June 1975
Height: 5ft 6in **Weight:** 11st
Nickname: Knotty, Grub, Grot, Pigmy, Imp
County debut: 1995
1st-Class catches: 12
1st-Class stumpings: 2
Place in batting averages: 223rd av. 17.16 (1997 217th av. 19.66)

Parents: Alan and Janet
Marital status: Single
Family links with cricket: 'Dad played a bit'
Education: Herne Church of England Primary School; Dane Court Grammar School; City of Westminster College
Qualifications: 10 GCSEs, 2 A-levels, 2 GNVQ level 3s, basic basketball and cricket coach
Off-season: 'House-hunting and coaching'
Overseas tours: Canterbury District U15 to Holland
Overseas teams played for: Wayerley, Sydney, 1993-94; Pinelands CC, Cape Town 1996-98
Cricketers particularly admired: Graham Gooch, David Boon, Mike Atherton and 'I guess my old man helped me out a bit'

Young players to look out for: Chris Read
Other sports followed: Football (West Ham United)
Relaxations: 'Love movies (video and cinema). Enjoy reading, spending time with good friends, and of course a night out with the Surrey boys'
Extras: 'Shortest ever basketball captain at school.' Has never won a trophy through cricket but has won several through football
Opinions on cricket: 'Need to get youngsters playing a higher standard of cricket earlier. Need to start producing more players of Test calibre and introduce them early to it.'
Best batting: 49* Surrey v South Africa A, The Oval 1996

1998 Season

	M	Inns	NO	Runs	HS	Avge	100s	50s	Ct	St	O	M	Runs	Wkts	Avge	Best	5wl	10wM
Test																		
All First	5	9	3	103	41 *	17.16	-	-	1	-	1	0	2	0	-	-	-	-
1-day Int																		
NatWest																		
B & H																		
Sunday	4	4	0	109	98	27.25	-	1	4	-	1	0	7	0	-	-	-	

35. Who captained New Zealand in the 1987 World Cup?

FICA

333

Career Performances

	M	Inns	NO	Runs	HS	Avge	100s	50s	Ct	St	Balls	Runs	Wkts	Avge	Best	5wl	10wM
Test																	
All First	12	20	7	273	49 *	21.00	-	-	12	2	6	2	0	-	-	-	-
1-day Int																	
NatWest																	
B & H	2	1	0	10	10	10.00	-	-	6	-							
Sunday	8	7	0	132	98	18.85	-	1	9	-	6	7	0	-	-	-	

KRIKKEN, K. M. Derbyshire

Name: Karl Matthew Krikken
Role: Right-hand bat, wicket-keeper,
county vice-captain
Born: 9 April 1969, Bolton
Height: 5ft 10in **Weight:** 13st
Nickname: Krikk
County debut: 1987 (one-day),
1989 (first-class)
County cap: 1992
1st-Class 50s: 18
1st-Class 100s: 1
1st-Class catches: 419
1st-Class stumpings: 27
Place in batting averages: 192nd av. 19.95
(1997 173rd av. 24.26)
Parents: Brian and Irene
Wife and date of marriage:
Leesha, 3 October 1998
Children: Harry Evan, 20 December 1996
'and another one in December'

Family links with cricket: Father played for Lancashire and Worcestershire
Education: Horwich Parish Church School; Rivington and Blackrod High School and
Sixth Form College
Qualifications: 6 O-levels, 3 A-levels, advanced cricket coach
Career outside cricket: 'Dad'
Off-season: Coaching for Derbyshire
Overseas tours: Derbyshire to Bermuda 1993, to Torremolinos 1995
Overseas teams played for: CBC Old Boys, Kimberley, South Africa 1988-89; Green
Island, Dunedin, New Zealand 1990-91; United, Cape Town 1992-93; Rivertonians,
Cape Town 1993-94
Cricketers particularly admired: Kim Barnett, Alan Hill, Bob Taylor

Young players to look out for: Kevin Dean
Other sports followed: Football (Bolton FC, Wigan FC)
Injuries: Two weeks out with a fractured cheekbone
Relaxations: 'Spending time with wife and family'
Extras: Derbyshire Supporters' Player of the Year 1991 and 1996, Derbyshire Clubman of the Year 1993. Derbyshire vice-captain for the 1998 season
Best batting: 104 Derbyshire v Lancashire, Old Trafford 1996

1998 Season

	M	Inns	NO	Runs	HS	Avge	100s	50s	Ct	St	O	M	Runs	Wkts	Avge	Best	5wI	10wM
Test																		
All First	17	27	5	439	83	19.95	-	3	37	2								
1-day Int																		
NatWest	4	2	1	10	8 *	10.00	-	-	2	1								
B & H	4	3	1	23	22 *	11.50	-	-	1	1								
Sunday	12	7	3	49	16	12.25	-	-	16	5								

Career Performances

	M	Inns	NO	Runs	HS	Avge	100s	50s	Ct	St	Balls	Runs	Wkts	Avge	Best	5wI	10wM
Test																	
All First	168	248	51	4496	104	22.82	1	18	419	27	36	40	0	-	-	-	-
1-day Int																	
NatWest	18	11	5	166	55	27.66	-	1	14	1							
B & H	27	19	8	275	42 *	25.00	-	-	26	3							
Sunday	103	68	24	768	44 *	17.45	-	-	114	18							

FIGA

36. At Albury in the 1992 World Cup, Graeme Hick was bowled for a duck by an old schoolfriend. Who was he?

LACEY, S. J.   Derbyshire

Name: Simon James Lacey
Role: Right-hand bat, off-spin bowler
Born: 9 March 1975, Nottingham
Height: 5ft 11in **Weight:** 12st 11lbs
Nickname: Bone ('apparently I'm supposed to be bone idle'), Junior Champion
County debut: 1997
1st-Class 50s: 1
1st-Class catches: 2
Strike rate: 132.00 (career 99.27)
Parents: Phil and Anne
Marital status: Engaged to Keleigh
Education: Mundy Street School, Heanor; Aldercar Comprehensive School, Langley Mill; Mill Hill Sixth Form, Ripley
Education: 6 GCSEs, senior coaching award
Career outside cricket: Police force or PE teacher
Off-season: Coaching for the club
Cricketers particularly admired: Alec Stewart, Kim Barnett
Young players to look out for: Chris Schofield, Ian Blackwell
Other sports played/followed: Football ('a very big fan of the "Rams", Derby County. I also follow Ilkeston Town who play in the Dr Martens League'), snooker, ('I play for South East Derbyshire Snooker Club')
Relaxations: Listening to music, 'Ocean Colour Scene, Bluetones and Oasis being particular favourites, although I do listen to anything'
Extras: Was a member of the England Junior Volleyball squad in 1991. Captained the NAYC at U19 level against ESCA at Lord's in 1994
Opinions on cricket: 'Play far too many games. There isn't enough time to practise and develop techniques once the season is under way. The third umpire should be used for all possible decisions that it can be used for. The technology is there so it might as well be used.'
Best batting: 50 Derbyshire v Somerset, Derby 1997
Best bowling: 3-97 Derbyshire v Essex, Southend 1997

---

37. Which country bowled out West Indies for 93
at Pune on 29 February 1996?

FICA

1998 Season

	M	Inns	NO	Runs	HS	Avge	100s	50s	Ct	St	O	M	Runs	Wkts	Avge	Best	5wI	10wM
Test																		
All First	3	3	0	28	17	9.33	-	-	1	-	88	19	274	4	68.50	2-89	-	-
1-day Int																		
NatWest																		
B & H																		
Sunday	1	0	0	0	0	-	-	-	-	-	8	0	50	1	50.00	1-50	-	

Career Performances

	M	Inns	NO	Runs	HS	Avge	100s	50s	Ct	St	Balls	Runs	Wkts	Avge	Best	5wI	10wM
Test																	
All First	9	11	4	157	50	22.42	-	1	2	-	1092	565	11	51.36	3-97	-	-
1-day Int																	
NatWest																	
B & H																	
Sunday	4	1	0	9	9	9.00	-	-	-	-	114	112	2	56.00	1-38	-	

LAMPITT, S. R. Worcestershire

Name: Stuart Richard Lampitt
Role: Right-hand bat, right-arm
medium bowler
Born: 29 July 1966, Wolverhampton
Height: 5ft 11in **Weight:** 14st
Nickname: Jed
County debut: 1985
County cap: 1989
50 wickets in a season: 6
1st-Class 50s: 17
1st-Class 100s: 1
1st-Class 5 w. in innings: 17
1st-Class catches: 125
One-Day 5 w. in innings: 3
Place in batting averages: 165th av. 22.90
(1997 136th av. 27.70)
Place in bowling averages: 60th av. 26.60
(1997 108th av. 37.20)
Strike rate: 49.92 (career 55.24)
Parents: Joseph Charles and Muriel Ann
Education: Kingswinford Secondary School; Dudley College of Technology
Qualifications: 7 O-levels, Diploma in Business Studies, NCA advanced coach

Career outside cricket: Youth development coach at Worcestershire CCC
Off-season: Coaching in schools around the Worcs area
Overseas tours: NCA U19 to Bermuda; Worcestershire to Bahamas 1990, to Zimbabwe 1990-91, to South Africa 1991-92, to Barbados 1996
Overseas teams played for: Mangere, Auckland 1986-88; University CC, Perth 1991-93
Cricketers particularly admired: Ian Botham, Malcolm Marshall
Young players to look out for: 'The good ones'
Other sports played: Golf, fishing
Other sports followed: Football (Wolves FC)
Relaxations: 'Spending time with our Clare'
Extras: Took five wickets and made 42 for Stourbridge in final of the William Younger Cup at Lord's in 1986. One of the Whittingdale Young Players of the Year 1990. 'Must be the only bowler to be hit for six first ball by Adrian Jones and Phil Tufnell (two master batsmen)'
Opinions on cricket: 'Good game, good game!!'
Best batting: 122 Worcestershire v Middlesex, Lord's 1994
Best bowling: 5-32 Worcestershire v Kent, Worcester 1989

1998 Season

	M	Inns	NO	Runs	HS	Avge	100s	50s	Ct	St	O	M	Runs	Wkts	Avge	Best	5wI	10wM
Test																		
All First	18	28	7	481	48	22.90	-	-	8	-	416	97	1330	50	26.60	5-33	4	
1-day Int																		
NatWest	1	1	0	54	54	54.00	-	1	-	-	12	1	44	2	22.00	2-44	-	
B & H	4	3	0	35	22	11.66	-	-	1	-	29	2	133	3	44.33	1-28	-	
Sunday	15	11	0	124	39	11.27	-	-	6	-	86.4	4	397	15	26.46	4-33	-	

Career Performances

	M	Inns	NO	Runs	HS	Avge	100s	50s	Ct	St	Balls	Runs	Wkts	Avge	Best	5wI	10wM
Test																	
All First	194	252	56	4700	122	23.97	1	17	125	-	26629	14494	482	30.07	5-32	17	-
1-day Int																	
NatWest	23	16	4	217	54	18.08	-	1	7	-	1223	885	35	25.28	5-22	1	
B & H	39	22	7	277	41	18.46	-	-	11	-	2056	1363	63	21.63	6-26	1	
Sunday	153	90	30	1163	41 *	19.38	-	-	46	-	5308	4272	168	25.42	5-67	1	

LANEY, J. S.   Hampshire

Name: Jason Scott Laney
Role: Right-hand bat, off-spin bowler
Born: 27 April 1973, Winchester
Height: 5ft 10in **Weight:** 12st 7lbs
Nickname: Chucky, The Rimmer, Wasp
County debut: 1993 (one-day),
1995 (first-class)
County cap: 1996
1000 runs in a season: 1
1st-Class 50s: 15
1st-Class 100s: 5
1st-Class catches: 38
One-Day 100s: 1
Place in batting averages: 222nd av. 17.23
(1997 11th av. 32.61)
Parents: Geoff and Pam
Marital status: Single
Family links with cricket: Grandfather
played good club cricket.

Education: Pewsey Vale Comprehensive; St John's, Marlborough; Leeds Metropolitan
University
Qualifications: 8 GCSEs, 2 A-levels, BA(Hons) in Human Movement Studies
Off-season: 'Yes, I know. Don't remind me!'
Overseas tours: England U18 to Canada 1991
Overseas teams played for: Waikato, New Zealand 1994-95; Matabeleland and Old
Miltonians, Zimbabwe 1995-96; DHS Old Boys, South Africa 1996-97
Cricketers particularly admired: Michael Slater, Courtney Walsh, Robin Smith,
Malcolm Marshall, Ian Botham, Paul Baker, Gary Sobers
Young players to look out for: Alex Morris and Dimitri Mascarenhas ('for their
cricket and spit-roasting abilities'), Graham Napier, John Rickard Jnr
Other sports played: Golf (10 handicap)
Other sports followed: Football
Relaxations: 'Playing golf with Ferret whilst ignoring the constant drivel he comes
out with. Socialising, drinking, laughing, "Jackpot Cafe", music'
Extras: Hampshire Young Cricketer of the Year 1995. Only Hampshire cricketer to
score a century before lunch on debut in the NatWest trophy
Opinions on cricket: 'Great game. Fantastic bunch of lads. How did a team that
finished top half in the Sunday League and County Championship and reach the
NatWest semi-finals not have any players on any winter tour? North Walls is the best
cricket wicket I have ever played on.'
Best batting: 112 Hampshire v Oxford University, The Parks 1996

1998 Season

	M	Inns	NO	Runs	HS	Avge	100s	50s	Ct	St	O	M	Runs	Wkts	Avge	Best	5wI	10wM
Test																		
All First	8	13	0	224	101	17.23	1	1	10	-	3	0	15	0	-	-	-	-
1-day Int																		
NatWest	3	3	0	72	47	24.00	-	-	1	-								
B & H	4	4	0	32	12	8.00	-	-	2	-								
Sunday	6	6	0	38	18	6.33	-	-	3	-								

Career Performances

	M	Inns	NO	Runs	HS	Avge	100s	50s	Ct	St	Balls	Runs	Wkts	Avge	Best	5wI	10wM
Test																		
All First	51	91	2	2808	112	31.55	5	15	38	-	150	98	0	-	-	-	-
1-day Int																		
NatWest	8	8	0	412	153	51.50	1	1	3	-							
B & H	12	12	0	180	41	15.00	-	-	3	-							
Sunday	37	37	0	870	69	23.51	-	4	11	-							

LANGER, J. L.   Middlesex

Name: Justin Lee Langer
Role: Left-hand bat, right-arm medium
bowler, county vice-captain
Born: 21 November 1970, Subiaco,
Western Australia
Height: 5ft 8in **Weight:** 12st 4lbs
Nickname: JL
County debut: 1998
County cap: 1998
Test debut: 1992-93
Tests: 8
One-Day Internationals: 8
1000 runs in a season: 1
1st-Class 50s: 33
1st-Class 100s: 19
1st-Class 200s: 5
1st-Class catches: 79
One-Day 100s: 1
Place in batting averages: 5th av. 62.95
(1997 37th av. 44.57)
Strike rate: (career 88.00)
Parents: Colin and Joy-Anne

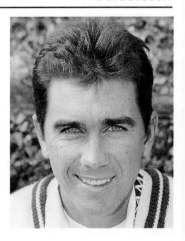

Wife and date of marriage: Sue, 13 April 1996
Children: Jessica, 28 March 1997; second 'due November 1998'
Family links with cricket: Uncle, Robbie Langer, played Sheffield Shield cricket for Western Australia and World Series for Australia
Education: Liwara Catholic School; Aquinas College, Perth; University of Western Australia
Career outside cricket: Writing, stockbroking
Off-season: Playing in Australia
Overseas tours: Australia to New Zealand 1992-93, to South Africa 1996-97, to England 1997, to Pakistan 1998-99; Young Australia to England 1995
Overseas teams played for: Western Australia 1990 –
Cricketers particularly admired: Graham Gooch, Mike Gatting, Graeme Hick, Allan Border, David Boon, Dennis Lillee
Young players to look out for: 'Ace' Shah, Jamie Hewitt
Other sports played: Tennis, golf, Aussie rules, martial arts (has black belts in judo and taekwondo)
Other sports followed: Football (Man Utd), Aussie rules (West Coast Eagles)
Relaxations: Family, writing
Extras: A prolific run-scorer for Western Australia in recent years, Justin Langer was drafted into the Australia 1992-93 side after Damien Martyn suffered an injury during the practice session for the match against the West Indies. He scored an heroic 54 in the face of some aggressive bowling by the West Indies but played in only another five Tests over the next three years until he forced his way back into the Test side in 1996-97 – ironically against the West Indies. Scored 233* on first-class debut for Middlesex at Lord's v Somerset 1998. With Mike Gatting, took part in an opening stand of 372 v Essex at Southgate in 1998, setting a new county record for the first wicket; during his innings of 166 he became the first batsman to reach 1000 first-class runs for the 1998 season. Scored maiden Test century (116) v Pakistan at Peshawar in 1998. Has contributed articles to the Australian Cricket Board website. Awarded county cap 1998. Appointed Middlesex vice-captain for 1999
Best batting: 274* Western Australia v South Australia, Perth 1996-97
Best bowling: 2-17 Australia A v South Africa, Brisbane 1997-98
Stop press: Scored 179* and 52 in the third Test v England at Adelaide 1998-99, receiving Man of the Match award. Selected for Australia's tour of West Indies 1998-99

1998 Season

	M	Inns	NO	Runs	HS	Avge	100s	50s	Ct	St	O	M	Runs	Wkts	Avge	Best	5wI	10wM
Test																		
All First	15	28	5	1448	233 *	62.95	4	6	12	-	13	5	34	1	34.00	1-10	-	-
1-day Int																		
NatWest	3	3	1	218	114 *	109.00	1	1	-	-	5	0	45	1	45.00	1-45	-	
B & H	5	5	0	136	71	27.20	-	1	3	-								
Sunday	12	12	1	427	87 *	38.81	-	3	6	-	16.2	0	96	4	24.00	3-51	-	

Career Performances

	M	Inns	NO	Runs	HS	Avge	100s	50s	Ct	St	Balls	Runs	Wkts	Avge	Best	5wI	10wM
Test	8	12	0	272	69	22.66	-	3	2	-							
All First	104	182	24	8443	274 *	53.43	24	33	79	-	264	109	3	36.33	2-17	-	-
1-day Int	8	7	2	160	36	32.00	-	-	2	1							
NatWest	3	3	1	218	114 *	109.00	1	1	-	-	30	45	1	45.00	1-45	-	
B & H	5	5	0	136	71	27.20	-	1	3	-							
Sunday	12	12	1	427	87 *	38.81	-	3	6	-	98	96	4	24.00	3-51	-	

LARA, B. C. — Warwickshire

Name: Brian Charles Lara
Role: Left-hand bat, leg-spin bowler
Born: 2 May 1969, Port of Spain, Trinidad
County debut: 1994
County cap: 1994
Test debut: 1990-91
Tests: 54
One-Day Internationals: 130
1000 runs in a season: 2
1st-Class 50s: 55
1st-Class 100s: 29
1st-Class 200s: 3
1st-Class 300s: 1
1st-Class 500s: 1
1st-Class catches: 197
One-Day 100s: 14
Place in batting averages: 41st av. 39.73
Strike rate: (career 212.50)

Overseas tours: West Indies to Pakistan 1990-91, to England 1991, to Australia 1992-93, to Sri Lanka 1993-94, to India 1994-95, to New Zealand 1994-95, to England 1995, to Australia 1995-96, to India and Pakistan (World Cup) 1996-97, to Australia 1996-97, to Sharjah 1997-98, to Pakistan 1997-98, to Bangladesh 1998-99, to South Africa 1998-99
Overseas teams played for: Trinidad & Tobago 1987-88 –
Extras: In an amazing few weeks in 1994, he broke the record for the highest Test score (375) against England at Antigua, and the highest first-class score (501*) for Warwickshire against Durham at Edgbaston. He also passed 1000 runs in an English season in only seven innings, equalling the record held by Don Bradman, scoring a record seven centuries in his first eight innings. He also created a record by scoring centuries in his first four Championship innings. Was one of *Wisden*'s Cricketers of the Year 1995. Appointed captain of Trinidad 1995-96. Rejoined Warwickshire for the

1998 season after an absence of four years and was appointed captain for the 1998 season. He replaced Courtney Walsh as West Indies captain for the series against England in 1997-98. Released by Warwickshire at end of 1998 season
Best batting: 501* Warwickshire v Durham, Edgbaston 1994
Best bowling: 1-14 Trinidad & Tobago v Windward Islands, Dominica 1996-97

1998 Season

	M	Inns	NO	Runs	HS	Avge	100s	50s	Ct	St	O	M	Runs	Wkts	Avge	Best	5wl	10wM
Test																		
All First	15	26	0	1033	226	39.73	3	3	15	-	5	0	44	0	-	-	-	-
1-day Int																		
NatWest	3	3	0	147	133	49.00	1	-	1	-								
B & H	5	5	1	242	101	60.50	1	-	1	-								
Sunday	14	13	1	285	60	23.75	-	2	5	-								

Career Performances

	M	Inns	NO	Runs	HS	Avge	100s	50s	Ct	St	Balls	Runs	Wkts	Avge	Best	5wl	10wM
Test	54	91	3	4550	375	51.70	10	23	75	-	60	28	0	-	-	-	-
All First	155	255	7	12676	501 *	51.11	34	55	197	-	425	358	2	179.00	1-14	-	-
1-day Int	130	128	12	5448	169	46.96	12	36	62	-	30	34	2	17.00	2-5	-	
NatWest	8	8	0	305	133	38.12	1	1	4	-							
B & H	8	8	1	354	101	50.57	1	1	1	-							
Sunday	28	27	1	649	75	24.96	-	5	11	-							

38. What is the World Cup claim to fame
of N. E. Clarke of the Netherlands?

FIGA

LARAMAN, A. W. — Middlesex

Name: Aaron William Laraman
Role: Right-hand bat, right-arm fast bowler
Born: 10 January 1979, Enfield
Height: 6ft 5in **Weight:** 13st 5lbs
Nickname: Lazza
County debut: 1998 (one-day)
Parents: William and Lynda
Marital status: Single
Education: St Paul's C of E School; Enfield Grammar School
Qualifications: 8 GCSEs
Off-season: Coaching, and playing in Christchurch, New Zealand
Overseas tours: England U17 to Holland 1995; England U19 to South Africa 1997-98
Cricketers particularly admired: Viv Richards, Ian Botham
Young players to look out for: Robert Key, Stephen Peters
Other sports followed: Football (Arsenal)
Injuries: Lower left leg and lower back
Relaxations: Working out at the gym, football, golf
Extras: Enfield Grammar School cap at the age of 13. Middlesex Colts county cap. Seaxe 2nd XI Player of the Year 1997
Opinions on cricket: 'In the game today, I feel that a high level of fitness is required. The game is becoming much more exciting and much more of a spectator sport.'

1998 Season

	M	Inns	NO	Runs	HS	Avge	100s	50s	Ct	St	O	M	Runs	Wkts	Avge	Best	5wI	10wM
Test																		
All First	1	0	0	0	0	-	-	-	-	-								
1-day Int																		
NatWest																		
B & H																		
Sunday	2	1	0	3	3	3.00	-	-	2	-	3.3	0	24	0	-		-	-

FIGA

39. In which World Cup tournament was the current
50 overs per innings format adopted?

Career Performances

	M	Inns	NO	Runs	HS	Avge	100s	50s	Ct	St	Balls	Runs	Wkts	Avge	Best	5wl	10wM
Test																	
All First	1	0	0	0	0	-	-	-	-	-							
1-day Int																	
NatWest																	
B & H																	
Sunday	2	1	0	3	3	3.00	-	-	2	-	21	24	0	-	-	-	-

LATHWELL, M. N.   Somerset

Name: Mark Nicholas Lathwell
Role: Right-hand bat, right-arm medium and off-break bowler
Born: 26 December 1971, Bletchley, Bucks
Height: 5ft 8in **Weight:** 12st
Nickname: Lathers, Rowdy, Trough
County debut: 1991
County cap: 1992
Test debut: 1993
Tests: 2
1000 runs in a season: 4
1st-Class 50s: 48
1st-Class 100s: 11
1st-Class 200s: 1
1st-Class catches: 92
One-Day 100s: 4
Place in batting averages: 100th av. 30.21
(1997 137th av. 27.63)
Strike rate: 30.00 (career 84.76)
Parents: Derek Peter and Valerie
Wife: Lisa

Children: Jason, 16 January 1995
Family links with cricket: Brother plays local club cricket; father is a 'retired' club cricketer and now senior coach
Education: Overstone Primary, Wing, Bucks; Southmead Primary, Braunton, North Devon; Braunton Comprehensive
Qualifications: 5 GCSEs
Overseas tours: England A to Australia 1992-93, to South Africa 1993-94
Cricketers particularly admired: Ian Botham, Graham Gooch
Other sports followed: Snooker, darts
Relaxations: Cooking and eating

Extras: Spent one season on Lord's groundstaff. Played for England U19 v Australia U19 1991. PCA Young Player of the Year and Somerset Player of the Year 1992. Cricket Writers' Club Young Cricketer of the Year 1993

Opinions on cricket: 'The size of the lunches at most grounds just cannot sustain you all day in the field.'

Best batting: 206 Somerset v Surrey, Bath 1994

Best bowling: 2-21 Somerset v Sussex, Hove 1994

1998 Season

	M	Inns	NO	Runs	HS	Avge	100s	50s	Ct	St	O	M	Runs	Wkts	Avge	Best	5wI	10wM
Test																		
All First	12	19	0	574	106	30.21	1	5	7	-								
1-day Int																		
NatWest	2	1	0	6	6	6.00	-	-	2	-								
B & H																		
Sunday	14	13	2	345	87	31.36	-	2	3	-								

Career Performances

	M	Inns	NO	Runs	HS	Avge	100s	50s	Ct	St	Balls	Runs	Wkts	Avge	Best	5wI	10wM
Test	2	4	0	78	33	19.50	-	-	-	-							
All First	134	237	9	7768	206	34.07	12	48	92	-	1102	684	13	52.61	2-21	-	-
1-day Int																	
NatWest	18	17	0	465	103	27.35	1	2	7	-	66	23	1	23.00	1-23	-	
B & H	21	21	0	821	121	39.09	2	6	7	-	25	50	0	-	-	-	
Sunday	104	102	5	2645	117	27.26	1	16	25	-	102	85	0	-	-	-	

LAW, D. R. C.   Essex

Name: Danny Richard Charles Law
Role: Right-hand bat, right-arm fast bowler
Born: 15 July 1975, Lambeth, London
Height: 6ft 5in **Weight:** 13st 7lbs
Nickname: Decas, Desperate
County debut: 1993 (Sussex), 1997 (Essex)
County cap: 1996 (Sussex)
1st-Class 50s: 8
1st-Class 100s: 1
1st-Class 5 w. in innings: 4
1st-Class catches: 34
Place in batting averages: 209th av. 18.64 (1997 237th av. 16.96)
Place in bowling averages: 121st av. 36.03 (1997 80th av. 31.25)
Strike rate: 51.27 (career 51.61)

Parents: Richard (deceased) and Claudette
Marital status: 'Attached'
Education: Wolverton Hall School; Steyning Grammar School
Qualifications: Cricket coach
Overseas tours: Sussex Schools U16 to Jersey 1991; England U18 to South Africa 1992-93, to Denmark 1993; England U19 to Sri Lanka 1993-94
Cricketers particularly admired: Michael Holding, Allan Donald, Courtney Walsh, Franklyn Stephenson, John North, Chris Tugwell
Other sports followed: Most sports
Relaxations: Listening to music, spending time at home
Extras: Left Sussex during the 1996 off-season and joined Essex for the 1997 season

on a three-year contract. Took Championship hat-trick v Durham at Riverside 1998
Opinions on cricket: 'The 2nd XI Championship should be increased from a three-day game to a four-day game so that younger players are used to playing four-day cricket and are not thrown in at the deep end if they progress to first-class cricket.'
Best batting: 115 Sussex v Young Australia, Hove 1995
Best bowling: 5-33 Sussex v Durham, Hove 1996

1998 Season

	M	Inns	NO	Runs	HS	Avge	100s	50s	Ct	St	O	M	Runs	Wkts	Avge	Best	5wI	10wM
Test																		
All First	14	25	0	466	65	18.64	-	3	10	-	247.5	34	1045	29	36.03	5-46	1	-
1-day Int																		
NatWest	2	1	0	47	47	47.00	-	-	-	-	3	0	15	0	-	-	-	-
B & H	3	3	1	49	36*	24.50	-	-	-	-								
Sunday	16	11	2	208	50	23.11	-	1	3	-	22	0	117	3	39.00	1-36	-	

Career Performances

	M	Inns	NO	Runs	HS	Avge	100s	50s	Ct	St	Balls	Runs	Wkts	Avge	Best	5wI	10wM
Test																	
All First	61	97	0	1836	115	18.92	1	8	34	-	5833	3754	113	33.22	5-33	4	-
1-day Int																	
NatWest	11	7	0	112	47	16.00	-	-	3	-	99	95	1	95.00	1-2	-	
B & H	9	8	1	95	36*	13.57	-	-	1	-	96	76	1	76.00	1-44	-	
Sunday	58	48	10	1029	82	27.07	-	5	13	-	857	822	25	32.88	3-34	-	

LAW, S. G.   Essex

Name: Stuart Grant Law
Role: Right-hand bat, right-arm medium bowler
Born: 18 October 1968, Herston, Brisbane, Australia
Height: 6ft 2in
County debut: 1996
County cap: 1996
Test debut: 1995-96
Tests: 1
One-Day Internationals: 51
1000 runs in a season: 3
1st-Class 50s: 54
1st-Class 100s: 30
1st-Class 5 w. in innings: 1
1st-Class catches: 161
One-Day 100s: 10
Place in batting averages: 38th av. 40.91
(1997 9th av. 57.00)
Strike rate: (career 99.52)
Education: Craigslea State High School
Off-season: Playing for Queensland and Australia
Overseas tours: Young Australia to England 1995; Australia to India and Pakistan (World Cup) 1995-96, to Sri Lanka, India and South Africa 1996-97, to New Zealand 1997-98
Overseas teams played for: Queensland 1988 –
Extras: Made his first-class debut for Queensland as a 19-year-old scoring 179 in only his second appearance, still his highest first-class score. Made his Test debut for Australia against Sri Lanka at Perth in 1995-96 and scored an unbeaten 54. Played in all 17 One-Day Internationals for Australia in 1995-96. Man of the Match in the 1997 NatWest final at Lord's. One of *Wisden*'s five Cricketers of the Year 1998
Best batting: 179 Queensland v Tasmania, Brisbane 1988-89
Best bowling: 5-39 Queensland v Tasmania, Brisbane 1995-96

---

40. Three Hadlees played for New Zealand in the
1975 World Cup. Name them.

1998 Season

	M	Inns	NO	Runs	HS	Avge	100s	50s	Ct	St	O	M	Runs	Wkts	Avge	Best	5wI	10wM
Test																		
All First	14	26	2	982	165	40.91	2	3	19	-								
1-day Int																		
NatWest	2	1	0	2	2	2.00	-	-	2	-	3	1	12	0	-		-	-
B & H	7	6	0	139	46	23.16	-	-	7	-	15.2	0	79	5	15.80	2-13	-	
Sunday	15	14	1	487	126	37.46	1	2	12	-	3	0	22	1	22.00	1-10	-	

Career Performances

	M	Inns	NO	Runs	HS	Avge	100s	50s	Ct	St	Balls	Runs	Wkts	Avge	Best	5wI	10wM
Test	1	1	1	54	54*	-	-	1	1	-	18	9	0	-	-	-	-
All First	153	259	27	10753	179	46.34	30	54	161	-	6668	3150	67	47.01	5-39	1	-
1-day Int	51	48	4	1206	110	27.40	1	7	12	-	795	627	12	52.25	2-22	-	
NatWest	11	10	1	626	107	69.55	3	3	8	-	385	302	7	43.14	2-36	-	
B & H	16	15	0	545	116	36.33	1	2	10	-	354	320	9	35.55	2-13	-	
Sunday	44	43	2	1562	126	38.09	5	5	24	-	760	682	20	34.10	4-37	-	

LAW, W. L.   Glamorgan

Name: Wayne Lincoln Law
Role: Right-hand bat
Born: 4 September 1978, Swansea
Height: 5ft 10in **Weight:** 11st 4lbs
Nickname: Sods, Alien
County debut: 1997
1st-Class 50s: 2
1st-Class 100s: 1
1st-Class catches: 4
Place in batting averages: 54th av. 37.00
Strike rate: 46.00 (career 46.00)
Parents: Lincoln and Barbara
Marital status: Single
Education: Halfway School, Llanelli; Graig
School, Llanelli
Qualifications: 1 GCSE, NCA senior and
advanced coaching awards
Off-season: Coaching
Overseas tours: Dyfed U15 to Zimbabwe
1994
Cricketers particularly admired: Steve James, Anthony Cottey, Matthew Maynard,
Philip George

Young players to look out for: Philip George, John Derrick, Michael Powell, Owen Parkin ('only 26 years old')
Other sports followed: Football
Injuries: Out for two weeks with a hamstring injury
Relaxations: Squash, running and reading
Extras: Scored first-class century (131) v Lancashire at Colwyn Bay in 1998 in only his second Championship match
Best batting: 131 Glamorgan v Lancashire, Colwyn Bay 1998
Best bowling: 2-29 Glamorgan v Cambridge University, Fenner's 1998

1998 Season

	M	Inns	NO	Runs	HS	Avge	100s	50s	Ct	St	O	M	Runs	Wkts	Avge	Best	5wI	10wM
Test																		
All First	9	14	2	444	131	37.00	1	2	4	-	23	2	85	3	28.33	2-29	-	-
1-day Int																		
NatWest																		
B & H																		
Sunday	4	4	1	41	24	13.66	-	-	2	-								

Career Performances

	M	Inns	NO	Runs	HS	Avge	100s	50s	Ct	St	Balls	Runs	Wkts	Avge	Best	5wI	10wM
Test																	
All First	10	15	3	482	131	40.16	1	2	4	-	138	85	3	28.33	2-29	-	-
1-day Int																	
NatWest																	
B & H																	
Sunday	6	6	1	64	24	12.80	-	-	3	-							

LAZENBURY, P. S.   Gloucestershire

Name: Paul Stuart Lazenbury
Role: Left-hand bat, leg-spin bowler
Born: 10 August 1978, Bath
Height: 6ft **Weight:** 12st 2lbs
Nickname: Lazers
County debut: No first-team appearance
Parents: Elizabeth and Stuart
Marital status: Single
Family links with cricket: Father played local club cricket
Education: Malmesbury Church of England; Malmesbury Comprehensive
Qualifications: 9 GCSEs, 1 GNVQ
Career outside cricket: Working in sports retail

Off-season: Going to New Zealand to play club cricket
Overseas tours: Gloucestershire Gypsies to Cape Town 1997-98
Cricketers particularly admired: Mike Atherton
Young players to look out for: Dom Hewson, Matt Windows, Jon Lewis
Other sports played: Golf, 'I like to have a go at most sports'
Other sports followed: Football (Bristol Rovers), 'I enjoy watching most sports'
Relaxations: Eating out, 'and having a few drinks with the lads'
Extras: Scored 1000 2nd XI runs in debut season
Opinions on cricket: '2nd XI matches should be four days and games to be played on main

county grounds all of the time. Lunches should be one hour and teas 30 minutes.'

LEATHERDALE, D. A. Worcestershire

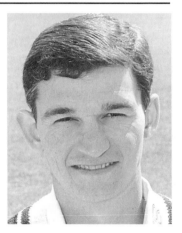

Name: David Anthony Leatherdale
Role: Right-hand bat, right-arm medium bowler, cover fielder
Born: 26 November 1967, Bradford
Height: 5ft 10in **Weight:** 11st
Nickname: Lugsy, Spock
County debut: 1988
County cap: 1994
1000 runs in a season: 1
1st-Class 50s: 36
1st-Class 100s: 10
1st-Class 5 w. in innings: 2
1st-Class catches: 120
Place in batting averages: 70th av. 33.36 (1997 17th av. 52.11)
Place in bowling averages: 13th av. 19.80 (1997 60th av. 28.53)
Strike rate: 31.90 (career 52.35)
Parents: Paul and Rosalyn
Wife's name: Vanessa
Children: Callum Edward, 6 July 1990

Family links with cricket: Father played local cricket; brother plays for East Bierley in Bradford League; brother-in-law played for England YC in 1979
Education: Bolton Royd Primary School; Pudsey Grangefield Secondary School
Qualifications: 8 O-levels, 2 A-levels; NCA coaching award (stage 1)
Overseas tours: England Indoor to Australia and New Zealand 1994-95
Overseas teams played for: Pretoria Police, South Africa 1987-88
Cricketers particularly admired: Mark Scott, George Batty, Peter Kippax
Other sports followed: Football, American football
Relaxations: Golf
Opinions on cricket: '2nd XI wickets need upgrading as many outgrounds are not up to standard, especially if four-day cricket is extended into the 2nd XI Championship.'
Best batting: 157 Worcestershire v Somerset, Worcester 1991
Best bowling: 5-20 Worcestershire v Gloucestershire, Worcester 1998

1998 Season

	M	Inns	NO	Runs	HS	Avge	100s	50s	Ct	St	O	M	Runs	Wkts	Avge	Best	5wl	10wM
Test																		
All First	18	32	2	1001	137	33.36	2	4	9	-	111.4	22	416	21	19.80	5-20	1	-
1-day Int																		
NatWest	1	1	0	3	3	3.00	-	-	2	-	5	0	29	0	-	-	-	-
B & H	4	4	1	31	25	10.33	-	-	2	-	16.2	1	68	2	34.00	2-18	-	
Sunday	16	14	3	176	36 *	16.00	-	-	5	-	51	1	314	14	22.42	4-19	-	

Career Performances

	M	Inns	NO	Runs	HS	Avge	100s	50s	Ct	St	Balls	Runs	Wkts	Avge	Best	5wl	10wM
Test																	
All First	143	225	26	6778	157	34.06	10	36	120	-	3560	2063	68	30.33	5-20	2	-
1-day Int																	
NatWest	20	17	1	300	43	18.75	-	-	7	-	166	135	3	45.00	3-14	-	
B & H	28	23	5	298	66	16.55	-	1	6	-	380	256	11	23.27	4-13	-	
Sunday	127	104	18	1571	62 *	18.26	-	6	61	-	917	831	43	19.32	4-19	-	

LEHMANN, D. S.   Yorkshire

Name: Darren Scott Lehmann
Role: Left-hand bat, slow left-arm bowler
Born: 5 February 1970, Gawler, Australia
County debut: 1997
County cap: 1997
Test debut: 1997-98
Tests: 1
One-Day Internationals: 24
1000 runs in a season: 1
1st-Class 50s: 56
1st-Class 100s: 28
1st-Class 200s: 5
1st-Class catches: 78
One-Day 100s: 3
Place in batting averages: 7th av. 60.56
(1997 5th av. 63.00)
Strike rate: 57.00 (career 107.10)
Off-season: Playing for South Australia
Overseas tours: Australia to Sri Lanka

1996-97, to New Zealand 1997-98, to Sharjah 1997-98, to India 1997-98, to Pakistan
1998-99, to Bangladesh 1998-99
Overseas teams played for: South Australia 1987-1990; Victoria 1990-93; South
Australia 1993 –
Extras: Played for Australia in their successful Carlton Union One-Day International
series win 1997-98. Relased by Yorkshire at end of 1998 season
Best batting: 255 South Australia v Queensland, Adelaide 1996-97
Best bowling: 4-42 Yorkshire v Kent, Maidstone 1998

1998 Season

	M	Inns	NO	Runs	HS	Avge	100s	50s	Ct	St	O	M	Runs	Wkts	Avge	Best	5wl	10wM
Test																		
All First	10	16	0	969	200	60.56	3	4	4	-	57	16	124	6	20.66	4-42	-	-
1-day Int																		
NatWest	2	1	0	1	1	1.00	-	-	1	-	7	2	14	1	14.00	1-14	-	
B & H	6	6	2	380	119	95.00	2	1	2	-	13	0	55	4	13.75	2-17	-	
Sunday	11	11	0	455	99	41.36	-	4	3	-	25	0	125	3	41.66	2-24	-	

Career Performances

	M	Inns	NO	Runs	HS	Avge	100s	50s	Ct	St	Balls	Runs	Wkts	Avge	Best	5wI	10wM
Test	1	1	0	52	52	52.00	-	1	2	-	42	27	1	27.00	1-27	-	-
All First	133	228	11	11288	255	52.01	33	56	78	-	2035	1047	19	55.10	4-42	-	-
1-day Int	24	23	4	542	70	28.52	-	3	6	-	234	200	5	40.00	2-11	-	
NatWest	5	4	0	133	105	33.25	1	-	1	-	48	19	1	19.00	1-14	-	
B & H	11	11	2	546	119	60.66	2	2	3	-	96	77	4	19.25	2-17	-	
Sunday	27	27	3	1098	99	45.75	-	10	7	-	226	210	7	30.00	3-43	-	

LEWIS, C. C. Leicestershire

Name: Christopher Clairmonte Lewis
Role: Right-hand bat, right-arm
fast-medium bowler, county vice-captain
Born: 14 February 1968, Georgetown,
Guyana
Height: 6ft 2in **Weight:** 13st
Nickname: Carl
County debut: 1987 (Leics), 1992 (Notts),
1996 (Surrey)
County cap: 1990 (Leics), 1994 (Notts),
1996 (Surrey)
Test debut: 1990
Tests: 32
One-Day Internationals: 53
50 wickets in a season: 2
1st-Class 50s: 32
1st-Class 100s: 7
1st-Class 5w. in innings: 20
1st-Class 10 w. in match: 3
1st-Class catches: 141
One-Day 5 w. in innings: 2

Place in batting averages: 71st av. 33.36 (1997 189th av. 22.88)
Place in bowling averages: 47th av. 24.92 (1997 66th av. 29.39)
Strike rate: 41.02 (career 58.20)
Parents: Philip and Patricia
Marital status: Single
Education: Willesden High School
Qualifications: 2 O-levels
Overseas tours: England YC to Australia (Youth World Cup) 1987-88; England A to
Kenya and Zimbabwe 1989-90; England to West Indies 1989-90, to Australia 1990-91,
to New Zealand 1991-92, to India and Sri Lanka 1992-93, to West Indies 1993-94,
to Australia 1994-95

Cricketers particularly admired: Graham Gooch, Robin Smith
Other sports followed: Snooker, football, darts, American football, basketball
Relaxations: Music, sleeping
Extras: Joined England's tour of West Indies in 1989-90 as a replacement for Ricky Ellcock. Suffers from Raynaud's disease, a problem of blood circulation, and has to spend one night in hospital every two months to have the disease treated. Left Leicestershire at the end of 1991 season and signed for Nottinghamshire. Hit first Test century v India at Madras on 1992-93 tour to India and Sri Lanka. Joined England tour party in Australia 1994-95 following injury to Darren Gough. Suffered a compressed fracture in the ball of his hip joint which prevented him from playing any Championship cricket in 1995. Left Nottinghamshire and joined Surrey for the 1996 season. Played for an England XI in the Cricket Max tournament in 1997. Rejoined Leicestershire as vice-captain for the 1998 season and captained the club for much of the season in the absence through injury of James Whitaker. Scored 71* in 33 balls as Leicestershire made 204 in 19 overs and one ball to beat Northamptonshire at Grace Road in 1998
Best batting: 247 Nottinghamshire v Durham, Chester-le-Street 1993
Best bowling: 6-22 Leicestershire v Oxford University, The Parks 1988

1998 Season

	M	Inns	NO	Runs	HS	Avge	100s	50s	Ct	St	O	M	Runs	Wkts	Avge	Best	5wl	10wM
Test																		
All First	13	14	3	367	71 *	33.36	-	4	10	-	266.4	53	972	39	24.92	6-60	2	-
1-day Int	2	2	1	26	16	26.00	-	-	-	-	18.4	2	88	1	88.00	1-42	-	
NatWest	4	1	0	9	9	9.00	-	-	3	-	25.4	4	63	8	7.87	5-19	1	
B & H	8	4	2	55	55 *	27.50	-	1	5	-	67	5	289	12	24.08	4-40	-	
Sunday	10	10	2	266	56 *	33.25	-	1	4	-	45.3	4	183	7	26.14	2-14	-	

Career Performances

	M	Inns	NO	Runs	HS	Avge	100s	50s	Ct	St	Balls	Runs	Wkts	Avge	Best	5wl	10wM
Test	32	51	3	1105	117	23.02	1	4	25	-	6852	3490	93	37.52	6-111	3	-
All First	174	255	32	6806	247	30.52	7	32	141	-	30267	15338	520	29.49	6-22	20	3
1-day Int	53	40	14	374	33	14.38	-	-	20	-	2625	1942	66	29.42	4-30	-	
NatWest	23	18	2	370	89	23.12	-	2	14	-	1216	689	32	21.53	5-19	1	
B & H	43	30	12	549	55 *	30.50	-	1	18	-	2271	1534	65	23.60	5-46	1	
Sunday	111	96	23	2043	93 *	27.98	-	9	37	-	4205	3044	117	26.01	4-13	-	

LEWIS, J. Gloucestershire

Name: Jonathan Lewis
Role: Right-hand bat,
right-arm medium-fast bowler
Born: 26 August 1975, Aylesbury
Height: 6ft 2in **Weight:** 13st
Nickname: JJ, Nugget, Stupid
County debut: 1995
County cap: 1998
50 wickets in a season: 2
1st-Class 50s: 1
1st-Class 5 w. in innings: 6
1st-Class catches: 11
Place in batting averages: 256th av. 13.44
(1997 233rd av. 17.54)
Place in bowling averages: 42nd av. 24.52
(1997 37th av. 25.94)
Strike rate: 47.00 (career 51.38)
Parents: John and Jane
Marital status: Single
Education: Lawn Junior School;
Churchfields Comprehensive School; Swindon College
Qualifications: 9 GCSEs, BTEC in Leisure and Hospitality
Overseas tours: Bath Schools to New South Wales, Australia 1993
Overseas teams played for: Marist, Christchurch, New Zealand 1994-95;
Richmond City, Melbourne 1995-96
Cricketers particularly admired: Dom Hewson, Jack Russell, Courtney Walsh, Jon
Summer, Alan Biggins, Paul Rignall
Other sports followed: 'Gurning'
Extras: Was on Northamptonshire staff in 1994 but made no first-team appearance.
Awarded Gloucestershire county cap 1998
Best batting: 54* Gloucestershire v Derbyshire, Chesterfield 1998
Best bowling: 6-48 Gloucestershire v Derbyshire, Chesterfield 1998

1998 Season

	M	Inns	NO	Runs	HS	Avge	100s	50s	Ct	St	O	M	Runs	Wkts	Avge	Best	5wI	10wM
Test																		
All First	18	31	2	390	54 *	13.44	-	1	5	-	462.1	108	1447	59	24.52	6-48	3	-
1-day Int																		
NatWest	2	2	1	3	2 *	3.00	-	-	1	-	19	2	85	1	85.00	1-42	-	
B & H	5	4	2	47	33 *	23.50	-	-	-	-	45	2	247	5	49.40	2-49	-	
Sunday	14	10	2	90	26 *	11.25	-	-	2	-	90	4	470	16	29.37	3-45	-	

Career Performances

	M	Inns	NO	Runs	HS	Avge	100s	50s	Ct	St	Balls	Runs	Wkts	Avge	Best	5wI	10wM
Test																	
All First	46	69	12	705	54 *	12.36	-	1	11	-	7348	3903	143	27.29	6-48	6	-
1-day Int																	
NatWest	5	4	2	10	6 *	5.00	-	-	2	-	266	169	6	28.16	3-27	-	
B & H	7	4	2	47	33 *	23.50	-	-	-	-	384	352	9	39.11	3-31	-	
Sunday	43	24	12	137	26 *	11.41	-	-	7	-	1713	1449	45	32.20	3-27	-	

LEWIS, J. J. B.   Durham

Name: Jonathan James Benjamin Lewis
Role: Right-hand bat, right-arm
slow-medium net bowler
Born: 21 May 1970, Middlesex
Height: 5ft 9in **Weight:** 11st 5lbs
Nickname: JJ, Judge, Mouse
County debut: 1990 (Essex), 1997 (Durham)
County cap: 1994 (Essex)
1000 runs in a season: 1
1st-Class 50s: 29
1st-Class 100s: 6
1st-Class 200s: 1
1st-Class catches: 69
One-Day 100s: 1
Place in batting averages: 164th av. 23.03
(1997 35th av. 44.71)
Strike rate: 48.00 (career 120.00)
Parents: Graham Edward and Regina Mary
Marital status: Single
Family links with cricket: Father played county schools. Uncle is a lifelong Somerset
supporter. Sister is right-arm medium-fast bowler for NorTel
Education: King Edward VI School, Chelmsford; Roehampton Institute of Higher
Education
Qualifications: 5 O-levels, 3 A-levels, BSc (Hons) Sports Science, NCA Senior Coach
Career outside cricket: 'I'm working on it – slowly'
Off-season: 'Working for a firm of precision engineers – all enquiries welcome at
Tees Precision in Thoraby'
Overseas teams played for: Old Hararians, Zimbabwe 1991-92; Taita District, New
Zealand 1992-93; Eshoue and Zululand 1994-95; Richards Bay 1996-97; Empangeni,
Natal 1997-98
Cricketers particularly admired: John Childs, Greg Matthews, Alan Walker

Young players to look out for: Steve Harmison
Other sports followed: Soccer (West Ham United), rugby, basketball, 'most sports really'
Injuries: Out for about two weeks with a slight hamstring tear
Relaxations: 'Pubs with real ale and "Trotters Wine Bar"'
Extras: Hit century on first-class debut in Essex's final Championship match of the 1990 season. Joined Durham for the 1997 season – 'I am slowly learning the local dialect'. Scored a double century on his debut for Durham (210* v Oxford University), placing him in a unique club, alongside Peter Bowler and Neil Taylor, of players who have scored centuries on debut for two different counties
Opinions on cricket: 'In order to raise the standard to produce better Test players, the quality of first-class pitches has to be looked at. Even in a very wet summer like 1998 too many games do not reach the final sessions.'
Best batting: 210* Durham v Oxford University, The Parks 1997
Best bowling: 1-73 Durham v Surrey, Riverside 1998

1998 Season

	M	Inns	NO	Runs	HS	Avge	100s	50s	Ct	St	O	M	Runs	Wkts	Avge	Best	5wI	10wM
Test																		
All First	15	28	1	622	72	23.03	-	4	10	-	8	0	73	1	73.00	1-73	-	-
1-day Int																		
NatWest	2	2	0	33	18	16.50	-	-	-	-								
B & H	5	5	0	168	67	33.60	-	1	-	-								
Sunday	13	11	1	247	67 *	24.70	-	3	-	-	1	0	31	0	-		-	-

Career Performances

	M	Inns	NO	Runs	HS	Avge	100s	50s	Ct	St	Balls	Runs	Wkts	Avge	Best	5wI	10wM
Test																	
All First	91	161	19	4833	210 *	34.03	7	29	69	-	120	121	1	121.00	1-73	-	-
1-day Int																	
NatWest	9	9	1	109	24 *	13.62	-	-	1	-							
B & H	14	14	1	339	67	26.07	-	1	3	-							
Sunday	71	59	13	1162	102	25.26	1	8	14	-	8	35	0	-		-	-

LEWRY, J. D.   Sussex

Name: Jason David Lewry
Role: Left-hand bat, left-arm
fast-medium bowler
Born: 2 April 1971, Worthing, West Sussex
Height: 6ft 3in **Weight:** 14st 6lbs
Nickname: Urco ('thanks Ath')
County debut: 1994
County cap: 1996
50 wickets in a season: 1
1st-Class 5 w. in innings: 10
1st-Class 10 w. in match: 1
1st-Class catches: 3
Place in batting averages: 291st av. 5.73
Place in bowling averages: 34th av. 22.72
Strike rate: 44.66 (career 46.22)
Parents: David and Veronica
Wife and date of marriage:
Naomi Madeleine, 18 August 1997
Children: William Jason Joseph,
14 February 1998

Family links with cricket: Father coaches
Education: Thomas à Becket, Worthing; Durrington High School, Worthing; Worthing
Sixth Form College
Qualifications: 6 O-levels, 3 GCSEs, City & Guilds, NCA Award Course
Career outside cricket: 'Still looking'
Off-season: England A tour to Zimbabwe and South Africa
Overseas tours: 'Goring CC to Isle of Wight 1992, 1993'; England A to Zimbabwe
and South Africa 1998-99
Cricketers particularly admired: The Sussex staff, David Gower, Wasim Akram,
Martin Andrews
Young players to look out for: 'Swing bowlers'
Other sports followed: Football (West Ham United), golf, squash, 'kicking on … zzz'
Injuries: Out for two weeks with shoulder strain
Relaxations: Golf, eating out, 'kicking on with Stan and annoying the wife'
Extras: Missed all 1997 season – two screws in back
Opinions on cricket: 'Play each game as if it is your last.'
Best batting: 34 Sussex v Kent, Hove 1995
Best bowling: 6-43 Sussex v Worcestershire, Eastbourne 1995

1998 Season

	M	Inns	NO	Runs	HS	Avge	100s	50s	Ct	St	O	M	Runs	Wkts	Avge	Best	5wI	10wM
Test																		
All First	17	23	0	132	24	5.73	-	-	1	-	461.3	112	1409	62	22.72	6-72	3	-
1-day Int																		
NatWest	1	1	0	9	9	9.00	-	-	-	-	12	0	42	4	10.50	4-42	-	
B & H	3	2	0	16	13	8.00	-	-	-	-	29	0	142	4	35.50	2-51	-	
Sunday	7	6	3	21	10 *	7.00	-	-	1	-	52	1	245	12	20.41	3-19	-	

Career Performances

	M	Inns	NO	Runs	HS	Avge	100s	50s	Ct	St	Balls	Runs	Wkts	Avge	Best	5wI	10wM
Test																	
All First	43	63	11	434	34	8.34	-	-	3	-	7258	3913	157	24.92	6-43	10	1
1-day Int																	
NatWest	5	4	3	19	9	19.00	-	-	-	-	324	224	11	20.36	4-42	-	
B & H	7	4	2	38	14 *	19.00	-	-	-	-	366	316	4	79.00	2-51	-	
Sunday	29	15	6	43	10 *	4.77	-	-	5	-	1180	939	41	22.90	4-29	-	

LLONG, N. J. — Kent

Name: Nigel James Llong
Role: Left-hand bat, off-spin bowler
Born: 11 February 1969, Ashford, Kent
Height: 6ft **Weight:** 11st 6lbs
Nickname: Nidge, Lloydie
County debut: 1991
County cap: 1993
1st-Class 50s: 16
1st-Class 100s: 6
1st-Class 5 w. in innings: 2
1st-Class catches: 59
One-Day 100s: 1
Place in batting averages:
(1997 226th av. 18.28)
Strike rate: (career 64.94)
Parents: Richard and Peggy (deceased)
Wife and date of marriage:
Rosemary Ann, 29 February 1996
Family links with cricket: Father and
brother play club cricket
Education: Newtown County Primary; North School for Boys
Qualifications: 6 CSEs, NCA coaching award

Career outside cricket: Snooker table technician and groundsman
Overseas tours: Kent to Zimbabwe 1992-93
Overseas teams played for: Ashburton, Melbourne 1988-90, 1996-97; Green Point, Cape Town 1990-95
Cricketers particularly admired: David Gower
Other sports followed: Golf, football, Aussie rules and fishing
Relaxations: 'Watching any sport'
Extras: Kent Supporters Club Young Player of the Year Award 1993
Opinions on cricket: 'All teams prepare pitches to suit their own strengths and the situation of pitches being reported could be stopped if the ECB took full control of all pitch conditions (i.e. by employing groundsmen). This would ensure that good quality pitches are played on. Test match pitches are prepared as well as possible so why not first-class games? All 2nd XI cricket should be played on first-class grounds, with practice facilities so that young, up-and-coming players have the facilities to work at their skills.'
Best batting: 130 Kent v Hampshire, Canterbury 1996
Best bowling: 5-21 Kent v Middlesex, Canterbury 1996

1998 Season

	M	Inns	NO	Runs	HS	Avge	100s	50s	Ct	St	O	M	Runs	Wkts	Avge	Best	5wI	10wM
Test																		
All First	2	4	1	32	16	10.66	-	-	2	-								
1-day Int																		
NatWest																		
B & H																		
Sunday	7	5	1	96	35 *	24.00	-	-	1	-	14	0	91	2	45.50	1-32	-	

Career Performances

	M	Inns	NO	Runs	HS	Avge	100s	50s	Ct	St	Balls	Runs	Wkts	Avge	Best	5wI	10wM
Test																	
All First	68	108	11	3024	130	31.17	6	16	59	-	2273	1259	35	35.97	5-21	2	-
1-day Int																	
NatWest	6	6	3	261	115 *	87.00	1	1	3	-	134	96	6	16.00	3-36	-	
B & H	17	14	1	320	75	24.61	-	2	4	-	204	175	3	58.33	2-38	-	
Sunday	94	76	16	1222	70	20.36	-	5	27	-	703	702	25	28.08	4-24	-	

LLOYD, G. D. Lancashire

Name: Graham David Lloyd
Role: Right-hand bat, right-arm medium
bowler
Born: 1 July 1969, Accrington
Height: 5ft 9in **Weight:** 12st 9lbs
Nickname: G
County debut: 1988
County cap: 1992
One-Day Internationals: 5
1000 runs in a season: 4
1st-Class 50s: 51
1st-Class 100s: 17
1st-Class 200s: 3
1st-Class catches: 106
One-Day 100s: 3
Place in batting averages: 45th av. 39.57
(1997 24th av. 48.77)
Strike rate: (career 139.50)
Parents: David and Susan

Wife and date of marriage: Sharon, 11 October 1997
Family links with cricket: Father played for Lancashire and England
Education: Hollins County High School, Accrington
Qualifications: 3 O-levels, NCA coaching certificate
Career outside cricket: 'Don't know yet'
Off-season: 'Start with Lancs on 1 December'
Overseas tours: England A to Australia 1992-93; Lancashire CCC to Guernsey 1995;
England to Bangladesh (Wills International Cup) 1998
Overseas teams played for: Maroochydore, Queensland 1988-89 and 1991-95
Cricketers particularly admired: Gordon Parsons, David Millns, Nigel Briers
Young players to look out for: Andrew Flintoff
Other sports played: Football
Other sports followed: Football (Manchester United)
Relaxations: Eating out and racing
Extras: His school did not play cricket, so he learnt at Accrington, playing in the same
team as his father. Won the EDS Walter Lawrence Trophy for the fastest century of the
year (for the second year running) – 100 off 73 balls against Leicestershire on 2 June
1997. Played for England in the 1997 Hong Kong Sixes tournament in which England
were runners-up to Pakistan
Opinions on cricket: 'More floodlit matches.'
Best batting: 241 Lancashire v Essex, Chelmsford 1996
Best bowling: 1-4 Lancashire v Warwickshire, Edgbaston 1996

1998 Season

	M	Inns	NO	Runs	HS	Avge	100s	50s	Ct	St	O	M	Runs	Wkts	Avge	Best	5wI	10wM
Test																		
All First	15	22	1	831	212 *	39.57	2	3	11	-	7.3	1	49	0	-	-	-	-
1-day Int																		
NatWest	5	4	2	108	40	54.00	-	-	-	-								
B & H	6	6	1	95	38	19.00	-	-	1	-								
Sunday	15	15	3	292	38	24.33	-	-	7	-								

Career Performances

	M	Inns	NO	Runs	HS	Avge	100s	50s	Ct	St	Balls	Runs	Wkts	Avge	Best	5wI	10wM
Test																	
All First	160	258	25	9137	241	39.21	20	51	106	-	279	340	2	170.00	1-4	-	-
1-day Int	5	4	1	39	22	13.00	-	-	2	-							
NatWest	21	19	2	536	96	31.52	-	3	3	-	30	35	1	35.00	1-23	-	
B & H	41	35	10	707	81 *	28.28	-	3	6	-	30	50	0	-	-	-	
Sunday	141	131	19	3514	134	31.37	3	19	34	-	12	18	0	-	-	-	

LOGAN, R. J.   Northamptonshire

Name: Richard James Logan
Role: Right-hand bat, right-arm fast bowler
Born: 28 January 1980, Stone, Staffs
Height: 6ft 1in **Weight:** 13st 7lbs
Nickname: Gus, Logie, Loges
County debut: No first-team appearance
Parents: Robert and Margaret
Marital status: Girlfriend Sarah
Family links with cricket: Father played for local club Cannock as batsman/wicket-keeper
Education: Walhouse C of E School, Cannock; Wolverhampton Grammar School
Qualifications: 10 GCSEs
Off-season: England U19 to New Zealand
Overseas tours: England U17 to Bermuda 1997 (International Youth Tournament); England U19 to South Africa 1997-98, to New Zealand 1998-99
Cricketers particularly admired:
Curtly Ambrose, Allan Donald
Young players to look out for: Graeme Swann, Paul Franks, John Blain, Stephen Peters
Other sports played: Hockey (Cannock – 'also played for Staffordshire from age 9 to

present day. Played for Midlands U14 but had to decline Midlands training due to commitment to cricket')

Other sports followed: Football (Wolverhampton Wanderers)
Injuries: Out for two weeks with back injury
Relaxations: Spending time with girlfriend. Cinema, keeping fit, socialising
Extras: Played for Staffordshire at every level from U11 to U19, and as captain from U13 to U17. Played for Midlands U14 and U15 (both as captain), HMC Schools U15. 1995 *Daily Telegraph*/Lombard U15 Midlands Bowler and Batsman of the Year. Played for Northamptonshire U17 and U19 national champions in 1997. Has played for England U15, U17 and U19
Opinions on cricket: 'I feel that if two divisions were introduced to the Championship, then the gap between the two divisions would grow and therefore we would end up with all the best players in the country in the top division getting paid the best money, and the bottom division would have the weaker players in, earning less money.'

LOYE, M. B. Northamptonshire

Name: Malachy Bernard Loye
Role: Right-hand bat, off-spin bowler
Born: 27 September 1972, Northampton
Height: 6ft 2in **Weight:** 13st 7lbs
Nickname: Mal, Mad Jack, Fruit Bat, Slugs
County debut: 1991
County cap: 1994
1000 runs in a season: 1
1st-Class 50s: 25
1st-Class 100s: 9
1st-Class 200s: 1
1st-Class 300s: 1
1st-Class catches: 55
One-Day 100s: 2
Place in batting averages: 8th av. 59.90
(1997 99th av. 34.33)
Parents: Patrick and Anne
Marital status: Single
Family links with cricket: Father and
brother both played for Cogenhoe CC in Northampton
Education: Brixworth Primary School; Moulton Comprehensive School
Qualifications: GCSEs and senior coaching certificate
Overseas tours: England U18 to Canada 1991; England U19 to Pakistan 1991-92; England A to South Africa 1993-94, to Zimbabwe and South Africa 1998-99

Overseas teams played for: Riccarton and Canterbury B, New Zealand 1992-93; Onslow, Wellington, New Zealand 1995-96

Cricketers particularly admired: Gordon Greenidge, Wayne Larkins, Curtly Ambrose

Young players to look out for: David Roberts, David Sales, Alec Swann, Kevin Innes, Tobin Bailey

Other sports followed: Football (Liverpool and Northampton Town), golf, basketball and boxing

Relaxations: Watching films, listening to music, singing and having a good night out with friends

Extras: Played for England U19 in the home series against Australia U19 in 1991 and against Sri Lanka U19 1992. Voted Professional Cricketers' Association's Young Player of the Year 1993 and Whittingdale Young Player of the Year 1993. Shared a record opening stand of 375 with Richard Montgomerie versus Yorkshire in 1996. His 322* v Glamorgan in 1998 is the highest individual first-class score for the county, beating Raman Subba Row's 300. During his innings, Loye put on 401 for the fifth wicket with David Ripley, setting a new fifth wicket record for first-class cricket in England. Voted the PCA's Player of the Year in 1998. Signed a new four-year contract with Northamptonshire in November 1998

Opinions on cricket: 'Tea time is too short. For such a great game it is so poorly marketed, which is why we are so far behind other sports. Cricketers should have nine-month contracts beginning January: this I'm sure will encourage better preparation and commitment before a season.'

Best batting: 322* Northamptonshire v Glamorgan, Northampton 1998

1998 Season

	M	Inns	NO	Runs	HS	Avge	100s	50s	Ct	St	O	M	Runs	Wkts	Avge	Best	5wI	10wM
Test																		
All First	15	22	2	1198	322 *	59.90	4	4	7	-	2	0	42	0	-	-	-	-
1-day Int																		
NatWest	1	1	0	40	40	40.00	-	-	-	-								
B & H	4	4	1	69	41	23.00	-	-	1	-								
Sunday	15	15	1	650	108 *	46.42	1	4	3	-								

Career Performances

	M	Inns	NO	Runs	HS	Avge	100s	50s	Ct	St	Balls	Runs	Wkts	Avge	Best	5wI	10wM
Test																	
All First	97	155	17	5305	322 *	38.44	11	25	55	-	13	43	0	-	-	-	-
1-day Int																	
NatWest	13	12	3	258	65	28.66	-	1	4	-							
B & H	21	21	5	475	68 *	29.68	-	2	7	-							
Sunday	76	72	7	2150	122	33.07	2	12	15	-							

LUCAS, D.   Nottinghamshire

Name: David Lucas
Role: Right-hand bat, left-arm medium
swing bowler
Born: 19 August 1978, Nottingham
Height: 6ft 2in   **Weight:** 13st
Nickname: Muc, Gary, Mucus, Carcinogen,
Conquistador
County debut: No first-team appearance
Parents: Mary and Terry
Marital status: Single
Family links with cricket: 'Dad played local
cricket'
Qualifications: 6 GCSEs, pass in
Computer-Aided Design
Off-season: 'Playing indoor cricket for
England in the World Cup in Melbourne.
Also, playing for Nottingham Bulldogs in the
Indoor Cricket National League'
Overseas teams played for: Bankstown

Canterbury Bulldogs, Sydney 1996-97
Cricketers particularly admired: Steve and Mark Waugh, Wasim Akram, Allan
Donald, Chris Murden, Rick Smith ('particularly for his catching'), Joe Thorpe
Young players to look out for: 'The Pikelets and Galas!', Stephen Randall, Matt
Whiley, Chris Read, Noel Gie, Rick Smith
Other sports played: 'I have played a good standard of local football', indoor cricket,
indoor golf
Other sports followed: Football (Arsenal), rugby league (Wigan)
Relaxations: Eating, going out, films, sleeping, going to the gym
Extras: Was selected to represent England at Indoor Cricket World Cup in Australia in
October 1998. Won Yorkshire League with Rotherham in 1996
Opinions on cricket: 'There should be more day/night games, and also cheerleaders.'

---

41. Who captained India in the 1979 World Cup?

FICA

LUGSDEN, S.   Hampshire

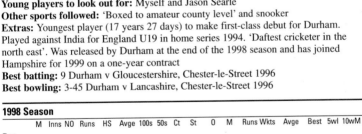

Name: Steven Lugsden
Role: Right-hand bat, right-arm fast bowler
Born: 10 July 1976, Gateshead
Height: 6ft 3in **Weight:** 13st
Nickname: 8-ball, Lugsy, Dime Bar,
Bluntest-tool-in-the-box
County debut: 1993
1st-Class catches: 2
Strike rate: 54.25 (career 70.08)
Parents: William and Nora
Wife and date of marriage:
Janette, 19 December 1997
Children: John James, 21 December 1997
Education: St Edmund Campion RC School,
Wrekenton, Gateshead
Qualifications: 7 GCSEs, BTEC Business
and Finance
Career outside cricket: Landscape gardener
and model ('clothed')
Overseas tours: England U19 to West Indies 1994-95
Cricketers particularly admired: Geoff Cook, Allan Donald
Young players to look out for: Myself and Jason Searle
Other sports followed: 'Boxed to amateur county level' and snooker
Extras: Youngest player (17 years 27 days) to make first-class debut for Durham.
Played against India for England U19 in home series 1994. 'Daftest cricketer in the
north east'. Was released by Durham at the end of the 1998 season and has joined
Hampshire for 1999 on a one-year contract
Best batting: 9 Durham v Gloucestershire, Chester-le-Street 1996
Best bowling: 3-45 Durham v Lancashire, Chester-le-Street 1996

1998 Season

	M	Inns	NO	Runs	HS	Avge	100s	50s	Ct	St	O	M	Runs	Wkts	Avge	Best	5wI	10wM
Test																		
All First	3	5	2	15	8 *	5.00	-	-	1	-	72.2	7	325	8	40.62	3-67	-	-
1-day Int																		
NatWest																		
B & H																		
Sunday																		

Career Performances

	M	Inns	NO	Runs	HS	Avge	100s	50s	Ct	St	Balls	Runs	Wkts	Avge	Best	5wl	10wM
Test																	
All First	13	18	7	45	9	4.09	-	-	2	-	1752	1172	25	46.88	3-45	-	-
1-day Int																	
NatWest																	
B & H																	
Sunday	1	0	0	0	0	-	-	-	-	-	48	55	1	55.00	1-55	-	

LYE, D.   Middlesex

Name: David Lye
Role: Right-hand bat
Born: 11 April 1979, Exeter
Height: 5ft 8in **Weight:** 12st 7lbs
County debut: No first-team appearance
Parents: Gerald and Marilyn
Marital status: Single
Family links with cricket: Dad plays cricket locally
Education: Stockland Primary School; Honiton Secondary School
Qualifications: 'Going through the stages to become a coach'
Career outside cricket: 'Left school to play cricket'
Cricketers particularly admired: Ian Botham, Graham Gooch, Allan Border
Other sports followed: Football (Manchester United) and indoor cricket (Honiton)
Relaxations: Field sports
Extras: Devon Young Cricketer of the Year in 1996. Devon U17 Player of the Season in 1995 and 1996

MACMILLAN, G. I.   Gloucestershire

Name: Gregor Innes Macmillan
Role: Right-hand bat, off-spin bowler
Born: 7 August 1969, Guildford
Height: 6ft 5in **Weight:** 13st 2lbs
County debut: 1994 (Leics, one-day),
1995 (Leics, first-class), 1998 (Glos)
1st-Class 50s: 11
1st-Class 100s: 3
1st-Class catches: 55
Place in batting averages: 197th av. 19.55
(1997 242nd av. 16.60)
Strike rate: (career 91.78)
Parents: Angus and Evelyn
Marital status: Single
Family links with cricket: 'Father plays club
cricket at Odiham and Greywell and
Hampshire Maniacs. Mother takes a mean
video. Her mother makes a great tea. Great-
uncle played a match at Kroonstad on Queen
Victoria's Jubilee Day'
Education: Guildford County School; Charterhouse; Southampton University; Keble
College, Oxford University
Qualifications: 'A few O- and A-levels', BA (Hons) Philosophy and Politics (Soton),
Dip. Soc Admin (Oxon), M Litt Politics at Oxford
Overseas teams played for: Harvinia, Orange Free State 1988-89, 1993-94 'plus the
odd game whenever they ask me'
Cricketers particularly admired: 'Those like Jim Bovill who put up with me without
often complaining. Mickey Carr. Gordon Parsons for being tidy and Richard
Montgomerie for being less tidy than I am'
Other sports followed: Football (Liverpool FC) and 'Scotland at anything except
rugby union and curling'
Extras: Captained Southampton University to the UAU final 1991. Played for Surrey
from U11 to U19. Captain of Oxford University for 1995 season. Played in Oxford's
last two Varsity match victories, plus the victory in the first one-day match between the
two Universities in 1995. Captained both Oxford and Combined Universities ('a good
way to stay thin'). Scored a century on Championship debut for Leics 1995. Released at
end of 1997 season and joined Glos. Released by Glos at end of the 1998 season
Opinions on cricket: 'You'll have to give me time before I become judgmental.
That's not something you lightly ask a philosopher to do.'
Best batting: 122 Leicestershire v Surrey, Leicester 1995
Best bowling: 3-13 Oxford University v Cambridge University, Lord's 1993

1998 Season

	M	Inns	NO	Runs	HS	Avge	100s	50s	Ct	St	O	M	Runs	Wkts	Avge	Best	5wI	10wM
Test																		
All First	5	9	0	176	53	19.55	-	2	4	-	5	2	14	0	-		-	-
1-day Int																		
NatWest																		
B & H																		
Sunday	6	6	0	85	31	14.16	-	-	2	-	3	0	18	0	-		-	-

Career Performances

	M	Inns	NO	Runs	HS	Avge	100s	50s	Ct	St	Balls	Runs	Wkts	Avge	Best	5wI	10wM
Test																	
All First	53	85	9	2024	122	26.63	3	11	55	-	2111	1217	23	52.91	3-13	-	-
1-day Int																	
NatWest	1	1	0	9	9	9.00	-	-	-	-	18	13	1	13.00	1-13	-	
B & H	15	14	2	339	77	28.25	-	2	4	-	107	109	2	54.50	1-18	-	
Sunday	29	28	2	463	58	17.80	-	1	9	-	114	94	3	31.33	2-37	-	

MADDY, D. L.   Leicestershire

Name: Darren Lee Maddy
Role: Right-hand bat, right-arm medium bowler
Born: 23 May 1974, Leicester
Height: 5ft 9in ('One inch taller than Dominic Williamson, two inches taller than Tim Mason') **Weight:** 11st
Nickname: Roaster, Stompie, St George
County debut: 1993 (one-day), 1994 (first-class)
County cap: 1996
One-Day Internationals: 2
1000 runs in a season: 1
1st-Class 50s: 15
1st-Class 100s: 8
1st-Class 200s: 1
1st-Class catches: 72
One-Day 100s: 5
Place in batting averages: 155th av. 23.70 (1997 84th av. 36.10)
Strike rate: 102.00 (career 104.50)
Parents: William Arthur and Hilary Jean
Marital status: Single

Family links with cricket: Father and younger brother, Greg, play club cricket
Education: Herrick Junior School, Leicester; Roundhills, Thurmaston;
Wreake Valley, Syston
Qualifications: 8 GCSEs
Off-season: Touring Zimbabwe and South Africa with England A
Overseas tours: Leicestershire to Bloemfontein 1995, to Western Transvaal 1996, to
Durban 1997; Leicestershire CCC to Barbados 1998; England A to Kenya and Sri
Lanka 1997-98, to Zimbabwe and South Africa 1998-99
Overseas teams played for: Wanderers, Johannesburg 1992-93; Northern Free State,
Orange Free State 1993-95; Rhodes University, South Africa 1995-97
Cricketers particularly admired: Brian Lara, Michael Atherton, Richard Hadlee,
Viv Richards, 'Babe Ruth' Dakin
Young players to look out for: Iain Sutcliffe, Darren Stevens, Jimmy Ormond
Other sports played: 5-a-side football, golf, squash
Other sports followed: Rugby (Leicester Tigers), football (Leicester City), baseball,
golf, boxing – 'most sports really except for horse racing and motor racing'
Injuries: Fractured knuckle and broken finger
Relaxations: 'Going to the gym, playing sport, spending time with my girlfriend Justine,
listening to music, watching TV, going on holiday, scuba diving, bunjee jumping'
Extras: 'Voted having the biggest thighs in Leicester by team-mates.' Set a new 2nd
XI Championship run aggregate record (1498) beating the previous one which had
stood since 1961. Rapid Cricketline 2nd XI Player of the Year 1994. Scored his
maiden first-class 200 against Kenya at Nairobi on England A's 1997-98 tour and was
leading run-scorer on the tour with 687 runs at 68.7. Set a new record for the number
of runs scored in the B&H competition in one season, previously held by Graham
Gooch. Also set a record for the most B&H gold awards won in one season.
Opinions on cricket: 'Counties should employ players on a nine-month basis.
NatWest should be reduced to 50 overs – 60 overs is too long. The over-rate fine
system is still too severe. The third umpire should be used in all one-day competitions.
To prevent teams from preparing wickets to give home advantage, perhaps the visiting
team could automatically choose the right to bat or bowl first, depending on the
condition of the wicket. This will mean that clubs will have to start preparing good
cricket wickets.'
Best batting: 202 England A v Kenya, Nairobi 1997-98
Best bowling: 2-21 Leicestershire v Lancashire, Old Trafford 1996

1998 Season

	M	Inns	NO	Runs	HS	Avge	100s	50s	Ct	St	O	M	Runs	Wkts	Avge	Best	5wI	10wM
Test																		
All First	18	26	2	569	162	23.70	2	-	17	-	34	9	130	2	65.00	1-9	-	-
1-day Int	2	1	0	1	1	1.00	-	-	-	-								
NatWest	4	3	0	36	30	12.00	-	-	3	-	2	0	18	1	18.00	1-18	-	
B & H	8	8	3	629	151	125.80	3	2	3	-	4	0	31	1	31.00	1-11	-	
Sunday	15	14	0	133	38	9.50	-	-	5	-	14	0	82	4	20.50	3-34	-	

Career Performances

	M	Inns	NO	Runs	HS	Avge	100s	50s	Ct	St	Balls	Runs	Wkts	Avge	Best	5wI	10wM
Test																	
All First	76	121	6	3657	202	31.80	9	15	72	-	836	446	8	55.75	2-21	-	-
1-day Int	2	1	0	1	1	1.00	-	-	-	-							
NatWest	9	8	0	98	34	12.25	-	-	4	-	144	127	5	25.40	2-38	-	
B & H	22	22	4	1126	151	62.55	4	5	7	-	150	143	6	23.83	3-32	-	
Sunday	73	64	5	1547	106 *	26.22	1	12	28	-	822	821	28	29.32	3-11	-	

MALCOLM, D. E.   Northamptonshire

Name: Devon Eugene Malcolm
Role: Right-hand bat, right-arm fast bowler
Born: 22 February 1963, Kingston, Jamaica
Height: 6ft 2in **Weight:** 15st
Nickname: Dude
County debut: 1984 (Derbyshire),
1998 (Northamptonshire)
County cap: 1989 (Derbyshire)
Benefit: 1997 (Derbyshire)
Test debut: 1989
Tests: 40
One-Day Internationals: 10
50 wickets in a season: 6
1st-Class 50s: 1
1st-Class 5 w. in innings: 33
1st-Class 10 w. in match: 7
1st-Class catches: 36
One-Day 5 w. in innings: 2
Place in batting averages: 271st av. 10.36
(1997 302nd av. 6.13)
Place in bowling averages: 107th av. 33.27 (1997 27th av. 23.48)
Strike rate: 50.10 (career 51.09)
Parents: Albert and Brendalee (deceased)
Wife and date of marriage: Jennifer, October 1989
Children: Erica Cian, 11 June 1991; Natile Jade, 25 June 1993
Education: St Elizabeth Technical High School; Richmond College;
Derby College of Higher Education
Qualifications: College certificates, O-levels, coaching certificate
Overseas tours: England to West Indies 1989-90, to Australia 1990-91, to India and
Sri Lanka 1992-93, to West Indies 1993-94, to Australia 1994-95, to South Africa
1995-96; England A to Bermuda and West Indies 1991-92

Overseas teams played for: Ellerslie, Auckland 1985-87
Cricketers particularly admired: Michael Holding, Richard Hadlee, Malcolm Marshall, Alan Warner, Viv Richards
Other sports followed: Football, boxing
Relaxations: Music and movies, eating
Extras: Played league cricket for Sheffield Works and Sheffield United. Became eligible to play for England in 1987. Took 10 for 137 v West Indies in Port-of-Spain Test, 1989-90. Took 9-57 v South Africa at The Oval in 1994; received the 'Century of Bottles' Award for this best performance against the touring South Africans. Was one of *Wisden*'s Cricketers of the Year 1995. Struck down with chickenpox early in the England tour to Australia 1994-95. Joined Northamptonshire for 1998
Best batting: 51 Derbyshire v Surrey, Derby 1989
Best bowling: 9-57 England v South Africa, The Oval 1994

1998 Season

	M	Inns	NO	Runs	HS	Avge	100s	50s	Ct	St	O	M	Runs	Wkts	Avge	Best	5wI	10wM
Test																		
All First	14	16	5	114	42	10.36	-	-	3	-	334	48	1331	40	33.27	6-54	2	-
1-day Int																		
NatWest	1	1	0	1	1	1.00	-	-	-	-	12	0	55	2	27.50	2-55	-	
B & H	4	3	2	16	16	16.00	-	-	1	-	40	7	149	4	37.25	2-50	-	
Sunday	1	0	0	0	0	-	-	-	-	-	8	0	40	0	-	-	-	

Career Performances

	M	Inns	NO	Runs	HS	Avge	100s	50s	Ct	St	Balls	Runs	Wkts	Avge	Best	5wI	10wM
Test	40	58	19	236	29	6.05	-	-	7	-	8480	4748	128	37.09	9-57	5	2
All First	246	293	91	1638	51	8.10	-	1	36	-	42565	25578	833	30.70	9-57	33	7
1-day Int	10	5	2	9	4	3.00	-	-	1	-	526	404	16	25.25	3-40	-	
NatWest	22	11	1	30	10 *	3.00	-	-	1	-	1379	902	35	25.77	7-35	1	
B & H	36	20	6	104	16	7.42	-	-	4	-	2039	1469	54	27.20	5-27	1	
Sunday	65	25	10	134	42	8.93	-	-	7	-	2875	2468	87	28.36	4-21	-	

MARSH, S. A.   Kent

Name: Steven Andrew Marsh
Role: Right-hand bat, wicket-keeper
Born: 27 January 1961, Westminster
Height: 5ft 11in **Weight:** 13st
Nickname: Marshy
County debut: 1982
County cap: 1986
Benefit: 1995
1st-Class 50s: 53
1st-Class 100s: 9
1st-Class catches: 660
1st-Class stumpings: 54
Place in batting averages: 137th av. 29.83
(1997 65th av. 39.85)
Strike rate: (career 101.00)
Parents: Melvyn Graham and Valerie Ann
Wife and date of marriage:
Julie, 27 September 1986
Children: Hayley Ann, 15 May 1987;
Christian James Robert, 20 November 1990
Family links with cricket: Father played local cricket for Lordswood. Father-in-law,
Bob Wilson, played for Kent 1954-66
Education: Walderslade Secondary School for Boys; Mid-Kent College of Higher and
Further Education
Qualifications: 6 O-levels, 2 A-levels, OND in Business Studies, 'Cycling proficiency'
Off-season: 'Trying to play as much golf as possible'
Overseas tours: Fred Rumsey XI to Barbados 1986-87
Overseas teams played for: Avendale CC, Cape Town 1985-86
Cricketers particularly admired: Robin Smith, Graham Cowdrey, Ian Botham, Colin
Johns, Mark Bradley
Young players to look out for: Robert Key, Ben Phillips
Other sports followed: Golf, football (Chelsea FC)
Injuries: Out for one week with injury to lower back
Extras: Appointed Kent vice-captain in 1991. In the match v Middlesex at Lord's in
1991 he held a world record eight catches in an innings and scored 113*. Took over as
Kent captain during 1996 season after injury to Mark Benson and held post until end
of 1998 season.
Opinions on cricket: 'The majority of county cricketers know and believe that our
game needs change. Why don't they listen to us?'
Best batting: 142 Kent v Sussex, Horsham 1997
Best bowling: 2-20 Kent v Warwickshire, Edgbaston 1990

1998 Season

	M	Inns	NO	Runs	HS	Avge	100s	50s	Ct	St	O	M	Runs	Wkts	Avge	Best	5wI	10wM
Test																		
All First	16	28	4	620	92	25.83	-	5	42	4								
1-day Int																		
NatWest																		
B & H	5	4	3	57	37 *	57.00	-	-	10	2								
Sunday	17	7	3	57	30 *	14.25	-	-	15	-								

Career Performances

	M	Inns	NO	Runs	HS	Avge	100s	50s	Ct	St	Balls	Runs	Wkts	Avge	Best	5wI	10wM
Test																	
All First	276	407	67	9632	142	28.32	9	53	660	54	202	240	2	120.00	2-20	-	-
1-day Int																	
NatWest	23	16	3	209	55	16.07	-	1	33	4	3	3	1	3.00	1-3	-	
B & H	64	48	14	641	71	18.85	-	1	78	6							
Sunday	195	136	42	1820	59	19.36	-	4	183	22							

MARTIN, N. D. Middlesex

Name: Neil Donald Martin
Role: Right-hand bat, right-arm
fast-medium bowler
Born: 19 August 1979, Enfield
Height: 5ft 10in **Weight:** 13st
Nickname: Nelly
County debut: 1997 (one-day),
1998 (first-class)
Strike rate: 108.00 (career 108.00)
Parents: Cliff and Jill
Marital status: Single
Family links with cricket: Father plays local
club cricket for North Mimms and is a
playing member of the MCC
Education: Wheatfields, St Albans;
Verulam, St Albans
Qualifications: 9 GCSEs, NCA coaching award
Overseas tours: England U19 to Pakistan
1996-97
Cricketers particularly admired: Allan Donald, Darren Gough
Other sports followed: Football (Tottenham Hotspur)

Relaxations: Socialising with friends, 'winding up team mates, talking breeze to anyone who will listen'
Best bowling: 1-22 Middlesex v Oxford University, The Parks 1998

1998 Season

	M	Inns	NO	Runs	HS	Avge	100s	50s	Ct	St	O	M	Runs	Wkts	Avge	Best	5wI	10wM
Test																		
All First	2	0	0	0	0	-	-	-	-	-	18	2	83	1	83.00	1-22	-	-
1-day Int																		
NatWest																		
B & H																		
Sunday	1	0	0	0	0	-	-	-	1	-	6	0	28	2	14.00	2-28	-	

Career Performances

	M	Inns	NO	Runs	HS	Avge	100s	50s	Ct	St	Balls	Runs	Wkts	Avge	Best	5wI	10wM
Test																	
All First	2	0	0	0	0	-	-	-	-	-	108	83	1	83.00	1-22	-	-
1-day Int																	
NatWest																	
B & H																	
Sunday	2	0	0	0	0	-	-	-	1	-	72	57	3	19.00	2-28	-	

MARTIN, P. J.   Lancashire

Name: Peter James Martin
Role: Right-hand bat, right-arm fast-medium bowler
Born: 15 November 1968, Accrington
Height: 6ft 5in **Weight:** 15st 4lbs
Nickname: Digger, Long John
County debut: 1989
County cap: 1994
Test debut: 1995
Tests: 8
One-Day Internationals: 19
50 wickets in a season: 1
1st-Class 50s: 5
1st-Class 100s: 1
1st-Class 5 w. in innings: 7
1st-Class 10 w. in match: 1
1st-Class catches: 36
One-Day 5 w. in innings: 4

Place in batting averages: 240th av. 15.40 (1997 223rd av. 18.73)
Place in bowling averages: 32nd av. 22.12 (1997 22nd av. 23.13)
Strike rate: 48.50 (career 63.41)
Parents: Keith and Catherine Lina
Marital status: Single
Education: Danum School, Doncaster
Qualifications: 6 O-levels, 2 A-levels
Off-season: To Bangladesh with England one-day squad for Wills International Cup
Overseas tours: England YC to Australia (Youth World Cup) 1987-88; 'and various other tours with English Schools and NAYC'; England to South Africa 1995-96, to India and Pakistan (World Cup) 1995-96, to Sharjah 1997-98 (Champions Trophy), to Bangladesh (Wills International Cup) 1998-99
Overseas teams played for: Southern Districts, Queensland 1988-89; South Launceston, Tasmania 1989-90; South Canberra, ACT 1990-92
Cricketers particularly admired: 'Too many to mention'
Other sports followed: Football (Manchester United), rugby league (St Helens), golf
Relaxations: Music, painting, golf, cooking, walking, rugby league
Extras: Plays district football and basketball for Doncaster. Played for England A v Sri Lankans 1991. Was originally selected for the England A tour to Pakistan in 1995-96, but was drafted on to the senior tour after the withdrawal of Richard Johnson
Opinions on cricket: 'Should only be six-hour days with 100 overs a day.'
Best batting: 133 Lancashire v Durham, Gateshead Fell 1992
Best bowling: 8-32 Lancashire v Middlesex, Uxbridge 1997

1998 Season

	M	Inns	NO	Runs	HS	Avge	100s	50s	Ct	St	O	M	Runs	Wkts	Avge	Best	5wl	10wM
Test																		
All First	14	15	5	154	26	15.40	-	-	3	-	388	94	1062	48	22.12	4-21	-	-
1-day Int	3	3	1	5	3	2.50	-	-	-	-	27	1	141	2	70.50	1-34	-	
NatWest	5	2	1	17	12	17.00	-	-	-	-	54.5	7	192	15	12.80	5-30	1	
B & H	6	2	1	4	4	4.00	-	-	2	-	56	3	267	8	33.37	2-20	-	
Sunday	14	3	2	6	3 *	6.00	-	-	5	-	84.4	8	334	20	16.70	4-22	-	

Career Performances

	M	Inns	NO	Runs	HS	Avge	100s	50s	Ct	St	Balls	Runs	Wkts	Avge	Best	5wl	10wM
Test	8	13	0	115	29	8.84	-	-	6	-	1452	580	17	34.11	4-60	-	-
All First	148	169	43	2470	133	19.60	1	5	36	-	24667	11476	389	29.50	8-32	7	1
1-day Int	19	13	7	38	6	6.33	-	-	1	-	1000	751	27	27.81	4-44	-	
NatWest	19	6	4	44	16	22.00	-	-	1	-	1154	635	38	16.71	5-30	1	
B & H	25	8	6	32	10 *	16.00	-	-	8	-	1389	986	33	29.87	3-31	-	
Sunday	95	28	17	155	35 *	14.09	-	-	17	-	3628	2675	122	21.92	5-21	3	

MARTIN-JENKINS, R. S. C.   Sussex

Name: Robin Simon Christopher Martin-Jenkins
Role: Right-hand bat, right-arm medium-fast bowler
Born: 28 October 1975, Guildford
Height: 6ft 5in **Weight:** 14st
Nickname: Tucker, Crazy MF
County debut: 1995
1st-Class 50s: 3
1st-Class 5 w. in innings: 1
1st-Class catches: 5
Place in batting averages: 107th av. 29.41
Place in bowling averages: 15th av. 19.86
Strike rate: 38.68 (career 55.67)
Parents: Christopher and Judy
Marital status: Single
Family links with cricket: Father is *Daily Telegraph* cricket correspondent and *TMS* commentator. Brother captains the Radley Rangers
Education: Cranleigh Prep School, Surrey; Radley College, Oxon; Durham University
Qualifications: 10 GCSEs, 3 A-levels, 1 AS-level, Grade 3 bassoon, BA (Hons) Social Sciences
Career outside cricket: Coach
Off-season: Coaching in Durham
Overseas tours: Radley College to Barbados 1992; Sussex U19 to Sri Lanka 1995; Durham University to Vienna 1995
Overseas teams played for: Lima CC, Peru 1994
Cricketers particularly admired: Angus Fraser, Robin Smith
Young players to look out for: Jim Chaplin, Jon Bond, Jonny Box
Other sports played: Hockey, fives
Other sports followed: Tennis, skiing, football (Liverpool FC)
Injuries: Various pulled muscles, but not much time off required
Relaxations: Travelling, TV
Extras: European Player of the Year, Vienna 1995. Played for ESCA from U15 to U19. *Daily Telegraph* Bowling Award 1994. Best Performance Award for Sussex 1998
Opinions on cricket: 'England so nearly there. Just need one quality all-rounder ("preferably blond and 6ft 5in") and one more quick bowler. ECB should buy floodlights and transport them to matches – Super Cup a perfect opportunity. Minimum wage for first-class cricketers should be £30,000; maximum £40,000. Excluding Oxford and Cambridge!'

Best batting: 78 Sussex v Glamorgan, Hove 1998
Best bowling: 7-54 Sussex v Glamorgan, Hove 1998

1998 Season

	M	Inns	NO	Runs	HS	Avge	100s	50s	Ct	St	O	M	Runs	Wkts	Avge	Best	5wI	10wM
Test																		
All First	8	13	1	353	78	29.41	-	2	3	-	141.5	43	437	22	19.86	7-54	1	-
1-day Int																		
NatWest																		
B & H	5	4	0	53	39	13.25	-	-	-	-	40.5	5	199	8	24.87	3-39	-	
Sunday	9	9	0	155	44	17.22	-	-	3	-	57	7	215	7	30.71	2-12	-	

Career Performances

	M	Inns	NO	Runs	HS	Avge	100s	50s	Ct	St	Balls	Runs	Wkts	Avge	Best	5wI	10wM
Test																	
All First	15	22	3	500	78	26.31	-	3	5	-	1559	790	28	28.21	7-54	1	-
1-day Int																	
NatWest																	
B & H	11	9	0	89	39	9.88	-	-	-	-	549	475	17	27.94	4-57	-	
Sunday	21	17	1	172	44	10.75	-	-	3	-	762	597	13	45.92	2-12	-	

MARU, R. J. — Hampshire

Name: Rajesh Jamnadass Maru
Role: Right-hand bat, slow left-arm bowler, part-time wicket-keeper
Born: 28 October 1962, Nairobi, Kenya
Height: 5ft 6in **Weight:** 12st
Nickname: Raj
County debut: 1980 (Middlesex), 1984 (Hampshire)
County cap: 1986 (Hampshire)
50 wickets in a season: 4
1st-Class 50s: 7
1st-Class 5 w. in innings: 15
1st-Class 10 w. in match: 1
1st-Class catches: 254
Strike rate: 144.00 (career 75.97)
Parents: Jamnadass and Prabhavati
Wife and date of marriage:
Amanda Jane, 21 September 1991

Children: Christopher Patrick, 21 January 1993; Daniel James, 7 January 1996
Family links with cricket: Father played in Kenya and in England for North London Polytechnic. Brother Pradip played for Wembley CC in the Middlesex League and has played for Middlesex 2nd XI, Middlesex U19 and for Middlesex Colts & Schools
Education: Oakington Manor, Wembley; Rooks Heath High School, Harrow; Pinner Sixth Form College
Qualifications: ECB staff coach
Career outside cricket: Coach
Off-season: '… and then next summer: coaching for Hampshire CCC on a full-time contract'
Overseas tours: England YC South to Canada 1979; England YC to West Indies 1979-80; Middlesex to Zimbabwe 1980; Hampshire to Barbados 1987,1988,1990, to Anguilla 1997, to Dubai 1989; Barbican International XI to Dubai 1981; MCC to Leeward Islands 1992, to Far East 1995
Overseas teams played for: Marlborough CA, Blenheim, New Zealand 1985-87
Cricketers particularly admired: Phil Edmonds, Bishen Bedi, Malcolm Marshall, Shane Warne, Brian Lara, Sachin Tendulkar
Young players to look out for: Derek Kenway, Simon Francis
Other sports played: Squash, swimming, 'play any sport'
Other sports followed: Football, rugby union (Wasps and England), 'any sport'
Injuries: 'Not enough opportunity to bowl and play'
Relaxations: Music, playing 'and spending time with my family'
Extras: Played for Middlesex 1980-83; reached 500 first-class wickets in 1995. Awarded benefit for 1998. Retired from first-class cricket at end of 1998 season and has joined Hampshire coaching staff
Opinions on cricket: 'England will not produce Test cricket until the standard of wickets improves at all levels below Test cricket. Younger players should be given the opportunity to play at higher levels if they are good enough. Give younger players the experience at a younger age, so when they step up they should be able to deal with situations. Take the game back to grass roots.'
Best batting: 74 Hampshire v Gloucestershire, Gloucester 1988
Best bowling: 8-41 Hampshire v Kent, Southampton 1989

1998 Season

	M	Inns	NO	Runs	HS	Avge	100s	50s	Ct	St	O	M	Runs	Wkts	Avge	Best	5wI	10wM
Test																		
All First	2	3	1	27	14	13.50	-	-	2	-	48	9	167	2	83.50	2-101	-	-
1-day Int																		
NatWest																		
B & H																		
Sunday																		

Career Performances

	M	Inns	NO	Runs	HS	Avge	100s	50s	Ct	St	Balls	Runs	Wkts	Avge	Best	5wI	10wM
Test																	
All First	229	232	58	2965	74	17.04	-	7	254	-	40038	17714	527	33.61	8-41	15	1
1-day Int																	
NatWest	16	6	2	44	22	11.00	-	-	12	-	948	586	13	45.07	3-46	-	
B & H	15	6	3	38	10 *	12.66	-	-	6	-	771	511	15	34.06	3-46	-	
Sunday	71	32	19	184	33 *	14.15	-	-	27	-	2527	2192	55	39.85	4-29	-	

MASCARENHAS, D. A.   Hampshire

Name: Dimitri Adrian Mascarenhas
Role: Right-hand bat, right-arm
medium bowler
Born: 30 October 1977, Chiswick, London
Height: 6ft 2in **Weight:** 11st 7lbs
Nickname: Dimmie, Genii, Gibson
County debut: 1996
County cap: 1998
1st-Class 50s: 6
1st-Class 5 w. in innings: 2
1st-Class catches: 11
Place in batting averages: 118th av. 28.04
(1997 292nd av. 8.33)
Place in bowling averages: 108th av. 33.33
Strike rate: 95.00 (career 54.66)
Parents: Malik and Pauline
Marital status: Single

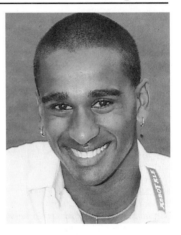

Family links with cricket: Uncle played in
Sri Lanka and brothers both play for Melville
CC in Perth, WA
Education: Our Lady's Primary, Melbourne; Trinity College, Perth
Overseas teams played for: Melville CC, Perth 1991-97
Cricketers particularly admired: Viv Richards, Malcolm Marshall, the Waugh twins
Young players to look out for: Ben Hollioake
Other sports followed: Aussie rules (Collingwood)
Relaxations: Aussie rules, tennis, golf, 'occasional scenario'
Extras: Played for Western Australia at U17 and U19 level as captain. Awarded
county cap 1998
Opinions on cricket: 'Great game'
Best batting: 89 Hampshire v Nottinghamshire, Portsmouth 1998
Best bowling: 6-88 Hampshire v Glamorgan, Southampton 1996

1998 Season

	M	Inns	NO	Runs	HS	Avge	100s	50s	Ct	St	O	M	Runs	Wkts	Avge	Best	5wI	10wM
Test																		
All First	17	25	2	645	89	28.04	-	6	11	-	280.5	58	1000	30	33.33	4-31	-	-
1-day Int																		
NatWest	4	4	2	145	73	72.50	-	1	1	-	24	0	86	4	21.50	3-28	-	
B & H	5	5	1	139	53	34.75	-	2	-	-	23	1	97	4	24.25	4-28	-	
Sunday	17	16	2	278	65	19.85	-	2	6	-	52.5	2	254	14	18.14	3-9	-	

Career Performances

	M	Inns	NO	Runs	HS	Avge	100s	50s	Ct	St	Balls	Runs	Wkts	Avge	Best	5wI	10wM
Test																		
All First	25	35	3	719	89	22.46	-	6	11	-	2997	1714	54	31.74	6-88	2	-
1-day Int																		
NatWest	4	4	2	145	73	72.50	-	1	1	-	144	86	4	21.50	3-28	-	
B & H	7	7	1	160	53	26.66	-	2	-	-	240	189	4	47.25	4-28	-	
Sunday	23	20	3	302	65	17.76	-	2	8	-	511	474	19	24.94	3-9	-	

MASON, T. J.   Leicestershire

Name: Timothy James Mason
Role: Right-hand bat, off-spin bowler
Born: 12 April 1975, Leicester
Height: 5ft 8in **Weight:** 10st 4lbs
Nickname: Perry, Biffa, Stone
County debut: 1994
1st-Class catches: 4
Strike rate: (career 166.00)
Parents: Phillip John and Anthea Jane
Marital status: Single
Family links with cricket: Father plays club
cricket and is manager of Leicestershire
Schools U11
Education: Brookvale High School,
Leicester; Denstone College
Qualifications: 9 GCSEs, 3 A-levels
Overseas tours: Denstone College to South
Africa 1993; England U19 to Sri Lanka 1993-
94; Westgold CC to Northern Transvaal 1996
Overseas teams played for: Eastern Freestate, South Africa 1994-95; Westgold CC,
Western Transvaal 1995-97
Cricketers particularly admired: Allan Lamb, Malcolm Marshall, Jon Dakin, Darren
'Roasting' Maddy

Young players to look out for: Darren Maddy, Jon Dakin 'and of course myself'
Other sports followed: Rugby union (Leicester Tigers), football (Leicester City)
Relaxations: Going out with friends and girlfriend, Nicole. Listening to music
Extras: Captained Leicestershire Schools at all age levels. 1992 *Daily Telegraph* U19 Midlands Bowler of the Year; 1993 *Daily Telegraph* U19 National Bowler of the Year; 1993 Gray-Nicolls Outstanding Schoolboy Player of the Year. Dislocated shoulder prevented him from going on England U18 tour to South Africa 1992-93. Played in the winning Bain Hogg team in 1996
Opinions on cricket: 'Great game, but 2nd XI grounds have to be better. This will definitely make young players better – especially young bowlers.'
Best batting: 4 Leicestershire v Australia, Leicester 1997
Best bowling: 2-21 Leicestershire v Australia, Leicester 1997

1998 Season

	M	Inns	NO	Runs	HS	Avge	100s	50s	Ct	St	O	M	Runs	Wkts	Avge	Best	5wI	10wM
Test																		
All First	2	0	0	0	0	-	-	-	-	-	45.2	9	139	0	-		-	-	-
1-day Int																		
NatWest	1	0	0	0	0	-	-	-	-	-								
B & H	3	0	0	0	0	-	-	-	1	-	19	0	85	5	17.00	3-41	-	
Sunday	9	7	3	22	11	5.50	-	-	3	-	38.1	2	201	7	28.71	4-12	-	

Career Performances

	M	Inns	NO	Runs	HS	Avge	100s	50s	Ct	St	Balls	Runs	Wkts	Avge	Best	5wI	10wM
Test																	
All First	5	2	0	7	4	3.50	-	-	4	-	498	262	3	87.33	2-21	-	-
1-day Int																	
NatWest	5	3	0	71	36	23.66	-	-	3	-	288	164	3	54.66	3-29	-	
B & H	8	4	2	61	30	30.50	-	-	2	-	378	271	10	27.10	3-41	-	
Sunday	31	20	8	107	17 *	8.91	-	-	6	-	929	836	21	39.80	4-12	-	

42. Which former Worcestershire player opened the bowling
for New Zealand on a number of occasions
in the 1992 World Cup?

FICA

MASTERS, D. D.   Kent

Name: David Daniel Masters
Role: Right-hand bat, right-arm
medium-fast bowler
Born: 22 April 1978, Chatham
Height: 6ft 3ins **Weight:** 12st 9lbs
Nickname: Hod, Hodlit
County debut: No first-team appearance
Parents: Kevin and Tracey
Marital status: Single
Family links with cricket:
Father played for Kent and Surrey
Education: Luton Junior School; Fort Luton
High School; Mid-Kent College
Qualifications: 8 GCSEs, GNVQ in Leisure
and Toursim, qualified football coach,
bricklayer and plasterer
Career outside cricket: Builder
Off-season: 'Going to Perth'
Cricketers particularly admired: 'My
father', Ian Botham
Young players to look out for: 'My brother Daniel Masters', Buster Gibbons, Peter
Stock
Other sports played: Football ('Tonbridge Angels in semi-pro'), 'and all other sports'
Other sports followed: Football (Manchester United)
Relaxations: Playing football, 'going out with my mates'
Opinions on cricket: 'Great game. Can only get better.'

MAUNDERS, J. K.   Middlesex

Name: John Kenneth Maunders
Role: Left-hand bat
Born: 4 April 1981, Ashford, Middlesex
Height: 5ft 10in **Weight:** 12st
Nickname: Johnny, Johnboy
County debut: No first-team appearance
Parents: Kenny and Lynn
Marital status: Single
Family links with cricket: 'Grandad and two uncles play club cricket'
Education: Ashford Park Primary School; Ashford High Secondary School;
Spelthorne College of Further Education

Qualifications: 9 GCSEs, Duke of Edinburgh Bronze and Silver Awards
Career outside cricket: Student
Off-season: Touring with England U19 'and keeping fit training with Middlesex'
Overseas tours: England U19 to New Zealand 1998-99
Cricketers particularly admired: Alec Stewart, Justin Langer, Graham Thorpe, Angus Fraser
Young players to look out for: Mark Wallace
Other sports played: Hockey
Other sports followed: Football (Liverpool)
Relaxations: Socialising with friends, playing sports, listening to music
Extras: Awarded junior county cap at the age of 12. Represented England U17

Opinions on cricket: 'Tea should be extended so that players have more time to recoup and get ready for the last session's play.'

MAY, M. R.   Derbyshire

Name: Michael Robert May
Role: Right-hand bat, off-spin bowler
Born: 22 July 1971, Chesterfield, Derbyshire
Height: 5ft 9in **Weight:** 14st 3lbs
Nickname: Maggie, Boonie, Maggo, Mazzey
County debut: 1996
1st-Class 50s: 5
1st-Class 100s: 3
1st-Class catches: 7
Place in batting averages: 194th av. 19.70 (1997 69th av. 39.20)
Parents: Michael and Christine
Wife and date of marriage: Sasha, 14 January 1996
Children: Benjamin Michael, 6 May 1998
Family links with cricket: Brother Paul has played 2nd XI cricket for Derbyshire
Education: Duckmanton Primary School; The Bolsover School; North East Derbyshire College

Qualifications: 4 O-levels, City and Guilds in Recreation and Leisure, NCA cricket coach
Off-season: Playing cricket in Australia for Donvale CC and coaching
Overseas teams played for: Marist, New Zealand 1987-88; Johannesburg Municipals 1991-93; Sandringham CC, Melbourne 1994-96; St Kilda CC, Australia 1996-97; Donvale, Australia 1997-99
Cricketers particularly admired: Steve Waugh, Ian Botham
Young players to look out for: Kevin Dean, Ben Spendlove
Other sports played: Football, tennis, golf
Other sports followed: Football (Chesterfield), Australian rules (Essendon), rugby league (Melbourne Storm)
Injuries: Out for two weeks with a sprained ankle
Relaxations: 'Spending time with my family. Listening to music and reading'
Opinions on cricket: 'Should be more coaching provided for the younger age groups in schools (create more interest).'
Best batting: 116 Derbyshire v Glamorgan, Chesterfield 1997

1998 Season

	M	Inns	NO	Runs	HS	Avge	100s	50s	Ct	St	O	M	Runs	Wkts	Avge	Best	5wI	10wM
Test																		
All First	13	24	0	473	101	19.70	1	1	4	-	3	0	51	0	-		-	-	-
1-day Int																		
NatWest																		
B & H																		
Sunday																		

Career Performances

	M	Inns	NO	Runs	HS	Avge	100s	50s	Ct	St	Balls	Runs	Wkts	Avge	Best	5wI	10wM
Test																	
All First	25	45	4	1221	116	29.78	3	5	7	-	61	120	0	-		-	-	-
1-day Int																	
NatWest	1	1	0	5	5	5.00	-	-	-	-							
B & H																	
Sunday																	

MAYNARD, M. P. Glamorgan

Name: Matthew Peter Maynard
Role: Right-hand bat, occasional
wicket-keeper, county captain
Born: 21 March 1966, Oldham, Lancashire
Height: 5ft 11in **Weight:** 13st
Nickname: Ollie
County debut: 1985
County cap: 1987
Benefit: 1996
Test debut: 1988
Tests: 4
One-Day Internationals: 10
1000 runs in a season: 10
1st-Class 50s: 107
1st-Class 100s: 40
1st-Class 200s: 3
1st-Class catches: 301
1st-Class stumpings: 5
One-Day 100s: 10
Place in batting averages: 111th av. 28.74 (1997 3rd av. 65.00)
Strike rate: (career 166.66)
Parents: Ken (deceased) and Pat
Wife and date of marriage: Susan, 27 September 1986
Children: Tom, 25 March 1989; Ceri Lloyd, 5 August 1993
Family links with cricket: Father played for many years for Duckinfield. Brother
Charles plays for St Fagans
Education: Ysgol David Hughes, Menai Bridge, Anglesey
Qualifications: Cricket coach
Off-season: 'Staying at home/touring with MCC to Kenya as captain February-March
1999'
Overseas tours: North Wales XI to Barbados 1982; Glamorgan to Barbados 1982, to
South Africa 1993; unofficial England XI to South Africa 1989-90; HKCC (Australia)
to Bangkok and Hong Kong, 1990; England VI to Hong Kong Sixes 1992 and 1994;
England to West Indies 1993-94
Overseas teams played for: St Joseph's, Whakatane, New Zealand 1986-88;
Gosnells, Perth, Western Australia 1988-89; Papakura and Northern Districts, New
Zealand 1990-92; Morrinsville College and Northern Districts 1991-92; Otago, New
Zealand 1996-97
Cricketers particularly admired: Ian Botham, Viv Richards, David Gower
Young players to look out for: Dean Cosker, Ben Spendlove
Other sports followed: Football (Manchester City), golf and squash

Injuries: Out for five weeks with a torn adductor

Relaxations: Spending time with my wife and family and relaxing

Extras: Scored century on first-class debut v Yorkshire at Swansea in 1985, when he became the youngest centurion for Glamorgan, and scored 1000 runs in first full season. In 1987 scored the fastest ever 50 for Glamorgan (14 mins) v Yorkshire and was youngest player to be awarded Glamorgan cap. Voted Young Cricketer of the Year 1988 by the Cricket Writers' Club. Banned from Test cricket for five years for joining 1989-90 tour of South Africa, ban remitted 1992. Scored 987 runs in July 1991, including a century in each innings v Gloucestershire at Cheltenham. Captained Glamorgan for most of 1992 in Alan Butcher's absence. Second child was born on the morning of the fifth Test against Australia at Edgbaston 1993 – he had a daughter and a duck on the same day. Awarded benefit for 1996. Voted Wombwell Cricket Lovers' Society captain of the year for 1997. He captained an England XI in the Cricket Max tournament in New Zealand in 1997-98. Has been Glamorgan's captain since the 1996 season. Was one of *Wisden*'s five Cricketers of the Year 1998

Opinions on cricket: 'I believe that people want to "tinker" with the Championship to see what may happen. That is a huge gamble. Just look at the state of Welsh rugby at the minute. Leave the Championship as it is. Tinker with the one-day national league.'

Best batting: 243 Glamorgan v Hampshire, Southampton 1991

Best bowling: 3-21 Glamorgan v Oxford University, The Parks 1987

1998 Season

	M	Inns	NO	Runs	HS	Avge	100s	50s	Ct	St	O	M	Runs	Wkts	Avge	Best	5wl	10wM
Test																		
All First	17	29	2	776	99	28.74	-	5	21	-	5.4	0	46	0	-	-	-	-
1-day Int																		
NatWest	2	2	0	98	66	49.00	-	1	2	-								
B & H	2	2	0	65	55	32.50	-	1	-	-								
Sunday	11	11	0	367	90	33.36	-	2	7	-	4	0	20	0	-	-	-	

Career Performances

	M	Inns	NO	Runs	HS	Avge	100s	50s	Ct	St	Balls	Runs	Wkts	Avge	Best	5wl	10wM
Test	4	8	0	87	35	10.87	-	-	3	-							
All First	309	509	54	19496	243	42.84	43	107	301	5	1000	829	6	138.16	3-21	-	-
1-day Int	10	10	1	153	41	17.00	-	-	2	-							
NatWest	36	35	3	1472	151 *	46.00	2	12	15	-	18	8	0	-	-	-	-
B & H	48	48	6	1802	151 *	42.90	4	9	17	-	30	38	0	-	-	-	-
Sunday	186	178	13	5094	132	30.87	4	32	74	-	46	51	0	-	-	-	-

McCAGUE, M. J.   Kent

Name: Martin John McCague
Role: Right-hand bat, right-arm fast bowler
Born: 24 May 1969, Larne, Northern Ireland
Height: 6ft 5in **Weight:** 17st
Nickname: Pigsy, Macca, Mad Mick
County debut: 1991
County cap: 1992
Test debut: 1993
Tests: 3
50 wickets in a season: 4
1st-Class 50s: 4
1st-Class 5 w. in innings: 24
1st-Class 10 w. in match: 2
1st-Class catches: 66
One-Day 5 w. in innings: 3
Place in batting averages: 182nd av. 20.75
(1997 234th av. 17.27)
Place in bowling averages: 70th av. 28.07
(1997 26th av. 23.43)
Strike rate: 52.25 (career 49.10)
Parents: Mal and Mary
Wife and date of marriage: Leigh-Anne, 8 February 1997
Children: Monte Frederick, 15 September 1998
Education: Hedland Senior High School
Qualifications: Electrician
Overseas tours: England A to South Africa 1993-94; England to Australia 1994-95;
Kent Cricket Board XI to West Indies 1998-99
Overseas teams played for: Western Australia 1990-91
Cricketers particularly admired: Paul Strang, Courtney Walsh
Young players to look out for: Ben Phillips, David Sales
Other sports followed: Football (Crystal Palace FC), golf and snooker
Relaxations: Playing golf
Extras: Kent Player of the Year in 1996
Best batting: 63* Kent v Surrey, The Oval 1996
Best bowling: 9-86 Kent v Derbyshire, Derby 1994

---

43. Who kept wicket for South Africa in the 1996 World Cup?

FICA

1998 Season

	M	Inns	NO	Runs	HS	Avge	100s	50s	Ct	St	O	M	Runs	Wkts	Avge	Best	5wI	10wM
Test																		
All First	10	15	7	166	38	20.75	-	-	8	-	235.1	45	758	27	28.07	4-40	-	-
1-day Int																		
NatWest	2	1	0	19	19	19.00	-	-	-	-	22	4	73	1	73.00	1-28	-	
B & H																		
Sunday	11	4	1	34	13	11.33	-	-	-	-	53.1	3	267	7	38.14	2-20	-	

Career Performances

	M	Inns	NO	Runs	HS	Avge	100s	50s	Ct	St	Balls	Runs	Wkts	Avge	Best	5wI	10wM
Test	3	5	0	21	11	4.20	-	-	1	-	593	390	6	65.00	4-121	-	-
All First	116	161	43	1857	63 *	15.73	-	4	66	-	20574	11127	419	26.55	9-86	24	2
1-day Int																	
NatWest	14	11	6	119	31 *	23.80	-	-	3	-	786	510	22	23.18	5-26	1	
B & H	30	19	8	169	30	15.36	-	-	7	-	1532	1186	39	30.41	5-43	1	
Sunday	88	46	14	286	22 *	8.93	-	-	15	-	3319	2901	116	25.00	5-40	1	

McGRATH, A. *Yorkshire*

Name: Anthony McGrath
Role: Right-hand bat, right-arm medium bowler
Born: 6 October 1975, Bradford
Height: 6ft 1in **Weight:** 14st
Nickname: Gripper, Mags
County debut: 1995
1st-Class 50s: 12
1st-Class 100s: 5
1st-Class catches: 34
One-Day 100s: 1
Place in batting averages: 146th av. 24.48 (1997 95th av. 34.66)
Strike rate: 84.00 (career 91.00)
Parents: Terry and Kathleen
Marital status: Single
Family links with cricket: Brother Dermot plays in the Bradford League. 'Sisters Anne and Catherine could have played for England Ladies. Nephews Aidan, Thomas and Niall are future stars'
Education: St Winefrides; St Blaize; Yorkshire Martyrs Collegiate School
Qualifications: 9 GCSEs, BTEC National Diploma in Leisure Studies, senior coaching award

Off-season: Playing in Melbourne
Overseas tours: England U19 to West Indies 1994-95; England A to Pakistan 1995-96, to Australia 1996-97
Overseas teams played for: Deep Dene, Melbourne 1998-99
Cricketers particularly admired: Darren Lehmann, Nasser Hussain, Ronnie Irani, Robin Smith
Young players to look out for: Matthew Wood, Ian Fisher, Alex Morris
Other sports played: Football (Green Man FC)
Other sports followed: Football (Manchester United)
Injuries: Gout
Relaxations: Watching football. Music. Socialising with friends
Extras: Captained Yorkshire Schools U13, U14, U15 and U16; captained English Schools U17. Bradford League Young Cricketer of the Year 1992 and 1993. Played for England U17, and for England U19 in home series against India 1994. Appeared as 12th man for England in the First Test against West Indies at Headingley in 1995. Scored his maiden first-class century on the England A tour to Pakistan
Opinions on cricket: 'I think cricket's going the right way with two divisions and floodlit cricket. Eventually the Championship should also become two divisions, keeping competitiveness all the way through the season.'
Best batting: 141 Yorkshire v Worcestershire, Headingley 1997
Best bowling: 2-33 Yorkshire v Lancashire, Headingley 1998

1998 Season

	M	Inns	NO	Runs	HS	Avge	100s	50s	Ct	St	O	M	Runs	Wkts	Avge	Best	5wI	10wM
Test																		
All First	17	28	3	612	63 *	24.48	-	3	5	-	42	10	159	3	53.00	2-33	-	-
1-day Int																		
NatWest	2	1	0	25	25	25.00	-	-	1	-								
B & H	6	6	0	151	55	25.16	-	1	5	-								
Sunday	14	13	1	282	55 *	23.50	-	3	1	-	18	1	82	4	20.50	2-20	-	

Career Performances

	M	Inns	NO	Runs	HS	Avge	100s	50s	Ct	St	Balls	Runs	Wkts	Avge	Best	5wI	10wM
Test																	
All First	66	112	7	3048	141	29.02	5	12	34	-	455	288	5	57.60	2-33	-	-
1-day Int																	
NatWest	9	8	1	140	34	20.00	-	-	4	-							
B & H	19	18	1	482	109 *	28.35	1	1	7	-	12	10	2	5.00	2-10	-	
Sunday	45	40	7	890	72	26.96	-	7	11	-	108	82	4	20.50	2-20	-	

McKEOWN, P. C.   Lancashire

Name: Patrick Christopher McKeown
Role: Right-hand bat
Born: 1 June 1976, Liverpool
Height: 6ft 3in **Weight:** 13st
Nickname: Paddy
County debut: 1996
1st-Class 50s: 1
1st-Class catches: 9
Place in batting averages: 128th av. 26.57
(1997 191st av. 22.50)
Parents: Paddy and Cathy
Marital status: Single
Education: St Mary's College, Crosby;
Rossall School (Blackpool)
Qualifications: 7 GCSEs, 3 A-levels
Overseas tours: Rossall School to Australia
1994-95

Overseas teams played for: Subiaco-Floriat,
Perth, Australia 1995-96
Cricketers particularly admired: Graeme Hick and Neil Fairbrother
Other sports followed: Football (Liverpool)
Relaxations: 'Playing most sports, especially football and rugby. I enjoy spending
time on the golf course'
Extras: Represented England Schools U19, and U18 versus India. Played for
Development of Excellence U19, National Cricket Association U19, Headmasters'
Conference U19. Awarded 2nd XI cap in 1996. Scored 307 in less than a day for
Lancashire 2nd XI v Gloucestershire 2nd XI at Bristol in 1998, the highest individual
score ever made for Lancashire 2nd XI
Best batting: 64 Lancashire v Warwickshire, Edgbaston 1996

1998 Season

	M	Inns	NO	Runs	HS	Avge	100s	50s	Ct	St	O	M	Runs	Wkts	Avge	Best	5wI	10wM
Test																		
All First	5	7	0	186	42	26.57	-	-	6	-								
1-day Int																		
NatWest																		
B & H																		
Sunday	5	5	0	43	20	8.60	-	-	-	-								

	M	Inns	NO	Runs	HS	Avge	100s	50s	Ct	St	Balls	Runs	Wkts	Avge	Best	5wI	10wM
Test																	
All First	11	15	0	394	64	26.26	-	1	9	-							
1-day Int																	
NatWest	1	1	0	42	42	42.00	-	-	-	-	60	51	0	-	-	-	-
B & H	1	1	0	10	10	10.00	-	-	-	-							
Sunday	14	14	0	199	69	14.21	-	1	5	-							

McLEAN, N. A. M.   Hampshire

Name: Nixon Alexei McNamara McLean
Role: Left-hand bat, right-arm fast bowler
Born: 28 July 1973, Stubbs, St Vincent
Height: 6ft 5in
Nickname: Nicko
County debut: 1998
County cap: 1998
Test debut: 1997-98
Tests: 4
One-Day Internationals: 8
50 wickets in a season: 1
1st-Class 50s: 1
1st-Class 5 w. in innings: 4
1st-Class catches: 8
Place in batting averages: 247th av. 14.40
Place in bowling averages: 49th av. 25.40
Strike rate: 50.20 (career 56.52)
Marital status: Single
Off-season: Touring South Africa with West Indies

Overseas tours: West Indies to Australia 1996-97, to Bangladesh 1998-99, to South Africa 1998-99
Best batting: 52 Windward Islands v Barbados, St George's 1997-98
Best bowling: 6-28 West Indies A v Eastern Province, Port Elizabeth 1997-98

---

44. Which New Zealand bowler had figures of 2-105
v England in the opening match of the 1983 World Cup?

FIGA

1998 Season

	M	Inns	NO	Runs	HS	Avge	100s	50s	Ct	St	O	M	Runs	Wkts	Avge	Best	5wl	10wM
Test																		
All First	16	22	2	288	43	14.40	-	-	5	-	518.5	105	1575	62	25.40	6-101	2-	
1-day Int																		
NatWest	4	4	2	89	36	44.50	-	-	-	-	35.4	2	141	6	23.50	2-23	-	
B & H	4	3	1	31	28 *	15.50	-	-	2	-	37.3	2	198	1	198.00	1-54	-	
Sunday	17	12	1	135	30	12.27	-	-	1	-	106	3	516	22	23.45	3-39	-	

Career Performances

	M	Inns	NO	Runs	HS	Avge	100s	50s	Ct	St	Balls	Runs	Wkts	Avge	Best	5wl	10wM
Test	4	4	1	22	11	7.33	-	-	1	-	468	203	5	40.60	2-46	-	
All First	41	62	13	858	52	17.51	-	1	8	-	6613	3458	117	29.55	6-28	4	-
1-day Int	8	3	0	8	7	2.66	-	-	2	-	306	222	6	37.00	3-44	-	
NatWest	4	4	2	89	36	44.50	-	-	-	-	214	141	6	23.50	2-23	-	
B & H	4	3	1	31	28 *	15.50	-	-	2	-	225	198	1	198.00	1-54	-	
Sunday	17	12	1	135	30	12.27	-	-	1	-	636	516	22	23.45	3-39	-	

MIDDLEBROOK, J. D.   Yorkshire

Name: James Daniel Middlebrook
Role: Right-hand bat, off-spin bowler
Born: 13 May 1977, Leeds
Height: 6ft 1in **Weight:** 13st
Nickname: Midi, Midders, Midhouse
County debut: 1998
1st-Class catches: 7
Place in batting averages: 251st av. 13.90
Place in bowling averages: 99th av. 32.46
Strike rate: 75.76 (career 75.76)
Parents: Ralph and Mavis
Marital status: Single
Family links with cricket: 'Dad is a senior staff coach/Cricket Development Officer for Leeds and Manager, Yorkshire Cricket School'
Education: Greenside, Pudsey ('same class as Paul Hutchison'); Crawshaw, Pudsey
Qualifications: NVQ Level 2 in Sport and Recreation, ECB senior coach
Off-season: 'Third year as pro at Stokes Valley CC, Wellington, New Zealand'
Overseas tours: Yorkshire CCC to Guernsey

Overseas teams played for: Stokes Valley CC, New Zealand; Gold Coast Dolphins, Brisbane; Surfers Paradise CC, Brisbane

Cricketers particularly admired: John Emburey, Ian Botham

Young players to look out for: Matthew Wood, Matthew Hoggard, 'Me!'

Other sports played: Golf, tennis, squash, badminton

Other sports followed: Football (Leeds United), athletics

Relaxations: 'Any music – MTV – sleeping, socialising, catching up with old friends'

Extras: Played for Pudsey Congs since age of seven. Played for Yorkshire at all age levels U11 to 1st XI. Awarded Yorkshire 2nd XI cap 1998

Opinions on cricket: 'Great fun. More day/night cricket – four segments of 20 overs: bat/bowl/bat/bowl. Sunday League should be 40 overs.'

Best batting: 41 Yorkshire v Lancashire, Headingley 1998

Best bowling: 3-20 Yorkshire v Worcestershire, Worcester 1998

1998 Season

	M	Inns	NO	Runs	HS	Avge	100s	50s	Ct	St	O	M	Runs	Wkts	Avge	Best	5wI	10wM
Test																		
All First	8	12	2	139	41	13.90	-	-	7	-	164.1	45	422	13	32.46	3-20	-	-
1-day Int																		
NatWest																		
B & H																		
Sunday	1	1	0	5	5	5.00	-	-	-	-	2	0	19	0	-		-	-

Career Performances

	M	Inns	NO	Runs	HS	Avge	100s	50s	Ct	St	Balls	Runs	Wkts	Avge	Best	5wI	10wM
Test																	
All First	8	12	2	139	41	13.90	-	-	7	-	985	422	13	32.46	3-20	-	-
1-day Int																	
NatWest																	
B & H																	
Sunday	1	1	0	5	5	5.00	-	-	-	-	12	19	0	-		-	-

MILLNS, D. J. — Leicestershire

Name: David James Millns
Role: Left-hand bat, right-arm fast-medium bowler
Born: 27 February 1965, Mansfield, Nottinghamshire
Height: 6ft 3in **Weight:** 14st 7lbs
Nickname: Rocket Man
County debut: 1988 (Nottinghamshire), 1990 (Leicestershire)
County cap: 1991
50 wickets in a season: 4
1st-Class 50s: 7
1st-Class 100s: 3
1st-Class 5 w. in innings: 21
1st-Class 10 w. in match: 4
1st-Class catches: 68
Place in batting averages: 16th av. 48.16 (1997 96th av. 34.53)
Place in bowling averages: 40th av. 24.02 (1997 50th av. 27.36)
Strike rate: 42.97 (career 48.51)

Parents: Bernard and Brenda
Wife and date of marriage: Wanda Marie, 25 September 1993
Children: Dylan, 17 April 1998
Family links with cricket: Andy Pick, former Notts CCC player, is brother-in-law. Brother Paul and his son Matthew play for Clipstone MWCC
Education: Samuel Barlow Junior; Garibaldi Comprehensive; North Notts College of Further Education; Nottingham Trent Polytechnic
Qualifications: Advanced coach
Career outside cricket: 'Hopefully should stay involved with the game'
Off-season: 'Testimonial year'
Overseas tours: England A to Australia 1992-93; Leicestershire to South Africa 1994 and 1995, to Holland 1994 and 1996, to Barbados 1998
Overseas teams played for: Uitenhage, Port Elizabeth, South Africa 1988-89; Birkenhead, Auckland 1989-91; Tasmania, Australia 1994-95; Boland, South Africa 1996-97
Cricketers particularly admired: Vince Wells, Aftab Habib
Young players to look out for: Ben Smith, Carl Crowe, Paul Franks
Other sports followed: Football (Leicester City), rugby union (Leicester Tigers), golf ('taking money off J.J. Whitaker on the golf course gives me great pleasure')
Injuries: Out for ten weeks with a virus

Relaxations: Computers and property development
Extras: Harold Larwood Bowling Award 1984. Asked to be released by
Nottinghamshire at the end of 1989 season and joined Leicestershire in 1990. Finished
third in national bowling averages in 1990. Britannic Assurance Player of the Month in
August 1991 after taking 9-37 v Derbyshire, the best Leicestershire figures since
George Geary's 10-18 v Glamorgan in 1929. Players' representative on Cricketers'
Association Executive for Leicestershire. Leicestershire Cricketer of the Year 1992.
Leicestershire Bowling Award 1990, 1991, 1992 and 1994. Granted a benefit for 1999
Opinions on cricket: 'Some of our young players are put into Test cricket before they
have sorted out the first-class game. This is not good for the future if you have already
destroyed a player's confidence at 19.'
Best batting: 121 Leicestershire v Northamptonshire, Northampton 1997
Best bowling: 9-37 Leicestershire v Derbyshire, Derby 1991

1998 Season

	M	Inns	NO	Runs	HS	Avge	100s	50s	Ct	St	O	M	Runs	Wkts	Avge	Best	5wI	10wM
Test																		
All First	11	10	4	289	99	48.16	-	1	4	-	243.3	55	817	34	24.02	4-60	-	-
1-day Int																		
NatWest																		
B & H	5	1	1	3	3*	-	-	-	-	-	30	2	152	2	76.00	1-27	-	
Sunday	1	1	0	6	6	6.00	-	-	-	-	3	0	26	0	-		-	-

Career Performances

	M	Inns	NO	Runs	HS	Avge	100s	50s	Ct	St	Balls	Runs	Wkts	Avge	Best	5wI	10wM
Test																	
All First	156	181	55	2744	121	21.77	3	7	68	-	24208	13790	499	27.63	9-37	21	4
1-day Int																	
NatWest	11	5	3	49	29*	24.50	-	-	2	-	648	423	12	35.25	3-22	-	
B & H	27	14	8	103	39*	17.16	-	-	5	-	1244	908	29	31.31	4-26	-	
Sunday	41	20	10	110	20*	11.00	-	-	9	-	1530	1349	31	43.51	2-11	-	

FIGA

45. Who scored an unbeaten 138 to help set up victory for
West Indies in the 1979 World Cup final?

MIRZA, M. M. Worcestershire

Name: Maneer Mohammed Mirza
Role: Right-hand bat, right-arm fast bowler
Born: 1 April 1978, Birmingham
Height: 5ft 10in **Weight:** 11st 9lbs
Nickname: Mo
County debut: 1997
1st-Class catches: 1
Place in bowling averages:
(1997 85th av. 32.63)
Strike rate: (career 48.21)
Parents: Mirza Sherbaz (deceased) and
Zarda Bi
Marital status: Single
Family links with cricket: 'My brother
Parvaz played for Worcestershire CCC
1993-1995'

Education: Wyndcliffe Primary School;
Sheldon Heath Secondary School;
Bourneville College of Further Education
Qualifications: 5 GCSEs and 2 A-levels
Career outside cricket: Studying for a degree in Business Management and Sports
Studies
Overseas tours: England U15 to South Africa 1993; Birmingham Schools to India and
Pakistan 1996
Cricketers particularly admired: Parvaz (brother), Imran Khan, Wasim Akram,
Malcolm Marshall, Ian Botham
Other sports followed: Boxing and basketball
Relaxations: Sleeping and spending time with friends and family
Opinions on cricket: 'The standard of wickets could be improved to produce better
players. Contracts should be extended to nine months instead of six.'
Best batting: 10* Worcestershire v Warwickshire, Edgbaston 1997
Best bowling: 4-51 Worcestershire v Warwickshire, Edgbaston 1997

FIGA

46. Who holds the record for the most runs
in a World Cup tournament?

1998 Season (did not make any first-class or one-day appearances)

Career Performances

	M	Inns	NO	Runs	HS	Avge	100s	50s	Ct	St	Balls	Runs	Wkts	Avge	Best	5wI	10wM
Test																	
All First	6	7	4	17	10 *	5.66	-	-	1	-	916	620	19	32.63	4-51	-	-
1-day Int																	
NatWest																		
B & H																		
Sunday	4	0	0	0	0	-	-	-	1	-	96	113	1	113.00	1-31	-	

MONTGOMERIE, R. R. Sussex

Name: Richard Robert Montgomerie
Role: Right-hand opening bat, off-spin bowler
Born: 3 July 1971, Rugby
Height: 5ft 10in **Weight:** 12st 7lbs
Nickname: Monty, Sheep's Head
County debut: 1991 (Northamptonshire)
County cap: 1995 (Northamptonshire)
1000 runs in a season: 2
1st-Class 50s: 27
1st-Class 100s: 9
1st-Class catches: 84
One-Day 100s: 1
Place in batting averages: 184th av. 20.61 (1997 105th av. 33.60)
Parents: Robert and Gillian
Marital status: Single
Family links with cricket: Father captained Oxfordshire
Education: Rugby School; Worcester College, Oxford University
Qualifications: 12 O-levels, 4 A-levels, BA in Chemistry
Overseas tours: Oxford University to Namibia 1991
Overseas teams played for: Sydney University CC 1995-96
Cricketers particularly admired: Many
Other sports followed: Golf, rackets, real tennis and many others
Relaxations: Any sport, good television, reading and 'occasionally testing my brain'
Extras: Scored unbeaten 50 in each innings of 1991 Varsity match and was Oxford captain in 1994. Oxford rackets Blue 1990. Captained Combined Universities 1994. Released by Northants at the end of the 1998 season and has joined Sussex for 1999

Opinions on cricket: 'Four-day cricket is in its infancy. It produces good quality matches and deserves time to mature in the present structure. An Under-21 first-class side should be considered and paid for by the ECB.'

Best batting: 192 Northamptonshire v Kent, Canterbury 1995

1998 Season

	M	Inns	NO	Runs	HS	Avge	100s	50s	Ct	St	O	M	Runs	Wkts	Avge	Best	5wl	10wM
Test																		
All First	10	16	3	268	54	20.61	-	1	4	-								
1-day Int																		
NatWest																		
B & H	2	1	0	9	9	9.00	-	-	-	-								
Sunday	2	2	0	18	12	9.00	-	-	-	-								

Career Performances

	M	Inns	NO	Runs	HS	Avge	100s	50s	Ct	St	Balls	Runs	Wkts	Avge	Best	5wl	10wM
Test																	
All First	98	170	19	4943	192	32.73	9	27	84	-	102	66	0	-	-	-	-
1-day Int																	
NatWest	7	7	1	300	109	50.00	1	2	3	-							
B & H	17	15	2	421	75	32.38	-	2	2	-	6	0	0	-	-	-	
Sunday	37	36	1	1058	86 *	30.22	-	10	10	-							

MOODY, T. M.   Worcestershire

Name: Thomas Masson Moody
Role: Right-hand bat, right-arm medium bowler, county captain
Born: 2 October 1965, Adelaide
Height: 6ft 7in **Weight:** 16st
Nickname: Moods, Tex
County debut: 1990 (Warwickshire), 1991 (Worcestershire)
County cap: 1990 (Warwickshire), 1991 (Worcestershire)
Test debut: 1989-90
Tests: 8
One-Day Internationals: 58
1000 runs in a season: 5
1st-Class 50s: 89
1st-Class 100s: 59
1st-Class 200s: 4
1st-Class 5 w. in innings: 9
1st-Class 10 w. in match: 2
1st-Class catches: 276

One-Day 100s: 15
Place in batting averages: 31st av. 42.19
(1997 25th av. 48.65)
Place in bowling averages: 81st av. 29.25
(1997 128th av. 43.63)
Strike rate: 55.81 (career 67.09)
Parents: John and Janet
Wife and date of marriage:
Helen, 3 March 1993
Children: Jackson, 5 March 1995
Family links with cricket: Father played A
Grade cricket in South Australia
Education: Guildford Grammar School,
Western Australia
Qualifications: HSE
Career outside cricket: Sports shop owner
Overseas tours: Australia to India and
Pakistan (World Cup) 1987-88, to England
1989, to India 1989-90, to Sri Lanka 1992-93, to New Zealand 1997-98, to Sharjah
1997-98, to India 1997-98
Overseas teams played for: Midland Guildford, Perth, Western Australia;
Western Australia 1985 –
Cricketers particularly admired: Dennis Lillee, Allan Border, Viv Richards, Rod Marsh
Other sports followed: Aussie rules football (West Coast Eagles), football, golf, tennis
Relaxations: Golf, sleeping and films
Extras: Scored 150s in both innings of 1988-89 Sheffield Shield final for Western
Australia v Queensland; has scored a total of four centuries in Sheffield Shield finals.
Hit a century against Warwickshire during Australia's 1989 tour and signed a one-year
contract with them for 1990. Hit centuries in first three first-class matches for
Warwickshire, and seven in first eight matches – a unique achievement. Scored the
(then) fastest ever first-class century v Glamorgan in 26 minutes – taking advantage of
declaration bowling. Reached 1000 first-class runs in first season of county cricket in
only 12 innings – another record. Released by Warwickshire at the end of the 1990
season after they had chosen Allan Donald as their one overseas player and was signed
by Worcestershire for 1991 when Graeme Hick was no longer considered an overseas
player. Not re-signed for 1993 season because he was expected to be touring with the
Australian team, although in the event he was not selected. Returned for 1994 season.
Scored 180* and shared record unbroken partnership with Tim Curtis in the semi-final
of the NatWest Trophy 1994. Appointed Worcestershire's captain in 1996 after
replacing Tim Curtis halfway through the 1995 season. Reclaimed a place in the
Australian one-day side for the World Series against West Indies and Pakistan in 1996-
97. Became the fastest player to score 4000 runs in the Sunday League, achieving the
feat in only 100 innings. Represented Australia in the World Series against South
Africa and New Zealand in 1997-98
Opinions on cricket: 'We need more quality not quantity.'

Best batting: 272 Western Australia v Tasmania, Hobart 1994-95
Best bowling: 7-38 Western Australia v Tasmania, Hobart 1995-96

1998 Season

	M	Inns	NO	Runs	HS	Avge	100s	50s	Ct	St	O	M	Runs	Wkts	Avge	Best	5wl	10wM
Test																		
All First	13	23	2	886	132	42.19	4	2	10	-	251.1	73	790	27	29.25	5-64	1	-
1-day Int																		
NatWest	1	1	0	4	4	4.00	-	-	-	-	12	3	55	2	27.50	2-55	-	
B & H	4	4	0	96	51	24.00	-	1	-	-	31	5	127	8	15.87	4-24	-	
Sunday	12	12	0	343	80	28.58	-	2	4	-	64	2	286	12	23.83	3-17	-	

Career Performances

	M	Inns	NO	Runs	HS	Avge	100s	50s	Ct	St	Balls	Runs	Wkts	Avge	Best	5wl	10wM
Test	8	14	0	456	106	32.57	2	3	9	-	432	147	2	73.50	1-17	-	-
All First	279	465	41	20143	272	47.50	63	89	276	-	21335	9879	318	31.06	7-38	9	2
1-day Int	58	52	5	1013	89	21.55	-	8	16	-	2017	1470	37	39.72	3-39	-	
NatWest	16	16	3	860	180*	66.15	3	3	10	-	631	363	11	33.00	2-33	-	
B & H	38	36	7	1555	110*	53.62	2	14	17	-	972	587	23	25.52	4-24	-	
Sunday	118	116	10	4565	160	43.06	10	30	37	-	2715	1934	71	27.23	4-46	-	

MOORES, P.   Sussex

Name: Peter Moores
Role: Right-hand bat, wicket-keeper
Born: 18 December 1962,
Macclesfield, Cheshire
Height: 6ft **Weight:** 13st
Nickname: Billy
County debut: 1983 (Worcestershire),
1985 (Sussex)
County cap: 1989 (Sussex)
Benefit: 1998
1st-Class 50s: 31
1st-Class 100s: 7
1st-Class catches: 502
1st-Class stumpings: 44
Place in batting averages:
(1997 203rd av. 21.14)
Parents: Bernard and Winifred
Wife and date of marriage:
Karen Jane, 28 September 1989

Children: Natalie Marie, 4 August 1993
Family links with cricket: Brothers, Anthony, Stephen and Robert, all play club cricket
Education: King Edward VI School, Macclesfield
Qualifications: 7 O-levels, 3 A-levels, advanced cricket coach
Career outside cricket: Sussex 1st XI coach
Overseas tours: Christians in Sport to India 1989-90; MCC to Namibia 1990-91, to Leeward Islands 1991-92, to Bahrain 1994-95
Overseas teams played for: Orange Free State, South Africa 1988-89
Cricketers particularly admired: Bob Taylor, Alan Knott, Clive Lloyd
Other sports followed: Football, golf
Relaxations: Golf, wine and old films
Extras: On MCC groundstaff in 1982 before joining Worcestershire in latter half of 1982 season. Joined Sussex in 1985. Captain 1997. Retired part-way through the 1998 season to concentrate on his role as first-team coach
Best batting: 185 Sussex v Cambridge University, Hove 1996

1998 Season

	M	Inns	NO	Runs	HS	Avge	100s	50s	Ct	St	O	M	Runs	Wkts	Avge	Best	5wI	10wM
Test																		
All First	3	3	2	56	36	56.00	-	-	2	-								
1-day Int																		
NatWest																		
B & H	2	1	0	14	14	14.00	-	-	2	-								
Sunday	3	3	0	7	4	2.33	-	-	3	-								

Career Performances

	M	Inns	NO	Runs	HS	Avge	100s	50s	Ct	St	Balls	Runs	Wkts	Avge	Best	5wI	10wM
Test																	
All First	231	345	43	7351	185	24.34	7	31	502	44	18	16	0	-	-	-	-
1-day Int																	
NatWest	28	19	4	231	45	15.40	-	-	36	3							
B & H	37	28	4	343	76	14.29	-	1	31	5							
Sunday	171	139	37	1934	89 *	18.96	-	7	148	23							

MORRIS, A. C.   Hampshire

Name: Alexander Corfield Morris
Role: Left-hand bat, right-arm
medium-fast bowler
Born: 4 October 1976, Barnsley
Height: 6ft 4in **Weight:** 12st 7lbs
County debut: 1995 (Yorkshire),
1998 (Hampshire)
50 wickets in a season: 1
1st-Class 50s: 2
1st-Class catches: 18
Place in batting averages: 172nd av. 21.90
(1997 290th av. 13.00)
Place in bowling averages: 18th av. 20.24
Strike rate: 37.68 (career 46.27)
Parents: Chris and Janet
Marital status: Single
Education: Wilthorpe Primary School;
Holgate School, Barnsley; Barnsley College
Qualifications: 4 GCSEs, BTEC National
Diploma in Sports Science, NCA coaching award
Overseas tours: England U19 to West Indies 1994-95, to Zimbabwe 1995-96;
England VI to Hong Kong 1996
Cricketers particularly admired: Ian Botham, Martyn Moxon
Young players to look out for: Anthony McGrath, Michael Vaughan
Other sports followed: Football (Barnsley FC)
Relaxations: Listening to music, relaxing with mates
Extras: Played for Yorkshire U11-U19. Played for England U15 against Barbados
and in 1994 for both England U17 and U19 against India. Played junior football with
both Barnsley and Rotherham and had trials for Nottingham Forest and Leeds. Left
Yorkshire and signed for Hampshire along with his brother Zac for the 1998 season
Opinions on cricket: 'More coloured clothing cricket.'
Best batting: 60 Yorkshire v Lancashire, Old Trafford 1996
Best bowling: 4-30 Hampshire v Durham, Southampton 1998

---

47. The World Cup match at Old Trafford on 14 June 1979
produced only 91 runs. Who were the teams
involved and what was the result?

1998 Season

	M	Inns	NO	Runs	HS	Avge	100s	50s	Ct	St	O	M	Runs	Wkts	Avge	Best	5wI	10wM
Test																		
All First	12	15	5	219	51	21.90	-	1	6	-	314	65	1012	50	20.24	4-30	-	-
1-day Int																		
NatWest																		
B & H																		
Sunday	1	1	1	3	3 *	-	-	-	-	-	5	0	19	0	-		-	-

Career Performances

	M	Inns	NO	Runs	HS	Avge	100s	50s	Ct	St	Balls	Runs	Wkts	Avge	Best	5wI	10wM
Test																	
All First	28	38	7	581	60	18.74	-	2	18	-	2730	1520	59	25.76	4-30	-	-
1-day Int																	
NatWest	1	1	1	1	1 *	-	-	-	-	-	48	43	1	43.00	1-43	-
B & H	1	0	0	0	0	-	-	-	1	-	6	4	0	-		-
Sunday	24	16	4	211	48 *	17.58	-	-	5	-	432	381	15	25.40	4-49	-

MORRIS, J. E.   Durham

Name: John Edward Morris
Role: Right-hand bat, right-arm
medium bowler
Born: 1 April 1964, Crewe
Height: 5ft 10in **Weight:** 13st 6lbs
Nickname: Animal
County debut: 1982 (Derbyshire),
1994 (Durham)
County cap: 1986 (Derbyshire)
Test debut: 1990
Tests: 3
One-Day Internationals: 8
1000 runs in a season: 11
1st-Class 50s: 93
1st-Class 100s: 45
1st-Class 200s: 2
1st-Class catches: 139
One-Day 100s: 9
Place in batting averages: 64th av. 34.86
(1997 94th av. 34.79)
Strike rate: (career 142.57)
Parents: George (Eddie) and Jean

Wife and date of marriage: Sally, 30 September 1990
Children: Thomas Edward, 27 June 1991
Family links with cricket: Father played for Crewe for many years as an opening bowler
Education: Shavington Comprehensive School; Dane Bank College of Further Education
Qualifications: O-levels
Overseas tours: England to Australia 1990-91; Romany to South Africa 1993: MCC to Bahrain 1994-95
Overseas teams played for: Umbilo, Durban, South Africa 1982-84; Alex Old Boys, Pietermaritzburg, South Africa 1984-85; Subiaco-Floriat, Western Australia 1986-87; Griqualand West, South Africa 1988-89, 1993-94; Protea, Johannesburg, South Africa 1993
Other sports followed: Golf, football (Derby County)
Relaxations: The golf course and home life
Extras: Youngest player to score a Sunday League century. Awarded a benefit in 1999
Best batting: 229 Derbyshire v Gloucestershire, Cheltenham 1993
Best bowling: 1-6 Derbyshire v Cambridge University, Fenner's 1993

1998 Season

	M	Inns	NO	Runs	HS	Avge	100s	50s	Ct	St	O	M	Runs	Wkts	Avge	Best	5wl	10wM
Test																		
All First	13	24	2	767	163	34.86	3	1	5	-								
1-day Int																		
NatWest	2	2	0	34	23	17.00	-	-	-	-								
B & H	3	3	0	40	21	13.33	-	-	1	-								
Sunday	10	9	0	260	66	28.88	-	2	4	-								

Career Performances

	M	Inns	NO	Runs	HS	Avge	100s	50s	Ct	St	Balls	Runs	Wkts	Avge	Best	5wl	10wM
Test	3	5	2	71	32	23.66	-	-	3	-							
All First	326	551	33	19506	229	37.65	47	93	139	-	998	913	7	130.42	1-6	-	-
1-day Int	8	8	1	167	63 *	23.85	-	1	2	-							
NatWest	29	28	3	846	109	33.84	1	5	9	-							
B & H	58	54	6	1481	145	30.85	3	7	13	-	24	14	0	-	-	-	
Sunday	207	197	12	4790	134	25.89	5	21	48	-	9	8	0	-	-	-	

FIGA

48. Which Indian spin wizard took 1-6 from 12 overs
v East Africa in the 1975 World Cup?

MORRIS, Z. C.   Hampshire

Name: Zachary Clegg Morris
Role: Right-hand bat, slow left-arm bowler
Born: 4 September 1978, Barnsley
Height: 6ft **Weight:** 12st 7lbs
Nickname: Cleggy
County debut: 1998
Parents: Lance and Janet
Marital status: Single
Family links with cricket: 'Lance runs local
junior team and Janet is a cricket nut'
Education: Wilthorpe Primary School;
Holgate Secondary School;
'The University of Life'
Qualifications: NCA coaching award
Overseas tours: England U19 to Pakistan
1996-97

Cricketers particularly admired:
Alex Wharf, Gareth Batty, Craig Dudley,
Dave Lyons
Young players to look out for: Ben Spendlove, Stephen Peters, Robert Key
Other sports followed: 'Coinidje, three man Chinese off-spin, Barnsley FC'
Relaxations: 'Visiting commercial places. Watching Keysi and Ralph dance. Black
jack. *The Jerry Springer Show*'
Extras: 'Pretty useful groundsman!' Moved to Hampshire in the 1997-98 close season
along with his brother, Alex. Represented England U19 v Pakistan U19 1998
Opinions on cricket: 'Enjoyable but could also do with a bit more pzazz.'
Best batting: 10 Hampshire v Gloucestershire, Southampton 1998

1998 Season

	M	Inns	NO	Runs	HS	Avge	100s	50s	Ct	St	O	M	Runs	Wkts	Avge	Best	5wI	10wM
Test																		
All First	1	2	0	10	10	5.00	-	-	-	-	1	0	5	0	-	-	-	-
1-day Int																		
NatWest																		
B & H																		
Sunday																		

Career Performances

	M	Inns	NO	Runs	HS	Avge	100s	50s	Ct	St	Balls	Runs	Wkts	Avge	Best	5wl	10wM
Test																	
All First	1	2	0	10	10	5.00	-	-	-	-	6	5	0	-	-	-	-
1-day Int																	
NatWest																	
B & H																	
Sunday																	

MUAZAM ALI   Durham

Name: Muazam Ali
Role: Right-hand bat, right-arm leg-spin bowler
Born: 23 October 1979, Whipps Cross, London
Height: 5ft 7in **Weight:** 10st 6lbs
Nickname: Muz
County debut: No first-team appearance
Parents: Masroor and Elean
Marital status: Single
Family links with cricket: Father's brother played first-class cricket in Pakistan
Education: St Aubyn's; Chigwell School
Qualifications: 10 GCSEs, 3 A-levels
Off-season: 'Between training in the gym and nets, working in London for solicitors'
Overseas tours: Essex U14 to Hong Kong 1993; Essex U15 to Barbados 1994
Cricketers particularly admired:
Martin Crowe, Steve Waugh, Dean Jones, Sachin Tendulkar
Young players to look out for: Carl Greenidge, Michael Gough, Owais Shah
Other sports followed: Football (Tottenham Hotspur), tennis
Injuries: Out for eight weeks after breaking collarbone in May
Relaxations: Listening to various types of music. Socialising with friends. Reading
Extras: MCC Young Cricketer of the Year 1993 (U13), 1995 (U15), 1997 (U19). Man of the Tour, Essex U15 to Barbados 1994

MULLALLY, A. D.   Leicestershire

Name: Alan David Mullally
Role: Right-hand bat, left-arm fast bowler
Born: 12 July 1969, Southend
Height: 6ft 5in **Weight:** 14st
Nickname: Bob, Bryan, Eric, Spider,
'too many to mention'
County debut: 1988 (Hampshire),
1990 (Leicestershire)
County cap: 1993 (Leicestershire)
Test debut: 1996
Tests: 9
One-Day Internationals: 8
50 wickets in a season: 4
1st-Class 50s: 2
1st-Class 5 w. in innings: 16
1st-Class 10 w. in match: 3
1st-Class catches: 31
One-Day 5 w. in innings: 2
Place in batting averages: 245th av. 14.66
(1997 295th av. 7.16)
Place in bowling averages: 9th av. 18.80 (1997 100th av. 35.18)
Strike rate: 44.86 (career 63.59)
Parents: Michael and Ann
Marital status: Single
Education: Cannington High School and Primary, Perth, Australia; Wembley and
Carlisle Technical College
Qualifications: 'This and that'
Career outside cricket: Musician
Overseas tours: Western Australia to India; Leicestershire to Jamaica 1992-93; England
to Zimbabwe and New Zealand 1996-97, to Australia 1998-99
Overseas teams played for: Western Australia 1987-90; Victoria 1990-91
Cricketers particularly admired: Geoff Marsh, Dermot Reeve
Young players to look out for: Darren Maddy
Other sports followed: Australian rules football, basketball, most sports
Relaxations: Music
Extras: English-qualified as he was born in Southend, he made his first-class debut for
Western Australia in the 1987-88 Sheffield Shield final, and played for Australian YC
1988-89. Played one match for Hampshire in 1988 before joining Leicestershire
Opinions on cricket: 'Good fun.'
Best batting: 75 Leicestershire v Middlesex, Leicester 1996
Best bowling: 7-55 Leicestershire v Nottinghamshire, Worksop 1998

Stop press: Claimed first five-wicket haul in Tests (5-105) in Australia's first innings at Brisbane 1998-99

1998 Season

	M	Inns	NO	Runs	HS	Avge	100s	50s	Ct	St	O	M	Runs	Wkts	Avge	Best	5wl	10wM
Test																		
All First	15	11	2	132	38 *	14.66	-	-	3	-	448.4	156	1128	60	18.80	7-55	3	1
1-day Int	3	2	1	2	1 *	2.00	-	-	-	-	27	1	90	4	22.50	2-20	-	
NatWest	4	0	0	0	0	-	-	-	-	-	48	9	125	11	11.36	5-18	1	
B & H	8	1	0	1	1	1.00	-	-	1	-	71	10	255	13	19.61	3-34	-	
Sunday	9	4	2	6	3 *	3.00	-	-	1	-	61	6	176	10	17.60	3-32	-	

Career Performances

	M	Inns	NO	Runs	HS	Avge	100s	50s	Ct	St	Balls	Runs	Wkts	Avge	Best	5wl	10wM
Test	9	12	4	79	24	9.87	-	-	1	-	2379	927	28	33.10	3-44	-	-
All First	157	170	44	1166	75	9.25	-	2	31	-	28807	13736	453	30.32	7-55	16	3
1-day Int	11	5	1	24	20	6.00	-	-	3	-	558	366	14	26.14	3-29	-	
NatWest	18	8	5	42	19 *	14.00	-	-	2	-	1152	622	29	21.44	5-18	1	
B & H	40	15	5	34	11	3.40	-	-	1	-	2206	1386	41	33.80	3-33	-	
Sunday	89	38	18	187	38	9.35	-	-	17	-	3857	2839	93	30.52	5-15	1	

MUNTON, T. A.   Warwickshire

Name: Timothy Alan Munton
Role: Right-hand bat, right-arm
fast-medium bowler
Born: 30 July 1965, Melton Mowbray
Height: 6ft 6in **Weight:** 15st 7lbs
Nickname: Harry, Captain Sensible
County debut: 1985
County cap: 1990
Benefit: 1998
Test debut: 1991
Tests: 2
50 wickets in a season: 5
1st-Class 50s: 2
1st-Class 5 w. in innings: 29
1st-Class 10 w. in match: 6
1st-Class catches: 68
One-Day 5 w. in innings: 2
Place in batting averages: 285th av. 7.20
Place in bowling averages: 11th av. 19.13

Strike rate: 45.21 (career 59.12)
Parents: Alan and Brenda
Wife and date of marriage: Helen, 20 September 1986
Children: Camilla Dallas, 13 August 1988; Harrison George Samuel, 17 February 1992
Family links with cricket: Father played for Buckminster CC
Education: Sarson High School; King Edward VII Upper School, Melton Mowbray
Qualifications: CSE grade 1, 9 O-levels, 1 A-level
Overseas tours: England A to Pakistan 1990-91, to Bermuda and West Indies 1991-92, to Pakistan 1995-96
Overseas teams played for: Victoria University, Wellington, New Zealand 1985-86; Witwatersrand University, Johannesburg, South Africa 1986-87
Cricketers particularly admired: Richard Hadlee, David Gower
Other sports followed: Basketball, soccer, golf
Relaxations: 'Playing golf, spending time with my family'
Extras: Appeared for Leicestershire 2nd XI 1982-84. Second highest wicket-taker in 1990 with 78. Called into England A squad to tour Bermuda and West Indies 1991-92 when Dermot Reeve replaced the injured Angus Fraser on the senior tour. Was voted Warwickshire Player of the Season 1990, 1991 and 1994. Was one of *Wisden*'s Cricketers of the Year 1995. Missed the first six months of the 1995 season recovering from a back operation. He was flown out to Pakistan as a replacement for the injured Mike Smith on the England A tour to Pakistan in 1995-96, and played in the second 'Test' less than a week after his arrival. Assumed the Warwickshire captaincy after the retirement of Dermot Reeve in 1996 but replaced by Brian Lara for the 1998 season after missing the whole of the 1997 season through injury. Made Championship comeback v Glamorgan in 1998, taking 3-41 in the first innings
Best batting: 54* Warwickshire v Worcestershire, Worcester 1992
Best bowling: 8-89 Warwickshire v Middlesex, Edgbaston 1991

1998 Season

	M	Inns	NO	Runs	HS	Avge	100s	50s	Ct	St	O	M	Runs	Wkts	Avge	Best	5wI	10wM
Test																		
All First	9	12	2	72	20	7.20	-	-	-	-	278.5	71	708	37	19.13	7-66	3	-
1-day Int																		
NatWest	1	0	0	0	0	-	-	-	-	-	12	1	79	1	79.00	1-79	-	
B & H	1	0	0	0	0	-	-	-	-	-	10	0	49	0	-	-	-	
Sunday	4	1	0	1	1	1.00	-	-	-	-	29	1	132	3	44.00	1-21	-	

49. Who were England's two opening batsmen
in the 1983 World Cup?

FICA

Career Performances

	M	Inns	NO	Runs	HS	Avge	100s	50s	Ct	St	Balls	Runs	Wkts	Avge	Best	5wI	10wM
Test	2	2	1	25	25 *	25.00	-	-	-	-	405	200	4	50.00	2-22	-	-
All First	214	218	87	1411	54 *	10.77	-	2	68	-	37328	16285	631	25.80	8-89	29	6
1-day Int																	
NatWest	33	10	6	11	5	2.75	-	-	5	-	2044	1029	36	28.58	3-36	-	
B & H	32	14	9	58	13	11.60	-	-	6	-	1954	1143	36	31.75	4-35	-	
Sunday	146	36	25	129	15 *	11.72	-	-	28	-	6293	4101	144	28.47	5-23	2	

MURALITHARAN, M.   Lancashire

Name: Muttiah Muralitharan
Role: Right-hand bat, off-spin bowler
Born: 17 April 1972, Kandy, Sri Lanka
Nickname: Murali
County debut: No first-team appearance
Test debut: 1992-93
Tests: 43
One-Day Internationals: 102
1st-Class 5 w. in innings: 38
1st-Class 10 w. in match: 7
One-Day 5 w. in innings: 3
Place in bowling averages: 1st av. 13.61
Strike rate: 39.97 (career 51.23)
Education: St Anthony's College, Kandy
Overseas tours: Sri Lanka to England 1991,
to India 1993-94, to Zimbabwe 1994-95, to
New Zealand 1994-95, 1996-97, to South

Africa 1994-95 (Mandela Cup), to Sharjah
1994-95, 1995-96, 1996-97, 1998-99 (One-Day tournaments), to Pakistan 1995-96, to
India and Pakistan (World Cup) 1995-96, to Singapore 1995-96 (Singer Cup), to
Australia 1995-96, to West Indies 1996-97, to Kenya 1996-97 (KCA Centenary
Tournament), to India (Independence Cup) 1996-97, to India 1997-98, to South Africa
1997-98, to Pakistan (Independence Cup) 1997-98, to England 1998, to Bangladesh
1998-99 (Wills International Cup), to Australia (CUB series) 1998-99
Overseas teams played for: Tamil Union Cricket and Athletic Club
Extras: Took 16-220 from 113.5 overs v England at The Oval 1998, the fifth best
bowling analysis in Test cricket; included 9-65 in England's second innings, in which
he took his 200th Test victim (Dominic Cork) in 42 Tests. His bowling action has
attracted controversy – including calls for throwing – but was studied by the ICC in
1996 and cleared
Best batting: 39 Sri Lanka v India, Colombo 1997-98
Best bowling: 9-65 Sri Lanka v England, The Oval 1998

1998 Season

	M	Inns	NO	Runs	HS	Avge	100s	50s	Ct	St	O	M	Runs	Wkts	Avge	Best	5wI	10wM
Test	1	1	0	30	30	30.00	-	-	1	-	113.5	41	220	16	13.75	9-65	2	1
All First	3	4	2	47	30	23.50	-	-	1	-	226.3	77	463	34	13.61	9-65	5	2
1-day Int	3	2	0	22	18	11.00	-	-	1	-	30	1	118	6	19.66	5-34	1	
NatWest																		
B & H																		
Sunday																		

Career Performances

	M	Inns	NO	Runs	HS	Avge	100s	50s	Ct	St	Balls	Runs	Wkts	Avge	Best	5wI	10wM
Test	43	58	24	488	39	14.35	-	-	23	-	13724	5684	219	25.95	9-65	18	3
All First	94	113	39	901	39	12.17	-	-	56	-	23465	9589	458	20.93	9-65	38	7
1-day Int	102	44	20	157	18	6.54	-	-	52	-	5573	3911	141	27.73	5-23	3	
NatWest																	
B & H																	
Sunday																	

MUSHTAQ AHMED   Somerset

Name: Mushtaq Ahmed
Role: Right-hand bat, leg-break bowler
Born: 28 June 1970, Sahiwal, Pakistan
Height: 5ft 4in **Weight:** 13st
Nickname: Mushy
County debut: 1993
County cap: 1993
Test debut: 1991-92
Tests: 38
One-Day Internationals: 130
50 wickets in a season: 3
1st-Class 50s: 9
1st-Class 5w. in innings: 52
1st-Class 10w. in match: 15
1st-Class catches: 81
One-Day 5 w. in innings: 3
Place in batting averages: 241st av. 15.12
(1997 273rd av. 12.42)
Place in bowling averages: 82nd av. 29.35
(1997 56th av. 28.14)
Strike rate: 58.28 (career 52.20)
Marital status: Married

Career outside cricket: Banking
Overseas tours: Pakistan to Australia 1989-90, 1995-96, to New Zealand and Australia (World Cup) 1991-92, to England 1992, 1996, Australia and South Africa 1992-93, to New Zealand 1993-94, 1995-96, to Sri Lanka 1994-95, 1996-97, to India and Sri Lanka (World Cup) 1995-96, to New Zealand and Australia 1996-97, to Sharjah 1996-97, to Sri Lanka 1996-97, to South Africa 1997-98, to Zimbabwe 1997-98
Overseas teams played for: United Bank, Pakistan 1986-87 –
Cricketers particularly admired: Viv Richards, Waqar Younis
Other sports followed: Football (Brazil), hockey
Relaxations: Watching videos, eating, spending time with family
Extras: Took 6-81 against England for Punjab Chief Minister's XI 1987. Finished second to Wasim Akram as Pakistan's highest wicket-taker in the World Cup 1991-92 with 16 wickets. Received specialist coaching from Intikhab Alam. Named Somerset Player of the Year 1993. Replaced as overseas player by Shane Lee for the 1996 season due to Pakistan's tour of England, but returned for the 1997 season. Was one of *Wisden*'s five Cricketers of the Year 1997. Released by Somerset at end of 1998 season
Opinions on cricket: 'I like the four-day county championship because it gives spin bowlers a good chance to bowl long spells. One-day cricket is exciting to watch and play in. A good cricketer can play all types of cricket successfully. Most of those against that view have never played it.'
Best batting: 90 Somerset v Sussex, Taunton 1993
Best bowling: 9-93 Multan v Peshawar, Sahiwal 1986-87

1998 Season

	M	Inns	NO	Runs	HS	Avge	100s	50s	Ct	St	O	M	Runs	Wkts	Avge	Best	5wI	10wM
Test																		
All First	6	9	1	121	37	15.12	-	-	1	-	136	40	411	14	29.35	3-26	-	-
1-day Int																		
NatWest	2	1	1	8	8*	-	-	-	1	-	24	6	49	7	7.00	5-26	1	
B & H	3	2	1	32	26	32.00	-	-	-	-	22	1	119	3	39.66	2-33	-	
Sunday	10	7	2	94	41	18.80	-	-	-	-	51.3	5	226	10	22.60	3-18	-	

Career Performances

	M	Inns	NO	Runs	HS	Avge	100s	50s	Ct	St	Balls	Runs	Wkts	Avge	Best	5wI	10wM
Test	38	54	11	518	59	12.04	-	2	17	-	9543	4426	160	27.66	7-56	10	3
All First	168	213	27	2648	90	14.23	-	9	81	-	38686	18770	741	25.33	9-93	52	15
1-day Int	130	69	31	343	26	9.02	-	-	28	-	6723	4842	144	33.62	5-36	1	
NatWest	11	7	3	100	35	25.00	-	-	4	-	754	362	22	16.45	5-26	1	
B & H	14	10	1	119	31	13.22	-	-	-	-	738	443	20	22.15	7-24	1	
Sunday	56	42	12	345	41	11.50	-	-	5	-	2366	1654	55	30.07	3-17	-	

NAPIER, G. R. Essex

Name: Graham Richard Napier
Role: Right-hand bat, right-arm medium bowler
Born: 6 January 1980, Colchester
Height: 5ft 10in **Weight:** 12st 7lbs
Nickname: Baldrick, Terry, Napes, Mensa
County debut: 1997
Strike rate: 54.00 (career 42.00)
Parents: Roger and Carol
Marital status: Single
Family links with cricket: Father played for Palmers Boys School 1st XI (1965-68), Essex Police divisional teams, and Harwich Immigration CC. 'Now makes guest appearances on Walton beach'
Education: Myland School, Colchester; Gilberd School, Colchester
Qualifications: NCA coaching award
Career outside cricket: 'On the dole'
Overseas tours: England U17 to Bermuda; England U19 to South Africa (including Youth World Cup) 1997-98
Cricketers particularly admired: Peter Such, Stuart Law, Barry Richards, Viv Richards
Young players to look out for: Michael Carberry, James Foster
Other sports followed: Football (Ipswich Town and Wimbledon FC)
Injuries: Out for eight weeks with intercostal injury. Three months off bowling with stress fracture
Relaxations: 'Going out and having a good time with my mates. I enjoy a good sleep, too, just after eating during the day'
Opinions on cricket: 'I have only played in a small handful of games at first-class level and I feel that I don't have the experience to comment on the game in its current state. But I would love to play more games at this level and become successful.'
Best batting: 35* Essex v Nottinghamshire, Worksop 1997
Best bowling: 2-25 Essex v Cambridge University, Fenner's 1997

50. Who replaced the injured Salim Yousuf behind the stumps during the Pakistan v Australia World Cup semi-final in 1987?

1998 Season

	M	Inns	NO	Runs	HS	Avge	100s	50s	Ct	St	O	M	Runs	Wkts	Avge	Best	5wI	10wM
Test																		
All First	2	3	0	15	7	5.00	-	-	-	-	18	4	76	2	38.00	2-59	-	-
1-day Int																		
NatWest																		
B & H	2	0	0	0	0	-	-	-	-	-	9	0	62	0	-		-	-
Sunday	6	3	0	33	16	11.00	-	-	1	-	12	1	49	6	8.16	3-22	-

Career Performances

	M	Inns	NO	Runs	HS	Avge	100s	50s	Ct	St	Balls	Runs	Wkts	Avge	Best	5wI	10wM
Test																	
All First	4	5	2	54	35 *	18.00	-	-	-	-	210	141	5	28.20	2-25	-	-
1-day Int																	
NatWest																	
B & H	2	0	0	0	0	-	-	-	-	-	54	62	0	-		-	-
Sunday	9	5	0	50	16	10.00	-	-	2	-	138	128	6	21.33	3-22	-

NASH, D. C.   Middlesex

Name: David Charles Nash
Role: Right-hand bat, wicket-keeper
Born: 19 January 1978, Chertsey, Surrey
Height: 5ft 8in **Weight:** 11st 3lbs
Nickname: Nashy
County debut: 1995 (one-day),
1997 (first-class)
1st-Class 50s: 2
1st-Class 100s: 2
1st-Class catches: 18
Place in batting averages: 179th av. 21.26
(1997 11th av. 55.33)
Strike rate: (career 19.00)
Parents: David and Christine
Marital status: Single
Family links with cricket: 'Father played
club cricket, and brother Glen is a very
talented left-hand bat and off-spinner. Mother
is an avid watcher and tea lady'

Education: Chennestone County Middle; Sunbury Manor; Malvern College,
Worcestershire
Qualifications: 10 GCSEs, 1 A-level, NCA coaching award, qualified football referee

Career outside cricket: 'Any ideas are welcome'

Off-season: 'Working hard on my game and fitness'

Overseas tours: England U15 to South Africa 1993; British Airways Youth Team to West Indies 1993-94; England U19 to Zimbabwe 1995-96, to Pakistan 1996-97; England A to Kenya and Sri Lanka 1997-98

Cricketers particularly admired: George Simons and Gareth Rees 'for their big hearts', 'the whole victorious Sunbury CC squad', and Angus Fraser 'for always smiling and enjoying his cricket, however unlucky he is!'

Young players to look out for: Owais Shah, David Sales

Other sports played: Football ('played for Millwall U15s and my district side') rugby, snooker ('always getting beaten by Richard Johnson')

Other sports followed: Football (Brentford), rugby union (London Irish) – 'in fact I follow all sports'

Injuries: 'Earache listening to Messrs Shah, Hewitt and Martin'

Relaxations: 'I enjoy playing golf, listening to music, going out with my mates, and visiting friends at uni in Leeds and Nottingham'

Extras: Represented Middlesex at all ages. Played for England U14, U15, U17 and U19. Once took six wickets in six balls when aged 11 – 'when I could bowl!'. *Daily Telegraph* Southern England Batting Award 1993. Seaxe Young Player of the Year 1993

Opinions on cricket: '2nd XI cricket should mirror the first-class game – i.e. four-day games, decent wickets and facilities. Floodlit cricket is great for the game and two divisions is a must. At least four players under the age of 23 should play on Sundays to give youngsters some experience. The 2nd XI rain rule should be abolished. The game needs to be marketed better to bring in the crowds and create interest. Transfer fees should be introduced to make it a more player-friendly market. Read entries of Shah and Johnson because these will be 100 per cent correct!'

Best batting: 114 Middlesex v Somerset, Lord's 1998

Best bowling: 1-8 Middlesex v Essex, Chelmsford 1997

1998 Season

	M	Inns	NO	Runs	HS	Avge	100s	50s	Ct	St	O	M	Runs	Wkts	Avge	Best	5wl	10wM
Test																		
All First	14	19	0	404	114	21.26	1	1	8	1	0.1	0	0	0	-	-	-	-
1-day Int																		
NatWest																		
B & H	4	2	2	10	9 *	-	-	-	2	-								
Sunday	12	10	0	171	36	17.10	-	-	8	-								

Career Performances

	M	Inns	NO	Runs	HS	Avge	100s	50s	Ct	St	Balls	Runs	Wkts	Avge	Best	5wI	10wM
Test																	
All First	22	30	2	757	114	27.03	2	2	18	1	19	19	1	19.00	1-8	-	-
1-day Int																	
NatWest																	
B & H	4	2	2	10	9 *	-	-	-	2	-							
Sunday	19	15	0	240	36	16.00	-	-	15	1							

NEWELL, K.   Glamorgan

Name: Keith Newell
Role: Right-hand bat, occasional right-arm
medium bowler
Born: 25 March 1972, Crawley
Height: 6ft **Weight:** 12st 7lbs
Nickname: Ede, Butcher, Wheelies
County debut: 1993 (one-day, Sussex),
1995 (first-class, Sussex)
1st-Class 50s: 9
1st-Class 100s: 4
1st-Class catches: 13
One-Day 5 w. in innings: 1
Place in batting averages: 83rd av. 31.84
(1997 132nd av. 28.51)
Place in bowling averages:
(1997 120th av. 39.63)
Strike rate: 78.80 (career 93.47)
Parents: Peter Charles and Julie Anne
Marital status: Single

Family links with cricket: Brother Mark was on the Sussex staff. Brother Jonathan
plays for Sussex U17 and U19
Education: Gossops Green Junior School; Ifield Community College
Qualifications: 'A few GCSEs', coaching certificate
Career outside cricket: Cricket coach
Off-season: Playing for Randwick CC, Sydney
Overseas teams played for: Zimbabwe Universals 1989-90; Bulawayo Athletic Club
1991-92, 1995-96; Riverside CC, Wellington 1992-93; Randwick CC, Sydney 1998-99
Cricketers particularly admired: Ian Botham
Young players to look out for: James Kirtley
Other sports played: Table tennis, football (Henfield FC)
Other sports followed: Football (Spurs)

Injuries: Out for five weeks with broken finger
Relaxations: Going to the cinema
Extras: Released by Sussex at end of 1998 season and has joined Glamorgan for 1999
Opinions on cricket: 'Still too much cricket played. Slightly less cricket would help guarantee the players' enthusiasm to get out there and play.'
Best batting: 135 Sussex v West Indies, Hove 1995
Best bowling: 4-61 Sussex v Kent, Horsham 1997

1998 Season

	M	Inns	NO	Runs	HS	Avge	100s	50s	Ct	St	O	M	Runs	Wkts	Avge	Best	5wI	10wM
Test																		
All First	11	19	6	414	84	31.84	-	3	7	-	65.4	22	190	5	38.00	3-23	-	-
1-day Int																		
NatWest																			
B & H	3	2	1	67	62 *	67.00	-	1	-	-	10	0	67	0	-		-	-
Sunday	12	10	2	257	97	32.12	-	1	1	-	59	1	272	10	27.20	5-33	1	

Career Performances

	M	Inns	NO	Runs	HS	Avge	100s	50s	Ct	St	Balls	Runs	Wkts	Avge	Best	5wI	10wM
Test																	
All First	44	80	11	2039	135	29.55	4	9	13	-	1589	837	17	49.23	4-61	-	-
1-day Int																	
NatWest	6	4	1	152	52	50.66	-	1	1	-	210	148	2	74.00	1-61	-	
B & H	10	8	1	193	62 *	27.57	-	1	1	-	205	182	2	91.00	1-25	-	
Sunday	46	39	4	706	97	20.17	-	2	9	-	828	690	18	38.33	5-33	1	

52. Who kept wicket for Australia in the 1987 World Cup?

FIGA

NEWELL, M. Sussex

Name: Mark Newell
Role: Right-hand bat, right-arm
fast-medium bowler
Born: 19 December 1973, Crawley
Height: 6ft 1in **Weight:** 12st
Nickname: Little Ede
County debut: 1996
1st-Class 50s: 3
1st-Class 100s: 3
1st-Class catches: 16
Place in batting averages: 103rd av. 29.69
(1997 192nd av. 22.42)
Parents: Peter Charles and Julie Anne
Marital status: Single
Family links with cricket: Brother Keith
was on the Sussex staff and is now at
Glamorgan, younger brother Jonathan plays
for Sussex Young Cricketers

Education: Hazelwick Comprehensive; City
of Westminster College
Qualifications: 9 GCSEs, GNVQ Advanced Leisure and Tourism, NCA senior
coaching award
Overseas tours: Sussex U18 to India 1990-91; Sussex U19 to Barbados (as captain)
1993-94
Overseas teams played for: Bulawayo Athletic Club, Zimbabwe 1991-92; Marist CC,
Whangerei, New Zealand 1996-97
Cricketers particularly admired: Curtly Ambrose, Allan Donald, Allan Border,
Graham Gooch
Other sports followed: 'A bit of football every now and then (support West Ham)'
Relaxations: 'Building a nest in the changing-room and sleeping in it.' Films and the
film industry
Extras: MCC Young Cricketer in 1994. Was on a sponsored scholarship at Arundel
Castle which enabled him and two others to work, play and coach all over Sussex for
two years. Played Sussex youth cricket from the age of nine. 'Bagged them, first-class
debut versus Worcestershire – thanks "G"'. Released by Sussex at end of 1998 season
Opinions on cricket: 'Four-day cricket in 2nd XI.'
Best batting: 135* Sussex v Derbyshire, Horsham 1998

1998 Season

	M	Inns	NO	Runs	HS	Avge	100s	50s	Ct	St	O	M	Runs	Wkts	Avge	Best	5wI	10wM
Test																		
All First	10	14	1	386	135 *	29.69	2	-	6	-	2	0	15	0	-	-	-	-
1-day Int																		
NatWest	1	1	1	63	63 *	-	-	1	-	-								
B & H																			
Sunday	12	11	1	204	77	20.40	-	1	-	-								

Career Performances

	M	Inns	NO	Runs	HS	Avge	100s	50s	Ct	St	Balls	Runs	Wkts	Avge	Best	5wI	10wM
Test																	
All First	23	38	2	857	135 *	23.80	3	3	16	-	12	15	0	-	-	-	-
1-day Int																	
NatWest	5	4	2	249	79	124.50	-	3	-	-							
B & H	2	2	0	147	87	73.50	-	2	-	-							
Sunday	30	29	3	627	77	24.11	-	3	7	-							

NEWELL, M.   Nottinghamshire

Name: Michael Newell
Role: Right-hand opening bat, leg-break bowler, occasional wicket-keeper
Born: 25 February 1965, Blackburn
Height: 5ft 10in **Weight:** 11st
Nickname: Mugly, Tricky, Animal
County debut: 1984
County cap: 1987
1000 runs in a season: 1
1st-Class 50s: 24
1st-Class 100s: 5
1st-Class 200s: 1
1st-Class catches: 93
1st-Class stumpings: 1
One-Day 100s: 1
Parents: Barry and Janet
Wife and date of marriage:
Jayne, 23 September 1989
Children: Elizabeth Rose, 1 September 1993
Family links with cricket: Father chairman of Notts Unity CC and brother, Paul, is the captain
Education: West Bridgford Comprehensive

Qualifications: 8 O-levels, 3 A-levels, NCA advanced coach
Cricketers particularly admired: Matthew Dowman, Dominic Cork, James Hindson
Young players to look out for: Paul Franks, Andy Oram, Guy Welton
Other sports followed: Rugby union, football, darts
Relaxations: Football, studying, being at home
Extras: Awarded a benefit in 1999
Opinions on cricket: 'Why do players who become journalists forget all that is good and just criticise? For some reason they change opinions and moan about things that they never criticised whilst they were playing. We should be playing in two divisions and four-day cricket should be played in the 2nd XI. Smaller staffs of a minimum of 20 would be more competitive.'
Best batting: 203* Nottinghamshire v Derbyshire, Derby 1987
Best bowling: 2-38 Nottinghamshire v Sri Lankans, Trent Bridge 1988

1998 Season (did not make any first-class or one-day appearances)

Career Performances

	M	Inns	NO	Runs	HS	Avge	100s	50s	Ct	St	Balls	Runs	Wkts	Avge	Best	5wI	10wM
Test																	
All First	102	178	26	4636	203 *	30.50	6	24	93	1	363	282	7	40.28	2-38	-	-
1-day Int																	
NatWest	5	5	0	136	60	27.20	-	1	3	-	6	10	0	-		-	-
B & H	10	10	1	205	39	22.77	-	-	2	-							
Sunday	24	21	4	611	109 *	35.94	1	3	8	-							

NEWPORT, P. J.   Worcestershire

Name: Philip John Newport
Role: Right-hand bat, right-arm
fast-medium bowler, outfielder
Born: 11 October 1962, High Wycombe
Height: 6ft 2in **Weight:** 13st 7lbs
Nickname: Schnozz, Newps
County debut: 1982
County cap: 1986
Benefit: 1998
Test debut: 1988
Tests: 3
50 wickets in a season: 8
1st-Class 50s: 21
1st-Class 5 w. in innings: 35
1st-Class 10 w. in match: 3

1st-Class catches: 76
One-Day 5 w. in innings: 3
Place in batting averages: 181st av. 20.76
(1997 258th av. 15.16)
Place in bowling averages: 46th av. 24.80
(1997 24th av. 23.36)
Strike rate: 55.86 (career 52.65)
Parents: John and Sheila Diana (deceased)
Wife and date of marriage:
Christine Anne, 26 October 1985
Children: Nathan Alexander, 10 May 1989
Family links with cricket: Brother Stewart
is captain of Octopus CC in North London
Education: Royal Grammar School, High
Wycombe; Portsmouth University
Qualifications: 8 O-levels, 3 A-levels,
BA (Hons) Geography, advanced coaching
qualification
Overseas tours: NCA to Denmark 1981; England A to Pakistan 1990-91;
England to Australia 1990-91
Overseas teams played for: Vogeltown, New Plymouth, New Zealand 1986; Boland,
South Africa 1987-88; Ginnenderra and ACT, Australia 1991; Northern Transvaal,
South Africa 1992-93
Other sports followed: American football, basketball, golf, football (QPR)
Extras: Had trial as schoolboy for Southampton FC. Played cricket for NAYC
England Schoolboys 1981 and for Buckinghamshire in Minor Counties Championship
in 1981 and 1982. Selected for cancelled England tour to India 1988-89 and selected
as a replacement for England's tour to Australia in 1990-91. Winner of
Worcestershire's Dick Lygon Award 1992 and voted Worcestershire Player of the Year
1992 and 1993. Finished 3rd in the Whyte and Mackay bowling ratings in 1995. Has
announced that he will retire at end of 1999 season
Best batting: 98 Worcestershire v New Zealanders, Worcester 1990
Best bowling: 8-52 Worcestershire v Middlesex, Lord's 1988

1998 Season

	M	Inns	NO	Runs	HS	Avge	100s	50s	Ct	St	O	M	Runs	Wkts	Avge	Best	5wI	10wM
Test																		
All First	13	16	3	270	56	20.76	-	1	4	-	335.1	117	893	36	24.80	4-44	-	-
1-day Int																		
NatWest	1	0	0	0	0	-	-	-	-	-	11	1	46	1	46.00	1-46	-	
B & H	4	3	1	33	28 *	16.50	-	-	-	-	34	6	95	8	11.87	4-36	-	
Sunday	8	4	4	17	9 *	-	-	-	1	-	45	4	198	7	28.28	2-17	-	

Career Performances

	M	Inns	NO	Runs	HS	Avge	100s	50s	Ct	St	Balls	Runs	Wkts	Avge	Best	5wI	10wM
Test	3	5	1	110	40 *	27.50	-	-	1	-	669	417	10	41.70	4-87	-	-
All First	279	323	90	5715	98	24.52	-	21	76	-	44704	22990	849	27.07	8-52	35	3
1-day Int																	
NatWest	32	16	5	134	25	12.18	-	-	4	-	1731	1086	42	25.85	4-30	-	
B & H	56	29	8	239	28 *	11.38	-	-	10	-	3293	1770	87	20.34	5-22	2	
Sunday	169	72	29	457	26 *	10.62	-	-	33	-	6580	4644	177	26.23	5-32	1	

NIXON, P. A. Leicestershire

Name: Paul Andrew Nixon
Role: Left-hand bat, wicket-keeper
Born: 21 October 1970, Carlisle
Height: 6ft **Weight:** 12st 6lbs
Nickname: Nico, Nobby
County debut: 1989
1000 runs in a season: 1
1st-Class 50s: 20
1st-Class 100s: 10
1st-Class catches: 423
1st-Class stumpings: 36
Place in batting averages: 52nd av. 37.52
(1997 40th av. 44.25)
Parents: Brian and Sylvia
Marital status: 'Engaged to Jen'
Family links with cricket: 'Grandad and
father played local league cricket. Mom made
the teas for Edenhall CC, Penrith'
Education: Langwathby Primary;
Ullswater High
Qualifications: Coaching certificates
Career outside cricket: Coaching
Off-season: Doing up new home, going on holiday and keeping very fit
Overseas tours: Cumbria U16 to Denmark 1985; Leicestershire to Holland 1991, to
Montego Bay 1992, to Bloemfontein 1994 and 1995, to Sri Lanka 1999; England A to
India 1994-95
Overseas teams played for: Melville and North Fremantle, Perth, Western Australia
1989-92; Mitchells Rain, Cape Town 1993; Primrose CC, Cape Town 1995-96
Cricketers particularly admired: Darren Maddy, Phil Simmons, Ian Healy
Young players to look out for: Jon Dakin, James Ormond
Other sports followed: Football (Leicester City, Carlisle United, Liverpool), rugby
(Leicester Tigers)

Relaxations: 'Studying positive books'

Extras: Youngest person to score a century against Yorkshire (at U15). Played for England U15 and played in Minor Counties Championship for Cumberland at 16. MCC Young Pro in 1988. Took eight catches in debut match v Warwickshire at Hinckley in 1989. Played for Carlisle United and 'once got lost in South African township at 3.30am'. Leicester Young Player of the Year two years running. Second Leicester wicket-keeper to score 1000 runs in a season. Voted Cumbrian Sports Personality of the Year 1994-95. Was selected to represent England in the cancelled World Super Max 8s originally scheduled to take place in Perth in October 1998. Has signed a contract that will keep him at Grace Road until the year 2000

Opinions on cricket: 'The players are being listened to, slowly!'

Best batting: 131 Leicestershire v Hampshire, Leicester 1994

1998 Season

	M	Inns	NO	Runs	HS	Avge	100s	50s	Ct	St	O	M	Runs	Wkts	Avge	Best	5wI	10wM
Test																		
All First	19	21	4	638	101 *	37.52	2	1	41	5								
1-day Int																		
NatWest	4	3	3	22	11 *	-	-	-	9	-								
B & H	8	4	3	97	36 *	97.00	-	-	12	2								
Sunday	16	15	3	324	60 *	27.00	-	3	20	2								

Career Performances

	M	Inns	NO	Runs	HS	Avge	100s	50s	Ct	St	Balls	Runs	Wkts	Avge	Best	5wI	10wM
Test																	
All First	163	227	52	5441	131	31.09	10	20	423	36	12	4	0	-	-	-	-
1-day Int																	
NatWest	20	17	7	241	39	24.10	-	-	27	5							
B & H	26	20	5	320	53	21.33	-	1	29	6							
Sunday	125	106	18	1822	84	20.70	-	9	103	23							

NOON, W. M. Nottinghamshire

Name: Wayne Michael Noon
Role: Right-hand bat, wicket-keeper
Born: 5 February 1971, Grimsby
Height: 5ft 9in **Weight:** 11st 7lbs
Nickname: Noonie, Spain Boon
County debut: 1988 (one-day, Northants),
1989 (first-class, Northants),
1994 (Nottinghamshire)
County cap: 1995 (Nottinghamshire)
1st-Class 50s: 12
1st-Class catches: 177
1st-Class stumpings: 20
Place in batting averages:
(1997 154th av. 25.80)
Parents: Trafford and Rosemary
Marital status: Engaged
Education: Caistor Grammar School
Qualifications: 5 O-levels
Career outside cricket:
Manager of G. Atkins (bookmakers)

Overseas tours: Lincolnshire U15 to Pakistan 1984; England YC to Australia
1989-90; Rutland tourists to South Africa 1988; Northamptonshire to Durban 1992, to
Cape Town 1993
Overseas teams played for: Burnside West, Christchurch, New Zealand 1989-90 and
1993-96; Rivertonians, Cape Town 1993-94; Canterbury, Christchurch 1994-95
Cricketers particularly admired: Ian Botham
Young players to look out for: Guy Welton
Other sports followed: Football (Lincoln City), horse racing (flat)
Relaxations: Having a bet. Eating out and having a pint
Extras: Played for England YC v New Zealand YC 1989; captain v Australian YC
1989-90 and Pakistan YC 1990. Was the 1000th player to appear in the Sunday League
competition. Broke the Northants record for most 2nd XI hundreds in one season in 1993
Best batting: 83 Nottinghamshire v Northamptonshire, Northampton 1997

FIGA

53. Who finished England's challenge in the 1979 World Cup
final with a burst of 5-4 in 11 balls?

1998 Season

	M	Inns	NO	Runs	HS	Avge	100s	50s	Ct	St	O	M	Runs	Wkts	Avge	Best	5wI	10wM
Test																		
All First	4	5	1	22	16 *	5.50	-	-	9	-								
1-day Int																		
NatWest																		
B & H	5	3	1	58	46	29.00	-	-	2	-								
Sunday	5	5	0	39	17	7.80	-	-	5	1								

Career Performances

	M	Inns	NO	Runs	HS	Avge	100s	50s	Ct	St	Balls	Runs	Wkts	Avge	Best	5wI	10wM
Test																	
All First	85	133	22	2445	83	22.02	-	12	177	20	30	34	0	-	-	-	-
1-day Int																	
NatWest	7	4	1	73	34	24.33	-	-	4	2							
B & H	18	11	3	152	46	19.00	-	-	9	4							
Sunday	79	51	14	460	38	12.43	-	-	60	14							

ORAM, A. R. Nottinghamshire

Name: Andrew Richard Oram
Role: Right-hand bat, right-arm
medium-fast bowler
Born: 7 March 1975, Northampton
Height: 6ft 2in **Weight:** 12st
Nickname: Tonto, Rustler, Dick, Maro
County debut: 1997
1st-Class catches: 6
Place in batting averages: 295th av. 3.54
Place in bowling averages: 95th av. 31.25
(1997 40th av. 26.30)
Strike rate: 59.19 (career 56.05)
Parents: Richard and Anne
Marital status: Single
Family links with cricket: Father played
cricket for local club sides in Northampton
leagues and is now groundsman for Horton
House CC
Education: Hackleton Primary School;
Roade Comprehensive
Qualifications: 10 GCSEs, 4 A-levels, 1 AS-level, NCA coaching award
Overseas teams played for: Wanneroo Districts CC 1993-94, 1997-98

Cricketers particularly admired: Allan Donald, Glenn McGrath, Paul Taylor
Young players to look out for: Graeme Swann, David Sales, Stephen Randall
Other sports followed: Hockey, golf, football (Northampton Town, Liverpool FC) and rugby union (Northampton Saints)
Relaxations: Eating out, playing golf, travelling, socialising with friends, wine tasting and watching sport
Best batting: 13 Nottinghamshire v Surrey, Trent Bridge 1998
Best bowling: 4-37 Nottinghamshire v Surrey, Trent Bridge 1998

1998 Season

	M	Inns	NO	Runs	HS	Avge	100s	50s	Ct	St	O	M	Runs	Wkts	Avge	Best	5wI	10wM
Test																		
All First	11	19	8	39	13	3.54	-	-	-	-	305.5	75	969	31	31.25	4-37	-	-
1-day Int																		
NatWest																		
B & H	5	1	1	1	1*	-	-	-	3	-	47.4	8	215	5	43.00	1-19	-	
Sunday	5	1	0	0	0	0.00	-	-	2	-	30.2	2	168	7	24.00	3-44	-	

Career Performances

	M	Inns	NO	Runs	HS	Avge	100s	50s	Ct	St	Balls	Runs	Wkts	Avge	Best	5wI	10wM
Test																	
All First	19	28	13	53	13	3.53	-	-	6	-	3195	1653	57	29.00	4-37	-	-
1-day Int																	
NatWest	1	0	0	0	0	-	-	-	-	-	66	51	1	51.00	1-51	-	
B & H	5	1	1	1	1*	-	-	-	3	-	286	215	5	43.00	1-19	-	
Sunday	14	3	2	0	0*	0.00	-	-	2	-	535	451	17	26.52	4-45	-	

ORMOND, J. Leicestershire

Name: James Ormond
Role: Right-hand bat, right-arm fast bowler
Born: 20 August 1977, Walsgrave, Coventry
Height: 6ft 3in **Weight:** 14st 7lbs
Nickname: Stavros, Horse, Fred, Del, Bob
County debut: 1995
1st-Class 5 w. in innings: 5
1st-Class catches: 7
Place in batting averages: (1997 297th av. 6.90)
Place in bowling averages: 4th av. 16.36 (1997 43rd av. 26.40)
Strike rate: 42.15 (career 45.15)
Parents: Richard and Margaret
Marital status: Single

Family links with cricket: 'Dad plays local club cricket'
Education: St Anthony's, Bedworth; St Thomas More, Nuneaton; North Warwickshire College of Further Education
Qualifications: 6 GCSEs
Overseas tours: England U19 to Zimbabwe 1995-96; England A to Kenya and Sri Lanka 1997-98
Overseas teams played for: Sydney University CC 1996-97
Cricketers particularly admired: Allan Donald, Ian Botham, Richard Hadlee
Young players to look out for: Darren Maddy, Lee Westwood
Other sports followed: Football (Coventry City)

Relaxations: Music and seeing my friends
Extras: Played for the Development of Excellence side and England U19 against South Africa U19 in 1995. Was forced to return home after one day of the England U19 tour to Zimbabwe in 1995-96 through injury. Played for England U19 against New Zealand U19 in 1996. Won Leicestershire's 2nd XI bowling award
Best batting: 49 England A v President's XI, Colombo 1997-98
Best bowling: 6-54 Leicestershire v Australia, Leicester 1997

1998 Season

	M	Inns	NO	Runs	HS	Avge	100s	50s	Ct	St	O	M	Runs	Wkts	Avge	Best	5wI	10wM
Test																		
All First	6	5	0	15	9	3.00	-	-	-	-	133.3	51	311	19	16.36	6-33	2	-
1-day Int																		
NatWest	1	0	0	0	0	-	-	-	-	-	10	1	58	1	58.00	1-58	-	
B & H	2	0	0	0	0	-	-	-	-	-	17	0	89	4	22.25	3-31	-	
Sunday	6	4	3	18	11 *	18.00	-	-	2	-	47	7	139	16	8.68	4-12	-	

Career Performances

	M	Inns	NO	Runs	HS	Avge	100s	50s	Ct	St	Balls	Runs	Wkts	Avge	Best	5wI	10wM
Test																	
All First	25	21	2	208	49	10.94	-	-	7	-	3612	1911	80	23.88	6-33	5	-
1-day Int																	
NatWest	1	0	0	0	0	-	-	-	-	-	60	58	1	58.00	1-58	-	
B & H	2	0	0	0	0	-	-	-	-	-	102	89	4	22.25	3-31	-	
Sunday	18	12	8	90	18	22.50	-	-	3	-	618	410	26	15.76	4-12	-	

OSTLER, D. P.   Warwickshire

Name: Dominic Piers Ostler
Role: Right-hand bat, right-arm
medium bowler, wicket-keeper
Born: 15 July 1970, Solihull
Height: 6ft 2in **Weight:** 12st
Nickname: Ossie
County debut: 1990
County cap: 1991
1000 runs in a season: 4
1st-Class 50s: 50
1st-Class 100s: 9
1st-Class 200s: 1
1st-Class catches: 185
One-Day 100s: 1
Place in batting averages: 201st av. 19.22
(1997 213th av. 19.95)
Parents: Mike and Ann
Marital status: Single
Family links with cricket: Brother used to
play for Knowle and Dorridge
Education: Our Lady of the Wayside; Princethorpe College; Solihull College of
Technology
Qualifications: 4 O-levels, A-levels, City and Guilds Recreation Course
Career outside cricket: Company director
Off-season: 'In business'
Overseas tours: Gladstone Small's Benefit Tour to Barbados, 1991; England A to
Pakistan 1995-96; England Cricket Max Tour to New Zealand 1997, Andy Moles'
Benefit Tour to Barbados 1997
Overseas teams played for: Avendale CC, Cape Town 1991-92
Cricketers particularly admired: Simon Millington, Graeme Welch, Tony Frost,
Ashley Giles, Gladstone Small, Jason Ratcliffe, Ed Giddins, Chris Adams
Young players to look out for: 'Simon George Ostler'
Other sports played: 'Snooker – Shirley Social Club'
Other sports followed: Football (Birmingham City)
Injuries: One week out with a bad finger
Relaxations: Snooker and golf
Extras: Played club cricket for Moseley in the Birmingham League; made his
Warwickshire 2nd XI debut in 1989 and was a member of Warwickshire U19 side that
won Esso U19 County Festivals in 1988 and 1989. Has collected winner's medals for
B&H Cup, County Championship, NatWest Trophy and Sunday League. Played for an
England XI in the Cricket Max tournament in New Zealand in 1997

Opinions on cricket: 'I love it.'
Best batting: 208 Warwickshire v Surrey, Edgbaston 1995

1998 Season

	M	Inns	NO	Runs	HS	Avge	100s	50s	Ct	St	O	M	Runs	Wkts	Avge	Best	5wl	10wM
Test																		
All First	6	10	1	173	133*	19.22	1	-	6	-	3	0	13	0	-		-	-
1-day Int																		
NatWest	2	2	0	37	30	18.50	-	-	-	-	1	0	6	0	-		-	-
B & H																		
Sunday	10	9	2	151	62	21.57	-	1	4	-								

Career Performances

	M	Inns	NO	Runs	HS	Avge	100s	50s	Ct	St	Balls	Runs	Wkts	Avge	Best	5wl	10wM
Test																	
All First	153	256	21	7832	208	33.32	10	50	185	-	197	201	0	-		-	-
1-day Int																	
NatWest	32	31	3	885	104	31.60	1	6	16	-	15	10	1	10.00	1-4	-	
B & H	30	29	4	1055	87	42.20	-	9	16	-							
Sunday	128	119	17	3163	91*	31.00	-	23	33	-	6	4	0	-		-	-

PARKER, B. Yorkshire

Name: Bradley Parker
Role: Right-hand bat, right-arm medium
bowler, cover point fielder
Born: 23 June 1970, Mirfield
Height: 5ft 10in **Weight:** 12st 7lbs
Nickname: Nesty, Ceefax, Floyd
County debut: 1992
1st-Class 50s: 9
1st-Class 100s: 2
1st-Class catches: 19
Place in batting averages: 168th av. 22.50
(1997 115th av. 32.24)
Parents: Diane and David
Marital status: Single
Family links with cricket: Father played
club cricket and Lincolnshire U23
Education: Bingley Grammar School
Qualifications: 'None worth mentioning
from school.' Cricket coaching awards

Overseas teams played for: Ellerslie, Auckland 1988-90
Cricketers particularly admired: Chris Spence, Alec Stewart, Graham Thorpe
Other sports followed: Rugby league, boxing
Relaxations: Films, eating out, drinking and socialising
Opinions on cricket: 'Far too much cricket played in too short a time.'
Best batting: 138* Yorkshire v Oxford University, The Parks 1997

1998 Season

	M	Inns	NO	Runs	HS	Avge	100s	50s	Ct	St	O	M	Runs	Wkts	Avge	Best	5wl	10wM
Test																		
All First	8	10	2	180	41	22.50	-	-	3	-								
1-day Int																		
NatWest	2	1	0	2	2	2.00	-	-	-	-								
B & H	6	5	2	81	19 *	27.00	-	-	3	-								
Sunday	16	14	1	235	40	18.07	-	-	1	-	2	0	18	0	-		-	-

Career Performances

	M	Inns	NO	Runs	HS	Avge	100s	50s	Ct	St	Balls	Runs	Wkts	Avge	Best	5wl	10wM
Test																	
All First	44	71	10	1839	138 *	30.14	2	9	19	-	6	3	0	-		-	-
1-day Int																	
NatWest	5	3	0	71	69	23.66	-	1	-	-							
B & H	10	7	2	154	58	30.80	-	1	3	-							
Sunday	54	47	6	715	42	17.43	-	-	7	-	12	18	0	-		-	-

PARKIN, O. T.   Glamorgan

Name: Owen Thomas Parkin
Role: Right-hand bat, right-arm
medium-fast bowler
Born: 24 August 1972, Coventry
Height: 6ft 3in **Weight:** 12st
Nickname: Parky, Buddy, Longterm
County debut: 1994
1st-Class 5 w. in innings: 2
1st-Class catches: 7
One-Day 5 w. in innings: 1
Place in batting averages: 280th av. 9.44
Place in bowling averages: 33rd av. 22.26
Strike rate: 53.02 (career 63.43)
Parents: Vernon Cyrus and Sarah Patricia
Marital status: Single

Family links with cricket: Younger brother Morgan plays for the county in his age group
Education: Bournemouth Grammar School; Bath University
Qualifications: 9 GCSEs, 4 A-levels, 1 S-level, BSc (Hons) in Mathematics
Career outside cricket: Teacher (Mathematics)
Off-season: 'In Australia playing for Balmain Tigers, Sydney'
Overseas tours: Dorset Youth to Denmark
Overseas teams played for: Kew, Melbourne 1992-93; North Balwyn, Melbourne 1993-94, Balmain Tigers, Sydney 1998-99
Cricketers particularly admired: Malcolm Marshall, Richard Hadlee
Young players to look out for: Wayne Law, Mike Powell
Other sports followed: Rugby, football (Nottingham Forest), golf
Injuries: Out for two weeks with a shoulder problem; insect bite – 'missed Sunday League game!'
Relaxations: 'Spending time with my girlfriend, Diane, and almost doing the *Telegraph* crossword'
Extras: Played for Dorset in the NatWest Trophy 1992 and 1993. ASW Young Player of the Month July 1994. Took 5 for 28 on debut in Sunday League at Hove – a club record
Opinions on cricket: 'The reverse sweep should be banned – as bowlers you have to tell the batsman which hand you are going to use and which side of the wicket you are going to bowl, yet as a right-handed batsman you play this shot and become a left-handed player whenever you like – it would be a refreshing change to have a rule brought in that was not in favour of the batsman.'
Best batting: 24* Glamorgan v Essex, Chelmsford 1998
Best bowling: 5-24 Glamorgan v Somerset, Cardiff, 1998

1998 Season

	M	Inns	NO	Runs	HS	Avge	100s	50s	Ct	St	O	M	Runs	Wkts	Avge	Best	5wl	10wM
Test																		
All First	11	13	4	85	24*	9.44	-	-	2	-	300.3	99	757	34	22.26	5-24	2	-
1-day Int																		
NatWest	2	1	0	2	2	2.00	-	-	1	-	19	1	74	0	-	-	-	
B & H																		
Sunday	11	3	1	3	2	1.50	-	-	1	-	78.3	2	264	14	18.85	3-24	-	

433

Career Performances

	M	Inns	NO	Runs	HS	Avge	100s	50s	Ct	St	Balls	Runs	Wkts	Avge	Best	5wI	10wM
Test																	
All First	24	28	14	152	24 *	10.85	-	-	7	-	3679	1787	58	30.81	5-24	2	-
1-day Int																	
NatWest	5	3	1	3	2	1.50	-	-	3	-	234	151	3	50.33	3-23	-	
B & H	4	2	0	15	8	7.50	-	-	1	-	192	149	5	29.80	3-42	-	
Sunday	24	8	4	5	2	1.25	-	-	2	-	975	699	30	23.30	5-28	1	

PARSONS, K. A. Somerset

Name: Keith Alan Parsons
Role: Right-hand bat, right-arm
medium bowler
Born: 2 May 1973, Taunton
Height: 6ft 1in **Weight:** 13st 10lbs
Nickname: Pilot, Pars, Orv
County debut: 1992
1st-Class 50s: 15
1st-Class 100s: 2
1st-Class catches: 49
Place in batting averages: 227th av. 16.68
(1997 82nd av. 36.41)
Strike rate: 97.00 (career 92.91)
Parents: Alan and Lynne
Marital status: Single
Family links with cricket: Identical twin
brother, Kevin, was on the Somerset staff
1992-94 and now captains the Somerset
Board XI. Father played six seasons for

Somerset 2nd XI and captained National Civil Service XI
Education: Bishop Henderson Primary School; The Castle School, Taunton; Richard
Huish Sixth Form College, Taunton
Qualifications: 8 GCSEs, 3 A-levels, NCA coaching award
Career outside cricket: Unknown
Off-season: Working in the indoor school at Taunton – 'coaching etc'
Overseas tours: Castle School to Barbados 1989
Overseas teams played for: Kapiti Old Boys, New Zealand 1992-93; Harowhenera,
New Zealand 1992-93; Taita District, Wellington, New Zealand 1993-96; Wembley
Downs CC, Perth 1998-99
Cricketers particularly admired: Viv Richards, Richard Hadlee, Robin Smith
Other sports followed: Rugby union (Bath RFC), football (Nottingham Forest FC),
golf, horse racing

Relaxations: Playing golf, watching movies, listening to music 'and the odd social pint of beer'

Extras: Captained two National Cup winning sides – Taunton St Andrews in National U15 Club Championship and Richard Huish College in National U17 School Championship. Represented English Schools at U15 and U19 level. Somerset Young Player of the Year 1993

Opinions on cricket: 'It's good to see more counties taking the initiative and setting up day/night fixtures whenever possible. It has to be the way to attract greater audiences to our great game.'

Best batting: 105 Somerset v Young Australia, Taunton 1995

Best bowling: 2-4 Somerset v Oxford University, Taunton 1997

1998 Season

	M	Inns	NO	Runs	HS	Avge	100s	50s	Ct	St	O	M	Runs	Wkts	Avge	Best	5wI	10wM
Test																		
All First	14	23	1	367	101 *	16.68	1	1	17	-	129.2	34	412	8	51.50	2-26	-	-
1-day Int																		
NatWest	2	1	0	42	42	42.00	-	-	-	-	9	1	35	0	-		-	-
B & H	4	4	1	51	32 *	17.00	-	-	2	-	5	0	44	0	-		-	-
Sunday	16	13	2	249	55	22.63	-	1	7	-	64	5	282	6	47.00	2-17	-	

Career Performances

	M	Inns	NO	Runs	HS	Avge	100s	50s	Ct	St	Balls	Runs	Wkts	Avge	Best	5wI	10wM
Test																	
All First	57	97	9	2206	105	25.06	2	15	49	-	2137	1263	23	54.91	2-4	-	-
1-day Int																	
NatWest	10	9	3	200	51	33.33	-	1	1	-	318	225	8	28.12	3-34	-	
B & H	10	9	4	119	33 *	23.80	-	-	5	-	168	215	3	71.66	2-60	-	
Sunday	59	45	8	797	56	21.54	-	4	27	-	1320	1046	28	37.35	3-36	-	

FIGA

54. After the round-robin stage in the 1992 World Cup, who topped the table with seven wins from eight games?

PATEL, D.   Worcestershire

Name: Depesh Patel
Role: Right-hand bat, right-arm fast bowler
Born: 23 September 1981, Wolverhampton
Height: 6ft 4in **Weight:** 11st
Nickname: Dip, Dippy, Petal
County debut: No first-team appearance
Parents: Balvant and Mena
Marital status: Single
Family links with cricket: 'Dad played for
Thompsons CC for 18 years. Brother Vijay
has just started playing cricket for
Wolverhampton CC'
Education: Wilkinson Park Primary School;
Mosely Park GM School; Bilston Community
College
Qualifications: GCSEs
Career outside cricket: Studying GNVQ
(Advanced) Leisure and Tourism
Off-season: Studying, keeping fit
Cricketers particularly admired: Allan Donald, Sachin Tendulkar, Glenn McGrath
Young players to look out for: Vikram Solanki
Other sports followed: Football (Wolverhampton Wanderers)
Relaxations: Keeping fit, playing snooker, watching television
Extras: Scored 120 aged 15 against Cheshire playing for Staffordshire. Has best
bowling of 7 for 1 playing against Glamorgan U11 for Staffordshire U11
Opinions on cricket: 'One-day cricket is played at a faster pace than five years ago.'

PATEL, M. M.   Kent

Name: Minal Mahesh Patel
Role: Right-hand bat, slow left-arm bowler
Born: 7 July 1970, Bombay, India
Height: 5ft 7in **Weight:** 9st 10lbs
Nickname: Spin, Geezer, Diamond, Ho-Chi
County debut: 1989
County cap: 1994
Test debut: 1996
Tests: 2
50 wickets in a season: 2

1st-Class 50s: 4
1st-Class 5 w. in innings: 16
1st-Class 10 w. in match: 7
1st-Class catches: 50
Place in batting averages: 188th av. 20.20
Place in bowling averages: 103rd av. 33.02
Strike rate: 73.85 (career 72.89)
Parents: Mahesh and Aruna
Wife and date of marriage:
Karuna, 8 October 1995
Family links with cricket: Father played good club cricket in Africa, India and England

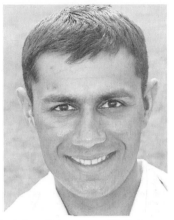

Education: Maypole CP; Dartford Grammar School; Erith College of Technology; Manchester Polytechnic
Qualifications: 6 O-levels, 3 A-levels, BA (Hons) in Economics
Off-season: MCC tour to East and Central Africa before Christmas; possibly India after Christmas
Overseas tours: Dartford GS to Barbados 1988; England A to India and Bangladesh 1994-95; MCC to Malta 1996, to Fiji, Sydney and Hong Kong 1997
Overseas teams played for: St Augustine's, Cape Town 1993-94; Alberton, Johannesburg 1997-98
Cricketers particularly admired: Derek Underwood, Sachin Tendulkar, Aravinda De Silva
Young players to look out for: Rob Key
Other sports followed: Football (Tottenham Hotspur), American football and basketball
Relaxations: Music, DJ-ing
Extras: Played for English Schools 1988, 1989 and NCA England South 1989. Was voted Kent League Young Player of the Year 1987 while playing for Blackheath. First six overs in NatWest Trophy were all maidens. Whittingdale Young Player of the Year 1994
Opinions on cricket: 'Domestic cricket is in need of change – quality not quantity.'
Best batting: 58* Kent v Hampshire, Canterbury 1998
Best bowling: 8-96 Kent v Lancashire, Canterbury 1994

55. Who is the all-time leading World Cup wicket-taker?

FIGA

1998 Season

	M	Inns	NO	Runs	HS	Avge	100s	50s	Ct	St	O	M	Runs	Wkts	Avge	Best	5wI	10wM
Test																		
All First	14	20	5	303	58 *	20.20	-	2	7	-	418.3	102	1123	34	33.02	5-73	1	-
1-day Int																		
NatWest																			
B & H	3	1	0	7	7	7.00	-	-	1	-	20	0	110	3	36.66	2-59	-	
Sunday	1	0	0	0	0	-	-	-	-	-	5	0	32	1	32.00	1-32	-	

Career Performances

	M	Inns	NO	Runs	HS	Avge	100s	50s	Ct	St	Balls	Runs	Wkts	Avge	Best	5wI	10wM
Test	2	2	0	45	27	22.50	-	-	2	-	276	180	1	180.00	1-101	-	-
All First	94	134	30	1534	58 *	14.75	-	4	50	-	20702	9241	284	32.53	8-96	16	7
1-day Int																	
NatWest	6	2	1	9	5 *	9.00	-	-	5	-	386	200	7	28.57	2-29	-	
B & H	13	7	5	46	18 *	23.00	-	-	4	-	576	437	9	48.55	2-29	-	
Sunday	7	2	0	6	5	3.00	-	-	1	-	206	223	7	31.85	3-50	-	

PATTERSON, M. W.   Surrey

Name: Mark William Patterson
Role: Right-hand bat, right-arm
fast-medium bowler
Born: 2 February 1974, Belfast
Height: 6ft 1in **Weight:** 'Summer 12st 6lbs,
winter 13st!!'
Nickname: Patto, Irish, 'and "Sorry can't
understand you"'
County debut: 1996
1st-Class 5 w. in innings: 1
Strike rate: (career 23.57)
Parents: Billy and Phyllis
Marital status: 'Some might say "whipped"'
Family links with cricket: Dad has always
played club cricket. Younger brother plays for
Ireland as a wicket-keeper batsman and has
ambitions to play county cricket. Was on
Surrey staff for 1998 season
Education: Carnmoney Primary School;
Belfast Royal Academy; University of Ulster
Qualifications: 9 GCSEs, 3 A-levels, BA (Hons) in Sport and Leisure Studies.

Qualified coach in soccer, cricket, rugby, hockey, basketball, swimming and squash. 'Now also a football referee for Surrey FA - hoping to pursue much further'
Off-season: Working for an insurance claims handling company called Network Property Services in Kent
Overseas tours: Ireland U19 to Denmark for International Youth Tournament 1993; Ireland to Denmark for European Championships 1996
Overseas teams played for: Mount Maunganui, Bay of Plenty, New Zealand 1994-95
Cricketers particularly admired: Malcolm Marshall, John Solanky 'our first club professional in Ireland'
Young players to look out for: Ian Ward, Rupesh Amin, Ben Phillips
Other sports followed: Football (Linfield FC and Northern Ireland – 'the British champions!')
Injuries: Problems all season with injury to sacroiliac joint in the back
Relaxations: 'Learning from Joey Benjamin at the "School of Life". Spending time with girlfriend Shavarne. Clubbing with younger bro. Gambling poorly!'
Extras: 1993 Irish Young Cricketer of the Year. In 1996 took 6 for 80 against South Africa A – the best ever figures by a Surrey bowler on debut. Represented Ireland in the ICC Trophy in Kuala Lumpur in March 1997; Ireland finished fourth. Represented Northern Ireland at the 1998 Commonwealth Games, also in Kuala Lumpur
Opinions on cricket: 'Two divisions needed – urgently. England players on central contracts. More day/night cricket. County cricketers contracted nine months a year, helping with cricket development in winter.'
Best batting: 4 Surrey v South Africa A, The Oval 1996
Best bowling: 6-80 Surrey v South Africa A, The Oval 1996

1998 Season (did not make any first-class or one-day appearances)

Career Performances

	M	Inns	NO	Runs	HS	Avge	100s	50s	Ct	St	Balls	Runs	Wkts	Avge	Best	5wl	10wM
Test																	
All First	1	2	0	6	4	3.00	-	-	-	-	165	124	7	17.71	6-80	1	-
1-day Int																	
NatWest	2	1	0	1	1	1.00	-	-	-	-	138	154	4	38.50	3-66	-	
B & H	7	5	1	23	9	5.75	-	-	-	-	342	330	10	33.00	3-48	-	
Sunday																	

PEIRCE, M. T. E.   Sussex

Name: Michael Toby Edward Peirce
Role: Left-hand bat, slow left-arm bowler
Born: 14 June 1973, Maidenhead
Height: 5ft 10in **Weight:** 11st 12lbs
Nickname: Carrot, Juice, Johnny Bravo, Lieutenant Dan
County debut: 1994 (one-day), 1995 (first-class)
1st-Class 50s: 9
1st-Class 100s: 1
1st-Class catches: 22
Place in batting averages: 152nd av. 24.00 (1997 164th av. 25.04)
Strike rate: 258.00 (career 433.00)
Parents: Mike and Kate
Marital status: Single
Education: Ardingly College; Durham University

Qualifications: GCSEs and A-levels, BA (Hons) Dunelm
Career outside cricket: 'Several'
Off-season: Coaching in Stellenbosch, South Africa. MCC tour to New Zealand, February 1999
Overseas tours: Ardingly College to India 1988-89; Sussex Schools U14 to Barbados 1987; Sussex Schools U18 to India 1990-91
Overseas teams played for: Kilbirnie, Wellington, New Zealand 1991-92; Wellington B, New Zealand 1991-92; Van der Stel CC, Stellenbosch, South Africa 1996-98
Cricketers particularly admired: David Gower, David Smith, Phil Edmonds
Young players to look out for: 'All the Sussex lot'
Other sports played: Golf
Other sports followed: Football (Brighton & Hove Albion), 'all sports'
Relaxations: Eating and drinking in good company, playing golf
Opinions on cricket: 'That there isn't quite as much wrong with English cricket as everyone seems to think'
Best batting: 104 Sussex v Hampshire, Southampton 1997
Best bowling: 1-16 Sussex v Warwickshire, Hove 1998

---

56. Which former Northants and Durham batsman made his One-Day International debut for England v New Zealand in the 1979 World Cup semi-finals?

FIGA

1998 Season

	M	Inns	NO	Runs	HS	Avge	100s	50s	Ct	St	O	M	Runs	Wkts	Avge	Best	5wI	10wM
Test																		
All First	19	32	1	744	96	24.00	-	5	7	-	43	18	99	1	99.00	1-16	-	-
1-day Int																		
NatWest	1	1	0	1	1	1.00	-	-	-	-								
B & H	1	1	0	16	16	16.00	-	-	1	-								
Sunday	6	6	1	74	29	14.80	-	-	-	-								

Career Performances

	M	Inns	NO	Runs	HS	Avge	100s	50s	Ct	St	Balls	Runs	Wkts	Avge	Best	5wI	10wM
Test																	
All First	38	67	1	1563	104	23.68	1	9	22	-	433	205	1	205.00	1-16	-	-
1-day Int																	
NatWest	1	1	0	1	1	1.00	-	-	-	-							
B & H	6	6	0	150	44	25.00	-	-	2	-							
Sunday	9	9	1	94	29	11.75	-	-	2	-							

PENBERTHY, A. L.　　　Northamptonshire

Name: Anthony Leonard Penberthy
Role: Left-hand bat, right-arm
medium bowler
Born: 1 September 1969, Troon, Cornwall
Height: 6ft 1in **Weight:** 12st
Nickname: Berth, Penbers, Sir Leonard,
Denzil
County debut: 1989
County cap: 1994
1st-Class 50s: 21
1st-Class 100s: 3
1st-Class 5 w. in innings: 3
1st-Class catches: 72
One-Day 5 w. in innings: 2
Place in batting averages: 40th av. 39.73
(1997 149th av. 26.26)
Strike rate: (career 70.88)
Parents: Gerald and Wendy
Wife and date of marriage:
Rebecca, 9 November 1996
Children: Georgia Lily, 4 March 1998
Family links with cricket: Father played in local leagues in Cornwall and is now a
qualified umpire instructor

Education: Troon County Primary; Camborne Comprehensive
Qualifications: 3 O-levels, 3 CSEs, coaching certificate
Career outside cricket: Coaching
Off-season: Coaching in state schools in Bedfordshire
Overseas tours: Druids to Zimbabwe 1988; Northants to Durban 1992, to Cape Town 1993, to Zimbabwe 1995, 1998, to Johannesburg 1996
Cricketers particularly admired: Ian Botham, David Gower, Dennis Lillee, Viv Richards, Eldine Baptiste
Young players to look out for: Graeme Swann, Jason Brown
Other sports played: Football, golf
Other sports followed: Football (West Ham United), rugby (Northampton Saints)
Relaxations: Listening to music, watching films and comedy programmes, 'walking my Irish setter'
Extras: Had football trials for Plymouth Argyle but came to Northampton for cricket trials instead. Took wicket with first ball in first-class cricket – Mark Taylor caught behind, June 1989. Played for England YC v New Zealand YC 1989. Scored maiden Championship century (102*) v Middlesex at Northampton in June 1998
Opinions on cricket: 'Day/night cricket is a must. Umpires are under too much pressure at big matches. I don't believe that decisions should be shown again and again on big screens. If this must be done, then surely the third umpire should pass judgment on all decisions.'
Best batting: 128 Northamptonshire v Warwickshire, Northampton 1998
Best bowling: 5-37 Northamptonshire v Glamorgan, Swansea 1993

1998 Season

	M	Inns	NO	Runs	HS	Avge	100s	50s	Ct	St	O	M	Runs	Wkts	Avge	Best	5wI	10wM
Test																		
All First	14	21	2	755	128	39.73	2	4	14	-	65	13	204	0	-	-	-	-
1-day Int																		
NatWest	1	1	0	0	0	0.00	-	-	-	-	8	1	33	0	-	-	-	
B & H	5	5	2	214	62	71.33	-	2	1	-	42.2	1	165	7	23.57	3-22	-	
Sunday	15	14	4	316	79 *	31.60	-	2	5	-	79	2	365	9	40.55	2-23	-	

Career Performances

	M	Inns	NO	Runs	HS	Avge	100s	50s	Ct	St	Balls	Runs	Wkts	Avge	Best	5wI	10wM
Test																	
All First	115	172	21	3765	128	24.93	3	21	72	-	10917	6052	154	39.29	5-37	3	-
1-day Int																	
NatWest	20	13	1	320	79	26.66	-	3	7	-	865	616	17	36.23	5-56	1	
B & H	29	23	5	529	62	29.38	-	2	7	-	1250	890	25	35.60	3-22	-	
Sunday	110	87	17	1577	81 *	22.52	-	8	23	-	3489	3038	97	31.31	5-36	1	

PENNEY, T. L. — Warwickshire

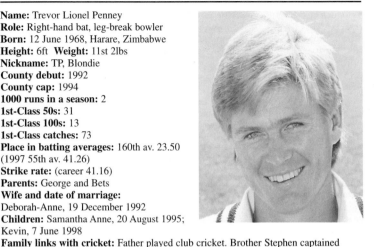

Name: Trevor Lionel Penney
Role: Right-hand bat, leg-break bowler
Born: 12 June 1968, Harare, Zimbabwe
Height: 6ft **Weight:** 11st 2lbs
Nickname: TP, Blondie
County debut: 1992
County cap: 1994
1000 runs in a season: 2
1st-Class 50s: 31
1st-Class 100s: 13
1st-Class catches: 73
Place in batting averages: 160th av. 23.50
(1997 55th av. 41.26)
Strike rate: (career 41.16)
Parents: George and Bets
Wife and date of marriage:
Deborah-Anne, 19 December 1992
Children: Samantha Anne, 20 August 1995;
Kevin, 7 June 1998
Family links with cricket: Father played club cricket. Brother Stephen captained
Zimbabwe schools
Education: Blakiston Junior School; Prince Edward Boys High School, Zimbabwe
Qualifications: 3 O-levels
Career outside cricket: Tobacco buyer. Zimbabwe B cricket coach
Off-season: Coaching Zimbabwe B and playing club cricket. Getting fit
Overseas tours: Zimbabwe U24 to England 1984; Zimbabwe to Sri Lanka 1987; ICC
Associates team to Australia (Youth World Cup) 1987-88
Overseas teams played for: Old Hararians, Zimbabwe 1983-89 and 1992-98;
Scarborough, Perth 1989-90; Boland, South Africa 1991-92; Avendale, South Africa
1990-91
Cricketers particularly admired: Colin Bland, Ian Botham, Allan Donald, Steve
Waugh
Young players to look out for: Shaun Pollock
Other sports played: Hockey (Zimbabwe and Africa), squash, tennis, golf and white
water rafting
Other sports followed: Basketball (Chicago Bulls), American football (San Francisco
49ers), Formula 1 motor racing
Injuries: Out for four weeks with a knee injury
Relaxations: 'Playing golf and drinking cold Castles on Lake Kariba. Spending time
with my family'
Extras: Captained the ICC Associates team at the Youth World Cup in 1987-88.

Played for Zimbabwe against Sri Lanka in 1987. Played hockey for Zimbabwe from 1984-87 and also made the African team who played Asia in 1987. Qualified to play for England in 1992

Opinions on cricket: 'Two divisions. Better wickets so four-day games last four days.'

Best batting: 151 Warwickshire v Middlesex, Lord's 1992

Best bowling: 3-18 Mashonaland v Mashonaland U24, Harare 1993-94

1998 Season

	M	Inns	NO	Runs	HS	Avge	100s	50s	Ct	St	O	M	Runs	Wkts	Avge	Best	5wl	10wM
Test																		
All First	9	16	2	329	53 *	23.50	-	1	5	-								
1-day Int																		
NatWest	3	3	1	53	45 *	26.50	-	-	2	-								
B & H	5	5	2	138	57 *	46.00	-	1	3	-								
Sunday	13	11	4	185	64 *	26.42	-	1	2	-								

Career Performances

	M	Inns	NO	Runs	HS	Avge	100s	50s	Ct	St	Balls	Runs	Wkts	Avge	Best	5wl	10wM
Test																	
All First	124	198	37	6717	151	41.72	13	31	73	-	247	183	6	30.50	3-18	-	-
1-day Int																	
NatWest	27	25	6	512	90	26.94	-	2	15	-	13	16	1	16.00	1-8	-	
B & H	28	25	6	581	57 *	30.57	-	3	11	1							
Sunday	105	90	31	1684	83 *	28.54	-	7	38	-	6	2	0	-	-	-	

PETERS, S. D.   Essex

Name: Stephen David Peters

Role: Right-hand bat, leg-break bowler

Born: 10 December 1978, Harold Wood

Height: 5ft 11in **Weight:** 11st

Nickname: Geezer, Pedro, Hot Rod

County debut: 1996

1st-Class 50s: 3

1st-Class 100s: 2

1st-Class catches: 15

Place in batting averages: 163rd av. 23.04 (1997 209th av. 23.66)

Parents: Brian and Lesley

Marital status: Single

Family links with cricket: 'Father plays for Upminster, as does brother-in-law'

Education: Upminster Junior School; Coopers, Coborn and Company School

Qualifications: 9 GCSEs

Off-season: 'Enjoying Xmas and New Year at home ("Jaks", "Chicagos" and "Dukes")'

Overseas tours: Essex U14 to Hong Kong; Essex U15 to Barbados; England U19 to Pakistan 1996-97, to South Africa 1997-98

Cricketers particularly admired: 'Anyone who has played at the top level'

Young players to look out for: Tim Phillips, Graeme Swann, Robert Key, Barry Hyam

Other sports played: Golf, rugby, football

Other sports followed: Football (West Ham United)

Injuries: Back injury, but no time off needed

Relaxations: Music, theme bars, TV

Extras: The Sir John Hobbs Jubilee Memorial Prize 1994, a *Daily Telegraph* regional batting award 1994, represented

England at U14, U15, U17 and U19. Essex Young Player of the Year 1996. Scored a century (107) in the U19 World Cup final in South Africa 1997-98

Opinions on cricket: 'Short leg fielders should be paid more!'

Best batting: 110 Essex v Cambridge University, Fenner's 1996

1998 Season

	M	Inns	NO	Runs	HS	Avge	100s	50s	Ct	St	O	M	Runs	Wkts	Avge	Best	5wI	10wM
Test																		
All First	13	23	2	484	64	23.04	-	3	7	-								
1-day Int																		
NatWest	1	1	0	6	6	6.00	-	-	1	-								
B & H	7	5	2	86	58 *	28.66	-	1	2	-								
Sunday	15	11	0	94	54	8.54	-	1	5	-								

Career Performances

	M	Inns	NO	Runs	HS	Avge	100s	50s	Ct	St	Balls	Runs	Wkts	Avge	Best	5wI	10wM
Test																	
All First	20	33	4	761	110	26.24	2	3	15	-							
1-day Int																	
NatWest	1	1	0	6	6	6.00	-	-	1	-							
B & H	7	5	2	86	58 *	28.66	-	1	2	-							
Sunday	19	14	0	112	54	8.00	-	1	5	-							

PHILLIPS, B. J.   Kent

Name: Ben James Phillips
Role: Right-hand bat, right-arm
fast-medium bowler
Born: 30 September 1975, Lewisham
Height: 6ft 6in **Weight:** 15st 2lbs
Nickname: Bus, Action, Barbie Doll, Bomb,
Golden Arm
County debut: 1996
1st-Class 50s: 2
1st-Class 100s: 1
1st-Class 5 w. in innings: 2
1st-Class catches: 8
Place in batting averages: 265th av. 11.94
(1997 163rd av. 25.06)
Place in bowling averages: 141st av. 54.58
(1997 9th av. 19.93)
Strike rate: 103.76 (career 56.87)
Parents: Trevor and Glynis
Marital status: Single
Family links with cricket: Father and brother keen club cricketers
Education: St Joseph's Primary, Bromley; Langley Park School for Boys,
Beckenham; Langley Park Sixth Form
Qualifications: 9 GCSEs and 3 A-levels
Career outside cricket: 'Keeping my options open, but hopefully something sports
related. Almost joined Met Police before I was offered contract with Kent'
Off-season: Playing and coaching at University of Western Australia, Perth
Overseas teams played for: University of Queensland, Australia 1993-94; Cape
Technikon Greenpoint, Cape Town, South Africa 1994-95, 1996-98, University of
Western Australia, Perth 1998-99
Cricketers particularly admired: Carl Hooper, Courtney Walsh, Dennis Lillee
Young players to look out for: Rob Key
Other sports followed: Football (West Ham United) and basketball (Chicago Bulls)
Injuries: Out for one game with torn chest muscle
Relaxations: 'Enjoy watching a decent film or listening to music. Slothing it on a
beach somewhere sunny in the off-season'
Extras: Represented England U19 Schools in 1993-94. Holds Langley Park School
record for the fastest half century, off 11 balls
Opinions on cricket: 'The problem with English cricket is the lack of adequate off-
season structure in place to improve playing standards. I would like to see 12-month
contracts therefore allowing players to develop aspects of their game during the off-
season.'

446

Best batting: 100* Kent v Lancashire, Old Trafford 1997
Best bowling: 5-47 Kent v Sussex, Horsham 1997

1998 Season

	M	Inns	NO	Runs	HS	Avge	100s	50s	Ct	St	O	M	Runs	Wkts	Avge	Best	5wI	10wM
Test																		
All First	11	17	0	203	54	11.94	-	1	1	-	294	55	928	17	54.58	3-66	-	-
1-day Int																		
NatWest	2	1	1	9	9*	-	-	-	1	-	15	3	67	3	22.33	3-14	-	
B & H	4	2	1	1	1*	1.00	-	-	1	-	25.2	5	103	6	17.16	3-13	-	
Sunday	11	3	0	15	13	5.00	-	-	2	-	55.5	1	272	11	24.72	3-31	-	

Career Performances

	M	Inns	NO	Runs	HS	Avge	100s	50s	Ct	St	Balls	Runs	Wkts	Avge	Best	5wI	10wM
Test																	
All First	27	39	4	584	100*	16.68	1	2	8	-	3697	1914	65	29.44	5-47	2	-
1-day Int																	
NatWest	2	1	1	9	9*	-	-	-	1	-	90	67	3	22.33	3-14	-	
B & H	4	2	1	1	1*	1.00	-	-	1	-	152	103	6	17.16	3-13	-	
Sunday	17	8	2	49	29	8.16	-	-	7	-	520	418	16	26.12	3-31	-	

PHILLIPS, N. C.   Durham

Name: Nicholas Charles Phillips
Role: Right-hand bat, off-spin bowler
Born: 10 May 1974, Pembury, Kent
Height: 6ft **Weight:** 11st 4lbs
Nickname: Milky, Spoons, Beastie, Nicky P
County debut: 1994 (Sussex),
1998 (Durham)
1st-Class 50s: 3
1st-Class 5 w. in innings: 1
1st-Class catches: 17
Place in batting averages: 275th av. 9.86
Place in bowling averages: 134th av. 43.42
Strike rate: 91.21 (career 99.21)
Parents: Robert and Joan
Marital status: Single
Family links with cricket: Father plays club cricket for Hastings. Represents Sussex Over 50s and has represented Kent 2nd XI, Kent League XI and has scored over 100 club 100s

Education: Hilden Grange School, Tonbridge; St Thomas's School, Winchelsea; William Parker School, Hastings
Qualifications: 8 GCSEs, NCA coaching award
Overseas tours: Sussex U18 to India 1990-91
Overseas teams played for: Maris CC, Auckland 1996-97
Cricketers particularly admired: Eddie Hemmings, Derek Randall
Other sports followed: Hockey, football
Relaxations: Spending time with friends and girlfriend. Listening to music. Eating out and socialising with fellow players
Extras: Represented England U19 in home series against West Indies U19 in 1993. Has played hockey for Sussex U14 and U16. Released by Sussex at the end of the 1997 season and joined Durham
Best batting: 53 Sussex v Young Australia, Hove 1995
Best bowling: 5-56 Durham v Derbyshire, Derby 1998

1998 Season

	M	Inns	NO	Runs	HS	Avge	100s	50s	Ct	St	O	M	Runs	Wkts	Avge	Best	5wl	10wM
Test																		
All First	17	25	2	227	35	9.86	-	-	8	-	425.4	101	1216	28	43.42	5-56	1	-
1-day Int																		
NatWest	2	1	0	1	1	1.00	-	-	-	-	23	4	59	2	29.50	2-16	-	
B & H	1	1	0	13	13	13.00	-	-	-	-	10	0	47	2	23.50	2-47	-	
Sunday	12	8	0	65	37	8.12	-	-	3	-	69	1	381	11	34.63	4-24	-	

Career Performances

	M	Inns	NO	Runs	HS	Avge	100s	50s	Ct	St	Balls	Runs	Wkts	Avge	Best	5wl	10wM
Test																	
All First	36	51	12	677	53	17.35	-	3	17	-	5457	2859	55	51.98	5-56	1	-
1-day Int																	
NatWest	3	2	0	22	21	11.00	-	-	-	-	138	59	2	29.50	2-16	-	
B & H	7	6	1	34	13	6.80	-	-	2	-	295	257	7	36.71	3-48	-	
Sunday	31	21	5	175	38*	10.93	-	-	6	-	935	845	18	46.94	4-24	-	

57. Who captained Zimbabwe in the 1983 World Cup?

FICA

PHILLIPS, T. J. — Essex

Name: Timothy James Phillips
Role: Left-hand bat, slow left-arm bowler
Born: 13 March 1981, Cambridge
Height: 6ft 1in **Weight:** 11st 1lb
Nickname: Timmy P
County debut: No first-team appearance
Parents: Martin (deceased) and Carolyn
Marital status: Single
Family links with cricket: Father played for Manchester Grammar School and subsequently in Lancashire League. On moving south, captained and played for local village sides. Brother has represented Essex Schools U14 and U15. 'Mother once represented Felsted Mothers!!'
Education: Felsted Preparatory School; Felsted School
Qualifications: 10 GCSEs, currently studying for 3 A-levels
Career outside cricket: Studying
Overseas tours: Felsted School to Australia 1995-96
Cricketers particularly admired: David Gower, Graham Gooch, Phil Tufnell
Young players to look out for: Jamie Foster, Justin Bishop
Other sports played: 'Played rugby and hockey at school and have represented Essex at hockey. Also play squash and golf'
Other sports followed: Football (Cambridge united FC), rugby league (Wigan)
Relaxations: Socialising with friends and going out
Extras: Winner of *Daily Telegraph* National Bowling Award 1995. Holmwoods School Cricketer of the Year runner-up 1997 and 1998
Opinions on cricket: 'One-day game needs to be more appealing to people – will then get the younger generation involved. More needs to be done to keep cricket going in state schools.'

58. Only two individual centuries were recorded by Australia in the 1992 World Cup. Who scored them?

FICA

PIERSON, A. R. K.   Somerset

Name: Adrian Roger Kirshaw Pierson
Role: Right-hand bat, off-spin bowler
Born: 21 July 1963, Enfield, Middlesex
Height: 6ft 4in **Weight:** 12st
Nickname: Skirlog, Stick, Bunny, Logga
County debut: 1985 (Warwickshire), 1993
(Leicestershire), 1998 (Somerset)
County cap: 1995 (Leicestershire)
50 wickets in a season: 1
1st-Class 50s: 4
1st-Class 100s: 1
1st-Class 5 w. in innings: 14
1st-Class catches: 78
One-Day 5 w. in innings: 1
Place in batting averages: 138th av. 25.76
(1997 241st av. 16.62)
Place in bowling averages: 131st av. 40.09
(1997 117th av. 38.89)

Strike rate: 73.76 (career 72.48)
Parents: Patrick and Patricia
Wife and date of marriage: Helen Majella, 28 September 1990
Children: Eleanor, 7 February 1997
Education: Lochinver House, Potters Bar, Herts; Kent College, Canterbury;
Hatfield Polytechnic
Qualifications: 8 O-levels, 2 A-levels, ECB advanced coach, private pilot's licence
Career outside cricket: 'Marketing account handler, picture framing, sub-editing,
coaching, liaison officer for World Masters tournaments etc'
Off-season: Liaison officer for West Indian World Masters team tour to South Africa.
MCC tour to Kenya 1999. Hour-building towards basic commercial pilot's licence
Overseas tours: Warwickshire to Barbados, St Lucia, Trinidad; Leicestershire to
Jamaica, Bloemfontein and Durban
Overseas teams played for: Walmer CC, Port Elizabeth 1985-90; Manicaland,
Zimbabwe 1990-91
Cricketers particularly admired: Tony Greig, Phil Edmonds, John Emburey
Young players to look out for: Marcus Trescothick, Darren Maddy, Matthew Brimson
Other sports played: Golf – 'won the County Cricketers' Golf Society Silver Salver
with my mate Colin Metson and won the *Daily Mail* "Mijas" trophy with Chris
Balderstone in 1996'
Other sports followed: 'Any sport except horse racing, but especially Formula 1
motor racing'
Injuries: Out for five weeks with a broken thumb

Relaxations: Flying, driving, reading, chess 'and playing with my daughter'

Extras: On Lord's groundstaff 1984-85 and on Warwickshire staff from 1985-91. First Championship wicket was Viv Richards. Won two Gold Awards in the Benson and Hedges. Released by Leicestershire at the end of the 1997 season and joined Somerset for 1998

Opinions on cricket: 'If cricket is weighted too much in favour of batsmen –i.e. only five fielders on the leg, only two outside the circle in first 15 overs, only two warnings for running on the wicket, but batsmen only get "asked" to stay off, can't be lbw if the ball hits the pad outside the line if playing a shot (even though it's simulated) – then there won't be many lining up to learn to bowl. And there are many more restrictions!'

Best batting: 108* Somerset v Sussex, Hove 1998

Best bowling: 8-42 Leicestershire v Warwickshire, Edgbaston 1994

1998 Season

	M	Inns	NO	Runs	HS	Avge	100s	50s	Ct	St	O	M	Runs	Wkts	Avge	Best	5wl	10wM
Test																		
All First	13	20	3	438	108 *	25.76	1	1	6	-	258.1	53	842	21	40.09	5-117	1	-
1-day Int																		
NatWest	1	1	0	9	9	9.00	-	-	-	-	11	0	32	0	-	-	-	-
B & H	3	2	2	10	8 *	-	-	-	1	-	14	1	54	2	27.00	2-19	-	
Sunday	6	3	0	16	8	5.33	-	-	2	-	11	0	51	2	25.50	2-32	-	

Career Performances

	M	Inns	NO	Runs	HS	Avge	100s	50s	Ct	St	Balls	Runs	Wkts	Avge	Best	5wl	10wM
Test																	
All First	160	200	63	2386	108 *	17.41	1	4	78	-	24862	12657	343	36.90	8-42	14	-
1-day Int																	
NatWest	12	7	2	42	20 *	8.40	-	-	2	-	734	377	9	41.88	3-20	-	
B & H	20	14	10	57	11	14.25	-	-	6	-	950	584	14	41.71	3-34	-	
Sunday	74	38	14	218	29 *	9.08	-	-	33	-	2613	2145	63	34.04	5-36	1	

FIGA

59. Who scored 107* and took 3-42 to win the Man of the Match award in the 1996 World Cup final?

PIPE, D. J.

Worcestershire

Name: David James Pipe
Role: Right-hand bat, wicket-keeper
Born: 16 December 1977, Bradford
Height: 5ft 10in **Weight:** 11st 7lbs
Nickname: Pipes, Pipey, Pip
County debut: 1998
1st-Class catches: 2
1st-Class stumpings: 1
Parents: David and Dorothy
Marital status: Single
Family links with cricket: 'My dad and uncle played in the local league'
Education: Stocks Lane Primary School; Hainsworth Moor Middle School; Queensbury School; BICC
Qualifications: 8 GCSEs, BTEC National in Business and Finance, HND Leisure Studies, senior coaching award
Career outside cricket: Coaching and studying
Off-season: Playing and training in Perth, Western Australia
Cricketers particularly admired: 'Any player that consistently puts in 100 per cent effort for both their preparation and participation in the game of cricket'
Young players to look out for: Matthew Wood
Other sports followed: 'Most sports, but in particular rugby league (Bradford Bulls), football (Bradford City), boxing, golf'
Relaxations: Playing golf, watching sport
Extras: Made first-class debut for Worcestershire in 1998. MCC School of Merit Wilf Slack Memorial Trophy winner 1995
Opinions on cricket: 'All 2nd XI Championship games should be played over four days. Nine-month contracts instead of six-month would be beneficial.'

1998 Season

	M	Inns	NO	Runs	HS	Avge	100s	50s	Ct	St	O	M	Runs	Wkts	Avge	Best	5wI	10wM
Test																		
All First-	1	0	0	0	0	-	-	-	2	1								
1-day Int																		
NatWest																		
B & H																		
Sunday																		

	M	Inns	NO	Runs	HS	Avge	100s	50s	Ct	St	Balls	Runs	Wkts	Avge	Best	5wl	10wM
Test																	
All First	1	0	0	0	0	-	-	-	2	1							
1-day Int																	
NatWest																	
B & H																	
Sunday																	

PIPER, K. J. Warwickshire

Name: Keith John Piper
Role: Right-hand bat, wicket-keeper
Born: 18 December 1969, Leicester
Height: 5ft 7in **Weight:** 10st 8lbs
Nickname: Tubbsy, Garden Boy
County debut: 1989
County cap: 1992
1st-Class 50s: 9
1st-Class 100s: 2
1st-Class catches: 400
1st-Class stumpings: 27
Place in batting averages: 238th av. 15.72
(1997 264th av. 13.87)
Strike rate: (career 28.00)
Parents: John and Charlotte
Marital status: Single
Family links with cricket: Father plays club
cricket in Leicester
Education: Seven Sisters Junior;
Somerset Senior
Qualifications: Senior coaching award, basketball coaching award, volleyball
coaching award
Overseas tours: Haringey Cricket College to Barbados 1986, to Trinidad 1987, to
Jamaica 1988; Warwickshire to La Manga 1989, to St Lucia 1990; England A to India
1994-95, to Pakistan 1995-96
Overseas teams played for: Desmond Haynes's XI, Barbados v Haringey Cricket College
Cricketers particularly admired: Jack Russell, Alec Stewart, Dermot Reeve, Colin
Metson
Other sports followed: Snooker, football, tennis
Relaxations: Music, eating
Extras: London Young Cricketer of the Year 1989 and in the last five 1992. Played for

England YC 1989. Was batting partner (116*) to Brian Lara when he reached his 501*, v Durham, Edgbaston 1994
Best batting: 116* Warwickshire v Durham, Edgbaston 1994
Best bowling: 1-57 Warwickshire v Nottinghamshire, Edgbaston 1992

1998 Season

	M	Inns	NO	Runs	HS	Avge	100s	50s	Ct	St	O	M	Runs	Wkts	Avge	Best	5wI	10wM
Test																		
All First	13	23	5	283	44 *	15.72	-	-	28	3								
1-day Int																		
NatWest	3	1	0	19	19	19.00	-	-	4	1								
B & H	5	3	2	37	13 *	37.00	-	-	10	2								
Sunday	12	6	4	61	24 *	30.50	-	-	8	3								

Career Performances

	M	Inns	NO	Runs	HS	Avge	100s	50s	Ct	St	Balls	Runs	Wkts	Avge	Best	5wI	10wM
Test																	
All First	151	214	34	3480	116 *	19.33	2	9	400	27	28	57	1	57.00	1-57	-	-
1-day Int																	
NatWest	28	13	6	123	19	17.57	-	-	41	3							
B & H	24	16	6	99	13 *	9.90	-	-	33	3							
Sunday	89	48	24	363	30	15.12	-	-	85	21							

POLLARD, P. R.   Worcestershire

Name: Paul Raymond Pollard
Role: Left-hand opening bat, right-arm medium bowler
Born: 24 September 1968, Carlton, Nottinghamshire
Height: 5ft 11in **Weight:** 12st
Nickname: Polly, Sugar Ray
County debut: 1987 (Nottinghamshire)
County cap: 1992 (Nottinghamshire)
1000 runs in a season: 3
1st-Class 50s: 40
1st-Class 100s: 13
1st-Class catches: 148
One-Day 100s: 5
Place in batting averages: 220th av. 17.28 (1997 63rd av. 40.00)
Strike rate: (career 68.50)
Parents: Eric (deceased) and Mary
Wife and date of marriage: Kate, 14 March 1992
Education: Gedling Comprehensive

Overseas teams played for: Southern Districts, Brisbane 1988; North Perth 1990
Cricketers particularly admired: David Gower, Derek Randall, Ian Botham, Graham Gooch
Other sports followed: Football, golf, ice hockey
Relaxations: Watching videos, playing golf and music
Extras: Made debut for Nottinghamshire 2nd XI in 1985. Worked in Nottinghamshire CCC office on a Youth Training Scheme. Shared stands of 222 and 282 with Tim Robinson in the same game v Kent 1989. Youngest player to reach 1000 runs for Nottinghamshire. Released by Notts at end of 1998 season and has joined Worcestershire for 1999
Opinions on cricket: 'The one bouncer rule should be abolished.'

Best batting: 180 Nottinghamshire v Derbyshire, Trent Bridge 1993
Best bowling: 2-79 Nottinghamshire v Gloucestershire, Bristol 1993

1998 Season

	M	Inns	NO	Runs	HS	Avge	100s	50s	Ct	St	O	M	Runs	Wkts	Avge	Best	5wI	10wM
Test																		
All First	4	7	0	121	69	17.28	-	1	3	-								
1-day Int																		
NatWest																		
B & H	5	5	0	117	50	23.40	-	1	2	-								
Sunday	5	5	0	64	25	12.80	-	-	2	-								

Career Performances

	M	Inns	NO	Runs	HS	Avge	100s	50s	Ct	St	Balls	Runs	Wkts	Avge	Best	5wI	10wM
Test																	
All First	157	275	20	8347	180	32.73	13	40	148	-	274	268	4	67.00	2-79	-	-
1-day Int																	
NatWest	13	13	2	369	96	33.54	-	2	4	-	18	9	0	-	-	-	
B & H	32	31	2	863	104	29.75	1	7	11	-							
Sunday	100	90	9	2730	132 *	33.70	4	13	40	-							

POOLEY, J. C. Middlesex

Name: Jason Calvin Pooley
Role: Left-hand bat, right-arm slow bowler
Born: 8 August 1969, Hammersmith
Height: 6ft **Weight:** 13st 7lbs
County debut: 1989
County cap: 1995
1000 runs in a season: 1
1st-Class 50s: 17
1st-Class 100s: 8
1st-Class catches: 81
One-Day 100s: 1
Place in batting averages:
(1997 187th av. 22.92)
Parents: Dave and Kath
Wife and date of marriage:
Justine, 30 September 1995
Children: Jake Aaron, 29 March 1997
Family links with cricket: Father and older
brother play club cricket. Younger brother
Gregg has played for Middlesex YC, Middlesex 2nd XI and Derbyshire 2nd XI
Education: Acton High School
Overseas tours: England A to Pakistan 1995-96
Overseas teams played for: St George's, Sydney 1988-89; Western Suburbs, Sydney
1991-92
Cricketers particularly admired: David Gower, Desmond Haynes
Young players to look out for: John Maunders
Other sports followed: 'All sports, support Portsmouth FC'
Relaxations: 'Eating out with my wife Justine'
Extras: Voted Rapid Cricketline 2nd XI Player of the Year in 1989, his first year on the
Middlesex staff. Called up as a late replacement on the England A tour to Pakistan
1995-96 after the withdrawal of Andrew Symonds. Released by Middlesex at end of
1998 season
Opinions on cricket: 'Coaching is still not of a high enough standard. Too many
chiefs, not enough Indians'
Best batting: 138* Middlesex v Cambridge University, Fenner's 1996

FICA

60. Who is England's all-time leading
World Cup run-scorer?

1998 Season

	M	Inns	NO	Runs	HS	Avge	100s	50s	Ct	St	O	M	Runs	Wkts	Avge	Best	5wI	10wM
Test																		
All First	1	0	0	0	0	-	-	-	-	-								
1-day Int																		
NatWest	1	1	0	8	8	8.00	-	-	-	-								
B & H	5	5	0	163	48	32.60	-	-	-	-								
Sunday	8	8	1	151	94	21.57	-	1	3	-								

Career Performances

	M	Inns	NO	Runs	HS	Avge	100s	50s	Ct	St	Balls	Runs	Wkts	Avge	Best	5wI	10wM
Test																	
All First	82	137	12	3811	138 *	30.48	8	17	81	-	60	68	0	-	-	-	-
1-day Int																	
NatWest	9	9	1	212	79 *	26.50	-	1	1	-							
B & H	23	23	1	514	50 *	23.36	-	2	5	-							
Sunday	65	62	7	1505	109	27.36	1	11	21	-							

POWELL, J. C.   Essex

Name: Jonathan Christopher Powell
Role: Right-hand bat, off-spin bowler
Born: 13 June 1979, Harold Wood
Height: 5ft 11in **Weight:** 11st 2lbs
Nickname: Ralphy, Powelly
County debut: 1996 (one-day),
1997 (first-class)
Strike rate: 234.00 (career 234.00)
Parents: Geoff and Joan
Marital status: Single
Family links with cricket: Brother Mark
was on the Essex staff for two years and now
plays Minor Counties cricket for Norfolk.
Father plays local cricket
Education: St Peter's C of E Primary School,
Brentwood; Brentwood County High;
Chelmsford College
Qualifications: 9 GCSEs, NCA coaching
award (level 2)
Off-season: 'Getting fit. Working at game'
Overseas tours: Essex U14 to Barbados, to Hong Kong; England U19 to Pakistan
1996-97, to South Africa 1997-98; England A to Kenya and Sri Lanka 1997-98

Cricketers particularly admired: Ronnie Irani
Young players to look out for: Robert Key, Chris Read, Stephen Peters
Other sports played: Golf
Other sports followed: Football (Arsenal FC)
Injuries: Troubled all year by back injury, so played as a batsman
Relaxations: Music, TV and going out
Extras: Winner of the *Daily Telegraph* U15 Bowling Award in 1994. Was a member of the England U19 side that won the Youth World Cup 1997-98
Opinions on cricket: '2nd XI games should be played on first-class grounds. Lunch and tea should be longer.'
Best batting: 4* Essex v Leicestershire, Leicester 1997
Best bowling: 1-109 Essex v Leicestershire, Leicester 1997

1998 Season (did not make any first-class or one-day appearances)

Career Performances

	M	Inns	NO	Runs	HS	Avge	100s	50s	Ct	St	Balls	Runs	Wkts	Avge	Best	5wI	10wM
Test																	
All First	1	1	1	4	4*	-	-	-	-	-	234	109	1	109.00	1-109	-	-
1-day Int																	
NatWest																	
B & H																	
Sunday	6	3	1	4	2	2.00	-	-	1	-	114	125	4	31.25	2-10	-	

---

61. Which Australian bowler took 6-14 v England at Headingley in the 1975 World Cup semi-finals?

FIÇA

458

POWELL, M. J.   Northamptonshire

Name: Mark John Powell
Role: Right-hand bat, off-spin bowler
Born: 4 November 1980, Northampton
Height: 5ft 10in **Weight:** 10st 10lbs
Nickname: Powelly
County debut: No first-team appearance
Parents: David and Philippa
Marital status: Single
Education: Flore Primary, Northants;
Campion School, Bugbrooke, Northants
Qualifications: 10 GCSEs,
'studying for A-levels'
Career outside cricket: Student
Cricketers particularly admired:
Graham Thorpe, Mark and Steve Waugh
Young players to look out for:
Graeme Swann, Richard Logan
Other sports played: Football, golf, tennis
Other sports followed: Football (Tottenham
Hotspur), rugby (Northampton Saints)
Relaxations: Listening to music, going to the cinema, 'socialising with mates'
Extras: Played for England U15 in inaugural Youth World Cup 1996; knocked out in
semi-finals by Pakistan at Headingley
Opinions on cricket: 'The game is improving with players taking a more professional
attitude, and with the increase in floodlit cricket it is becoming more of a spectacle.'

---

62. What was the significance of India's World Cup victory over
West Indies at Old Trafford on 9/10 June 1983?

FICA

POWELL, M. J.   Warwickshire

Name: Michael James Powell
Role: Right-hand bat, right-arm
medium bowler
Born: 5 April 1975, Bolton
Height: 5ft 10in **Weight:** 11st
Nickname: Powelly, Arthur, (Rat and Parrot)
County debut: 1996
1st-Class 50s: 3
1st-Class 100s: 1
1st-Class catches: 17
Place in batting averages: 148th av. 24.33
(1997 216th av. 22.75)
Strike rate: 48.00 (career 40.00)
Parents: Terry and Pat
Wife and date of marriage:
Sarah, 26 October 1996
Family links with cricket: 'Father is
fanatical about the game.' Brother played for
Warwickshire youth teams

Education: Horwich Parish C of E School; Rivington and Blackrod High School,
Horwich; Lawrence Sheriff Grammar School, Rugby; 'Neal Abberley School of Hard
Knocks'
Qualifications: 6 GCSEs, 2 A-levels, basic and senior coaching awards
Career outside cricket: Coaching – 'anywhere, any time'
Off-season: Coaching in schools around Warwickshire
Overseas tours: England U18 (captain) to South Africa 1992-93, to Denmark
(captain) 1993; England U19 to Sri Lanka 1993-94
Overseas teams played for: Avendale CC, Cape Town 1994-95, 1996-97
Cricketers particularly admired: Roger Twose, Dermot Reeve, Graeme Hick, Ian
Botham
Young players to look out for: Ian Bell
Other sports followed: Rugby (Rugby Lions), football (Manchester United)
Relaxations: 'Golf, golf and golf'
Extras: 2nd XI Player of the Month June 1996. Scored a career-best 210 against
Somerset 2nd XI in July 1996. Became first uncapped Warwickshire player for 49
years to carry his bat, against Nottinghamshire at Edgbaston, June 1998
Opinions on cricket: 'Reduce first team games to 12 four-day matches on Test
standard pitches. Increase second team games to four days and play on quality wickets
that will eventually take spin. Then we may find quality spinners coming through to
play for England.'
Best batting: 132 Warwickshire v Sussex, Hove 1998
Best bowling: 2-16 Warwickshire v Oxford University, The Parks 1998

1998 Season

	M	Inns	NO	Runs	HS	Avge	100s	50s	Ct	St	O	M	Runs	Wkts	Avge	Best	5wI	10wM
Test																		
All First	13	22	1	511	132	24.33	1	3	13	-	16	5	46	2	23.00	2-16	-	-
1-day Int																		
NatWest																		
B & H																		
Sunday																		

Career Performances

	M	Inns	NO	Runs	HS	Avge	100s	50s	Ct	St	Balls	Runs	Wkts	Avge	Best	5wI	10wM
Test																	
All First	18	31	1	713	132	23.76	1	3	17	-	120	64	3	21.33	2-16	-	-
1-day Int																	
NatWest																	
B & H																	
Sunday																	

POWELL, M. J. Glamorgan

Name: Michael John Powell
Role: Right-hand bat
Born: 3 February 1977, Abergavenny, South Wales
Height: 6ft 1in **Weight:** 14st 4lbs
Nickname: Powelly
County debut: 1997
1st-Class 50s: 5
1st-Class 100s: 1
1st-Class 200s: 1
1st-Class catches: 11
Place in batting averages: 62nd av. 35.00
Parents: John and Linda
Family links with cricket: 'My dad played for Abergavenny CC and my uncle played for Glamorgan 2nd XI'
Education: Crickhowell Primary School; Crickhowell Secondary School; Pontypool College
Qualifications: 5 GCSEs, BTEC National Sports Science, NCA coaching award
Off-season: Playing in Auckland
Overseas teams played for: Western Suburbs, Brisbane 1997-98

Cricketers particularly admired: Stuart Law, Gareth Meredith
Young players to look out for: Dean Cosker, Mark Wagh
Relaxations: 'Going out with my girlfriend Emma and my friends'
Extras: Scored 200 not out on his first-class debut. Scored 1210 runs at 75.63 in the 1997 2nd XI Championship, the second-highest ever total behind Alan Brazier's 1212 for Surrey 2nd XI in 1948
Opinions on cricket: 'Play more day/night cricket.'
Best batting: 200* Glamorgan v Oxford University, The Parks 1997

1998 Season

	M	Inns	NO	Runs	HS	Avge	100s	50s	Ct	St	O	M	Runs	Wkts	Avge	Best	5wI	10wM
Test																		
All First	16	27	3	840	106	35.00	1	5	10	-	0.2	0	8	0	-	-	-	-
1-day Int																		
NatWest	2	2	0	15	11	7.50	-	-	-	-								
B & H																		
Sunday	15	15	1	305	55	21.78	-	1	5	-								

Career Performances

	M	Inns	NO	Runs	HS	Avge	100s	50s	Ct	St	Balls	Runs	Wkts	Avge	Best	5wI	10wM
Test																	
All First	21	35	6	1126	200 *	38.82	2	5	11	-	8	11	0	-	-	-	-
1-day Int																	
NatWest	2	2	0	15	11	7.50	-	-	-	-							
B & H																	
Sunday	18	18	1	390	55	22.94	-	1	5	-							

PRATT, A.   Durham

Name: Andrew Pratt
Role: Left-hand bat, wicket-keeper
Born: 4 March 1975, Bishop Auckland
Height: 6ft **Weight:** 11st 3lbs
County debut: 1997
1st-Class catches: 4
Parents: Gordon and Brenda
Marital status: Single
Family links with cricket: Brother was with MCC Young Cricketers for four years. Younger brother plays for Durham County Schools and father played in local leagues
Education: Parkside Comprehensive School; Durham New College
Qualifications: 9 GCSEs, Advanced Diploma in Information Technology, cricket coaching certificate

Cricketers particularly admired:
Alan Knott, Jack Russell
Young players to look out for: Jimmy Daley
Other sports followed: Golf and football
(Middlesbrough FC)
Extras: Played for Durham County Schools
at all levels and for the North of England
U15. Played for MCC Young Cricketers for
three years
Opinions on cricket: 'I think that the
English game is very demanding both
physically and mentally. England should take
note of Australia and play less matches,
especially one-day games. I also think that
the better young English players should be
given more of a chance to play for their
country.'
Best batting: 34 Durham v Lancashire,
Riverside 1998

1998 Season

	M	Inns	NO	Runs	HS	Avge	100s	50s	Ct	St	O	M	Runs	Wkts	Avge	Best	5wl	10wM
Test																		
All First	2	3	0	40	34	13.33	-	-	4	-								
1-day Int																		
NatWest																		
B & H																		
Sunday	1	1	1	5	5*	-	-	-	3	-								

Career Performances

	M	Inns	NO	Runs	HS	Avge	100s	50s	Ct	St	Balls	Runs	Wkts	Avge	Best	5wl	10wM
Test																	
All First	3	3	0	40	34	13.33	-	-	4	-							
1-day Int																	
NatWest																	
B & H																	
Sunday	1	1	1	5	5*	-	-	-	3	-							

PRICHARD, P. J. — Essex

Name: Paul John Prichard
Role: Right-hand bat,
cover/mid-wicket fielder
Born: 7 January 1965, Brentwood, Essex
Height: 5ft 10in **Weight:** 13st
Nickname: Pablo
County debut: 1984
County cap: 1986
1000 runs in a season: 8
1st-Class 50s: 86
1st-Class 100s: 26
1st-Class 200s: 3
1st-Class catches: 185
One-Day 100s: 6
Place in batting averages: 258th av. 13.16
(1997 27th av. 47.36)
Strike rate: (career 144.50)
Parents: John and Margaret
Marital status: Separated
Children: Danielle Jade, 23 April 1993; Alexander James, 16 August 1995
Family links with cricket: Father played club cricket in Essex
Education: Warley Primary School; Brentwood County High School
Qualifications: NCA coaching certificate
Off-season: Sales PR with Ridleys Brewery
Overseas tours: England A to Australia 1992-93
Overseas teams played for: VOB Cavaliers, Cape Town 1981-82; Sutherland, Sydney 1984-87; Waverley, Sydney 1987-92
Cricketers particularly admired: Malcolm Marshall, Allan Border, David Gower, Mark Waugh, Greg Matthews
Young players to look out for: Andrew Flintoff, Steve Harmison, Melvyn Betts
Other sports followed: Football (West Ham), rugby union (London Irish) and rugby league (London Broncos)
Injuries: Out for four months with stress fracture and pulled tendons in left shin
Relaxations: Sleeping, being with family, watching West Ham
Extras: Shared county record second wicket partnership of 403 with Graham Gooch v Leicestershire in 1990. Britannic Assurance Cricketer of the Year 1992. Essex joint Player of the Year 1993. Appointed Essex captain for 1995. Awarded benefit for 1996. Won the last ever B&H Gold Award for his 92 from 113 balls v Leicestershire in the 1998 final at Lord's. Resigned as Essex captain at end of 1998 season
Opinions on cricket: 'Floodlit cricket with one or two minor alterations should become a regular spectacle in county cricket as well as international in this country.'

Best batting: 245 Essex v Leicestershire, Chelmsford 1990
Best bowling: 1-28 Essex v Hampshire, Chelmsford 1991

1998 Season

	M	Inns	NO	Runs	HS	Avge	100s	50s	Ct	St	O	M	Runs	Wkts	Avge	Best	5wI	10wM
Test																		
All First	10	18	0	237	24	13.16	-	-	7	-								
1-day Int																		
NatWest	2	2	1	55	55 *	55.00	-	1	1	-								
B & H	1	1	0	92	92	92.00	-	1	-	-								
Sunday	9	8	1	276	99 *	39.42	-	2	1	-								

Career Performances

	M	Inns	NO	Runs	HS	Avge	100s	50s	Ct	St	Balls	Runs	Wkts	Avge	Best	5wI	10wM
Test																	
All First	290	472	46	15006	245	35.22	29	86	185	-	289	497	2	248.50	1-28	-	-
1-day Int																	
NatWest	34	33	5	1112	94	39.71	-	9	14	-							
B & H	56	53	8	1480	114	32.88	2	8	14	-							
Sunday	178	159	10	4019	107	26.97	4	19	50	-							

RAMPRAKASH, M. R.   Middlesex

Name: Mark Ravindra Ramprakash
Role: Right-hand bat, right-arm
off-spin bowler, county captain
Born: 5 September 1969, Bushey, Herts
Height: 5ft 10in **Weight:** 12st 4lbs
Nickname: Ramps, Bloodaxe
County debut: 1987
County cap: 1990
Test debut: 1991
Tests: 29
One-Day Internationals: 13
1000 runs in a season: 8
1st-Class 50s: 72
1st-Class 100s: 40
1st-Class 200s: 4
1st-Class catches: 134
One-Day 100s: 7
One-Day 5 w. in innings: 1

Place in batting averages: 29th av. 42.56 (1997 10th av. 55.88)
Strike rate: 62.80 (career 97.88)
Parents: Deonarine and Jennifer
Date of marriage: 24 September 1993
Family links with cricket: Father played club cricket in Guyana
Education: Gayton High School; Harrow Weald Sixth Form College
Qualifications: 6 O-levels, 2 A-levels
Career outside cricket: 'Any ideas welcome'
Off-season: Touring Australia with England
Overseas tours: England YC to Sri Lanka 1986-87, to Australia (Youth World Cup) 1987-88; England A to Pakistan 1990-91, to West Indies 1991-92, to India (vice-captain) 1994-95; Lion Cubs to Barbados 1993; England to New Zealand 1991-92, to West Indies 1993-94, to Australia 1994-95, to South Africa 1995-96, to West Indies 1997-98, to Australia 1998-99
Overseas teams played for: Nairobi Jafferys, Kenya 1988; North Melbourne 1989
Cricketers particularly admired: 'All the great all-rounders'
Other sports followed: Snooker, football
Relaxations: 'Being at home with the family, going to movies, eating out'
Extras: Did not begin to play cricket until he was nine years old; played for Bessborough CC at age 13, played for Middlesex 2nd XI aged 16 and made first-team debut for Middlesex aged 17. Scored 204* in NCA Guernsey Festival Tournament and in 1987 made 186* on his debut for Stanmore CC. Voted Best U15 Schoolboy of 1985 by Cricket Society, Best Young Cricketer of 1986 and Most Promising Player of the Year in 1988. Played for England YC v New Zealand YC in 1989. Man of the Match in Middlesex's NatWest Trophy final win in 1988, on his debut in the competition. While on tour with England A in India 1994-95 was called up as replacement for Graeme Hick on the senior tour to Australia. Finished top of the Whyte and Mackay batting ratings in 1995 and again in 1997. Scored maiden Test 100 (154) v West Indies at Bridgetown 1997-98, sharing in a record England v West Indies sixth wicket Test partnership (205) with Graham Thorpe and receiving Man of the Match award; took first Test wicket (Roland Holder) in same game. Achieved feat of scoring a century against all other first-class counties with his 128* v Glamorgan in 1998
Best batting: 235 Middlesex v Yorkshire, Headingley 1995
Best bowling: 3-32 Middlesex v Glamorgan, Lord's 1998
Stop press: During 1998-99 Ashes tour, put on 377 for England with Graham Thorpe in an unbroken fifth wicket stand v South Australia in Adelaide, the highest stand by any touring team in Australia

---

63. Two Joneses played in the 1992 World Cup.
What were their forenames and who did they represent?

FICA

1998 Season

	M	Inns	NO	Runs	HS	Avge	100s	50s	Ct	St	O	M	Runs	Wkts	Avge	Best	5wI	10wM
Test	6	11	1	344	67*	34.40	-	2	5	-	10	0	41	0	-	-	-	-
All First	15	26	3	979	128*	42.56	4	2	10	-	52.2	8	153	5	30.60	3-32	-	-
1-day Int																		
NatWest	3	3	0	31	17	10.33	-	-	1	-	7	1	24	2	12.00	2-24	-	
B & H	5	5	1	160	55*	40.00	-	1	3	-	19	1	72	6	12.00	2-7	-	
Sunday	7	7	1	168	57	28.00	-	2	1	-	4	0	10	1	10.00	1-10	-	

Career Performances

	M	Inns	NO	Runs	HS	Avge	100s	50s	Ct	St	Balls	Runs	Wkts	Avge	Best	5wI	10wM
Test	29	51	3	1195	154	24.89	1	5	20	-	571	308	3	102.66	1-2	-	-
All First	244	398	52	15964	235	46.13	44	76	134	-	2545	1455	26	55.96	3-32	-	-
1-day Int	13	13	3	265	51	26.50	-	1	6	-	12	14	0	-	-	-	
NatWest	27	26	1	765	104	30.60	1	3	10	-	324	193	8	24.12	2-15	-	
B & H	40	39	8	1290	119*	41.61	2	7	17	-	240	166	9	18.44	3-35	-	
Sunday	137	130	24	4457	147*	42.04	4	32	40	-	313	319	14	22.78	5-38	1	

RANDALL, S. J.   Nottinghamshire

Name: Stephen John Randall
Role: Right-hand bat, right-arm
off-spin bowler
Born: 9 June 1980, Nottingham
Height: 5ft 10in **Weight:** 10st 7lbs
Nickname: Rags, Rago, Portland
County debut: No first-team appearance
Parents: Rob and Glenda
Marital status: Single
Family links with cricket: 'Dad played
league cricket for 15 years'
Education: Heyman; The West Bridgford
School; 'to be advised'
Qualifications: 9 GCSEs
Career outside cricket: 'Not yet known'
Off-season: 'Getting fit. Fine-tuning my
batting with Paul Franks. Visiting Ibiza for a
week's relaxation'
Overseas tours: England U17 to Bermuda
1997; Nottinghamshire to South Africa 1998
Cricketers particularly admired: Robert Croft, Paul Johnson, Eddie Hemmings,
Peter Such, Paul Franks

Young players to look out for: 'The Pikelets, aka [Chris] Read, [Paul] Franks, [Stephen] Randall, [Matthew] Whiley, [David] Lucas'
Other sports played: Golf ('when I can find my ball')
Other sports followed: Football (Notts County FC), ice hockey (Nottingham Panthers)
Relaxations: Socialising with friends
Opinions on cricket: 'The game needs more advertising to bring in more spectators to the game at county level.'

RAO, R. K. Sussex

Name: Rajesh Krishnakant Rao
Role: Right-hand bat, right-arm leg-spin bowler
Born: 9 December 1974, London
Height: 5ft 10in **Weight:** 12st 7lbs
Nickname: Harry, 2pac
County debut: 1996
1st-Class 50s: 5
1st-Class catches: 6
One-Day 100s: 1
Place in batting averages: 186th av. 20.31 (1997 215th av. 19.73)
Strike rate: 204.00 (career 134.00)
Parents: Krishnakant and Meena
Marital status: Single
Family links with cricket: 'Dad played for Ugandan national side and East Africa. Brother Rishi represented Middlesex youth regional sides. All my cousins play club cricket'
Education: Lyon Park Junior School; Alperton High School; City of Westminster College; Manchester Metropolitan University
Qualifications: 7 GCSEs, GNVQ Advanced Leisure and Tourism, basic coaching award, currently studying for BSc in Sports Science
Career outside cricket: Coach, personal fitness adviser 'anything related to sport'
Off-season: Studying and keeping fit
Overseas tours: Sussex to Spain 1996
Cricketers particularly admired: 'My Dad, Sachin Tendulkar, Shane Warne'
Young players to look out for: 'Too many to mention'
Other sports played: Football (Bedfont Eagles), tennis, badminton
Other sports followed: Football (Liverpool), boxing

Relaxations: Music – soul, R&B, hip-hop; reading biographies of famous sportsmen – 'Dennis Rodman *Bad as I wanna be* highly recommended'

Extras: Played for England at all youth levels from U11 to U18. MCC Lord's Taverners Player of the Year 1989 (at Under 14). Sussex 2nd XI Player of the Year 1998. Achieved highest one-day score by Sussex player – 158 v Derbyshire in the NatWest competition 1997

Opinions on cricket: 'The introduction of day/night games can only better the promotion of cricket to a wider audience.'

Best batting: 89 Sussex v Essex, Hove 1997
Best bowling: 1-1 Sussex v Yorkshire, Hove 1998

1998 Season

	M	Inns	NO	Runs	HS	Avge	100s	50s	Ct	St	O	M	Runs	Wkts	Avge	Best	5wI	10wM
Test																		
All First	10	17	1	325	76	20.31	-	2	-	-	34	3	136	1	136.00	1-1	-	-
1-day Int																		
NatWest																			
B & H																			
Sunday	9	9	0	91	38	10.11	-	-	-	-	7	1	45	2	22.50	1-22	-	

Career Performances

	M	Inns	NO	Runs	HS	Avge	100s	50s	Ct	St	Balls	Runs	Wkts	Avge	Best	5wI	10wM
Test																	
All First	23	40	3	787	89	21.27	-	5	6	-	402	243	3	81.00	1-1	-	-
1-day Int																	
NatWest	2	2	0	158	158	79.00	1	-	2	-							
B & H	2	2	0	76	61	38.00	-	1	1	-							
Sunday	32	32	1	650	91	20.96	-	5	9	-	126	127	5	25.40	3-31	-	

RASHID, U. B. A. Sussex

Name: Umer Bin Abdul Rashid
Role: Left-hand bat, slow left-arm bowler
Born: 6 February 1976, Southampton
Height: 6ft 3in **Weight:** 12st 7lbs
Nickname: Umie, Looney, Bin
County debut: 1995 (one-day, Middlesex), 1996
(first-class, Middlesex)
Parents: Mirza and Sebea
Marital status: Single
Education: Southfield Combined First and
Middle School; Ealing Green High; Ealing
Tertiary College; South Bank University
Qualifications: 7 GCSEs, 2 A-levels,
'currently studying for BA (Hons) in
Business Studies'
Cricketers particularly admired: Carl
Hooper, Aamir Sohail
Young players to look out for: Vikram
Solanki, Owais Shah, David Nash, David
Sales, Anurag Singh

Other sports followed: Football (Southampton FC), Formula 1 motor racing
Relaxations: 'Chilling out with family and friends, playing Nintendo and computer
games. A keen reader of books by John Grisham'
Extras: Lord's Taverners' Cricketer of the Year 1994-95. Played England U19 against
South Africa in 1995. Played for the Combined Universities side in the B & H Cup.
Released by Middlesex at end of 1998 season and has joined Sussex for the 1999
season on a two-year contract
Best batting: 9 Middlesex v Gloucestershire, Lord's 1996

1998 Season

	M	Inns	NO	Runs	HS	Avge	100s	50s	Ct	St	O	M	Runs	Wkts	Avge	Best	5wI	10wM
Test																		
All First	1	0	0	0	0	-	-	-	-	-								
1-day Int																		
NatWest																		
B & H																		
Sunday	1	0	0	0	0	-	-	-	1	-	7	0	35	1	35.00	1-35	-	

Career Performances

	M	Inns	NO	Runs	HS	Avge	100s	50s	Ct	St	Balls	Runs	Wkts	Avge	Best	5wI	10wM
Test																	
All First	2	2	0	15	9	7.50	-	-	-	-	36	17	0	-		-	-	-
1-day Int																	
NatWest																	
B & H	12	11	2	246	82	27.33	-	1	3	-	663	543	9	60.33	2-57	-	
Sunday	8	4	0	14	8	3.50	-	-	1	-	282	270	8	33.75	2-34	-	

RATCLIFFE, J. D. *Surrey*

Name: Jason David Ratcliffe
Role: Right-hand opening bat, right-arm medium/off-spin bowler, slip fielder
Born: 19 June 1969, Solihull
Height: 6ft 4in **Weight:** 14st 7lbs
Nickname: Ratters, Fridge
County debut: 1988 (Warwickshire), 1995 (Surrey)
1st-Class 50s: 36
1st-Class 100s: 5
1st-Class catches: 60
One-Day 100s: 1
Place in batting averages: 81st av. 32.07 (1997 117th av. 31.62)
Strike rate: (career 95.50)
Parents: David and Sheila
Wife and date of marriage: Andrea, 7 January 1995
Family links with cricket: Father (D.P. Ratcliffe) played for Warwickshire 1956-62
Education: Meadow Green Primary School; Sharmans Cross Secondary School; Solihull Sixth Form College
Qualifications: 6 O-levels, 3 A-levels; NCA staff coach
Career outside cricket: Sports PR and marketing
Off-season: Working for PCA management in London
Overseas tours: NCA (South) to Ireland 1988; Warwickshire to South Africa 1991-92
Overseas teams played for: West End, Kimberley, South Africa 1987-88; Belmont, Newcastle, NSW 1990-91; Penrith, Sydney 1992-94
Cricketers particularly admired: 'Too many to name'
Young players to look out for: Ben Hollioake, Alex Tudor, Chris Read, Paul Franks, Andrew Flintoff, Martin Bicknell

Other sports followed: Football, tennis, golf
Relaxations: Music, reading, eating out
Extras: Scored a century against Boland on Warwickshire tour to South Africa 1991-92. Is treasurer of the Professional Cricketers' Association
Best batting: 135 Surrey v Worcestershire, Worcester 1997
Best bowling: 2-26 Surrey v Yorkshire, Middlesbrough 1996

1998 Season

	M	Inns	NO	Runs	HS	Avge	100s	50s	Ct	St	O	M	Runs	Wkts	Avge	Best	5wI	10wM
Test																		
All First	9	15	1	449	100	32.07	1	2	2	-	2	1	4	0	-	-	-	-
1-day Int																		
NatWest	3	3	0	90	71	30.00	-	1	-	-								
B & H	7	6	0	69	41	11.50	-	-	5	-								
Sunday	14	12	0	198	80	16.50	-	1	3	-	8.3	2	48	2	24.00	1-9	-	

Career Performances

	M	Inns	NO	Runs	HS	Avge	100s	50s	Ct	St	Balls	Runs	Wkts	Avge	Best	5wI	10wM
Test																	
All First	120	218	12	6115	135	29.68	5	36	60	-	955	582	10	58.20	2-26	-	-
1-day Int																	
NatWest	14	14	1	469	105	36.07	1	3	1	-	30	20	0	-	-	-	-
B & H	12	10	1	125	41	13.88	-	-	6	-	48	42	2	21.00	2-42	-	-
Sunday	48	42	3	765	82	19.61	-	4	14	-	328	319	9	35.44	2-11	-	

RAWNSLEY, M. J.   Worcestershire

Name: Matthew James Rawnsley
Role: Right-hand bat, slow left-arm bowler
Born: 8 June 1976, Birmingham
Height: 6ft 3in **Weight:** 12st 8lbs
Nickname: Scrawny, Dog
County debut: 1996
1st-Class 5 w. in innings: 2
1st-Class 10 w. in match: 1
1st-Class catches: 8
Place in batting averages: 287th av. 6.87
Place in bowling averages: 80th av. 29.23
Strike rate: 60.76 (career 71.71)
Parents: Christopher (deceased) and June
Marital status: Single
Family links with cricket: 'Brother sometimes turns out for Old Griffinians RFC's

cricket section's 3rd XI Sunday irregulars'
Education: Northfield Manor Primary
School, Birmingham; Bourneville Secondary
School, Birmingham; Brynteg
Comprehensive, Bridgend
Qualifications: 9 GCSEs and 4 A-levels,
NCA coaching award, qualified canoe
instructor
Off-season: 'The Scrawny World Tour'
Overseas tours: Worcestershire CCC to
Zimbabwe 1997
Overseas teams played for: Kumeu,
Auckland 1995-96; Sunrise Sports Club,
Harare, Zimbabwe 1996-97
Cricketers particularly admired: Richard
Illingworth, Dave Houghton
Young players to look out for:
Vikram Solanki
Other sports played: Rugby (Old Griffinians RFC)
Other sports followed: Rugby
Relaxations: TV, eating
Extras: Holds the record for the most wickets at the Oxford festival (27).
Warwickshire U19 Player of the Year in 1995. Took ten wickets and scored 133 not
out against Gloucestershire 2nd XI in 1997
Opinions on cricket: 'I have faith in the ECB's new proposals. We need to come
round to a more Australian way of thinking, i.e. less cricket but of a higher quality,
thus putting more pressure on players to perform.'
Best batting: 26 Worcestershire v Essex, Chelmsford 1997
Best bowling: 6-44 Worcestershire v Oxford University, The Parks 1998

1998 Season

	M	Inns	NO	Runs	HS	Avge	100s	50s	Ct	St	O	M	Runs	Wkts	Avge	Best	5wI	10wM
Test																		
All First	6	8	0	55	21	6.87	-	-	7	-	172.1	46	497	17	29.23	6-44	2	1
1-day Int																		
NatWest																			
B & H																			
Sunday	6	4	0	7	5	1.75	-	-	3	-	31	0	133	1	133.00	1-26	-	

64. Who replaced Craig White in England's 1996 World Cup
squad after he was injured v UAE?

FICA

Career Performances

	M	Inns	NO	Runs	HS	Avge	100s	50s	Ct	St	Balls	Runs	Wkts	Avge	Best	5wl	10wM
Test																	
All First	14	14	3	130	26	11.81	-	-	8	-	2008	934	28	33.35	6-44	2	1
1-day Int																	
NatWest	1	0	0	0	0	-	-	-	-	-	66	50	2	25.00	2-50	-	
B & H																		
Sunday	11	8	1	19	7	2.71	-	-	3	-	353	285	5	57.00	2-29	-	

READ, C. M. W. — Nottinghamshire

Name: Christopher Mark Wells Read
Role: Right-hand bat, wicket-keeper
Born: 10 August 1978, Paignton, Devon
Height: 5ft 8in **Weight:** 11st
Nickname: Readie, Little Eddie, Lambchops, Wells Road, Bouch
County debut: 1997 (one-day, Glos), 1998 (Notts)
1st-Class 50s: 1
1st-Class catches: 46
1st-Class stumpings: 3
Place in batting averages: 141st av. 25.06
Parents: Geoffrey and Carolyn
Marital status: Single
Family links with cricket: Father played local club cricket and is an avid fan
Education: Roselands Primary School; Torquay Boys' Grammar School; University of Bath
Qualifications: 9 GCSEs, 4 A-levels, senior coaching award
Career outside cricket: 'Unsure'
Off-season: England A tour to Zimbabwe and South Africa
Overseas tours: West of England U13 to Holland 1991; West of England U15 to West Indies 1992-93; England U17 to Holland (International Youth tournament) 1995; England U19 to Pakistan 1996-97; England A to Kenya and Sri Lanka 1997-98, to Zimbabwe and South Africa 1998-99
Cricketers particularly admired: Alan Knott, Jack Russell
Young players to look out for: Graeme Swann, Matt Whiley
Other sports played: Hockey, table tennis
Other sports followed: Football (Torquay United)
Relaxations: Reading, listening to music, keeping fit and going out with friends

Extras: Represented Devon in Minor Counties Championship and NatWest in 1995, 1996 and 1997, the county winning the Minor Counties Championship three years running. Played for England U18 against New Zealand U19 in 1996. Has also played hockey for Devon U18 and U21 and for West of England U17. Played for England U19 in the series against Zimbabwe U19. He was selected for the England A tour to Kenya and Sri Lanka aged 18 and without having played a first-class game. Asked to be released by Gloucestershire whilst still on tour with England A. Joined Nottinghamshire for 1998 season

Opinions on cricket: 'I believe there is a wealth of talent in this country, but I feel it is not being harnessed properly since we do not have enough time to work at our game. I feel that if we did not play as much county cricket, it would give us more time to prepare for each match and iron out any technical faults. In my opinion this would help to raise the standard of cricket in this country.'

Best batting: 76 Nottinghamshire v Middlesex, Trent Bridge 1998

1998 Season

	M	Inns	NO	Runs	HS	Avge	100s	50s	Ct	St	O	M	Runs	Wkts	Avge	Best	5wI	10wM
Test																		
All First	13	22	6	401	76	25.06	-	2	39	3								
1-day Int																		
NatWest	3	3	2	21	8	21.00	-	-	1	1								
B & H																		
Sunday	11	7	3	67	19	16.75	-	-	10	2								

Career Performances

	M	Inns	NO	Runs	HS	Avge	100s	50s	Ct	St	Balls	Runs	Wkts	Avge	Best	5wI	10wM
Test																	
All First	17	25	6	462	76	24.31	-	2	46	3							
1-day Int																	
NatWest	6	5	2	61	37	20.33	-	-	2	2							
B & H																	
Sunday	12	8	3	67	19	13.40	-	-	10	2							

REEVE, D. A.   Somerset

Name: Dermot Alexander Reeve
Role: Right-hand bat, right-arm medium
bowler
Born: 2 April 1963, Hong Kong
Height: 6ft **Weight:** 12st 7lbs
Nickname: Legend
County debut: 1983 (Sussex),
1988 (Warwicks), 1998 (one-day, Somerset)
County cap: 1986 (Sussex),
1989 (Warwicks)
Benefit: 1996 (Warwicks)
Test debut: 1991-92
Tests: 3
One-Day Internationals: 29
1000 runs in a season: 2
50 wickets in a season: 2
1st-Class 50s: 52
1st-Class 100s: 6
1st-Class 200s: 1
1st-Class 5 w. in innings: 8
1st-Class catches: 200

One-Day 100s: 1
Strike rate: (career 128.6)
Parents: Alexander James and Monica
Marital status: 'Engaged to Donna'
Children: Emily Kaye, 14 September 1988
Family links with cricket: 'Brother Mark struggling along with Stanmore IIIs. Mum
scored for England when Clem Driver fell ill on India tour. Fiancée Donna keeps
wicket for Taunton Ladies and the league side'
Education: King George V School, Kowloon, Hong Kong
Qualifications: 7 O-levels
Career outside cricket: After-dinner speaker
Off-season: 'Playing football and getting fit for another comeback. Six weeks in Perth
visiting my daughter. Playing golf and coaching'
Overseas tours: England to New Zealand 1991-92, to India and Pakistan (World Cup)
1995-96
Overseas teams played for: Hong Kong
Cricketers particularly admired: 'Too many to mention, but in the last two years
you can add Butcher, Knight, Wells (Vince) and Caddick, plus the obvious ones'
Young players to look out for: 'Trescothick, Maddy, Key, Harmison, Flintoff'
Other sports played: Football (North Curry FC), golf ('when allowed')

Other sports followed: Football (Man United)

Injuries: Out for four and a half months with a knee injury and operation

Relaxations: Swimming, golf, eating out, music, movies and popcorn. 'Have two great dogs which I have to walk occasionally'

Extras: Formerly on Lord's groundstaff. Hong Kong Cricketer of the Year 1980-81 and Hong Kong's Cricket Sports Personality of the Year 1981. Represented Hong Kong in ICC Trophy June 1982. Twice Western Australian CA Cricketer of the Year. Man of the Match in 1986 NatWest final for Sussex and 1989 final for Warwickshire. Originally selected for England A tour to Bermuda and West Indies 1991-92 but promoted to senior tour to New Zealand when Angus Fraser was ruled out by injury. Appointed Warwickshire captain for 1993 and was voted their Player of the Year 1993 after leading them to victory in the NatWest Trophy. On the Sky Sports commentary team for the England tour of Australia 1994-95. Now holds the record for the number of Man of the Match awards in the NatWest final with three. During his three years as Warwickshire captain they won six trophies. Called up for the World Cup in India and Pakistan 1995-96 as a replacement for the injured Craig White. Awarded the OBE in New Year Honours list 1996. One of *Wisden*'s five Cricketers of the Year 1996. Was forced to retire from first-class cricket during the 1996 season due to an arthritic hip and joined Somerset as director of cricket in 1997. Played one-day cricket in 1998. His book *Winning Ways* was published in 1996

Opinions on cricket: 'Fielding, lower-order batting, overall fitness and professionalism have definitely improved since I started in 1983. Too many ex-players point out negatives and suggest cricket has not improved. They're talking rubbish. County cricket is far more competitive in four-day mode than three-day, and I haven't seen any so-called "soft cricket" for years. Everyone should stop knocking the sport and support it and the national team. Day/night cricket has been a hit and we must invest in a new competition to make the sport more exciting and appealing to youngsters. How about two zonal leagues of nine teams playing eight midweek matches in the middle of summer, culminating in a floodlit final for the two league winners? Each match is 20 overs per side and you can lose 20 wickets per innings. Batsman must run in and out at the fall of a wicket to keep the game flowing. No taking guard and limited run-ups for the bowlers. You would get a faster, more exciting spectacle with lots of athletic fielding, run-outs and aggressive batting; loads of music and colour, face painting and gift packs etc for kids. Starting at 6pm, all over by 9pm; no need for expensive lights. We must grab youngsters' attention and then help them graduate to understanding and loving the longer game as well. The day/night games finish too late for parents to bring their children on a regular basis. Three hours is long enough for kids' attention span and you would get more close finishes to add to the excitement.'

Best batting: 202* Warwickshire v Northamptonshire, Northampton 1990

Best bowlng: 7-37 Sussex v Lancashire, Lytham 1987

1998 Season

	M	Inns	NO	Runs	HS	Avge	100s	50s	Ct	St	O	M	Runs	Wkts	Avge	Best	5wI	10wM
Test																		
All First																		
1-day Int																		
NatWest																		
B & H	4	3	1	88	60	44.00	-	1	2	-	30	1	132	2	66.00	1-29	-	
Sunday	2	0	0	0	0	-	-	-	2	-	10.4	0	36	1	36.00	1-24	-	

Career Performances

	M	Inns	NO	Runs	HS	Avge	100s	50s	Ct	St	Balls	Runs	Wkts	Avge	Best	5wI	10wM
Test	3	5	0	124	59	24.80	-	1	1	-	149	60	2	30.00	1-4	-	-
All First	241	322	77	8541	202 *	34.86	7	52	200	-	29533	12232	456	26.82	7-37	8	-
1-day Int	29	21	9	291	35	24.25	-	-	12	-	1147	820	20	41.00	3-20	-	
NatWest	43	33	12	784	81 *	37.33	-	4	16	-	2452	1247	49	25.44	4-20	-	
B & H	48	38	14	655	80	27.29	-	2	18	-	2471	1680	57	29.47	4-23	-	
Sunday	174	127	33	2352	100	25.02	1	9	51	-	6129	4558	165	27.62	5-23	1	

RENSHAW, S. J.   Hampshire

Name: Simon John Renshaw
Role: Right-hand bat, right-arm
fast-medium bowler
Born: 6 March 1974, Bebington, Wirral
Height: 6ft 3in **Weight:** 14st 4lbs
Nickname: Rennie Arnoux, Toady
County debut: 1996
1st-Class 50s: 1
1st-Class 5 w. in innings: 1
1st-Class catches: 6
One-Day 5 w. in innings: 1
1st-Class catches: 3
Place in batting averages:
(1997 193rd av. 22.41)
Place in bowling averages:
(1997 99th av. 34.54)
Strike rate: 51.00 (career 66.46)
Parents: Michael and Barbara
Wife and date of marriage:
Tracy, 26 September 1998

Family links with cricket: Father and brother play in local league competitions
Education: Birkenhead Prep School; Birkenhead; Leeds University

Qualifications: 9 GCSEs, 4 A-levels, BSc in Microbiology, Grade 1 coach
Career outside cricket: 'Lying on the sofa'
Off-season: Coaching in Southampton
Overseas teams played for: Mulgrave, Melbourne 1995-96; Ashwood, Melbourne 1996-97
Cricketers particularly admired: Ian Botham, Viv Richards
Young players to look out for: Alex Tudor, Michael Powell
Other sports followed: Football (Everton FC)
Injuries: Out for three weeks with sprained ankle; for two weeks with disc wear and tear; for two months with ruptured ankle ligaments
Relaxations: 'Finding things to do while injured'
Extras: His 6-25 against Surrey in 1997 is the best bowling by a Hampshire bowler in the Benson and Hedges Cup
Opinions on cricket: 'Current County Championship is stagnating. Two divisions with promotion and relegation would increase interest. There should be a greater liaison between minor counties and major ones. There is no structured development plan for any boy who lives outside the major county catchment area, which means that many players of county standard are ignored.'
Best batting: 56 Hampshire v Surrey, Guildford 1997
Best bowling: 5-110 Hampshire v Derbyshire, Chesterfield 1997

1998 Season

	M	Inns	NO	Runs	HS	Avge	100s	50s	Ct	St	O	M	Runs	Wkts	Avge	Best	5wl	10wM
Test																		
All First	2	1	1	10	10 *	-	-	-	-	-	17	5	24	2	12.00	1-9	-	-
1-day Int																		
NatWest																		
B & H	2	2	1	25	23	25.00	-	-	-	-	20	0	120	3	40.00	2-51	-	
Sunday	1	0	0	0	0	-	-	-	-	-	8	0	44	4	11.00	4-44	-	

Career Performances

	M	Inns	NO	Runs	HS	Avge	100s	50s	Ct	St	Balls	Runs	Wkts	Avge	Best	5wl	10wM
Test																	
All First	23	28	13	289	56	19.26	-	1	6	-	3722	2236	56	39.92	5-110	1	-
1-day Int																	
NatWest	4	2	0	5	4	2.50	-	-	1	-	186	133	4	33.25	2-20	-	
B & H	12	8	3	28	23	5.60	-	-	2	-	708	532	21	25.33	6-25	1	
Sunday	23	14	9	111	25	22.20	-	-	1	-	876	774	29	26.68	4-44	-	

---

65. Who is Australia's all-time leading
World Cup wicket-taker?

FICA

RHODES, S. J.   Worcestershire

Name: Steven John Rhodes
Role: Right-hand bat, wicket-keeper
Born: 17 June 1964, Bradford,
West Yorkshire
Height: 5ft 8in **Weight:** 12st 4lbs
Nickname: Bumpy, Wilf
County debut: 1981 (Yorkshire),
1985 (Worcestershire)
County cap: 1986 (Worcestershire)
Benefit: 1996
Test debut: 1994
Tests: 11
One-Day Internationals: 9
1000 runs in a season: 2
1st-Class 50s: 63
1st-Class 100s: 10
1st-Class catches: 863
1st-Class stumpings: 110
Place in batting averages: 60th av. 35.71
(1997 98th av. 34.35)
Parents: William Ernest and Norma Kathleen
Wife and date of marriage: Judy Ann, 6 March 1993
Children: Holly Jade, 20 August 1985; George Harry, 26 October 1993;
Lily Amber, 3 March 1995
Family links with cricket: Father played for Nottinghamshire 1959-64
Education: Bradford Moor Junior School; Lapage St Middle; Carlton-Bolling
Comprehensive, Bradford
Qualifications: 4 O-levels, advanced coach
Career outside cricket: Marketing department at Worcestershire CCC
Off-season: As above plus MCC tour to Kenya, February/March 1999
Overseas tours: England A to Sri Lanka 1986; England A to Zimbabwe and Kenya
1989-90, to Pakistan 1990-91, to West Indies 1991-92, to South Africa 1993-94;
England to Australia 1994-95; MCC to Kenya 1999
Overseas teams played for: Past Bros, Bundaberg, Queensland; Avis Vogeltown,
New Plymouth, New Zealand; Melville, Perth, Australia
Cricketers particularly admired: Graeme Hick, Richard Hadlee, Courtney Walsh
Young players to look out for: Paul Franks
Other sports followed: Horse racing and golf
Relaxations: Horse racing
Extras: Played for England YC v Australia YC in 1983 and holds record for most
victims in an innings for England YC. Youngest wicket-keeper to play for Yorkshire.

Released by Yorkshire to join Worcestershire at end of 1984 season. Selected for cancelled England tour to India 1988-89 and was one of four players put on stand-by as reserves for 1992 World Cup squad. Writes a weekly cricket column for a Birmingham newspaper. One of *Wisden*'s Cricketers of the Year 1995. Overtook David Bairstow as the wicket-keeper with the most dismissals in the Sunday League

Opinions on cricket: 'As long as English cricket is tough and competitive I see no reason why England shouldn't be one of the top two Test-playing cricketing nations. To be this, we must remain fresh with the right balance between rest and competition.'

Best batting: 122* Worcestershire v Young Australia, Worcester 1995

1998 Season

	M	Inns	NO	Runs	HS	Avge	100s	50s	Ct	St	O	M	Runs	Wkts	Avge	Best	5wI	10wM
Test																		
All First	18	33	5	1000	104 *	35.71	1	6	43	2								
1-day Int																		
NatWest	1	1	0	6	6	6.00	-	-	1	-								
B & H	4	3	1	50	37 *	25.00	-	-	5	1								
Sunday	16	11	3	88	18	11.00	-	-	19	6								

Career Performances

	M	Inns	NO	Runs	HS	Avge	100s	50s	Ct	St	Balls	Runs	Wkts	Avge	Best	5wI	10wM
Test	11	17	5	294	65 *	24.50	-	1	46	3							
All First	346	483	131	11837	122 *	33.62	10	63	863	110	6	30	0	-	-	-	-
1-day Int	9	8	2	107	56	17.83	-	1	9	2							
NatWest	40	31	11	400	61	20.00	-	2	48	7	6	1	0	-	-	-
B & H	66	47	8	575	51 *	14.74	-	1	90	10							
Sunday	214	130	34	1700	48 *	17.70	-	-	225	64							

RICHARDSON, A.   Warwickshire

Name: Alan Richardson
Role: Right-hand bat, right-arm medium-fast bowler
Born: 6 May 1975, Newcastle-under-Lyme
Height: 6ft 2in **Weight:** 13st 6lbs
Nickname: Richo
County debut: 1995 (Derbyshire)
Parents: Roy and Sandra
Marital status: Single
Family links with cricket: Father played for and captained Littlestoke 3rd XI
Education: Manor Hill First School; Walton Priory Middle School; Alleyne's High School, Stone; Stafford College of Further Education
Qualifications: 8 GCSEs, 2 A-levels, 2 AS-levels, Advanced Cricket Coach
Off-season: Playing for Hawkesbury in Sydney Grade competition
Overseas teams played for: Northern Natal, South Africa 1994-96; Hawkesbury CC, Australia 1997-99
Cricketers particularly admired: Angus Fraser, Darren Gough, Tim Parmenter, Andrew Power ('for his dedication and enthusiasm in training')
Young players to look out for: Chris Lowndes, Denton Brock, Steve Dean
Other sports played: Golf, volleyball, football
Other sports followed: Football ('ardent Stoke City fan')
Relaxations: Movies, socialising, going to the beach
Extras: *The Cricketer*/Slazenger Cricketer of the Month June 1991. *Cricket World* award for best bowling performance in Oxford U19 Festival (8-60 v Devon). Topped Minor Counties bowling averages 1998
Opinions on cricket: 'Too many games; not enough time given to training. Tea breaks need to be longer.'
Best batting: 4 Derbyshire v Oxford University, The Parks 1995
Best bowling: 3-27 Derbyshire v Oxford University, The Parks 1995

---

66. Which fast bowler helped Deryck Murray add 64 for the last wicket to bring West Indies victory over Pakistan at Edgbaston in the 1975 World Cup?

1998 Season

	M	Inns	NO	Runs	HS	Avge	100s	50s	Ct	St	O	M	Runs	Wkts	Avge	Best	5wI	10wM
Test																		
All First																		
1-day Int																		
NatWest	1	1	0	3	3	3.00	-	-	-	-	12	2	48	1	48.00	1-48	-	
B & H	3	2	1	2	1*	2.00	-	-	-	-	12	1	48	1	48.00	1-16	-	
Sunday																		

Career Performances

	M	Inns	NO	Runs	HS	Avge	100s	50s	Ct	St	Balls	Runs	Wkts	Avge	Best	5wI	10wM
Test																	
All First	1	1	0	4	4	4.00	-	-	-	-	114	60	3	20.00	3-27	-	-
1-day Int																	
NatWest	3	3	0	3	3	1.00	-	-	-	-	168	116	1	116.00	1-48	-	
B & H	3	2	1	2	1*	2.00	-	-	-	-	72	48	1	48.00	1-16	-	
Sunday	1	0	0	0	0	-	-	-	-	-	36	41	0	-	-	-	-

RIDGWAY, P. M.   Lancashire

Name: Paul Mathew Ridgway
Role: Right-hand bat, right-arm
fast-medium bowler
Born: 13 February 1977, Keighley, Yorkshire
Height: 6ft 3in **Weight:** 15st 2lbs
Nickname: Ridgeback
County debut: 1997
Strike rate: 27.00 (career 57.00)
Parents: Peter and Judith
Marital status: Single
Family links with cricket: Father is first
cousin to Don Wilson (Yorkshire and
England)
Education: Hellifield Primary School;
Settle High School
Qualifications: GCSEs, BTEC Business and
Finance
Off-season: 'We start training on 1 December'
Cricketers particularly admired: Ian Austin, Wasim Akram
Young players to look out for: 'All Lancashire 2nd XI'
Other sports followed: Motorcycle racing, rugby, football (Bradford City FC)
Injuries: Out for first part of season – 'broke a bone off my spine'
Relaxations: Motorbikes

Extras: Awarded 2nd XI cap 1998
Opinions on cricket: 'Longer break at tea. More music and fun for the crowd.'
Best batting: 35 Lancashire v Durham, Riverside 1998
Best bowling: 3-51 Lancashire v Durham, Riverside 1998

1998 Season

	M	Inns	NO	Runs	HS	Avge	100s	50s	Ct	St	O	M	Runs	Wkts	Avge	Best	5wI	10wM
Test																		
All First	1	2	0	39	35	19.50	-	-	-	-	18	2	83	4	20.75	3-51	-	-
1-day Int																		
NatWest																			
B & H																			
Sunday																			

Career Performances

	M	Inns	NO	Runs	HS	Avge	100s	50s	Ct	St	Balls	Runs	Wkts	Avge	Best	5wI	10wM
Test																	
All First	3	4	1	39	35	13.00	-	-	-	-	342	246	6	41.00	3-51	-	-
1-day Int																	
NatWest	2	1	1	47	47 *	-	-	-	1	-	120	103	5	20.60	4-62	-	
B & H																	
Sunday																	

RIPLEY, D.   Northamptonshire

Name: David Ripley
Role: Right-hand bat, wicket-keeper, county vice-captain
Born: 13 September 1966, Leeds
Height: 5ft 11in **Weight:** 12st
Nickname: Rips, Spud
County debut: 1984
County cap: 1987
1st-Class 50s: 26
1st-Class 100s: 6
1st-Class 200s: 1
1st-Class catches: 556
1st-Class stumpings: 74
Place in batting averages: 39th av. 40.25 (1997 48th av. 42.88)
Strike rate: (career 30.00)
Parents: Arthur and Brenda

Wife and date of marriage: Jackie, 24 September 1988
Children: Joe David, 11 October 1989; George William, 5 March 1994
Education: Woodlesford Primary; Royds High, Leeds
Qualifications: 5 O-levels, NCA advanced coach
Career outside cricket: Coaching
Off-season: Working for the club in youth development
Overseas tours: England YC to West Indies 1984-85; Northants to Durban 1991-92, to Cape Town 1992-93, to Zimbabwe 1994-95, to Johannesburg 1996, to Zimbabwe 1998
Overseas teams played for: Marists and Poverty Bay, New Zealand 1985-87
Cricketers particularly admired: Alan Knott, Bob Taylor 'and many other keepers', Clive Radley, Ian Botham, Geoff Boycott, Dennis Lillee
Young players to look out for: 'Sales, Davies, Swann'
Other sports played: Football (locally), golf
Other sports followed: Football (Leeds United), rugby league (Castleford), golf
Relaxations: 'Eating out, and sampling different bitters'
Extras: Finished top of wicket-keepers' dismissals list for 1988 and 1992 and was voted Wombwell Cricket Lovers' Society Best Wicket-keeper 1992. Played for England YC v Sri Lanka 1986. Northamptonshire Player of the Year in 1988 and 1997. Put on 401 for the fifth wicket with Mal Loye v Glamorgan 1998, setting a new fifth wicket partnership record for first-class cricket in England and registering a career best 209. Appointed vice-captain of Northants for 1999
Opinions on cricket: 'Two divisions in the Championship. Groundsmen should be employed by the ECB, or visiting team should have choice to bat or bowl first to try to get better four-day pitches.'
Best batting: 209 Northamptonshire v Glamorgan, Northampton 1998
Best bowling: 2-89 Northamptonshire v Essex, Ilford 1987

1998 Season

	M	Inns	NO	Runs	HS	Avge	100s	50s	Ct	St	O	M	Runs	Wkts	Avge	Best	5wI	10wM
Test																		
All First	17	22	2	805	209	40.25	1	5	30	1								
1-day Int																		
NatWest																		
B & H	5	4	2	58	25*	29.00	-	-	7	-								
Sunday	5	2	1	34	27*	34.00	-	-	2	-								

Career Performances

	M	Inns	NO'	Runs	HS	Avge	100s	50s	Ct	St	Balls	Runs	Wkts	Avge	Best	5wI	10wM
Test																	
All First	264	345	89	7054	209	27.55	7	26	556	74	60	103	2	51.50	2-89	-	-
1-day Int																	
NatWest	35	20	9	130	27*	11.81	-	-	36	3							
B & H	47	31	12	383	36*	20.15	-	-	51	6							
Sunday	142	85	37	901	52*	18.77	-	1	98	13							

ROBERTS, D. J. — Northamptonshire

Name: David James Roberts
Role: Right-hand bat
Born: 29 December 1976, Truro, Cornwall
Height: 5ft 11in **Weight:** 12st 7lbs
Nickname: Robbo, Chips, Maverick
County debut: 1996
1st-Class 50s: 2
1st-Class 100s: 1
1st-Class catches: 4
Place in batting averages:
(1997 125th av. 29.61)
Parents: Dennis and Pam
Marital status: Single
Family links with cricket: Cousin, Chris Bullen, played for Surrey. Father played cricket for local club and is also a youth coach. 'Mother is a keen supporter!'
Education: Mullion County Primary; Mullion Comprehensive
Qualifications: 9 GCSEs, senior cricket coach
Career outside cricket: Coaching
Overseas tours: West of England to Barbados, Trinidad and Tobago 1990-91 and 1991-92 (captain)
Cricketers particularly admired: Graeme Hick, Mal Loye, David Gower
Young players to look out for: John Blain, Graeme Swann, Richard Logan
Other sports followed: Football (Manchester United), NBA basketball and all sports
Relaxations: Watching television, listening to music, playing football
Extras: Played for English Schools since the age of 14, including matches against South Africa in 1992. Represented England U17 against India U17 in 1994
Opinions on cricket: 'Tea is too short. 2nd XI cricket should be played at first-class grounds instead of club grounds.'
Best batting: 117 Northamptonshire v Essex, Northampton 1997

1998 Season

	M	Inns	NO	Runs	HS	Avge	100s	50s	Ct	St	O	M	Runs	Wkts	Avge	Best	5wI	10wM
Test																		
All First	1	2	0	39	39	19.50	-	-	3	-								
1-day Int																		
NatWest																		
B & H																		
Sunday																		

Career Performances

	M	Inns	NO	Runs	HS	Avge	100s	50s	Ct	St	Balls	Runs	Wkts	Avge	Best	5wI	10wM
Test																	
All First	12	22	0	678	117	30.81	1	2	4	-							
1-day Int																	
NatWest																	
B & H																	
Sunday																	

ROBERTS, G. M.   Derbyshire

Name: Glenn Martin Roberts
Role: Left-hand bat, slow left-arm bowler
Born: 4 November 1973, Huddersfield
Height: 5ft 11in **Weight:** 12st
Nickname: Robbo
County debut: 1996
1st-Class 50s: 1
1st-Class catches: 7
Place in batting averages: 156th av. 23.70
Strike rate: 123.33 (career 136.20)
Parents: Tony and Margaret
Marital status: Single
Family links with cricket: 'Major influence was my grandfather who played Huddersfield League cricket. My parents took me everywhere to play and support me'
Education: King James's School; Greenhead College, Huddersfield; Carnegie College, Leeds Metropolitan University
Qualifications: 8 GCSEs, 4 A-levels, BEd (Hons) Physical Education, FA Teaching Certificate, NCA advanced coach
Career outside cricket: PE teacher
Off-season: PE teaching in Huddersfield
Overseas tours: Roses CC (Yorkshire) to Menorca 1995, 1996
Overseas teams played for: Easts, Brisbane 1997-98
Cricketers particularly admired: Kim Barnett, Phil DeFreitas, Phil Carrick
Young players to look out for: Matthew Wood, Gavin Hamilton, Steve Griffiths, Tim Tweats
Other sports followed: Rugby league (Huddersfield Giants) and football
Relaxations: Jogging, fitness, gym work, socialising
Extras: Played for Yorkshire from U14 to U19 and captained the U16s and the U19s.

Was a member of the Yorkshire Academy for two years. Scored 50 batting at No. 9 on his Championship debut for Derbyshire and featured in a then-record eighth-wicket stand for Derbyshire of 118 with Karl Krikken

Opinions on cricket: 'Introduce fitness trainers, sports psychologists, dieticians, nutritionists and other support systems to maintain and enhance the performance of county and international players. Optional schemes for players to obtain professional qualifications during the off-season – e.g. sports coaching, PE teaching, etc.'

Best batting: 52 Derbyshire v Somerset, Taunton 1996
Best bowling: 4-105 Derbyshire v Durham, Derby 1998

1998 Season

	M	Inns	NO	Runs	HS	Avge	100s	50s	Ct	St	O	M	Runs	Wkts	Avge	Best	5wI	10wM
Test																		
All First	8	13	3	237	44	23.70	-	-	6	-	185	27	729	9	81.00	4-105	-	-
1-day Int																		
NatWest	3	0	0	0	0	-	-	-	-	-	22	7	41	1	41.00	1-30	-	
B & H																		
Sunday	10	5	1	14	7	3.50	-	-	2	-	69	3	305	17	17.94	3-34	-	

Career Performances

	M	Inns	NO	Runs	HS	Avge	100s	50s	Ct	St	Balls	Runs	Wkts	Avge	Best	5wI	10wM
Test																	
All First	11	17	4	334	52	25.69	-	1	7	-	1362	810	10	81.00	4-105	-	-
1-day Int																	
NatWest	3	0	0	0	0	-	-	-	-	-	132	41	1	41.00	1-30	-	
B & H	5	3	1	15	12	7.50	-	-	2	-	276	228	9	25.33	3-45	-	
Sunday	21	12	5	39	9	5.57	-	-	5	-	837	698	23	30.34	3-34	-	

ROBINSON, D. D. J.   Essex

Name: Darren David John Robinson
Role: Right-hand opening bat, occasional right-arm medium bowler
Born: 2 March 1973, Braintree, Essex
Height: 5ft 10in **Weight:** 14st
Nickname: Pie Shop, Robbo
County debut: 1993
County cap: 1997
1st-Class 50s: 14
1st-Class 100s: 4
1st-Class catches: 58
One-Day 100s: 3
Place in batting averages: 213th av. 17.84 (1997 92nd av. 35.00)

Parents: David and Dorothy
Marital status: Engaged
Children: Kalli, 20 July 1998
Family links with cricket: Father plays club cricket for Halstead
Education: Tabor High School, Braintree; Chelmsford College of Further Education
Qualifications: 5 GCSEs, BTEC National Diploma in Building and Construction
Career outside cricket: Civil engineering and surveying
Off-season: 'Work for my car sponsor, P.J. Tarrant Ltd, Site Investigators'
Overseas tours: England U18 to Canada 1991; England U19 to Pakistan 1991-92
Overseas teams played for: Waverley, Sydney 1992-94; Eden Roshill CC, Auckland 1995-96
Cricketers particularly admired: David Denny
Young players to look out for: Steve Hale ('huge potential')
Other sports followed: Golf, football, rugby, swimming
Injuries: Out for three weeks with two broken fingers
Relaxations: Reading crime novels, music, eating out, pubs
Extras: *Daily Telegraph* batting award 1988 and International Youth Tournament in Canada batting award 1991
Opinions on cricket: 'Cricket's a great game when everything is going well, but a pain in the arse when it's not.'
Best batting: 148 Essex v Worcestershire, Chelmsford 1997

1998 Season

	M	Inns	NO	Runs	HS	Avge	100s	50s	Ct	St	O	M	Runs	Wkts	Avge	Best	5wI	10wM
Test																		
All First	14	25	0	446	85	17.84	-	1	11	-								
1-day Int																		
NatWest	1	1	1	37	37 *	-	-	-	-	-								
B & H	6	5	1	251	137 *	62.75	2	-	-	-								
Sunday	12	11	1	351	129 *	35.10	1	2	3	-								

> 67. Which New Zealand spinner made his One-Day International debut v Pakistan at Edgbaston in the 1983 World Cup?

FIGA

Career Performances

	M	Inns	NO	Runs	HS	Avge	100s	50s	Ct	St	Balls	Runs	Wkts	Avge	Best	5wl	10wM
Test																	
All First	60	107	3	2781	148	26.74	4	14	58	-	36	31	0	-	-	-	-
1-day Int																	
NatWest	13	11	1	239	62	23.90	-	2	4	-							
B & H	17	15	3	451	137 *	37.58	2	-	2	-							
Sunday	58	57	7	1324	129 *	26.48	1	5	17	-	17	26	1	26.00	1-7	-	

ROBINSON, M. A. Sussex

Name: Mark Andrew Robinson
Role: Right-hand bat, right-arm medium-fast bowler
Born: 23 November 1966, Hull
Height: 6ft 3in **Weight:** 13st 3lbs
Nickname: Jessy, Coddy, Scoope, Tiger, Stormy, Storm
County debut: 1987 (Northamptonshire), 1991 (Yorkshire), 1996 (Sussex)
County cap: 1990 (Northamptonshire), 1992 (Yorkshire)
1st-Class 5 w. in innings: 9
1st-Class 10 w. in match: 2
1st-Class catches: 36
Place in batting averages: 297th av. 3.07 (1997 296th av. 7.12)
Place in bowling averages: 61st av. 26.80 (1997 67th av. 29.70)
Strike rate: 59.45 (career 66.36)
Parents: Malcolm and Joan
Wife and date of marriage: Julia, 8 October 1994
Children: Samuel Lewes, 11 January 1996
Family links with cricket: Grandfather a prominent local cricketer and 'father was hostile bowler in the back garden'
Education: Fifth Avenue Primary; Endike Junior High; Hull Grammar School
Qualifications: 6 O-levels, 2 A-levels, advanced cricket coach, badminton coach, rugby union coach
Career outside cricket: Self-employed cricket coach
Overseas tours: England U19 North to Bermuda; Yorkshire to Cape Town 1991-92, 1992-93, to West Indies 1993-94
Overseas teams played for: East Shirley, Canterbury, New Zealand 1987-89; Canterbury, New Zealand 1989-98

Cricketers particularly admired: Dennis Lillee
Young players to look out for: 'The boys from Joe Duffy's junior set-up at Hull CC'
Injuries: 'General niggles, but stayed fit thanks to a hard-working physio'
Extras: Took hat-trick with first three balls of innings in Yorkshire League playing for Hull v Doncaster. First player to win Yorkshire U19 Bowler of the Season in two successive years. Northamptonshire Uncapped Player of the Year in 1989. Endured a world record 11 innings without scoring a run in 1990. Currently trying to open an eight-lane indoor cricket stadium. Sussex Clubman of the Year 1997 and 1998
Opinions on cricket: 'A batsman should have the same penalties as a bowler when he continues to run down the wicket. What goes around comes around. Beware the wolf in sheep's clothing.'
Best batting: 27 Sussex v Lancashire, Old Trafford 1997
Best bowling: 9-37 Yorkshire v Northamptonshire, Harrogate 1993

1998 Season

	M	Inns	NO	Runs	HS	Avge	100s	50s	Ct	St	O	M	Runs	Wkts	Avge	Best	5wI	10wM
Test																		
All First	16	21	8	40	7	3.07	-	-	1	-	416.1	107	1126	42	26.80	4-72	-	-
1-day Int																		
NatWest	1	1	0	4	4	4.00	-	-	-	-	10	2	36	1	36.00	1-36	-	
B & H	3	1	0	0	0	0.00	-	-	-	-	30	3	150	6	25.00	4-53	-	
Sunday	16	8	3	10	3 *	2.00	-	-	1	-	113.1	4	431	17	25.35	3-24	-	

Career Performances

	M	Inns	NO	Runs	HS	Avge	100s	50s	Ct	St	Balls	Runs	Wkts	Avge	Best	5wI	10wM
Test																	
All First	188	207	85	466	27	3.81	-	-	36	-	30463	14611	459	31.83	9-37	9	2
1-day Int																	
NatWest	23	9	6	11	4	3.66	-	-	3	-	1560	869	33	26.33	4-32	-	
B & H	27	12	6	6	3 *	1.00	-	-	5	-	1516	914	33	27.69	4-53	-	
Sunday	127	50	22	87	9 *	3.10	-	-	14	-	5399	3943	111	35.52	4-23	-	

ROBINSON, P. E. — Leicestershire

Name: Phillip Edward Robinson
Role: Right-hand bat, left-arm
'declaration' bowler
Born: 3 August 1963, Keighley,
West Yorkshire
Height: 5ft 9in **Weight:** 13st 10lbs
Nickname: Roundbat, Brigadier, F.B.,
Skip, Robbo, Red
County debut: 1984 (Yorkshire),
1992 (Leicestershire)
County cap: 1988 (Yorkshire)
1000 runs in a season: 3
1st-Class 50s: 51
1st-Class 100s: 7
1st-Class catches: 130
One-Day 100s: 1
Parents: Keith and Lesley
Wife and date of marriage: Jane, 19
September 1986
Family links with cricket: Father and brother played in Bradford League. Dad now
an umpire
Education: Long Lee Primary; Hartington Middle; Greenhead Comprehensive
Qualifications: 2 O-levels
Overseas tours: Southland CC to Tasmania 1987; Yorkshire to St Lucia and Barbados
1988; Leicestershire to Jamaica 1993, to South Africa 1994-95
Overseas teams played for: Southland, New Zealand 1987; Eastern Southland cricket
coach 1987; Eden Roskill, Auckland 1989-90; Riverside, Wellington 1990-91
Cricketers particularly admired: Geoff Boycott, Richard Hadlee, Michael Holding
Other sports followed: Football (Manchester United), rugby league (Keighley
Cougars)
Relaxations: War-gaming, eating out
Extras: Made the highest score by a Yorkshire 2nd XI player with 233 in 1983.
Scored most runs by an overseas player in the Auckland Cricket League for Eden
Roskill 1989-90 (1200 runs). Hit the fastest televised 50 in the Sunday League (19
balls) v Derbyshire at Chesterfield 1991. Released by Yorkshire at his own request at
the end of the 1991 season. Played for Cumberland in 1992 and could play only
limited-overs for Leicestershire in 1992 (apart from one match) but on full contract
from 1993. Captain of Leicestershire 2nd XI. Led the team to Bain Hogg win in 1995
Opinions on cricket: 'Cricket should be played on uncovered pitches over three days.
Alternatively, four-day games should be played Wednesday to Saturday, with the
Sunday League game after. Also, second-class cricket should be played Wednesday to

Friday to allow the younger players to work with the senior players during the season.'
Best batting: 189 Yorkshire v Lancashire, Scarborough 1991
Best bowling: 1-10 Yorkshire v Somerset, Scarborough 1990

1998 Season (did not make any first-class or one-day appearances)

Career Performances

	M	Inns	NO	Runs	HS	Avge	100s	50s	Ct	St	Balls	Runs	Wkts	Avge	Best	5wl	10wM
Test																	
All First	159	261	35	7617	189	33.70	7	51	130	-	296	329	3	109.66	1-10	-	-
1-day Int																	
NatWest	17	13	0	421	73	32.38	-	3	5	-							
B & H	33	29	4	684	73 *	27.36	-	4	12	-							
Sunday	145	140	14	3111	104	24.69	1	14	59	-							

ROBINSON, R.   Durham

Name: Ryan Robinson
Role: Right-hand bat, right-arm medium bowler
Born: 19 October 1976, Huddersfield, West Yorkshire
Height: 6ft 2in **Weight:** 12st
Nickname: Robbo
County debut: No first-team appearance
Parents: Peter and Jennifer
Marital status: Single
Family links with cricket: 'Dad plays in local village side. Cousin used to play a bit'
Education: Emley First; Kirkburton Middle; Shelley High and Sixth Form
Qualifications: 9 GCSEs
Off-season: Playing football
Overseas teams played for: Darling, Cape Town 1995-96
Cricketers particularly admired: Jacques Kallis
Other sports played: Football (Emley FC – Unibond Premier)
Other sports followed: Football (Liverpool)
Injuries: Eight weeks off bowling with rib muscle injury
Relaxations: Fishing, DJ-ing

Opinions on cricket: 'If floodlights and coloured clothes are needed to encourage more spectators, then they should continue being used.'

ROBINSON, R. T. Nottinghamshire

Name: Robert Timothy Robinson
Role: Right-hand opening bat
Born: 21 November 1958,
Sutton-in-Ashfield, Nottinghamshire
Height: 6ft **Weight:** 12st 7lbs
Nickname: Robbo
County debut: 1978
County cap: 1983
Benefit: 1992 (£90,040)
Test debut: 1984-85
Tests: 29
One-Day Internationals: 26
1000 runs in a season: 14
1st-Class 50s: 137
1st-Class 100s: 60
1st-Class 200s: 3
1st-Class catches: 247
One-Day 100s: 9
Place in batting averages: 65th av. 34.56
(1997 112th av. 32.48)
Strike rate: (career 64.75)
Parents: Eddy and Christine
Marital status: Separated
Children: Philip Thomas; Alex James
Family links with cricket: Father, uncle, cousin and brother all play or played local cricket
Education: Dunstable Grammar School; High Pavement College, Nottingham; Sheffield University
Qualifications: BA (Hons) in Accountancy and Financial Management
Career outside cricket: Director of sports retail business
Off-season: Working in own business
Overseas tours: England to India and Sri Lanka 1984-85, to West Indies 1985-86, to India and Pakistan (World Cup) 1987-88, to New Zealand 1987-88; to Australia 1987-88; unofficial English XI to South Africa 1989-90
Cricketers particularly admired: Clive Rice, Geoffrey Boycott
Young players to look out for: Matt Whiley
Other sports played: Golf, squash
Other sports followed: Football (Nottingham Forest, Notts County)

Injuries: Out for seven weeks with broken wrist

Relaxations: 'Spending time with my children'

Extras: Played for Northamptonshire 2nd XI in 1974-75 and for Nottinghamshire 2nd XI in 1977. Had soccer trials with Portsmouth, Chelsea and QPR. One of *Wisden*'s Five Cricketers of the Year 1986. Banned from Test cricket for joining 1989-90 tour of South Africa, remitted in 1992. Handed over captaincy to Paul Johnson in 1995 to give more time to business

Opinions on cricket: 'Decision-makers should listen to the views of the participants and the spectators!!'

Best batting: 220* Nottinghamshire v Yorkshire, Trent Bridge 1990

Best bowling: 1-22 Nottinghamshire v Northamptonshire, Northampton 1982

1998 Season

	M	Inns	NO	Runs	HS	Avge	100s	50s	Ct	St	O	M	Runs	Wkts	Avge	Best	5wI	10wM
Test																		
All First	11	18	2	553	114	34.56	1	4	6	-								
1-day Int																		
NatWest	2	2	0	57	46	28.50	-	-	-	-								
B & H	4	3	0	36	17	12.00	-	-	1	-								
Sunday	4	3	0	35	25	11.66	-	-	3	-								

Career Performances

	M	Inns	NO	Runs	HS	Avge	100s	50s	Ct	St	Balls	Runs	Wkts	Avge	Best	5wI	10wM
Test	29	49	5	1601	175	36.38	4	6	8	-	6	0	0	-	-	-	-
All First	413	717	84	27046	220 *	42.72	63	137	247	-	259	289	4	72.25	1-22	-	-
1-day Int	26	26	0	597	83	22.96	-	3	6	-							
NatWest	43	43	3	1652	139	41.30	2	8	17	-							
B & H	78	75	9	2567	120	38.89	3	18	17	-							
Sunday	233	226	27	6603	119 *	33.18	4	44	75	-							

ROLLINS, A. S. Derbyshire

Name: Adrian Stewart Rollins
Role: Right-hand bat, occasional
wicket-keeper
Born: 8 February 1972, Barking, Essex
Height: 6ft 5in **Weight:** 16st 10lbs
Nickname: Rollie, Ainsley Harriott ('but I
don't like this one, so don't call me it')
County debut: 1993
County cap: 1995
1000 runs in a season: 3
1st-Class 50s: 28
1st-Class 100s: 8
1st-Class 200s: 1
1st-Class catches: 71
1st-Class stumpings: 1
One-Day 100s: 1
Place in batting averages: 74th av. 32.52
(1997 41st av. 43.92)
Strike rate: (career 90.00)
Parents: Marva
Marital status: Engaged to Debbie
Children: Stepdaughter Gemma (5 yrs)
Family links with cricket: 'Uncles play club cricket. Robert (bruv) at Essex. Gary
(other bruv) should be playing county cricket'
Education: Avenue Primary, Manor Park, London; Little Ilford Secondary, Manor
Park, London
Qualifications: 10 GCSEs, 4 A-levels, NCA coaching award, Diploma in Sports
Psychology, 'I am also doing a course in business management at present'
Career outside cricket: 'Business – probably sports-related or media'
Off-season: 'Coaching with Karl "The Fidget" Krikken. He's aaaallriiight'
Overseas tours: London Federation of Boys Clubs to Barbados 1987
Overseas teams played for: Kaponga, New Zealand 1993-94
Cricketers particularly admired: Viv Richards, Clive Lloyd, David Gower, Ian
Botham, Malcolm Marshall, Desmond Haynes, Gordon Greenidge
Young players to look out for: 'Whether it's in the present, past or future, it doesn't
matter if you play for Derbyshire, Northants, Notts, Glamorgan. Just look at the usual
teams you look at and you'll find the chosen ones'
Other sports played: 'Used to goalkeep and play basketball. To be honest my school
footie team was crap. Good individuals who wouldn't pass the bloody ball'
Other sports followed: Football (West Ham United; 'Ian Wright, Wright, Wright'), 'I
follow the NBA, athletics and boxing (that Naseem lad's all right)'

Injuries: Two months out with back disc problems. 'Came back in the NatWest final. That made a lot of difference'

Relaxations: 'Music, lots of music. Chilling with my better half. Chilling with my "boys". Not shy of a few dance moves in the "P.C."'

Extras: Made Championship debut on same day as brother. Became 500th first-class player for Derbyshire, for whom he was named Young Player of the Year 1993. Was the 100th Derbyshire player to score a hundred. Holds record for the highest score by a Derbyshire opener to carry his bat and his 200 not out against Gloucestershire was the longest innings by a Derbyshire player. He became the youngest English-qualified Derbyshire double centurion. Voted Derbyshire Player of the Year for 1995. Took part in record third wicket partnership for Derbyshire with Kim Barnett against Leicestershire 1997. Scored century before lunch against Glamorgan at Chesterfield August 1997

Opinions on cricket: 'Super cup is a joke. A one-day competition where qualification is based upon the results of the four-day competition. Baffling! Two divisions in AXA is good idea; but who decided on playing out of your division? What a brainless concept. Test pitches will produce Test cricketers. I think a lot of people know what I'm saying. Do selectors look at the playing conditions of every county before picking potential Test cricketers, or do they just pick media-friendly pretty boys? Ian Austin should have been in the one-day side five years ago. He may have been picked back in 1993 if he was marketable.'

Best batting: 210 Derbyshire v Hampshire, Chesterfield 1997
Best bowling: 1-19 Derbyshire v Essex, Chelmsford 1995

1998 Season

	M	Inns	NO	Runs	HS	Avge	100s	50s	Ct	St	O	M	Runs	Wkts	Avge	Best	5wI	10wM
Test																		
All First	10	19	0	618	107	32.52	1	4	10	-								
1-day Int																		
NatWest	2	2	0	59	58	29.50	-	1	2	-								
B & H	4	4	1	103	70 *	34.33	-	1	-	-								
Sunday	9	9	0	76	23	8.44	-	-	2	-								

Career Performances

	M	Inns	NO	Runs	HS	Avge	100s	50s	Ct	St	Balls	Runs	Wkts	Avge	Best	5wI	10wM
Test																	
All First	86	159	15	5056	210	35.11	9	28	71	1	90	122	1	122.00	1-19	-	-
1-day Int																	
NatWest	9	9	0	190	58	21.11	-	2	5	-							
B & H	11	11	1	262	70 *	26.20	-	2	2	-							
Sunday	54	48	4	815	126 *	18.52	1	1	23	-	12	15	0	-	-	-	-

ROLLINS, R. J.   Essex

Name: Robert John Rollins
Role: Right-hand bat, wicket-keeper
Born: 30 January 1974, Plaistow, London
Height: 5ft 9in **Weight:** 14st
Nickname: Walter, Rollie
County debut: 1992
County cap: 1995
1st-Class 50s: 11
1st-Class 100s: 1
1st-Class catches: 152
1st-Class stumpings: 20
Place in batting averages: 249th av. 14.25
(1997 161st av. 25.11)
Parents: 'Mrs Marva Rollins BEd, MA'
Marital status: 'Engaged to Kerry-Ann'
Children: Lawren and Ellisee
Family links with cricket: 'Big brother
(Adrian) plays for Derbyshire, middle brother
(Gary) is an aspiring fast bowler (if anyone is
interested, please call me)'
Education: Avenue Primary School, Manor Park; Little Ilford Comprehensive School;
'School of Hard Knocks'
Qualifications: 6 GCSEs, senior coach NVQ Level 2
Off-season: Getting fit for the next season
Overseas tours: England U18 to Canada 1991; England U19 to Pakistan 1991-92,
to India 1992-93
Overseas teams played for: MOB Pietermaritzburg, South Africa 1995-96; Shell
Harbour, New South Wales 1996-97
Cricketers particularly admired: Adrian Rollins, Gary Rollins, Ash, Keith Hurst,
John French
Young players to look out for: Ryan Hurst, Carl Hurst, Benjamin Hurst,
Dominic Hurst ('my little cousins')
Other sports played: Loxford Youth Club pool team – district winners 1992
Other sports followed: Football (West Ham United)
Injuries: Out for two months with patella tendonitis
Relaxations: Reading, playing golf, playing PlayStation
Extras: Named Essex Young Player of the Year 1992 and awarded his 2nd XI cap in
September of that year. Made Championship debut on the same day as his brother
Adrian. Both kept wicket in the same Sunday League game
Opinions on cricket: 'The game continues to be a great leveller.'
Best batting: 133* Essex v Glamorgan, Swansea 1995

1998 Season

	M	Inns	NO	Runs	HS	Avge	100s	50s	Ct	St	O	M	Runs	Wkts	Avge	Best	5wI	10wM
Test																		
All First	8	12	0	171	42	14.25	-	-	13	-								
1-day Int																		
NatWest	2	1	0	10	10	10.00	-	-	4	-								
B & H	7	5	0	43	28	8.60	-	-	5	2								
Sunday	11	7	0	73	36	10.42	-	-	4	3								

Career Performances

	M	Inns	NO	Runs	HS	Avge	100s	50s	Ct	St	Balls	Runs	Wkts	Avge	Best	5wI	10wM
Test																	
All First	66	107	9	2193	133 *	22.37	1	11	152	20							
1-day Int																	
NatWest	14	11	4	258	67 *	36.85	-	3	8	3							
B & H	19	11	2	89	28	9.88	-	-	17	4							
Sunday	66	51	9	516	38	12.28	-	-	55	16							

ROSE, F. A. — Northamptonshire

Name: Franklyn Albert Rose
Role: Right-hand bat, right-arm
fast bowler
Born: 1 February 1972, St Ann's Bay,
Jamaica
Height: 6ft 5in **Weight:** 15st
Nickname: Bap-Bap
County debut: 1998
Test debut: 1996-97
Tests: 10
One-Day Internationals: 13
50 wickets in a season: 1
1st-Class 50s: 1
1st-Class 5 w. in innings: 9
1st-Class 10 w. in match: 2
1st-Class catches: 8
One-Day 5 w. in innings: 1
Place in batting averages: 281st av. 8.86
Place in bowling averages: 66th av. 27.34
Strike rate: 44.80 (career 44.78)
Parents: Herma Hardware and Franklyn Rose Senior
Education: Ocho Rios Secondary; Holmwood Technical High School

Overseas tours: West Indies to Sharjah 1995-96, to India and Pakistan (World Cup) 1995-96, to Pakistan 1997-98, to Bangladesh 1998-99, to South Africa 1998-99
Cricketers particularly admired: C.E.L. Ambrose, I.V.A. Richards
Young players to look out for: L.V. (Leon) Garrick of Jamaica
Other sports played: Basketball, football
Relaxations: Music, swimming
Extras: Became the first West Indian fast bowler to claim six wickets (6-100) in a Test innings at the first attempt in the first Test against India at Kingston, Jamaica, 1997. Claimed 5-14, the best ever figures by a Northants bowler in the Benson and Hedges Cup, on B&H debut against Minor Counties 1998. Released by Northants at end of 1998 season
Opinions on cricket: 'Too much cricket in general'
Best batting: 96 Jamaica v Leeward Islands, Anguilla 1996-97
Best bowling: 7-39 Northamptonshire v Worcestershire, Worcester 1998
Stop press: Took 7-84 in South Africa's first innings in the third Test at Durban 1998-99, the best Test innings figures at the ground by a visiting bowler

1998 Season

	M	Inns	NO	Runs	HS	Avge	100s	50s	Ct	St	O	M	Runs	Wkts	Avge	Best	5wI	10wM
Test																		
All First	14	17	2	133	21	8.86	-	-	-	-	373.2	59	1367	50	27.34	7-39	3	1
1-day Int																		
NatWest	1	1	0	19	19	19.00	-	-	1	-	12	1	43	3	14.33	3-43	-	
B & H	5	5	0	20	15	4.00	-	-	1	-	45.1	5	204	12	17.00	5-14	1	
Sunday	13	4	1	13	9 *	4.33	-	-	2	-	87.1	6	380	15	25.33	2-19	-	

Career Performances

	M	Inns	NO	Runs	HS	Avge	100s	50s	Ct	St	Balls	Runs	Wkts	Avge	Best	5wI	10wM
Test	10	12	2	97	34	9.70	-	-	1	-	1471	738	27	27.33	6-100	1	-
All First	53	69	12	736	96	12.91	-	1	8	-	8420	4703	188	25.01	7-39	9	2
1-day Int	13	11	2	83	24	9.22	-	-	2	-	606	517	10	51.70	3-25	-	
NatWest	1	1	0	19	19	19.00	-	-	1	-	72	43	3	14.33	3-43	-	
B & H	5	5	0	20	15	4.00	-	-	1	-	271	204	12	17.00	5-14	1	
Sunday	13	4	1	13	9 *	4.33	-	-	2	-	523	380	15	25.33	2-19	-	

ROSE, G. D. — Somerset

Name: Graham David Rose
Role: Right-hand bat, right-arm fast-medium bowler, first slip
Born: 12 April 1964, Tottenham
Height: 6ft 4in **Weight:** 15st 7lbs
Nickname: Rosie, Hagar, Yid
County debut: 1985 (Middlesex), 1987 (Somerset)
County cap: 1988 (Somerset)
Benefit: 1997 (£91,500)
1000 runs in a season: 1
50 wickets in a season: 5
1st-Class 50s: 39
1st-Class 100s: 8
1st-Class 5 w. in innings: 14
1st-Class 10 w. in match: 1
1st-Class catches: 110
One-Day 100s: 2
Place in batting averages: 140th av. 25.25 (1997 20th av. 50.11)
Place in bowling averages: 62nd av. 26.90 (1997 31st av. 24.80)
Strike rate: 55.44 (career 55.03)
Parents: William and Edna
Wife and date of marriage: Teresa Julie, 19 September 1987
Children: Georgina Charlotte, 6 December 1990; Felix William Michael, 11 August 1997
Family links with cricket: Father and brothers have played club cricket
Education: Northumberland Park School, Tottenham
Qualifications: 6 O-levels, 4 A-levels, NCA coaching certificate
Off-season: 'That old chestnut!'
Overseas teams played for: Carey Park, Bunbury, Western Australia 1984-85; Fremantle, Perth 1986-87; Paarl, Cape Town 1988-89
Cricketers particularly admired: Richard Hadlee, Jimmy Cook, Mushtaq Ahmed
Young players to look out for: Matthew Bulbeck
Other sports followed: Football, rugby, golf
Injuries: None – 'not bad for an old 'un!'
Relaxations: Wine, golf, 'Georgina and Felix'
Extras: Played for England YC v Australia YC 1983. Took 6-41 on Middlesex debut in 1985, then scored 95 on debut for Somerset in 1987. Completed double of 1000 runs and 50 wickets in first-class cricket in 1990 and scored fastest recorded centuries in NatWest Trophy (v Devon) and Sunday League (v Glamorgan). Cricket Society's All-rounder of the Year 1997

Opinions on cricket: 'Not sure that a two-divisional split at county level will produce a better Test team – didn't the all-play-all format produce the likes of Gower, Gatting, Gooch, Botham et al? Surely haven't we got to focus on the bottom half of the pyramid – school and club cricket – to produce a better product at the apex?'
Best batting: 191 Somerset v Sussex, Taunton 1997
Best bowling: 7-47 Somerset v Nottinghamshire, Taunton 1996

1998 Season

	M	Inns	NO	Runs	HS	Avge	100s	50s	Ct	St	O	M	Runs	Wkts	Avge	Best	5wl	10wM
Test																		
All First	17	26	2	606	76	25.25	-	4	3	-	480.3	132	1399	52	26.90	5-48	2	-
1-day Int																		
NatWest	2	1	0	1	1	1.00	-	-	-	-	19.5	6	65	2	32.50	2-5	-	
B & H	4	4	0	97	38	24.25	-	-	1	-	32	4	120	3	40.00	2-10	-	
Sunday	16	14	4	202	59	20.20	-	1	2	-	105.2	7	423	16	26.43	3-33	-	

Career Performances

	M	Inns	NO	Runs	HS	Avge	100s	50s	Ct	St	Balls	Runs	Wkts	Avge	Best	5wl	10wM
Test																	
All First	221	310	56	7776	191	30.61	8	39	110	-	30547	16148	555	29.09	7-47	14	1
1-day Int																	
NatWest	24	20	3	348	110	20.47	1	1	4	-	1306	851	27	31.51	3-11	-	
B & H	54	48	4	911	79	20.70	-	4	12	-	2932	1950	67	29.10	4-21	-	
Sunday	181	158	32	3434	148	27.25	1	18	46	-	7034	5226	180	29.03	4-26	-	

ROSEBERRY, M. A.   Middlesex

Name: Michael Anthony Roseberry
Role: Right-hand bat, right-arm medium-fast bowler
Born: 28 November 1966, Houghton-le-Spring, Sunderland
Height: 6ft 2in **Weight:** 14st 7lbs
Nickname: Micky
County debut: 1985 (Middlesex), 1995 (Durham)
County cap: 1990 (Middlesex)
1000 runs in a season: 4
1st-Class 50s: 53
1st-Class 100s: 19
1st-Class catches: 146
One-Day 100s: 6
Place in batting averages: 123rd av. 26.81 (1997 265th av. 13.83)
Strike rate: (career 127.75)
Parents: Matthew and Jean

Wife and date of marriage:
Helen Louise, 22 February 1991
Children: Jordan Louise, 29 May 1992;
Lauren Ella, 19 February 1994
Family links with cricket: Brother Andrew
played for Glamorgan and Leicestershire;
father is director of Durham CCC
Education: Tonstall Preparatory School,
Sunderland; Durham School
Qualifications: 5 O-levels, 1 A-level,
advanced cricket coach
Career outside cricket: 'Coaching cricket.
Director in our business'
Overseas tours: England YC to West Indies
1984-85; England A to Australia 1992-93;
England XI and Lord's Taverners to Hong
Kong 'on numerous occasions'; MCC
to West Africa 1993-94; Durham CCC
to South Africa 1994-95
Overseas teams played for: Fremantle, Western Australia 1986; Melville, Perth 1988;
Alberton, Johannesburg 1994-96
Cricketers particularly admired: 'Desmond Haynes for the obvious and his
generosity on the golf course'
Other sports followed: 'Played rugby union at a good level when at school,
representing Durham County at all levels except the senior side. Follow golf and very
loyal supporter of Sunderland FC'
Relaxations: 'Eating out and spending time with my family which is limited during
the summer'
Extras: Won Lord's Taverners/MCC Cricketer of the Year 1983, Cricket Society
award for Best Young Cricketer of the Year 1984 and twice won Cricket Society award
for best all-rounder in schools cricket. Played in Durham League as a professional
while still at school. At age 16, playing for Durham School v St Bees, he hit 216 in
160 minutes. In 1992 scored 2044 runs in 1992 – joint highest in first-class cricket
with Peter Bowler and was named Middlesex Player of the Year and Lucozade Player
of the Year. Left Middlesex at end of 1994 to return to his native Durham as captain
for the 1995 season but relinquished the captaincy during the 1996 season
Best batting: 185 Middlesex v Leicestershire, Lord's 1993
Best bowling: 1-1 Middlesex v Sussex, Hove 1988

FICA

68. Who is India's all-time leading
World Cup run-scorer?

1998 Season

	M	Inns	NO	Runs	HS	Avge	100s	50s	Ct	St	O	M	Runs	Wkts	Avge	Best	5wI	10wM
Test																		
All First	6	11	0	295	97	26.81	-	2	2	-								
1-day Int																		
NatWest	1	1	1	23	23 *	-	-	-	-	-								
B & H	3	3	0	19	11	6.33	-	-	-	-								
Sunday	8	8	1	91	28	13.00	-	-	2	-								

Career Performances

	M	Inns	NO	Runs	HS	Avge	100s	50s	Ct	St	Balls	Runs	Wkts	Avge	Best	5wI	10wM
Test																	
All First	202	343	37	10498	185	34.30	19	53	146	-	511	406	4	101.50	1-1	-	-
1-day Int																	
NatWest	17	17	1	703	121	43.93	3	1	7	-	36	42	1	42.00	1-22	-	
B & H	33	31	3	707	84	25.25	-	6	7	-	6	2	0	-	-	-	-
Sunday	126	120	15	3317	119 *	31.59	3	23	47	-	4	7	0	-	-	-	-

RUSSELL, R. C. — Gloucestershire

Name: Robert Charles Russell
Role: Left-hand bat, wicket-keeper
Born: 15 August 1963, Stroud
Height: 5ft 8¹/₄in **Weight:** 9st 9lbs
Nickname: Jack
County debut: 1981
County cap: 1985
Benefit: 1994
Test debut: 1988
Tests: 54
One-Day Internationals: 39
1000 runs in a season: 1
1st-Class 50s: 72
1st-Class 100s: 7
1st-Class catches: 973
1st-Class stumpings: 110
One-Day 100s: 2
Place in batting averages: 187th av. 20.26
(1997 30th av. 45.60)
Strike rate: (career 56.00)
Parents: John and Jennifer
Wife and date of marriage: Aileen Ann, 6 March 1985
Children: Stepson, Marcus Anthony 1980; Elizabeth Ann, March 1988;

Victoria, 1989; Charles David, 1991; Katherine Jane, 1996
Education: Uplands County Primary School; Archway Comprehensive School; Bristol Polytechnic ('walked out after two months of accountancy course. Couldn't understand the sociology and economics – wanted to play cricket instead')
Qualifications: 7 O-levels, 2 A-levels
Career outside cricket: Professional artist
Off-season: Working on new commissions and exhibitions at Jack Russell Gallery
Overseas tours: England A to Australia 1992-93; England to Pakistan 1987-88, to India and West Indies 1989-90, to Australia 1990-91, to New Zealand 1991-92, to West Indies 1993-94, to Australia 1994-95, to South Africa 1995-96, to Pakistan and India (World Cup) 1995-96, to Zimbabwe and New Zealand 1996-97, to West Indies 1997-98, to Bangladesh (Wills International Cup) 1998-99
Cricketers particularly admired: Alan Knott, Bob Taylor, Ian Botham, Rodney Marsh 'and other greats'
Other sports followed: Football (Tottenham Hotspur), rugby (England), snooker, 'anything competitive'
Relaxations: Playing cricket and painting pictures. 'I love comedians and comedies. Life is too short, you need to laugh as much as you can'
Extras: Spotted at age nine by Gloucestershire coach, Graham Wiltshire. Youngest Gloucestershire wicket-keeper (17 years 307 days) and set record for most dismissals in a match on first-class debut: 8 (7 caught, 1 stumped) for Gloucestershire v Sri Lankans at Bristol, 1981. Hat-trick of catches v Surrey at The Oval 1986. Represented England YC v West Indies YC in 1982. Was chosen as England's Man of the Test Series, England v Australia 1989 and was one of *Wisden*'s five Cricketers of the Year 1990. Appointed vice-captain to Martyn Moxon on the England A tour to Australia 1992-93. Called up as stand-by wicket-keeper for the England tour to Australia 1994-95 when Alec Stewart broke his finger for the second time on the tour. Opened Jack Russell Gallery in Chipping Sodbury, South Gloucestershire in 1995 where he displays original oil paintings and limited edition prints of cricketing scenes, landscapes, wildlife etc. Books of his that have been published include *A Cricketer's Art – Sketches by Jack Russell* (1988), *Sketches of a Season – illustrated by Jack Russell* (1989), *Jack Russell's Sketch Book* (1996) and *Jack Russell – Unleashed*, an autobiography which made the top ten bestsellers in 1997. Commissioned by Dean of Gloucester to do a drawing of Gloucester Cathedral to raise funds for 900th Anniversary. Still turns out for his original club, Stroud CC, whenever he can. Keen military enthusiast, 'We must never forget'. His paintings are sold and displayed in museums and private collections all around the world. Loves England, 'To me, it's the greatest place of all to play and paint.' Captain of Gloucestershire and Player of the Year 1995. Broke Bob Taylor's long-standing world record for the number of dismissals in a Test match with 11 in the second Test v South Africa at Johannesburg 1995-96; his 27 Test dismissals in the series is a record for England. Awarded MBE in 1996 for services to cricket. Was the Whyte and Mackay wicket-keeper/batsman of the year 1995, 1996, 1997. He also has his own website: http://www.jackrussell.co.uk. Announced his retirement from international cricket in October 1998 after the Wills International Cup in Bangladesh

Best batting: 129* England v Boland, Paarl 1995-96
Best bowling: 1-4 Gloucestershire v West Indians, Bristol 1991

1998 Season

	M	Inns	NO	Runs	HS	Avge	100s	50s	Ct	St	O	M	Runs	Wkts	Avge	Best	5wI	10wM
Test																		
All First	16	28	2	527	63 *	20.26	-	2	56	-								
1-day Int																		
NatWest	2	2	1	76	49 *	76.00	-	-	5	-								
B & H	5	5	1	231	119*	57.75	1	1	9	-								
Sunday	14	11	0	198	40	18.00	-	-	11	2								

Career Performances

	M	Inns	NO	Runs	HS	Avge	100s	50s	Ct	St	Balls	Runs	Wkts	Avge	Best	5wI	10wM
Test	54	86	16	1897	128*	27.10	2	6	153	12							
All First	392	579	123	13648	129*	29.92	7	72	973	110	56	68	1	68.00	1-4	-	-
1-day Int	39	30	7	404	50	17.56	-	1	41	6							
NatWest	40	28	8	530	59 *	26.50	-	1	57	9							
B & H	66	49	17	1007	119*	31.46	1	3	67	12							
Sunday	209	159	34	2797	108	22.37	1	10	169	31							

SACHDEVA, A.   Leicestershire

Name: Atul Sachdeva
Role: Right-hand bat, leg-spin bowler
Born: 22 August 1980, Preston, Lancs
Height: 5ft 9in **Weight:** 10st 7lbs
Nickname: Sach
County debut: No first-team appearance
Parents: Anju and Surendra
Marital status: Single
Education: Queen's Drive County Primary,
Preston; St Pius X School, Preston; King
Edward VII School, Lytham; Lancaster RGS;
Leicester University
Qualifications: 10 GCSEs, 4 A-levels
Career outside cricket: Medical student
Off-season: Studying
Overseas tours: Lancaster RGS to Barbados
1998; Leicestershire to Holland 1998
Cricketers particularly admired:
Viv Richards, Shane Warne

Young players to look out for: Chris Schofield
Other sports played: Rugby union, badminton, golf
Other sports followed: Rugby, football, golf
Relaxations: Sport – golf
Extras: Represented Lancashire at U15, U17, U19 level. Played for Northern League U18 representative side
Opinions on cricket: 'In favour of two divisions.'

SAGGERS, M. J. Durham

Name: Martin John Saggers
Role: Right-hand bat, right-arm fast-medium bowler
Born: 23 May 1972, King's Lynn
Height: 6ft 2in **Weight:** 14st
Nickname: Saggs, Pony
County debut: 1996
1st-Class 5 w. in innings: 2
1st-Class catches: 3
Strike rate: 50.00 (career 49.62)
Parents: Brian and Edna
Marital status: Single
Education: Roseberry Avenue Primary School; Springwood High School; University of Huddersfield
Qualifications: BA (Hons) Architectural Studies
Career outside cricket: Architectural technician/consultant
Overseas teams played for: Randburg CC, Johannesburg, South Africa 1996-97
Cricketers particularly admired: Neil Foster, Richard Hadlee
Young players to look out for: Robert Ferley, Richard Saddleton
Other sports followed: Football (Tottenham Hotspur), golf, tiddlywinks, seven-card stud poker
Relaxations: Egyptology, sleeping
Extras: Released by Durham at end of 1998 season
Best batting: 18 Durham v Somerset, Weston-super-Mare 1996
Best bowling: 6-65 Durham v Glamorgan, Chester-le-Street 1996

1998 Season

	M	Inns	NO	Runs	HS	Avge	100s	50s	Ct	St	O	M	Runs	Wkts	Avge	Best	5wl	10wM
Test																		
All First	2	4	2	25	10	12.50	-	-	1	-	58.2	14	149	7	21.28	3-47	-	-
1-day Int																		
NatWest	1	0	0	0	0	-	-	-	-	-	9.4	1	42	2	21.00	2-42	-	
B & H																		
Sunday	6	4	3	13	8 *	13.00	-	-	2	-	39	3	167	8	20.87	3-35	-	

Career Performances

	M	Inns	NO	Runs	HS	Avge	100s	50s	Ct	St	Balls	Runs	Wkts	Avge	Best	5wl	10wM
Test																	
All First	10	17	5	128	18	10.66	-	-	3	-	1340	769	27	28.48	6-65	2	-
1-day Int																	
NatWest	2	1	0	0	0	0.00	-	-	-	-	118	98	2	49.00	2-42	-	
B & H	5	5	3	58	34 *	29.00	-	-	2	-	246	247	5	49.40	2-49	-	
Sunday	13	6	4	31	13	15.50	-	-	3	-	522	367	17	21.58	4-35	-	

SALES, D. J.   Northamptonshire

Name: David John Sales
Role: Right-hand bat, right-arm occasional bowler
Born: 3 December 1977, Carshalton, Surrey
Height: 6ft **Weight:** 13st
Nickname: Jumble
County debut: 1994 (one-day), 1996 (first-class)
1st-Class 50s: 4
1st-Class 100s: 1
1st-Class 200s: 1
1st-Class catches: 23
Place in batting averages: 219th av. 17.30 (1997 139th av. 27.40)
Strike rate: 66.00 (career 114.00)
Parents: John and Daphne
Marital status: Single
Family links with cricket: Father played club cricket
Education: Cumnor House Prep School, Croydon; Caterham Boys' School
Qualifications: 7 GCSEs, cricket coach
Overseas tours: England U15 to South Africa 1993; England U19 to West Indies

1994-95, to Zimbabwe 1995-96, to Pakistan 1996-97; England A to Kenya and Sri Lanka 1997-98

Cricketers particularly admired: Graham Gooch

Young players to look out for: Owais Shah

Other sports followed: Football (Crystal Palace), golf

Relaxations: Golf and fishing

Extras: Youngest batsman to score a 50 in the Sunday League. The first Englishman to score a double century on his Championship debut and the youngest ever to score a double century

Best batting: 210* Northamptonshire v Worcestershire, Kidderminster 1996

Best bowling: 1-28 Northamptonshire v Glamorgan, Northampton 1998

1998 Season

	M	Inns	NO	Runs	HS	Avge	100s	50s	Ct	St	O	M	Runs	Wkts	Avge	Best	5wI	10wM
Test																		
All First	14	21	1	346	60	17.30	-	2	10	-	11	2	36	1	36.00	1-28	-	-
1-day Int																		
NatWest	1	1	0	42	42	42.00	-	-	-	-
B & H	4	4	0	52	26	13.00	-	-	2	-
Sunday	15	13	1	231	36	19.25	-	-	4	-

Career Performances

	M	Inns	NO	Runs	HS	Avge	100s	50s	Ct	St	Balls	Runs	Wkts	Avge	Best	5wI	10wM
Test																	
All First	37	57	5	1352	210 *	26.00	2	4	23	-	114	64	1	64.00	1-28	-	-
1-day Int																	
NatWest	3	3	0	95	53	31.66	-	1	1	-
B & H	5	5	0	67	26	13.40	-	-	2	-
Sunday	33	29	5	515	70 *	21.45	-	1	8	-

SALISBURY, I. D. K.   Surrey

Name: Ian David Kenneth Salisbury
Role: Right-hand bat, leg-break bowler
Born: 21 January 1970, Northampton
Height: 5ft 11in **Weight:** 12st
Nickname: Sals
County debut: 1989 (Sussex), 1997 (Surrey)
County cap: 1991 (Sussex), 1998 (Surrey)
Test debut: 1992
Tests: 12
One-Day Internationals: 4
50 wickets in a season: 4
1st-Class 50s: 13
1st-Class 5 w. in innings: 28
1st-Class 10 w. in match: 4
1st-Class catches: 139
One-Day 5 w. in innings: 1
Place in batting averages: 195th av. 19.62
(1997 283rd av. 10.60)
Place in bowling averages: 54th av. 25.89
(1997 79th av. 31.20)
Strike rate: 62.89 (career 64.48)
Parents: Dave and Margaret
Wife and date of marriage: Emma Louise, 25 September 1993
Family links with cricket: 'Dad is vice-president of my first club, Brixworth'
Education: Moulton Comprehensive, Northampton
Qualifications: 7 O-levels, NCA coaching certificate
Overseas tours: England A to Pakistan 1990-91, to Bermuda and West Indies
1991-92, to India 1994-95, to Pakistan 1995-96; England to India and Sri Lanka
1992-93, to West Indies 1993-94; World Masters XI v Indian Masters XI November
1996 ('Masters aged 26?')
Cricketers particularly admired: 'Any that keep performing day in, day out, for both
country and county'
Young players to look out for: Ben Hollioake, Owais Shah, Vasbert Drakes
Other sports followed: Most sports
Relaxations: 'Spending time with wife, Emma, meeting friends and relaxing with
them and eating out – with good wine'
Extras: Picked to play two Tests for England against Pakistan in 1992, 'proudest
moments of my career'. Originally selected for England A tour to Australia 1992-93
but was asked to stay on in India and played in the first two Tests of the series. In
1992 was named Young Player of the Year by both the Wombwell Cricket Lovers and
the Cricket Writers. One of *Wisden*'s five Cricketers of the Year 1993. Left Sussex

during the 1996-97 off-season to join Surrey

Opinions on cricket: 'Players should be asked for their opinion on changes in the game, before authorities make the changes themselves.'

Best batting: 86 England A v Pakistan A, Rawalpindi 1995-96

Best bowling: 8-75 Sussex v Essex, Chelmsford 1996

1998 Season

	M	Inns	NO	Runs	HS	Avge	100s	50s	Ct	St	O	M	Runs	Wkts	Avge	Best	5wI	10wM
Test	3	5	0	29	23	5.80	-	-	2	-	50.5	10	192	1	192.00	1-86	-	-
All First	15	18	2	314	61	19.62	-	3	8	-	387.5	109	958	37	25.89	7-65	2	-
1-day Int																		
NatWest	2	2	1	38	34 *	38.00	-	-	-	-	16.5	2	58	3	19.33	2-28	-	
B & H	7	3	2	25	12	25.00	-	-	1	-	60.1	3	248	12	20.66	3-32	-	
Sunday	10	7	1	87	33	14.50	-	-	5	-	48	2	280	8	35.00	3-15	-	

Career Performances

	M	Inns	NO	Runs	HS	Avge	100s	50s	Ct	St	Balls	Runs	Wkts	Avge	Best	5wI	10wM
Test	12	22	2	284	50	14.20	-	1	5	-	2078	1346	19	70.84	4-163	-	-
All First	193	252	52	3649	86	18.24	-	13	139	-	35210	18243	546	33.41	8-75	28	4
1-day Int	4	2	1	7	5	7.00	-	-	1	-	186	177	5	35.40	3-41	-	
NatWest	21	15	4	140	34 *	12.72	-	-	5	-	1313	720	26	27.69	3-28	-	
B & H	33	19	7	154	19	12.83	-	-	13	-	1809	1275	43	29.65	4-53	-	
Sunday	112	72	21	710	48 *	13.92	-	-	37	-	4182	3504	102	34.35	5-30	1	

69. Who blazed 82 off 44 balls to help bring Sri Lanka victory over England in the 1996 World Cup quarter-finals?

FICA

SAQLAIN MUSHTAQ   Surrey

Name: Saqlain Mushtaq
Role: Right-hand bat, off-spin bowler
Born: 27 November 1976, Lahore, Pakistan
County debut: 1997
County cap: 1998
Test debut: 1995-96
Tests: 15
One-Day Internationals: 79
50 wickets in a season: 1
1st-Class 50s: 4
1st-Class 5 w. in innings: 18
1st-Class 10 w. in match: 6
1st-Class catches: 29
One-Day 5 w. in innings: 4
Place in batting averages: 217th av. 17.60
(1997 165th av. 24.85)
Place in bowling averages: 8th av. 17.76
(1997 7th av. 19.28)
Strike rate: 45.23 (career 52.66)
Overseas tours: Pakistan to Australia 1995-96, to Sharjah 1995-96, 1996-97, 1997-98,
to Singapore 1995-96, to England 1996, to Sri Lanka 1996-97, to Toronto and Nairobi
1996-97, to Australia 1996-97, to India 1996-97, to South Africa 1997-98,
to Zimbabwe 1997-98, to Sri Lanka 1997-98, to Toronto 1997-98, 1998-99,
to Bangladesh 1998-99
Overseas teams played for: PIA, Islamabad 1994-1998
Extras: Has reportedly developed a 'mystery ball' – a leg break bowled with an off-
break action
Best batting: 79 Pakistan v Zimbabwe, Shekhupura 1996-97
Best bowling: 8-65 Surrey v Derbyshire, The Oval 1998
Stop press: Returned match figures of 10-187 (5-94 and 5-93) in first Test v India at
Madras 1998-99; won Man of the Series award

1998 Season

	M	Inns	NO	Runs	HS	Avge	100s	50s	Ct	St	O	M	Runs	Wkts	Avge	Best	5wI	10wM
Test																		
All First	12	15	5	176	45 *	17.60	-	-	7	-	475	136	1119	63	17.76	8-65	3	3
1-day Int																		
NatWest	2	1	0	6	6	6.00	-	-	-	-	23	3	57	3	19.00	2-24	-	
B & H	4	2	0	17	11	8.50	-	-	2	-	36.4	2	174	7	24.85	4-46	-	
Sunday	6	4	1	14	9 *	4.66	-	-	1	-	39.1	0	166	5	33.20	2-34	-	

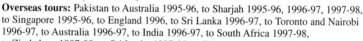

Career Performances

	M	Inns	NO	Runs	HS	Avge	100s	50s	Ct	St	Balls	Runs	Wkts	Avge	Best	5wl	10wM
Test	15	22	5	306	79	18.00	-	2	5	-	4298	1959	58	33.77	5-54	3	-
All First	61	88	25	1003	79	15.92	-	4	29	-	13746	5820	261	22.29	8-65	18	6
1-day Int	79	48	14	362	30 *	10.64	-	-	22	-	4133	2965	155	19.12	5-29	4	
NatWest	4	2	1	12	6 *	12.00	-	-	-	-	259	150	7	21.42	3-30	-	
B & H	6	2	0	17	11	8.50	-	-	2	-	322	228	9	25.33	4-46	-	
Sunday	15	8	2	75	29 *	12.50	-	-	3	-	568	442	17	26.00	3-31	-	

SAVIDENT, L. Hampshire

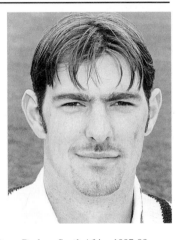

Name: Lee Savident
Role: Right-hand bat, right-arm medium-fast
bowler
Born: 22 October 1976, Guernsey
Height: 6ft 5in **Weight:** 16st
Nickname: Sav
County debut: 1997
1st-Class catches: 1
Strike rate: 84.00 (career 84.00)
Parents: Nev and Sue
Marital status: Single
Family links with cricket: None
Education: Castel Primary School; Guernsey
Grammar School; Guernsey College of
Further Education
Qualifications: 5 GCSEs and 1 A-level.
Assistant physio
Off-season: 'South Africa until Xmas.
Getting fit??'
Overseas teams played for: Glenwood Old Boys, Durban, South Africa 1997-98
Cricketers particularly admired: Malcolm Marshall, Mark Waugh
Young players to look out for: Dimitri Mascarenhas, Dale Benkenstein,
Philip Tucker
Other sports played: '"Hearts", "Turbo's", "Zulu Warriors"'
Other sports followed: Football (Tottenham Hotspur)
Injuries: 'Cartilage op, fractured metatarsal, stress-fractured tibia, slipped disc in back
– nothing major'
Relaxations: 'Sleeping, music, TV, quiet beverage, cards'
Extras: First person from the Channel Islands to play first-class cricket
Opinions on cricket: 'Top game.'
Best batting: 6 Hampshire v Yorkshire, Portsmouth 1997
Best bowling: 2-86 Hampshire v Yorkshire, Portsmouth 1997

1998 Season

	M	Inns	NO	Runs	HS	Avge	100s	50s	Ct	St	O	M	Runs	Wkts	Avge	Best	5wI	10wM
Test																		
All First																		
1-day Int																		
NatWest																		
B & H																		
Sunday	2	2	0	52	39	26.00	-	-	-	-								

Career Performances

	M	Inns	NO	Runs	HS	Avge	100s	50s	Ct	St	Balls	Runs	Wkts	Avge	Best	5wI	10wM
Test																		
All First	3	4	1	15	6	5.00	-	-	1	-	336	247	4	61.75	2-86	-	-
1-day Int																		
NatWest																		
B & H																		
Sunday	5	4	2	60	39	30.00	-	-	1	-	115	104	6	17.33	3-41	-	

SCHOFIELD, C. P.   Lancashire

Name: Chris Paul Schofield
Role: Left-hand bat, leg-break bowler
Born: 6 October 1978, Birch Hill,
Wardle, Rochdale
Height: 6ft 1in **Weight:** 11st 5lbs
Nickname: Scoey, Junior, Scoffer
County debut: 1998
1st-Class catches: 1
Place in bowling averages: 84th av. 29.90
Strike rate: 47.80 (career 47.80)
Parents: David and Judith
Marital status: Single
Family links with cricket: Father played
with local club team Whittles and brother
plays with local team Littleborough
Education: St John's; Wardle High School
Qualifications: 4 GCSEs, NVQ Levels
2 and 3 in Information Technology
Off-season: Touring Australia and playing
other sports to keep fit. Also pre-season tour
Overseas tours: England U17 to Bermuda 1997; England U19 to South Africa 1997-98
Cricketers particularly admired: Shane Warne, Stuart Law

Young players to look out for: Graeme Swann, Robert Key
Other sports played: Football (Littleborough FC, Whittles FC), snooker (Wardle Con Club –Littleborough League champions; individual knockout semi-finalist)
Other sports followed: Football ('like watching Liverpool FC')
Injuries: Out for five weeks with snapped ligament in right thumb
Relaxations: Listening to music, playing snooker, socialising
Extras: Was on England U17 unbeaten tour to Bermuda. Was part of England U19 World Cup winning set-up 1998. Won double twice in two years with Littleborough CC (Wood Cup and Lancashire Cup 1997; League and Wood Cup 1998). Awarded 2nd XI cap 1998. Was employed as net leg-spinner by England party touring Australia 1998-99
Opinions on cricket: 'The day/night game was very enjoyable over in South Africa and I think that it also took off very well over here – I think there should be more games.'
Best batting: 4* Lancashire v Glamorgan, Colwyn Bay 1998
Best bowling: 4-56 Lancashire v Gloucestershire, Old Trafford 1998

1998 Season

	M	Inns	NO	Runs	HS	Avge	100s	50s	Ct	St	O	M	Runs	Wkts	Avge	Best	5wI	10wM
Test																		
All First	2	3	2	5	4 *	5.00	-	-	1	-	79.4	9	299	10	29.90	4-56	-	-
1-day Int																		
NatWest																			
B & H																			
Sunday																			

Career Performances

	M	Inns	NO	Runs	HS	Avge	100s	50s	Ct	St	Balls	Runs	Wkts	Avge	Best	5wI	10wM
Test																	
All First	2	3	2	5	4 *	5.00	-	-	1	-	478	299	10	29.90	4-56	-	-
1-day Int																	
NatWest																	
B & H																	
Sunday																	

Name: Darren Anthony Scott
Role: Left-hand bat, off-spin bowler
Born: 26 August 1972, Canterbury
Height: 6ft 2in **Weight:** 13st
Nickname: Stav, El Greco, Spic
County debut: 1998
Parents: Anthony and Linda
Marital status: 'Engaged to Julia'
Education: St Stephens Primary School, Canterbury; Geoffrey Chaucer Grammar School, Canterbury; Christ Church College, Canterbury
Qualifications: 7 GCSEs, 3 A-levels, BA Business Studies/Sports Science, part-qualified accountant, Level 2 cricket coach
Career outside cricket: Accountancy
Off-season: Working as an accountant for a local firm of accountants
Overseas teams played for: Fishoek CC, Cape Town 1991-92
Cricketers particularly admired: David Gower, John Emburey, Michael Holding, Edward Stanford
Young players to look out for: Robert Key, Owais Shah, James Hockley
Other sports played: Football, badminton
Other sports followed: Football (Nottingham Forest)
Relaxations: Watching sport on TV. Listening to music. 'Studying spread-betting indexes with Min Patel'
Extras: Represented the ECB in the Triple Crown 1998. Awarded 2nd XI cap 1998
Opinions on cricket: 'Local counties need to merge so that the level of competition is increased with the best players competing against each other on a regular basis. Players need to be employed on ten-month contracts so that they can be monitored throughout the winter.'
Best batting: 17* Kent v Oxford University, Canterbury 1998
Best bowling: 1-48 Kent v Warwickshire, Edgbaston 1998

---

70. Name the losing semi-finalists in the 1992 World Cup.

FICA

1998 Season

	M	Inns	NO	Runs	HS	Avge	100s	50s	Ct	St	O	M	Runs	Wkts	Avge	Best	5wl	10wM
Test																		
All First	2	3	3	22	17 *	-	-	-	-	-	48	14	124	1	124.00	1-48	--	
1-day Int																		
NatWest																		
B & H																		
Sunday																		

Career Performances

	M	Inns	NO	Runs	HS	Avge	100s	50s	Ct	St	Balls	Runs	Wkts	Avge	Best	5wl	10wM
Test																		
All First-	2	3	3	22	17 *	-	-	-	-	-	288	124	1	124.00	1-48	-	-
1-day Int																		
NatWest																		
B & H																		
Sunday																		

SEARLE, J. P.   Durham

Name: Jason Paul Searle
Role: Right-hand bat, off-spin bowler
Born: 16 May 1976, Chippenham
Height: 5ft 8in **Weight:** 11st
Nickname: Shaggy, Village, Dumb, Elf
County debut: 1994
1st-Class catches: 2
Strike rate: 51.40 (career 68.42)
Parents: Paul and Chris
Marital status: Single
Family links with cricket: Father played for Chippenham and Wiltshire
Education: John Bentley School, Calne; Wiltshire and Swindon Building College
Qualifications: Bricklayer, farmer
Overseas tours: England U19 to West Indies 1994-95; Durham to South Africa 1994-95
Cricketers particularly admired: Steve Lugsden, Martin Robinson
Young players to look out for: 'Me'
Other sports followed: Football (Man Utd)
Relaxations: 'Music and the fairer sex'

Extras: Released by Durham at the end of the 1998 season
Best batting: 5* Durham v Lancashire, Stockton 1994
Best bowling: 3-92 Durham v Lancashire, Riverside 1998

1998 Season

	M	Inns	NO	Runs	HS	Avge	100s	50s	Ct	St	O	M	Runs	Wkts	Avge	Best	5wI	10wM
Test																		
All First	2	2	0	0	0	0.00	-	-	2	-	42.5	9	158	5	31.60	3-92	-	-
1-day Int																		
NatWest																		
B & H																		
Sunday																		

Career Performances

	M	Inns	NO	Runs	HS	Avge	100s	50s	Ct	St	Balls	Runs	Wkts	Avge	Best	5wI	10wM
Test																	
All First	4	6	3	7	5 *	2.33	-	-	2	-	479	291	7	41.57	3-92	-	-
1-day Int																	
NatWest																	
B & H	1	0	0	0	0	-	-	-	-	-							
Sunday	1	0	0	0	0	-	-	-	-	-	12	19	0	-		-	-

SHADFORD, D. J.   Lancashire

Name: Darren James Shadford
Role: Right-hand bat, right-arm
medium-fast bowler
Born: 4 March 1975, Oldham, Lancashire
Height: 6ft 1in **Weight:** 14st
Nickname: Shaddy, Shed Head
County debut: 1994 (one-day),
1995 (first-class)
1st-Class 5 w. in innings: 1
1st-Class catches: 6
Place in batting averages:
(1997 258th av. 15.14)
Place in bowling averages:
(1997 125th av. 41.36)
Strike rate: 185.00 (career 54.69)
Parents: Ken and Susan
Marital status: Single
Family links with cricket: Father and

brother play club cricket for Oldham CC. Andrew plays with LSCA U19

Education: Roundthorn Primary School; Breeze Hill High School; Oldham College of Technology

Career outside cricket: Travelling the world

Overseas tours: Lancashire to Jamaica 1995-96, to South Africa 1997

Overseas teams played for: Sandgate CC, Brisbane 1993-94

Cricketers particularly admired: Jamie Haynes

Young players to look out for: Mark Chilton

Other sports followed: Football (Manchester United), squash, golf, snooker, 'the lot really'

Relaxations: Socialising, shopping, listening to music, playing on my Sony PlayStation and going for a couple of curries every now and then'

Extras: 'Coaching award in cricket and canoeing first star'

Opinions on cricket: 'Second team should play four-day cricket to prepare the players for first-class cricket. Tea should be extended by 10 to 15 minutes.'

Best batting: 30 Lancashire v Hampshire, Southampton 1997

Best bowling: 5-80 Lancashire v Warwickshire, Blackpool 1997

1998 Season

	M	Inns	NO	Runs	HS	Avge	100s	50s	Ct	St	O	M	Runs	Wkts	Avge	Best	5wI	10wM
Test																		
All First	1	1	1	13	13*	-	-	-	-	-	30.5	5	90	1	90.00	1-56	-	-
1-day Int																		
NatWest																		
B & H																		
Sunday	1	0	0	0	0	-	-	-	-	-	5	0	29	0	-	-	-	

Career Performances

	M	Inns	NO	Runs	HS	Avge	100s	50s	Ct	St	Balls	Runs	Wkts	Avge	Best	5wI	10wM
Test																	
All First	11	13	5	120	30	15.00	-	-	6	-	1258	983	23	42.73	5-80	1	-
1-day Int																	
NatWest	1	0	0	0	0	-	-	-	-	-	42	31	0	-	-	-	
B & H																	
Sunday	11	3	2	3	2	3.00	-	-	4	-	330	317	11	28.81	3-30	-	

SHAH, O. A.   Middlesex

Name: Owais Alam Shah
Role: Right-hand bat, off-spin bowler
Born: 22 October 1978, Karachi, Pakistan
Height: 6ft 1in **Weight:** 12st
Nickname: Ace
County debut: 1995 (one-day),
1996 (first-class)
1st-Class 50s: 8
1st-Class 100s: 3
1st-Class catches: 26
Place in batting averages: 47th av. 39.30
(1997 70th av. 39.14)
Strike rate: 107.00 (career 74.50)
Parents: Jamshed and Mehjabeen
Marital status: Single
Family links with cricket: Father played for
his college side
Education: Berkley's Junior School;
Isleworth and Syon School; Lampton School;
part-time course at Westminster University, Harrow
Qualifications: 7 GCSEs, 2 A-levels, starting Business Administration degree
Off-season: Gym, studying
Overseas tours: England U19 to Zimbabwe 1995-96, to South Africa 1997-98;
England A to Australia 1996-97, to Kenya and Sri Lanka 1997-98
Cricketers particularly admired: Viv Richards, Wasim Akram
Young players to look out for: Stephen Peters, Paul Franks, Robert Key,
Matthew Wood, Graeme Swann
Other sports played: Snooker
Other sports followed: Football (Man Utd)
Relaxations: 'Spend time with friends. Gym. Music'
Extras: Middlesex Sports Federation Award winner. Man of the Series in U17 Test
series against India 1994. Played for Middlesex U13, Ken Barrington Trophy (National
Champions) and Middlesex U15, county competition winners, as captain. Scored
record 232 for England U15 against England U16. Man of the Series for England U17
against India U17. Awarded 2nd XI cap in 1996. Captained the England U19 side to
success in the U19 World Cup in South Africa, scoring 54 not out in the final in 1997-
98. Captain of England U19 against Pakistan U19 (one-day and 'Test' matches) 1998
Opinions on cricket: 'There is too much cricket played in this country. This is the
reason why all county cricketers love the sight of rain.'
Best batting: 140 Middlesex v Yorkshire, Lord's 1998
Best bowling: 1-24 Middlesex v Somerset, Uxbridge 1996

1998 Season

	M	Inns	NO	Runs	HS	Avge	100s	50s	Ct	St	O	M	Runs	Wkts	Avge	Best	5wI	10wM
Test																		
All First	15	23	3	786	140	39.30	2	4	10	-	17.5	1	79	1	79.00	1-46	-	-
1-day Int																		
NatWest	3	3	0	44	37	14.66	-	-	-	-								
B & H	5	4	0	74	43	18.50	-	-	5	-	1.2	0	2	2	1.00	2-2	-	
Sunday	14	14	2	305	87 *	25.41	-	2	5	-	5	0	35	1	35.00	1-24	-	

Career Performances

	M	Inns	NO	Runs	HS	Avge	100s	50s	Ct	St	Balls	Runs	Wkts	Avge	Best	5wI	10wM
Test																	
All First	34	53	6	1633	140	34.74	3	8	26	-	149	122	2	61.00	1-24	-	-
1-day Int																	
NatWest	7	7	1	101	37	16.83	-	-	1	-							
B & H	8	7	1	126	43	21.00	-	-	5	-	8	2	2	1.00	2-2	-	
Sunday	37	34	7	753	87 *	27.88	-	5	11	-	49	68	2	34.00	1-4	-	

SHAHID, N.   Surrey

Name: Nadeem Shahid
Role: Right-hand bat, leg-spin bowler
Born: 23 April 1969, Karachi
Height: 6ft **Weight:** 12st
Nickname: Nad, Gonads, National Hero,
Maggie, 'far too many to mention'
County debut: 1989 (Essex), 1995 (Surrey)
1000 runs in a season: 1
1st-Class 50s: 26
1st-Class 100s: 7
1st-Class catches: 102
One-Day 100s: 1
Place in batting averages: 58th av. 35.94
(1997 228th av. 18.00)
Strike rate: 48.00 (career 70.00)
Parents: Ahmed and Salma
Marital status: Single
Family links with cricket: Brother plays in
the local Two Counties League for Felixstowe
Education: Stoke High; Northgate High; Ipswich School; Plymouth Polytechnic
Qualifications: 6 O-levels, 1 A-level, coaching certificate
Overseas tours: Ipswich School to Barbados (Sir Garfield Sobers Trophy) 1987;

England (South) to N Ireland (Youth World Tournament) 1988
Overseas teams played for: Gosnells, Perth, Western Australia 1989-91; Fairfield, Sydney 1992-93
Cricketers particularly admired: Ian Botham, Shane Warne, Graham Thorpe and Nasser Hussain
Young players to look out for: Ben Hollioake, Alex Tudor
Other sports followed: Golf, tennis, badminton, squash, most ball sports
Extras: Youngest Suffolk player aged 17. Played for HMC, MCC Schools, ESCA U19, NCA Young Cricketers (Lord's and International Youth tournament in Belfast), England U25 and at every level for Suffolk. TSB Young Player of the Year 1987, winner of the *Daily Telegraph* Bowling Award 1987 and 1988, Cricket Society's All-rounder of the Year 1988 and Laidlaw Young Player of the Year for Essex 1993. Essex Society Player of the Year 1993. Released by Essex at end of 1994 season and signed for Surrey. Member of the Surrey Sunday League-winning side of 1996
Opinions on cricket: 'Players should be allowed to have fun on the field, and be allowed to express themselves in order to bring the best out of them. Players can and should work a lot harder at their game. I favour the two-divisional system in order to improve the standard of English cricket. It would allow players more time off the field and more time to work on skills, fitness etc. All first-class cricketers should be presented with a gold card which would allow them into any night club.'
Best batting: 139 Surrey v Yorkshire, The Oval 1995
Best bowling: 3-91 Essex v Surrey, The Oval 1990

1998 Season

	M	Inns	NO	Runs	HS	Avge	100s	50s	Ct	St	O	M	Runs	Wkts	Avge	Best	5wI	10wM
Test																		
All First	12	22	3	683	126 *	35.94	2	3	13	-	16	1	66	2	33.00	1-19	-	-
1-day Int																		
NatWest	2	2	0	12	12	6.00	-	-	-	-	9	1	30	3	10.00	3-30	-	
B & H	4	3	1	33	16	16.50	-	-	1	-								
Sunday	13	12	1	226	58	20.54	-	2	3	-	4	0	20	0	-		-	-

Career Performances

	M	Inns	NO	Runs	HS	Avge	100s	50s	Ct	St	Balls	Runs	Wkts	Avge	Best	5wI	10wM
Test																	
All First	110	176	24	4878	139	32.09	7	26	102	-	3010	1993	43	46.34	3-91	-	-
1-day Int																	
NatWest	9	7	1	163	85 *	27.16	-	1	5	-	72	30	4	7.50	3-30	-	
B & H	22	15	5	271	65 *	27.10	-	2	3	-	150	131	1	131.00	1-59	-	
Sunday	90	77	12	1533	101	23.58	1	4	27	-	60	63	0	-		-	-

SHAW, A. D.   Glamorgan

Name: Adrian David Shaw
Role: Right-hand bat, wicket-keeper
Born: 17 February 1972, Neath
Height: 5ft 11in **Weight:** 12st 12lbs
Nickname: Shawsy, Wham, Dale, Redknapp,
Midfield General, John Inman
County debut: 1992 (one-day),
1994 (first-class)
1st-Class 50s: 5
1st-Class catches: 115
1st-Class stumpings: 9
Place in batting averages: 229th av. 16.53
(1997 171st av. 24.31)
Parents: David Colin and Christina
Marital status: Single
Education: Catwg; Llangatwg
Comprehensive; Neath Tertiary College
Qualifications: 9 O-levels, 3 A-levels,
advanced coach

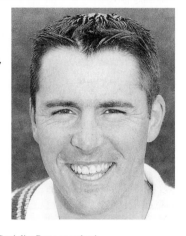

Career outside cricket: 'Politics hopefully. Socialist Party member'
Off-season: 'In the pursuit of gratification of any kind whatsoever in that highly upper-class part of S. Wales that is Neath. However, I never ever drink Budweiser'
Overseas tours: Welsh Schools U17 to Barbados 1987; England YC to New Zealand 1990-91
Overseas teams played for: Welkom Police, Orange Free State 1995-96
Cricketers particularly admired: 'I admire anyone who has had to endure persecution from uninformed "supposed" sports journalists!!!'
Young players to look out for: 'Anyone who can make you laugh!!'
Other sports played: Rugby (Neath RFC)
Other sports followed: Rugby (Neath RFC), darts ('The Bronze Adonis – Steve Beaton'), football (Notts Forest – 'due to Parkin')
Injuries: Out for six weeks with mystery virus and broken finger
Relaxations: 'I spend a lot of time developing new fashion accessories and clothes, much to the amusement of Cottey and Croft'
Extras: One of youngest players (18 years 7 days) to play first-class rugby for Neath. Played for Neath against Swansea six days after playing against Zimbabwe for Glamorgan, and had the 'pleasure' of marking Scott Gibbs. Neath RFC Back of the Year 1993-94. Hopes to become the first player for a number of years to play against South Africa in two sports when Neath play them. 'Hoping to be awarded Glamorgan 2nd XI's first benefit after 10 years in the "Stiffs"!' Voted Glamorgan 2nd XI Player of the Year and Glamorgan Young Player of the Year in 1995. 2nd XI Player of the

Month, June 1996. Claimed 12 victims in 2nd XI game v Gloucestershire at Usk in 1998, a record for 2nd XI cricket. 'Anything notable I've ever achieved is sadly wallowing in the recesses of my mind as I try to come to terms with my increasing years'

Opinions on cricket: 'A fine game that throws together fine individuals. People like Wayne Law, Andrew Davies, Robert Croft, Tony Cottey. These people epitomise all that is alive and well in this noble game of ours. P.S. Life is too short to be too serious!!'

Best batting: 74 Glamorgan v Surrey, Cardiff 1996

1998 Season

	M	Inns	NO	Runs	HS	Avge	100s	50s	Ct	St	O	M	Runs	Wkts	Avge	Best	5wI	10wM
Test																		
All First	11	16	1	248	71	16.53	-	2	26	-	1	0	7	0	-	-	-	-
1-day Int																		
NatWest	2	2	0	48	47	24.00	-	-	4	-								
B & H	4	4	1	38	25	12.66	-	-	4	3								
Sunday	8	8	2	113	40	18.83	-	-	4	-								

Career Performances

	M	Inns	NO	Runs	HS	Avge	100s	50s	Ct	St	Balls	Runs	Wkts	Avge	Best	5wI	10wM
Test																	
All First	47	62	9	956	74	18.03	-	5	115	9	6	7	0	-	-	-	-
1-day Int																	
NatWest	6	6	1	112	47	22.40	-	-	8	-							
B & H	8	7	1	64	25	10.66	-	-	9	4							
Sunday	34	24	7	291	48	17.11	-	-	14	5							

FIGA

71. Which current county all-rounder scored 73 and took 3-65 for Zimbabwe in their second match v India in the 1983 World Cup?

SHEIKH, M. A. — Warwickshire

Name: Mohammed Avez Sheikh
Born: 2 July 1973, Birmingham
Role: Left-hand bat, right-arm medium bowler
Nickname: Sheikhy
Education: Broadway School
County debut: 1997
Strike rate: 62.66 (career 45.83)
Overseas teams played for:
Western Province CC 1997-98
Extras: Has also played for Warwickshire U19 and played for both Worcestershire and Essex 2nd XIs in 1995
Best batting: 30 Warwickshire v Oxford University, The Parks 1998
Best bowling: 2-14 Warwickshire v Middlesex, Edgbaston 1997

1998 Season

	M	Inns	NO	Runs	HS	Avge	100s	50s	Ct	St	O	M	Runs	Wkts	Avge	Best	5wI	10wM
Test																		
All First	2	3	0	56	30	18.66	-	-	-	-	31.2	7	74	3	24.66	2-18	-	-
1-day Int																		
NatWest	1	1	0	5	5	5.00	-	-	-	-	11	2	38	0	-		-	-
B & H																		
Sunday	5	4	1	13	8	4.33	-	-	1	-	37	3	144	12	12.00	3-28	-	

Career Performances

	M	Inns	NO	Runs	HS	Avge	100s	50s	Ct	St	Balls	Runs	Wkts	Avge	Best	5wI	10wM
Test																	
All First	3	4	0	80	30	20.00	-	-	-	-	275	98	6	16.33	2-14	-	-
1-day Int																	
NatWest	1	1	0	5	5	5.00	-	-	-	-	66	38	0	-		-	-
B & H																	
Sunday	7	5	1	14	8	3.50	-	-	1	-	222	144	12	12.00	3-28	-	

SHERIYAR, A.   Worcestershire

Name: Alamgir Sheriyar
Role: Right-hand bat, left-arm fast bowler
Born: 15 November 1973, Birmingham
Height: 6ft 1in **Weight:** 13st
Nickname: Sheri
County debut: 1993 (one-day, Leics),
1994 (first-class, Leics), 1996 (Worcs)
50 wickets in a season: 1
1st-Class 5 w. in innings: 7
1st-Class 10 w. in match: 2
1st-Class catches: 12
Place in batting averages: 268th av. 11.00
(1997 284th av. 10.44)
Place in bowling averages: 130th av. 40.08
(1997 33rd av. 25.40)

Strike rate: 71.54 (career 54.44)
Parents: Mohammed Zaman (deceased) and
Safia Sultana
Marital status: Single
Family links with cricket: Brothers play a bit
Education: George Dixon Secondary School, Birmingham; Joseph Chamberlain Sixth
Form College, Birmingham; Oxford Brookes University
Qualifications: 6 O-levels, studying for BEng (Hons) Combined Engineering
Overseas tours: Leicestershire to South Africa 1995; Worcestershire to
Barbados 1996
Cricketers particularly admired: Wasim Akram
Other sports followed: Football, basketball
Injuries: Out for most of season with side strain
Relaxations: Time at home, music
Extras: Played for English Schools U17 and has also played in the Indoor National
League. Became only the second player to take a hat-trick on his first-class debut.
Asked to be released by Leicestershire at the end of the 1995 season and joined
Worcestershire for 1996
Opinions on cricket: 'It's a batsman's game.'
Best batting: 21 Worcestershire v Pakistan A, Worcester 1997
Best bowling: 6-19 Worcestershire v Sussex, Arundel 1997

---

72. Which Indian batsman scored his first
One-Day International hundred in 85 balls
FIGA   v New Zealand at Nagpur in the 1987 World Cup?

1998 Season

	M	Inns	NO	Runs	HS	Avge	100s	50s	Ct	St	O	M	Runs	Wkts	Avge	Best	5wI	10wM
Test																		
All First	12	10	4	66	20	11.00	-	-	1	-	286.1	70	962	24	40.08	5-85	1	-
1-day Int																		
NatWest																			
B & H	4	3	1	27	15	13.50	-	-	-	-	24	2	102	2	51.00	1-24	-	
Sunday	7	5	3	13	5 *	6.50	-	-	-	-	35.2	1	173	10	17.30	3-32	-	

Career Performances

	M	Inns	NO	Runs	HS	Avge	100s	50s	Ct	St	Balls	Runs	Wkts	Avge	Best	5wI	10wM
Test																	
All First	58	53	20	285	21	8.63	-	-	12	-	8874	5397	163	33.11	6-19	7	2
1-day Int																	
NatWest	3	2	0	10	10	5.00	-	-	-	-	120	109	2	54.50	1-35	-	
B & H	8	4	2	28	15	14.00	-	-	-	-	355	275	8	34.37	3-40	-	
Sunday	36	13	9	49	19	12.25	-	-	3	-	979	891	30	29.70	4-18	-	

SHINE, K. J. Somerset

Name: Kevin James Shine
Role: Right-hand bat, right-arm fast-medium
bowler
Born: 22 February 1969, Bracknell, Berks
Height: 6ft 3in **Weight:** 15st 7lbs
Nickname: Wookie, Kenny
County debut: 1989 (Hampshire),
1994 (Middlesex), 1996 (Somerset)
50 wickets in a season: 1
1st-Class 5 w. in innings: 12
1st-Class 10 w. in match: 2
1st-Class catches: 21
Place in batting averages:
(1997 300th av. 6.40)
Place in bowling averages:
(1997 72nd av. 30.50)
Strike rate: 86.50 (career 55.81)
Parents: Joe and Clair
Wife and date of marriage:
Bethan Clare, 3 October 1998

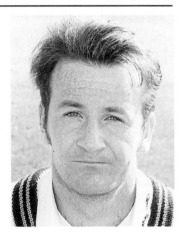

Education: Winnersh County Primary; Maiden Erlegh Comprehensive
Qualifications: 5 O-levels, ECB staff coach, qualified free weight training instructor

Career outside cricket: Personal fitness centre manager for John Neal Training
Off-season: 'Working for John Neal Training and some coaching and moving into our new home with my gorgeous wife, and two lunatic labradors, Jaffa and Mac'
Overseas teams played for: Merewether CC, Newcastle, NSW 1990
Cricketers particularly admired: Peter Bowler, Graham Rose, Adi Aymes
Young players to look out for: Richard Johnson – 'he hits the bat as hard as anyone when he gets it right, but he still can't beat me in a 200m sprint'
Other sports followed: Football (Reading)
Injuries: Out for four months with hip and back problems
Relaxations: 'Walking the dogs and going to the cinema with Bethan. Listening to Luke Sutton's weekend antics'
Extras: Took 8-47 including a hat-trick against Lancashire at Old Trafford in May 1992. Has written (with Jason Harris) a weekly column for the *Reading Chronicle*. 'Told I was released by Middlesex four days before major surgery on left ankle.' Joined Somerset for the 1996 season
Opinions on cricket: 'I keep saying it. It's still too easy for the batters. The old dino doesn't know how easy he's got it.'
Best batting: 40 Somerset v Surrey, Taunton 1996
Best bowling: 8-47 Hampshire v Lancashire, Old Trafford 1992

1998 Season

	M	Inns	NO	Runs	HS	Avge	100s	50s	Ct	St	O	M	Runs	Wkts	Avge	Best	5wI	10wM
Test																		
All First	3	5	2	44	18	14.66	-	-	-	-	57.4	10	216	4	54.00	2-40	-	-
1-day Int																		
NatWest																		
B & H																		
Sunday																		

Career Performances

	M	Inns	NO	Runs	HS	Avge	100s	50s	Ct	St	Balls	Runs	Wkts	Avge	Best	5wI	10wM
Test																	
All First	102	96	37	564	40	9.55	-	-	21	-	13897	8988	249	36.09	8-47	12	2
1-day Int																	
NatWest	2	0	0	0	0	-	-	-	-	-	129	92	3	30.66	3-31	-	
B & H	7	2	1	38	38 *	38.00	-	-	-	-	308	329	6	54.83	4-68	-	
Sunday	23	5	4	8	3	8.00	-	-	2	-	913	846	26	32.53	4-31	-	

SIDEBOTTOM, R. J. Yorkshire

Name: Ryan Jay Sidebottom
Role: Left-hand bat, left-arm
fast-medium bowler
Born: 15 January 1978, Huddersfield
Height: 6ft 4in **Weight:** 13st
Nickname: Sexual Chocolate,
Ginger Spice, Curly
County debut: 1997
1st-Class 50s: 1
1st-Class catches: 3
One-Day 5 w. in innings: 1
Strike rate: 79.33 (career 67.83)
Parents: Arnie and Gillian
Marital status: Single
Family links with cricket: Father played for
Yorkshire and England and football for
Manchester United and Huddersfield Town
Education: Almondbury Primary,
Huddersfield; Lepton Middle; King James
Grammar School, Almondbury
Qualifications: 5 GCSEs
Career outside cricket: Promoting cricket in schools around Yorkshire
Off-season: Coaching, getting fitter and stronger for the next season, 'relaxing with mates'
Overseas tours: England U17 to Holland 1995
Overseas teams played for: Ringwood, Melbourne
Cricketers particularly admired: Darren Gough, Wayne Morton, Bradley Parker
Young players to look out for: John Inglis, Paul Hutchison, Matthew Wood, Gary Fellows
Other sports played: Football (Sheffield United), 'all sports'
Other sports followed: Football (Huddersfield Town FC)
Injuries: Hernia and groin injury
Relaxations: 'Going out with Paul Hutchison. Socialising and meeting women. Music. Buying clothes to keep up with Michael Vaughan – he's cool'
Best batting: 54 Yorkshire v Glamorgan, Cardiff 1998
Best bowling: 3-13 Yorkshire v Durham, Riverside 1998

---

73. Who is Australia's all-time leading
World Cup run-scorer?

1998 Season

	M	Inns	NO	Runs	HS	Avge	100s	50s	Ct	St	O	M	Runs	Wkts	Avge	Best	5wl	10wM
Test																		
All First	5	4	2	84	54	42.00	-	1	3	-	119	25	390	9	43.33	3-13	-	-
1-day Int																		
NatWest	1	0	0	0	0	-	-	-	-	-	4	1	15	3	5.00	3-15	-	
B & H	1	1	0	4	4	4.00	-	-	-	-	10	0	42	2	21.00	2-42	-	
Sunday	11	4	3	2	2 *	2.00	-	-	1	-	62.4	4	308	14	22.00	6-40	1	

Career Performances

	M	Inns	NO	Runs	HS	Avge	100s	50s	Ct	St	Balls	Runs	Wkts	Avge	Best	5wl	10wM
Test																	
All First	6	5	3	86	54	43.00	-	1	3	-	814	461	12	38.41	3-13	-	-
1-day Int																	
NatWest	1	0	0	0	0	-	-	-	-	-	24	15	3	5.00	3-15	-	
B & H	1	1	0	4	4	4.00	-	-	-	-	60	42	2	21.00	2-42	-	
Sunday	14	4	3	2	2 *	2.00	-	-	2	-	490	411	15	27.40	6-40	1	

SILVERWOOD, C. E. W.   Yorkshire

Name: Christopher Eric Wilfred Silverwood
Role: Right-hand bat, right-arm
fast-medium bowler
Born: 5 March 1975, Pontefract
Height: 6ft 1in **Weight:** 12st 9lbs
Nickname: Spoons, Silvers, Chubby
County debut: 1993
Test debut: 1996-97
Tests: 1
One-Day Internationals: 6
1st-Class 50s: 3
1st-Class 5 w. in innings: 11
1st-Class 10 w. in match: 1
1st-Class catches: 16
One-Day 5 w. in innings: 1
Place in batting averages: 154th av. 23.90
(1997 202nd av. 21.47)
Place in bowling averages: 37th av. 23.39
(1997 42nd av. 26.39)
Strike rate: 48.77 (career 50.30)
Parents: Brenda
Wife and date of marriage: Emma, 3 October 1997

Family links with cricket: 'Dad played a bit'
Education: Gibson Lane School, Kippax; Garforth Comprehensive
Qualifications: 8 GCSEs, City and Guilds in Leisure and Recreation
Off-season: To Bangladesh with England one-day squad for Wills International Cup
Overseas tours: England A to Kenya and Sri Lanka 1997-98; England to Zimbabwe and New Zealand 1996-97, to West Indies 1997-98, to Bangladesh (Wills International Cup) 1998-99
Overseas teams played for: Wellington, Cape Town 1993-94, 1995-96
Cricketers particularly admired: Ian Botham, Allan Donald
Other sports followed: Rugby league (Castleford), karate
Relaxations: Listening to music, watching videos, 'riding my motorbike'
Extras: Black belt in karate. Attended the Yorkshire Cricket Academy. Represented Yorkshire at athletics. Played for England U19 in the home series against India in 1994. Made his Test debut against Zimbabwe in the first Test at Bulawayo in 1996-97. Called up to the England tour of West Indies 1997-98 after the withdrawal of Darren Gough through injury
Best batting: 58 Yorkshire v Lancashire, Old Trafford 1997
Best bowling: 7-93 Yorkshire v Kent, Headingley 1997

1998 Season

	M	Inns	NO	Runs	HS	Avge	100s	50s	Ct	St	O	M	Runs	Wkts	Avge	Best	5wI	10wM
Test																		
All First	13	13	3	239	57 *	23.90	-	1	2	-	390.1	99	1123	48	23.39	5-13	3	-
1-day Int																		
NatWest	2	1	1	12	12 *	-	-	-	-	-	18.3	2	37	3	12.33	2-23	-	
B & H	6	1	0	6	6	6.00	-	-	2	-	44	3	203	10	20.30	3-38	-	
Sunday	11	6	2	34	12	8.50	-	-	1	-	70.3	9	277	13	21.30	2-5	-	

Career Performances

	M	Inns	NO	Runs	HS	Avge	100s	50s	Ct	St	Balls	Runs	Wkts	Avge	Best	5wI	10wM
Test	1	1	0	0	0	0.00	-	-	1	-	150	71	4	17.75	3-63	-	-
All First	70	92	22	1068	58	15.25	-	3	16	-	11017	6127	219	27.97	7-93	11	1
1-day Int	6	4	0	17	12	4.25	-	-	3	-	252	201	3	67.00	2-27	-	
NatWest	10	4	3	23	12 *	23.00	-	-	3	-	527	301	11	27.36	3-24	-	
B & H	17	5	0	17	8	3.40	-	-	4	-	832	605	32	18.90	5-28	1	
Sunday	58	28	15	120	14 *	9.23	-	-	5	-	2283	1726	70	24.65	4-26	-	

SIMMONS, P. V. — Leicestershire

Name: Philip Verant Simmons
Role: Right-hand bat, right-arm
medium bowler
Born: 18 April 1963, Port-of-Spain, Trinidad
County debut: 1994
County cap: 1994
Test debut: 1988
Tests: 26
One-Day Internationals: 130
1000 runs in a season: 1
50 wickets in a season: 1
1st-Class 50s: 60
1st-Class 100s: 21
1st-Class 200s: 2
1st-Class 5 w. in innings: 5
1st-Class catches: 225
One-Day 100s: 10
One-Day 5 w. in innings: 2
Place in batting averages: 147th av. 24.42
(1997 16th av. 56.54)
Place in bowling averages: 24th av. 21.34 (1997 5th av. 18.23)
Strike rate: 44.56 (career 61.91)
Overseas tours: West Indies YC to England 1982; West Indies B to Zimbabwe 1983
and 1986; West Indies to India and Pakistan (World Cup) 1987-88, to England 1988,
to Sharjah and India (Nehru Cup) 1989-90, to Sharjah 1991-92, to Australia and South
Africa 1992-93, to Sharjah, India (Hero Cup) and Sri Lanka 1993-94, to India
1994-95, to England 1995, to Australia 1995-96, to India and Pakistan (World Cup)
1995-96, to Australia 1996-97, to Sharjah 1997-98, to Pakistan 1997-98,
to Bangladesh 1998-99
Overseas teams played for: Crompton, Trinidad; Trinidad and Tobago 1983 –;
Eastern Transvaal 1996-97
Extras: Suffered a bad head injury on West Indies tour to England in 1988. Appointed
captain of Trinidad in 1989. Scored record 261 on his debut for Leicestershire in 1994.
Scored 1186 runs and took 56 wickets in the 1996 County Championship. Was one of
Wisden's five Cricketers of the Year 1997. Returned to Leicestershire in 1998 as their
overseas player after a year's absence. Captained the club for the latter part of the
1998 season
Best batting: 261 Leicestershire v Northamptonshire, Leicester 1994
Best bowling: 7-49 Leicestershire v Durham, Darlington 1998

1998 Season

	M	Inns	NO	Runs	HS	Avge	100s	50s	Ct	St	O	M	Runs	Wkts	Avge	Best	5wI	10wM
Test																		
All First	17	19	0	464	194	24.42	1	2	23	-	170.5	44	491	23	21.34	7-49	1	-
1-day Int																		
NatWest	4	4	2	217	107 *	108.50	1	1	4	-	26	2	117	1	117.00	1-35	-	
B & H	8	8	4	276	89	69.00	-	1	5	-	58.1	1	333	10	33.30	5-33	1	
Sunday	16	16	1	463	114	30.86	1	2	8	-	81	4	420	13	32.30	2-27	-	

Career Performances

	M	Inns	NO	Runs	HS	Avge	100s	50s	Ct	St	Balls	Runs	Wkts	Avge	Best	5wI	10wM
Test	26	47	2	1002	110	22.26	1	4	26	-	624	257	4	64.25	2-34	-	-
All First	193	322	15	11095	261	36.14	23	60	225	-	11950	5563	193	28.82	7-49	5	-
1-day Int	130	128	10	3503	122	29.68	5	18	52	-	3367	2479	72	34.43	4-3	-	
NatWest	10	10	2	410	107 *	51.25	1	2	7	-	468	360	9	40.00	3-31	-	
B & H	12	12	4	412	89	51.50	-	3	7	-	511	467	11	42.45	5-33	1	
Sunday	49	49	2	1938	140	41.23	4	12	23	-	1589	1344	44	30.54	5-37	1	

SINGH, A.   Warwickshire

Name: Anurag Singh
Role: Right-hand bat, off-spin bowler
Born: 9 September 1975, Kanpur, India
Height: 5ft 10in **Weight:** 11st
Nickname: Ragga, Ragi, Ragstar, Rood
County debut: 1995
1st-Class 50s: 4
1st-Class 100s: 4
1st-Class catches: 14
One-Day 100s: 1
Place in batting averages: 57th av. 36.16
(1997 140th av. 27.30)
Parents: Vijay and Rajul
Marital status: Single
Education: King Edward's School,
Birmingham; Gonville and Caius College,
Cambridge
Qualifications: 12 GCSEs, 4 A-levels
Overseas tours: England U19 to West Indies
1994-95; Warwickshire U21 to South Africa; Warwickshire CCC to South Africa
Cricketers particularly admired: Trevor Penney, Graeme Welch, Brian Lara,
Allan Donald, Mohammed Azharuddin

Young players to look out for: Darren Altree, Vikram Solanki
Other sports followed: Football (Wimbledon FC and Aston Villa)
Relaxations: 'Spending time with my family. Going out with friends and girlfriend, Louise'
Extras: Broke school record for number of runs in a season (1102). *Daily Telegraph* regional award for batting (twice) and bowling (once). Tiger Smith Memorial Award for Warwickshire Most Promising Young Cricketer 1994, Coney Edmonds Trophy for Warwickshire Best U19 Cricketer 1994, Lord's Taverners Trophy for Best Young Cricketer 1994, Gray-Nicolls Len Newbery Award for ESCA U19 Best Player 1994. Scored two centuries for England U19 against India U19 in 1994. Scored one century against West Indies U20 and was Man of the Series 1994-95. Scored 128 for Warwickshire 2nd XI v Gloucestershire 2nd XI in 1994. Awarded 2nd XI cap in 1995
Best batting: 157 Cambridge University v Sussex, Hove 1996

1998 Season

	M	Inns	NO	Runs	HS	Avge	100s	50s	Ct	St	O	M	Runs	Wkts	Avge	Best	5wl	10wM
Test																		
All First	10	12	0	434	117	36.16	1	2	2	-	2	0	21	0	-		-	-
1-day Int																		
NatWest																		
B & H	5	5	0	94	56	18.80	-	1	2	-								
Sunday	1	1	0	0	0	0.00	-	-	-	-								

Career Performances

	M	Inns	NO	Runs	HS	Avge	100s	50s	Ct	St	Balls	Runs	Wkts	Avge	Best	5wl	10wM
Test																	
All First	33	50	3	1519	157	32.31	4	4	14	-	54	45	0	-		-	-
1-day Int																	
NatWest																	
B & H	15	15	1	432	123	30.85	1	3	3	-							
Sunday	7	7	0	114	86	16.28	-	1	1	-							

SLATER, M. J. Derbyshire

Name: Michael Jonathon Slater
Role: Right-hand bat, leg-spin bowler
Born: 21 February 1970,
Wagga Wagga, New South Wales
Height: 5ft 9in
Nickname: Slats
County debut: 1998
County cap: 1998
Test debut: 1993
Tests: 37
One-Day Internationals: 42
1st-Class 50s: 51
1st-Class 100s: 19
1st-Class 200s: 2
1st-Class catches: 62
Place in batting averages: 61st av. 35.33
Strike rate: (career 31.00)
Education: Wagga Wagga High School, NSW

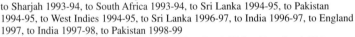

Overseas tours: Australia to England 1993,
to Sharjah 1993-94, to South Africa 1993-94, to Sri Lanka 1994-95, to Pakistan
1994-95, to West Indies 1994-95, to Sri Lanka 1996-97, to India 1996-97, to England
1997, to India 1997-98, to Pakistan 1998-99
Overseas teams played for: University of New South Wales; New South Wales
1991-92 –
Extras: Has published autobiography – *Slats Opens Up*. Joined Derbyshire in 1998 as
overseas player
Best batting: 219 Australia v Sri Lanka, Perth 1995-96
Best bowling: 1-4 Australia v Pakistan, Rawalpindi 1994-95
Stop press: Scored three Test 100s against the 1998-99 England tourists, his 123 at
Sydney (the third) accounting for 66 per cent of Australia's second innings total of
184; only Australia's Charles Bannerman made a higher percentage of a side's innings
total in a Test match. Selected for Australia's tour of West Indies 1998-99

1998 Season

	M	Inns	NO	Runs	HS	Avge	100s	50s	Ct	St	O	M	Runs	Wkts	Avge	Best	5wI	10wM
Test																		
All First	14	24	0	848	185	35.33	1	3	10	-								
1-day Int																		
NatWest	5	5	0	146	82	29.20	-	1	1	-								
B & H																		
Sunday	10	10	0	429	110	42.90	1	3	2	-								

Career Performances

	M	Inns	NO	Runs	HS	Avge	100s	50s	Ct	St	Balls	Runs	Wkts	Avge	Best	5wl	10wM
Test	37	65	3	2817	219	45.43	7	11	11	-	7	4	1	4.00	1-4	-	-
All First	124	218	11	9286	219	44.85	21	51	62	-	31	26	1	26.00	1-4	-	-
1-day Int	42	42	1	987	73	24.07	-	9	9	-	12	11	0	-	-	-	-
NatWest	5	5	0	146	82	29.20	-	1	1	-							
B & H																	
Sunday	10	10	0	429	110	42.90	1	3	2	-							

SMALL, G. C. Warwickshire

Name: Gladstone Cleophas Small
Role: Right-hand bat, right-arm
fast-medium bowler
Born: 18 October 1961, St George, Barbados
Height: 5ft 11in **Weight:** 12st
Nickname: Gladys, Glad, Stoney
County debut: 1980
County cap: 1982
Benefit: 1992 (£129,500)
Test debut: 1986
Tests: 17
One-Day Internationals: 53
50 wickets in a season: 6
1st-Class 50s: 7
1st-Class 5 w. in innings: 29
1st-Class 10 w. in match: 2
1st-Class catches: 93
One-Day 5 w. in innings: 5
Strike rate: 100.00 (career 58.17)
Parents: Chelston and Gladys
Wife and date of marriage: Lois, 19 September 1987
Children: Zak, Marcus and Zoe
Family links with cricket: Cousin Milton Small toured England with West Indies in 1988
Education: Moseley School; Hall Green Technical College, Birmingham
Qualifications: 2 O-levels, NCA senior coaching award
Career outside cricket: Sports marketing consultant
Overseas tours: Warwickshire to Cape Town, to Zimbabwe, to Trinidad; England YC to New Zealand 1979-80; England to Australia 1986-87, to India and Pakistan (World Cup) 1987-88, to India and West Indies 1989-90, to Australia 1990-91, to Australia and New Zealand (World Cup) 1991-92
Overseas teams played for: Balwyn, Melbourne 1982-83, 1984-85; West Torrens, Adelaide 1985-86; South Australia 1985-86

Cricketers particularly admired: Malcolm Marshall, Richard Hadlee, Allan Donald, Brian Lara, Robin Smith
Other sports followed: Golf, tennis, football (Aston Villa FC)
Relaxations: 'Home with family, tending my vegetable garden, wining and dining with friends'
Extras: Was called up for England Test squad v Pakistan at Edgbaston, July 1982, but did not play. Bowled 18-ball over v Middlesex in August 1982, with 11 no-balls. Grandfather watched him take eight wickets in the Barbados Test v West Indies in 1989-90 on his return to the land of his birth. Was Andy Lloyd's best man. Has announced that he will retire at the end of the 1999 season
Best batting: 70 Warwickshire v Lancashire, Old Trafford 1988
Best bowling: 7-15 Warwickshire v Nottinghamshire, Edgbaston 1988

1998 Season

	M	Inns	NO	Runs	HS	Avge	100s	50s	Ct	St	O	M	Runs	Wkts	Avge	Best	5wI	10wM
Test																		
All First																		
1-day Int																		
NatWest	2	0	0	0	0	-	-	-	1	-	17.1	2	59	1	59.00	1-40	-	
B & H	4	3	2	26	19	26.00	-	-	-	-	32	0	110	2	55.00	2-39	-	
Sunday	11	3	1	23	20	11.50	-	-	3	-	53.4	1	207	14	14.78	5-18	1	

Career Performances

	M	Inns	NO	Runs	HS	Avge	100s	50s	Ct	St	Balls	Runs	Wkts	Avge	Best	5wI	10wM
Test	17	24	7	263	59	15.47	-	1	9	-	3927	1871	55	34.01	5-48	2	-
All First	314	403	97	4409	70	14.40	-	7	93	-	49411	24324	851	28.58	7-15	29	2
1-day Int	53	24	9	98	18 *	6.53	-	-	7	-	2793	1942	58	33.48	4-31	-	
NatWest	50	30	9	256	33	12.19	-	-	9	-	2931	1550	54	28.70	3-22	-	
B & H	68	40	12	210	22	7.50	-	-	11	-	3764	2194	81	27.08	5-23	1	
Sunday	202	88	32	452	40 *	8.07	-	-	43	-	8328	6131	254	24.13	5-18	4	

SMETHURST, M. P.   Lancashire

Name: Michael Paul Smethurst
Role: Right-hand bat, right-arm
fast-medium bowler
Born: 11 October 1976, Oldham
Height: 6ft 5in **Weight:** 13st 7lbs
County debut: No first-team appearance
Parents: Julie Martin (Mum)
Marital status: Single
Education: Middleton Parish Primary
School; Hulme Grammar School, Oldham;
University of Salford
Qualifications: 9 GCSEs, 4 A-levels,
BA (Hons) Leisure Management
Off-season: 12-month contract with
Lancashire
Other sports followed: Football
(Manchester United)

SMITH, A. M.   Gloucestershire

Name: Andrew Michael Smith
Role: Right-hand bat, left-arm
fast-medium bowler
Born: 1 October 1967, Dewsbury,
West Yorks
Height: 5ft 9in **Weight:** 12st 3lbs
Nickname: Smudge, Charlie Babbitt
County debut: 1991
Test debut: 1997
Tests: 1
50 wickets in a season: 4
1st-Class 50s: 4
1st-Class 5 w. in innings: 17
1st-Class 10 w. in match: 5
1st-Class catches: 20
Place in batting averages: 167th av. 22.58
(1997 287th av. 9.70)
Place in bowling averages: 22nd av. 21.17
(1997 3rd av. 17.63)

Strike rate: 46.10 (career 49.43)
Parents: Hugh and Margaret
Wife and date of marriage: Sarah, 2 October 1993
Children: William James, 9 October 1994; Amelia, 14 June 1997
Family links with cricket: Father (Birstall club), brother (East Ardsley club) and uncle all play or played club cricket in Yorkshire
Education: Queen Elizabeth Grammar School, Wakefield; Exeter University; University of West of England
Qualifications: 9 O-levels, 4 A-levels, BA (Hons) French and German
Off-season: Studying Law at UWE. Touring New Zealand with MCC
Overseas tours: Queen Elizabeth Grammar School to Holland 1985; Bradford Junior Cricket League to Barbados 1986; Exeter University to Barbados 1987; Gloucestershire to Kenya 1990, to Sri Lanka 1992-93, to Zimbabwe 1996; England A to Pakistan 1995-96; MCC to New Zealand 1999
Overseas teams played for: Waimea, New Zealand 1990; WTTU, New Zealand 1991
Cricketers particularly admired: Richard Hadlee, Allan Donald, Jonty Rhodes, Sanath Jayasuriya, Wasim Akram, Courtney Walsh
Young players to look out for: Rob Cunliffe
Other sports played: Football, golf
Other sports followed: Football (Leeds United)
Injuries: Out for two Sunday games with sore hip
Relaxations: Looking after the kids ('hardly relaxing!'). Crosswords. Computers
Extras: Played for English Schools U19, NAYC and represented Combined Universities in the B&H Cup in 1988 and 1990. Persistent side strain forced him to fly home from the England A tour of Pakistan in 1995-96. Finished the 1997 season as leading first-class wicket-taker with 83 first-class wickets. Gloucestershire Player of the Year 1997
Opinions on cricket: 'Pitches still aren't good enough for four-day cricket (although as a bowler I'm not really complaining!). Bob Willis on Sky TV is, in my opinion, often discourteous and unfair to players – didn't he ever make a mistake? He should take an example from Messrs Nicholas, Benaud and Botham who are very positive and constructive in their criticism.'
Best batting: 61 Gloucestershire v Yorkshire, Gloucester 1998
Best bowling: 8-73 Gloucestershire v Middlesex, Lord's 1996

1998 Season

	M	Inns	NO	Runs	HS	Avge	100s	50s	Ct	St	O	M	Runs	Wkts	Avge	Best	5wI	10wM
Test																		
All First	18	30	13	384	61	22.58	-	2	5	-	522.3	139	1440	68	21.17	6-32	4	-
1-day Int																		
NatWest	2	2	1	7	6 *	7.00	-	-	2	-	23	2	71	5	14.20	4-46	-	
B & H	5	1	1	9	9 *	-	-	-	-	-	48	7	196	5	39.20	2-17	-	
Sunday	13	4	2	28	14	14.00	-	-	2	-	81.1	4	339	12	28.25	4-29	-	

Career Performances

	M	Inns	NO	Runs	HS	Avge	100s	50s	Ct	St	Balls	Runs	Wkts	Avge	Best	5wl	10wM
Test	1	2	1	4	4 *	4.00	-	-	-	-	138	89	0	-	-	-	-
All First	110	145	37	1428	61	13.22	-	4	20	-	18141	9356	367	25.49	8-73	17	5
1-day Int																	
NatWest	16	9	5	51	13	12.75	-	-	5	-	913	561	21	26.71	4-46	-	
B & H	37	21	11	90	15 *	9.00	-	-	7	-	2126	1443	48	30.06	6-39	1	
Sunday	107	52	30	289	26 *	13.13	-	-	15	-	4132	3253	113	28.78	4-29	-	

SMITH, B. F. Leicestershire

Name: Benjamin Francis Smith
Role: Right-hand bat, right-arm medium bowler
Born: 3 April 1972, Corby
Height: 5ft 8in **Weight:** 11st
Nickname: Smudge, The Ferret
County debut: 1990
County cap: 1995
1000 runs in a season: 2
1st-Class 50s: 27
1st-Class 100s: 10
1st-Class 200s: 1
1st-Class catches: 54
One-Day 100s: 1
Place in batting averages: 6th av. 62.00
(1997 36th av. 44.57)
Strike rate: (career 130.50)
Parents: Keith and Janet
Wife and date of marriage:
Lisa, 10 October 1998
Family links with cricket: 'Dad, grandad and both uncles played club, colts and England U15s'
Education: Tugby Primary; Kibworth High; Robert Smyth, Market Harborough
Qualifications: 5 O-levels, NCA coaching certificate
Off-season: 'At home. Maybe a couple of months in New Zealand'
Overseas tours: England YC to New Zealand 1990-91; Rutland Tourists to South Africa 1992
Overseas teams played for: Alexandria, Zimbabwe 1990; Bankstown Canterbury, Sydney 1993-96; Central Hawke's Bay CC, New Zealand 1997-98
Cricketers particularly admired: David Gower, Viv Richards
Young players to look out for: Michael Jones

Other sports played: Tennis, golf
Other sports followed: Football (Leicester City), rugby union (Leicester Tigers)
Relaxations: 'Eating out. Nights in. Nights out. Watching films. Listening to good music'
Extras: Played tennis for Leicestershire aged 12. Cricket Society Young Player of the Year 1991. Took part in Leicestershire record fourth-wicket partnership with Phil Simmons
Best batting: 204 Leicestershire v Surrey, The Oval 1998
Best bowling: 1-5 Leicestershire v Essex, Ilford 1991

1998 Season

	M	Inns	NO	Runs	HS	Avge	100s	50s	Ct	St	O	M	Runs	Wkts	Avge	Best	5wI	10wM
Test																		
All First	19	24	4	1240	204	62.00	4	4	13	-	5	0	11	0	-		-	-
1-day Int																		
NatWest	4	4	0	120	60	30.00	-	1	2	-								
B & H	8	8	1	248	90	35.42	-	2	3	-								
Sunday	16	16	1	441	87	29.40	-	3	6	-								

Career Performances

	M	Inns	NO	Runs	HS	Avge	100s	50s	Ct	St	Balls	Runs	Wkts	Avge	Best	5wI	10wM
Test																	
All First	128	191	29	5966	204	36.82	11	27	54	-	261	205	2	102.50	1-5	-	-
1-day Int																	
NatWest	13	12	1	290	63 *	26.36	-	2	5	-							
B & H	27	25	1	666	90	27.75	-	5	12	-							
Sunday	112	110	12	2638	115	26.91	1	11	29	-	18	15	0	-		-	-

SMITH, E. T.   Kent

Name: Edward Thomas Smith
Role: Right-hand bat, right-arm
medium bowler
Born: 19 July 1977, Pembury, Kent
Height: 6ft 2in **Weight:** 13st
Nickname: Jazzer
County debut: 1996
1000 runs in a season: 1
1st-Class 50s: 11
1st-Class 100s: 4
1st-Class catches: 9
Place in batting averages: 144th av. 24.82
(1997 47th av. 43.07)
Parents: Jonathan and Gillie
Marital status: Single
Family links with cricket: Father Jonathan
wrote *Good Enough?* with Chris Cowdrey
Education: Tonbridge School; Peterhouse,
Cambridge University
Qualifications: 11 GCSEs, 3 A-levels
Cricketers particularly admired: Greg Chappell, Martin Crowe, Graham Cowdrey
amd Michael Slater
Young players to look out for: Will House, Anurag Singh, Owais Shah
Other sports followed: Football (Arsenal FC)
Relaxations: Reading, theatre, cinema, socialising
Extras: Scored a century (101) on his first-class debut against Glamorgan and in
doing so became the youngest player to score a century on debut for Cambridge
University. He is also the first person to score 50 or more in each of his first five first-
class games. Cambridge Blue in 1996. Played for England U19 against New Zealand
U19 in 1996
Opinions on cricket: 'Cricket is not 50 per cent head, 50 per cent heart and nothing to
do with technique. English players should have greater ambition in their own
performance – technical and temperamental. The system encourages them to settle for
enough; which is not enough at the highest level.'
Best batting: 190 Cambridge University v Leicestershire, Fenner's 1997

---

75. In what unusual way did Javed Miandad react to a run-out appeal
by India's Kiran More at Sydney in the 1992 World Cup?

FICA

1998 Season

	M	Inns	NO	Runs	HS	Avge	100s	50s	Ct	St	O	M	Runs	Wkts	Avge	Best	5wI	10wM
Test																		
All First	11	18	1	422	58	24.82	-	1	1	-								
1-day Int																		
NatWest																		
B & H																		
Sunday	5	4	0	89	31	22.25	-	-	-	-								

Career Performances

	M	Inns	NO	Runs	HS	Avge	100s	50s	Ct	St	Balls	Runs	Wkts	Avge	Best	5wI	10wM
Test																	
All First	36	60	4	2161	190	38.58	4	11	9	-	12	22	0	-	-	-	-
1-day Int																	
NatWest																	
B & H	4	4	0	61	43	15.25	-	-	3	-							
Sunday	9	7	2	235	72 *	47.00	-	2	2	-							

SMITH, N. M. K. Warwickshire

Name: Neil Michael Knight Smith
Role: Right-hand bat, off-spin bowler,
county captain
Born: 27 July 1967, Solihull
Height: 6ft **Weight:** 14st
Nickname: Gert
County debut: 1987
County cap: 1993
One-Day Internationals: 7
1000 runs in a season: 1
1st-Class 50s: 24
1st-Class 100s: 4
1st-Class 5 w. in innings: 16
1st-Class catches: 46
One-Day 100s: 2
One-Day 5 w. in innings: 3
Place in batting averages: 34th av. 41.75
(1997 104th av. 33.78)
Place in bowling averages: 129th av. 39.87
(1997 123rd av. 40.23)
Strike rate: 82.37 (career 75.81)
Parents: Mike (M.J.K.) and Diana

Wife and date of marriage: Rachel, 4 December 1993
Family links with cricket: Father captained Warwickshire and England
Education: Warwick School
Qualifications: 3 O-levels (Maths, English, French), cricket coach Grade 1
Career outside cricket: Sports teacher
Off-season: Teaching sport at Warwick School
Overseas tours: England to South Africa 1995-96, to India and Pakistan (World Cup) 1995-96
Overseas teams played for: Phoenix, Perth, Western Australia 1989-90
Cricketers particularly admired: Allan Donald, Tim Munton, David Gower
Young players to look out for: Mark Wagh, Anurag Singh, Tony Frost
Other sports played: Golf
Other sports followed: Rugby union, golf, football
Relaxations: Travel
Extras: Played for England in the one-day series against South Africa in 1995-96 and was then selected for the squad to play in the World Cup in India and Pakistan. Followed in his father's footsteps when he led his side out against Northamptonshire in the Sunday League – the first time both father and son have captained Warwickshire. Played for an England XI in the Cricket Max tournament in New Zealand in 1997-98. Reached 100 v Durham at Edgbaston at 4.09pm on 17 April 1998, thereby scoring the earliest century in County Championship history. Was selected to represent England in the cancelled World Super Max 8s originally scheduled to take place in Perth in October 1998. Appointed Warwickshire captain for 1999
Opinions on cricket: 'Pitches must improve.'
Best batting: 161 Warwickshire v Yorkshire, Headingley 1989
Best bowling: 7-42 Warwickshire v Lancashire, Edgbaston 1994

1998 Season

	M	Inns	NO	Runs	HS	Avge	100s	50s	Ct	St	O	M	Runs	Wkts	Avge	Best	5wI	10wM
Test																		
All First	18	29	5	1002	147	41.75	2	6	2	-	329.3	84	957	24	39.87	5-128	1	-
1-day Int																		
NatWest	3	3	0	57	52	19.00	-	1	-	-	14	0	71	2	35.50	2-60	-	
B & H	5	5	0	32	18	6.40	-	-	-	-	32.3	1	124	7	17.71	3-36	-	
Sunday	15	14	0	312	80	22.28	-	1	4	-	61	4	268	12	22.33	2-8	-	

Career Performances

	M	Inns	NO	Runs	HS	Avge	100s	50s	Ct	St	Balls	Runs	Wkts	Avge	Best	5wI	10wM
Test																	
All First	145	211	30	5086	161	28.09	4	24	46	-	21910	10921	289	37.78	7-42	16	-
1-day Int	7	6	1	100	31	20.00	-	-	1	-	261	190	6	31.66	3-29	-	
NatWest	35	31	6	536	72	21.44	-	4	11	-	1426	884	38	23.26	5-17	1	
B & H	35	29	2	580	125	21.48	1	3	5	-	1307	987	34	29.02	3-29	-	
Sunday	154	127	18	2740	111 *	25.13	1	16	55	-	4902	3788	142	26.67	6-33	2	

Name: Robin Arnold Smith
Role: Right-hand bat, slip fielder, county captain
Born: 13 September 1963, Durban, South Africa
Height: 6ft **Weight:** 15st
Nickname: The Judge
County debut: 1982
County cap: 1985
Benefit: 1996
Test debut: 1988
Tests: 62
One-Day Internationals: 71
1000 runs in a season: 10
1st-Class 50s: 109
1st-Class 100s: 55
1st-Class 200s: 1
1st-Class catches: 202
One-Day 100s: 27
Place in batting averages: 53rd av. 37.08 (1997 52nd av. 41.72)
Strike rate: 63.00 (career 77.21)
Parents: John and Joy
Wife and date of marriage: Katherine, 21 September 1988
Children: Harrison Arnold, 4 December 1991; Margaux Elizabeth, 28 July 1994
Family links with cricket: Grandfather played for Natal in Currie Cup. Brother Chris played for Natal, Hampshire and England
Education: Northlands Boys High, Durban
Qualifications: Matriculation, '62 England caps'
Career outside cricket: Director of Judge Tours. Set up Masuri Helmets and Chase Bats with former county cricketer Jon Hardy. Is partner in a chain of sports theme bars
Overseas tours: England to India and West Indies 1989-90, to Australia 1990-91, to Australia and New Zealand (World Cup) 1991-92, to India and Sri Lanka 1992-93, to West Indies 1993-94, to South Africa 1995-96, to India and Pakistan (World Cup) 1995-96
Overseas teams played for: Natal 1980-84; Perth, Australia 1984-85 (grade cricket)
Cricketers particularly admired: Malcolm Marshall, Brian Lara, Graeme Hick, Graham Gooch, Allan Lamb
Other sports followed: Soccer, athletics, rugby, golf, racing
Relaxations: 'Reading (Leslie Thomas in particular), trout fishing, assembling a good wine cellar, keeping fit and spending as much time as possible with my lovely wife Katherine and my children'

Extras: Played rugby for Natal Schools and for Romsey RFC as a full-back. Held 19 school athletics records and two South African schools records in shot putt and 100-metre hurdles. One of *Wisden*'s Five Cricketers of the Year 1990. First child was born while he was on tour in Australia. Played for an England XI in the Cricket Max tournament in New Zealand in 1997-98. Was appointed Hampshire captain for the 1998 season. Raises funds for physically handicapped children at Cedar School, Nursling

Opinions on cricket: 'I enjoy playing cricket for Hampshire and particularly enjoy the camaraderie of the county circuit.'

Best batting: 209* Hampshire v Essex, Southampton 1987

Best bowling: 2-11 Hampshire v Surrey, Southampton 1985

1998 Season

	M	Inns	NO	Runs	HS	Avge	100s	50s	Ct	St	O	M	Runs	Wkts	Avge	Best	5wI	10wM
Test																		
All First	17	25	2	853	138	37.08	3	2	10	-	21	1	197	2	98.50	1-63	-	-
1-day Int																		
NatWest	3	3	1	152	144 *	76.00	1	-	-	-								
B & H	5	5	0	81	45	16.20	-	-	1	-								
Sunday	15	15	1	537	103	38.35	1	3	4	-								

Career Performances

	M	Inns	NO	Runs	HS	Avge	100s	50s	Ct	St	Balls	Runs	Wkts	Avge	Best	5wI	10wM
Test	62	112	15	4236	175	43.67	9	28	39	-	24	6	0	-	-	-	-
All First	350	593	80	22498	209 *	43.85	56	109	202	-	1081	965	14	68.92	2-11	-	-
1-day Int	71	70	8	2419	167 *	39.01	4	15	26	-							
NatWest	38	38	11	2106	158	78.00	8	8	20	-	17	13	2	6.50	2-13	-	
B & H	57	54	8	2186	155 *	47.52	5	9	22	-	6	2	0	-	-	-	
Sunday	169	162	17	5768	131	39.77	10	35	68	-	2	0	1	0.00	1-0	-	

SMITH, T. M.   Derbyshire

Name: Trevor Mark Smith
Role: Left-hand bat, right-arm
fast-medium bowler
Born: 18 January 1977, Derby
Height: 6ft 3in **Weight:** 13st 7lbs
Nickname: Tricky
County debut: 1997
1st-Class 5 w. in innings: 2
1st-Class catches: 1
Place in batting averages: 270th av. 10.44

Place in bowling averages: 35th av. 23.04
Strike rate: 43.00 (career 45.95)
Parents: Graham and Marilyn
Marital status: Single
Family links with cricket: Brothers all play for Sandiacre Town CC
Education: Cloudside Junior School, Sandiacre; Friesland School, Sandiacre; Broxtowe College of Further Education, Chilwell, Notts

Qualifications: 9 GCSEs, BTEC National Diploma in Business and Finance, NCA basic coach
Career outside cricket: 'Still working on one'
Off-season: Training, working, playing football
Cricketers particularly admired: Ian Botham, Allan Donald
Young players to look out for: Ben Spendlove
Other sports played: Football, golf
Other sports followed: Football (Derby County)
Injuries: Out for three weeks with groin strain
Relaxations: Music, football and golf
Opinions on cricket: 'Nice way to make a living.'
Best batting: 29 Derbyshire v Essex, Derby 1998
Best bowling: 6-32 Derbyshire v Essex, Derby 1998

1998 Season

	M	Inns	NO	Runs	HS	Avge	100s	50s	Ct	St	O	M	Runs	Wkts	Avge	Best	5wI	10wM
Test																		
All First	7	10	1	94	29	10.44	-	-	-	-	150.3	42	484	21	23.04	6-32	2	-
1-day Int																		
NatWest																		
B & H																		
Sunday	1	1	0	6	6	6.00	-	-	1	-	4.3	0	31	0	-	-	-	-

Career Performances

	M	Inns	NO	Runs	HS	Avge	100s	50s	Ct	St	Balls	Runs	Wkts	Avge	Best	5wI	10wM
Test																	
All First	8	10	1	94	29	10.44	-	-	1	-	1011	535	22	24.31	6-32	2	-
1-day Int																	
NatWest																	
B & H																	
Sunday	1	1	0	6	6	6.00	-	-	1	-	27	31	0	-	-	-	-

SNAPE, J. N. — Gloucestershire

Name: Jeremy Nicholas Snape
Role: Right-hand bat, off-spin bowler
Born: 27 April 1973, Stoke-on-Trent, Staffordshire
Height: 5ft 8in **Weight:** 12st
Nickname: Snapey, Coot, Jez
County debut: 1992 (Northamptonshire)
1st-Class 50s: 7
1st-Class 5 w. in innings: 1
1st-Class catches: 34
One-Day 5 w. in innings: 1
Place in batting averages:
(1997 182nd av. 23.53)
Place in bowling averages:
(1997 131st av. 48.26)
Strike rate: (career 84.58)
Parents: Keith and Barbara
Marital status: Single
Family links with cricket: Brother Jonathan
plays local club cricket in North Staffs and South Cheshire League for Kidsgrove, 'Dad only umpired once as he was the only person to appeal for a caught behind – off my bowling in the U13'
Education: Denstone College; Durham University
Qualifications: 8 GCSEs, 3 A-levels
Career outside cricket: 'Open to suggestions'
Overseas tours: England U18 to Canada 1991 (captain); England U19 to Pakistan 1991-92; Durham University to South Africa 1993; Northamptonshire to Cape Town 1993; Christians in Sport to Zimbabwe 1994-95; Durham University to Vienna (Indoor European Championships) 1994; Troubadours to South Africa 1997
Overseas teams played for: Petone, Wellington, New Zealand 1994-95; Wainuiamata, Wellington, New Zealand 1995-96
Cricketers particularly admired: Allan Lamb, Carl Hooper, Anil Kumble
Other sports followed: Golf, rugby union, shove ha'penny, white-water rafting, Bangalore kabadi team, yarding
Relaxations: Good food and drink, listening to music, travelling
Extras: Sir Jack Hobbs award (U15 Schoolboy 1988), Gold Award winner for Combined Universities v Worcestershire 1992 (3-34) at The Parks. Player of the Tournament at European Indoor 6-a-side Championships in 1994. Released by Northants at end of 1998 season and has joined Gloucestershire for 1999
Opinions on cricket: 'Definitely in favour of four-day cricket as it induces a more disciplined approach, although I equally enjoy the challenges of one-day cricket.

Counties should work harder to maximise the potential of their individual players while encouraging the teamwork essential to competition.'

Best batting: 87 Northamptonshire v Mashonaland Select XI, Harare 1994-95
Best bowling: 5-65 Northamptonshire v Durham, Northampton 1995

1998 Season

	M	Inns	NO	Runs	HS	Avge	100s	50s	Ct	St	O	M	Runs	Wkts	Avge	Best	5wI	10wM
Test																		
All First																		
1-day Int																		
NatWest	1	1	0	35	35	35.00	-	-	-	-	11	1	47	1	47.00	1-47	-	
B & H	5	5	0	54	31	10.80	-	-	2	-	39	1	193	5	38.60	3-44	-	
Sunday	15	12	5	242	77 *	34.57	-	1	6	-	92.4	1	452	20	22.60	3-39	-	

Career Performances

	M	Inns	NO	Runs	HS	Avge	100s	50s	Ct	St	Balls	Runs	Wkts	Avge	Best	5wI	10wM
Test																	
All First	39	56	11	1139	87	25.31	-	7	34	-	5498	2931	65	45.09	5-65	1	-
1-day Int																	
NatWest	8	7	2	134	54	26.80	-	1	3	-	355	235	6	39.16	2-43	-	
B & H	20	17	4	264	52	20.30	-	1	9	-	1032	714	23	31.04	5-32	1	
Sunday	54	35	15	484	77 *	24.20	-	1	17	-	1738	1420	54	26.29	4-31	-	

FIGA

76. Who took 7-51 for West Indies v Australia
at Headingley in the 1983 World Cup?

SOLANKI, V. S. Worcestershire

Name: Vikram Singh Solanki
Role: Right-hand bat, off-spin bowler
Born: 1 April 1976, Udaipur, India
Height: 6ft 1in **Weight:** 12st
Nickname: Mowgli, Vik
County debut: 1993 (one-day),
1995 (first-class)
County cap: 1998
1st-Class 50s: 13
1st-Class 100s: 3
1st-Class 5 w. in innings: 3
1st-Class 10 w. in match: 1
1st-Class catches: 57
Place in batting averages: 113th av. 28.54
(1997 133rd av. 28.11)
Strike rate: 78.75 (career 74.90)
Parents: Vijay Singh and Florabell
Marital status: Single
Family links with cricket: 'Father played in
India. Brother Vishal (9 yrs) is keen cricketer'

Education: St Luke's, Udaipur; Merridale, Wolverhampton;
Regis School, Wolverhampton
Qualifications: 9 GCSEs, 3 A-levels
Off-season: England A tour to South Africa and Zimbabwe
Overseas tours: England U18 to South Africa 1992-93, to Denmark 1994 (ICC Youth
Tournament); England U19 to West Indies 1994-95; Worcestershire CCC to Barbados
1996, to Zimbabwe 1997; England A to South Africa and Zimbabwe 1998-99
Overseas teams played for: Midland Guildford, Perth, Western Australia
Cricketers particularly admired: Sachin Tendulkar, Graeme Hick, Tom Moody
Other sports followed: 'Enjoy playing most sports'
Injuries: Knee operation, but no time off required
Relaxations: 'Spending time with friends and family'
Extras: Awarded county cap in August 1998
Opinions on cricket: 'Clubs should prepare wickets to produce good cricket and good
cricketers and not result wickets which often see games over in two or three days. This
defeats the object of four-day cricket.'
Best batting: 170 Worcestershire v Derbyshire, Derby 1998
Best bowling: 5-69 Worcestershire v Middlesex, Lord's 1996

1998 Season

	M	Inns	NO	Runs	HS	Avge	100s	50s	Ct	St	O	M	Runs	Wkts	Avge	Best	5wI	10wM
Test																		
All First	19	36	1	999	170	28.54	2	4	28	-	105	22	375	8	46.87	2-22	-	-
1-day Int																		
NatWest	1	1	0	1	1	1.00	-	-	-	-								
B & H	4	4	0	41	25	10.25	-	-	3	-								
Sunday	16	15	2	461	120 *	35.46	1	1	4	-								

Career Performances

	M	Inns	NO	Runs	HS	Avge	100s	50s	Ct	St	Balls	Runs	Wkts	Avge	Best	5wI	10wM
Test																	
All First	54	89	6	2516	170	30.31	3	13	57	-	2996	1925	40	48.12	5-69	3	1
1-day Int																	
NatWest	6	5	0	95	50	19.00	-	1	1	-	183	142	2	71.00	1-48	-	
B & H	9	9	0	131	25	14.55	-	-	4	-	18	17	1	17.00	1-17	-	
Sunday	56	43	7	879	120 *	24.41	1	3	16	-	132	141	4	35.25	1-9	-	

SPEAK, N. J.   Durham

Name: Nicholas Jason Speak
Role: Right-hand opening bat,
leg-spin bowler, county vice-captain
Born: 21 November 1966, Manchester
Height: 6ft **Weight:** 12st 6lbs
Nickname: Speaky, Judge
County debut: 1986-87 (Lancashire),
1997 (Durham)
County cap: 1992 (Lancashire)
1000 runs in a season: 3
1st-Class 50s: 50
1st-Class 100s: 12
1st-Class 200s: 1
1st-Class catches: 99
One-Day 100s: 1
Place in batting averages: 131st av. 26.32
(1997 181st av. 23.66)
Strike rate: (career 90.50)
Parents: John and Irene
Wife and date of marriage: Michele Frances, 29 March 1993
Children: Kenneth John, 24 September 1995; Ella Frances, 13 July 1997
Family links with cricket: Father and uncle were league professionals in Lancashire
and Yorkshire

Education: Broad Oak, Didsbury; Parrs Wood High School, Manchester; Sixth Form College, Didsbury, Manchester

Qualifications: 6 O-levels, NCA coaching award, Farming diploma

Career outside cricket: Coaching/farming

Off-season: Victoria, Australia. Checking on the farm

Overseas tours: Lancashire to Jamaica 1986-87, 1993, to Zimbabwe 1989, to Perth 1990-91, to Johannesburg 1992

Overseas teams played for: South Canberra 1989-90; North Canberra 1991-93; Hawthorn, Melbourne 1994-96; Dandenong 1997-99

Cricketers particularly admired: Mark Waugh, Shane Warne

Young players to look out for: Kenneth Speak, Melvyn Betts

Other sports played: Golf, lacrosse, football, Aussie Rules

Other sports followed: All sports – Manchester City FC

Injuries: Out for five weeks with groin injury

Relaxations/interests: 'Two children under the age of three not a relaxation.' Golf

Extras: Scored century for Australian Capital Territories v England A at Canberra 1992-93. Released by Lancashire at the end of the 1996 season and joined Durham for 1997. Appointed Durham vice-captain for 1999

Opinions on cricket: 'Tea should be ten minutes longer.'

Best batting: 232 Lancashire v Leicestershire, Leicester 1992

Best bowling: 1-0 Lancashire v Warwickshire, Old Trafford 1991

1998 Season

	M	Inns	NO	Runs	HS	Avge	100s	50s	Ct	St	O	M	Runs	Wkts	Avge	Best	5wI	10wM
Test																		
All First	15	27	2	658	77 *	26.32	-	6	9	-	2	0	13	0	-		-	-	-
1-day Int																		
NatWest	2	2	1	130	73	130.00	-	2	-	-								
B & H	5	5	0	71	23	14.20	-	-	-	-								
Sunday	9	9	1	235	90 *	29.37	-	1	4	-								

Career Performances

	M	Inns	NO	Runs	HS	Avge	100s	50s	Ct	St	Balls	Runs	Wkts	Avge	Best	5wI	10wM
Test																	
All First	150	262	26	8484	232	35.94	13	50	99	-	181	191	2	95.50	1-0	-	-
1-day Int																	
NatWest	10	10	1	353	83	39.22	-	4	2	-	24	31	0	-		-	-
B & H	25	23	2	587	82	27.95	-	4	1	-							
Sunday	86	80	9	1910	102 *	26.90	1	8	20	-							

SPEIGHT, M. P.   Durham

Name: Martin Peter Speight
Role: Right-hand bat, wicket-keeper
Born: 24 October 1967, Walsall
Height: 5ft 10in **Weight:** 12st 7lbs
Nickname: Sprog, Badger
County debut: 1986 (Sussex),
1997 (Durham)
County cap: 1991 (Sussex)
1000 runs in a season: 2
1st-Class 50s: 42
1st-Class 100s: 13
1st-Class catches: 212
One-Day 100s: 3
Place in batting averages: 145th av. 24.56
(1997 188th av. 22.92)
Strike rate: (career 10.50)
Parents: Peter John and Valerie
Wife and date of marriage:
Lisa Irene, 27 September 1997
Education: The Windmills School, Hassocks; Hurstpierpoint College Junior and
Senior Schools; Durham University (St Chad's College)
Qualifications: 13 O-levels, 3 A-levels, BA (Hons) Archaeology/Ancient History
Career outside cricket: Artist
Off-season: Painting commissions
Overseas tours: NCA U19 to Bermuda 1984; Hurstpierpoint to India 1986;
England YC to Sri Lanka 1986-87
Overseas teams played for: Karori, Wellington, New Zealand 1989-90; University
CC, Wellington 1990-93; North City, Wellington 1995-96; Wellington CA 1989-90,
1992-93, 1995-96
Cricketers particularly admired: David Gower, Viv Richards
Young players to look out for: Stephen Harmison
Other sports played: Hockey, squash
Other sports followed: Rugby, football (Walsall FC)
Injuries: Out for one week with strained ankle ligament
Relaxations: Music, art, cinema, nice food and wine
Extras: Member of Durham University UAU winning side 1987; played for
Combined Universities in B&H Cup 1987 and 1988; Sussex Most Promising Player
1989. Fastest first-class 100 in 1992 v Lancashire. Scored 47-ball Sunday League 100
v Somerset at Taunton 1993. Has won two Gold Awards in the Benson and Hedges
competition. Painted an oil painting of the maiden first-class game at Arundel Castle
between Sussex and Hampshire which was later auctioned to raise £1200 for the

Sussex YC tour to India 1990-91, and of which a limited edition has also been printed and sold. Has done paintings of Hove, Southampton and The Oval for the benefits of Messrs Pigott, Parks and Greig. Member of Durham University's men's hockey team to Barbados 1988. Book of his paintings, *A Cricketer's View*, a collection of 54 paintings and commentary, published in 1995. Various commissions and a print of Abergavenny CC published in 1997. Joined Durham from Sussex for the 1997 season

Opinions on cricket: 'The A1 north of the M18 is still only two lanes and should be three! Cricket should not be played if the temperature drops below a certain (agreed on) level.'

Best batting: 184 Sussex v Nottinghamshire, Eastbourne 1993
Best bowling: 1-2 Sussex v Middlesex, Hove 1988

1998 Season

	M	Inns	NO	Runs	HS	Avge	100s	50s	Ct	St	O	M	Runs	Wkts	Avge	Best	5wI	10wM
Test																		
All First	17	29	4	614	97 *	24.56	-	4	58	3								
1-day Int																		
NatWest	2	1	0	32	32	32.00	-	-	4	1								
B & H	5	5	0	82	55	16.40	-	1	7	1								
Sunday	14	13	0	221	45	17.00	-	-	7	5								

Career Performances

	M	Inns	NO	Runs	HS	Avge	100s	50s	Ct	St	Balls	Runs	Wkts	Avge	Best	5wI	10wM
Test																	
All First	157	263	22	8001	184	33.19	13	42	212	3	21	32	2	16.00	1-2	-	-
1-day Int																	
NatWest	19	17	1	391	50	24.43	-	1	10	1							
B & H	40	37	1	820	83	22.77	-	4	31	2							
Sunday	126	116	6	3103	126	28.20	3	15	46	7							

SPENDLOVE, B. L. — Derbyshire

Name: Benjamin Lee Spendlove
Role: Right-hand bat, off-spin bowler
Born: 4 November 1978, Belper, Derbyshire
Height: 6ft 1in **Weight:** 12st 7lbs
Nickname: Silky, Sick Boy
County debut: 1997
1st-Class catches: 6
Place in batting averages: 199th av. 19.44
Parents: Lee and Chris
Marital status: Single

Family links with cricket: Father played local leagues and was professional cricket coach at Trent College

Education: Harrington Junior School, Long Eaton; Trent College, Long Eaton

Qualifications: 9 GCSEs

Career outside cricket: Entrepreneur

Off-season: 'Training hard, working on my game, and enjoying myself'

Overseas tours: England U17 to Holland (International Youth Tournament) 1995

Overseas teams played for: Gold Coast CC, Queensland, Australia 1995-96

Cricketers particularly admired: Graham Gooch, Alec Stewart, Robin Smith

Young players to look out for: Owais Shah ('he's cuttin' it')

Other sports played: Hockey (Derbyshire U15), rugby (Midlands trialist)

Other sports followed: Football (Derby County)

Injuries: Out for one month with stress fracture of left ankle

Relaxations: Listening to music. Going out to restaurants

Extras: Represented England at U15, U17 and U19. Fielded as 12th man for England in Test match v South Africa at Edgbaston 1998, taking two catches (G. Liebenberg and W. Cronje) off bowling of Dominic Cork. Played in a Lord's final aged 19 ('I really enjoyed that')

Opinions on cricket: 'It's good to see all the people I grew up playing with are all getting a good chance at the counties they are at. It's always good to see my mates do well.'

Best batting: 49 Derbyshire v Somerset, Taunton 1998

1998 Season

	M	Inns	NO	Runs	HS	Avge	100s	50s	Ct	St	O	M	Runs	Wkts	Avge	Best	5wI	10wM
Test																		
All First	10	19	1	350	49	19.44	-	-	4	-								
1-day Int																		
NatWest	5	4	0	119	58	29.75	-	1	1	-								
B & H	2	2	0	16	11	8.00	-	-	1	-								
Sunday	8	7	0	82	25	11.71	-	-	3	-								

Career Performances

	M	Inns	NO	Runs	HS	Avge	100s	50s	Ct	St	Balls	Runs	Wkts	Avge	Best	5wI	10wM
Test																	
All First	12	22	2	377	49	18.85	-	-	6	-							
1-day Int																	
NatWest	5	4	0	119	58	29.75	-	1	1	-							
B & H	2	2	0	16	11	8.00	-	-	1	-							
Sunday	9	8	0	86	25	10.75	-	-	3	-							

SPIRING, K. R. Worcestershire

Name: Karl Reuben Spiring
Role: Right-hand opening bat
Born: 13 November 1974, Southport
Height: 5ft 10in **Weight:** 12st
Nickname: Ginga, Caspa, Faceless,
Jesse James
County debut: 1993 (one-day),
1994 (first-class)
1000 runs in a season: 1
1st-Class 50s: 13
1st-Class 100s: 4
1st-Class catches: 19
Place in batting averages:
(1997 91st av. 35.04)
Parents: Peter and June
Marital status: Engaged to Jess
Children: Dai Rhys and Blodwyn, 8 October
1997 ('twins')
Education: Monmouth School;
Durham University
Qualifications: 9 GCSEs, 3 A-levels, NCA Senior Coach
Career outside cricket: 'Lawnmower man'
Off-season: 'Going to Venice with Jess. Spending more time with Scott Ellis'
Overseas tours: Worcestershire to Barbados 1996
Overseas teams played for: Fremantle/Mosman Park Pirates, Perth, Western Australia
1995-97
Cricketers particularly admired: Scott Ellis, Steve Rhodes
Other sports played: 'Frisbee with Raggy and Zig'
Other sports followed: Women's rugby
Injuries: Out all season with knee injury followed by a brain illness
Relaxations: 'Smoking in the toilets at Worcester CCC. Everything to do with Venice'

Extras: Father was a professional footballer. Rapid Cricketline 2nd XI Player of the Month June 1994. Worcestershire Uncapped Player of the Year 1994
Opinions on cricket: 'Cricket is life – you never know what you're gonna get.'
Best batting: 150 Worcestershire v Essex, Chelmsford 1997

1998 Season (did not make any first-class or one-day appearances)

Career Performances

	M	Inns	NO	Runs	HS	Avge	100s	50s	Ct	St	Balls	Runs	Wkts	Avge	Best	5wl	10wM
Test																	
All First	37	64	9	2072	150	37.67	4	13	19	-	12	10	0	-	-	-	-
1-day Int																	
NatWest	4	4	0	141	53	35.25	-	1	2	-							
B & H	12	10	1	202	35	22.44	-	-	4	-							
Sunday	29	25	10	518	58 *	34.53	-	1	9	-							

STEMP, R. D. Nottinghamshire

Name: Richard David Stemp
Role: Right-hand bat, slow left-arm bowler
Born: 11 December 1967, Erdington, Birmingham
Height: 6ft **Weight:** 12st 4lbs
Nickname: Stempy, Sherriff, Badger
County debut: 1990 (Worcestershire), 1993 (Yorkshire)
County cap: 1996 (Yorkshire)
1st-Class 50s: 2
1st-Class 5 w. in innings: 13
1st-Class 10 w. in match: 1
1st-Class catches: 59
Place in batting averages: 205th av. 19.00 (1997 281st av. 11.00)
Place in bowling averages: 122nd av. 37.07 (1997 87th av. 32.83)

Strike rate: 90.88 (career 80.08)
Parents: Arnold and Rita Homer
Marital status: Single
Family links with cricket: Father played Birmingham League cricket for Old Hill
Education: Britannia High School, Rowley Regis
Qualifications: NCA coaching award
Overseas tours: England A to India 1994-95, to Pakistan 1995-96

Overseas teams played for: Pretoria Technikon 1988-89
Cricketers particularly admired: Ian Botham, Phil Tufnell
Other sports followed: Indoor cricket, American football (New England Patriots)
Relaxations: Ornithology, music, driving
Extras: Played for England indoor cricket team v Australia in ManuLife 'Test' series 1990. Moved to Yorkshire at end of 1992 season (first English non-Yorkshireman to be signed for the county). Included in England Test squad against New Zealand in 1994. Released by Yorkshire at the end of the 1998 season and has joined Notts for 1999
Opinions on cricket: 'Groundsmen should prepare cricket wickets, not wickets made for corporate hospitality.'
Best batting: 65 Yorkshire v Durham, Chester-le-Street 1996
Best bowling: 6-37 Yorkshire v Durham, Durham University 1994

1998 Season

	M	Inns	NO	Runs	HS	Avge	100s	50s	Ct	St	O	M	Runs	Wkts	Avge	Best	5wI	10wM
Test																		
All First	12	16	9	133	43 *	19.00	-	-	6	-	409	141	1001	27	37.07	5-191	1	-
1-day Int																		
NatWest	1	1	0	0	0	0.00	-	-	-	-	10	1	37	0	-	-	-	-
B & H																		
Sunday	10	4	2	10	9	5.00	-	-	1	-	66	2	342	9	38.00	2-19	-	

Career Performances

	M	Inns	NO	Runs	HS	Avge	100s	50s	Ct	St	Balls	Runs	Wkts	Avge	Best	5wI	10wM
Test																	
All First	136	161	53	1425	65	13.19	-	2	59	-	25548	10868	319	34.06	6-37	13	1
1-day Int																	
NatWest	11	3	2	1	1 *	1.00	-	-	1	-	666	406	14	29.00	4-45	-	
B & H	19	4	1	3	2	1.00	-	-	-	-	1062	679	19	35.73	3-22	-	
Sunday	69	23	8	118	23 *	7.86	-	-	16	-	2667	2190	73	30.00	4-25	-	

STEPHENSON, J. P.   Hampshire

Name: John Patrick Stephenson
Role: Right-hand opening bat, right-arm medium bowler
Born: 14 March 1965, Stebbing, Essex
Height: 6ft 1in **Weight:** 12st 7lbs
Nickname: Stan
County debut: 1985 (Essex), 1995 (Hants)
County cap: 1989 (Essex)
Test debut: 1989

Tests: 1
1000 runs in a season: 5
1st-Class 50s: 70
1st-Class 100s: 22
1st-Class 200s: 1
1st-Class 5 w. in innings: 9
1st-Class catches: 149
One-Day 100s: 7
One-Day 5 w. in innings: 3
Place in batting averages: 104th av. 29.60
(1997 101st av. 34.08)
Place in bowling averages: 98th av. 32.08
(1997 121st av. 40.00)
Strike rate: 71.66 (career 62.59)
Parents: Pat and Eve
Wife and date of marriage: Fiona Maria,
24 September 1994
Children: Emma-Lydia, 19 May 1997
Family links with cricket: Father was member of Rugby Meteors Cricketer Cup-winning side in 1973. Three brothers played in Felsted 1st XI; Guy played for Essex 2nd XI and now plays for Teddington
Education: Felsted Prep School; Felsted Senior School; Durham University
Qualifications: 7 O-levels, 3 A-levels, BA General Arts (Dunelm)
Off-season: 'Working with Grist – specialist IT and financial recruitment consultancy'
Overseas tours: English Schools U19 to Zimbabwe 1982-83; England A to Kenya and Zimbabwe 1989-90, to Bermuda and West Indies 1991-92
Overseas teams played for: Fitzroy, Melbourne 1982-83, 1987-88; Boland, South Africa 1988-89; Gold Coast Dolphins and Bond University, Australia 1990-91; St George's, Argentina 1994-95; Belgrano, Argentina 1994-95; Victoria CC, South Africa 1995-96
Cricketers particularly admired: Brian Hardie
Relaxations: Watching cricket, reading (*Sunday Telegraph*, *Wisden*, *The Cricketer*), alternative music
Extras: Awarded 2nd XI cap in 1984 when leading run-scorer with Essex 2nd XI. Essex Young Player of the Year, 1985. Captained Durham University to victory in UAU Championship 1986 and captain of Combined Universities team 1987 in the first year that it was drawn from all universities. Called up to replace the injured Michael Atherton on England A tour to Bermuda and West Indies 1991-92 and was leading wicket-taker. Scored two not out centuries v Somerset at Taunton in 1992 and was on the field for the whole game (the first Essex player to achieve this). First Essex player to achieve 500 runs and 20 wickets in Sunday League season 1993. Took over the captaincy of Hampshire in 1996, but relinquished it at the end of the 1997 season. Founded the One Test Wonder Club in 1996
Opinions on cricket: 'Leave the Championship as it is and change the structure of one-day cricket if change has to happen.'

Best batting: 202* Essex v Somerset, Bath 1990
Best bowling: 7-51 Hampshire v Middlesex, Lord's 1995

1998 Season

	M	Inns	NO	Runs	HS	Avge	100s	50s	Ct	St	O	M	Runs	Wkts	Avge	Best	5wl	10wM
Test																		
All First	16	24	1	681	114	29.60	2	4	14	-	286.4	71	770	24	32.08	4-29	-	-
1-day Int																		
NatWest	4	4	0	36	21	9.00	-	-	2	-	28	2	98	5	19.60	3-25	-	
B & H	3	3	0	73	53	24.33	-	1	2	-	27	3	95	4	23.75	2-18	-	
Sunday	15	15	1	323	77 *	23.07	-	3	2	-	78	4	382	17	22.47	3-38	-	

Career Performances

	M	Inns	NO	Runs	HS	Avge	100s	50s	Ct	St	Balls	Runs	Wkts	Avge	Best	5wl	10wM
Test	1	2	0	36	25	18.00	-	-	-	-							
All First	253	429	42	13198	202 *	34.10	23	70	149	-	17402	9541	278	34.32	7-51	9	-
1-day Int																	
NatWest	27	25	1	806	107	33.58	1	7	11	-	997	775	25	31.00	5-34	1	
B & H	45	40	5	1471	142	42.02	2	11	11	-	1504	1060	42	25.23	3-22	-	
Sunday	163	145	19	3541	110 *	28.10	4	16	65	-	4796	3771	154	24.48	6-33	2	

STEVENS, D. I. Leicestershire

Name: Darren Ian Stevens
Role: Right-hand bat, right-arm medium bowler
Born: 30 April 1976, Leicester
Height: 5ft 11in **Weight:** 12st 7lbs
Nickname: Beetroot, JJ Junior
County debut: 1997
1st-Class catches: 1
Strike rate: (career 12.00)
Parents: Robert and Madeleine
Marital status: Single
Family links with cricket: Father and grandfather played club cricket in local leagues
Education: Richmond Primary School; Mount Grace High School; John Cleavland College, Hinckley
Qualifications: 4 GCSEs, BTEC in Sports Studies

Overseas tours: Leicestershire U19 to South Africa 1994-95
Overseas teams played for: Wanderers CC, Johannesburg, South Africa 1995-97; Rhodes University, Grahamstown, South Africa 1997-98
Cricketers particularly admired: Ian Botham, Graham Thorpe, David Gower
Young players to look out for: Darren Maddy, Tim 'Biffa' Mason, Jon 'Babe Ruth' Dakin, Dominic 'Yoda' Williamson
Other sports followed: Football (Leicester City), rugby (Leicester Tigers), golf, squash
Relaxations: Socialising, going out with friends, clubbing, spending time with girlfriend Clare. 'Having a round of golf – not walking around but on a buggy'
Opinions on cricket: 'Great game.'
Best batting: 27 Leicestershire v Cambridge University, Fenner's 1997
Best bowling: 1-5 Leicestershire v Sussex, Eastbourne 1997

1998 Season

	M	Inns	NO	Runs	HS	Avge	100s	50s	Ct	St	O	M	Runs	Wkts	Avge	Best	5wI	10wM
Test																		
All First	1	2	0	3	2	1.50	-	-	-	-								
1-day Int																		
NatWest																		
B & H																		
Sunday	4	4	1	39	21	13.00	-	-	-	-								

Career Performances

	M	Inns	NO	Runs	HS	Avge	100s	50s	Ct	St	Balls	Runs	Wkts	Avge	Best	5wI	10wM
Test																	
All First	3	4	0	38	27	9.50	-	-	1	-	12	5	1	5.00	1-5	-	-
1-day Int																	
NatWest																	
B & H																	
Sunday	6	6	1	46	21	9.20	-	-	1	-							

STEWART, A. J.   Surrey

Name: Alec James Stewart
Role: Right-hand bat, wicket-keeper,
honorary club captain
Born: 8 April 1963, Merton
Height: 5ft 11in **Weight:** 13st
Nickname: Stewie, Ming
County debut: 1981
County cap: 1985
Benefit: 1994 (£202,187)
Test debut: 1989-90
Tests: 81
One-Day Internationals: 105
1000 runs in a season: 8
1st-Class 50s: 120
1st-Class 100s: 40
1st-Class 200s: 2
1st-Class catches: 506
1st-Class stumpings: 17
One-Day 100s: 16

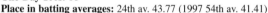

Place in batting averages: 24th av. 43.77 (1997 54th av. 41.41)
Strike rate: (career 156.33)
Parents: Michael and Sheila
Wife and date of marriage: Lynn, 28 September 1991
Children: Andrew James, 21 May 1993; Emily Elizabeth, 6 September 1996
Family links with cricket: Father played for England (1962-64), Surrey (1954-72)
and Malden Wanderers. Brother Neil captains Malden Wanderers
Education: Tiffin Boys School
Qualifications: 'Streetwise'
Off-season: Ashes tour with England
Overseas tours: England to India (Nehru Cup) 1989-90, to West Indies 1989-90, to
Australia 1990-91, to Australia and New Zealand (World Cup) 1991-92, to India and
Sri Lanka 1992-93, to West Indies 1993-94, to Australia 1994-95; to South Africa
1995-96, to Pakistan and India (World Cup) 1996, to Zimbabwe and New Zealand
1996-97, to Sharjah 1997-98 (Champions Trophy), to West Indies 1997-98, to
Australia 1998-99 (captain)
Overseas teams played for: Midland Guildford, Perth, Western Australia 1981-89
Cricketers particularly admired: Graham Monkhouse, Graham Gooch, Alan Knott,
Geoff Arnold, K Gartrell
Young players to look out for: Ben Hollioake
Other sports followed: Football (Chelsea)
Relaxations: 'Spending as much time with my family as possible'

Extras: Captained England in a Test match for the first time v India at Madras 1992-93 and has acted as vice-captain to both Graham Gooch and Mike Atherton. One of *Wisden*'s five Cricketers of the Year 1993. First Englishman to score a century in each innings against West Indies, at Barbados 1994. He was the leading scorer in Test cricket in the 1996 calendar year (with 793 runs) ahead of Saeed Anwar (701). Appointed captain of England 1998. Awarded MBE in HM The Queen's birthday honours list 1998. Scored 164 in England's second innings v South Africa at Old Trafford in 1998, the highest Test score by a captain/wicket-keeper. Is contracted to Surrey until 2003

Opinions on cricket: 'Improve the level of pitches and practice pitches.'

Best batting: 271* Surrey v Yorkshire, The Oval 1997

Best bowling: 1-7 Surrey v Lancashire, Old Trafford 1989

1998 Season

	M	Inns	NO	Runs	HS	Avge	100s	50s	Ct	St	O	M	Runs	Wkts	Avge	Best	5wI	10wM
Test	6	12	1	499	164	45.36	1	1	26	-								
All First	14	24	2	963	164	43.77	1	5	41	-								
1-day Int	6	6	1	201	52	40.20	-	2	9	-								
NatWest	3	3	0	189	97	63.00	-	2	8	-								
B & H	7	7	0	277	108	39.57	1	-	3	7								
Sunday	6	6	0	118	58	19.66	-	1	5	1								

Career Performances

	M	Inns	NO	Runs	HS	Avge	100s	50s	Ct	St	Balls	Runs	Wkts	Avge	Best	5wI	10wM
Test	81	146	10	5652	190	41.55	11	28	144	7	20	13	0	-	-	-	-
All First	356	590	65	21466	271 *	40.88	42	120	506	17	469	417	3	139.00	1-7	-	-
1-day Int	105	100	8	3013	116	32.75	2	18	92	11							
NatWest	39	36	6	1545	125 *	51.50	3	11	48	2							
B & H	65	65	10	2598	167 *	47.23	4	18	47	11							
Sunday	168	152	16	4211	125	30.96	7	24	132	11	4	8	0	-	-	-	

FIGA

77. Who was England's leading run-scorer in the 1992 World Cup?

STRANG, P. A. Nottinghamshire

Name: Paul Andrew Strang
Role: Right-hand bat, leg-spin bowler
Born: 28 July 1970, Bulawayo, Zimbabwe
Height: 5ft 9in **Weight:** 11st 7lbs
Nickname: Stump
County debut: 1997 (Kent),
1998 (Nottinghamshire)
50 wickets in a season: 1
1st-Class 50s: 13
1st-Class 100s: 2
1st-Class 5 w. in innings: 16
1st-Class 10 w. in match: 2
1st-Class catches: 75
One-Day 5 w. in innings: 2
Place in batting averages: 191st av. 20.00
(1997 168th av. 24.58)
Place in bowling averages: 102nd av. 32.76
(1997 74th av. 30.61)
Strike rate: 70.70 (career 69.95)
Parents: Ronald Charles and Jennifer Joan
Marital status: Single

Family links with cricket: Father is a first-class umpire. Brother Bryan plays for
Zimbabwe
Education: Falcon College, Esigodini, Zimbabwe; University of Cape Town,
South Africa
Qualifications: A-levels, BSocSc (Econ), advanced coach
Overseas tours: Zimbabwe U19 to New Zealand 1989; Zimbabwe to India and
Pakistan (World Cup) 1995-96, to Pakistan 1996-97, to Sri Lanka 1996-97, 1997-98,
to Sharjah 1997-98, to New Zealand 1997-98, to Bangladesh 1998-99
Cricketers particularly admired: David Houghton and John Traicos
Young players to look out for: Brian Murphy
Other sports followed: Most international sport. 'Liverpool FC. I always keep an eye
on Nick Price (golf) and Byron Black (tennis).' Played hockey for Zimbabwe U19
Relaxations: 'I like to relax with mates watching sport'
Extras: Captained Zimbabwe U19 (1989-90). Shared all ten wickets with brother
Bryan in a local game. Played in the Birmingham League for Aston Manor (1989) and
Barnt Green (1996). Became only the 18th player to score a century and take five
wickets in an innings in a Test match against Pakistan at Shekhupura. Made his first-
class debut in Zimbabwe against Kent. Signed a two-year contract as overseas player
for Nottinghamshire starting from 1998
Opinions on cricket: 'Lbws for balls pitching outside leg would be nice!'

Best batting: 106* Zimbabwe v Pakistan, Shekhupura 1996-97
Best bowling: 7-75 Mashonaland Country Districts v Mashonaland U24, Harare South 1994-95

1998 Season

	M	Inns	NO	Runs	HS	Avge	100s	50s	Ct	St	O	M	Runs	Wkts	Avge	Best	5wI	10wM
Test																		
All First	13	18	3	300	48	20.00	-	-	19	-	353.3	105	983	30	32.76	5-166	1	-
1-day Int																		
NatWest	3	3	0	66	40	22.00	-	-	1	-	35	4	128	4	32.00	2-33	-	
B & H	5	4	2	37	23 *	18.50	-	-	2	-	50	5	188	6	31.33	4-49	-	
Sunday	14	12	3	143	35	15.88	-	-	7	-	95	4	452	17	26.58	6-32	1	

Career Performances

	M	Inns	NO	Runs	HS	Avge	100s	50s	Ct	St	Balls	Runs	Wkts	Avge	Best	5wI	10wM
Test	20	34	7	747	106 *	27.66	1	2	12	-	4849	2158	57	37.85	5-106	3	-
All First	82	123	24	2685	106 *	27.12	2	13	75	-	18147	8345	262	31.85	7-75	16	2
1-day Int	59	51	17	816	47	24.00	-	-	19	-	2815	1952	63	30.98	5-21	1	
NatWest	4	4	0	72	40	18.00	-	-	1	-	282	190	4	47.50	2-33	-	
B & H	13	11	7	123	38 *	30.75	-	-	6	-	711	410	18	22.77	4-27	-	
Sunday	31	24	4	308	40	15.40	-	-	12	-	1239	983	33	29.78	6-32	1	

STRAUSS, A. J. Middlesex

Name: Andrew John Strauss
Role: Left-hand bat
Born: 2 March 1977, Johannesburg, South Africa
Height: 5ft 11in **Weight:** 12st 7lbs
Nickname: Johann, Mousey
County debut: 1997 (one-day), 1998 (first-class)
1st-Class 50s: 1
1st-Class catches: 3
Place in batting averages: 149th av. 24.33
Parents: David and Dawn
Marital status: Single
Education: Caldicott Prep School; Radley College; University of Durham
Qualifications: 4 A-levels
Cricketers particularly admired: Brian Lara, Allan Donald

Young players to look out for: Luke Sutton
Other sports played/followed: Rugby, golf
Relaxations: Macroeconomics
Best batting: 83 Middlesex v Hampshire, Southampton 1998

1998 Season

	M	Inns	NO	Runs	HS	Avge	100s	50s	Ct	St	O	M	Runs	Wkts	Avge	Best	5wI	10wM
Test																		
All First	3	6	0	146	83	24.33	-	1	3	-								
1-day Int																		
NatWest																		
B & H	2	2	1	47	29	47.00	-	-	-	-								
Sunday	3	3	0	24	15	8.00	-	-	1	-								

Career Performances

	M	Inns	NO	Runs	HS	Avge	100s	50s	Ct	St	Balls	Runs	Wkts	Avge	Best	5wI	10wM
Test																	
All First	3	6	0	146	83	24.33	-	1	3	-							
1-day Int																	
NatWest																	
B & H	3	3	1	48	29	24.00	-	-	-	-							
Sunday	5	5	0	31	15	6.20	-	-	2	-							

STRONG, M.   Sussex

Name: Michael Strong
Role: Left-hand bat, right-arm fast-medium bowler
Born: 28 June 1974, Cuckfield, West Sussex
Height: 6ft 1in **Weight:** 12st 10lbs
Nickname: Strongbow, Stella, Sleazy
County debut: 1997
Parents: David and Gillian
Marital status: Single ('just')
Family links with cricket: Father and brother both played club cricket in Sussex
Education: St Peter's School, Burgess Hill; Brighton College; Brunel University College (formerly West London Institute)
Qualifications: 9 GCSEs, 3 A-levels, BA/BSc (QTS) PE and Geography
Career outside cricket: 'PE teacher and lager drinker'
Off-season: Playing and coaching in South Africa
Overseas tours: Brighton College to India 1991-92
Overseas teams played for: Umbilo CC, Durban 1992-93, 1997-99
Cricketers particularly admired: 'WG', Ranjitsinhji

Young players to look out for:
William Lewry
Other sports played: Two-touch football, hockey, touch rugby, golf
Other sports followed: Football (Chelsea FC – 'the best team in London')
Injuries: Out for a couple of weeks with metatarsal ligament injury ('little toe!') and shoulder muscle impingement
Relaxations: 'Going out with the boys to the "Big P", playing golf, sleeping, lying on the beach in Durban or Cape Town'
Extras: 'Would like to thank the master in charge of cricket at Brighton College, John Spencer, for all the time he spent coaching me from the age of ten.' 'Caused much amusement in an AON Trophy match at The Oval when going for an important caught-and-bowled chance. Having flattened all three stumps, fallen over, dived and got one hand to the ball, I dropped it! Roy Palmer found it particularly amusing. Luckily we went on to win the match'

Opinions on cricket: 'Day/night cricket is definitely a good thing. Four-day cricket at 2nd XI level is a must (on first-class wickets). Jazz-hat cricket should be abolished! Some adjustments need to be made to the listing methods.'
Best batting: 2* Sussex v South Africa, Arundel 1998

1998 Season

	M	Inns	NO	Runs	HS	Avge	100s	50s	Ct	St	O	M	Runs	Wkts	Avge	Best	5wI	10wM
Test																		
All First	1	1	1	2	2 *	-	-	-	-	-	11	2	41	0	-	-	-	-
1-day Int																		
NatWest																			
B & H																			
Sunday																			

Career Performances

	M	Inns	NO	Runs	HS	Avge	100s	50s	Ct	St	Balls	Runs	Wkts	Avge	Best	5wI	10wM
Test																	
All First	1	1	1	2	2 *	-	-	-	-	-	66	41	0	-	-	-	-
1-day Int																	
NatWest																		
B & H																		
Sunday	3	3	1	4	2 *	2.00	-	-	-	-	92	97	0	-	-	-	

STUBBINGS, S. D. Derbyshire

Name: Stephen David Stubbings
Role: Left-hand bat
Born: 31 March 1978, Huddersfield
Height: 6ft 4in **Weight:** 14st 1lb
Nickname: Stubbo
County debut: 1997
Parents: David and Marie-Anne
Marital status: Single
Family links with cricket: 'Father played the odd game'
Education: Frankston High School, Victoria
Qualifications: Completed Year 12
Overseas teams played for: Frankston-Finchley CC, Victoria 1993-1998
Cricketers particularly admired: Mark Taylor, Ricky Ponting, Steve Waugh, Michael Atherton
Young players to look out for:

Ian Blackwell, Kevin Dean, Ben Spendlove
Other sports followed: Aussie rules (Essendon Bombers), football (Cambridge United)
Relaxations: Golf, eating, drinking and television
Extras: Has also played for Victoria at U17, Colts and U21 level
Best batting: 22 Derbyshire v Worcestershire, Worcester 1997

1998 Season

	M	Inns	NO	Runs	HS	Avge	100s	50s	Ct	St	O	M	Runs	Wkts	Avge	Best	5wl	10wM
Test																		
All First																		
1-day Int																		
NatWest																		
B & H	2	2	0	8	7	4.00	-	-	-	-								
Sunday	1	1	0	4	4	4.00	-	-	-	-								

Career Performances

	M	Inns	NO	Runs	HS	Avge	100s	50s	Ct	St	Balls	Runs	Wkts	Avge	Best	5wl	10wM
Test																	
All First	1	2	0	27	22	13.50	-	-	-	-							
1-day Int																	
NatWest																	
B & H	2	2	0	8	7	4.00	-	-	-	-							
Sunday	1	1	0	4	4	4.00	-	-	-	-							

SUCH, P. M.   Essex

Name: Peter Mark Such
Role: Right-hand bat, off-spin bowler
Born: 12 June 1964, Helensburgh, Scotland
Height: 6ft **Weight:** 11st 7lbs
Nickname: Suchy
County debut: 1982 (Nottinghamshire),
1987 (Leicestershire), 1990 (Essex)
County cap: 1991 (Essex)
Test debut: 1993
Tests: 8
50 wickets in a season: 5
1st-Class 50s: 2
1st-Class 5 w. in innings: 41
1st-Class 10 w. in innings: 7
1st-Class catches: 103
One-Day 5 w. in innings: 3
Place in batting averages: 204th av. 19.00
(1997 303rd av. 5.72)
Place in bowling averages: 126th av. 38.81
(1997 41st av. 26.34)
Strike rate: 82.89 (career 66.58)
Parents: John and Margaret
Marital status: Engaged
Family links with cricket: Father and brother both village cricketers
Education: Lantern Lane Primary; Harry Carlton Comprehensive, East Leake, Notts
Qualifications: 9 O-levels, 3 A-levels, advanced cricket coach
Off-season: Touring Australia with England
Overseas tours: England A to Australia 1992-93, to South Africa 1993-94, to
Australia 1996-97; England to Australia 1998-99
Overseas teams played for: Kempton Park, South Africa 1982-83; Bathurst, Australia
1985-86; Matabeleland, Zimbabwe 1989-92
Cricketers particularly admired: Bob White, Eddie Hemmings, Graham Gooch,
John Childs
Young players to look out for: Ashley Cowan, Robert Rollins, Andrew Harris
Injuries: Out for three weeks with torn intercostal
Relaxations: Gardening
Extras: Played for England YC v Australian YC 1983 and for TCCB XI v New
Zealand, 1985. Left Nottinghamshire at end of 1986 season; joined Leicestershire in
1987 and released at end of 1989; signed by Essex for 1990. Played in one-day games
for England A v Sri Lanka 1991. Joint winner with J.H. Childs of the Essex Player of
the Year Award 1992 and shared the award again in 1993. Took 6-67 on Test debut v

Australia 1993 – best figures by England Test debutant since John Lever in India 1976-77. Holds the record for the most overs bowled in a County Championship innings when he bowled 86 overs against Leicestershire in August 1997 – he ended up with figures of 4 for 96. Is vice-chairman of the Professional Cricketers' Association

Best batting: 54 Essex v Worcestershire, Chelmsford 1993
54 Essex v Nottinghamshire, Chelmsford 1996
Best bowling: 8-93 Essex v Hampshire, Colchester 1995

1998 Season

	M	Inns	NO	Runs	HS	Avge	100s	50s	Ct	St	O	M	Runs	Wkts	Avge	Best	5wl	10wM
Test																		
All First	16	25	18	133	25	19.00	-	-	5	-	525	128	1475	38	38.81	5-73	2	-
1-day Int																		
NatWest	2	1	1	3	3 *	-	-	-	-	-	15	4	22	2	11.00	2-10	-	
B & H	7	2	2	15	8 *	-	-	-	3	-	52.3	2	208	2	104.00	1-34	-	
Sunday	12	4	2	17	13 *	8.50	-	-	1	-	69	2	292	14	20.85	3-18	-	

Career Performances

	M	Inns	NO	Runs	HS	Avge	100s	50s	Ct	St	Balls	Runs	Wkts	Avge	Best	5wl	10wM
Test	8	11	4	65	14 *	9.28	-	-	2	-	2177	805	22	36.59	6-67	1	-
All First	255	265	99	1339	54	8.06	-	2	103	-	48072	21275	722	29.46	8-93	41	7
1-day Int																	
NatWest	24	9	5	21	8 *	5.25	-	-	3	-	1512	828	25	33.12	3-56	-	
B & H	38	14	8	46	10 *	7.66	-	-	7	-	1947	1207	32	37.71	4-43	-	
Sunday	126	49	29	184	19 *	9.20	-	-	32	-	4925	3814	128	29.79	5-29	3	

SUTCLIFFE, I. J.   Leicestershire

Name: Iain John Sutcliffe
Role: Left-hand bat, leg-spin bowler
Born: 20 December 1974, Leeds
Height: 6ft 1in **Weight:** 12st
Nickname: Sooty, Bertie, Ripper
County debut: 1995
1st-Class 50s: 15
1st-Class 100s: 4
1st-Class catches: 29
One-Day 100s: 2
Place in batting averages: 85th av. 31.72 (1997 59th av. 40.38)
Strike rate: 54.00 (career 50.40)
Parents: John and Valerie
Marital status: Single

Education: Leeds Grammar School;
Oxford University
Qualifications: 10 GCSEs, 4 A-levels,
2:1 PPE degree
Overseas tours: Leeds GS to Kenya
Cricketers particularly admired:
David Gower, Brian Lara, Saeed Anwar
Other sports followed: Boxing
(Mike Tyson), football (Liverpool)
Relaxations: Listening to music, eating out
Extras: Played NCA England U14 and NCA
Development Team U18/U19. Oxford boxing
Blue 1994 and 1995, British Universities
Light-middleweight Champion 1993. Highest
partnership (283) with C. Gupte for Oxford
University against a first-class county in
which he scored 163*

Best batting: 167 Leicestershire v
Middlesex, Leicester 1998
Best bowling: 2-21 Oxford University v Cambridge University, Lord's 1996

1998 Season

	M	Inns	NO	Runs	HS	Avge	100s	50s	Ct	St	O	M	Runs	Wkts	Avge	Best	5wI	10wM
Test																		
All First	19	26	4	698	167	31.72	1	2	11	-	9	0	51	1	51.00	1-17	-	-
1-day Int																		
NatWest	3	3	1	78	39 *	39.00	-	-	1	-								
B & H	8	8	1	270	105 *	38.57	1	2	2	-								
Sunday	4	4	0	42	21	10.50	-	-	-	-								

Career Performances

	M	Inns	NO	Runs	HS	Avge	100s	50s	Ct	St	Balls	Runs	Wkts	Avge	Best	5wI	10wM
Test																	
All First	60	88	11	2734	167	35.50	4	15	29	-	252	200	5	40.00	2-21	-	-
1-day Int																	
NatWest	7	7	2	354	103 *	70.80	1	2	2	-							
B & H	14	14	1	425	105 *	32.69	1	3	2	-							
Sunday	12	12	1	238	96	21.63	-	1	4	-							

SUTTON, L. D.   Somerset

Name: Luke David Sutton
Role: Right-hand bat, 'right-arm fast bowler',
wicket-keeper
Born: 4 October 1976, Keynsham
Height: 5ft 11in **Weight:** 13st
Nickname: Suts, Duke
County debut: 1997
1st-Class catches: 10
Parents: David and Molly
Marital status: Single
Family links with cricket: 'Unknown'
Education: Edgarley Hall; Millfield School;
Durham University
Qualifications: 9 GCSEs, 4 A-levels,
2:1 degree in Economics, 'some sort of
cricket coaching award, Grade 1'
Career outside cricket: None
Off-season: 'Spending the winter in Sydney
playing cricket'
Overseas tours: Various Somerset Schools tours to Holland; West of England U15
to West Indies 1991; Millfield School to Zimbabwe 1993, to Sri Lanka 1994; Durham
University to Zimbabwe 1997
Cricketers particularly admired: Ian Healy, Steve Waugh, Paul Nixon
Young players to look out for: Mark Chilton, Tom Paltridge, Robert Key, Will Hale,
Colin Wells, Julian Wyatt
Other sports played: Football, hockey, 'Temper-Temper Trophy golf'
Other sports followed: 'Follow most sports, especially football'
Relaxations: Keeping fit, 'visiting "Sturms"/"Dellers"'
Extras: Captain of the England U15 side that played against South Africa and also
played for England U18 and U19. Won John Hobbs Award for the U16 Cricketer of
the Year in 1992 and the Gray Nicolls Award for the English Schools Cricketer of the
Year in 1995
Opinions on cricket: 'Love playing the game and am looking forward to playing
cricket at the highest level I can for as long as I can.'
Best batting: 16* Somerset v Sri Lanka, Taunton 1998

---

78. What is the World Cup claim to fame of
Sri Lanka's S. P. Pasqual?

FICA

1998 Season

	M	Inns	NO	Runs	HS	Avge	100s	50s	Ct	St	O	M	Runs	Wkts	Avge	Best	5wI	10wM
Test																		
All First	2	4	2	24	16 *	12.00	-	-	5	-								
1-day Int																		
NatWest																		
B & H	4	4	1	105	60	35.00	-	1	-	-								
Sunday																		

Career Performances

	M	Inns	NO	Runs	HS	Avge	100s	50s	Ct	St	Balls	Runs	Wkts	Avge	Best	5wI	10wM
Test																	
All First	3	6	3	41	16 *	13.66	-	-	10	-							
1-day Int																	
NatWest																	
B & H	4	4	1	105	60	35.00	-	1	-	-							
Sunday																	

SWANN, A. J. — Northamptonshire

Name: Alec James Swann
Role: Right-hand opening bat, occasional wicket-keeper
Born: 26 October 1976, Northampton
Height: 6ft 2in **Weight:** 12st 6lbs
Nickname: Ron, Swanny
County debut: 1996
1st-Class 50s: 2
1st-Class 100s: 1
1st-Class catches: 7
Place in batting averages: 244th av. 14.70
Parents: Ray and Mavis
Marital status: Single
Family links with cricket: Dad played for Northumberland, Bedfordshire, Northants II and England Amateurs. Still plays local league cricket. Brother Graeme selected for England A (winter 1998-99)
Education: Sponne Comprehensive, Towcester
Qualifications: 9 GCSEs, 4 A-levels, NCA coaching award
Off-season: Playing in Cape Town for Montrose CC

Overseas tours: Northants to Zimbabwe 1998
Overseas teams played for: Wallsend, NSW, Australia 1995-96, 1997-98; Montrose CC, Cape Town 1998-99
Cricketers particularly admired: Mark and Steve Waugh, Robin Smith, Russell Warren
Young players to look out for: John Blain, Richard Logan
Other sports played: 'Used to play football; now just golf every now and then'
Other sports followed: Most sports except athletics
Relaxations: 'I enjoy gambling on horses and sometimes on football or cricket', reading political thrillers, watching films
Extras: Played for England Schools U15 and U19. Opened batting for Bedfordshire (with father in Minor Counties game). *Daily Telegraph* U15 Young Cricketer of the Year 1992. Midlands Club Cricket Conference Young Cricketer of the Year 1992. Played for England U19 against New Zealand in 1996
Opinions on cricket: 'I like the idea of a national one-day league, one cup competition and a two-divisional championship. County cricket is not as soft or as uncompetitive as people seem to believe, but some slight adjustments to the system could improve county cricket for the better. Day/night cricket should be given an increased priority.'
Best batting: 136 Northamptonshire v Warwickshire, Edgbaston 1997

1998 Season

	M	Inns	NO	Runs	HS	Avge	100s	50s	Ct	St	O	M	Runs	Wkts	Avge	Best	5wI	10wM
Test																		
All First	11	17	0	250	85	14.70	-	1	6	-	6.3	0	59	0	-	-	-	-
1-day Int																		
NatWest																		
B & H																		
Sunday																		

Career Performances

	M	Inns	NO	Runs	HS	Avge	100s	50s	Ct	St	Balls	Runs	Wkts	Avge	Best	5wI	10wM
Test																		
All First	16	25	1	512	136	21.33	1	2	7	-	69	74	0	-	-	-	-
1-day Int																		
NatWest																		
B & H																		
Sunday																		

SWANN, G. P.   Northamptonshire

Name: Graeme Peter Swann
Role: Right-hand bat, off-spin bowler
Born: 24 March 1979, Northampton
Height: 6ft **Weight:** 11st 7lbs
Nickname: Swanny, Flymo, G-spot,
Guppy, Shark
County debut: 1997 (one-day),
1998 (first-class)
1st-Class 50s: 2
1st-Class 100s: 1
1st-Class 5 w. in innings: 1
1st-Class catches: 7
Place in batting averages: 67th av. 34.25
Place in bowling averages: 86th av. 30.27
Strike rate: 54.45 (career 54.45)
Parents: Raymond and Mavis
Marital status: Single
Family links with cricket: Dad has played
Minor Counties cricket for Bedfordshire and
Northumberland and also for England Amateurs. Brother is contracted to Northants
Education: Abington Vale Lower School; Sponne School, Towcester
Qualifications: 10 GCSEs, 4 A-levels, NCA coaching award
Off-season: England A tour to Zimbabwe and South Africa
Overseas tours: England U19 to South Africa 1997-98, England A to Zimbabwe and
South Africa 1998-99
Cricketers particularly admired: Mark and Steve Waugh, Don Bradman, Neil Foster
Young players to look out for: Jason Brown, Richard Logan, Alec Swann
Other sports followed: Football (Newcastle United), rugby (Northampton Saints)
Injuries: 'Out for two and a half hours with a sore knee'
Relaxations: 'Spending money, going out, watching TV, listening to music'
Extras: Played for England U14, U15, U17 and U19. *Daily Telegraph* regional
bowling award winner in 1994. Gray-Nicolls Len Newbery Schools Cricketer of the
Year in 1996. Took 8-118 for England U19 in second 'Test' v Pakistan U19, the best-
ever figures in an U19 'Test'. Scored 92 and 111 in Championship match v
Leicestershire at Grace Road in 1998
Best batting: 111 Northamptonshire v Leicestershire, Leicester 1998
Best bowling: 5-29 Northamptonshire v Sussex, Northampton 1998

1998 Season

	M	Inns	NO	Runs	HS	Avge	100s	50s	Ct	St	O	M	Runs	Wkts	Avge	Best	5wI	10wM
Test																		
All First	14	18	2	548	111	34.25	1	2	7	-	199.4	41	666	22	30.27	5-29	1	-
1-day Int																		
NatWest																		
B & H	1	0	0	0	0	-	-	-	-	-	6	0	14	1	14.00	1-14	-	
Sunday	6	2	1	16	10 *	16.00	-	-	1	-	18.3	0	146	5	29.20	2-5	-	

Career Performances

	M	Inns	NO	Runs	HS	Avge	100s	50s	Ct	St	Balls	Runs	Wkts	Avge	Best	5wI	10wM
Test																	
All First	14	18	2	548	111	34.25	1	2	7	-	1198	666	22	30.27	5-29	1	-
1-day Int																	
NatWest																	
B & H	1	0	0	0	0	-	-	-	-	-	36	14	1	14.00	1-14	-	
Sunday	10	4	2	16	10 *	8.00	-	-	1	-	303	274	10	27.40	2-5	-	

SYMINGTON, M. J. Durham

Name: Marc Joseph Symington
Role: Right-hand bat, right-arm medium bowler, all-rounder
Born: 10 January 1980, Newcastle-upon-Tyne
Height: 5ft 9in **Weight:** 10st 8lbs
Nickname: Simo
County debut: 1998
Parents: Keith and Sheila
Marital status: Single
Family links with cricket: Grandfather (Ron Symington) played 24 years in Northumberland League, then umpired in same league for 21 years. Father currently plays for Norton CC in NYSD League. Brother (Craig) plays for Norton CC and Cleveland county U15. Mother is fixtures secretary for Norton CC
Education: St Joseph's, Norton, Stockton-on-Tees; St Michael's, Billingham, Stockton-on-Tees; Stockton Sixth Form College
Qualifications: 5 GCSEs, cricket coaching award
Career outside cricket: Student

Off-season: Preparing for England U19 tour to New Zealand
Overseas tours: Durham U21 to Sri Lanka 1996; England U19 to New Zealand 1998-99
Cricketers particularly admired: Ian Botham, Graham Thorpe, Allan Donald
Young players to look out for: Michael Gough, Ian Hunter, John Inglis
Other sports followed: Football (Middlesbrough)
Injuries: Out for three weeks with a side strain
Relaxations: Playing snooker and golf
Opinions on cricket: 'Cameras are too involved with decisions. Umpires should be left to make up their own minds except in run-out situations.'
Best batting: 8* Durham v Cambridge University, Fenner's 1998
Best bowling: 3-55 Durham v Derbyshire, Derby 1998

1998 Season

	M	Inns	NO	Runs	HS	Avge	100s	50s	Ct	St	O	M	Runs	Wkts	Avge	Best	5wI	10wM
Test																		
All First	2	1	1	8	8*	-	-	-	1	-	36.2	7	148	6	24.66	3-55	--	
1-day Int																		
NatWest																		
B & H																		
Sunday	1	0	0	0	0	-	-	-	-	-								

Career Performances

	M	Inns	NO	Runs	HS	Avge	100s	50s	Ct	St	Balls	Runs	Wkts	Avge	Best	5wI	10wM
Test																		
All First	2	1	1	8	8*	-	-	-	1	-	218	148	6	24.66	3-55	-	-
1-day Int																		
NatWest																		
B & H																		
Sunday	2	1	0	7	7	7.00	-	-	1	-	42	51	1	51.00	1-51	-	

TAYLOR, J. P. Northamptonshire

Name: Jonathan Paul Taylor
Role: Left-hand bat, left-arm
fast-medium bowler
Born: 8 August 1964, Ashby-de-la-Zouch,
Leicestershire
Height: 6ft 2in **Weight:** 14st
Nickname: Roadie, PT
County debut: 1984 (Derbyshire),
1991 (Northamptonshire)
County cap: 1992 (Northamptonshire)
Test debut: 1992-93
Tests: 2
One-Day Internationals: 1
50 wickets in a season: 6
1st-Class 50s: 7
1st-Class 5 w. in innings: 16
1st-Class 10 w. in match: 3
1st-Class catches: 50

Place in batting averages: 173rd av. 21.82
(1997 272nd av. 12.70)
Place in bowling averages: 45th av. 24.75 (1997 58th av. 28.37)
Strike rate: 48.53 (career 55.55)
Parents: Derek (deceased) and Janet
Wife and date of marriage: Elaine Mary, 30 July 1993
Children: Christopher Paul, 8 July 1994; Danny Michael, 6 February 1997
Family links with cricket: Father and brother played local league cricket
Education: Pingle School, Swadlincote, Derbyshire
Qualifications: 6 O-levels, NCA senior coach
Off-season: 'Keeping out of mischief!!!'
Overseas tours: Midland Club Cricket Conference to Australia 1990-91; England to
India and Sri Lanka 1992-93; England A to South Africa 1993-94; Northamptonshire
to Natal 1993, to Zimbabwe 1995, 1998, to Johannesburg 1996
Overseas teams played for: Papakura, New Zealand 1984-85; Napier High School
Old Boys, New Zealand 1985-86; North Kalgoorlie, Western Australia 1990-91;
Great Boulder, Western Australia 1991-92; Montrose CC, Cape Town
Cricketers particularly admired: Dennis Lillee, Courtney Walsh, Curtly Ambrose
Young players to look out for: Jason Brown, Michael Davies, Graeme Swann
('the Spin Triplets'), Richard Logan
Other sports followed: Soccer, rugby, basketball
Relaxations: 'Looking after two hyperactive little lads. Relaxing...I think not;
enjoyable...definitely!!!'

Extras: Spent four seasons on the staff at Derbyshire 1984-87 and played Minor Counties cricket for Staffordshire 1989-90. Won Man of the Match in the Bain Clarkson Final in 1987 for Derbyshire, after being released. Played first game at Lord's in NatWest Trophy final 1992. Was voted Northamptonshire's Player of the Year in 1992. Called up as replacement during England A tour to South Africa 1993-94. Selected for England Indoor World Cup squad 1995

Opinions on cricket: 'Some way needs to be found to enable our international players to have sufficient rest in between games. One-day "Super Cup" for our top eight four-day sides – I think that sums up our game at the moment.'

Best batting: 86 Northamptonshire v Durham, Northampton 1995
Best bowling: 7-23 Northamptonshire v Hampshire, Bournemouth 1992

1998 Season

	M	Inns	NO	Runs	HS	Avge	100s	50s	Ct	St	O	M	Runs	Wkts	Avge	Best	5wl	10wM
Test																		
All First	15	20	3	371	58	21.82	-	3	5	-	436.5	105	1337	54	24.75	4-31	-	-
1-day Int																		
NatWest	1	1	1	3	3*	-	-	-	-	-	12	2	54	2	27.00	2-54	-	
B & H	3	3	0	26	14	8.66	-	-	1	-	30	3	170	3	56.66	2-57	-	
Sunday	12	4	1	20	19	6.66	-	-	6	-	80	6	356	13	27.38	2-18	-	

Career Performances

	M	Inns	NO	Runs	HS	Avge	100s	50s	Ct	St	Balls	Runs	Wkts	Avge	Best	5wl	10wM
Test	2	4	2	34	17*	17.00	-	-	-	-	288	156	3	52.00	1-18	-	-
All First	147	165	59	1568	86	14.79	-	7	50	-	25443	13306	458	29.05	7-23	16	3
1-day Int	1	1	0	1	1	1.00	-	-	-	-	18	20	0	-	-	-	
NatWest	27	11	6	34	9	6.80	-	-	6	-	1653	1070	37	28.91	4-34	-	
B & H	32	14	7	62	14	8.85	-	-	6	-	1797	1101	42	26.21	5-45	1	
Sunday	108	36	17	180	24	9.47	-	-	23	-	4656	3597	121	29.72	3-14	-	

79. What was unusual about Sunil Gavaskar's 36*
v England at Lord's in the 1975 World Cup?

FIGA

TAYLOR, N. R. Sussex

Name: Neil Royston Taylor
Role: Right-hand bat, occasional
off-spin bowler
Born: 21 July 1959, Farnborough, Kent
Height: 6ft 1in **Weight:** 15st
Nickname: Map
County debut: 1979 (Kent), 1997 (Sussex)
County cap: 1982 (Kent)
Benefit: 1992 (£131,000)
1000 runs in a season: 11
1st-Class 50s: 91
1st-Class 100s: 43
1st-Class 200s: 2
1st-Class catches: 158
One-Day 100s: 6
Place in batting averages: 75th av. 32.42
(1997 74th av. 38.25)
Strike rate: (career 98.43)
Parents: Leonard and Audrey
Marital status: Divorced; girlfriend Leigh
Children: Amy Louise, 7 November 1985; Lauren, 21 July 1988
Family links with cricket: Brother Colin played for Kent U19. Father played club cricket
Education: Cray Valley Technical High School
Qualifications: 8 O-levels, 2 A-levels, advanced cricket coach
Off-season: 'Looking for a full-time job'
Overseas tours: English Schools to India 1977-78; Kent to Canada 1978, to
Zimbabwe 1992-93; Fred Rumsey XI to West Indies 1988
Overseas teams played for: Randburg, Johannesburg 1979-85; St Stithian's College,
Johannesburg (as coach) 1980-85
Cricketers particularly admired: Chris Tavaré, Mark Benson, Mike Gatting,
Robin Smith
Other sports played: Golf
Other sports followed: Rugby union (Westcombe Park RFC), golf, football (Chelsea)
Injuries: Out for nine weeks with knee ligament problems
Relaxations: Music and reading (mainly biographies)
Extras: Made 110 on debut for Kent v Sri Lankans, 1979. Won four Man of the Match
awards in his first five matches and scored three successive centuries in the B&H.
Played for England B v Pakistan, 1982 and twice fielded as 12th man for England –
v India in 1982 and v West Indies in 1988, both matches at The Oval. Holds Kent first
and second wicket record partnerships with Mark Benson (300 v Derbyshire) and
Simon Hinks (366 v Middlesex). Only Kent player to score 200 and 100 in a match

twice (204 and 142 v Surrey, 111 and 203* v Sussex). Has scored 13 centuries at Canterbury, beating Frank Woolley and Colin Cowdrey. Provides a weekly contribution to Radio Kent through the summer. Joined Sussex for the 1997 season and scored a century on debut, placing him in a unique club alongside Peter Bowler (Somerset) and Jon Lewis (Durham) of players who have scored centuries on debut for two different counties. Retired at the end of the 1998 season

Best batting: 204 Kent v Surrey, Canterbury 1990
Best bowling: 2-20 Kent v Somerset, Canterbury 1985

1998 Season

	M	Inns	NO	Runs	HS	Avge	100s	50s	Ct	St	O	M	Runs	Wkts	Avge	Best	5wI	10wM
Test																		
All First	6	8	1	227	74*	32.42	-	2	4	-								
1-day Int																		
NatWest	1	1	0	1	1	1.00	-	-	1	-								
B & H																		
Sunday																		

Career Performances

	M	Inns	NO	Runs	HS	Avge	100s	50s	Ct	St	Balls	Runs	Wkts	Avge	Best	5wI	10wM
Test																	
All First	325	551	70	19031	204	39.56	45	91	158	-	1575	891	16	55.68	2-20	-	-
1-day Int																	
NatWest	36	35	1	891	86	26.20	-	5	8	-	143	86	6	14.33	3-29	-	
B & H	56	53	2	2122	137	41.60	6	8	14	-	12	5	0	-	-	-	
Sunday	155	149	15	4026	95	30.04	-	24	40	-							

80. Who holds the record for the highest score
by an England batsman in the World Cup?

FICA

THOMAS, I. J. Glamorgan

Name: Ian James Thomas
Role: Left-hand top-order bat,
off-spin bowler
Born: 9 May 1979
Height: 6ft **Weight:** 12st
Nickname: Bolts
County debut: 1998
1st-Class catches: 2
Parents: Mandy and Alun
Marital status: Single
Family links with cricket: Father plays local
league cricket
Education: Machen Primary School;
Bassaleg Comprehensive; UWIC
Qualifications: GCSEs, A-levels,
cricket coaching
Career outside cricket: Sports development
Off-season: Studying for a Sports
Development degree at UWIC

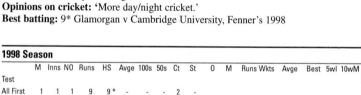

Overseas tours: Wales U16 to Isle of Wight 1994, to Jersey 1995
Cricketers particularly admired: Brian Lara, Hugh Morris
Young players to look out for: Wayne Law, Carwin James
Other sports played: Rugby, golf
Other sports followed: Rugby (Newport RFC)
Injuries: Out for six weeks after having part of a disc removed from back
Relaxations: Sleeping, watching sport and training
Extras: Released by Glamorgan at end of 1998 season
Opinions on cricket: 'More day/night cricket.'
Best batting: 9* Glamorgan v Cambridge University, Fenner's 1998

1998 Season

	M	Inns	NO	Runs	HS	Avge	100s	50s	Ct	St	O	M	Runs	Wkts	Avge	Best	5wI	10wM
Test																		
All First	1	1	1	9	9*	-	-	-	2	-								
1-day Int																		
NatWest																		
B & H																		
Sunday																		

Career Performances

	M	Inns	NO	Runs	HS	Avge	100s	50s	Ct	St	Balls	Runs	Wkts	Avge	Best	5wI	10wM
Test																	
All First	1	1	1	9	9*	-		-	-	2	-						
1-day Int																	
NatWest																	
B & H																	
Sunday																	

THOMAS, S. D. Glamorgan

Name: Stuart Darren Thomas
Role: Left-hand bat, right-arm medium-fast bowler
Born: 25 January 1975, Morriston
Height: 6ft **Weight:** 12st 9lbs
Nickname: Teddy, Tedrick, Thomo
County debut: 1992
50 wickets in a season: 2
1st-Class 50s: 7
1st-Class 5 w. in innings: 11
1st-Class catches: 27
One-Day 5 w. in innings: 3
Place in batting averages: 169th av. 22.04
(1997 212th av. 20.00)
Place in bowling averages: 43rd av. 24.63
(1997 49th av. 27.24)
Strike rate: 45.98 (career 51.64)
Parents: Stuart and Anne
Marital status: 'Courting Clare very strongly'
Family links with cricket: 'Dad played local cricket'
Education: Craig Comprehensive; Neath Tertiary College
Qualifications: 4 GCSEs, BTEC National Diploma in Sports Science, NCA coaching certificate
Overseas tours: England U18 to South Africa 1992-93; Glamorgan to South Africa 1992-93, to Portugal 1994, to Zimbabwe 1995; England U19 to Sri Lanka 1993-94; England A to Zimbabwe and South Africa 1998-99
Cricketers particularly admired: Dean Cosker 'for his natural length'
Young players to look out for: Alun 'face like a clock' Evans 'for his pulling ability'
Other sports followed: Rugby union and league (Warrington)
Relaxations: 'Talking smut with Dean Cosker. Spending a lot of time horseriding with my girlfriend. Surfing off the Gower coastline'

Extras: Youngest player to take five wickets on debut v Derbyshire in 1992 and finished eighth in national bowling averages. BBC Welsh Young Sports Personality 1992. Played last U19 'Test' against India at Edgbaston 1994. Broke Alan Wilkins' (Glamorgan) best Benson and Hedges bowling record on his debut in the competition with 6 for 20 in 1995. Took 7-16 v Surrey in the Sunday League in 1998, the best analysis by a Glamorgan bowler in the competition

Opinions on cricket: 'Best game in the world.'

Best batting: 78* Glamorgan v Gloucestershire, Abergavenny 1995

Best bowling: 5-24 Glamorgan v Sussex, Swansea 1997

Stop press: Took 8-50 for England A v Zimbabwe A on 1998-99 tour – the first eight-wicket haul by an England A tourist

1998 Season

	M	Inns	NO	Runs	HS	Avge	100s	50s	Ct	St	O	M	Runs	Wkts	Avge	Best	5wI	10wM
Test																		
All First	18	26	3	507	74	22.04	-	3	10	-	544.1	94	1749	71	24.63	5-84	3	-
1-day Int																		
NatWest	2	2	1	39	28 *	39.00	-	-	2	-	20.3	2	72	4	18.00	2-31	-	
B & H	4	3	0	54	29	18.00	-	-	-	-	22	0	131	3	43.66	2-53	-	
Sunday	11	11	0	98	21	8.90	-	-	1	-	66.5	1	347	20	17.35	7-16	1	

Career Performances

	M	Inns	NO	Runs	HS	Avge	100s	50s	Ct	St	Balls	Runs	Wkts	Avge	Best	5wI	10wM
Test																	
All First	71	95	22	1435	78 *	19.65	-	7	27	-	11361	7001	220	31.82	5-24	11	-
1-day Int																	
NatWest	7	5	1	54	28 *	13.50	-	-	2	-	435	334	12	27.83	5-74	1	
B & H	13	8	3	95	29	19.00	-	-	5	-	560	502	20	25.10	6-20	1	
Sunday	32	23	3	200	21	10.00	-	-	5	-	1070	932	35	26.62	7-16	1	

THOMPSON, J. B. de C.   Kent

Name: Julian Barton de Courcy Thompson

Role: Right-hand bat, right-arm fast-medium bowler

Born: 28 October 1968, Cape Town, South Africa

Height: 6ft 5in **Weight:** 13st 7lbs

Nickname: Doc, Bambi, Thommo

County debut: 1994

1st-Class 50s: 2

1st-Class 5 w. in innings: 2

1st-Class catches: 4

Place in batting averages: (1997 258th av. 15.14)

Place in bowling averages: 90th av. 30.45 (1997 62nd av. 28.70)
Strike rate: 52.18 (career 49.79)
Parents: John and Joyce
Wife and date of marriage: Tanya, 4 October 1997
Family links with cricket: 'Wife a keen supporter and follower (?!)'
Education: Holmewood House School, Tunbridge Wells, Kent; The Judd School, Tonbridge, Kent; Guy's Hospital Medical School, University of London
Qualifications: MBBS, basic coaching certificate
Career outside cricket: Doctor (Obstetrics and Gynaecology)
Off-season: Senior House Officer at Kent and Canterbury Hospital
Overseas tours: University of London to India 1991
Overseas teams played for: Northern Districts CC, Sydney 1987-88
Cricketers particularly admired: Courtney Walsh, Glenn McGrath, Allan Donald
Young players to look out for: Robert Key, Darren Scott
Other sports played: Squash, golf
Other sports followed: Football (Liverpool), golf
Injuries: Thigh strain, side strain, stress fracture of right fibula – 'season ended on 23 August'
Relaxations: Travel, good food, fine wines, cinema, quiet nights in
Extras: Dismissed Brian Lara twice for a duck in Kent's game against the West Indies in 1995 – Brian Lara's only pair in first-class cricket. Dismissed three England captains in first month of the 1996 season – Atherton, Gatting and Gooch
Opinions on cricket: 'Pitches should be better, preferably prepared by neutral groundsmen, with no influence from either team.'
Best batting: 65* Kent v Oxford University, Canterbury 1998
Best bowling: 5-72 Kent v Surrey, The Oval 1996

1998 Season

	M	Inns	NO	Runs	HS	Avge	100s	50s	Ct	St	O	M	Runs	Wkts	Avge	Best	5wI	10wM
Test																		
All First	4	6	4	89	65*	44.50	-	1	-	-	95.4	20	335	11	30.45	4-52	-	-
1-day Int																		
NatWest																		
B & H																		
Sunday	2	1	1	1	1*	-	-	-	-	-	11	3	27	2	13.50	2-16	-	

Career Performances

	M	Inns	NO	Runs	HS	Avge	100s	50s	Ct	St	Balls	Runs	Wkts	Avge	Best	5wI	10wM
Test																	
All First	22	29	10	370	65 *	19.47	-	2	4	-	2888	1838	58	31.68	5-72	2	
1-day Int																	
NatWest																	
B & H	4	3	2	17	12 *	17.00	-	-	-	-	180	114	6	19.00	3-29	-	
Sunday	29	16	9	75	30	10.71	-	-	3	-	928	723	22	32.86	3-17	-	

THORPE, G. P. Surrey

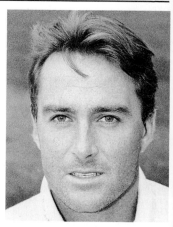

Name: Graham Paul Thorpe
Role: Left-hand bat, occasional right-arm
medium bowler
Born: 1 August 1969, Farnham
Height: 5ft 10in **Weight:** 12st
Nickname: Chalky
County debut: 1988
County cap: 1991
Test debut: 1993
Tests: 52
One-Day Internationals: 44
1000 runs in a season: 8
1st-Class 50s: 87
1st-Class 100s: 30
1st-Class 200s: 2
1st-Class catches: 186
One-Day 100s: 6
Place in batting averages: 134th av. 26.16
(1997 7th av. 61.05)
Strike rate: (career 89.24)
Parents: 'Mr and Mrs Thorpe'
Wife: Nicola
Family links with cricket: Both brothers play for Farnham, father also plays cricket
and mother is 'professional scorer'
Education: Weydon Comprehensive; Farnham Sixth Form College
Qualifications: 7 O-levels, PE Diploma
Overseas tours: England A to Zimbabwe and Kenya 1989-90, to Pakistan 1990-91,
to Bermuda and West Indies 1991-92, to Australia 1992-93; England to West Indies
1993-94, to Australia 1994-95, to South Africa 1995-96, to India and Pakistan
(World Cup) 1995-96, to Zimbabwe and New Zealand 1996-97, to Sharjah
(Champions Trophy) 1997-98, to West Indies 1997-98, to Australia 1998-99

Cricketers particularly admired: Viv Richards, Grahame Clinton, David Gower
Young players to look out for: Ben Hollioake
Other sports followed: Football (Chelsea FC), golf
Relaxations: Sleeping
Extras: Played for English Schools cricket U15 and U19 and England Schools football U18. Scored a century against Australia on his Test debut at Trent Bridge 1993. Arrived a few days late for the Zimbabwe leg of England's tour to attend the birth of his son. He scored hundreds in successive Tests during the winter tour to New Zealand. England's Player of the Series and leading run scorer in the 1997 Ashes campaign with 453 runs at an average of 50.33. Shared in a record England v West Indies sixth wicket Test partnership (205) with Mark Ramprakash at Bridgetown 1997-98. A back injury suffered during the 1997-98 West Indies tour affected his availability for England in the 1998 season. One of *Wisden*'s five Cricketers of the Year 1998. Named Cornhill England Player of the Year 1998
Best batting: 222 Surrey v Glamorgan, The Oval 1997
Best bowling: 4-40 Surrey v Australians, The Oval 1993
Stop press: During 1998-99 Ashes tour, put on 377 for England with Mark Ramprakash in an unbroken fifth wicket stand v South Australia in Adelaide, the highest stand by any touring team in Australia, finishing with a new career best 223*. Forced to return early from the 1998-99 Ashes tour with recurrence of back injury

1998 Season

	M	Inns	NO	Runs	HS	Avge	100s	50s	Ct	St	O	M	Runs	Wkts	Avge	Best	5wI	10wM
Test	3	6	0	63	43	10.50	-	-	-	-								
All First	9	13	1	314	114	26.16	1	1	10	-								
1-day Int																		
NatWest	1	1	0	17	17	17.00	-	-	-	-								
B & H	6	6	1	293	85 *	58.60	-	3	1	-								
Sunday	5	4	0	35	14	8.75	-	-	1	-								

Career Performances

	M	Inns	NO	Runs	HS	Avge	100s	50s	Ct	St	Balls	Runs	Wkts	Avge	Best	5wI	10wM
Test	52	95	11	3366	138	40.07	6	23	48	-	138	37	0	-	-	-	-
All First	233	390	54	14965	222	44.53	32	87	186	-	2231	1248	25	49.92	4-40	-	-
1-day Int	44	44	7	1482	89	40.05	-	14	24	-	120	97	2	48.50	2-15	-	-
NatWest	24	23	4	824	145 *	43.36	1	6	13	-	13	12	0	-	-	-	-
B & H	43	42	4	1532	103	40.31	1	11	20	-	168	131	4	32.75	3-35	-	
Sunday	113	103	14	3123	115 *	35.08	4	21	42	-	318	307	8	38.37	3-21	-	

TITCHARD, S. P.   Lancashire

Name: Stephen Paul Titchard
Role: Right-hand bat, right-arm medium
bowler
Born: 17 December 1967,
Warrington, Cheshire
Height: 6ft 3in **Weight:** 15st
Nickname: Titch, Stainy, Tyrone
County debut: 1990
1st-Class 50s: 25
1st-Class 100s: 4
1st-Class catches: 52
Place in batting averages:
(1997 211th av. 20.00)
Strike rate: 30.00 (career 78.00)
Parents: Alan and Margaret
Marital status: Single
Family links with cricket: Father, uncle and
two brothers have played for Grappenhall 1st
XI in the Manchester Association League.
Father also represented the Army
Education: Lymm County High School; Priestley College
Qualifications: 3 O-levels, NCA senior coaching award
Career outside cricket: Coach
Overseas tours: Lancashire to Tasmania and Western Australia 1990, to Western
Australia 1991, to Johannesburg 1992
Overseas teams played for: South Canberra, Australia 1991-92
Cricketers particularly admired: Graham Gooch, Malcolm Marshall
Other sports followed: Football (Manchester City) and rugby league (Warrington)
Relaxations: Snooker, golf, 'most sports'
Extras: Played for England U19. Made record scores for Manchester Association U18
(200*) and Cheshire Schools U19 (203*). Released by Lancashire at end of 1998
season
Best batting: 163 Lancashire v Essex, Chelmsford 1996
Best bowling: 1-11 Lancashire v Northamptonshire, Old Trafford 1997
           1-11 Lancashire v Kent, Old Trafford 1997

---

81. Which Australian batsman scored 110 on his World Cup
debut v India at Trent Bridge in 1983?

FICA

1998 Season

	M	Inns	NO	Runs	HS	Avge	100s	50s	Ct	St	O	M	Runs	Wkts	Avge	Best	5wI	10wM
Test																		
All First	1	0	0	0	0	-	-	-	-	-	-							
1-day Int																		
NatWest																		
B & H																		
Sunday																		

Career Performances

	M	Inns	NO	Runs	HS	Avge	100s	50s	Ct	St	Balls	Runs	Wkts	Avge	Best	5wI	10wM
Test																	
All First	76	131	8	3945	163	32.07	4	25	52	-	312	171	4	42.75	1-11	-	-
1-day Int																	
NatWest	3	3	0	116	92	38.66	-	1	1	-							
B & H	3	3	0	101	82	33.66	-	1	1	-							
Sunday	29	29	3	705	96	27.11	-	3	4	-							

TOLLEY, C. M.   Nottinghamshire

Name: Christopher Mark Tolley
Role: Right-hand bat, left-arm
medium bowler
Born: 30 December 1967, Kidderminster
Height: 5ft 9in **Weight:** 11st 12lbs
Nickname: Red Dog, Red'uns,
Ginger Warrior
County debut: 1989 (Worcestershire),
1996 (Nottinghamshire)
County cap: 1993 (Worcestershire)
1st-Class 50s: 10
1st-Class 5 w. in innings: 5
1st-Class catches: 40
One-Day 5 w. in innings: 1
Place in batting averages: 170th av. 22.00
(1997 146th av. 26.61)
Place in bowling averages: 72nd av. 28.23
(1997 63rd av. 28.71)
Strike rate: 57.26 (career 71.44)
Parents: Ray and Liz
Wife and date of marriage: Simone, 12 December 1998
Family links with cricket: Brother Richard plays in the Birmingham League for
Stourbridge

Education: Oldswinford Primary School; Redhill Comprehensive School; King Edward VI College, Stourbridge; Loughborough University
Qualifications: 9 O-levels, 3 A-levels, BSc (Hons) PE, Sports Science & Recreation Management, Dip SMT. Qualified teacher and level 2 hockey coach
Career outside cricket: PE teacher
Off-season: Working as sports massage therapist
Overseas tours: British Universities Sports Federation tour to Barbados, October 1989; Worcestershire to Zimbabwe and South Africa
Overseas teams played for: Lancaster Park, Christchurch, New Zealand 1996-97
Cricketers particularly admired: Ian Botham, Graeme Hick
Young players to look out for: Andy Oram, Jamie Hart
Other sports followed: Hockey
Injuries: Out for one month with torn calf
Relaxations: Food and wine
Extras: Played for English Schools U19 in 1986 and for the Combined Universities in B&H Cup. Asked to be released by Worcestershire at the end of the 1995 season and joined Nottinghamshire for the 1996 season. Took first-class hat-trick against Leicestershire in 1997
Best batting: 84 Worcestershire v Derbyshire, Derby 1994
Best bowling: 7-45 Nottinghamshire v Worcestershire, Kidderminster 1998

1998 Season

	M	Inns	NO	Runs	HS	Avge	100s	50s	Ct	St	O	M	Runs	Wkts	Avge	Best	5wl	10wM
Test																		
All First	11	19	2	374	78	22.00	-	2	5	-	324.3	76	960	34	28.23	7-45	3	-
1-day Int																		
NatWest	3	3	0	91	77	30.33	-	1	1	-	31	6	92	4	23.00	2-16	-	
B & H																		
Sunday	12	10	1	185	44	20.55	-	-	4	-	76	2	346	13	26.61	3-22	-	

Career Performances

	M	Inns	NO	Runs	HS	Avge	100s	50s	Ct	St	Balls	Runs	Wkts	Avge	Best	5wl	10wM
Test																	
All First	96	131	30	2337	84	23.13	-	10	40	-	12860	6317	180	35.09	7-45	5	-
1-day Int																	
NatWest	11	8	3	158	77	31.60	-	1	1	-	618	350	15	23.33	3-21	-	
B & H	20	17	2	355	77	23.66	-	3	3	-	978	633	9	70.33	1-12	-	
Sunday	72	44	11	553	44	16.75	-	-	24	-	2416	1962	75	26.16	5-16	1	

TOMLINSON, S. C. B. — Glamorgan

Name: Steven Charles Benjamin Tomlinson
Role: Right-hand bat, right-arm medium bowler
Born: 21 December 1978, Bridgetown, Barbados
Height: 5ft 11in **Weight:** 13st
Nickname: Tomo, Louise
County debut: 1998 (one-day)
Parents: Paul and Jan
Marital status: Single
Family links with cricket: Dad is chairman of The Crossbatters CC touring side
Education: The Oratory Prep School; The Oratory School, Reading; University of Wales Institute, Cardiff (Sports Science)
Qualifications: 9 GCSEs, 3 A-levels
Career outside cricket: Plays real tennis. Student

Off-season: University and training
Overseas tours: The Oratory School to Barbados 1996
Cricketers particularly admired: Viv Richards, Jonty Rhodes
Young players to look out for: Wayne Law, Tim Phillips
Other sports played: Real tennis (British and American U19 champion)
Other sports followed: Football (Spurs, Chester City)
Injuries: Out for three weeks with hip injury
Relaxations: Playing golf. Relaxing with friends
Extras: Represented England U14. HMC U15 and U19. Schoolboy All-rounder award 1996, 1997. Released by Glamorgan at end of 1998 season
Opinions on cricket: '1. All 2nd XI games should be played on 1st XI wickets. 2. There should be a 2nd XI Sunday league.'

1998 Season

	M	Inns	NO	Runs	HS	Avge	100s	50s	Ct	St	O	M	Runs	Wkts	Avge	Best	5wI	10wM
Test																		
All First																		
1-day Int																		
NatWest																		
B & H																		
Sunday	2	1	0	2	2	2.00	-	-	1	-	8	0	41	0	-	-	-	-

Career Performances

	M	Inns	NO	Runs	HS	Avge	100s	50s	Ct	St	Balls	Runs	Wkts	Avge	Best	5wl	10wM
Test																	
All First																	
1-day Int																	
NatWest																	
B & H																	
Sunday	2	1	0	2	2	2.00	-	-	1	-	48	41	0	-		-	-

TRAINOR, N. J. Gloucestershire

Name: Nicholas James Trainor
Role: Right-hand opening bat, off-spin
bowler
Born: 29 June 1975, Gateshead
Height: 6ft 2in **Weight:** 14st
Nickname: Big Red, Geordie
County debut: 1996
1st-Class 50s: 4
1st-Class 100s: 1
1st-Class catches: 12
One-Day 100s: 1
Place in batting averages: 253rd av. 13.62
(1997 208th av. 20.16)
Parents: Eric and Anna-Maria
Wife and date of marriage:
Sharyn, 7 March 1998
Family links with cricket: Father played
club cricket for Gateshead CC in the Durham
Senior League

Education: St Peters RC Primary School; St Edmund Campion Secondary School
Qualifications: 9 GCSEs, BTEC in Business and Finance, NCA cricket coach
Off-season: Playing in South Africa
Overseas teams played for: Triangle Rovers CC, South Africa 1994-95;
Zoo Lake CC, South Africa 1995-98; Marks Park, South Africa 1998-99
Cricketers particularly admired: Michael Atherton, Geoffrey Boycott, Robin Smith
Young players to look out for: Jon Lewis, Ben Gannon, N. Wake, J. Coetzee
Other sports played: Golf, tennis, squash, swimming
Other sports followed: Football (Newcastle United)
Injuries: Out for two months with twisted knee
Relaxations: 'Spending time with my wife and family'
Extras: Holds the record with Tony Wright for the highest partnership in the NatWest

competition with 311 against Scotland in 1997. Top run-scorer in South Africa Premier League for past two seasons

Opinions on cricket: 'Too much cricket is played. There is not enough time to have quality practice on good practice surfaces.'

Best batting: 121 Gloucestershire v Australia, Bristol 1997

1998 Season

	M	Inns	NO	Runs	HS	Avge	100s	50s	Ct	St	O	M	Runs	Wkts	Avge	Best	5wI	10wM
Test																		
All First	4	8	0	109	52	13.62	-	1	4	-								
1-day Int																		
NatWest																		
B & H	1	1	0	6	6	6.00	-	-	-	-								
Sunday	2	2	1	34	25	34.00	-	-	1	-								

Career Performances

	M	Inns	NO	Runs	HS	Avge	100s	50s	Ct	St	Balls	Runs	Wkts	Avge	Best	5wI	10wM
Test																		
All First	26	47	2	854	121	18.97	1	4	12	-	132	93	0	-	-	-	-
1-day Int																		
NatWest	3	3	0	186	143	62.00	1	-	1	-	48	49	2	24.50	2-25	-	
B & H	5	5	0	129	62	25.80	-	1	1	-	36	26	0	-	-	-	
Sunday	6	5	1	80	25	20.00	-	-	2	-	24	12	0	-	-	-	

<hr>

82. Who were the West Indies' opening bowlers
in the 1975 World Cup final?

FICA

TRESCOTHICK, M. E.   Somerset

Name: Marcus Edward Trescothick
Role: Left-hand bat, right-arm swing bowler,
reserve wicket-keeper, county vice-captain
Born: 25 December 1975, Keynsham, Bristol
Height: 6ft 3in **Weight:** 14st 7lbs
Nickname: Banger
County debut: 1993
1st-Class 50s: 21
1st-Class 100s: 4
1st-Class catches: 68
One-Day 100s: 2
Place in batting averages: 89th av. 31.37
(1997 199th av. 21.66)
Place in bowling averages: 124th av. 38.47
Strike rate: 68.29 (career 69.00)
Parents: Martyn and Lin
Marital status: Single
Family links with cricket: Father played for
Somerset 2nd XI; uncle played club cricket
Education: Sir Bernard Lovell School
Qualifications: 7 GCSEs
Career outside cricket: Playing abroad
Off-season: Playing in Perth for Melville CC
Overseas tours: England U18 to South Africa 1992-93; England U19 to Sri Lanka
1993-94, to West Indies (captain) 1994-95
Overseas teams played for: Melville CC, Perth 1997-99
Cricketers particularly admired: All my team-mates
Young players to look out for: Matt Bulbeck, Ben Trott
Other sports followed: Golf, football
Injuries: Prevented from bowling by disc problem in lower back
Relaxations: Playing golf, repairing and renovating cricket bats and listening to music
Extras: Member of England U19 squad for home series against West Indies 1993.
Man of the Series against India U19 in 1994, scoring most runs in the series.
Whittingdale Young Player of the Month, August 1994. Took a hat-trick against Young
Australia in 1995. Scored more than 1000 runs for England U19. Scored 322 in the
second innings of a 2nd XI game against Warwickshire in 1997 – Somerset were
chasing a target of 612 and Trescothick was the last man out with the score on 605!
Appointed vice-captain of Somerset for 1999
Opinions on cricket: 'There should be some sort of retainer contract.'
Best batting: 178 Somerset v Hampshire, Taunton 1996
Best bowling: 4-36 Somerset v Young Australia, Taunton 1995

1998 Season

	M	Inns	NO	Runs	HS	Avge	100s	50s	Ct	St	O	M	Runs	Wkts	Avge	Best	5wI	10wM
Test																		
All First	18	29	2	847	98	31.37	-	6	20	-	193.3	45	654	17	38.47	4-82	-	-
1-day Int																		
NatWest	2	1	0	22	22	22.00	-	-	-	-	15	1	64	2	32.00	2-49	-	
B & H	4	4	1	84	49	28.00	-	-	2	-	30	0	134	8	16.75	3-46	-	
Sunday	16	12	4	161	32	20.12	-	-	5	-	75	4	368	12	30.66	2-14	-	

Career Performances

	M	Inns	NO	Runs	HS	Avge	100s	50s	Ct	St	Balls	Runs	Wkts	Avge	Best	5wI	10wM
Test																	
All First	72	122	4	3312	178	28.06	4	21	68	-	1587	963	23	41.86	4-36	-	-
1-day Int																	
NatWest	6	5	0	211	116	42.20	1	-	2	-	108	92	2	46.00	2-49	-	
B & H	11	11	2	350	122	38.88	1	2	7	-	180	134	8	16.75	3-46	-	
Sunday	57	49	6	866	74	20.13	-	3	18	-	546	475	14	33.92	2-14	-	

TROTT, B. J.   Somerset

Name: Benjamin James Trott
Role: Right-hand bat, right-arm fast-medium bowler
Born: 14 March 1975, Wellington, Somerset
Height: 6ft 6in **Weight:** 14st 7lbs
Nickname: Trotty, Gallop
County debut: 1997
1st-Class catches: 1
Strike rate: 51.00 (career 37.71)
Parents: Alan Robert and Jane Elizabeth
Marital status: Single
Family links with cricket: Younger brother Thomas plays for Somerset youth teams
Education: Wellesley Park Primary School, Wellington; Court Fields Community School, Wellington; Richard Huish College, South Road, Taunton ('A-levels'); University College of St Mark and St John, Plymouth
Qualifications: 9 GCSEs, 3 A-levels, BEd (Hons)
Career outside cricket: Teacher of Physical Education
Off-season: 'Four months in Perth, Western Australia. Training hard for next season'

Overseas teams played for: Claremont Nedlands, Perth 1998-99
Cricketers particularly admired: Andrew Caddick, Graham Rose, Waqar Younis
Young players to look out for: Joe Tucker
Other sports followed: Football (Manchester United), rugby and basketball
Relaxations: Music, socialising, driving, swimming
Extras: Wellington Young Player of the Year in 1993. Wellington Players' Player of the Year in 1996
Opinions on cricket: 'There is an increased demand on improved mental and physical toughness.'
Best batting: 1* Somerset v Glamorgan, Taunton 1997
Best bowling: 3-74 Somerset v Glamorgan, Taunton 1997

1998 Season

	M	Inns	NO	Runs	HS	Avge	100s	50s	Ct	St	O	M	Runs	Wkts	Avge	Best	5wl	10wM
Test																		
All First	1	0	0	0	0	-	-	-	-	-	17	4	56	2	28.00	2-16	-	-
1-day Int																		
NatWest																		
B & H																		
Sunday																		

Career Performances

	M	Inns	NO	Runs	HS	Avge	100s	50s	Ct	St	Balls	Runs	Wkts	Avge	Best	5wl	10wM
Test																	
All First	3	2	1	1	1*	1.00	-	-	1	-	264	184	7	26.28	3-74	-	-
1-day Int																	
NatWest																	
B & H																	
Sunday	1	0	0	0	0	-	-	-	-	-	24	29	1	29.00	1-29	-

TUCKER, J.   Somerset

Name: Joe Tucker
Role: Right-hand bat, right-arm fast-medium bowler
Born: 14 September 1979, Bath
Height: 6ft 3in **Weight:** 13st
Nickname: Tucks, Smokey, Hugo, Farmer
County debut: No first-team appearance
Parents: Geoff and Chris
Marital status: Single
Family links with cricket: Father, brother and grandfather all played good club cricket

Education: Pensford Primary School, Bristol; Chew Valley and Colston Collegiate School, Bristol; Richard Huish College, Taunton

Qualifications: 9 GCSEs, NCA coaching award

Career outside cricket: Cricket coach

Overseas tours: West of England U16 to West Indies 1996; England U17 to Bermuda 1997; England U19 to South Africa (Youth World Cup) 1997-98

Young players to look out for: Stephen Peters, Paul Franks, Graham Napier, Owais Shah

Other sports followed: Football (Manchester United and Bristol City), squash, rugby (Bath RFC), basketball (Taunton Tigers) and 'my cousin, Martin, at motorcross'

Relaxations: Going to the gym. Going to the cinema and ten-pin bowling, listening to music. Spending time with my family, girlfriend and friends, eating out

Extras: Recorded the best bowling for Somerset 2nd XI in 1997 with 5 for 41 in the Bain Hogg Trophy against Worcestershire. Recorded the best bowling figures for England U17 in the International Youth tournament in Bermuda in 1997 with 4 for 41 against Holland. Made his 2nd XI debut for Somerset at the age of 15

Opinions on cricket: 'It's great that more and more youngsters are now getting into the game earlier and the game is becoming more competitive for places. It's also good to hear that we are trying to cut down on the number of games in the English summer so more people are more hungry for runs and wickets.'

83. Which member of the 1992 South Africa World Cup squad played for Derbyshire in 1990?

FICA

TUDOR, A. J. Surrey

Name: Alexander Jeremy Tudor
Role: Right-hand bat, right-arm fast bowler
Born: 23 October 1977,
West Brompton, London
Height: 6ft 4in **Weight:** 13st 7lbs
Nickname: Big Al, Bambi, Tudes
County debut: 1995
1st-Class 50s: 1
1st-Class 5 w. in innings: 3
1st-Class catches: 4
Place in batting averages: 226th av. 16.70
Place in bowling averages: 51st av. 25.41
(1997 103rd av. 35.70)
Strike rate: 38.13 (career 42.83)
Parents: Daryll and Jennifer
Marital status: Single
Family links with cricket: Brother was on
the staff at The Oval

Education: Wandle Primary, Earlsfield; St
Mark's C of E, Fulham; City of Westminster College
Overseas tours: England U15 to South Africa 1992-93; England U19 to Zimbabwe
1995-96, to Pakistan 1996-97; England to Australia 1998-99
Cricketers particularly admired: Curtly Ambrose, Brian Lara
Other sports followed: Basketball, football (QPR)
Relaxations: Listening to music
Extras: Played for London Schools at all ages from U8. Played for England U17
against India in 1994. MCC Young Cricketer. Had to return home from the England
U19 tour to Zimbabwe in 1995-96 through injury and subsequently missed the
majority of the 1996 season through injury. He toured Pakistan with England U19
in 1996-97
Best batting: 56 Surrey v Leicestershire, Leicester 1995
Best bowling: 6-101 Surrey v Gloucestershire, Gloucester 1997
Stop press: Made Test debut at Perth during 1998-99 Ashes tour, taking 4-89 in
Australia's first innings; his victims included both Waugh twins

---

FIGA

84. Who is West Indies' all-time leading
World Cup run-scorer?

1998 Season

	M	Inns	NO	Runs	HS	Avge	100s	50s	Ct	St	O	M	Runs	Wkts	Avge	Best	5wI	10wM
Test																		
All First	10	13	3	167	48	16.70	-	-	3	-	184.2	34	737	29	25.41	5-43	1	-
1-day Int																		
NatWest	1	1	0	1	1	1.00	-	-	-	-	10.3	1	39	4	9.75	4-39	-	
B & H																		
Sunday	4	3	0	8	3	2.66	-	-	1	-	19	0	112	6	18.66	3-38	-	

Career Performances

	M	Inns	NO	Runs	HS	Avge	100s	50s	Ct	St	Balls	Runs	Wkts	Avge	Best	5wI	10wM
Test																	
All First	24	33	9	399	56	16.62	-	1	4	-	2570	1664	60	27.73	6-101	3	-
1-day Int																	
NatWest	2	1	0	1	1	1.00	-	-	-	-	123	66	5	13.20	4-39	-	
B & H																	
Sunday	8	5	1	48	29 *	12.00	-	-	5	-	210	209	9	23.22	3-38	-	

TUFNELL, P. C. R.   Middlesex

Name: Philip Clive Roderick Tufnell
Role: Right-hand bat, slow left-arm spinner
Born: 29 April 1966, Hadley Wood, Hertfordshire
Height: 6ft **Weight:** 12st 7lbs
Nickname: The Cat
County debut: 1986
County cap: 1990
Test debut: 1990-91
Tests: 34
One-Day Internationals: 20
50 wickets in a season: 7
1st-Class 50s: 1
1st-Class 5 w. in innings: 41
1st-Class 10 w. in match: 5
1st-Class catches: 96
One-Day 5 w. in innings: 1
Place in batting averages: 276th av. 9.68 (1997 298th av. 6.73)
Place in bowling averages: 132nd av. 41.07 (1997 15th av. 21.90)
Strike rate: 97.23 (career 72.83)
Parents: Sylvia and Alan

Marital status: Divorced
Education: Highgate School; Southgate School
Qualifications: O-level in Art; City & Guilds Silversmithing
Overseas tours: England YC to West Indies 1984-85; England to Australia 1990-91, to New Zealand and Australia (World Cup) 1991-92, to India and Sri Lanka 1992-93, to West Indies 1993-94, to Australia 1994-95, to Zimbabwe and New Zealand 1996-97, to West Indies 1997-98
Overseas teams played for: Queensland University, Australia
Cricketers particularly admired: Jason Pooley
Other sports followed: American football
Relaxations: Sleeping
Extras: MCC Young Cricketer of the Year 1984 and Middlesex Uncapped Bowler of the Year 1987. Was originally a seam bowler and gave up cricket for three years in his mid-teens. Recalled to the England squad for winter tours to Zimbabwe and New Zealand in 1996-97 after an absence of two years and ensured himself a place on England's tour to West Indies with match figures of 11 for 93 in the final Test against Australia at The Oval in 1997 – picking up the Man of the Match award in the process. Awarded a benefit by Middlesex for 1999
Best batting: 67* Middlesex v Worcestershire, Lord's 1996
Best bowling: 8-29 Middlesex v Glamorgan, Cardiff 1993

1998 Season

	M	Inns	NO	Runs	HS	Avge	100s	50s	Ct	St	O	M	Runs	Wkts	Avge	Best	5wl	10wM
Test																		
All First	17	22	6	155	24	9.68	-	-	2	-	632	162	1602	39	41.07	4-24	-	-
1-day Int																		
NatWest																		
B & H																		
Sunday	3	2	1	5	5 *	5.00	-	-	1	-	22	1	99	3	33.00	2-39	-	

Career Performances

	M	Inns	NO	Runs	HS	Avge	100s	50s	Ct	St	Balls	Runs	Wkts	Avge	Best	5wl	10wM
Test	34	47	23	123	22 *	5.12	-	-	12	-	9230	3636	100	36.36	7-47	5	2
All First	248	266	104	1611	67 *	9.94	-	1	96	-	60311	24573	828	29.67	8-29	41	5
1-day Int	20	10	9	15	5 *	15.00	-	-	4	-	1020	699	19	36.78	4-22	-	
NatWest	8	1	0	8	8	8.00	-	-	4	-	570	323	10	32.30	3-29	-	
B & H	15	8	4	56	18	14.00	-	-	2	-	809	591	15	39.40	3-32	-	
Sunday	36	12	6	35	13 *	5.83	-	-	4	-	1524	1163	44	26.43	5-28	1	

TURNER, R. J.   Somerset

Name: Robert Julian Turner
Role: Right-hand bat, wicket-keeper
Born: 25 November 1967, Worcestershire
Height: 6ft 2in **Weight:** 13st 11lbs
Nickname: Noddy, Kingo, Turns
County debut: 1991
County cap: 1994
1000 runs in a season: 1
1st-Class 50s: 23
1st-Class 100s: 6
1st-Class catches: 315
1st-Class stumpings: 36
Place in batting averages: 119th av. 27.90
(1997 18th av. 50.90)
Parents: Derek Edward and Doris Lilian
Marital status: 'Engaged to Lucy'
Family links with cricket: 'My father and
two brothers Richard and Simon are closely
associated with Weston-Super-Mare CC.

Simon played for Somerset in 1984 in the 1st XI, as a wicket-keeper also'
Education: Uphill Primary School; Broadoak School, Weston-Super-Mare; Millfield
School; Magdalene College, Cambridge University
Qualifications: B Eng (Hons) in Engineering, Diploma in Computer Science,
NCA coaching award, SFA securities representative of the London Stock Exchange
Career outside cricket: Stockbroker with Rowan Dartington & Co in Bristol
Off-season: Working in Bristol with stockbrokers Rowan Dartington. MCC tour
to New Zealand
Overseas tours: Millfield School to Barbados, 1985; Combined Universities to
Barbados 1989; Qantas Airlines Tournament, Kuala Lumpur, Malaysia 1992-93;
English Lions Cricket Max tour to New Zealand 1997
Overseas teams played for: Claremont-Nedlands, Perth, Western Australia 1991-93
Cricketers particularly admired: Mushtaq Ahmed, Ian Healy, Alec Stewart,
Andy Caddick, Adam Nosher
Young players to look out for: Stuart Fawcett (Weston-Super-Mare CC)
Other sports followed: Football ('The Villa'), 'Taunton Ladies hockey and cricket
teams'
Injuries: Out for two months with tennis elbow
Relaxations: Eating and drinking with friends, 'sleeping a lot'
Extras: Captain of Cambridge University (Blue 1988-91) and Combined Universities
1991. Capped at end of 1994 season. Equalled Somerset record of six catches in an
innings in 1995 against West Indies and eight dismissals in a match against West

Indies and Durham. Holds the Somerset record seventh wicket partnership with Shane Lee of 278 against Worcestershire in 1996. Played for an England XI in the Cricket Max tournament in New Zealand in 1997-98. In 1997 became first wicket-keeper in 26 years to score 1000 runs in a season for Somerset

Opinions on cricket: 'I think the structure of two divisions for the Championship is a step in the right direction, thus giving more meaning to games at the end of the season – as long as there is a reasonable turnover of teams between divisions.'

Best batting: 144 Somerset v Kent, Taunton 1997

1998 Season

	M	Inns	NO	Runs	HS	Avge	100s	50s	Ct	St	O	M	Runs	Wkts	Avge	Best	5wI	10wM
Test																		
All First	14	22	2	558	105	27.90	1	2	43	-								
1-day Int																		
NatWest	1	0	0	0	0	-	-	-	1	-								
B & H	4	4	0	41	18	10.25	-	-	2	-								
Sunday	13	11	2	205	60	22.77	-	1	11	-								

Career Performances

	M	Inns	NO	Runs	HS	Avge	100s	50s	Ct	St	Balls	Runs	Wkts	Avge	Best	5wI	10wM
Test																	
All First	133	208	42	4989	144	30.05	6	23	315	36	19	29	0	-	-	-	-
1-day Int																	
NatWest	10	7	2	100	40	20.00	-	-	18	1							
B & H	25	23	9	516	70	36.85	-	1	24	1							
Sunday	76	63	19	942	67	21.40	-	2	68	10							

TWEATS, T. A.   Derbyshire

Name: Timothy Andrew Tweats
Role: Right-hand bat, off-spin bowler
Born: 18 April 1974, Stoke-on-Trent
Height: 6ft 3in **Weight:** 13st
County debut: 1992
1st-Class 50s: 4
1st-Class 100s: 2
1st-Class catches: 27
Place in batting averages: 210th av. 18.44 (1997 13th av. 53.63)
Strike rate: (career 74.50)
Parents: Malcolm and Linda
Marital status: Single

Family links with cricket: Father and two brothers, Jon and Simon, play for the local club, Leek, for whom he played before joining Derbyshire
Education: Endon High School; Stoke-on-Trent Sixth Form College; Staffordshire University
Qualifications: 5 GCSEs, 2 A-levels
Overseas tours: Kidsgrove and District Junior Cricket League to Australia 1991
Cricketers particularly admired: Robin Smith, Phil Tufnell
Other sports followed: Football
Best batting: 189 Derbyshire v Yorkshire, Derby 1997
Best bowling: 1-23 Derbyshire v Surrey, Derby 1995

1998 Season

	M	Inns	NO	Runs	HS	Avge	100s	50s	Ct	St	O	M	Runs	Wkts	Avge	Best	5wI	10wM
Test																		
All First	9	18	0	332	161	18.44	1	-	8	-	3	0	29	0	-	-	-	-
1-day Int																		
NatWest	2	1	0	5	5	5.00	-	-	-	-								
B & H	4	4	1	82	42 *	27.33	-	-	-	-								
Sunday	8	7	0	85	35	12.14	-	-	-	-								

Career Performances

	M	Inns	NO	Runs	HS	Avge	100s	50s	Ct	St	Balls	Runs	Wkts	Avge	Best	5wI	10wM
Test																	
All First	29	55	5	1384	189	27.68	2	4	27	-	298	237	4	59.25	1-23	-	-
1-day Int																	
NatWest	4	3	1	26	16	13.00	-	-	1	-							
B & H	6	5	1	92	42 *	23.00	-	-	-	-							
Sunday	22	17	2	185	35	12.33	-	-	9	-	24	27	0	-	-	-	

UDAL, S. D. Hampshire

Name: Shaun David Udal
Role: Right-hand bat, off-spin bowler,
'field in the deep', county vice-captain
Born: 18 March 1969, Farnborough
Height: 6ft 3in **Weight:** 13st 8lbs
Nickname: Shaggy
County debut: 1989
County cap: 1992
One-Day Internationals: 10
50 wickets in a season: 4
1st-Class 50s: 17
1st-Class 100s: 1
1st-Class 5 w. in innings: 20
1st-Class 10 w. in match: 4
1st-Class catches: 69
One-Day 5 w. in innings: 1
Place in batting averages: 95th av. 31.07
(1997 131st av. 28.57)
Place in bowling averages: 117th av. 34.31
(1997 139th av. 53.23)

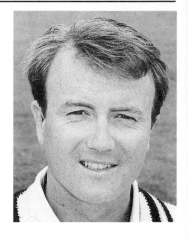

Strike rate: 71.75 (career 72.53)
Parents: Robin and Mary
Wife and date of marriage: Emma Jane, 5 October 1991
Children: Katherine Mary, 26 August 1992; Rebecca Jane, 17 November 1995
Family links with cricket: Father played for Surrey Colts and Camberley for 42
years; brother plays for Camberley 1st XI. Grandfather played for Leicestershire
and Middlesex
Education: Tower Hill Infant and Junior Schools; Cove Comprehensive School
Qualifications: 8 CSEs, qualified print finisher
Career outside cricket: Director of Omega Print Finishers
Off-season: Running my business
Overseas tours: England to Australia 1994-95; England A to Pakistan 1995-96
Overseas teams played for: Hamilton Wickham, Newcastle, NSW 1990-91
Cricketers particularly admired: Ian Botham, Robin Smith, Malcolm Marshall,
John Emburey
Young players to look out for: Ashley Cowan, Owais Shah
Other sports followed: Football (Aldershot Town) and golf (handicap of 14)
Relaxations: Good food and spending time with family
Extras: Has taken two hat-tricks in club cricket, scored a double hundred in a 40-over
club game and took 8-50 v Sussex in the first game of 1992 season, his seventh
Championship match. Man of the Match on NatWest debut against Berkshire 1991 and

named Hampshire Cricket Association Player of the Year 1993. Scored his maiden first-class century in 1997 against Warwickshire. Played for an England XI in the Cricket Max tournament in New Zealand in 1997-98. Appointed county vice-captain for the 1998 season

Opinions on cricket: 'Whatever the powers that be decide on our game, let's get on with it and just play the game.'

Best batting: 117* Hampshire v Warwickshire, Southampton 1997
Best bowling: 8-50 Hampshire v Sussex, Southampton 1992

1998 Season

	M	Inns	NO	Runs	HS	Avge	100s	50s	Ct	St	O	M	Runs	Wkts	Avge	Best	5wI	10wM
Test																		
All First	14	18	5	404	62	31.07	-	1	9	-	191.2	44	549	16	34.31	4-37	-	-
1-day Int																		
NatWest	4	2	1	23	12	23.00	-	-	4	-	21.3	3	76	6	12.66	4-20	-	
B & H	5	5	1	46	14 *	11.50	-	-	1	-	38	1	162	2	81.00	1-15	-	
Sunday	17	13	1	110	29	9.16	-	-	9	-	102.3	3	466	21	22.19	5-43	1	

Career Performances

	M	Inns	NO	Runs	HS	Avge	100s	50s	Ct	St	Balls	Runs	Wkts	Avge	Best	5wI	10wM
Test																	
All First	140	198	35	3756	117 *	23.04	1	17	69	-	26984	13483	372	36.24	8-50	20	4
1-day Int	10	6	4	35	11 *	17.50	-	-	1	-	570	371	8	46.37	2-37	-	
NatWest	21	10	5	125	39 *	25.00	-	-	11	-	1263	697	28	24.89	4-20	-	
B & H	35	20	5	188	34	12.53	-	-	10	-	2076	1343	42	31.97	4-40	-	
Sunday	128	82	24	907	78	15.63	-	5	42	-	5420	4483	152	29.49	5-43	1	

85. Who captained New Zealand in the 1979 World Cup?

FIGA

VAN TROOST, A. P. Somerset

Name: Adrianus Petrus van Troost
Role: Right-hand bat, right-arm fast bowler
Born: 2 October 1972, Schiedam, Holland
Height: 6ft 7in **Weight:** 16st 7lbs
Nickname: Rooster, Flap
County debut: 1991
1st-Class 5 w. in innings: 4
1st-Class catches: 10
One-Day 5 w. in innings: 1
Place in batting averages: 272nd av. 10.16
Place in bowling averages: 68th av. 27.66
Strike rate: 47.20 (career 57.86)
Parents: Aad and Anneke
Marital status: Single
Family links with cricket: Father plays
for Excelsior in Holland; brother plays for
Excelsior and Holland U23; grandfather
played for Excelsior and Holland

Education: Spieringshoek College, Schiedam
Qualifications: Finished Havo schooling – specialised in languages
Career outside cricket: 'Concentrating on cricket at the moment'
Off-season: Playing and training in Perth, Western Australia, from Christmas onwards
Overseas tours: Holland to Zimbabwe 1989, to Namibia 1990, to Dubai 1991,
to Canada, New Zealand and South Africa 1992
Overseas teams played for: Excelsior, Holland 1979-91; Alma Marist, Cape Town
1992-93; Griqualand West, South Africa 1994-96
Cricketers particularly admired: James 'batmaker' Parkhouse, Erik 'mac-attack'
van 't Zelfde, Jacob Jan Esmeyer, Wim 'the Skip' Bruning
Young players to look out for: Bas Zuiderent, Koos Oosterholt, JP
Other sports followed: Football, tennis and most other sports
Injuries: Out for five weeks with broken wrist
Relaxations: Reading, music, travelling
Extras: Played for Holland at age 15 and became third Dutch national to play
professional cricket. Took 6-3 v Durham 2nd XI in 1992 season
Opinions on cricket: 'Second XI cricket should be played on decent grounds, with
decent wickets and decent umpires, otherwise you might as well get rid of it.'
Best batting: 35 Somerset v Lancashire, Taunton 1993
Best bowling: 6-48 Somerset v Essex, Taunton 1992

1998 Season

	M	Inns	NO	Runs	HS	Avge	100s	50s	Ct	St	O	M	Runs	Wkts	Avge	Best	5wI	10wM
Test																		
All First	5	7	1	61	23	10.16	-	-	-	-	118	24	415	15	27.66	4-18	-	-
1-day Int																		
NatWest																		
B & H																		
Sunday																		

Career Performances

	M	Inns	NO	Runs	HS	Avge	100s	50s	Ct	St	Balls	Runs	Wkts	Avge	Best	5wI	10wM
Test																	
All First	71	85	27	461	35	7.94	-	-	10	-	8449	5614	146	38.45	6-48	4	-
1-day Int																	
NatWest	7	3	1	27	17 *	13.50	-	-	-	-	366	274	12	22.83	5-22	1	
B & H	3	3	1	19	9 *	9.50	-	-	-	-	172	172	4	43.00	2-38	-	
Sunday	17	6	3	29	9 *	9.66	-	-	2	-	639	532	17	31.29	4-23	-	

VAUGHAN, M. P. *Yorkshire*

Name: Michael Paul Vaughan
Role: Right-hand bat, off-spin bowler
Born: 29 October 1974, Eccles, Manchester
Height: 6ft 2in **Weight:** 11st 7lbs
Nickname: Virgil, Frankie, Chippo
County debut: 1993
County cap: 1995
1000 runs in a season: 4
1st-Class 50s: 27
1st-Class 100s: 12
1st-Class catches: 41
Place in batting averages: 35th av. 41.46
(1997 106th av. 33.56)
Strike rate: 78.77 (career 86.31)
Parents: Graham John and Dee
Marital status: Single
Family links with cricket: Father played
league cricket for Worsley CC. Brother plays
for Sheffield Collegiate. Mother is related to
the famous Tyldesley family (Lancashire and England)
Education: St Marks, Worsley, Manchester; Dore Juniors, Sheffield; Silverdale
Comprehensive, Sheffield

Qualifications: 7 GCSEs
Off-season: 'Touring Zimbabwe and South Africa with England A'
Overseas tours: England U19 to India 1992-93, to Sri Lanka 1993-94; Yorkshire to West Indies 1994, to South Africa 1995, to Zimbabwe 1996; England A to India 1994-95, to Australia 1996-97, to Zimbabwe and South Africa 1998-99 (captain)
Cricketers particularly admired: Glenn Chapple, Graham Lloyd, 'all the present Yorkshire team'
Young players to look out for: Matthew Wood, Matthew Hoggard
Other sports played: Football (Baslow FC), golf
Other sports followed: Football (Sheffield Wednesday), all golf
Relaxations: Most sports. 'Enjoy a good meal with friends'
Extras: Played club cricket for Sheffield Collegiate in the Yorkshire League. *Daily Telegraph* U15 Batsman of the Year, 1990. Maurice Leyland Batting Award 1990. Rapid Cricketline Player of the Month, June 1993. The Cricket Society's Most Promising Young Cricketer 1993. AA Thompson Memorial Trophy – The Roses Cricketer of the Year 1993. Whittingdale Cricketer of the Month, July 1994. Scored 1066 runs in first full season of first-class cricket in 1994. Captained England U19 in home series against India 1994. Awarded county cap at the end of the 1995 season
Best batting: 183 Yorkshire v Glamorgan, Cardiff 1996
Best bowling: 4-39 Yorkshire v Oxford University, The Parks 1994

1998 Season

	M	Inns	NO	Runs	HS	Avge	100s	50s	Ct	St	O	M	Runs	Wkts	Avge	Best	5wI	10wM
Test																		
All First	19	31	3	1161	177	41.46	2	5	10	-	118.1	30	412	9	45.77	3-73	-	-
1-day Int																		
NatWest	2	2	1	46	38 *	46.00	-	-	-	-	6	2	28	0	-		-	-
B & H	6	6	0	99	70	16.50	-	1	-	-	32	2	133	2	66.50	1-19	-	
Sunday	16	15	0	276	57	18.40	-	2	5	-	12	0	50	2	25.00	1-11	-	

Career Performances

	M	Inns	NO	Runs	HS	Avge	100s	50s	Ct	St	Balls	Runs	Wkts	Avge	Best	5wI	10wM
Test																	
All First	99	177	9	5840	183	34.76	12	27	41	-	6042	3533	70	50.47	4-39	-	-
1-day Int																	
NatWest	13	13	1	231	64	19.25	-	1	2	-	66	45	1	45.00	1-17	-	
B & H	22	22	1	722	88	34.38	-	6	4	-	333	237	6	39.50	1-0	-	
Sunday	61	59	3	1303	71 *	23.26	-	6	13	-	324	323	9	35.88	3-48	-	

WAGH, M. A.   Warwickshire

Name: Mark Anant Wagh
Role: Right-hand bat, off-spin bowler
Born: 20 October 1976, Birmingham
Height: 6ft 2in **Weight:** 12st 7lbs
Nickname: Waggy
County debut: 1997
1st-Class 50s: 8
1st-Class 100s: 6
1st-Class catches: 24
Place in batting averages: 73rd av. 32.66
(1997 64th av. 39.86)
Strike rate: 64.66 (career 115.56)
Parents: Mohan and Rita
Marital status: Single
Education: Harborne Junior School;
King Edward's School, Birmingham;
Keble College, Oxford
Qualifications: 12 GCSEs, 4 A-levels,
basic coaching

Overseas tours: Warwickshire U19 to South Africa 1992
Cricketers particularly admired: Carl Hooper, Brian Lara, David Gower,
Daryll Cullinan
Other sports followed: Hockey, snooker, football
Relaxations: Snooker and going out with friends
Best batting: 126 Warwickshire v Kent, Canterbury 1998
Best bowling: 4-11 Warwickshire v Middlesex, Lord's 1998

1998 Season

	M	Inns	NO	Runs	HS	Avge	100s	50s	Ct	St	O	M	Runs	Wkts	Avge	Best	5wI	10wM
Test																		.
All First	14	23	2	686	126	32.66	2	3	6	-	97	18	272	9	30.22	4-11	-	-
1-day Int																		
NatWest																		
B & H																		
Sunday																		

86. Which Kenyan batsman scored 65 v India
at Calcutta in the 1996 World Cup?

FICA

	M	Inns	NO	Runs	HS	Avge	100s	50s	Ct	St	Balls	Runs	Wkts	Avge	Best	5wI	10wM
Test																	
All First	43	67	7	2040	126	34.00	6	8	24	-	2889	1573	25	62.92	4-11	-	-
1-day Int																	
NatWest																	
B & H	3	3	1	36	23	18.00	-	-	-	-	174	119	3	39.66	1-39	-	
Sunday																	

WALKER, A. Durham

Name: Alan Walker
Role: Left-hand bat, right-arm
medium-fast bowler
Born: 7 July 1962, Emley, near Huddersfield
Height: 5ft 11in **Weight:** 13st 7lbs
Nickname: Wacky, Walks
County debut: 1983 (Northants),
1994 (Durham)
County cap: 1987 (Northants)
1st-Class 5 w. in innings: 6
1st-Class 10 w. in match: 1
1st-Class catches: 43
Place in batting averages: 294th av. 7.66
Place in bowling averages: 82nd av. 32.21
Strike rate: 143.00 (career 62.52)
Parents: Malcolm and Enid
Wife and date of marriage:
Nicky, 2 October 1994
Children: Jessica, 3 March 1988

Family links with cricket: Grandfather played in local league
Education: Emley Junior School; Kirkburton Middle School; Shelley High School
Qualifications: 2 O-levels, 4 CSEs, qualified coal-face worker
Career outside cricket: On Durham CCC coaching staff
Overseas tours: NCA North U19 to Denmark; Northamptonshire to Durban
Overseas teams played for: Uitenhage, South Africa 1984-85 and 1987-88;
Sunshine, Melbourne 1994-95
Cricketers particularly admired: Dennis Lillee, Richard Hadlee, Jeremy Snape 'for
his ability to see the funny side of things when things are not going well'
Other sports followed: Football (Huddersfield Town and Emley), rugby league
(Wakefield Trinity)
Relaxations: DIY, drinking, gardening

Extras: Recorded best bowling and match figures by a Durham bowler in 1995 (8 for 118 and 14 for 177). Retired at end of 1998 season and joined Durham coaching staff
Best batting: 41* Northamptonshire v Warwickshire, Edgbaston 1987
Best bowling: 8-118 Durham v Essex, Chester-le-Street 1995

1998 Season

	M	Inns	NO	Runs	HS	Avge	100s	50s	Ct	St	O	M	Runs	Wkts	Avge	Best	5wI	10wM
Test																		
All First	1	2	2	5	3*	-	-	-	-	-	23.5	5	51	1	51.00	1-51	-	-
1-day Int																		
NatWest																		
B & H																		
Sunday	1	0	0	0	0	-	-	-	1	-	3	0	23	0	-		-	-

Career Performances

	M	Inns	NO	Runs	HS	Avge	100s	50s	Ct	St	Balls	Runs	Wkts	Avge	Best	5wI	10wM
Test																	
All First	128	142	63	922	41*	11.67	-	-	43	-	18694	9667	299	32.33	8-118	6	1
1-day Int																	
NatWest	22	7	1	52	13	8.66	-	-	5	-	1311	770	24	32.08	4-7	-	
B & H	37	16	11	55	15*	11.00	-	-	7	-	1955	1418	44	32.22	4-42	-	
Sunday	151	44	19	278	30	11.12	-	-	36	-	6156	4908	168	29.21	4-18	-	

87. Who holds the all-time record for the most
World Cup appearances as captain?

FICA

WALKER, L. N. Nottinghamshire

Name: Lyndsay Nicholas Walker
Role: Right-hand bat, wicket-keeper
Born: 22 June 1974, Armidale, Australia
Height: 6ft 1in **Weight:** 13st
Nickname: Max
County debut: 1994
1st-Class catches: 19
1st-Class stumpings: 3
Parents: Graham (deceased) and Barbara
Wife and date of marriage:
Laurie, 17 June 1994
Children: Guy Lyndsay, 12 September 1995;
Chloe Ellen, 20 April 1997
Family links with cricket: 'Dad, brother
played good standard in Australia. My dog
Max has played in a benefit match. My son is
showing signs of addiction to the game'
Education: Garden Suburb Primary School;
Cardiff High School, New South Wales
Qualifications: Higher School Certificate, senior coaching award; bricklaying,
plumbing, landscape gardening
Career outside cricket: 'Cricket coach, building, Rex Hunt's fishing apprentice.
Building our aerobics business up'
Off-season: 'I'll spend four months coaching at Trent Bridge. I'll see if my dog can
learn to do some more housework; try to increase my business; show the kids that their
dad adores them; hopefully sell our house; propagate my cuttings and vegetables for
next summer; hope that my wife doesn't say she's expecting again'
Overseas teams played for: Wallsend, Newcastle, Australia 1987-91;
Johore, Malaysia 1992 (Malaysian youth coach for three months)
Cricketers particularly admired: Bruce French, Greg Geise, Jimmy Adams,
Mark Waugh, Allan Border, 'at times I've admired some of the things I've done'
Young players to look out for: John Shaw, Bilal Shafayat, 'players who have
tremendous self-belief and sheer determination'
Other sports played: Qualified for the NSW Amateur Open golf championship 1987.
'At high school, thanks to having many aborigines, I was a part of a great school
rugby league, Aussie Rules team'
Other sports followed: 'I love Aussie fishing, rugby league (Newcastle Knights),
Aussie Rules, triathlons'
Injuries: Out for the whole season with a thumb injury 'caused by a child falling on it
while coaching'

Relaxations: 'My faith and love of Jesus Christ, my Lord; Aussie fishing, walking my dog, calculating how many nappies my kids have ever worn, gardening'

Extras: Equalled the record for Nottinghamshire's most dismissals in an innings in 1996

Opinions on cricket: 'English cricket does not have enough intensity. There are only enough players who have the ability, the desire to go close or to push for international honours to fill 11 or 12 counties at present. If there were only 11 or 12 counties playing, players would then need to go about every aspect of their game to the maximum to do well, and that can only do English cricket good. There are a lot of very good young cricketers around. If they are brought up in an environment like this – i.e. the right physical and mental preparation – then the English game may then have enough class players to fill 18 counties. These are extreme measures, but English cricket is not as high up the ladder as it should be. Fifteen- and sixteen-year-olds should be exposed to 70-80-over games, and under the right supervison start going to the gym, swimming, cycling etc. There is a need for more physical and mental maturity at this age. Night cricket is the way forward. Cricket needs to go into the year 2000 now, not in 2080.'

Best batting: 42* Nottinghamshire v Oxford University, The Parks 1997

1998 Season (did not make any first-class or one-day appearances)

Career Performances

	M	Inns	NO	Runs	HS	Avge	100s	50s	Ct	St	Balls	Runs	Wkts	Avge	Best	5wI	10wM
Test																	
All First	12	15	3	233	42 *	19.41	-	-	19	3							
1-day Int																	
NatWest	1	1	0	1	1	1.00	-	-	-	-							
B & H																	
Sunday	2	2	0	24	22	12.00	-	-	-	-							

WALKER, M. J.   Kent

Name: Matthew Jonathan Walker
Role: Left-hand bat, right-arm medium-fast bowler
Born: 2 January 1974, Gravesend, Kent
Height: 5ft 7in **Weight:** 13st 11lbs
Nickname: Walks, Walkdog, Cheeky Monkey, Pumba, Ollie Reed
County debut: 1992-93
1st-Class 50s: 7
1st-Class 100s: 1
1st-Class 200s: 1
1st-Class catches: 22
One-Day 100s: 1
Place in batting averages: 133rd av. 26.23 (1997 218th av. 19.42)
Parents: Richard and June
Marital status: Engaged
Family links with cricket: Grandfather Jack played for Kent as a wicket-keeper. Father played for Kent and Middlesex 2nd XIs and was on Lord's groundstaff. Mother coached ex-England Ladies cricketer Megan Lear
Education: Shorne CE Primary School; King's School, Rochester
Qualifications: 9 GCSEs, 2 A-levels, advanced cricket coach
Career outside cricket: 'Yet to be decided'
Off-season: 'Buying a house with my fiancée, Claudia. Coaching cricket at Kent CCC. Playing hockey for Gore Court HC'
Overseas tours: Kent U17 to New Zealand 1991; England U19 to Pakistan 1991-92, to India 1992-93; Kent to Zimbabwe 1992-93
Cricketers particularly admired: Aravinda De Silva, John Crawley, Mark Ramprakash
Young players to look out for: Bob Key, Graeme Swann, Andy Flintoff
Other sports followed: Rugby, hockey, skiing, football
Other sports played: Hockey (England U14-U18 [captain U15-U17], Kent U14-U21, South East U16-U18), rugby (Kent U18), football (trials for Chelsea and Gillingham), athletics (Kent U15 javelin champion)
Other sports followed: Football (Charlton Athletic), hockey (Gore Court HC), rugby (Gravesend RFC)
Injuries: Out for four weeks with chipped bone in thumb
Relaxations: Music and films ('avid collector of both'). 'Spending as much time as I can with my family and my fiancée'
Extras: Captained England U19 tour to India 1992-93 and v West Indies in 1993

home series which England U19 won 2-0 in one-day matches and 1-0 in 'Test' series. Received Sir Jack Hobbs award for best young cricketer 1989, and *Daily Telegraph* U15 batting award 1989. Woolwich Kent League's Young Cricketer of the Year 1994. Scored 275 not out against Somerset in 1996 – the highest ever individual score by a Kent batsman at Canterbury – and was on the pitch for the whole game. Became an eminent Ruffensian in 1995

Opinions on cricket: 'You've got to be fit!!'

Best batting: 275* Kent v Somerset, Canterbury 1996

1998 Season

	M	Inns	NO	Runs	HS	Avge	100s	50s	Ct	St	O	M	Runs	Wkts	Avge	Best	5wI	10wM
Test																		
All First	8	14	1	341	68	26.23	-	2	6	-	12	0	51	0	-	-	-	-
1-day Int																		
NatWest																		
B & H	4	4	0	98	57	24.50	-	1	1	-								
Sunday	11	9	2	237	62 *	33.85	-	2	1	-								

Career Performances

	M	Inns	NO	Runs	HS	Avge	100s	50s	Ct	St	Balls	Runs	Wkts	Avge	Best	5wI	10wM
Test																	
All First	41	69	6	1756	275 *	27.87	2	7	22	-	78	70	0	-	-	-	-
1-day Int																	
NatWest	3	3	1	105	51	52.50	-	1	-	-							
B & H	22	21	3	709	117	39.38	1	5	9	-							
Sunday	58	54	8	1044	80	22.69	-	6	13	-							

FIGA

88. Who scored 130 for New Zealand
v Australia in the 1996 World Cup quarter-finals?

WALLACE, M. A. Glamorgan

Name: Mark Alex Wallace
Role: Left-hand bat, wicket-keeper
Born: 19 November 1981, Abergavenny,
South Wales
Height: 5ft 9in **Weight:** 11st
Nickname: Grom, Wally
County debut: No first-class appearance
Parents: Ryland and Alvine
Marital status: Single
Family links with cricket: Father plays for
Abergavenny
Education: Crickhowell Primary School;
Crickhowell High School
Qualifications: 10 GCSEs
Career outside cricket: Studying for
A-levels
Off-season: 'Hope to be selected for England
U19 tour of New Zealand; otherwise studying
for A-levels'

Overseas tours: Gwent U15 to South Africa 1996; Wales U16 to Jersey 1996, 1997;
England U19 to New Zealand 1998-99
Cricketers particularly admired: Ian Healy, Alec Stewart, Adrian Aymes,
Mark Taylor
Young players to look out for: Adam Davies, David Harrison, Ian Bell,
John Maunders, Ian Bird, Paul Franks
Other sports played: Football, rugby, golf
Other sports followed: Football (Merthyr Tydfil FC), rugby
Relaxations: PlayStation, sleep, golf, Merthyr Tydfil FC
Extras: Represented England U19 against Pakistan 1998
Opinions on cricket: 'Tea break should be extended by ten minutes to allow players
enough time to recuperate for the final session.'

WALSH, C. A.   Gloucestershire

Name: Courtney Andrew Walsh
Role: Right-hand bat, right-arm fast bowler
Born: 30 October 1962, Kingston, Jamaica
Height: 6ft 5¹/₂in **Weight:** 14st 7lbs
Nickname: Mark, Walshy, Cuddy, RP
County debut: 1984
County cap: 1985
Benefit: 1992
Test debut: 1984-85
Tests: 93
One-Day Internationals: 176
50 wickets in a season: 9
100 wickets in a season: 2
1st-Class 50s: 8
1st-Class 5 w. in innings: 96
1st-Class 10 w. in match: 19
1st-Class catches: 111
One-Day 5 w. in innings: 4
Place in batting averages: 282nd av. 8.53
Place in bowling averages: 7th av. 17.31
Strike rate: 35.83 (career 46.55)
Parents: Eric and Joan
Marital status: Single
Education: Excelsior High School
Qualifications: GCE and CXL
Overseas tours: West Indies YC to England 1982; West Indies B to Zimbabwe 1983-84; West Indies to England 1984, to Australia 1984-85, to Pakistan, Australia and New Zealand 1986-87, to India and Pakistan (World Cup) 1987-88, to England 1988, to Australia 1988-89, to Pakistan 1990-91, to England 1991, to Australia and South Africa 1992-93, to Sharjah, India (Hero Cup) and Sri Lanka 1993-94, to India and New Zealand 1994-95, to England 1995, to Australia 1995-96, to India and Pakistan (World Cup) 1995-96, to Australia 1996-97, to Sharjah 1997-98, to Pakistan 1997-98, to South Africa 1998-99
Overseas teams played for: Jamaica 1981-97
Relaxations: 'Being in my sports shop at home'
Extras: Took record 10-43 in Jamaican school cricket in 1979. On tour, he has a reputation as an insatiable collector of souvenirs. David Graveney, when captaining Gloucestershire, reckoned Walsh was the 'best old-ball bowler in the world'. One of *Wisden*'s Five Cricketers of the Year 1987. Took hat-trick for West Indies v Australia in 1988-89. Captain of Jamaica 1991-92 and 1993-94. Cricketers' Association Player of the Year and Wombwell Cricket Lovers' Cricketer of the Year 1993. Captain of

Gloucestershire 1993-94 and 1996. Took over captaincy of West Indies from Richie Richardson for Test series against India and New Zealand in 1994-95 and took full control in 1996. Was the leading wicket-taker in first-class cricket in 1996 with 85 wickets. Commitments with the West Indies side prevented him from playing for Gloucestershire in the 1997 season but returned in 1998. Surpassed Danny Morrison's unenviable record of the most ducks (25) in Test cricket on 24 June 1997 against Sri Lanka. Was replaced as West Indies captain by Brian Lara for the series against England in 1997-98. Became fifth West Indies cricketer to play 100 Tests, v England at Georgetown 1997-98. Was granted a testimonial by Gloucestershire in 1998. Received the International Award at the Variety Club's 25th Annual Sporting Awards 1998. Took 106 first-class wickets in the 1998 season. Gloucestershire contract not renewed for 1999
Opinions on cricket: 'Watch the changes.'
Best batting: 66 Gloucestershire v Kent, Cheltenham 1994
Best bowling: 9-72 Gloucestershire v Somerset, Bristol 1986
Stop press: Took his 377th Test wicket (Jacques Kallis) v South Africa at Johannesburg on 1998-99 tour, taking him past Malcolm Marshall's 376 and making him the leading West Indies Test wicket-taker of all time

1998 Season

	M	Inns	NO	Runs	HS	Avge	100s	50s	Ct	St	O	M	Runs	Wkts	Avge	Best	5wI	10wM
Test																		
All First	17	23	10	111	25	8.53	-	-	4	-	633	164	1835	106	17.31	6-36	7	2
1-day Int																		
NatWest	2	1	0	17	17	17.00	-	-	1	-	23	3	57	3	19.00	2-32	-	
B & H	4	2	1	16	16 *	16.00	-	-	1	-	37.3	4	166	5	33.20	3-36	-	
Sunday	13	5	3	7	2 *	3.50	-	-	1	-	80.4	6	335	23	14.56	5-23	1	

Career Performances

	M	Inns	NO	Runs	HS	Avge	100s	50s	Ct	St	Balls	Runs	Wkts	Avge	Best	5wI	10wM
Test	102	134	43	800	30 *	8.79	-	-	23	-	22032	9668	375	25.78	7-37	15	2
All First	386	489	132	4299	66	12.04	-	8	111	-	75464	35551	1621	21.93	9-72	96	19
1-day Int	185	68	29	292	30	7.48	-	-	27	-	9772	6312	204	30.94	5-1	1	
NatWest	23	15	3	153	37	12.75	-	-	3	-	1452	769	45	17.08	6-21	2	
B & H	27	17	6	130	28	11.81	-	-	2	-	1592	985	31	31.77	3-36	-	
Sunday	122	74	14	552	38	9.20	-	-	24	-	4920	3338	166	20.10	5-23	1	

WALSH, C. D. Kent

Name: Christopher David Walsh
Role: Right-hand bat, leg-spin bowler
Born: 6 November 1975, Pembury, Kent
Height: 6ft 1in **Weight:** 12st 8lbs
Nickname: Courtney, Spaceman
County debut: 1996
1st-Class 50s: 1
1st-Class catches: 3
Place in batting averages: 286th av. 7.00
Parents: David Robert and Carol Susan
Marital status: Single
Family links with cricket: Father played for
Oxford University 1967-69
Education: Yardley Court Prep School;
Tonbridge School; Exeter University
Qualifications: 11 GCSEs, 4 A-levels,
2 AO-levels, 2 S-levels, LLB
Career outside cricket: Law
Off-season: Playing and training in
Cape Town (Green Point CC)
Overseas tours: Tonbridge School to South Africa 1992-93
Overseas teams played for: Swanbourne CC, Perth 1995; Green Point CC,
Cape Town 1998-99
Cricketers particularly admired: David Gower, Carl Hooper, Mike Atherton
Young players to look out for: Robert Key, Jim Storey
Other sports played: Hockey (captain of Exeter University XI), rackets
(British U21 finalist)
Other sports followed: Football (Tottenham Hotspur), golf
Relaxations: Skiing, golf, good movies, 'drinking with "The Amigos"'
Extras: Scored three centuries in first 2nd XI championship season in 1995. *Daily
Telegraph* Batting Award in 1994. Kent CCC Blue Circle Award for The Most
Improved Uncapped Player 1995. Woolwich Kent League Young Player of the Year
1995. Member of the Kent U19 side which won the Hilda Overy Trophy at the
Oxford/Cambridge Festival in 1995. Scored century (105*) for Old Tonbridgians in
Cricketer Cup final 1998. Kent 2nd XI cap 1997
Opinions on cricket: 'Two division Championship cricket is the way forward – free
transfer system would mean all the best players would be playing in a higher quality
competition (Division 1).'
Best batting: 56* Kent v Oxford University, Canterbury 1996

1998 Season

	M	Inns	NO	Runs	HS	Avge	100s	50s	Ct	St	O	M	Runs	Wkts	Avge	Best	5wl	10wM
Test																		
All First	3	6	0	42	20	7.00	-	-	1	-								
1-day Int																		
NatWest																		
B & H																		
Sunday																		

Career Performances

	M	Inns	NO	Runs	HS	Avge	100s	50s	Ct	St	Balls	Runs	Wkts	Avge	Best	5wl	10wM
Test																		
All First	4	7	1	98	56 *	16.33	-	1	3	-	72	64	0	-	-	-	-
1-day Int																		
NatWest																		
B & H																		
Sunday	1	1	0	0	0	0.00	-	-	-	-	48	20	1	20.00	1-20	-	

WALTON, T. C.   Northamptonshire

Name: Timothy Charles Walton
Role: Right-hand bat, right-arm
medium bowler
Born: 8 November 1972, Low Lead,
North Yorkshire
Height: 6ft **Weight:** 12st 10lbs
Nickname: TC, Spadge
County debut: 1992 (one-day),
1994 (first-class)
1st-Class 50s: 7
1st-Class catches: 5
Place in batting averages:
(1997 155th av. 25.66)
Strike rate: (career 97.50)
Parents: Alan Michael and Sally Ann
Marital status: Single
Family links with cricket: Younger brother
Adam played Yorkshire Schools cricket and
is a good prospect
Education: Leeds Grammar School;
University of Northumbria, Newcastle
Qualifications: 7 GCSEs, 3 A-levels

Overseas tours: England U19 to Pakistan 1991-92
Overseas teams played for: Woolston Workingmens CC, New Zealand
Cricketers particularly admired: Viv Richards, Greg Blewett
Young players to look out for: David Sales, Jason Brown
Other sports followed: Rugby union ('long ago I played for England U16 at full-back') and league
Relaxations: Sketching and impersonating
Extras: Released by Northamptonshire at end of 1998 season
Opinions on cricket: 'Still too stiff. Needs loosening to make it interesting for all people i.e. Cricket Max in New Zealand.'
Best batting: 71 Northamptonshire v Somerset, Taunton 1995
Best bowling: 1-26 Northamptonshire v Kent, Northampton 1994

1998 Season

	M	Inns	NO	Runs	HS	Avge	100s	50s	Ct	St	O	M	Runs	Wkts	Avge	Best	5wI	10wM
Test																		
All First																		
1-day Int																		
NatWest	1	1	0	15	15	15.00	-	-	1	-								
B & H	2	2	0	28	26	14.00	-	-	1	-								
Sunday	12	11	4	209	51*	29.85	-	2	3	-								

Career Performances

	M	Inns	NO	Runs	HS	Avge	100s	50s	Ct	St	Balls	Runs	Wkts	Avge	Best	5wI	10wM
Test																	
All First	19	29	3	653	71	25.11	-	7	5	-	390	282	4	70.50	1-26	-	-
1-day Int																	
NatWest	4	3	0	21	15	7.00	-	-	2	-							
B & H	13	10	2	266	70*	33.25	-	1	6	-	36	27	1	27.00	1-27	-	
Sunday	59	51	10	1030	72	25.12	-	6	15	-	240	197	6	32.83	2-27	-	

89. Which current county captain was Man of the Match when England beat UAE in the 1996 World Cup?

FICA

WAQAR YOUNIS   Glamorgan

Name: Waqar Younis
Role: Right-hand bat, right-arm fast bowler
Born: 16 November 1971, Vehari, Pakistan
Height: 5ft 11in **Weight:** 12st
Nickname: Wicky
County debut: 1990 (Surrey),
1997 (Glamorgan)
County cap: 1990 (Surrey),
1997 (Glamorgan)
Test debut: 1989-90
Tests: 53
One-Day Internationals: 166
50 wickets in a season: 4
1st-Class 50s: 2
1st-Class 5 w. in innings: 56
1st-Class 10 w. in match: 14
1st-Class catches: 39
One-Day 5 w. in innings: 11
Place in batting averages: 289th av. 6.50
(1997 221st av. 19.33)
Place in bowling averages: 105th av. 33.08 (1997 18th av. 22.80)
Strike rate: 50.08 (career 39.81)
Marital status: Single
Education: Pakistani College, Sharjah; Government College, Vehari
Off-season: Playing for Pakistan
Overseas tours: Pakistan to India, Australia and Sharjah 1989-90, to England 1992,
to New Zealand, Australia, South Africa and West Indies 1992-93, to Sharjah 1993-94,
to New Zealand 1993-94, to South Africa, to Sri Lanka 1994-95, to Sri Lanka and
India (World Cup) 1995-96, to England 1996, to Australia 1996-97, to Kenya 1996-97,
to Sharjah 1996-97, to Toronto 1996-97, to Sharjah 1997-98, to South Africa 1997-98,
to Zimbabwe 1997-98
Overseas teams played for: United Bank, Pakistan 1988-89 –
Cricketers particularly admired: Imran Khan, Wasim Akram, Geoff Arnold,
Alec Stewart
Other sports followed: Football, badminton, squash
Injuries: Out for most of season with elbow injury
Relaxations: 'Sleeping and family get-togethers'
Extras: Made Test debut for Pakistan against India aged 17, taking 4 for 80 at
Karachi. Signed by Surrey during the 1990 season on recommendation of Imran Khan
who had first seen him bowling on television, and made his county debut in the
quarter-final of the B&H Cup. Martin Crowe described his bowling during Pakistan's

series with New Zealand as the best display of fast bowling he had ever seen. Named Professional Cricketers' Association Player of the Year 1991 and one of *Wisden*'s Cricketers of the Year 1992. Joined Glamorgan on a two-year contract from 1997. Took a hat-trick against Lancashire on 21 June – the first Glamorgan player to do so since Ossie Wheatley achieved the feat in 1968. Took his 250th Test wicket in his 51st Test, v South Africa at Port Elizabeth 1998. Not contracted by Glamorgan for 1999
Opinions on cricket: 'There should be no over-rate fines.'
Best batting: 55 Pakistan v Natal, Durban 1994-95
Best bowling: 8-17 Glamorgan v Sussex, Swansea 1997

1998 Season

	M	Inns	NO	Runs	HS	Avge	100s	50s	Ct	St	O	M	Runs	Wkts	Avge	Best	5wI	10wM
Test																		
All First	4	6	0	39	15	6.50	-	-	1	-	100.1	13	397	12	33.08	3-147	-	-
1-day Int																		
NatWest	1	0	0	0	0	-	-	-	-	-	12	2	46	4	11.50	4-46	-	
B & H	4	3	0	115	45	38.33	-	-	1	-	27	1	110	8	13.75	4-43	-	
Sunday	3	3	0	13	9	4.33	-	-	-	-	18.3	1	110	2	55.00	1-41	-	

Career Performances

	M	Inns	NO	Runs	HS	Avge	100s	50s	Ct	St	Balls	Runs	Wkts	Avge	Best	5wI	10wM
Test	53	69	12	556	45	9.75	-	-	7	-	10798	5748	267	21.52	7-76	21	5
All First	166	190	42	1857	55	12.54	-	2	39	-	29623	15884	744	21.34	8-17	56	14
1-day Int	171	85	31	538	37	9.96	-	-	19	-	8513	6496	281	23.11	6-26	9	
NatWest	14	5	2	75	34 *	25.00	-	-	2	-	931	603	33	18.27	5-40	1	
B & H	11	8	2	130	45	21.66	-	-	2	-	563	374	17	22.00	4-43	-	
Sunday	52	23	6	129	39	7.58	-	-	7	-	2313	1693	94	18.01	5-26	1	

90. Where was the final of the 1992 World Cup held?

FICA

WARD, I. J.   Surrey

Name: Ian James Ward
Role: Left-hand bat, right-arm
medium bowler
Born: 30 September 1973, Plymouth
Height: 5ft 8in **Weight:** 13st
Nickname: Stumpy, The Chimp, The Gnome,
Son of Baboon, Cocker
County debut: 1996
1st-Class 50s: 6
1st-Class catches: 16
Place in batting averages: 93rd av. 31.11
Parents: Tony and Mary
Wife and date of marriage:
Joanne, 15 February 1998
Children: Robert

Family links with cricket: Grandfather and
father played for Devon. 'Mother thinks
anything Mark Butcher does is "sexy". Wife
hates cricket ("Footballers are paid better")'
Education: Valley End; Millfield School; 'Ben Hollioake's School of Life';
'wife's cooking'
Qualifications: 8 GCSEs, 3 A-levels, NCA coaching award
Career outside cricket: 'John Wayne impersonator'
Off-season: In Perth, Western Australia
Overseas tours: Surrey U19 to Barbados 1990; Millfield to Barbados and Jamaica
1991; Malden Wanderers to Jersey 1994
Overseas teams played for: North Perth CC, Western Australia 1996-97; Perth CC,
Western Australia
Cricketers particularly admired: Graham Thorpe, Greg Kennis, Mark Wasley
(North Perth CC), Saqlain Mushtaq
Young players to look out for: Jon Batty, Mike Johnson (North Perth CC)
Other sports played: Golf
Other sports followed: Football (Liverpool), rugby (Richmond), golf
Relaxations: 'Spending time with my wife and listening to Ben Hollioake tell me all I
need to know'
Extras: Surrey 2nd XI cap at the age of 23
Opinions on cricket: 'Two divisions for County Championship. Floodlit cricket a
must also. England players contracted to ECB and then loaned back to counties if they
feel they need match practice – especially the bowlers.'
Best batting: 81* Surrey v Lancashire, Old Trafford 1998

1998 Season

	M	Inns	NO	Runs	HS	Avge	100s	50s	Ct	St	O	M	Runs	Wkts	Avge	Best	5wI	10wM
Test																		
All First	10	19	2	529	81 *	31.11	-	5	9	-								
1-day Int																		
NatWest	3	3	0	44	27	14.66	-	-	-	-								
B & H																			
Sunday	12	12	1	351	91	31.90	-	3	3	-	2	0	25	0	-	-	-	

Career Performances

	M	Inns	NO	Runs	HS	Avge	100s	50s	Ct	St	Balls	Runs	Wkts	Avge	Best	5wI	10wM
Test																	
All First	15	26	2	650	81 *	27.08	-	6	16	-	102	84	0	-	-	-	-
1-day Int																	
NatWest	4	4	0	58	27	14.50	-	-	-	-							
B & H																		
Sunday	25	23	5	434	91	24.11	-	3	5	-	35	66	0	-	-	-

WARD, T. R.   Kent

Name: Trevor Robert Ward
Role: Right-hand bat, occasional
off-spin bowler
Born: 18 January 1968, Farningham, Kent
Height: 5ft 11in **Weight:** 13st
Nickname: Wardy, Chikka
County debut: 1986
County cap: 1989
1000 runs in a season: 6
1st-Class 50s: 70
1st-Class 100s: 22
1st-Class 200s: 1
1st-Class catches: 188
One-Day 100s: 7
Place in batting averages: 207th av. 18.90
(1997 102nd av. 33.93)
Strike rate: (career 135.37)
Parents: Robert Henry and Hazel Ann
Wife and date of marriage:
Sarah Ann, 29 September 1990
Children: Holly Ann, 23 October 1995; Samuel Joseph, 25 April 1998
Family links with cricket: Father played club cricket

Education: Anthony Roper County Primary; Hextable Comprehensive
Qualifications: 7 O-levels, NCA coaching award
Overseas tours: NCA to Bermuda 1985; England YC to Sri Lanka 1986-87, to Australia (Youth World Cup) 1987-88
Overseas teams played for: Scarborough, Perth, Western Australia 1985; Gosnells, Perth 1993
Cricketers particularly admired: Ian Botham, Graham Gooch, Robin Smith
Other sports followed: Most sports
Relaxations: Fishing, watching television, golf
Extras: Was awarded £1000 for becoming the first player to score 400 runs in the Benson and Hedges Cup in 1995. Has been granted a benefit for 1999
Best batting: 235* Kent v Middlesex, Canterbury 1991
Best bowling: 2-10 Kent v Yorkshire, Canterbury 1996

1998 Season

	M	Inns	NO	Runs	HS	Avge	100s	50s	Ct	St	O	M	Runs	Wkts	Avge	Best	5wI	10wM
Test																		
All First	12	22	0	416	94	18.90	-	1	8	-	2	0	4	0	-	-	-	-
1-day Int																		
NatWest	2	2	1	70	61 *	70.00	-	1	2	-								
B & H	5	5	0	125	60	25.00	-	2	-	-								
Sunday	16	13	0	370	101	28.46	1	2	2	-								

Career Performances

	M	Inns	NO	Runs	HS	Avge	100s	50s	Ct	St	Balls	Runs	Wkts	Avge	Best	5wI	10wM
Test																	
All First	198	342	19	11657	235 *	36.08	23	70	188	-	1083	647	8	80.87	2-10	-	-
1-day Int																	
NatWest	22	22	1	915	120	43.57	1	8	4	-	156	129	2	64.50	1-28	-	
B & H	50	50	3	1647	125	35.04	2	12	11	-	12	10	0	-	-	-	
Sunday	160	155	6	4520	131	30.33	4	28	35	-	228	187	6	31.16	3-20	-	

WARREN, R. J.   Northamptonshire

Name: Russell John Warren
Role: Right-hand bat, wicket-keeper
Born: 10 September 1971, Northampton
Height: 6ft 2in **Weight:** 13st 7lbs
Nickname: Rabbit, Rabbs
County debut: 1992
County cap: 1995
1st-Class 50s: 15

1st-Class 100s: 2
1st-Class 200s: 1
1st-Class catches: 82
1st-Class stumpings: 3
One-Day 100s: 1
Place in batting averages: 294th av. 3.75
(1997 39th av. 44.26)
Parents: John and Sally
Marital status: Single
Family links with cricket: 'Dad likes a bet.
Mum follows scores on Teletext'
Education: Whitehills Lower School;
Kingsthorpe Middle and Upper Schools
Qualifications: 8 O-levels, 2 A-levels
Overseas tours: England YC to New
Zealand 1990-91; Northamptonshire to Cape
Town 1993, to Zimbabwe 1995,
to Johannesburg 1996

Overseas teams played for: Lancaster Park, Christchurch, and Canterbury B, New
Zealand 1991-93; Riverside CC, Lower Hutt, New Zealand 1994-95; Petone CC,
Wellington, New Zealand 1995-96; Alma Marist CC, Cape Town, South Africa
1997-98
Cricketers particularly admired: Wayne Larkins, Allan Lamb, Malachy Loye
Young players to look out for: David Roberts, Alec Swann, Graeme Swann, David
Sales, Richard Logan, John Blain, Richard Montgomerie, Tim Walton
Other sports followed: Football (Manchester United and Northampton Town), rugby
(Northampton Saints), golf, snooker and horse racing ('mostly Nick Cook and John
Hughes tips!')
Injuries: Out for six weeks with cartilage injury to left wrist; for two weeks with
fractured cheek bone
Relaxations: Sky television, fashion and training
Opinions on cricket: 'Fewer games, smaller staffs and increased wages. Too many
"ra-ras" in the game.'
Best batting: 201* Northamptonshire v Glamorgan, Northampton 1996

1998 Season

	M	Inns	NO	Runs	HS	Avge	100s	50s	Ct	St	O	M	Runs	Wkts	Avge	Best	5wI	10wM
Test																		
All First	5	8	0	30	11	3.75	-	-	7	-								
1-day Int																		
NatWest	1	1	0	7	7	7.00	-	-	1	-								
B & H																		
Sunday	11	10	0	222	39	22.20	-	-	10	1								

	M	Inns	NO	Runs	HS	Avge	100s	50s	Ct	St	Balls	Runs	Wkts	Avge	Best	5wI	10wM
Test																	
All First	61	100	12	2743	201 *	31.17	3	15	82	3							
1-day Int																	
NatWest	13	11	2	258	100 *	28.66	1	-	18	1							
B & H	12	11	1	95	23	9.50	-	-	11	-							
Sunday	63	52	9	911	71 *	21.18	-	3	54	9							

WASIM AKRAM Lancashire

Name: Wasim Akram
Role: Left-hand bat, left-arm
fast bowler
Born: 3 June 1966, Lahore, Pakistan
Height: 6ft 3in **Weight:** 12st 7lbs
Nickname: Waz
County debut: 1988
County cap: 1989
Benefit: 1998 (£100,000)
Test debut: 1984-85
Tests: 79
One-Day Internationals: 247
50 wickets in a season: 5
1st-Class 50s: 20
1st-Class 100s: 5
1st-Class 200s: 1
1st-Class 5 w. in innings: 64
1st-Class 10 w. in match: 15
1st-Class catches: 77
One-Day 5 w. in innings: 8
Place in batting averages: 90th av. 31.23
Place in bowling averages: 25th av. 21.35
Strike rate: 41.97 (career 47.63)
Parents: Choudhary Mohd. Akram and Irshad Begum
Wife's name: Huma Akram
Children: Tahmoor Akram (son), 21 August 1997
Education: Cathedral School, Lahore; Islamia College, Civil Lines, Lahore
Off-season: Playing for Pakistan
Overseas tours: Pakistan U23 to Sri Lanka 1984-85; Pakistan to New Zealand
1984-85, to Sri Lanka 1985-86, to India 1986-87, to England 1987, to West Indies
1987-88, to Australia 1989-90, to Australia and New Zealand (World Cup) 1991-92,

to England 1992, to New Zealand, Australia, South Africa and West Indies 1992-93, to New Zealand 1993-94, to South Africa 1994-95, to Sri Lanka 1994-95, to Australia 1995-96, to India and Sri Lanka (World Cup) 1995-96, to England 1996, to Kenya 1996-97, to Sharjah 1996-97, to Toronto 1996-97, to Australia 1996-97, to Sharjah 1997-98, to South Africa 1997-98, to Zimbabwe 1997-98, to Bangladesh 1998-99

Overseas teams played for: PACO 1984-86; Lahore Whites 1985-86

Cricketers particularly admired: Viv Richards, Imran Khan

Young players to look out for: Andrew Flintoff, Azhar Mahmood, Shoaib Akhtar

Other sports played: Golf, hunting, fishing, squash

Other sports followed: Golf, football (Manchester United)

Relaxations: TV, reading, golf

Extras: His second first-class match was playing for Pakistan on tour in New Zealand. Imran Khan wrote of him: 'I have great faith in Wasim Akram. I think he will become a great all-rounder, as long as he realises how much hard work is required. As a bowler he is extremely gifted, and has it in him to be the best left-armer since Alan Davidson.' Hit maiden Test 100 v Australia 1989-90 during stand of 191 with Imran Khan. One of *Wisden*'s five Cricketers of the Year 1993. Appointed captain of Pakistan 1992-93 and replaced by Salim Malik on tour to New Zealand 1993-94 but captained the tour to England in 1996. Alan Mullally became his 300th Test victim as the final wicket fell in the third Test at The Oval in 1996. Scored a career best 257 not out for Pakistan against Zimbabwe at Shekhupura in 1996-97 – the highest score batting at No. 8 in Test history. Lancashire captain in 1998. Lifetime Achievement Award and Pride of Performance from President of Pakistan. Released by Lancashire at end of 1998 season

Best batting: 257* Pakistan v Zimbabwe, Shekhupura 1996-97

Best bowling: 8-30 Lancashire v Somerset, Southport 1994

Stop press: Took 350th Test wicket (Neil Johnson) v Zimbabwe at Peshawar 1998. Took 363rd Test wicket (N. Mongia) v India at New Delhi 1998-99 in his 85th Test, taking him past Imran Khan's 362 in 88 Tests and making him Pakistan's highest Test wicket-taker

1998 Season

	M	Inns	NO	Runs	HS	Avge	100s	50s	Ct	St	O	M	Runs	Wkts	Avge	Best	5wI	10wM
Test																		
All First	13	18	1	531	155	31.23	1	2	8	-	335.5	75	1025	48	21.35	5-56	1	-
1-day Int																		
NatWest	3	2	1	37	37 *	37.00	-	-	1	-	31.4	1	132	6	22.00	3-50	-	
B & H	6	5	1	132	89 *	33.00	-	1	3	-	50.5	4	185	8	23.12	2-20	-	
Sunday	12	11	3	153	75 *	19.12	-	1	3	-	70	4	261	12	21.75	3-18	-	

Career Performances

	M	Inns	NO	Runs	HS	Avge	100s	50s	Ct	St	Balls	Runs	Wkts	Avge	Best	5wI	10wM
Test	79	109	15	2018	257 *	21.46	2	4	30	-	17922	7706	341	22.59	7-119	21	4
All First	217	298	34	5985	257 *	22.67	6	20	77	-	43201	19408	907	21.39	8-30	64	15
1-day Int	247	194	36	2384	86	15.08	-	5	59	-	12764	8117	356	22.80	5-15	5	
NatWest	20	16	4	229	50	19.08	-	1	6	-	1280	813	29	28.03	4-27	-	
B & H	37	29	6	670	89 *	29.13	-	4	5	-	2146	1393	67	20.79	5-10	2	
Sunday	106	86	22	1403	75 *	21.92	-	3	23	-	4480	3175	163	19.47	5-41	1	

WATKIN, S. L. Glamorgan

Name: Steven Llewellyn Watkin
Role: Right-hand bat, right-arm
fast-medium bowler
Born: 15 September 1964, Maesteg
Height: 6ft 3in **Weight:** 12st 8lbs
Nickname: Watty, Banger
County debut: 1986
County cap: 1989
Benefit: 1998
Test debut: 1991
Tests: 3
One-Day Internationals: 4
50 wickets in a season: 9
1st-Class 5 w. in innings: 25
1st-Class 10 w. in match: 4
1st-Class catches: 58
One-Day 5 w. in innings: 1
Place in batting averages:
(1997 282nd av. 10.61)
Place in bowling averages: 29th av. 21.83 (1997 19th av. 22.83)
Strike rate: 52.95 (career 57.72)
Parents: John (deceased) and Sandra
Marital status: Single
Family links with cricket: One brother plays local cricket; 'older brother a good watcher'
Education: Cymer Afan Comprehensive; Swansea College of Further Education;
South Glamorgan Institute of Higher Education
Qualifications: 8 O-levels, 2 A-levels, BA (Hons) in Human Movement Studies
Career outside cricket: Cricket development officer
Off-season: Finishing off benefit
Overseas tours: British Colleges to West Indies 1987; England A to Kenya and
Zimbabwe 1989-90, to Pakistan and Sri Lanka 1990-91, to Bermuda and West Indies
1991-92; England to West Indies 1993-94

Overseas teams played for: Potchefstroom University, South Africa 1987-88; Aurora, Durban, South Africa 1991-92
Cricketers particularly admired: Richard Hadlee, Dennis Lillee, Ian Botham
Young players to look out for: Matthew Hoggard, Wayne Law
Other sports followed: All sports except horse racing
Injuries: Out for five weeks with rib injury
Relaxations: Watching television, music, DIY, motor mechanics, 'a quiet pint'
Extras: Joint highest wicket-taker in 1989 with 94 wickets and took most (92) in 1993. Sister Lynda has played for Great Britain at hockey. Players' Player of the Year and Glamorgan Player of the Year 1993. One of *Wisden*'s five Cricketers of the Year 1994
Opinions on cricket: 'The amount of cricket must be reduced. It's not possible for players to perform at 100 per cent with present format. This surely affects Test performances as well.'
Best batting: 41 Glamorgan v Worcestershire, Worcester 1992
Best bowling: 8-59 Glamorgan v Warwickshire, Edgbaston 1988

1998 Season

	M	Inns	NO	Runs	HS	Avge	100s	50s	Ct	St	O	M	Runs	Wkts	Avge	Best	5wI	10wM
Test																		
All First	13	16	13	107	25 *	35.66	-	-	4	-	370.4	107	917	42	21.83	5-30	1	-
1-day Int																		
NatWest	2	1	0	0	0	0.00	-	-	-	-	24	4	69	4	17.25	3-25	-	
B & H	4	3	2	17	12 *	17.00	-	-	-	-	27	3	139	2	69.50	1-27	-	
Sunday	9	7	4	13	5 *	4.33	-	-	1	-	64.2	4	290	8	36.25	3-39	-	

Career Performances

	M	Inns	NO	Runs	HS	Avge	100s	50s	Ct	St	Balls	Runs	Wkts	Avge	Best	5wI	10wM
Test	3	5	0	25	13	5.00	-	-	1	-	534	305	11	27.72	4-65	-	-
All First	223	248	87	1638	41	10.17	-	-	58	-	44332	21637	768	28.17	8-59	25	4
1-day Int	4	2	0	4	4	2.00	-	-	-	-	221	193	7	27.57	4-49	-	
NatWest	29	13	4	53	13	5.88	-	-	2	-	1884	973	41	23.73	4-26	-	
B & H	37	21	11	89	15	8.90	-	-	8	-	2133	1417	48	29.52	4-31	-	
Sunday	133	53	19	252	31 *	7.41	-	-	21	-	5812	4202	156	26.93	5-23	1	

WATKINSON, M.   Lancashire

Name: Michael Watkinson
Role: Right-hand bat, right-arm medium or off-spin bowler
Born: 1 August 1961, Westhoughton
Height: 6ft 1½in **Weight:** 13st
Nickname: Winker
County debut: 1982
County cap: 1987
Benefit: 1996 (£209,000)
Test debut: 1995
Tests: 4
One-Day Internationals: 1
1000 runs in a season: 1
50 wickets in a season: 7
1st-Class 50s: 50
1st-Class 100s: 10
1st-Class 5 w. in innings: 27
1st-Class 10 w. in match: 3
1st-Class catches: 152
One-Day 100s: 1
One-Day 5 w. in innings: 3
Place in batting averages: 109th av. 28.90 (1997 130th av. 28.88)
Place in bowling averages: 112th av. 33.72 (1997 122nd av. 40.25)
Strike rate: 58.55 (career 64.62)
Parents: Albert and Marian
Wife and date of marriage: Susan, 12 April 1986
Children: Charlotte, 24 February 1989; Liam, 27 July 1991
Education: Rivington and Blackrod High School, Horwich
Qualifications: 8 O-levels, HTC Civil Engineering
Career outside cricket: Draughtsman
Overseas tours: England to South Africa 1995-96
Cricketers particularly admired: Clive Lloyd, Imran Khan
Other sports followed: Football
Relaxations: Watching Bolton Wanderers
Extras: Played for Cheshire in Minor Counties Championship and in NatWest Trophy (v Middlesex) 1982. Man of the Match in the first Refuge Assurance Cup final 1988 and in B&H Cup final 1990. Resigned the Lancashire captaincy during the 1997-98 off-season
Best batting: 161 Lancashire v Essex, Old Trafford 1995
Best bowling: 8-30 Lancashire v Hampshire, Old Trafford 1994

1998 Season

	M	Inns	NO	Runs	HS	Avge	100s	50s	Ct	St	O	M	Runs	Wkts	Avge	Best	5wI	10wM
Test																		
All First	10	12	1	318	87	28.90	-	2	6	-	175.4	22	607	18	33.72	5-45	1	-
1-day Int																		
NatWest	3	3	0	14	7	4.66	-	-	1	-	24	1	74	1	74.00	1-35	-	
B & H	1	1	0	34	34	34.00	-	-	1	-								
Sunday	8	8	1	161	56	23.00	-	1	-	-	10	0	60	1	60.00	1-32	-	

Career Performances

	M	Inns	NO	Runs	HS	Avge	100s	50s	Ct	St	Balls	Runs	Wkts	Avge	Best	5wI	10wM
Test	4	6	1	167	82 *	33.40	-	1	1	-	672	348	10	34.80	3-64	-	-
All First	300	446	48	10594	161	26.61	10	50	152	-	46984	24547	727	33.76	8-30	27	3
1-day Int	1	0	0	0	0	-	-	-	-	-	54	43	0	-	-	-	
NatWest	43	37	7	905	90	30.16	-	7	12	-	2555	1655	43	38.48	3-14	-	
B & H	71	51	12	819	76	21.00	-	4	22	-	3656	2565	86	29.82	5-44	2	
Sunday	222	177	38	3026	121	21.76	1	9	55	-	8268	6804	213	31.94	5-46	1	

WATSON, J. D.   Kent

Name: James David Watson
Role: Right-hand bat, right-arm fast bowler
Born: 21 April 1981, Ashford, Kent
Height: 6ft 7in **Weight:** 18st 7lbs
Nickname: Watto
County debut: No first-team appearance
Parents: David and Caroline
Marital status: Single
Family links with cricket: Grandfather Watson comes from famous Watson cricketing family of Hertfordshire. Father played Kent League cricket for Ashford and Wye CC. Grandfather Ireland played for Thornton Heath in the Surrey Championship
Education: Willesborough Junior School; Sutton Valence School
Qualifications: 5 GCSEs
Off-season: 'Studying for A-levels 1998. Winter 1999, playing for Sutherland in Australia'
Overseas tours: Kent U14 to Holland 1993; Sutton Valence to Barbados 1997
Cricketers particularly admired: Viv Richards, Richard Hadlee

Young players to look out for: 'My brother Alex', Leo Taylor
Other sports played: Rugby (school 1st XV), hockey (school 1st XI)
Other sports followed: Football (Arsenal)
Relaxations: Music, reading
Extras: U17 Kent county cap. Number of club awards
Opinions on cricket: 'Should be a Test match league. First-class cricket should be made more competitive with two leagues.'

WEEKES, P. N. Middlesex

Name: Paul Nicholas Weekes
Role: Left-hand bat, off-spin bowler
Born: 8 July 1969, Hackney, London
Height: 5ft 10in **Weight:** 12st 10lbs
Nickname: Weekesy, Twiddles
County debut: 1990
County cap: 1993
1000 runs in a season: 1
1st-Class 50s: 23
1st-Class 100s: 8
1st-Class 5 w. in innings: 3
1st-Class catches: 104
One-Day 100s: 3
Place in batting averages: 28th av. 43.00
(1997 225th av. 18.29)
Place in bowling averages: 140th av. 54.00
Strike rate: 109.38 (career 88.24)
Parents: Robert and Carol
Marital status: 'Partner Christine'
Children: Cherie, 4 September 1993; Shyann, 3 May 1998
Family links with cricket: Father played club cricket
Education: Homerton House Secondary School, Hackney; Hackney College
Qualifications: 3 O-levels, NCA and senior cricket coach
Career outside cricket: Coach for Middlesex MCB
Overseas tours: England A to India 1994-95; BWIA to Trinidad 1999
Overseas teams played for: Newcastle University, NSW 1989; Sunrise, Zimbabwe 1990
Cricketers particularly admired: Courtney Walsh
Young players to look out for: Stephen Peters
Other sports played: 'Try to play football. Best goal-hanger in the country – strike rate fantastic'
Other sports followed: Boxing
Relaxations: 'Don't get much time to relax. If possible, listening to music; having a good time with friends'

Extras: Scored 50 in debut innings for both 2nd and 1st teams. Took two catches whilst appearing as 12th man for England in the second Test against West Indies at Lord's in 1995. First English-qualified player to score more than 150 twice in the same match
Opinions on cricket: 'The game needs to be televised more. Needs more games under lights; something to boost the interest of youngsters.'
Best batting: 171* Middlesex v Somerset, Uxbridge 1996
Best bowling: 8-39 Middlesex v Glamorgan, Lord's 1996

1998 Season

	M	Inns	NO	Runs	HS	Avge	100s	50s	Ct	St	O	M	Runs	Wkts	Avge	Best	5wI	10wM
Test																		
All First	16	26	5	903	139	43.00	1	5	20	-	237	37	702	13	54.00	3-113	-	-
1-day Int																		
NatWest	3	3	1	31	18 *	15.50	-	-	-	-	25	0	112	2	56.00	1-37	-	
B & H	5	5	3	135	66 *	67.50	-	1	3	-	47	3	192	7	27.42	3-42	-	
Sunday	14	13	2	199	42 *	18.09	-	-	5	-	48.5	0	277	10	27.70	3-17	-	

Career Performances

	M	Inns	NO	Runs	HS	Avge	100s	50s	Ct	St	Balls	Runs	Wkts	Avge	Best	5wI	10wM
Test																	
All First	119	183	20	5328	171 *	32.68	9	23	104	-	11736	5607	133	42.15	8-39	3	-
1-day Int																	
NatWest	15	15	2	411	143 *	31.61	2	1	4	-	851	606	16	37.87	3-35	-	
B & H	31	28	6	723	77	32.86	-	5	9	-	1400	1009	28	36.03	3-32	-	
Sunday	122	100	14	2203	119 *	25.61	1	10	48	-	4060	3478	129	26.96	4-29	- -	

91. Who kept wicket for England in the 1983 World Cup?

FICA

WELCH, G. Warwickshire

Name: Graeme Welch
Role: Right-hand bat, right-arm
medium-fast bowler
Born: 21 March 1972, County Durham
Height: 6ft **Weight:** 13st
Nickname: Pop
County debut: 1992 (one-day),
1994 (first-class)
50 wickets in a season: 1
1st-Class 50s: 7
1st-Class 5 w. in innings: 3
1st-Class 10 w. in match: 1
1st-Class catches: 25
Place in batting averages: 198th av. 19.52
(1997 190th av. 22.75)
Place in bowling averages: 128th av. 39.84
(1997 32nd av. 25.00)
Strike rate: 75.48 (career 57.24)
Parents: Jean and Robert
Wife and date of marriage: Emma, 4 October 1997
Family links with cricket: Father Robert plays club cricket in Durham. Brother
Barrie plays club cricket in Leeds
Education: Hetton Primary; Hetton Comprehensive
Qualifications: 9 GCSEs, City & Guilds in Sports and Leisure, senior coaching award
Career outside cricket: 'Anything'
Off-season: Coaching at the indoor school at Edgbaston
Overseas tours: Warwickshire to Cape Town 1992 and 1993
Overseas teams played for: Avendale, Cape Town 1991-93; Wellington Collegians
1994-95; Johnsonville CC, New Zealand 1995-96; Wellington 1997
Cricketers particularly admired: Allan Donald, Andy Moles, Brian Lara, Dominic
Ostler, Tim Munton
Young players to look out for: Mark Wagh, Tony Frost
Other sports played: Football, 'Playstation'
Other sports followed: Football (Newcastle United)
Injuries: Out for three weeks with broken fingers; for eight weeks with Achilles
tendon injury
Relaxations: 'Few beers in "The Brook". Playing PlayStation. Spending time with
wife Emma'
Extras: Played for England YC v Australian YC 1991. Has taken two hat-tricks in the
2nd XI against Durham in 1992 and against Worcestershire. Axa Equity and Law
Winners Medal 1994. Britannic Assurance Winners Medal 1994. Warwickshire's most

improved player in 1994. Played for an England XI in the Cricket Max tournament in New Zealand in 1997-98

Opinions on cricket: 'There should be a first and second division. Sunday league should be kept exactly the same – 40 overs.'

Best batting: 84* Warwickshire v Nottinghamshire, Edgbaston 1994

Best bowling: 6-115 Warwickshire v Lancashire, Blackpool 1997

1998 Season

	M	Inns	NO	Runs	HS	Avge	100s	50s	Ct	St	O	M	Runs	Wkts	Avge	Best	5wI	10wM
Test																		
All First	12	18	1	332	54	19.52	-	1	7	-	314.3	71	996	25	39.84	4-94	-	-
1-day Int																		
NatWest	3	1	0	25	25	25.00	-	-	-	-	29	7	59	4	14.75	4-31	-	
B & H	5	4	1	21	16	7.00	-	-	1	-	34	5	110	9	12.22	3-20	-	
Sunday	11	6	2	24	10 *	6.00	-	-	2	-	56	2	260	5	52.00	1-11	-	

Career Performances

	M	Inns	NO	Runs	HS	Avge	100s	50s	Ct	St	Balls	Runs	Wkts	Avge	Best	5wI	10wM
Test																	
All First	57	80	11	1453	84 *	21.05	-	7	25	-	8587	4745	150	31.63	6-115	3	1
1-day Int																	
NatWest	11	7	2	77	25	15.40	-	-	-	-	582	302	8	37.75	4-31	-	
B & H	19	14	4	211	55 *	21.10	-	1	1	-	816	634	17	37.29	3-20	-	
Sunday	50	36	16	445	54	22.25	-	1	9	-	1683	1357	33	41.12	3-37	-	

92. Which pair of brothers hold the World Cup batting partnership record for any wicket?

FIGA

WELLS, A. P. Kent

Name: Alan Peter Wells
Role: Right-hand bat, right-arm
medium bowler
Born: 2 October 1961, Newhaven
Height: 6ft **Weight:** 'Going up'
Nickname: Morph, Bomber
County debut: 1981 (Sussex), 1997 (Kent)
County cap: 1986 (Sussex), 1997 (Kent)
Benefit: 1995
Test debut: 1995
Tests: 1
One-Day Internationals: 1
1000 runs in a season: 11
1st-Class 50s: 98
1st-Class 100s: 43
1st-Class 200s: 1
1st-Class catches: 223
One-Day 100s: 8

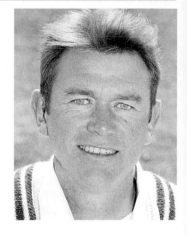

Place in batting averages: 120th av. 27.36
(1997 77th av. 37.33)
Strike rate: (career 115.30)
Parents: Ernest William Charles and Eunice Mae
Wife and date of marriage: Melanie Elizabeth, 26 September 1987
Children: Luke William Peter, 29 December 1990; Daniel Allan Christian, 24 June 1995
Family links with cricket: Father, Billy, played for many years for local club and had
trial for Sussex. Eldest brother Ray plays club cricket; brother Colin played for Sussex,
Derbyshire and Somerset
Education: Tideway Comprehensive, Newhaven
Qualifications: 5 O-levels, NCA coaching certificate
Career outside cricket: Family packaging business
Overseas tours: Unofficial England XI to South Africa 1989-90; England A to South
Africa 1993-94, to India (captain) 1994-95
Overseas teams played for: Border, South Africa 1981-82
Cricketers particularly admired: Graham Gooch
Young players to look out for: Giles Haywood
Other sports followed: Football (Tottenham Hotspur)
Relaxations: Good wine, cooking, spending time with family, reading books and
articles on wine
Extras: Played for England YC v India 1981. Banned from Test cricket for five years
in 1990 for joining tour of South Africa, suspension remitted in 1992. Scored a century
in each of his first two matches as acting-captain of Sussex and won both matches.

Won top batting award for Sussex 1989-93, 'much to David Smith's annoyance'. Vice-captain on England A tour to South Africa 1993-94 and captain for the highly successful tour to India 1994-95. Scored a century in both innings against Kent at Hove in 1995, the first Sussex player to do so since C.B. Fry. This was followed by a pair against Glamorgan at Swansea ('Funny old game!'). Left Sussex after 15 years during the 1996-97 off-season and joined Kent in 1997. Struck six sixes off successive deliveries v Durham in the AXA League at Canterbury 1998, of which five came from an over by Jon Lewis

Best batting: 253* Sussex v Yorkshire, Middlesbrough 1991
Best bowling: 3-67 Sussex v Worcestershire, Worcester 1987

1998 Season

	M	Inns	NO	Runs	HS	Avge	100s	50s	Ct	St	O	M	Runs	Wkts	Avge	Best	5wI	10wM
Test																		
All First	15	26	1	684	95	27.36	-	5	3	-								
1-day Int																		
NatWest	2	2	1	77	53 *	77.00	-	1	-	-								
B & H	5	4	1	139	111 *	46.33	1	-	2	-								
Sunday	10	8	2	277	118	46.16	1	-	3	-								

Career Performances

	M	Inns	NO	Runs	HS	Avge	100s	50s	Ct	St	Balls	Runs	Wkts	Avge	Best	5wI	10wM
Test	1	2	1	3	3 *	3.00	-	-	-	-							
All First	354	594	79	20312	253 *	39.44	44	98	223	-	1153	820	10	82.00	3-67	-	-
1-day Int	1	1	0	15	15	15.00	-	-	-	-							
NatWest	37	34	7	1038	119	38.44	3	5	13	-	6	1	0	-	-	-	-
B & H	67	63	8	1667	111 *	30.30	1	14	17	-	60	72	3	24.00	1-17	-	
Sunday	244	224	26	6080	127	30.70	4	36	72	-	62	69	4	17.25	1-0	-	

93. Who is the all-time leading World Cup run-scorer?

FIGA

WELLS, V. J. Leicestershire

Name: Vincent John Wells
Role: Right-hand bat, right-arm medium
bowler, occasional wicket-keeper
Born: 6 August 1965, Dartford
Height: 6ft **Weight:** 13st
Nickname: Vinny, Both
County debut: 1987 (Kent),
1992 (Leicestershire)
1000 runs in a season: 2
1st-Class 50s: 32
1st-Class 100s: 9
1st-Class 200s: 3
1st-Class 5 w. in innings: 3
1st-Class catches: 85
One-Day 100s: 4
One-Day 200s: 1
One-Day 5 w. in innings: 2
Place in batting averages: 56th av. 36.34

(1997 38th av. 44.44)
Place in bowling averages: 2nd av. 14.27 (1997 119th av. 39.47)
Strike rate: 33.19 (career 51.22)
Parents: Pat and Jack
Wife and date of marriage: Deborah Louise, 14 October 1989
Children: Harrison John, 25 January 1995; Molly Louise, 2 June 1996
Family links with cricket: Brother plays Kent league cricket
Education: Downs School, Dartford; Sir William Nottidge School, Whitstable
Qualifications: 1 O-level, 8 CSEs, junior and senior coaching certificates
Off-season: Cornwall CC, Auckland. England to Australia (CUB Series)
Overseas tours: Leicestershire to Jamaica 1993, to Bloemfontein 1994 and 1995,
to Western Transvaal 1996, to Durban 1997, to Barbados 1998; England to Australia
(CUB Series) 1998-99
Overseas teams played for: Parnell, Auckland 1986; Avendale, Cape Town 1986-89,
1990-91; Potchefstroom University, North West Transvaal 1996-97; Cornwall CC,
Auckland 1998-99
Cricketers particularly admired: James Whitaker, Phil Simmons, Robin Smith
Young players to look out for: 'Too many to mention from Leics'
Other sports followed: Most sports especially football
Injuries: Out for one week with tonsillitis
Relaxations: 'Spending time with family, pint of Guinness and good food'
Extras: Was a schoolboy footballer with Leyton Orient. Scored 100 not out on
NatWest debut v Oxfordshire. Left Kent at the end of 1991 season to join

Leicestershire. Missed 1992 NatWest final owing to viral infection. Hat-trick against Durham, 1994. Scored 201 not out against Berkshire in the 1996 NatWest Trophy. Was selected to represent England in the cancelled World Super Max 8s originally scheduled to take place in Perth in October 1998

Opinions on cricket: 'Would like to see all groundsmen employed by ECB to produce good, fair pitches all over the country. Sunday League should stay at 40 overs, with return to limited run-ups. Still believe there should be a smaller point gap between a draw and a win as with a few rain-affected games you can fall a long way behind sides finishing games.'

Best batting: 224 Leicestershire v Middlesex, Lord's 1997
Best bowling: 5-18 Leicestershire v Nottinghamshire, Worksop 1998

1998 Season

	M	Inns	NO	Runs	HS	Avge	100s	50s	Ct	St	O	M	Runs	Wkts	Avge	Best	5wl	10wM
Test																		
All First	17	25	2	836	171	36.34	3	3	10	-	199.1	66	514	36	14.27	5-18	1	-
1-day Int																		
NatWest	4	3	1	56	51 *	28.00	-	1	1	-	37	2	128	5	25.60	2-18	-	
B & H	6	3	0	38	19	12.66	-	-	3	-	55	7	194	9	21.55	6-25	1	
Sunday	15	15	0	368	77	24.53	-	1	2	-	81	9	313	13	24.07	4-18	-	

Career Performances

	M	Inns	NO	Runs	HS	Avge	100s	50s	Ct	St	Balls	Runs	Wkts	Avge	Best	5wl	10wM
Test																	
All First	132	207	16	6571	224	34.40	12	32	85	-	10758	5365	210	25.54	5-18	3	-
1-day Int																	
NatWest	17	16	4	483	201	40.25	2	1	1	-	743	442	19	23.26	3-30	-	
B & H	35	29	3	647	90	24.88	-	3	11	-	1456	1061	37	28.67	6-25	1	
Sunday	108	102	12	2414	101	26.82	2	10	24	-	3408	2729	99	27.56	5-10	1	

94. Who was Shaun Pollock's opening bowling partner in all but one of South Africa's 1996 World Cup matches?

FIGA

Name: Guy Edward Welton
Role: Right-hand opening bat
Born: 4 May 1978, Grimsby
Height: 6ft 1in **Weight:** 13st 7lbs
Nickname: Trigger, Welts
County debut: 1997
1st-Class 50s: 2
1st-Class catches: 4
Place in batting averages: 225th av. 16.88
(1997 141st av. 26.81)
Parents: Robert and Diana
Marital status: Single
Family links with cricket: Father is a
qualified cricket coach and keen club
cricketer
Education: Keelby Primary; Healing
Comprehensive; Grimsby College of
Technology
Qualifications: 9 GCSEs, BTEC in Business
and Finance, senior cricket coach
Off-season: Playing club cricket in Perth, Western Australia
Overseas tours: England U17 to Holland 1995
Overseas teams played for: Randfontein CC, Johannesburg, South Africa 1996-97;
Willetton CC, Perth, Western Australia 1997-98
Cricketers particularly admired: Viv Richards, Sachin Tendulkar, Mark Lavender
Young players to look out for: Shane Lavender
Other sports played: Football ('youth trainee at Grimsby Town Football Club 1994-96')
Injuries: Out for one month with a broken finger
Relaxations: Shopping, going to the gym, listening to music
Extras: Completed a two-year YTS with Grimsby Town Football Club where he made
one first-team appearance as a substitute. Played cricket for England U14, U15 and
U17. Won the Lord's Taverners Young Player Award in 1993 and MCC Young
Cricketer from 1994-95. Was 12th man for England at Lord's and The Oval against
West Indies in 1995
Opinions on cricket: 'More floodlit cricket.'
Best batting: 95 Nottinghamshire v Sussex, Hove 1997

---

95. Who was the first winner of the World Cup
Player of the Tournament award, and when?

1998 Season

	M	Inns	NO	Runs	HS	Avge	100s	50s	Ct	St	O	M	Runs	Wkts	Avge	Best	5wl	10wM
Test																		
All First	5	9	0	152	55	16.88	-	1	3	-								
1-day Int																		
NatWest																		
B & H																		
Sunday	1	1	0	2	2	2.00	-	-	-	-								

Career Performances

	M	Inns	NO	Runs	HS	Avge	100s	50s	Ct	St	Balls	Runs	Wkts	Avge	Best	5wl	10wM
Test																		
All First	11	20	0	447	95	22.35	-	2	4	-								
1-day Int																		
NatWest																		
B & H																		
Sunday	6	6	0	98	68	16.33	-	1	2	-								

WESTON, R. M. S.   Derbyshire

Name: Robin Michael Swann Weston
Role: Right-hand bat, leg-break bowler
Born: 7 June 1975, Durham
Height: 6ft **Weight:** 12st 6lbs
County debut: 1995 (Durham);
1998 (Derbyshire)
1st-Class 50s: 4
1st-Class catches: 16
Place in batting averages: 87th av. 31.58
(1997 236th av. 17.12)
Strike rate: (career 151.00)
Parents: Michael Philip and Kathleen Mary
Marital status: Single
Family links with cricket: Father played for
Durham (and played rugby union for
England); brother Philip plays for
Worcestershire
Education: Bow School; Durham School;
Loughborough University
Qualifications: 10 GCSEs, 4 A-levels, degree in Economics with Accountancy, basic
cricket coaching certificate
Off-season: Playing and training in Perth, Western Australia

Overseas tours: England U18 to South Africa 1992-93, to Denmark 1993; England U19 to Sri Lanka 1993-94

Overseas teams played for: Fremantle, Western Australia 1996-98

Cricketers particularly admired: 'Anyone at the highest level'

Young players to look out for: Kevin Dean, Melvyn Betts

Other sports played: Golf, rugby union (Loughborough Students 1994-96, England U18 1993)

Other sports followed: Football (Sunderland AFC)

Relaxations: Most sports, listening to music and socialising with friends

Extras: Youngest to play for Durham 1st XI, in Minor Counties competition, aged 15 in 1991. Played rugby for England U18. Released by Durham at the end of the 1997 season and joined Derbyshire

Opinions on cricket: 'Structure the season so that teams play no more than four Championship games without a decent rest (four to five days). That way people will stay fitter and still play the same number of games.'

Best batting: 97 Derbyshire v Kent, Derby 1998

Best bowling: 1-41 Durham v Somerset, Chester-le-Street 1995

1998 Season

	M	Inns	NO	Runs	HS	Avge	100s	50s	Ct	St	O	M	Runs	Wkts	Avge	Best	5wI	10wM
Test																		
All First	9	17	0	537	97	31.58	-	4	5	-								
1-day Int																		
NatWest	4	4	1	101	56	33.66	-	1	1	-								
B & H																			
Sunday	6	6	1	99	41	19.80	-	-	1	-								

Career Performances

	M	Inns	NO	Runs	HS	Avge	100s	50s	Ct	St	Balls	Runs	Wkts	Avge	Best	5wI	10wM
Test																	
All First	20	36	0	718	97	19.94	-	4	16	-	151	81	1	81.00	1-41	-	-
1-day Int																	
NatWest	4	4	1	101	56	33.66	-	1	1	-							
B & H																		
Sunday	9	9	1	131	41	16.37	-	-	2	-							

WESTON, W. P. C. Worcestershire

Name: William Philip Christopher Weston
Role: Left-hand bat, left-arm medium bowler
Born: 16 June 1973, Durham
Height: 6ft 4in **Weight:** 14st
Nickname: Sven, Junior, Reverend
County debut: 1991
County cap: 1995
1000 runs in a season: 3
1st-Class 50s: 34
1st-Class 100s: 12
1st-Class 200s: 1
1st-Class catches: 67
Place in batting averages: 105th av. 29.60
(1997 22nd av. 49.58)
Strike rate: (career 229.75)
Parents: Michael Philip and Kathleen Mary
Marital status: Single
Family links with cricket: Father played
Minor Counties cricket (and rugby union for

England). Brother played for England U19 and Durham CCC; now at Derbyshire
Education: Bow School, Durham; Durham School
Qualifications: 9 GCSEs, 4 A-levels, NCA coaching award
Overseas tours: England U18 to Canada; England YC to New Zealand 1990-91;
England U19 to Pakistan 1991-92 (captain); Worcestershire to Zimbabwe 1996
Overseas teams played for: Melville, Perth 1992-94 and 1996-97;
Swanbourne, Perth 1995-96
Cricketers particularly admired: 'Everyone who makes the most of their talent'
Other sports followed: Rugby union and football (Sunderland AFC)
Relaxations: Travelling. Beach life, hanging out with friends and family
Extras: Scored century for England YC v Australian YC 1991. Was appointed captain
of England U19 for their tour to Pakistan 1991-92 and told by Keble College, Oxford,
that he would not be accepted if he decided to tour; he chose to sacrifice his place at
Oxford. Downing College, Cambridge, offered him a place the following year, but by
then he was so disillusioned with universities that he turned down the offer and
decided to concentrate on his cricket. Played for Northants 2nd XI and Worcs 2nd XI
in 1989. Cricket Society's Most Promising Young Cricketer 1992. Worcestershire
Uncapped Player of the Year 1992. Member of Whittingdale Fringe Squad 1993
Opinions on cricket: 'Four-day cricket is good, better pitches are still needed and a
two-division championship would surely produce a more competitive finish to the
season. I cannot see the logic in rewarding four-day success with a one-day
tournament (two separate games now almost).'

Best batting: 205 Worcestershire v Northamptonshire, Northampton 1997
Best bowling: 2-39 Worcestershire v Pakistanis, Worcester 1992

1998 Season

	M	Inns	NO	Runs	HS	Avge	100s	50s	Ct	St	O	M	Runs	Wkts	Avge	Best	5wl	10wM
Test																		
All First	17	31	3	829	95	29.60	-	5	9	-	2	0	20	0	-	-	-	-
1-day Int																		
NatWest	1	1	0	6	6	6.00	-	-	-	-								
B & H	4	4	0	33	12	8.25	-	-	2	-								
Sunday	14	11	1	186	37	18.60	-	-	3	-								

Career Performances

	M	Inns	NO	Runs	HS	Avge	100s	50s	Ct	St	Balls	Runs	Wkts	Avge	Best	5wl	10wM
Test																	
All First	123	213	23	6862	205	36.11	13	34	67	-	919	599	4	149.75	2-39	-	-
1-day Int																	
NatWest	8	8	0	103	31	12.87	-	-	1	-								
B & H	21	20	2	234	54 *	13.00	-	1	9	-								
Sunday	64	53	8	1058	80 *	23.51	-	4	13	-	6	2	1	2.00	1-2	-	

WHARF, A. G. Nottinghamshire

Name: Alexander George Wharf
Role: Right-hand bat, right-arm
fast-medium bowler
Born: 4 June 1975, Bradford
Height: 6ft 4in **Weight:** 15st 10lbs
Nickname: Gangster, River
County debut: 1994 (Yorks), 1998 (Notts)
1st-Class 50s: 1
1st-Class catches: 8
Strike rate: 55.44 (career 62.65)
Parents: Derek and Jane
Marital status: Lives with girlfriend Shelley
Family links with cricket: Father played
local league cricket
Education: Marshfields First School;
Preistman Middle School; Buttershaw Upper
School; Thomas Danby College

Qualifications: 6 GCSEs, City and Guilds in Sports Management, NCA coaching award, junior football coaching award
Career outside cricket: Anything
Overseas tours: Yorkshire to Cape Town 1994-95, to Guernsey 1996
Overseas teams played for: Somerset West, Cape Town 1993-95; Johnsonville CC, Wellington, New Zealand 1996-97
Cricketers particularly admired: Ian Botham, Wasim Akram, Curtly Ambrose, Anthony McGrath, Bradley Parker, Chris Burns, 'King Ray!'
Young players to look out for: Alex and Zac Morris, Guy Welton, Ian Fisher
Other sports followed: Football (Manchester United)
Relaxations: Watching movies, eating out, spending time with friends outside cricket, clothes shopping
Extras: Attended Dennis Lillee coaching school, Madras, during winter 1997-98
Best batting: 62 Yorkshire v Glamorgan, Cardiff 1996
Best bowling: 4-29 Yorkshire v Lancashire, Old Trafford 1996

1998 Season

	M	Inns	NO	Runs	HS	Avge	100s	50s	Ct	St	O	M	Runs	Wkts	Avge	Best	5wl	10wM
Test																		
All First	5	6	1	8	3	1.60	-	-	6	-	83.1	14	333	9	37.00	3-25	-	-
1-day Int																		
NatWest																		
B & H	4	4	0	48	20	12.00	-	-	2	-	40	0	232	4	58.00	2-49	-	
Sunday	3	3	0	20	12	6.66	-	-	-	-	19	0	79	4	19.75	3-26	-	

Career Performances

	M	Inns	NO	Runs	HS	Avge	100s	50s	Ct	St	Balls	Runs	Wkts	Avge	Best	5wl	10wM
Test																	
All First	12	15	2	194	62	14.92	-	1	8	-	1253	787	20	39.35	4-29	-	-
1-day Int																	
NatWest																	
B & H	6	4	0	48	20	12.00	-	-	2	-	354	321	9	35.66	4-29	-	
Sunday	7	4	1	22	12	7.33	-	-	1	-	198	166	7	23.71	3-26	-	

WHILEY, M. J. A.   Nottinghamshire

Name: Matthew Jeffrey Allen Whiley
Role: Right-hand bat, left-arm
fast bowler
Born: 6 May 1980, Nottingham
Height: 6ft 5in **Weight:** 14st 9lbs
Nickname: The Fox, Ding, Whilas, Coyote,
Nod, Oggy
County debut: No first-team appearance
Parents: Paul and Barbara
Marital status: Single
Family links with cricket: 'Dad played club
cricket'
Education: Whitegate Primary School,
Clifton; Harry Carlton Comprehensive
School, East Leake

Qualifications: 8 GCSEs
Career outside cricket: 'None yet'
Off-season: Touring with England U19
Overseas tours: England U19 to New
Zealand 1998-99
Overseas teams played for: Foxton CC and Horo-Whenua District, both New
Zealand 1997-98
Cricketers particularly admired: Chris Tolley, Allan Donald, Wasim Akram,
Tim Robinson, Paul Franks, Noel Gie
Young players to look out for: Stephen Randall, David Lucas, Jack Daniels
Other sports followed: Football (Man Utd), rugby (Wellington Hurricanes –
Super 12)
Relaxations: 'Going out with the Pikelets, sleeping'
Opinions on cricket: 'What a wonderful game it is!'
Best batting: 62 Yorkshire v Glamorgan, Cardiff 1996
Best bowling: 4-29 Yorkshire v Lancashire, Old Trafford 1996

WHITAKER, J. J. — Leicestershire

Name: John James Whitaker
Role: Right-hand bat, off-spin bowler, county captain
Born: 5 May 1962, Skipton, North Yorkshire
Height: 6ft **Weight:** 13st
Nickname: Jimmy
County debut: 1983
County cap: 1986
Benefit: 1993
Test debut: 1986-87
Tests: 1
One-Day Internationals: 2
1000 runs in a season: 10
1st-Class 50s: 80
1st-Class 100s: 36
1st-Class 200s: 2
1st-Class catches: 171
One-Day 100s: 6
Place in batting averages: (1997 45th av. 43.76)
Strike rate: (career 89.00)
Parents: John and Ann
Marital status: Single

Family links with cricket: Father is a local league player
Education: Malsis Hall Prep School, Crosshills, Yorks; Uppingham School, Leics
Qualifications: 7 O-levels
Off-season: 'With ITC tour operator – Perth, Adelaide. Recovery/rehabilitation on knee'
Overseas tours: Uppingham to Australia 1980-81; England to Australia 1986-87, to Sharjah 1987; England A to Zimbabwe and Kenya 1989-90; Hong Kong Sixes 1991, 1992
Overseas teams played for: Glenelg, Australia 1982-83; Old Scotch, Tasmania 1983-84; Somerset West, Cape Town 1984-85
Cricketers particularly admired: Geoff Boycott, Dennis Amiss, Brian Davison, Maurice Hallam
Players to look out for: Darren Maddy, Ben Smith, Iain Sutcliffe, Aftab Habib, Paul Nixon, James Ormond
Other sports played: Squash, tennis
Other sports followed: Rugby (Leicester Tigers), football (Leicester City)
Injuries: Out for whole season with knee injury
Relaxations: Eating out, movies, watching sport

Extras: One of *Wisden*'s Five Cricketers of the Year 1987. Second in batting averages in 1986. Young Cricketer Award jointly in 1986. Appointed captain 1996, since when the county have lost only two first-class matches and won the Championship twice. Voted the Brian Sellars County Captain of the Year by the Wombwell Cricket Lovers' Society in 1996. His 218 v Yorkshire in 1996 at Bradford was the highest score by a Yorkshireman against his native county

Opinions on cricket: 'Get better pitches, more practice time, better practice facilities.'

Best batting: 218 Leicestershire v Yorkshire, Bradford 1996

Best bowling: 1-29 Leicestershire v Somerset, Leicester 1992

1998 Season

	M	Inns	NO	Runs	HS	Avge	100s	50s	Ct	St	O	M	Runs	Wkts	Avge	Best	5wl	10wM
Test																		
All First	1	0	0	0	0	-	-	-	-	-								
1-day Int																		
NatWest																		
B & H																		
Sunday	1	1	0	10	10	10.00	-	-	1	-								

Career Performances

	M	Inns	NO	Runs	HS	Avge	100s	50s	Ct	St	Balls	Runs	Wkts	Avge	Best	5wl	10wM
Test	1	1	0	11	11	11.00	-	-	1	-							
All First	310	490	51	17068	218	38.87	38	80	171	-	178	268	2	134.00	1-29	-	-
1-day Int	2	2	1	48	44 *	48.00	-	-	1	-							
NatWest	30	29	2	1077	155	39.88	1	6	1	-	24	9	0	-		-	-
B & H	58	53	3	1490	100	29.80	1	10	10	-							
Sunday	184	172	18	5035	132	32.69	4	31	53	-	2	4	0	-		-	-

WHITAKER, P. R.   Hampshire

Name: Paul Robert Whitaker

Role: Left-hand opening bat, right-arm off-spin bowler

Born: 28 June 1973, Keighley, West Yorkshire

Height: 5ft 10in **Weight:** 12st 4lbs 'and still rising'

Nickname: Tika, Pudsey Bear, Yorkie Bar, Big Boy

County debut: 1994

1st-Class 50s: 11

1st-Class 100s: 1

1st-Class catches: 15

Place in batting averages: 97th av. 30.90

Strike rate: 36.00 (career 73.46)

Parents: Robert and Maureen

Marital status: Single
Family links with cricket: Father coaches at Yorkshire School of Excellence and played in Bradford League for Bingley for over 20 years. Mother used to make nice cricket teas for Bingley U12s
Education: 8 GCSEs, 2 A-levels, NCA coaching award
Career outside cricket: Part-time cricket coach
Overseas tours: Represented England U17, U18 and U19
Overseas teams played for: Bedford, Perth, Australia 1992-93; Southern Hawke Bay, New Zealand 1993-97
Cricketers particularly admired: Ian Botham, Malcolm Marshall, Robin Smith, Phil Tufnell, Romesh Kaluwitharana
Young players to look out for: Daniel Vettori, Shahid Afridi, Alan Bigglewaite
Other sports followed: Rugby league (Bradford Bulls), football (Leeds United), horse racing
Relaxations: 'A quiet meal and a nice bottle of Liebfraumilch and then feeding the horse'
Extras: Hampshire Exiles Cricketer of the Year 1994-95. Released by Hampshire at end of 1998 season
Opinions on cricket: 'Leave cricket alone! Keep a full 2nd XI programme as this is the nearest thing we have and the smallest stepping stone to county cricket. England players and groundsmen should be contracted to the Board. Lunch should be 45 minutes and tea 30 minutes in order for a full three-course meal and a light snooze.'
Best batting: 119 Hampshire v Worcestershire, Southampton 1995
Best bowling: 3-36 Hampshire v Oxford University, The Parks 1996

1998 Season

	M	Inns	NO	Runs	HS	Avge	100s	50s	Ct	St	O	M	Runs	Wkts	Avge	Best	5wI	10wM
Test																		
All First	7	11	1	309	74	30.90	-	2	7	-	6	1	15	1	15.00	1-2	-	-
1-day Int																		
NatWest	2	2	0	1	1	0.50	-	-	-	-	1	0	7	0	-		-	-
B & H																		
Sunday	9	8	4	115	41 *	28.75	-	-	3	-								

Career Performances

	M	Inns	NO	Runs	HS	Avge	100s	50s	Ct	St		Balls	Runs	Wkts	Avge	Best	5wI	10wM
Test																		
All First	37	62	5	1734	119	30.42	1	11	15	-		955	561	13	43.15	3-36	-	-
1-day Int																		
NatWest	6	6	1	24	13	4.80	-	-	-	-		126	106	3	35.33	3-48	-	
B & H	9	8	0	149	53	18.62	-	1	1	-		216	155	4	38.75	2-33	-	
Sunday	38	35	6	575	97	19.82	-	2	11	-		332	303	10	30.30	3-44	-	

WHITE, C. Yorkshire

Name: Craig White
Role: Right-hand bat, right-arm fast-medium bowler, cover fielder
Born: 16 December 1969, Morley, Yorkshire
Height: 6ft 1in **Weight:** 11st 11lbs
Nickname: Chalky, Bassey
County debut: 1990
County cap: 1993
Test debut: 1994
Tests: 8
One-Day Internationals: 15
1st-Class 50s: 32
1st-Class 100s: 8
1st-Class 5 w. in innings: 7
1st-Class catches: 103
One-Day 100s: 2
Place in batting averages: 44th av. 39.58 (1997 129th av. 29.04)
Place in bowling averages: 3rd av. 15.64 (1997 71st av. 30.14)
Strike rate: 35.32 (career 50.02)
Parents: Fred Emsley and Cynthia Anne
Wife and date of marriage: Elizabeth Anne, 19 September 1992
Family links with cricket: Father played for Pudsey St Lawrence
Education: Kennington Primary; Flora Hill High School; Bendigo Senior High School (all Victoria, Australia)
Overseas tours: Australian YC to West Indies 1989-90; England to Australia 1994-95, to India and Pakistan (World Cup) 1995-96, to Zimbabwe and New Zealand 1996-97; England A to Pakistan 1995-96, to Australia 1996-97
Overseas teams played for: Victoria, Australia 1990-94
Cricketers particularly admired: Graeme Hick, Mark Waugh, Brian Lara

Other sports followed: Leeds RFC, motocross, golf, tennis
Relaxations: Playing guitar, reading, gardening and socialising
Extras: Recommended to Yorkshire by Victorian Cricket Academy, being eligible to play for Yorkshire as he was born in the county. 'Fred Trueman and I are the only Yorkshire players to debut in the 1st XI before the 2nd XI.' Formerly bowled off-spin. Had to fly home from the World Cup in 1995-96 with a side strain and was replaced by Dermot Reeve. Called up to England's tour to Zimbabwe and New Zealand in 1996-97 after a successful A tour to Australia as cover for the injured Ronnie Irani
Best batting: 181 Yorkshire v Lancashire, Headingley 1996
Best bowling: 8-55 Yorkshire v Gloucestershire, Gloucester 1998

1998 Season

	M	Inns	NO	Runs	HS	Avge	100s	50s	Ct	St	O	M	Runs	Wkts	Avge	Best	5wI	10wM
Test																		
All First	10	15	3	475	104 *	39.58	1	2	16	-	147.1	36	391	25	15.64	8-55	2	-
1-day Int																		
NatWest																		
B & H	6	5	0	52	27	10.40	-	-	4	-	47	5	165	6	27.50	4-29	-	
Sunday	10	10	0	130	35	13.00	-	-	2	-	43.1	4	141	6	23.50	2-17	-	

Career Performances

	M	Inns	NO	Runs	HS	Avge	100s	50s	Ct	St	Balls	Runs	Wkts	Avge	Best	5wI	10wM
Test	8	12	0	166	51	13.83	-	1	3	-	811	452	11	41.09	3-18	-	-
All First	145	219	33	6057	181	32.56	8	32	103	-	11505	6293	230	27.36	8-55	7	-
1-day Int	15	13	0	187	38	14.38	-	-	2	-	608	446	15	29.73	4-37	-	
NatWest	18	15	5	569	113	56.90	1	4	8	-	845	511	17	30.05	3-38	-	
B & H	28	24	5	381	57 *	20.05	-	1	9	-	1188	881	25	35.24	4-29	-	
Sunday	100	87	14	1888	148	25.86	1	6	35	-	2805	2152	79	27.24	4-18	-	

96. Who captained England in the 1975 World Cup?

FICA

WHITE, G. W. Hampshire

Name: Giles William White
Role: Right-hand bat, leg-break bowler
Born: 23 March 1972, Barnstaple, Devon
Height: 6ft **Weight:** 12st
Nickname: Chalky, Chilli
County debut: 1991 (Somerset), 1994 (Hampshire)
County cap: 1998 (Hampshire)
1000 runs in a season: 1
1st-Class 50s: 20
1st-Class 100s: 6
1st-Class catches: 59
Place in batting averages: 33rd av. 41.75 (1997 32nd av. 45.40)
Strike rate: 73.00 (career 165.00)
Parents: John and Tina
Marital status: Engaged (Samantha Donald)
Family links with cricket: Father played club cricket for Exeter CC

Education: Sandford Primary School, Devon; Exeter Cathedral School; Millfield School; Loughborough University
Qualifications: 10 O-levels, 3 A-levels, BA (Hons) in Sports Management, Computing diploma
Career outside cricket: 'Trying to find that out'
Off-season: Working in the marketing department at Hants CCC. House hunting. 'No doubt having to listen to Adi Aymes talking about his average (an annual treat for me)'
Overseas tours: Millfield School to Australia 1989; Hampshire to Anguilla, Cork and Guernsey
Overseas teams played for: Waverley, Sydney 1990-91; Tigers Parrow, Cape Town 1994-95; Techs Mutual CC, Cape Town 1995-96; Rygersdaal, Cape Town 1996-97; Waneroo, Perth 1997-98
Cricketers particularly admired: Wayne Larkins, Paul Terry, Cardigan Connor, Peter Hartley
Young players to look out for: Simon Francis, Derek Kenway, 'Bernard and Dimi'
Other sports played: Golf, football
Other sports followed: Football (Chelsea FC), golf (Fred Couples), *Gladiators* (Wolf)
Relaxations: Pubs, restaurants, travelling, painting, money-making schemes
Extras: Hants Exiles Young Player of the Year 1997. Played for Somerset before joining Hants. 'Beat "The Judge" in "Down a Stella Competition" – Bushwhackers, Worcs, 1998'. Scored 1000 runs in a season for the first time in 1998. Awarded Hampshire cap 1998

Opinions on cricket: 'Should be a greater/stricter control on the state of wickets. Surely the purpose of introducing four-day cricket was to play on wickets as close to Test quality as possible. I know everyone wants a result, but too many of the wickets have been "shockers". Still think tea should be 30 minutes.'
Best batting: 156 Hampshire v Sri Lanka, Southampton 1998
Best bowling: 1-4 Hampshire v Sri Lanka, Southampton 1998

1998 Season

	M	Inns	NO	Runs	HS	Avge	100s	50s	Ct	St	O	M	Runs	Wkts	Avge	Best	5wI	10wM
Test																		
All First	19	31	2	1211	156	41.75	4	5	12	-	12.1	2	51	1	51.00	1-4	-	-
1-day Int																		
NatWest	4	4	0	80	69	20.00	-	1	4	-								
B & H	5	5	0	62	47	12.40	-	-	1	-								
Sunday	16	16	2	426	76	30.42	-	4	8	-								

Career Performances

	M	Inns	NO	Runs	HS	Avge	100s	50s	Ct	St	Balls	Runs	Wkts	Avge	Best	5wI	10wM
Test																	
All First	69	117	10	3607	156	33.71	6	20	59	-	330	240	2	120.00	1-4	-	-
1-day Int																	
NatWest	7	7	0	92	69	13.14	-	1	6	-	72	45	1	45.00	1-45	-	
B & H	12	11	0	187	56	17.00	-	1	1	-							
Sunday	51	49	5	1180	76	26.81	-	8	16	-	12	14	0	-	-	-	

97. Who hit a straight six off Courtney Walsh in the final over as Pakistan beat West Indies at Lahore in the 1987 World Cup?

FIGA

WHITTICASE, P.   Leicestershire

Name: Philip Whitticase
Role: Right-hand bat, wicket-keeper
Born: 15 March 1965, Wythall, Birmingham
Height: 5ft 8in **Weight:** 11st
Nickname: Jasper, Tracy, Boggy, Rat
County debut: 1984
County cap: 1987
Benefit: 1997
1st-Class 50s: 17
1st-Class 100s: 1
1st-Class catches: 309
1st-Class stumpings: 14
Parents: Larry Gordon and Ann
Marital status: Single
Family links with cricket: Grandfather and
father played local club cricket (both were
wicket-keepers)
Education: Belle Vue Junior and Middle
School; Buckpool Secondary; Crestwood
Comprehensive

Qualifications: 5 O-levels, 4 CSEs, senior coaching certificate
Overseas teams played for: South Bunbury, Western Australia 1983-85
Cricketers particularly admired: Bob Taylor, Alan Knott, Dennis Amiss
Other sports followed: Football, rugby
Relaxations: Playing soccer, watching rugby and 'a good night out'
Extras: Played schoolboy football for Birmingham City. Was Derek Underwood's last
first-class victim. Lost seven teeth after being struck in the mouth by a bouncer from
Neil Williams in Leicestershire's game against Essex in April 1995
Best batting: 114* Leicestershire v Hampshire, Bournemouth 1991

1998 Season (did not make any first-class or one-day appearances)

Career Performances

	M	Inns	NO	Runs	HS	Avge	100s	50s	Ct	St	Balls	Runs	Wkts	Avge	Best	5wI	10wM
Test																	
All First	132	174	40	3113	114 *	23.23	1	17	309	14	5	7	0	-	-	-	-
1-day Int																	
NatWest	13	6	1	67	32	13.40	-	-	14	-							
B & H	29	19	7	313	45	26.08	-	-	29	4							
Sunday	69	45	9	413	38	11.47	-	-	56	4							

WIDDUP, S.   Yorkshire

Name: Simon Widdup
Role: Right-hand bat, off-spin bowler
Born: 10 November 1977, Doncaster,
South Yorks
Height: 6ft **Weight:** 11st 7lbs
Nickname: Widds, Knotty
County debut: No first-team appearance
Parents: Eric and Maggie
Marital status: Single
Family links with cricket: Great uncle
Richard Knowles Tyldesley played for Lancs
in 1920s and was *Wisden* Cricketer of the
Year 1925
Education: Saltersgate Infants/Middle
School, Doncaster; Ridgewood
Comprehensive School, Doncaster;
Danum Sixth Form School, Doncaster

Qualifications: 10 GCSEs, 1 A-level,
first coaching award
Off-season: Coaching in schools
Overseas tours: England U15 to South Africa 1993; England U17 to Holland
(ICC Youth Tournament) 1995
Overseas teams played for: Curtin University CC, Perth 1997-98
Cricketers particularly admired: Graeme Hick, Michael Atherton, Steve Waugh
Young players to look out for: James Smith
Other sports played: Golf (Amsterfield Golf Club), football (Sutton Rovers FC)
Other sports followed: Football (Arsenal FC, Doncaster Rovers FC), rugby
(Doncaster RUFC)
Relaxations: Golf, music (Oasis, Stone Roses)
Extras: Young *Telegraph* Cricketer of the Year 1992. Set Yorkshire League opening
partnership record 1994. Set Yorkshire 2nd XI opening partnership record 1998. Abbot
Ale Cup winner with Doncaster Town CC 1998
Opinions on cricket: 'Two division County Championship. Play-offs/grand final for
the top four teams with five-day games for semi-finals and final.'

WILKINSON, R.   Yorkshire

Name: Richard Wilkinson
Role: Right-hand bat, off-spin bowler
Born: 11 November 1977, Barnsley
Height: 5ft 11in **Weight:** 13st 10lbs
Nickname: Wilko, Sergeant, Tonker, Mongo
County debut: 1998
Strike rate: 90.00 (career 90.00)
Parents: Patricia Anne and Ronald Leslie
Marital status: Single
Family links with cricket: Father played for
Wombwell Main CC for 25 years
Education: Highfields Junior, Wombwell;
Wombwell High School; Worksop College
Qualifications: 6 GCSEs, 2 A-levels,
Level 1 coaching award
Career outside cricket: Cricket coaching
Off-season: 'Try and visit as many countries
as I can playing cricket'
Overseas teams played for:
Curtin University, Vic Park, Perth
Cricketers particularly admired: Robin Smith, Carl Hooper
Young players to look out for: Matthew Wood, Gary Fellows, 'Myself'
Other sports played: Rugby, hockey, football, 'silent Fizz Buzz (drinking game)'
Other sports followed: Football (Barnsley FC, Wombwell Main FC)
Relaxations: Drawing, listening to music of all types, 'playing with my PlayStation',
reading magazines
Extras: At 8 years old, became youngest player ever to play for Wombwell Main CC
1st XI. Represented Yorkshire from 11 years old, and England from 14 to 19.
Opinions on cricket: 'The use of the third umpire should be broadened to areas like
lbw and catches.'
Best batting: 9 Yorkshire v Cambridge University, Headingley 1998
Best bowling: 1-35 Yorkshire v Cambridge University, Headingley 1998

1998 Season

	M	Inns	NO	Runs	HS	Avge	100s	50s	Ct	St	O	M	Runs	Wkts	Avge	Best	5wl	10wM
Test																		
All First	1	1	0	9	9	9.00	-	-	-	-	15	3	35	1	35.00	1-35	-	-
1-day Int																		
NatWest																		
B & H																		
Sunday																		

	M	Inns	NO	Runs	HS	Avge	100s	50s	Ct	St	Balls	Runs	Wkts	Avge	Best	5wI	10wM
Test																	
All First	1	1	0	9	9	9.00	-	-	-	-	90	35	1	35.00	1-35	-	-
1-day Int																	
NatWest																	
B & H																	
Sunday																	

WILLIAMS, N. F. Essex

Name: Neil FitzGerald Williams
Role: Right-hand bat, right-arm
fast-medium bowler
Born: 2 July 1962, Hope Well,
St Vincent, West Indies
Height: 5ft 10in **Weight:** 11st 7lbs
Nickname: Joe
County debut: 1982 (Middlesex),
1995 (Essex)
County cap: 1984 (Middlesex), 1996 (Essex)
Benefit: 1994
Test debut: 1990
Tests: 1
50 wickets in a season: 3
1st-Class 50s: 13
1st-Class 5 w. in innings: 22
1st-Class 10 w. in match: 2
1st-Class catches: 67

Place in batting averages: 224th av. 17.10
Place in bowling averages: 101st av. 32.65 (1997 35th av. 25.84)
Strike rate: 56.96 (career 55.52)
Parents: Alexander and Aldreta
Marital status: Single
Family links with cricket: 'Uncle Joe plays first division cricket in St Vincent
and the Grenadines'
Education: Cane End Primary School, St Vincent; Acland Burghley School,
Tufnell Park
Qualifications: School Leaver's Certificate, 6 O-levels, 1 A-level
Overseas tours: English Counties to Zimbabwe 1984-85; MCC to Leeward Islands 1992
Overseas teams played for: St Vincent 1982-92; Windward Islands 1982-92;
Tasmania 1983-84

Cricketers particularly admired: Viv Richards, Desmond Haynes, David Gower
Other sports followed: Athletics
Relaxations: Music, 'useful DJ', cinema
Extras: Was on stand-by for England in New Zealand and Pakistan 1983-84. Joined Essex for the 1995 season. Released by Essex at the end of the 1998 season
Best batting: 77 Middlesex v Warwickshire, Edgbaston 1991
Best bowling: 8-75 Middlesex v Gloucestershire, Lord's 1992

1998 Season

	M	Inns	NO	Runs	HS	Avge	100s	50s	Ct	St	O	M	Runs	Wkts	Avge	Best	5wI	10wM
Test																		
All First	9	16	6	171	36	17.10	-	-	2	-	246.5	47	849	26	32.65	4-42	-	-
1-day Int																		
NatWest																		
B & H	2	1	1	20	20 *	-	-	-	-	-	17	0	86	3	28.66	2-26	-	
Sunday	2	2	1	0	0 *	0.00	-	-	1	-	11	0	57	2	28.50	2-39	-	

Career Performances

	M	Inns	NO	Runs	HS	Avge	100s	50s	Ct	St	Balls	Runs	Wkts	Avge	Best	5wI	10wM
Test	1	1	0	38	38	38.00	-	-	-	-	246	148	2	74.00	2-148	-	-
All First	255	302	63	4457	77	18.64	-	13	67	-	37479	20448	675	30.29	8-75	22	2
1-day Int																	
NatWest	23	13	6	73	11 *	10.42	-	-	5	-	1151	778	18	43.22	4-36	-	
B & H	58	32	8	279	29 *	11.62	-	-	7	-	3042	1965	61	32.21	3-16	-	
Sunday	127	57	21	455	43	12.63	-	-	32	-	5225	3917	139	28.17	4-39	-	

WILLIAMS, R. C. J.   Gloucestershire

Name: Richard Charles James Williams
Role: Left-hand bat, wicket-keeper
Born: 8 August 1969, Bristol
Height: 5ft 10in **Weight:** 11st
Nickname: Reg
County debut: 1990
County cap: 1996
1st-Class 50s: 5
1st-Class catches: 97
1st-Class stumpings: 15
Place in batting averages: (1997 256th av. 16.62)
Parents: Michael (deceased) and Angela
Marital status: Single
Family links with cricket: Father played local club cricket

Education: Clifton College Preparatory School; Millfield School
Qualifications: PE Diploma, NCA junior coaching award
Overseas tours: Gloucestershire to Namibia 1990, to Kenya 1991, to Sri Lanka 1992-93; Romany CC to Durban & Cape Town 1993; Gloucestershire Gypsies to Zimbabwe 1994-95, to South Africa 1995-96
Overseas teams played for: Manicaland, Zimbabwe 1990-91
Cricketers particularly admired: Andy Brassington, Jack Russell, David Gower
Other sports followed: Football, hockey, squash, snooker
Relaxations: 'Eating out, pubs and clubs, strutting my funky stuff'
Best batting: 90 Gloucestershire v Oxford University, Bristol 1995

1998 Season

	M	Inns	NO	Runs	HS	Avge	100s	50s	Ct	St	O	M	Runs	Wkts	Avge	Best	5wI	10wM
Test																		
All First	2	3	0	72	67	24.00	-	1	3	1								
1-day Int																		
NatWest																		
B & H	1	0	0	0	0	-	-	-	-	1	-							
Sunday	1	0	0	0	0	-	-	-	-	1	-							

Career Performances

	M	Inns	NO	Runs	HS	Avge	100s	50s	Ct	St	Balls	Runs	Wkts	Avge	Best	5wI	10wM
Test																		
All First	37	47	8	712	90	18.25	-	5	97	15							
1-day Int																		
NatWest																		
B & H	1	0	0	0	0	-	-	-	-	1	-						
Sunday	19	7	2	76	19	15.20	-	-	20	4							

WILLIAMSON, D.   Leicestershire

Name: Dominic Williamson
Role: Right-hand bat, right-arm
medium bowler
Born: 15 November 1975, Durham City
Height: 6ft 2in **Weight:** 11st
Nickname: Woky, Midge, Burt Picker, Watto
County debut: 1996
1st-Class catches: 3
One-Day 5 w. in innings: 2
Strike rate: 76.50 (career 65.22)
Parents: Dorothy and Gerard
Marital status: Single
Family links with cricket: 'Father still
playing for Kimblesworth CC at the tender
age of 50 and still scoring more runs than me
(averaging 70 last year). My brother Mark
also plays for KCC but can't decide whether
he's better than Richard Stemp or Ed Giddins'

Education: Easington C of E Primary School, Co. Durham; St Leonards RC
Comprehensive, Co. Durham; Durham Sixth Form Centre
Qualifications: 9 GCSEs, 3 A-levels
Career outside cricket: Property developer
Off-season: 'Training, resting, relaxing'
Overseas tours: Leicestershire CCC to Holland 1996, 1998, to Guernsey 1997, 1998
('returned home early to sort club house out'), to Barbados 1998
Overseas teams played for: Ashburton CC, Australia 1994, 1996; Klerksdorp CC,
South Africa 1996-97
Cricketers particularly admired: Brian McMillan, Shane Warne, Steve Waugh,
Glenn McGrath, Stuart Smith ('The Walrus')
Young players to look out for: Robson Smith ('slip fielder'), Totty and Michael Carr,
Mark Williamson ('left-arm tweaker'), 'Fitt Smitt'
Other sports played: Squash, golf, football 'and PlayStation'
Other sports followed: Football (Newcastle United)
Injuries: Cramps in calves
Relaxations: 'Mark, Bill and myself spending an evening chilling together'
Extras: Winner of the Leicestershire 2nd XI Bowler of the Year award in 1997. Most
Improved Uncapped Player of the Year award 1998
Opinions on cricket: 'Coaching and facilities must be improved in primary and
secondary schools.'
Best batting: 41* Leicestershire v Hampshire, Leicester 1998
Best bowling: 3-19 Leicestershire v Glamorgan, Leicester 1997

1998 Season

	M	Inns	NO	Runs	HS	Avge	100s	50s	Ct	St	O	M	Runs	Wkts	Avge	Best	5wI	10wM
Test																		
All First	2	3	1	95	41 *	47.50	-	-	3	-	51	10	183	4	45.75	3-110	-	-
1-day Int																		
NatWest	4	1	1	19	19 *	-	-	-	-	-	36	5	143	8	17.87	5-37	1	
B & H	3	1	0	11	11	11.00	-	-	-	-	19	0	112	2	56.00	2-49	-	
Sunday	16	13	3	126	32 *	12.60	-	-	6	-	92.5	4	367	23	15.95	3-12	-	

Career Performances

	M	Inns	NO	Runs	HS	Avge	100s	50s	Ct	St	Balls	Runs	Wkts	Avge	Best	5wI	10wM
Test																	
All First	4	4	1	98	41 *	32.66	-	-	3	-	587	318	9	35.33	3-19	-	-
1-day Int																	
NatWest	4	1	1	19	19 *	-	-	-	-	-	216	143	8	17.87	5-37	1	
B & H	5	2	0	17	11	8.50	-	-	-	-	198	203	3	67.66	2-49	-	
Sunday	34	25	10	179	32 *	11.93	-	-	12	-	1088	809	38	21.28	5-32	1	

WILLIS, S. C.   Kent

Name: Simon Charles Willis
Role: Right-hand bat, wicket-keeper
Born: 19 March 1974, Greenwich, London
Height: 5ft 8in **Weight:** 12st 7lbs
Nickname: Wilco
County debut: 1993
1st-Class 50s: 4
1st-Class catches: 27
1st-Class stumpings: 2
Parents: Ray and Janet
Wife and date of marriage:
Louise Clare, 12 October 1996
Family links with cricket: Father played in
Kent League. Father-in-law Alan Ealham
played for Kent 1962-82. Brother-in-law
Mark Ealham plays for Kent and England
Education: Fleetdown Primary School;
Wilmington Grammar School
Qualifications: 9 GCSEs, advanced coach
Off-season: Coaching
Overseas tours: Kent U17 to New Zealand 1990-91; Kent to Zimbabwe 1993
Overseas teams played for: Scarborough, Western Australia 1992-93

Cricketers particularly admired: Alan Knott, Robin Smith, Carl Hooper, Jack Russell
Young players to look out for: Richard Clinton, Rob Key, Ed Smith
Other sports followed: Golf, soccer (Arsenal FC), horse racing, squash
Relaxations: 'Playing golf, spending time with my wife'
Best batting: 82 Kent v Cambridge University, Folkestone 1995

1998 Season

	M	Inns	NO	Runs	HS	Avge	100s	50s	Ct	St	O	M	Runs	Wkts	Avge	Best	5wl	10wM
Test																		
All First	2	2	1	58	58	58.00	-	1	3	2								
1-day Int																		
NatWest	2	1	0	3	3	3.00	-	-	3	-								
B & H																		
Sunday																		

Career Performances

	M	Inns	NO	Runs	HS	Avge	100s	50s	Ct	St	Balls	Runs	Wkts	Avge	Best	5wl	10wM
Test																	
All First	12	15	4	389	82	35.36	-	4	27	2							
1-day Int																	
NatWest	3	2	1	22	19 *	22.00	-	-	4	-							
B & H	1	0	0	0	0	-	-	-	-	-							
Sunday	8	6	2	80	31 *	20.00	-	-	11	1							

WILSON, D. G.   Essex

Name: Daniel Graeme Wilson
Role: Right-hand bat, right-arm medium-fast bowler
Born: 18 February 1977, Paddington
Height: 6ft 2in **Weight:** 13st
Nickname: OJ, Juice, Juicy, Stan
County debut: 1996 (one-day), 1997 (first-class)
1st-Class catches: 1
Strike rate: 75.00 (career 60.75)
Parents: Tony and Margaret
Marital status: Single
Family links with cricket: 'Dad played for Trinidad Colts. Stepbrother Nick, brother Rob and stepdad John give it licks for the local village. Mum plays fantasy cricket'
Education: The Firs Primary School, Bishop's Stortford; St Mary's RC School; Cheltenham and Gloucester College of Higher Education (currently deferred course)
Qualifications: 10 GCSEs, 3 A-levels, Certificate of Higher Education
Overseas teams played for: Queen's Park CC, Trinidad 1997-98

Cricketers particularly admired: Stuart Law, Rob Wilson, Nick Malay, 'anyone who has been in the game for a long time'

Young players to look out for: Rupesh Amin, David Sales, Wayne Ritzema, Ed Smith, Mouhssin Ismail

Other sports followed: Football (Liverpool FC), American football, golf, skiing

Relaxations: 'Playing on my PlayStation, golf, a day at the races. Listening to sweet soul and swing music and riding the Groovy Train of the old skool'

Extras: Scored 52 not out on first-team debut against South Africa A in 1996. Took a wicket with his first ball in the Sunday League. Father used to play in the 70s band Hot Chocolate. Released by Essex at end of 1998 season

Best batting: 14* Essex v Durham, Riverside 1998

Best bowling: 1-22 Essex v Durham, Riverside 1998

1998 Season

	M	Inns	NO	Runs	HS	Avge	100s	50s	Ct	St	O	M	Runs	Wkts	Avge	Best	5wI	10wM
Test																		
All First	2	3	1	31	14 *	15.50	-	-	-	-	25	4	114	2	57.00	1-22	-	-
1-day Int																		
NatWest																			
B & H																			
Sunday	2	2	2	9	7 *	-	-	-	-	-	4	0	25	1	25.00	1-25	-	

Career Performances

	M	Inns	NO	Runs	HS	Avge	100s	50s	Ct	St	Balls	Runs	Wkts	Avge	Best	5wI	10wM
Test																	
All First	3	3	1	31	14 *	15.50	-	-	1	-	243	181	4	45.25	1-22	-	-
1-day Int																	
NatWest																		
B & H																		
Sunday	4	3	2	16	7 *	16.00	-	-	1	-	72	65	4	16.25	3-40	-	

WILSON, E. J. Worcestershire

Name: Elliot James Wilson
Role: Right-hand bat, right-arm
medium bowler
Born: 3 November 1976, London
Height: 6ft 2in **Weight:** 13st
County debut: 1998
Place in batting averages: 273rd av. 10.10
Parents: Alec and Faye
Marital status: Single
Family links with cricket: None
Education: Felsted Prep School; Felsted
School; University of Durham
Qualifications: 10 GCSEs, 3 A-levels
Overseas tours: Felsted to Australia 1995-96
Overseas teams played for: Pinetown CC,
Durban, South Africa 1995-96
Cricketers particularly admired: Nick
Knight

Young players to look out for: Tim Phillips
Other sports followed: Rugby, football and athletics, 'all sports really'
Relaxations: Sport and seeing friends
Extras: Scored 950 runs in ten 2nd XI championship games in 1996, while scoring
more than 3,000 runs in the season. Essex League Batsman of the Year in 1996. Broke
Nick Knight's school record with 1,200 runs in 16 innings at an average of 120. Art
scholar to Felsted School. Uncle Nev won yachting two-tonne World Cup
Championship and was New Zealand touring car champion. Great Grandad went to the
South Pole with Shackleton in 1907-09. Missed 1997 season after back operation
Opinions on cricket: 'Why are the young lads who have the temperament which
enables them to achieve in a match situation discarded to allow opportunities for other
young lads who simply look the part, but always seem to underachieve? Surely
technical abilities can be relatively easily developed through experience, while
temperament is a natural gift that cannot be learned.'
Best batting: 27 Worcestershire v Warwickshire, Worcester 1998

98. Who topped the batting averages in the 1996 World Cup?

1998 Season

	M	Inns	NO	Runs	HS	Avge	100s	50s	Ct	St	O	M	Runs	Wkts	Avge	Best	5wI	10wM
Test																		
All First	5	10	0	101	27	10.10	-	-	3	-								
1-day Int																		
NatWest																		
B & H																		
Sunday	5	4	0	28	15	7.00	-	-	1	-								

Career Performances

	M	Inns	NO	Runs	HS	Avge	100s	50s	Ct	St	Balls	Runs	Wkts	Avge	Best	5wI	10wM
Test																	
All First	5	10	0	101	27	10.10	-	-	3	-							
1-day Int																	
NatWest																	
B & H																	
Sunday	5	4	0	28	15	7.00	-	-	1	-							

WILTON, N.   Sussex

Name: Nicholas James Wilton
Role: Right-hand bat, wicket-keeper
Born: 23 September 1978, Pembury
Height: 5ft 11in **Weight:** 12st
Nickname: Rodders, Froggie, Pops
County debut: 1998
1st-Class catches: 5
Parents: Graham Robert and Susan Dawn
Marital status: Single
Family links with cricket:
Dad played local club cricket. Brother plays
for school and club
Education: St Johns C of E Primary School,
Crowborough; Beacon Community College;
Beacon Sixth Form College; City of
Westminster College
Qualifications: 10 GCSEs, CFS in Sports
Studies, Prevention of Sports Injury
Certificate, completed 1st year in Advanced
GNVQ in Leisure and Tourism, Pitman Computer Course Level 1
Off-season: Preparing for 1999 season ('fitness and own game')
Overseas tours: England U19 to South Africa (inc Youth World Cup) 1997-98

Cricketers particularly admired: Alan Knott, Ian Healy, Mark and Steve Waugh
Young players to look out for: Mike Yardy, Graeme Swann, Michael Gough, Morne van Wyk (South Africa U19)
Other sports played: Football (Sussex U10 and U11)
Other sports followed: Football (Arsenal FC)
Relaxations: Music, films, cinema, 'spending time with girlfriend Amy'
Extras: Played for Sussex Colts since the age of ten (U11 to U19). Played for Sussex 2nd XI in 1996. Retained and registered by Sussex in 1997 while spending a season with the MCC Young Cricketers. Has represented England at U14, U17 and U19 levels. Missed two-thirds of the 1997 season with a dislocated shoulder. Represented England at U14, U17 and U19 levels. Part of the England U19 squad which won the U19 World Cup in South Africa 1998
Opinions on cricket: 'Introduction of day/night cricket has proved to be a massive success and more should be played, maybe a separate league. All 2nd XI cricket should be four days and played at first-class grounds to narrow gap between the two standards of 1st and 2nd XI.'
Best batting: 19* Sussex v Hampshire, Hove 1998

1998 Season

	M	Inns	NO	Runs	HS	Avge	100s	50s	Ct	St	O	M	Runs	Wkts	Avge	Best	5wI	10wM
Test																		
All First	2	4	2	46	19 *	23.00	-	-	5	-								
1-day Int																		
NatWest																		
B & H																		
Sunday	1	1	0	3	3	3.00	-	-	3	-								

Career Performances

	M	Inns	NO	Runs	HS	Avge	100s	50s	Ct	St	Balls	Runs	Wkts	Avge	Best	5wI	10wM
Test																		
All First	2	4	2	46	19 *	23.00	-	-	5	-								
1-day Int																		
NatWest																		
B & H																		
Sunday	1	1	0	3	3	3.00	-	-	3	-								

WINDOWS, M. G. N. Gloucestershire

Name: Matthew Guy Newman Windows
Role: Right-hand bat, left-arm medium
bowler
Born: 5 April 1973, Clifton, Bristol
Height: 5ft 6in **Weight:** 11st 7lbs
Nickname: Steamy, Maggot
County debut: 1992
County cap: 1998
1000 runs in a season: 1
1st-Class 50s: 16
1st-Class 100s: 6
1st-Class catches: 48
Place in batting averages: 26th av. 43.44
(1997 167th av. 24.60)
Strike rate: (career 49.50)
Parents: Tony and Carolyn
Marital status: Single
Family links with cricket: Father (A.R.)
played for Gloucestershire (1960-69) and

Cambridge University. 'Brother is backbone of Clifton Nomads'
Education: Clifton Primary; Clifton College; Durham University
Qualifications: 9 GCSEs, 3 A-levels, BA (Hons) Sociology
Career outside cricket: Works for Sporting Index spread-betting firm
Off-season: England A tour
Overseas tours: Clifton College to Barbados 1991; England U19 to Pakistan 1991-92;
Durham University to South Africa 1992-93; England A to Zimbabwe and South
Africa 1998-99
Overseas teams played for: Gold Coast Dolphins, Queensland 1996-97
Cricketers particularly admired: Robin Smith, Mike Procter
Young players to look out for: Vikram Solanki
Other sports played: Rugby, rackets (British Open runner-up 1997)
Other sports followed: Football (Arsenal), rugby
Relaxations: Travel, keeping fit, 'having an ale'
Extras: Played for Lincolnshire and in England U19 home series v Sri Lanka 1992.
Scored 71 on county debut v Essex in 1992. Public schools rackets and fives
champion. 1994 Gloucestershire Young Player of the Year. Holds the record for highest
individual score for Durham University (218 not out). Gloucestershire Player of the
Year 1998. First Gloucestershire batsman to 1000 runs in 1998 season. Awarded
county cap 1998
Opinions on cricket: 'We have to bowl too many overs in a day resulting in a heavy
fine rate. The county circuit offers us great camaraderie.'

Best batting: 184 Gloucestershire v Warwickshire, Cheltenham 1996
Best bowling: 1-6 Combined Universities v West Indies, The Parks 1995

1998 Season

	M	Inns	NO	Runs	HS	Avge	100s	50s	Ct	St	O	M	Runs	Wkts	Avge	Best	5wI	10wM
Test																		
All First	16	29	2	1173	151	43.44	4	5	13	-	1	0	7	0	-	-	-	-
1-day Int																		
NatWest	2	2	0	29	25	14.50	-	-	1	-								
B & H	3	3	0	47	24	15.66	-	-	-	-								
Sunday	11	9	2	185	59	26.42	-	1	8	-								

Career Performances

	M	Inns	NO	Runs	HS	Avge	100s	50s	Ct	St	Balls	Runs	Wkts	Avge	Best	5wI	10wM
Test																	
All First	56	104	6	3237	184	33.03	6	16	48	-	99	97	2	48.50	1-6	-	-
1-day Int																	
NatWest	5	5	0	71	33	14.20	-	-	1	-							
B & H	4	4	1	63	24	21.00	-	-	-	-							
Sunday	49	43	4	795	72	20.38	-	3	15	-	48	49	0	-	-	-	-

WOOD, J.   Durham

Name: John Wood
Role: Right-hand bat, right-arm
fast-medium bowler
Born: 22 July 1970, Crofton, Wakefield
Height: 6ft 3in **Weight:** 16st
Nickname: Woody, Cone Head
County debut: 1992
50 wickets in a season: 1
1st-Class 50s: 2
1st-Class 5 w. in innings: 6
1st-Class catches: 17
Place in batting averages: 269th av. 10.72
Place in bowling averages: 92nd av. 30.80
(1997 134th av. 49.18)
Strike rate: 55.33 (career 54.81)
Parents: Brian and Anne
Wife and date of marriage:
Emma Louise, 30 October 1994

Children: Alexandra Mae, 7 April 1996; Joseph Samuel, 3 July 1998
Family links with cricket: 'Father and brother Ian play to good standard of league cricket, particularly Ian in Bradford League'
Education: Crofton Junior School; Crofton High School; Wakefield District College; Leeds Polytechnic
Qualifications: 6 O-levels, BTEC Diploma and HND in Electrical and Electronic Engineering, senior cricket coach
Career outside cricket: 'At the moment cricket coach'
Off-season: Coaching at Durham. Jobs around the house
Overseas tours: Durham CCC to South Africa 1994-95
Overseas teams played for: Griqualand West Cricket Union, South Africa 1989-90; TAWA, New Zealand 1993-95; Wellington B, New Zealand, 1993-94
Cricketers particularly admired: Ian Botham, Robin Smith, Wasim Akram, Malcolm Marshall
Young players to look out for: Matthew Wood, Stephen Harmison
Other sports played: Golf
Other sports followed: Football (Newcastle United)
Injuries: Sore shin, but no time out
Relaxations: Gardening, watching TV
Extras: Played in the Bradford League. Made his debut for Durham (Minor Counties) in 1991. Durham Players' Player of the Year 1998
Opinions on cricket: 'We need to improve the general standard of wickets. Still wish I could have been a football player.'
Best batting: 63* Durham v Nottinghamshire, Chester-le-Street 1993
Best bowling: 6-110 Durham v Essex, Stockton 1994

1998 Season

	M	Inns	NO	Runs	HS	Avge	100s	50s	Ct	St	O	M	Runs	Wkts	Avge	Best	5wl	10wM
Test																		
All First	17	26	4	236	37	10.72	-	-	3	-	571.5	113	1910	62	30.80	5-52	2	-
1-day Int																		
NatWest	2	1	1	8	8 *	-	-	-	-	-	23	1	84	2	42.00	2-40	-	
B & H	5	2	2	12	10 *	-	-	-	1	-	43.1	6	187	5	37.40	2-30	-	
Sunday	14	9	3	33	19 *	5.50	-	-	-	-	94.3	1	494	11	44.90	2-32	-	

Career Performances

	M	Inns	NO	Runs	HS	Avge	100s	50s	Ct	St	Balls	Runs	Wkts	Avge	Best	5wl	10wM
Test																	
All First	68	102	19	1015	63 *	12.22	-	2	17	-	10470	6790	191	35.54	6-110	6	-
1-day Int																	
NatWest	7	2	1	9	8 *	9.00	-	-	-	-	366	252	6	42.00	2-22	-	
B & H	11	6	2	48	27	12.00	-	-	1	-	607	411	10	41.10	3-50	-	
Sunday	46	32	10	198	28	9.00	-	-	4	-	1923	1685	43	39.18	4-17	-	

WOOD, M. J. Yorkshire

Name: Matthew James Wood
Role: Right-hand bat
Born: 6 April 1977, Huddersfield
Height: 5ft 10in **Weight:** 11st 10lbs
Nickname: Chuddy, Ronnie
County debut: 1997
1000 runs in a season: 1
1st-Class 50s: 5
1st-Class 100s: 3
1st-Class 200s: 1
1st-Class catches: 18
Place in batting averages: 19th av. 46.95
Parents: Roger and Kathryn
Marital status: Single
Family links with cricket: 'Father played for
local team Emley. Mum made the teas and
sister Caroline scored'

Education: Emley First School; Kirkburton
Middle School; Shelley High School
Qualifications: 9 GCSEs, 2 A-levels, NCA coaching award
Career outside cricket: 'None yet'
Off-season: 'Go on holiday. Rest and prepare for next season. Maybe play in
South Africa'
Overseas tours: England U19 to Zimbabwe 1995-96; Yorkshire CCC to West Indies
1996-97, to Cape Town 1998
Overseas teams played for: Somerset West CC, Cape Town 1995-96, Upper Hutt
United CC, Wellington, New Zealand 1997-98
Cricketers particularly admired: Martyn Moxon, 'all the Yorkshire CCC staff',
Michael Slater, 'especially Darren Lehmann'
Young players to look out for: Richard Dawson, Matthew Hoggard, Ben Heritage,
Alex Morris
Other sports played: Football (Kirkburton FC), 'occasional golfer'
Other sports followed: Football (Liverpool FC and Emley FC)
Relaxations: Socialising, eating out, watching a good film, playing football
Extras: Played for England U17 against India 1994. Spent two years at the Yorkshire
Academy before graduating to the full staff in 1996. Scored 81 on first-class debut v
Lancashire at Headingley in 1997. Made maiden first-class century v Derbyshire in
1998
Opinions on cricket: 'Twelve-month contracts should be introduced to help players
feel secure all year round.'
Best batting: 200* Yorkshire v Warwickshire, Headingley 1998

1998 Season

	M	Inns	NO	Runs	HS	Avge	100s	50s	Ct	St	O	M	Runs	Wkts	Avge	Best	5wI	10wM
Test																		
All First	19	29	6	1080	200 *	46.95	4	4	17	-								
1-day Int																		
NatWest	1	1	1	25	25 *	-	-	-	-	-								
B & H																		
Sunday	9	7	1	161	65 *	26.83	-	2	2	-								

Career Performances

	M	Inns	NO	Runs	HS	Avge	100s	50s	Ct	St	Balls	Runs	Wkts	Avge	Best	5wI	10wM
Test																	
All First	20	31	6	1182	200 *	47.28	4	5	18	-							
1-day Int																	
NatWest	1	1	1	25	25 *	-	-	-	-	-							
B & H																	
Sunday	9	7	1	161	65 *	26.83	-	2	2	-							

WOOD, N. T.   Lancashire

Name: Nathan Theodore Wood
Role: Left-hand opening bat
Born: 4 October 1974, Ossett, Yorkshire
Height: 5ft 7in **Weight:** 10st 5lbs
Nickname: Pecker, Rodders, Woderwick
County debut: 1996
1st-Class 50s: 4
1st-Class 100s: 1
1st-Class catches: 4
Place in batting averages: 112th av. 28.56
(1997 86th av. 36.07)
Parents: Barry and Janet
Marital status: Single
Family links with cricket: Father played
first-class and Test cricket (Yorkshire,
Derbyshire, Lancashire and England). Uncle
(Ron) played first-class cricket
(for Yorkshire)
Education: Altrincham Prep School;
William Hulme's Grammar School
Qualifications: 8 GCSEs, coaching awards
Off-season: Relaxing

Overseas tours: England U18 to South Africa 1992-93, to Denmark 1993; England U19 to Sri Lanka 1993-94; Lancashire CCC to India and South Africa 1997, to South Africa 1998

Cricketers particularly admired: Steve Titchard, John Crawley, Warren Hegg

Young players to look out for: Chris Schofield, Richard Green

Other sports played: Football

Other sports followed: Football (Manchester United)

Relaxations: Music

Extras: Played in junior One-Day Internationals against Zimbabwe, India, South Africa and Sri Lanka. Played in U19 Tests against West Indies and Sri Lanka. Holds highest opening partnership record for Lancashire 2nd XI of 340 with P.C. McKeown and highest first-wicket partnership for Lancashire against Surrey (259 with M.A. Atherton)

Opinions on cricket: 'There is a lot of nonsense spoken about the structure of the first-class programme. The standard of our domestic game would improve if we reduced the number of games and increased the prize money substantially. Think the introduction of 12-month contracts at Lancashire is a step forward. Do cricket's marketing men undersell the game?'

Best batting: 155 Lancashire v Surrey, The Oval 1997

1998 Season

	M	Inns	NO	Runs	HS	Avge	100s	50s	Ct	St	O	M	Runs	Wkts	Avge	Best	5wI	10wM
Test																		
All First	12	19	3	457	80 *	28.56	-	2	1	-	5.1	0	80	0	-	-	-	-
1-day Int																		
NatWest																		
B & H																		
Sunday	1	1	0	23	23	23.00	-	-	-	-								

Career Performances

	M	Inns	NO	Runs	HS	Avge	100s	50s	Ct	St	Balls	Runs	Wkts	Avge	Best	5wI	10wM
Test																	
All First	23	35	5	927	155	30.90	1	4	4	-	56	118	0	-	-	-	-
1-day Int																	
NatWest																	
B & H																	
Sunday	1	1	0	23	23	23.00	-	-	-	-							

WOOLLEY, A. P. Derbyshire

Name: Anthony Paul Woolley
Role: Right-hand bat, right-arm medium bowler
Born: 4 December 1971, Derby
Height: 6ft 2in **Weight:** 14st
Nickname: Gus
County debut: No first-team appearance
Parents: Gerry and Jean
Marital status: Single ('girlfriend Annie')
Education: St Werburgh's Primary, Spondon, Derby; Spondon School, Spondon, Derby; Broomfield College, Morley, Derby
Qualifications: 4 GCSEs, Phase I and II Greenkeeping
Career outside cricket: Engineering – machinist
Off-season: 'Going on holiday with girlfriend and returning to work'

Cricketers particularly admired:
Ian Botham, Viv Richards
Young players to look out for: Ian Blackwell, Ben Spendlove, Trevor Smith
Other sports played: Football ('played for Derby Boys when 15 years old'), golf
Other sports followed: Football (Derby County), cricket (Alvaston & Boulton CC)
Relaxations: 'Golf, football, general socialising'
Opinions on cricket: 'Not enough investment in the game. Would like to see players better rewarded financially.'

WRIGHT, A. J.   Gloucestershire

Name: Anthony John Wright
Role: Right-hand bat, off-spin bowler
Born: 27 July 1962, Stevenage, Hertfordshire
Height: 6ft **Weight:** 14st
Nickname: Billy
County debut: 1982
County cap: 1987
Benefit: 1996
1000 runs in a season: 6
1st-Class 50s: 67
1st-Class 100s: 18
1st-Class catches: 218
One-Day 100s: 4
Place in batting averages: 221st av. 17.25
(1997 197th av. 21.89)
Strike rate: (career 74.00)
Parents: Michael and Patricia
Wife and date of marriage:
Rachel, 21 December 1986
Children: Hannah, 3 April 1988; Beth, 19 August 1992; Joseph, 29 November 1993
Education: Alleyn's School, Stevenage
Qualifications: 6 O-levels
Overseas tours: Gloucestershire to Sri Lanka 1987 and 1993, to Barbados 1980, 1985, 1988, to Namibia 1990, to Kenya 1991
Cricketers particularly admired: Mike Gatting, Malcolm Marshall, Dermot Reeve, David Gower
Other sports followed: Soccer ('life-long Chelsea supporter'), rugby (Bristol RFC)
Relaxations: 'Celebrating any Arsenal defeat and hacking my way around a golf course'
Extras: Captain of Gloucestershire 1990-93. Retired at end of 1998 season
Opinions on cricket: 'I feel that it is vital that the game is introduced to as many youngsters as possible. Unless kids are at private schools they are unlikely to get a chance to participate – a shocking situation!'
Best batting: 193 Gloucestershire v Nottinghamshire, Bristol 1995
Best bowling: 1-16 Gloucestershire v Yorkshire, Harrogate 1989

99. Who was Player of the Tournament in the 1996 World Cup?

FICA

1998 Season

	M	Inns	NO	Runs	HS	Avge	100s	50s	Ct	St	O	M	Runs	Wkts	Avge	Best	5wI	10wM
Test																		
All First	11	20	0	345	57	17.25	-	1	5	-								
1-day Int																		
NatWest	2	2	0	33	28	16.50	-	-	-	-								
B & H	5	5	1	232	93	58.00	-	2	4	-								
Sunday	11	11	1	158	46	15.80	-	-	2	-								

Career Performances

	M	Inns	NO	Runs	HS	Avge	100s	50s	Ct	St	Balls	Runs	Wkts	Avge	Best	5wI	10wM
Test																	
All First	287	504	38	13440	193	28.84	18	67	218	-	74	68	1	68.00	1-16	-	-
1-day Int																	
NatWest	32	31	2	1293	177	44.58	3	9	11	-							
B & H	52	49	1	1582	123	32.95	1	10	14	-							
Sunday	194	183	18	4011	96	24.30	-	25	69	-	26	22	0	-		-	-

WRIGHT, A. S.   Leicestershire

Name: Ashley Spencer Wright
Role: Right-hand opening bat, right-arm medium bowler
Born: 21 October 1980, Grantham
Height: 5ft 11in **Weight:** 11st 7lbs
Nickname: Ash
County debut: No first-team appearance
Parents: Keith and Anna
Marital status: Single
Family links with cricket: Father very keen cricketer and senior coach
Education: Redmile Primary School; Belvoir High School; King Edward VII, Melton Mowbray
Qualifications: 10 GCSEs, coaching award
Career outside cricket: 'Cricket is the only thing I want to do'
Cricketers particularly admired: 'All the Leicestershire players'
Other sports played: Squash
Other sports followed: Football (Leicester City, Notts County, Notts Forest)
Relaxations: Music, cinema, going to gym

Extras: Hit a highest score of 158 against Staffordshire U15. Was in pre-Christmas squad of 22 for England U19 tour to New Zealand 1998-99
Opinions on cricket: 'Pleased to see more younger players given a chance to play at higher levels.'

YATES, G. Lancashire

Name: Gary Yates
Role: Right-hand bat, off-spin bowler
Born: 20 September 1967,
Ashton-under-Lyne
Height: 6ft 1in **Weight:** 12st 10lbs
Nickname: Sweatty, Yugo, Pearly,
Backyard, Zippy
County debut: 1990
County cap: 1994
1st-Class 50s: 4
1st-Class 100s: 3
1st-Class 5 w. in innings: 3
1st-Class catches: 28
Place in batting averages:
(1997 219th av. 19.40)
Place in bowling averages: 39th av. 24.00
(1997 89th av. 33.20)
Strike rate: 43.83 (career 76.45)
Parents: Alan and Patricia
Marital status: Single
Family links with cricket: Father played in Lancashire Leagues
Education: Manchester Grammar School
Qualifications: 6 O-levels, Australian Cricket Coaching Council coach
Career outside cricket: 'Rep with family business (Digical Ltd), selling diaries, calendars and business gifts'
Off-season: 'Working at Digical. Start back with Lancashire in December'
Overseas tours: Lancashire to Tasmania and Western Australia 1990, to Western Australia 1991, to Johannesburg 1992, to Barbados and St Lucia 1992, to Cape Town 1997-98, to Calcutta 1997
Overseas teams played for: South Barwon, Geelong, Australia 1987-88; Johnsonville, Wellington, New Zealand 1989-90; Western Suburbs, Brisbane 1991-92; Old Selbornian, East London, South Africa 1992-93; Hermanus CC, South Africa 1995-96
Cricketers particularly admired: Michael Atherton, Ian Botham, John Emburey
Young players to look out for: Mark Chilton, Andrew Flintoff
Other sports followed: All sports, especially football (Manchester City), golf, motor rallying

Relaxations: Playing golf, watching football and good films, eating
Extras: Played for Worcestershire 2nd XI in 1987. Made debut for Lancashire 2nd XI in 1988 and taken on to county staff in 1990. Scored century on Championship debut v Nottinghamshire at Trent Bridge. Rapid Cricketline Player of the Month April/May 1992
Opinions on cricket: 'Would like to see more points awarded for rained-off games or draws. This would hopefully help to abolish contrived matches. Hope four-day cricket is here to stay.'
Best batting: 134* Lancashire v Northamptonshire, Old Trafford 1993
Best bowling: 5-34 Lancashire v Hampshire, Old Trafford 1994

1998 Season

	M	Inns	NO	Runs	HS	Avge	100s	50s	Ct	St	O	M	Runs	Wkts	Avge	Best	5wl	10wM
Test																		
All First	4	6	1	174	55	34.80	-	1	2	-	131.3	26	432	18	24.00	4-64	-	-
1-day Int																		
NatWest	5	2	0	13	7	6.50	-	-	-	-	43	4	137	1	137.00	1-19	-	
B & H	6	4	1	37	16	12.33	-	-	-	-	48	1	219	7	31.28	2-35	-	
Sunday	15	8	5	53	24 *	17.66	-	-	4	-	71	0	380	11	34.54	3-35	-	

Career Performances

	M	Inns	NO	Runs	HS	Avge	100s	50s	Ct	St	Balls	Runs	Wkts	Avge	Best	5wl	10wM
Test																	
All First	70	93	35	1670	134 *	28.79	3	4	28	-	11851	6253	155	40.34	5-34	3	-
1-day Int																	
NatWest	17	9	5	82	34 *	20.50	-	-	1	-	1038	594	12	49.50	2-15	-	
B & H	32	14	3	134	26	12.18	-	-	6	-	1548	1081	35	30.88	3-42	-	
Sunday	89	39	21	305	38	16.94	-	-	23	-	3066	2595	87	29.82	4-34	-	

100. Where is the World Cup scheduled to be held in 2003?

FICA

How you **s&p**end it is up to you.

Save & Prosper and the PCA sponsor, Fleming Premier Banking, are both part
of the Fleming Group which manages worldwide assets of £64 billion.
We're delighted to be associated with the Professional Cricketers' Association.

save**&p**rosper

PEPs, Unit Trusts & ISAs
0800 829 400

THE UMPIRES

BALDERSTONE, J. C.

Name: John Christopher Balderstone
Born: 16 November 1940, Huddersfield
Height: 6ft 0½in
Nickname: Baldy
Appointed to 1st-Class list: 1988
First appointed to Test panel: 1994
One-Day Internationals umpired: 2
Counties as player: Yorkshire, Leicestershire
Role: Right-hand opening bat, slow
left-arm bowler
County debut: 1961 (Yorkshire),
1971 (Leicestershire)
County cap: 1973 (Leicestershire)
Test debut: 1976
Tests: 2
1000 runs in a season: 11
1st-Class 50s: 102
1st-Class 100s: 32
1st-Class 5 w. in innings: 5
1st-Class catches: 210
One-Day 100s: 5
Wife and date of marriage: Angela, January 1991
Children: Sally, 15 September 1970; Michael, 3 January 1973
Education: Paddock County School, Huddersfield
Career outside cricket: Professional footballer 1958-78, cricket and soccer coach
Off-season: Coaching cricket
Overseas tours: Leicestershire to Zimbabwe 1981, to Oman 1984
Cricketers particularly admired: Willie Watson, Brian Close, Fred Trueman,
David Gower, Ray Illingworth
Young players to look out for: Alec and Graeme Swann, Paul Franks
Other sports followed: All sports
Relaxations: Golf
Extras: Fourteen one-day Man of the Match Awards. Played a first-class cricket match
and football league game on the same day in 1975 (Leicestershire v Derbyshire,
Doncaster v Brentford). Was the first man to act as third umpire in Test in England, in
the second Test against Australia at Lord's in 1993 and has acted as third umpire in
'10-12' Tests in total. Umpired his first one-day international, England v South Africa
1994
Opinions on cricket: 'Still think the Championship is best as it is. The fact that in the
last three years Leicestershire (twice) and Glamorgan have beaten so-called bigger
clubs appeals to me.'

Best batting: 181* Leicestershire v Gloucestershire, Leicester 1984
Best bowling: 6-25 Leicestershire v Hampshire, Southampton 1978

First-Class Career Performances

	M	Inns	NO	Runs	HS	Avge	100s	Ct	St	Runs	Wkts	Avge	Best	5wI	10wM
Test	2	4	0	39	35	9.75	-	-	1	80	1	80.00	1-80	-	-
All First	390	619	61	19034	181*	34.11	32	210	-	8160	310	26.32	6-25	5	-

BURGESS, G. I.

Name: Graham Iefvion Burgess
Born: 5 May 1943,
Glastonbury, Somerset
Appointed to 1st-Class list: 1991
County as player: Somerset
Role: Right-hand bat, right-arm
medium bowler
County debut: 1966
County cap: 1968
Testimonial: 1977
1st-Class 100s: 2
1st-Class 5 w. in innings: 18
1st-Class 10 w. in match: 2
1st-Class catches: 120
Education: Millfield School
Extras: Played Minor Counties cricket for
Wilts 1981-82 and for Cambs 1983-84
Best batting: 129 Somerset v
Gloucestershire, Taunton 1973
Best bowling: 7-43 Somerset v Oxford University, The Parks 1975

First-Class Career Performances

	M	Inns	NO	Runs	HS	Avge	100s	Ct	St	Runs	Wkts	Avge	Best	5wI	10wM
Test															
All First	252	414	37	7129	129	18.90	2	120	-	13543	474	28.57	7-43	18	2

CLARKSON, A.

Name: Anthony Clarkson
Born: 5 September 1939, Killinghall,
North Yorkshire
Height: 6ft
Appointed to 1st-Class list: 1996
Counties as player: Yorkshire, Somerset
Role: Right-hand bat, right-arm off-spin
bowler
County debut: 1963 (Yorkshire),
1965 (Somerset)
County cap: 1969 (Somerset)
1000 runs in a season: 2
1st-Class 100s: 2
1st-Class catches: 52
Marital status: Engaged to Cheryl
Children: André, 5 September 1964;
Chantal, 27 May 1967; Pierre, 1 May 1969
Family links with cricket: Father was a
league professional

Education: Killinghall C of E; Harrogate Grammar School; Leeds College of
Building; Bradford Polytechnic; Brunel College, Bristol
Career outside cricket: Architectural, Civil Engineering and Surveying Consultant
Off-season: Working and completing the renovation of house
Other sports followed: Golf and rugby ('especially league')
Relaxations: Golf, DIY, and gardening
Extras: First English player to score a century in the Sunday League

First-Class Career Performances

	M	Inns	NO	Runs	HS	Avge	100s	Ct	St	Runs	Wkts	Avge	Best	5wI	10wM
Test															
All First	110	189	12	4458	131	25.18	2	52	-	367	13	28.23	3-51	-	-

CONSTANT, D. J.

Name: David John Constant
Born: 9 November 1941,
Bradford-on-Avon, Wiltshire
Height: 5ft 7in
Nickname: Connie
Appointed to 1st-Class list: 1969
First appointed to Test panel: 1971
Tests umpired: 36
One-Day Internationals umpired: 31
Counties as player: Kent, Leicestershire
Role: Left-hand bat, slow left-arm bowler
County debut: 1961 (Kent),
1965 (Leicestershire)
1st-Class 50s: 6
1st-Class catches: 33
Wife's name: Rosalyn
Children: Lisa, 6 July 1966;
Julie, 21 February 1969
Family links with cricket: Father-in-law,
G.E.E. Lambert, played for Gloucestershire
Education: Grove Park Secondary Modern
Off-season: Bowls
Other sports followed: Football (Millwall)
Interests/relaxations: 'Six grandchildren and bowls'
Extras: County bowls player for Gloucestershire 1984-86 (outdoors). Also represented
Somerset at indoor version of the game
Best batting: 80 Leicestershire v Gloucestershire, Bristol 1966

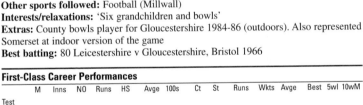

First-Class Career Performances

	M	Inns	NO	Runs	HS	Avge	100s	Ct	St	Runs	Wkts	Avge	Best	5wI	10wM
Test															
All First	61	93	14	1517	80	19.20	-	33	-	36	1	36.00	1-28	-	-

DUDLESTON, B.

Name: Barry Dudleston
Born: 16 July 1945, Bebington, Cheshire
Height: 5ft 9in
Nickname: Danny
Appointed to 1st-Class list: 1984
First appointed to Test panel: 1991
Tests umpired: 2
One-Day Internationals umpired: 2
Counties as player: Leicestershire,
Gloucestershire
Role: Right-hand opening bat, occasional
slow left-arm bowler, occasional
wicket-keeper
County debut: 1966 (Leicestershire),
1981 (Gloucestershire)
County cap: 1969 (Leicestershire)
Benefit: 1980 (£25,000)
1000 runs in a season: 8
1st-Class 100s: 31
1st-Class 200s: 1
1st-Class catches: 234
One-Day 100s: 4
Wife and date of marriage: Louise Wendy, 19 October 1994
Children: Sharon Louise, 29 October 1968; Matthew Barry, 12 September 1988;
Jack Nicholas, 29 April 1998
Family links with cricket: Father was a club cricketer
Education: Stockport School
Career outside cricket: Managing director of Sunsport Tours & Travel
(sports travel company)
Off-season: In South Africa, Australia and Zimbabwe on business
Overseas tours: Kent (as guest player) to West Indies 1972; D.H. Robins' XI
to West Indies 1973; Wisden XI to West Indies 1984; MCC to Kenya 1993
Overseas teams played for: Rhodesia 1975-80
Other sports played: Golf
Other sports followed: 'Follow all sports. Don't laugh – support Stockport County
and Manchester City'
Cricketers particularly admired: Gary Sobers, Tom Graveney
Cricketers particularly learnt from: Vinoo Mankad
Young players to look out for: Graeme Swann
Relaxations: 'TV, bridge, good red wine'
Extras: Played for England U25. Suffered badly from broken fingers, breaking fingers
on the same hand three times in 1978. Holder with John Steele of the highest first

wicket partnership for Leicestershire, 390 v Derbyshire in 1979. Fastest player in Rhodesian cricket history to 1000 first-class runs in Currie Cup; second fastest ever in Currie Cup. Has acted as third umpire in 15 Tests

Opinions on cricket: 'Too much emphasis on blanket fitness rather than being able to do your job mentally and physically. Too little attention to playing straight and bowling straight. A fear that if Colin Cowdrey and Colin Milburn turned up for a trial today, they would be sent away without ever holding a bat.'

Best batting: 202 Leicestershire v Derbyshire, Leicester 1979
Best bowling: 4-6 Leicestershire v Surrey, Leicester 1972

First-Class Career Performances

	M	Inns	NO	Runs	HS	Avge	100s	Ct	St	Runs	Wkts	Avge	Best	5wI	10wM
Test															
All First	295	501	47	14747	202	32.48	32	234	7	1365	47	29.04	4-6	-	-

HAMPSHIRE, J. H.

Name: John Harry Hampshire
Born: 10 February 1941, Thurnscoe, Yorkshire
Height: 6ft
Nickname: Hamp
Appointed to 1st-Class list: 1985
First appointed to Test panel: 1989
Tests umpired: 11
One-Day Internationals umpired: 8
Counties as player: Yorkshire, Derbyshire
Role: Right-hand bat, leg-spin bowler
County debut: 1961 (Yorkshire), 1982 (Derbyshire)
County cap: 1963 (Yorkshire), 1982 (Derbyshire)
Benefit: 1976
Test debut: 1969
Tests: 11
1000 runs in a season: 15
1st-Class 50s: 142
1st-Class 100s: 43
1st-Class 5 w. in innings: 2
1st-Class catches: 445
One-Day 100s: 7
Wife and date of marriage: Judith Ann, 5 September 1964
Children: Ian Christopher, 6 January 1969; Paul Wesley, 12 February 1972

Family links with cricket: Father (J.) and brother (A.W.) both played for Yorkshire
Education: Oakwood Technical High School, Rotherham
Overseas tours: MCC to Australia and New Zealand, 1970-71
Overseas teams played for: Tasmania, 1966-69, 1977-79
Cricketers particularly admired: Peter May, Gary Sobers
Other sports followed: Most sports
Relaxations: Gardening and cooking
Extras: Captained Yorkshire 1979-80. Scored a century (107) at Lord's in his first Test match (against West Indies 1969); the only England player to have done so. Appointed manager/coach of the Zimbabwe Test squad for their first Test matches against India and New Zealand. Umpired four Tests in Pakistan 1989-90
Best batting: 183* Yorkshire v Surrey, Hove 1971
Best bowling: 7-52 Yorkshire v Glamorgan, Cardiff 1963

First-Class Career Performances

	M	Inns	NO	Runs	HS	Avge	100s	Ct	St	Runs	Wkts	Avge	Best	5wl	10wM
Test	8	16	1	405	107	26.86	1	9	-						
All First	577	924	112	28059	183	*34.55	43	445	-	1637	30	54.56	7-52	2	-

HARRIS, J. H.

Name: John Henry Harris
Born: 13 February 1936, Taunton
Height: 5ft 11in
Nickname: Arry, Boater, JH
Appointed to 1st-Class list: 1983
County as player: Somerset
Role: Left-hand bat, right-arm fast-medium bowler
County debut: 1952
1st-Class catches: 6
Wife and date of marriage:
Morag Elspeth Jane, 20 October 1984
Children: Karen, Andrew, Mark and Tim
Family links with cricket: 'Grandfather (Harry Jernie) was head groundsman at Somerset CCC for 25 years'
Education: Priory School, Taunton; Coopers Lane, Grove Park, London
Career outside cricket: Devon League cricket inspector of grounds

Other sports played/followed: Golf ('poorly') and squash
Relaxations: DIY, Glenn Miller music, Bournemouth Symphony Orchestra, television

'and a few drinks with my friends at the D&E squash club'
Extras: Made his debut for Somerset aged 16 years 99 days. Played Minor Counties cricket for Suffolk (1960-62) and Devon (1975). Two overseas tours with the MCC as umpire. Umpired the first Masters Cup in Bombay. Stepped down as Chairman of the First-Class Cricket Umpires' Association after five years
Best batting: 41 Somerset v Worcestershire, Taunton 1957
Best bowling: 3-29 Somerset v Worcestershire, Bristol 1959

First-Class Career Performances

	M	Inns	NO	Runs	HS	Avge	100s	Ct	St	Runs	Wkts	Avge	Best	5wI	10wM
Test															
All First	15	18	4	154	41	11.00	-	6	-	609	19	32.05	3.29	-	-

HARRIS, M. J.

Name: Michael John Harris
Born: 25 May 1944, St Just-in-Roseland, Cornwall
Height: 6ft 1in
Nickname: Pasty
Appointed to 1st-Class list: 1998
Counties as player: Middlesex, Nottinghamshire
Role: Right-hand bat, leg-break bowler, wicket-keeper
County debut: 1964 (Middlesex), 1969 (Notts)
County cap: 1967 (Middlesex), 1970 (Notts)
1000 runs in a season: 11
1st-Class 50s: 98
1st-Class 100s: 40
1st-Class 200s: 1
1st-Class catches: 288
1st-Class stumpings: 14

Wife and date of marriage: Danielle Ruth, 10 September 1969
Children: Jodie, Richard
Education: Gerrans Comprehensive
Career outside cricket: Sports teacher
Other sports followed: Squash, golf
Cricketers particularly admired: Gary Sobers, Clive Rice
Cricketers particularly learnt from: Eric Russell (Middlesex)
Extras: Played for Eastern Province in the Currie Cup 1971-72 and for Wellington in the Shell Trophy 1975-76. Scored nine centuries in 1971 to equal Nottinghamshire

county record, scoring two centuries in a match twice and totalling 2238 for the season at an average of 50.86. Also shared Middlesex record first wicket partnership (312) with Eric Russell v Pakistanis at Lord's 1967

Best batting: 201* Nottinghamshire v Glamorgan, Trent Bridge 1973
Best bowling: 4-16 Nottinghamshire v Warwickshire, Trent Bridge 1969

First-Class Career Performances

	M	Inns	NO	Runs	HS	Avge	100s	Ct	St	Runs	Wkts	Avge	Best	5wI	10wM
Test															
All First	344	581	58	19196	201*	36.70	41	288	14	3459	79	43.78	4-16	-	-

HOLDER, J. W.

Name: John Wakefield Holder
Born: 19 March 1945,
St George, Barbados
Height: 6ft
Nickname: Benson, Hod
Appointed to 1st-Class list: 1983
First appointed to Test panel: 1988
Tests umpired: 10
One-Day Internationals umpired: 14
County as player: Hampshire
Role: Right-hand bat, right-arm
fast bowler
County debut: 1968
50 wickets in a season: 1
1st-Class 5 w. in innings: 5
1st-Class 10 w. in match: 1
1st-Class catches: 12
Wife: Glenda
Children: Christopher 1968; Nigel 1970
Family links with cricket: None
Education: St Giles Boys School; Combermere High School, Barbados;
Rochdale College
Off-season: 'Idling'
Young players to look out for: Alex Tudor
Other sports followed: Football (Manchester United)
Relaxations: Keeping fit and helping coach the Rochdale Indoor Cricket Team which plays in the National League in the winter
Extras: Umpired four Tests in Pakistan 1989-90
Best batting: 33 Hampshire v Sussex, Hove 1971
Best bowling: 7-79 Hampshire v Gloucestershire, Gloucester 1972

First-Class Career Performances

	M	Inns	NO	Runs	HS	Avge	100s	Ct	St	Runs	Wkts	Avge	Best	5wI	10wM
Test															
All First	47	49	14	374	33	10.68	-	12	-	3415	139	24.56	7-79	5	1

HOLDER, V. A.

Name: Vanburn Alonza Holder
Born: 8 October 1945,
St Michael, Barbados
Height: 6ft 3in
Nickname: Van
Appointed to 1st-Class list: 1991
County as player: Worcestershire
Role: Right-hand bat, right-arm
fast-medium bowler
County debut: 1968
County cap: 1970
Test debut: 1969
Tests: 40
1st-Class 50s: 4
1st-Class 100s: 1
1st-Class 5 w. in innings: 38
1st-Class 10 w. in match: 3
1st-Class catches: 98

Wife's name: Christine
Children: James Vanburn, 2 September 1981
Education: St Leonard's Secondary Modern; Community High
Off-season: 'Working'
Overseas tours: West Indies to England 1969, 1973, 1975 (World Cup), to India,
Sri Lanka and Pakistan 1974-75, to Australia 1975-76, to England 1976, to India and
Sri Lanka 1978-79 (as vice-captain); Rest of the World to Pakistan 1973-74
Overseas teams played for: Barbados
Other sports followed: Football (Liverpool)
Young players to look out for: Ben Hollioake, Alex Tudor, Steve Harmison
Relaxations: Music. Doing crosswords
Extras: Made his debut for Barbados in the Shell Shield competition in 1966-67. Won
John Player League with Worcestershire 1973 and County Championship 1974. Played
in West Indies 1975 World Cup winning side
Opinions on cricket: 'The English players have got to learn to back themselves.'
Best batting: 122 Barbados v Trinidad, Bridgetown 1973-74
Best bowling: 7-40 Worcestershire v Glamorgan, Cardiff 1974

First-Class Career Performances

	M	Inns	NO	Runs	HS	Avge	100s	Ct	St	Runs	Wkts	Avge	Best	5wI	10wM
Test	40	59	11	682	42	14.20	-	16	-	3627	109	33.27	6-28	3	-
All First	311	354	81	3559	122	13.03	1	98	-	23183	948	24.45	7-40	38	3

JESTY, T. E.

Name: Trevor Edward Jesty
Born: 2 June 1948, Gosport, Hampshire
Height: 5ft 9in
Nickname: Jets
Appointed to 1st-Class list: 1994
Counties as player: Hampshire, Surrey, Lancashire
Role: Right-hand bat, right-arm medium bowler
County debut: 1966 (Hampshire), 1985 (Surrey), 1988 (Lancashire)
County cap: 1971 (Hampshire), 1985 (Surrey)
Benefit: 1982
One-Day Internationals: 10
1000 runs in a season: 10
50 wickets in a season: 2
1st-Class 50s: 110
1st-Class 100s: 33
1st-Class 200s: 2
1st-Class 5 w. in innings: 19
1st-Class catches: 265
1st-Class stumpings: 1
One-Day 100s: 7
Wife and date of marriage: Jacqueline, 12 September 1970
Children: Graeme Barry, 27 September 1972; Lorna Samantha, 7 November 1976
Education: Privett County Secondary Modern, Gosport
Off-season: Coaching for Hampshire CCC from January to March
Overseas tours: International XI to West Indies 1982; joined England tour to Australia and New Zealand 1982-83; Lancashire to Zimbabwe 1989
Overseas teams played for: Border, South Africa 1973-74; Griqualand West 1974-76; Canterbury, New Zealand 1980-81
Cricketers particularly admired: Sir Garfield Sobers, Barry Richards
Young players to look out for: Graeme Swann, Alec Swann, Robert Key
Other sports followed: Football (Arsenal)

Relaxations: Gardening, reading
Extras: One of *Wisden*'s five Cricketers of the Year 1983. Left Hampshire at end of 1984 when not appointed captain and offered the captaincy of Surrey for 1985 season
Best batting: 248 Hampshire v Cambridge University, Fenner's 1984
Best bowling: 7-75 Hampshire v Worcestershire, Southampton 1976

First-Class Career Performances

	M	Inns	NO	Runs	HS	Avge	100s	Ct	St	Runs	Wkts	Avge	Best	5wI	10wM
Test															
All First	490	777	107	21916	248	32.71	35	265	1	16075	585	27.47	7-75	19	-

JONES, A. A.

Name: Alan Arthur Jones
Born: 9 December 1947, Horley, Surrey
Height: 6ft 3in
Nickname: Jonah, Buckets
Appointed to 1st-Class list: 1985
One-Day Internationals umpired: 1
Counties as player: Sussex, Somerset, Middlesex, Glamorgan
Role: Right-hand bat, right-arm fast-medium bowler
County debut: 1964 (Sussex), 1970 (Somerset), 1976 (Middlesex), 1980 (Glamorgan)
County cap: 1972 (Somerset), 1976 (Middlesex), 1980 (Glamorgan)
50 wickets in a season: 4
1st-Class 5 w. in innings: 23
1st-Class 10 w. in match: 3
1st-Class catches: 50

Wife: Marilyn
Children: Clare Michelle
Education: St John's College, Horsham
Overseas teams played for: Northern Transvaal 1971-72; Orange Free State 1976-77
Other sports followed: All sports
Cricketers particularly admired: Tom Cartwright, Brian Close
Young players to look out for: Darren Altree, Ashley Giles, Jason Laney
Other sports followed: Golf
Relaxations: Reading, cooking and travel
Extras: Won two Championship medals with Middlesex (1976 and 1977). He was the first person to play for four counties – only one other player has done so since

Best batting: 33 Middlesex v Kent, Canterbury 1978
Best bowling: 9-51 Somerset v Sussex, Hove 1976

First-Class Career Performances

	M	Inns	NO	Runs	HS	Avge	100s	Ct	St	Runs	Wkts	Avge	Best	5wI	10wM
Test															
All First	214	216	68	799	33	5-39	-	50	-	15414	549	28.07	9-51	23	3

JULIAN, R.

Name: Raymond Julian
Born: 23 August 1936,
Cosby, Leicestershire
Height: 5ft 11in
Nickname: Julie
Appointed to 1st-Class list: 1972
International panel: 1996
One-Day Internationals umpired: 3
County as player: Leicestershire
Role: Right-hand bat, wicket-keeper
County debut: 1953
County cap: 1961
1st-Class 50s: 2
1st-Class catches: 381
1st-Class stumpings: 40
Wife and date of marriage:
Megan, 3 April 1993
Children: Peter Raymond, 1 February 1958;
John Kelvin, 13 October 1960;
David Andrew, 15 October 1963; Paul Anthony, 22 September 1967
Family links with cricket: Father and two brothers all played local cricket. Two sons play local cricket
Education: Cosby Primary School, Leicestershire; Wigston Secondary Modern
Career outside cricket: Cricket coach, decorator and gardener
Off-season: Watching the England tour to Australia and the A team in Zimbabwe
Overseas tours: MCC to West Africa, 1975
Cricketers particularly admired: Gary Sobers, Keith Andrew
Young players to look out for: James Ormond, Paul Hutchison
Other sports followed: Football (Leicester City FC), boxing, rugby (Leicester Tigers)
Relaxations: Gardening, holidays, travel
Extras: Youngest wicket-keeper to make debut in first-class cricket, Leicestershire v Gloucestershire, Bristol 1953, aged 16. Took six catches in an innings, Leicestershire v Northants, Kettering 1965. Played for the Army 1955-57. Gave eight lbw decisions in

succession, Glamorgan v Sussex at Cardiff 1986. Stood in 1998 B&H final and has umpired three B&H semi-finals and one Gillette Cup semi-final. Has just completed 26 years on the first-class list. Has been the stand-by umpire in three Tests, has acted as third umpire in six Tests and has umpired three One-Day Internationals. Captained Leicestershire 2nd XI from 1968 to 1971. First-class football referee. One FA Cup match. Linesman in old Southern League 1960-72. Recipient of the Professional Cricketers' Association's Umpires Cup in 1998

Opinions on cricket: 'Good to have two divisions.'

Best batting: 51 Leicestershire v Worcestershire, Worcester 1962

First-Class Career Performances

	M	Inns	NO	Runs	HS	Avge	100s	Ct	St	Runs	Wkts	Avge	Best	5wI	10wM
Test															
All First	192	288	23	2581	51	9.73	-	381	40						

KITCHEN, M. J.

Name: Mervyn John Kitchen
Born: 1 August 1940,
Nailsea, Somerset
Appointed to 1st-Class list: 1982
First appointed to Test panel: 1990
International panel: 1995-
Tests umpired: 18
One-Day Internationals umpired: 25
County as player: Somerset
Role: Left-hand bat, right-arm
medium bowler
County debut: 1960
County cap: 1966
Testimonial: 1973
1000 runs in a season: 7
1st-Class 50s: 68
1st-Class 100s: 17
1st-Class catches: 157
One-Day 100s: 1
Education: Blackwell Secondary Modern, Nailsea
Extras: Was third umpire for two Tests in 1994
Best batting: 189 Somerset v Pakistanis, Taunton 1967

First-Class Career Performances

	M	Inns	NO	Runs	HS	Avge	100s	Ct	St	Runs	Wkts	Avge	Best	5wI	10wM
Test															
All First	354	612	32	15230	189	26.25	17	157	-	109	2	54.50	1-4	-	-

LEADBEATER, B.

Name: Barrie Leadbeater
Born: 14 August 1943, Leeds
Height: 6ft
Nickname: Leady
Appointed to 1st-Class list: 1981
One-Day Internationals umpired: 4
County as player: Yorkshire
Role: Right-hand opening bat, right-arm
medium bowler, slip fielder
County debut: 1966
County cap: 1969
Benefit: 1980 (joint benefit with G.A. Cope)
1st-Class 50s: 27
1st-Class 100s: 1
1st-Class catches: 82
Marital status: Widowed
Wife and date of marriage: Jacqueline
(deceased), 18 September 1971

Children: Richard Barrie, 23 November
1972; Michael Spencer, 21 March 1976; Daniel Mark Ronnie, 19 June 1981
Education: Brownhill County Primary; Harehills Secondary Modern, Leeds
Career outside cricket: HGV driver
Overseas tours: Duke of Norfolk's XI to West Indies 1970
Overseas teams played for: Johannesburg Municipals 1978-79
Other sports followed: Table tennis, golf, snooker, football (Leeds United)
Cricketers particularly admired: Colin Cowdrey, Clive Rice, Richard Hadlee,
Gary Sobers, Michael Holding
Cricketers particularly learnt from: Brian Close, Willie Watson, Arthur Mitchell,
Maurice Leyland
Relaxations: 'Taking care of my family'
Extras: Acted as third umpire in the fourth Test against Australia at Headingley 1993
Opinions on cricket: 'Disappointed in players who lack self-control and professional
pride and set bad examples to young players and public alike. Public should be
regularly and properly informed during stoppages in play. Stoppages for bad light
cause more frustration for public, players and, not least, umpires and a change in

regulations may be needed soon if the game is to retain its support and credibility. The recent theory of the wicket-keeper standing between the leg stump and the return crease when the slow left-arm bowler is operating over the wicket should be made illegal. It is grossly negative and against the spirit of the game.'

Best batting: 140* Yorkshire v Hampshire, Portsmouth 1976

First-Class Career Performances

	M	Inns	NO	Runs	HS	Avge	100s	Ct	St	Runs	Wkts	Avge	Best	5wI	10wM
Test															
All First	147	241	29	5373	140	*25.34	1	82	-	5	1	5.00	1-1	-	-

LLOYDS, J. W.

Name: Jeremy William Lloyds
Born: 17 November 1954, Penang, Malaya
Height: 5ft 11in
Nickname: Jerry
Appointed to 1st-Class list: 1998
Counties as player: Somerset, Gloucestershire
Role: Left-hand bat, off-spin bowler
County debut: 1979 (Somerset), 1985 (Gloucestershire)
County cap: 1982 (Somerset), 1985 (Gloucestershire)
1000 runs in a season: 3
1st-Class 50s: 62
1st-Class 100s: 10
1st-Class 5 w. in innings: 13
1st-Class 10 w. in match: 1
1st-Class catches: 229
Wife and date of marriage: Janine, 16 September 1997
Children: Kaeli, 16 November 1991
Family links with cricket: Father played cricket in Malaya. Brother Chris played for Somerset 2nd XI
Education: Curry Rivel Primary School; St Dunstan's Prep School; Blundell's School, Tiverton
Career outside cricket: Coaching and setting up Western Province Youth Programme 1992-95 in South Africa. Coach at St Stithian's, Johannesburg, 1995-98
Off-season: Working at home in Cape Town
Overseas tours: Somerset to Antigua 1982; Gloucestershire to Barbados 1985, to Sri Lanka 1987

Overseas teams played for: St Stithian's Old Boys, Johannesburg 1978-79; Toombull DCC, Brisbane 1980-82; North Sydney District 1982-83; Alberton, Johannesburg 1984; Preston CC, Melbourne 1986; Orange Free State 1987; Fish Hoek CC, Cape Town 1988-92

Young players to look out for: Chris Read

Other sports played: Golf (6 handicap)

Other sports followed: Golf, football (Tottenham Hotspur), American football (San Francisco 49ers), Formula 1 and saloon car racing, rugby (Bath)

Relaxations: 'Reading, music and spending time at home with my family'

Extras: Highest score in Brisbane Premier League 1980-81 (165). Britannic Player of the Month July 1987. Gloucestershire Player of the Year 1987. Leading run-scorer in Western Province Cricket League 1988, 1989

Opinions on cricket: 'The only way to produce good players is to play on good wickets. Maybe one way to stop wicket tampering is to let the away team have the choice of batting or bowling first.'

Best batting: 132* Somerset v Northamptonshire, Northampton 1982

Best bowling: 7-88 Somerset v Essex, Chelmsford 1982

First-Class Career Performances

	M	Inns	NO	Runs	HS	Avge	100s	Ct	St	Runs	Wkts	Avge	Best	5wl	10wM
Test															
All First	267	408	64	10679	132*	31.04	10	229	-	12943	333	38.86	7-88	13	1

MALLENDER, N. A.

Name: Neil Alan Mallender
Born: 13 August 1961, Doncaster
Height: 6ft
Appointed to 1st-Class list: 1999
Counties as player: Northamptonshire,
Somerset
Role: Right-hand bat, right-arm fast-medium
bowler
County debut: 1980 (Northamptonshire),
1987 (Somerset)
County cap: 1984 (Northamptonshire), 1987
(Somerset)

Test debut: 1992
Tests: 2
50 wickets in a season: 6
1st-Class 50s: 10
1st-Class 100s: 1
1st-Class 5 w. in innings: 36
1st-Class 10 w. in match: 5
1st-Class catches: 111
One-Day 5 w. in innings: 3
Children: Kirstie, 10; Dominic, 7; Jacob 2
Family links with cricket: Brother Graham used to play good representative cricket
before joining the RAF
Education: Beverley Grammar School
Overseas tours: England YC to West Indies 1979-80
Overseas teams played for: Kaikorai, Dunedin, New Zealand; University,
Wellington, New Zealand; Otago, New Zealand 1983-93
Young players to look out for: Marcus Trescothick, Simon Francis
Other sports played: Golf
Other sports followed: Most sports
Relaxations: Golf
Extras: Took 5-50 on Test debut v Pakistan at Headingley in 1992
Best batting: 100* Otago v Central Districts, Palmerston North 1991-92
Best bowling: 7-27 Otago v Auckland, Auckland 1984-85

First-Class Career Performances

	M	Inns	NO	Runs	HS	Avge	100s	Ct	St	Runs	Wkts	Avge	Best	5wI	10wM
Test	2	3	0	8	4	2.66	-	-	-	215	10	21.50	5-50	1	-
All First	345	396	122	4709	100*	17.18	1	111	-	24654	937	26.31	7-27	36	5

PALMER, K. E.

Name: Kenneth Ernest Palmer
Born: 22 April 1937, Winchester
Height: 5ft 10in
Nickname: Pedlar
Appointed to 1st-Class list: 1972
First appointed to Test panel: 1978
International panel: 1994
Tests umpired: 22
One-Day Internationals umpired: 20
County as player: Somerset
Role: Right-hand bat, right-arm
fast-medium bowler
County debut: 1955
County cap: 1958
Testimonial: 1968
Test debut: 1965
Tests: 1
1000 runs in a season: 1
50 wickets in a season: 2
100 wickets in a season: 4
1st-Class 50s: 27
1st-Class 100s: 2
1st-Class 5 w. in innings: 46
1st-Class 10 w. in match: 5
1st-Class catches: 156

Wife and date of marriage: Jacqueline, 24 September 1994
Children: Gary Vincent, 6 September 1961
Family links with cricket: Father played club cricket and did the cricketer's double
13 times. Son played for Somerset, as did brother Roy, also a Test umpire
Education: Southbroom Secondary Modern, Devizes
Overseas tours: Commonwealth XI to Pakistan 1962; International Cavaliers
to West Indies 1963-64
Cricketers particularly admired: Gary Sobers, Richard Hadlee, Viv Richards,
David Gower, Michael Holding, Malcolm Marshall
Cricketers particularly learnt from: Father and Maurice Tremlett
Other sports followed: Football (Manchester United) and rugby (Bath and England)
Relaxations: Car enthusiast
Extras: Called into Test side while coaching in South Africa 1964-65. Umpired two
B&H finals and two NatWest finals and was twice on World Cup panel in England.
Won Carling Single Wicket Competition 1961. Did the 'double' in 1961 (114 wickets,
1036 runs). With Bill Alley holds the Somerset record for sixth wicket partnership.

Has umpired five Benson and Hedges finals and five NatWest finals
Best batting: 125* Somerset v Northamptonshire, Northampton 1961
Best bowling: 9-57 Somerset v Nottinghamshire, Trent Bridge 1963

First-Class Career Performances

	M	Inns	NO	Runs	HS	Avge	100s	Ct	St	Runs	Wkts	Avge	Best	5wI	10wM
Test	1	1	0	10	10	10.00	-	-	-	189	1	189.00	1-113	-	-
All First	314	481	105	7771	125	*20.66	2	156	-	18485	866	21.34	9-57	46	5

PALMER, R.

Name: Roy Palmer
Born: 12 July 1942, Hampshire
Height: 6ft 3in
Nickname: Arp
Appointed to 1st-Class list: 1980
First appointed to Test panel: 1992
Tests umpired: 2
One-Day Internationals umpired: 8
County as player: Somerset
Role: Right-hand bat, right-arm
fast-medium bowler
County debut: 1965
50 wickets in a season: 1
1st-Class 50s: 1
1st-Class 5 w. in innings: 4
1st-Class catches: 25
Wife and date of marriage:
Alyne, 5 November 1983
Children: Nick, 7 October 1968
Family links with cricket: Brother of Ken Palmer, Test umpire and former
Somerset player; nephew Gary also played for Somerset
Education: Southbroom Secondary Modern, Devizes
Young players to look out for: Dean Cosker
Relaxations: DIY and reading
Extras: Won two Man of the Match Awards in the Gillette Cup
Best batting: 84 Somerset v Leicestershire, Taunton 1967
Best bowling: 6-45 Somerset v Middlesex, Lord's 1967

First-Class Career Performances

	M	Inns	NO	Runs	HS	Avge	100s	Ct	St	Runs	Wkts	Avge	Best	5wI	10wM
Test															
All First	74	110	32	1037	84	13.29	-	25	-	5439	172	31.62	6-45	4	-

PLEWS, N. T.

Name: Nigel Trevor Plews
Born: 5 September 1934, Nottingham
Height: 6ft 6in
Nickname: Plod, Sarge
Appointed to 1st-Class list: 1982
First appointed to Test panel: 1988
International panel: 1994-96
Tests umpired: 11
One-Day Internationals umpired: 16
County as player: Did not play first-class cricket (the only remaining first-class umpire not to have done so). Played local league and club cricket in Nottingham area
Role: Right-hand opening bat
Wife and date of marriage: Margaret, 24 September 1956
Children: Elaine, 24 February 1961; Douglas, 21 April 1964
Education: Mundella Grammar School, Nottingham

Career outside cricket: Nottingham City police for 25 years (Det Sgt in Fraud Squad for 15 years)
Off-season: Assisting MCC to update the laws of cricket. 'Trying to understand next season's playing conditions!'
Young players to look out for: 'I watch them all the time!! I hope they all have a good future'
Other sports played: Occasional bowls
Other sports followed: Football, rugby, table tennis, swimming
Relaxations: Hill-walking, reading, travel, cricket administration
Extras: Full member of Association of Cricket Umpires and Scorers. Has acted as third umpire in a total of 13 Tests and One-Day Internationals. Has umpired five Lord's finals and 11 major semi-finals; Asia Cup final, Sharjah; Singer Cup, Sharjah. Was Director of Umpires for the ICC Trophy 1997 in Kuala Lumpur. Toured Namibia as umpire with MCC 1991
Opinions on cricket: 'Not enough smiles on the field from the players. Have you forgotten how to enjoy the game?'

Did not play first-class cricket

SHARP, G.

Name: George Sharp
Born: 12 March 1950,
Hartlepool, County Durham
Height: 5ft 11in
Nickname: Blunt, Razor, Sharpie
Appointed to 1st-Class list: 1991
International panel: 1996-
Tests umpired: 8
One-Day Internationals umpired: 4
County as player: Northamptonshire
Role: Right-hand bat, wicket-keeper
County debut: 1967
County cap: 1972
1st-Class catches: 565
1st-Class stumpings: 90
Wife and date of marriage:
Audrey, 14 September 1974
Children: Gareth James, 27 June 1985
Education: Elwick Road, Hartlepool
Career outside cricket: Director of GSB Loams Ltd, suppliers of top dressings for all types of sports fields
Off-season: Working for GSB Loams Ltd. Umpiring as part of National Grid Panel (overseas)
Overseas tours: England Counties XI to Barbados and Trinidad 1975
Cricketers particularly admired: Alan Knott, Bob Taylor, Keith Andrew
Other sports played: Golf
Other sports followed: Football (Newcastle Utd), rugby league and union
Relaxations: Golf and watching most sports
Extras: Has acted as third umpire in one Test. Has umpired two B&H finals and one NatWest final. Stood in Singer Trophy (India, Sri Lanka, Pakistan), Singapore 1996. Umpired in tournament between Pakistan, Sri Lanka and New Zealand in Sharjah 1997
Best batting: 98 Northamptonshire v Yorkshire, Northampton 1983

First-Class Career Performances

	M	Inns	NO	Runs	HS	Avge	100s	Ct	St	Runs	Wkts	Avge	Best	5wI	10wM
Test															
All First	306	396	81	6254	98	19.85	-	565	90	70	1	70.00	1-47	-	-

SHEPHERD, D. R.

Name: David Robert Shepherd
Born: 27 December 1940,
Bideford, Devon
Height: 5ft 10in
Nickname: Shep
Appointed to 1st-Class list: 1981
First appointed to Test panel: 1985
International panel: 1994-
Tests umpired: 42
One-Day Internationals umpired: 65+
County as player: Gloucestershire
Role: Right-hand bat, right-arm
medium bowler
County debut: 1965
County cap: 1969
Benefit: 1978 (joint benefit with J. Davey)
1000 runs in a season: 2
1st-Class 50s: 55
1st-Class 100s: 12
1st-Class catches: 95
One-Day 100s: 2
Marital status: Single

Family links with cricket: Brother played for MCC Young Professionals and Devon
Education: Barnstaple Grammar School; St Luke's College, Exeter
Career outside cricket: Teacher. Family business – post office/newsagent
Off-season: ICC umpiring abroad
Other sports followed: Rugby, football
Cricketers particularly admired: Gary Sobers, Mike Procter
Relaxations: Stamp collecting
Extras: Played Minor Counties cricket for Devon 1959-64. Only Gloucestershire
player to score a century on his first-class debut. Umpired the MCC Bicentenary Test,
England v Rest of the World, at Lord's in 1987. With Dickie Bird and Steve Bucknor
was one of the first umpires officially sponsored by the ICC. Known for his
superstition regarding 'Nelson' score 111, and multiples – 222, 333 etc. Has stood in
each World Cup since 1983, including the 1996 final between Australia and Sri Lanka
in Lahore. Has umpired numerous domestic finals. Was awarded the MBE in 1997 for
services to cricket. Received National Grid/ICC 'bronze award' in March 1998 for
long-service as a Test umpire
Best batting: 153 Gloucestershire v Middlesex, Bristol 1968

	M	Inns	NO	Runs	HS	Avge	100s	Ct	St	Runs	Wkts	Avge	Best	5wI	10wM
Test															
All First	282	476	40	10672	153	24.47	12	95	-	106	2	53.00	1-1	-	-

STEELE, J. F.

Name: John Frederick Steele
Born: 23 July 1946, Stafford
Height: 5ft 10in
Nickname: Steely
Appointed to 1st-Class list: 1997
Counties as player: Leicestershire, Glamorgan
Role: Right-hand bat, slow left-arm bowler
County debut: Leicestershire (1970), Glamorgan (1984)
County cap: Leicestershire (1971), Glamorgan (1984)
1000 runs in a season: 6
1st-Class 100s: 21
1st-Class 5 w. in innings: 16
1st-Class catches: 414
Wife and date of marriage: Susan, 17 April 1977
Children: Sarah Jane, 2 April 1982; Robert Alfred, 10 April 1985
Family links with cricket: Uncle Stan played for Staffordshire. Brother David played for Northamptonshire and England. Cousin Brian Crump played for Northamptonshire and Staffordshire
Education: Endon School, Stoke-on-Trent; Stafford College
Career outside cricket: Work study officer. Fireman with Staffordshire Fire Brigade
Overseas teams played for: Springs HSOB, Northern Transvaal 1971-73; Pine Town CC, Natal 1973-74, 1982-83; Natal 1975-76, 1978-79
Other sports followed: Soccer (Stoke City, Port Vale), golf
Relaxations: Music and walking
Extras: Played for England U25. First wicket record partnership for Leicestershire of 390 with Barry Dudleston versus Derbyshire in 1979. Won two Man of the Match Awards in the Gillette Cup and four in the Benson and Hedges Cup. Won the award for the most catches in a season in 1984 and was voted Natal's Best Bowler in 1975-76
Best batting: 195 Leicestershire v Derbyshire, Leicester 1971
Best bowling: 7-29 Natal B v Griqualand West, Umzinto 1973-74
7-29 Leicestershire v Gloucestershire, Leicester 1980

First-class career performances

	M	Inns	NO	Runs	HS	Avge	100s	Ct	St	Runs	Wkts	Avge	Best	5wl	10wM
Test															
All First	379	605	85	15053	195	28.94	21	414	-	15793	584	27.04	7-29	16	-

WHITE, R. A.

Name: Robert Arthur White
Born: 6 October 1936, Fulham
Height: 5ft 9in
Nickname: Knocker
Appointed to 1st-Class list: 1982
Counties as player: Middlesex,
Nottinghamshire
Role: Left-hand bat, off-break bowler
County debut: 1958 (Middlesex),
1966 (Nottinghamshire)
County cap: 1963 (Middlesex),
1966 (Nottinghamshire)
Benefit: 1974
1000 runs in a season: 1
50 wickets in a season: 2
1st-Class 50s: 50
1st-Class 100s: 5
1st-Class 5 w. in innings: 28
1st-Class 10 w. in match: 4
1st-Class catches: 190

Wife: Janice – 'still married, must be a record in the modern game'
Children: Robin and Vanessa
Education: Chiswick Grammar School
Career outside cricket: Fireworks salesman
Off-season: Working
Other sports followed: All sports – golf, football, ice hockey and horse racing in
particular
Cricketers particularly admired: 'Gary Sobers more than anyone else'
Cricketers particularly learnt from: 'I tried to learn from everyone I encountered'
Young players to look out for: 'All of them'
Relaxations: Theatre-going
Extras: Made independent coaching trips to South Africa 1959, 1960, 1966, 1967,
1968. Together with M.J. Smedley broke the Nottinghamshire seventh wicket record
with 204 v Surrey at The Oval 1967
Opinions on cricket: 'There is so much verbal noise on the field these days (mainly

in my opinion to distract the batsman), that I, if still a player, would wear earphones and carry a Walkman so that I could listen to soothing music and obliterate the verbals. Those people who saw me play would no doubt say that I would have had time just to hear the "Minute Waltz".'

Best batting: 116* Nottinghamshire v Surrey, The Oval 1967
Best bowling: 7-41 Nottinghamshire v Derbyshire, Ilkeston 1971

First-Class Career Performances

	M	Inns	NO	Runs	HS	Avge	100s	Ct	St	Runs	Wkts	Avge	Best	5wI	10wM
Test															
All First	413	642	105	12452	116*	23.18	5	190	-	21138	693	30.50	7-41	28	4

WHITEHEAD, A. G. T.

Name: Alan Geoffrey Thomas Whitehead
Born: 28 October 1940, Butleigh, Somerset
Appointed to 1st-Class list: 1970
First appointed to Test panel: 1982
Tests umpired: 5
One-Day Internationals umpired: 13
County as player: Somerset
Role: Left-hand bat, slow left-arm bowler
County debut: 1957
1st-Class 5 w. in innings: 3
1st-Class catches: 20
Extras: Acted as third umpire in the fifth Test against Australia at Edgbaston 1993 and in two Tests in 1994
Best batting: 15 Somerset v Hampshire, Southampton 1959
Best bowling: 6-74 Somerset v Sussex, Eastbourne 1959

First-Class Career Performances

	M	Inns	NO	Runs	HS	Avge	100s	Ct	St	Runs	Wkts	Avge	Best	5wI	10wM
Test															
All First	38	49	25	137	15	5.70	-	20	-	2306	67	34.41	6-74	3	

WILLEY, P.

Name: Peter Willey
Born: 6 December 1949, Sedgefield,
County Durham
Height: 6ft 1in
Nickname: Will, 'many unprintable'
Appointed to 1st-Class list: 1993
International panel: 1996-
Tests umpired: 11
One-Day Internationals umpired: 7
Counties as player: Northamptonshire,
Leicestershire
Role: Right-hand bat, off-break bowler
County debut: 1966 (Northamptonshire),
1984 (Leicestershire)
County cap: 1971 (Northamptonshire),
1984 (Leicestershire)
Benefit: 1981 (£31,400)
Test debut: 1976
Tests: 26
One-Day Internationals: 26
1000 runs in a season: 10
50 wickets in a season: 2
1st-Class 50s: 101
1st-Class 100s: 43
1st-Class 200s: 1
1st-Class 5 w. in innings: 26
1st-Class 10 w. in match: 3
1st-Class catches: 235
One-Day 100s: 9
Wife and date of marriage: Charmaine, 23 September 1971
Children: Heather Jane, 11 September 1985; David, 28 February 1990
Family links with cricket: Father played local club cricket in County Durham
Education: Seaham Secondary School, County Durham
Overseas tours: England to Australia and India 1979-80, to West Indies 1980-81,
1985-86; with unofficial England XI to South Africa 1981-82
Overseas teams played for: Eastern Province, South Africa 1982-85
Cricketers particularly admired: Malcolm Marshall
Other sports followed: All sports
Relaxations: Gardening, dog walking
Extras: With Wayne Larkins, received 2016 pints of beer (seven barrels) from a
brewery in Northampton as a reward for their efforts in Australia with England in

1979-80. Youngest player ever to play for Northamptonshire at 16 years 180 days v Cambridge University in 1966. Banned from Test cricket for three years for joining England rebel tour of South Africa in 1982. Left Northamptonshire at end of 1983 and moved to Leicestershire as vice-captain. Appointed Leicestershire captain for 1987, but resigned after only one season. Released by Leicestershire at end of 1991 season to play for Northumberland in 1992. He was appointed to the first-class umpires list in 1993 and to the international panel in 1996. Umpired the 1996-97 Australia v West Indies series in Australia

Opinions on cricket: 'I think the fun has gone out of the game for many of the players. Not enough hard work and practice is done to improve playing standards throughout the first-class game. Players of average ability are being paid silly money in the modern game, by clubs, so they may not need to try and improve their standards. Why does the English game need overseas coaches? Why do we also need team managers?'

Best batting: 227 Northamptonshire v Somerset, Northampton 1976
Best bowling: 7-37 Northamptonshire v Oxford University, The Parks 1975

First-Class Career Performances

	M	Inns	NO	Runs	HS	Avge	100s	Ct	St	Runs	Wkts	Avge	Best	5wl	10wM
Test	26	50	6	1184	102	*26.90	2	3	-	456	7	65.14	2-73	-	-
All First	559	918	121	24361	227	30.56	44	235	-	23400	756	30.95	7-37	26	3

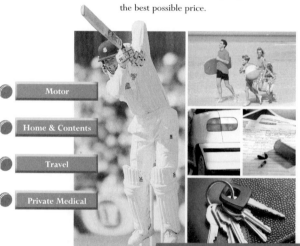

ROLL OF HONOUR
1998

ROLL OF HONOUR 1998

BRITANNIC ASSURANCE CHAMPIONSHIP

		P	W	L	D	T	Bt	Bl	Pts
1	Leicestershire (10)	17	11	0	6	0	47	51	292
2	Lancashire (11)	17	11	1	5	0	30	56	277
3	Yorkshire (6)	17	9	3	5	0	47	63	269
4	Gloucestershire (7)	17	11	5	1	0	23	65	267
5	Surrey (8)	17	10	5	2	0	38	57	261
6	Hampshire (14)	17	6	5	6	0	27	61	202
7	Sussex (18)	17	6	7	4	0	30	63	201
8	Warwickshire (4)	17	6	8	3	0	35	60	200
9	Somerset (12)	17	6	7	4	0	30	54	192
10	Derbyshire (16)	17	6	7	4	0	28	55	191
11	Kent (2)	17	5	5	7	0	18	59	178
12	Worcestershire (3)	17	4	6	7	0	32	59	176
12	Glamorgan (1)	17	4	6	7	0	36	55	176
14	Durham (17)	17	3	9	5	0	30	65	158
15	Northamptonshire* (15)	17	4	5	8	0	31	52	146
16	Nottinghamshire (13)	17	3	10	4	0	20	60	140
17	Middlesex (4)	17	2	9	6	0	28	52	130
18	Essex (8)	17	2	11	4	0	16	58	118

1997 positions in brackets. * Northamptonshire were deducted 25 points for an unfit pitch. The top eight counties qualify for the Super Cup in 1999

NATWEST TROPHY

Winners: Lancashire
Runners-up: Derbyshire

BENSON AND HEDGES CUP

Winners: Essex
Runners-up: Leicestershire

AXA LEAGUE

		P	W	L	T	NR	Pts
1	Lancashire (3)	17	12	2	0	3	54
2	Warwickshire (1)	17	9	5	0	3	42
3	Essex (7)	17	9	5	1	2	42
4	Leicestershire (4)	17	9	6	0	2	40
5	Kent (2)	17	8	6	0	3	38
6	Gloucestershire (11)	17	7	6	0	4	36
7	Worcestershire (8)	17	7	6	1	3	36
8	Hampshire (15)	17	8	8	0	1	34
9	Yorkshire (10)	17	8	8	0	1	34
10	Glamorgan (13)	17	7	8	0	2	32
11	Nottinghamshire (12)	17	7	8	1	1	32
12	Middlesex (9)	17	7	8	0	2	32
13	Northamptonshire (9)	17	6	7	1	3	32
14	Somerset (6)	17	6	8	1	2	30
15	Derbyshire (14)	17	6	8	0	3	30
16	Sussex (18)	17	6	9	0	2	28
17	Durham (17)	17	4	9	1	3	24
18	Surrey (5)	17	3	12	0	2	16

1997 positions in brackets. The league will be divided into two
divisions in 1999, operating a promotion and relegation system

NO ONE DOES MORE TO PROTECT CRICKET'S MOST VALUABLE ASSETS

FIRST-CLASS AVERAGES
1998

1998 AVERAGES (all first-class matches)

BATTING AVERAGES - including fielding
Qualifying requirements : 6 completed innings

Name	Matches	Inns	NO	Runs	HS	Avge	100s	50s	Ct	St
J P Crawley	18	28	3	1851	239	74.04	8	5	7	-
W J Cronje	11	12	2	704	195	70.40	2	4	6	-
D J Cullinan	12	17	4	900	200*	69.23	2	6	9	-
G Kirsten	12	19	5	892	210	63.71	4	2	8	-
J L Langer	15	28	5	1448	233*	62.95	4	6	12	-
B F Smith	19	24	4	1240	204	62.00	4	4	13	-
D S Lehmann	10	16	0	969	200	60.56	3	4	4	-
M B Loye	15	22	2	1198	322*	59.90	4	4	7	-
A Habib	19	22	5	952	198	56.00	3	3	12	-
J H Kallis	10	14	3	612	132	55.63	2	3	9	-
M G Bevan	12	19	2	935	149*	55.00	3	4	10	-
M S Atapattu	4	7	1	316	114	52.66	1	2	1	-
N H Fairbrother	12	17	2	759	138	50.60	3	3	11	-
S P James	15	28	1	1339	227	49.59	4	5	9	-
A D Brown	15	22	1	1036	155	49.33	4	6	20	-
D J Millns	11	10	4	289	99	48.16	-	1	4	-
S T Jayasuriya	5	9	1	382	213	47.75	1	-	4	-
K J Barnett	17	32	6	1229	162	47.26	1	7	8	-
M J Wood	19	29	6	1080	200*	46.95	4	4	17	-
G F J Liebenberg	10	17	3	642	104*	45.85	1	5	11	-
C L Hooper	15	28	1	1215	203	45.00	6	1	15	-
N V Knight	15	26	2	1069	192	44.54	4	4	19	-
M W Gatting	17	29	3	1139	241	43.80	2	7	19	-
A J Stewart	14	24	2	963	164	43.77	1	5	41	-
G A Hick	17	30	0	1304	166	43.46	7	2	24	-
M G N Windows	16	29	2	1173	151	43.44	4	5	13	-
J N Rhodes	11	14	1	562	123	43.23	2	3	4	-
P N Weekes	16	26	5	903	139	43.00	1	5	20	-
M R Ramprakash	15	26	3	979	128*	42.56	4	2	10	-
W S Kendall	8	11	3	340	78*	42.50	-	2	8	-
T M Moody	13	23	2	886	132	42.19	4	2	10	-
C J Adams	18	29	1	1174	170	41.92	4	4	30	-
G W White	19	31	2	1211	156	41.75	4	5	12	-
N M K Smith	18	29	5	1002	147	41.75	2	6	2	-
M P Vaughan	19	31	3	1161	177	41.46	2	5	10	-
D C Boon	16	29	4	1024	139*	40.96	3	5	12	-
M A Butcher	16	26	1	1024	116	40.96	3	6	11	-
S G Law	14	26	2	982	165	40.91	2	3	19	-
D Ripley	17	22	2	805	209	40.25	1	5	30	1
A L Penberthy	14	21	2	755	128	39.73	2	4	14	-
B C Lara	15	26	0	1033	226	39.73	3	3	15	-
M A Atherton	13	24	2	874	152	39.72	2	3	9	-
H P Tillekeratne	6	9	1	317	120	39.62	1	1	5	-

Name	Matches	Inns	NO	Runs	HS	Avge	100s	50s	Ct	St
C White	10	15	3	475	104*	39.58	1	2	16	-
G D Lloyd	15	22	1	831	212*	39.57	2	3	11	-
I Mohammed	6	7	1	237	136	39.50	1	-	-	-
O A Shah	15	23	3	786	140	39.30	2	4	10	-
P Johnson	15	26	1	976	139	39.04	2	4	14	-
R P Arnold	5	9	1	312	209	39.00	1	-	1	-
M W Alleyne	18	33	2	1189	137	38.35	3	6	24	-
T H C Hancock	18	34	2	1227	220*	38.34	2	7	16	-
P A Nixon	19	21	4	638	101*	37.52	2	1	41	5
R A Smith	17	25	2	853	138	37.08	3	2	10	-
W L Law	9	14	2	444	131	37.00	1	2	4	-
W K Hegg	15	21	4	628	85	36.94	-	6	34	3
V J Wells	17	25	2	836	171	36.34	3	3	10	-
A Singh	10	12	0	434	117	36.16	1	2	2	-
N Shahid	12	22	3	683	126*	35.94	2	3	13	-
A N Aymes	18	27	6	754	133	35.90	2	3	53	2
S J Rhodes	18	33	5	1000	104*	35.71	1	6	43	2
M J Slater	14	24	0	848	185	35.33	1	3	10	-
M J Powell	16	27	3	840	106	35.00	1	5	10	-
P A Cottey	19	32	3	1012	123	34.89	2	5	20	-
J E Morris	13	24	2	767	163	34.86	3	1	5	-
R T Robinson	11	18	2	553	114	34.56	1	4	6	-
R J Bailey	16	24	2	759	188	34.50	1	2	10	-
G P Swann	14	18	2	548	111	34.25	1	2	7	-
A J Hollioake	15	22	2	684	112	34.20	1	4	15	-
K D James	18	26	9	570	57	33.52	-	3	6	-
D A Leatherdale	18	32	2	1001	137	33.36	2	4	9	-
C C Lewis	13	14	3	367	71*	33.36	-	4	10	-
G R Haynes	12	21	5	532	86	33.25	-	4	2	-
M A Wagh	14	23	2	686	126	32.66	2	3	6	-
A S Rollins	10	19	0	618	107	32.52	1	4	10	-
N R Taylor	6	8	1	227	74*	32.42	-	2	4	-
T Frost	8	14	2	389	111*	32.41	1	1	21	-
R C Irani	18	33	2	1001	127*	32.29	2	2	6	-
K M Curran	18	26	4	709	90*	32.22	-	6	23	-
A Dale	19	33	1	1028	92	32.12	-	9	7	-
G M Hamilton	15	19	1	578	79	32.11	-	6	3	-
J D Ratcliffe	9	15	1	449	100	32.07	1	2	2	-
B W Byrne	8	12	4	256	69*	32.00	-	1	4	-
K Newell	11	19	6	414	84	31.84	-	3	7	-
D P Fulton	17	31	1	954	207	31.80	1	7	21	-
I J Sutcliffe	19	26	4	698	167	31.72	1	2	11	-
J A Daley	12	22	2	634	157	31.70	1	1	5	-
R M S Weston	9	17	0	537	97	31.58	-	4	5	-
R K Illingworth	15	21	6	473	84	31.53	-	3	5	-
M E Trescothick	18	29	2	847	98	31.37	-	6	20	-
Wasim Akram	13	18	1	531	155	31.23	1	2	8	-
D Byas	18	28	1	842	116	31.18	4	3	20	-
S M Pollock	6	8	2	187	50	31.16	-	1	3	-

Name	Matches	Inns	NO	Runs	HS	Avge	100s	50s	Ct	St
I J Ward	10	19	2	529	81*	31.11	-	5	9	-
N Hussain	10	19	0	591	105	31.10	1	4	9	-
S D Udal	14	18	5	404	62	31.07	-	1	9	-
Q J Hughes	6	7	0	217	84	31.00	-	1	4	-
P R Whitaker	7	11	1	309	74	30.90	-	2	7	-
P D Collingwood	19	33	6	833	105	30.85	1	5	16	-
K R Brown	17	25	6	576	59*	30.31	-	2	40	5
M N Lathwell	12	19	0	574	106	30.21	1	5	7	-
D R Brown	16	27	4	691	81*	30.04	-	5	9	-
A W Evans	8	14	1	386	125	29.69	1	1	7	-
M Newell	10	14	1	386	135*	29.69	2	-	6	-
J P Stephenson	16	24	1	681	114	29.60	2	4	14	-
W P C Weston	17	31	3	829	95	29.60	-	5	9	-
D P M Jayawardena	6	10	1	266	90	29.55	-	2	7	-
R S C Martin-Jenkins	8	13	1	353	78	29.41	-	2	3	-
W J House	8	11	0	322	65	29.27	-	3	3	-
M Watkinson	10	12	1	318	87	28.90	-	2	6	-
W G Khan	18	30	1	837	125	28.86	1	6	5	-
M P Maynard	17	29	2	776	99	28.74	-	5	21	-
N T Wood	12	19	3	457	80*	28.56	-	2	1	-
V S Solanki	19	36	1	999	170	28.54	2	4	28	-
A F Giles	14	21	4	485	83	28.52	-	3	8	-
R A Kettleborough	12	22	4	512	92*	28.44	-	3	7	-
M A Gough	10	18	0	508	123	28.22	1	2	12	-
G F Archer	13	23	0	647	107	28.13	1	5	23	-
A D Mascarenhas	17	25	2	645	89	28.04	-	6	11	-
R J Turner	14	22	2	558	105	27.90	1	2	43	-
A P Wells	15	26	1	684	95	27.36	-	5	3	-
M E Cassar	17	31	5	708	121	27.23	1	5	4	-
J E R Gallian	14	25	3	592	113*	26.90	1	3	8	-
M A Roseberry	6	11	0	295	97	26.81	-	2	2	-
J A M Molins	7	10	0	268	73	26.80	-	3	2	-
M J Foster	8	13	1	321	76*	26.75	-	2	2	-
R W T Key	13	23	0	612	115	26.60	2	1	11	-
S C Ecclestone	5	7	0	186	94	26.57	-	1	4	-
P C McKeown	5	7	0	186	42	26.57	-	-	6	-
M Burns	10	17	0	450	96	26.47	-	3	15	1
M J Chilton	3	6	0	158	47	26.33	-	-	-	-
N J Speak	15	27	2	658	77*	26.32	-	6	9	-
P D Bowler	18	32	2	789	104	26.30	2	3	18	-
M J Walker	8	14	1	341	68	26.23	-	2	6	-
G P Thorpe	9	13	1	314	114	26.16	1	1	10	-
G P Butcher	9	14	2	311	85	25.91	-	2	5	-
D L Hemp	15	26	1	646	102	25.84	1	4	15	-
S A Marsh	16	28	4	620	92	25.83	-	5	42	4
A R K Pierson	13	20	3	438	108*	25.76	1	1	6	-
U Afzaal	17	30	3	686	109*	25.40	2	4	7	-
G D Rose	17	26	2	606	76	25.25	-	4	3	-
C M W Read	13	22	6	401	76	25.06	-	2	39	3

Name	Matches	Inns	NO	Runs	HS	Avge	100s	50s	Ct	St
P C L Holloway	16	28	3	624	123	24.96	1	1	7	-
D J Goodchild	7	14	1	324	105	24.92	1	2	1	-
E T Smith	11	18	1	422	58	24.82	-	1	1	-
M P Speight	17	29	4	614	97*	24.56	-	4	58	3
A McGrath	17	28	3	612	63*	24.48	-	3	5	-
P V Simmons	17	19	0	464	194	24.42	1	2	23	-
M J Powell	13	22	1	511	132	24.33	1	3	13	-
A J Strauss	3	6	0	146	83	24.33	-	1	3	-
A Flintoff	17	25	0	608	124	24.32	1	3	23	-
M A Ealham	12	22	3	461	121	24.26	1	2	2	-
M T E Peirce	19	32	1	744	96	24.00	-	5	7	-
M Keech	12	14	0	335	70	23.92	-	3	12	-
C E W Silverwood	13	13	3	239	57*	23.90	-	1	2	-
D L Maddy	18	26	2	569	162	23.70	2	-	17	-
G M Roberts	8	13	3	237	44	23.70	-	-	6	-
M C J Ball	18	30	5	592	67*	23.68	-	3	22	-
M V Fleming	17	30	4	612	51	23.53	-	1	9	-
D R Hewson	12	22	3	447	78*	23.52	-	3	4	-
T L Penney	9	16	2	329	53*	23.50	-	1	5	-
M V Boucher	11	10	1	211	46	23.44	-	-	43	1
I N Flanagan	6	11	0	254	61	23.09	-	2	9	-
S D Peters	13	23	2	484	64	23.04	-	3	7	-
J J B Lewis	15	28	1	622	72	23.03	-	4	5	-
S R Lampitt	18	28	7	481	48	22.90	-	-	8	-
R D B Croft	13	22	7	343	63*	22.86	-	1	9	-
A M Smith	18	30	13	384	61	22.58	-	2	5	-
B Parker	8	10	2	180	41	22.50	-	-	3	-
S D Thomas	18	26	3	507	74	22.04	-	3	10	-
C M Tolley	11	19	2	374	78	22.00	-	2	5	-
D G Cork	16	27	4	506	102*	22.00	1	3	11	-
A C Morris	12	15	5	219	51	21.90	-	1	6	-
J P Taylor	15	20	3	371	58	21.82	-	3	5	-
P A J DeFreitas	14	23	3	435	87	21.75	-	2	6	-
P J Franks	12	20	2	390	66*	21.66	-	2	6	-
M P Bicknell	17	21	1	433	81	21.65	-	1	5	-
R J Blakey	17	23	2	448	67*	21.33	-	3	69	2
J M Dakin	6	6	0	128	79	21.33	-	1	2	-
D C Nash	14	19	0	404	114	21.26	1	1	8	1
I D Austin	12	16	4	255	64	21.25	-	2	7	-
P J Newport	13	16	3	270	56	20.76	-	1	4	-
M J McCague	10	15	7	166	38	20.75	-	-	8	-
J N Batty	16	19	2	351	63	20.64	-	2	39	6
R R Montgomerie	10	16	3	268	54	20.61	-	1	4	-
B C Hollioake	17	26	3	469	60	20.39	-	2	8	-
R K Rao	10	17	1	325	76	20.31	-	2	-	-
R C Russell	16	28	2	527	63*	20.26	-	2	56	-
M M Patel	14	20	5	303	58*	20.20	-	2	7	-
J A Claughton	5	8	1	140	45	20.00	-	-	1	-
R J Kirtley	18	26	10	320	59	20.00	-	1	2	-

Name	Matches	Inns	NO	Runs	HS	Avge	100s	50s	Ct	St
P A Strang	13	18	3	300	48	20.00	-	-	19	-
K M Krikken	17	27	5	439	83	19.95	-	3	37	2
B M McMillan	6	6	0	119	54	19.83	-	1	8	-
M R May	13	24	0	473	101	19.70	1	1	4	-
I D K Salisbury	15	18	2	314	61	19.62	-	3	8	-
M P Dowman	13	24	1	451	63	19.60	-	2	7	-
G I Macmillan	5	9	0	176	53	19.55	-	2	4	-
G Welch	12	18	1	332	54	19.52	-	1	7	-
B L Spendlove	10	19	1	350	49	19.44	-	-	4	-
K J Dean	15	21	13	154	27*	19.25	-	-	1	-
D P Ostler	6	10	1	173	133*	19.22	1	-	6	-
D Gough	11	15	1	269	89	19.21	-	2	1	-
B J Hyam	10	19	3	307	47*	19.18	-	-	32	2
P M Such	16	25	18	133	25	19.00	-	-	5	-
R D Stemp	12	16	9	133	43*	19.00	-	-	6	-
A R Caddick	17	25	8	322	37	18.94	-	-	5	-
T R Ward	12	22	0	416	94	18.90	-	1	8	-
G Chapple	14	18	3	282	69	18.80	-	1	7	-
D R Law	14	25	0	466	65	18.64	-	3	10	-
T A Tweats	9	18	0	332	161	18.44	1	-	8	-
P W Jarvis	5	7	1	110	39	18.33	-	-	4	-
T P Hodgson	7	13	0	236	54	18.15	-	1	4	-
D D J Robinson	14	25	0	446	85	17.84	-	1	11	-
A Hafeez	10	18	1	303	55	17.82	-	1	6	-
M N Bowen	10	13	5	142	32	17.75	-	-	2	-
I Dawood	7	12	1	194	40	17.63	-	-	19	1
Saqlain Mushtaq	12	15	5	176	45*	17.60	-	-	7	-
A P Cowan	8	13	0	228	94	17.53	-	2	4	-
D J G Sales	14	21	1	346	60	17.30	-	2	10	-
P R Pollard	4	7	0	121	69	17.28	-	1	3	-
A J Wright	11	20	0	345	57	17.25	-	1	5	-
J S Laney	8	13	0	224	101	17.23	1	1	10	-
J A Knott	5	9	3	103	41*	17.16	-	-	1	-
N F Williams	9	16	6	171	36	17.10	-	-	2	-
G E Welton	5	9	0	152	55	16.88	-	1	3	-
A J Tudor	10	13	3	167	48	16.70	-	-	3	-
K A Parsons	14	23	1	367	101*	16.68	1	1	17	-
D W Headley	14	21	5	265	81	16.56	-	1	5	-
A D Shaw	11	16	1	248	71	16.53	-	2	26	-
A P Grayson	17	31	0	509	59	16.41	-	4	9	-
J A G Fulton	8	12	1	180	78	16.36	-	1	4	-
N A Gie	4	8	0	128	50	16.00	-	1	3	-
P M Hutchison	17	16	8	127	30	15.87	-	-	4	-
R J Harden	12	21	2	301	63	15.84	-	2	15	-
P Aldred	7	9	3	95	37*	15.83	-	-	6	-
J P Hewitt	15	19	2	268	53	15.76	-	1	5	-
D R Lockhart	7	11	0	173	35	15.72	-	-	6	-
K J Piper	13	23	5	283	44*	15.72	-	-	28	3
R J Cunliffe	12	22	0	339	53	15.40	-	2	14	-

Name	Matches	Inns	NO	Runs	HS	Avge	100s	50s	Ct	St
P J Martin	14	15	5	154	26	15.40	-	-	3	-
Mushtaq Ahmed	6	9	1	121	37	15.12	-	-	1	-
J P Pyemont	6	7	0	105	54	15.00	-	1	3	-
G R Loveridge	7	9	1	118	41	14.75	-	-	-	-
A J Swann	11	17	0	250	85	14.70	-	1	6	-
A D Mullally	15	11	2	132	38*	14.66	-	-	3	-
J O Grove	4	7	1	88	33	14.66	-	-	-	-
N A M McLean	16	22	2	288	43	14.40	-	-	5	-
M T Brimson	18	14	6	115	54*	14.37	-	1	3	-
R J Rollins	8	12	0	171	42	14.25	-	-	13	-
I D Blackwell	11	18	0	254	57	14.11	-	2	6	-
J D Middlebrook	8	12	2	139	41	13.90	-	-	7	-
J R Carpenter	9	16	0	222	65	13.87	-	1	3	-
N J Trainor	4	8	0	109	52	13.62	-	1	4	-
S Humphries	14	22	1	286	66	13.61	-	1	25	-
R I Dawson	8	15	2	177	46	13.61	-	-	3	-
J Lewis	18	31	2	390	54*	13.44	-	1	5	-
R L Johnson	14	21	3	242	43	13.44	-	-	5	-
P J Prichard	10	18	0	237	24	13.16	-	-	7	-
R J Chapman	11	16	8	102	43*	12.75	-	-	2	-
C J Batt	9	14	2	150	43	12.50	-	-	1	-
S J Harmison	14	22	4	223	36	12.38	-	-	2	-
P J Hartley	13	16	3	160	29	12.30	-	-	3	-
M M Betts	12	18	7	135	29*	12.27	-	-	3	-
M J Church	4	7	0	85	30	12.14	-	-	5	-
B J Phillips	11	17	0	203	54	11.94	-	1	1	-
G J Kennis	3	6	0	71	49	11.83	-	-	5	-
M C Ilott	17	30	4	307	38	11.80	-	-	3	-
A Sheriyar	12	10	4	66	20	11.00	-	-	1	-
J Wood	17	26	4	236	37	10.72	-	-	3	-
T M Smith	7	10	1	94	29	10.44	-	-	-	-
D E Malcolm	14	16	5	114	42	10.36	-	-	3	-
A P van Troost	5	7	1	61	23	10.16	-	-	-	-
E T Wilson	5	10	0	101	27	10.10	-	-	3	-
K P Evans	9	13	0	129	36	9.92	-	-	3	-
N C Phillips	17	25	2	227	35	9.86	-	-	8	-
P C R Tufnell	17	22	6	155	24	9.68	-	-	2	-
A R C Fraser	14	19	5	134	32	9.57	-	-	1	-
V P Clarke	4	7	0	67	26	9.57	-	-	4	-
J E Benjamin	8	9	3	57	18*	9.50	-	-	1	-
O T Parkin	11	13	4	85	24*	9.44	-	-	2	-
F A Rose	14	17	2	133	21	8.86	-	-	-	-
C A Walsh	17	23	10	111	25	8.53	-	-	4	-
N E Batson	3	6	0	50	18	8.33	-	-	-	-
J J Bates	4	7	0	54	38	7.71	-	-	4	-
T A Munton	9	12	2	72	20	7.20	-	-	-	-
C D Walsh	3	6	0	42	20	7.00	-	-	1	-
M J Rawnsley	6	8	0	55	21	6.87	-	-	7	-
D A Cosker	15	21	3	123	37	6.83	-	-	11	-

Waqar Younis	4	6	0	39	15	6.50	-	-	1	-
M J Birks	6	7	1	38	13	6.33	-	-	5	2
J D Lewry	17	23	0	132	24	5.73	-	-	1	-
M J Hoggard	9	10	3	35	13*	5.00	-	-	3	-
A D Edwards	4	7	0	30	10	4.28	-	-	3	-
R J Warren	5	8	0	30	11	3.75	-	-	7	-
A R Oram	11	19	8	39	13	3.54	-	-	-	-
E S H Giddins	18	23	9	47	11*	3.35	-	-	4	-
M A Robinson	16	21	8	40	7	3.07	-	-	1	-
J F Brown	8	11	5	18	6*	3.00	-	-	1	-
D Follett	5	7	1	13	7	2.16	-	-	2	-

BOWLING AVERAGES
Qualifying requirements : 10 wickets taken

Name	Overs	Mdns	Runs	Wkts	Avge	Best	5wI	10wM
M Muralitharan	226.3	77	463	34	13.61	9-65	5	2
V J Wells	199.1	66	514	36	14.27	5-18	1	-
C White	147.1	36	391	25	15.64	8-55	2	-
J Ormond	133.3	51	311	19	16.36	6-33	2	-
T H C	68	16	214	13	16.46	3-5	-	-
P L	92.3	26	207	12	17.25	5-60	1	-
C A	633	164	1835	106	17.31	6-36	7	2
Saqlain Mushtaq	475	136	1119	63	17.76	8-65	3	3
A D Mullally	448.4	156	1128	60	18.80	7-55	3	1
M P L Bulbeck	154.4	28	609	32	19.03	4-40	-	-
T A Munton	278.5	71	708	37	19.13	7-66	3	-
J J Bates (Sussex)	102.5	24	273	14	19.50	5-67	2	-
D A Leatherdale	111.4	22	416	21	19.80	5-20	1	-
A R Caddick	687.2	156	2082	105	19.82	8-64	10	3
R S C Martin-Jenkins	141.5	43	437	22	19.86	7-54	1	-
A R C Fraser	480.3	122	1224	61	20.06	6-23	4	1
A A Donald	302.2	89	785	39	20.12	6-56	5	-
A C Morris	314	65	1012	50	20.24	4-30	-	-
G M Hamilton	415	100	1212	59	20.54	7-50	4	2
M P Bicknell	494.1	141	1340	65	20.61	5-27	2	-
M J Foster	113	23	351	17	20.64	4-41	-	-
A M Smith	522.3	139	1440	68	21.17	6-32	4	-
K J Dean	465.3	96	1572	74	21.24	6-63	5	1
P V Simmons	170.5	44	491	23	21.34	7-49	1	-
Wasim Akram	335.5	75	1025	48	21.35	5-56	1	-
G Chapple	313	57	942	44	21.40	5-49	1	-
D W Headley	410.2	88	1175	54	21.75	6-71	4	-
M J Hoggard	258	51	895	41	21.82	5-57	1	-
S L Watkin	370.4	107	917	42	21.83	5-30	1	-
J F Brown	280.2	68	726	33	22.00	6-53	4	1
M M Betts	363	81	1061	48	22.10	6-83	4	-
P J Martin	388	94	1062	48	22.12	4-21	-	-
O T Parkin	300.3	99	757	34	22.26	5-24	2	-
J D Lewry	461.3	112	1409	62	22.72	6-72	3	-

Name	Overs	Mdns	Runs	Wkts	Avge	Best	5wI	10wM
T M Smith	150.3	42	484	21	23.04	6-32	2	-
M C Ilott	506.5	138	1345	58	23.18	6-20	2	-
C E W Silverwood	390.1	99	1123	48	23.39	5-13	3	-
E S H Giddins	668.2	161	2006	84	23.88	6-79	5	1
G Yates	131.3	26	432	18	24.00	4-64	-	-
D J Millns	243.3	55	817	34	24.02	4-60	-	-
P M Hutchison	474.3	119	1432	59	24.27	7-31	3	-
J Lewis	462.1	108	1447	59	24.52	6-48	3	-
S D Thomas	544.1	94	1749	71	24.63	5-84	3	-
S M Pollock	266.5	87	594	24	24.75	5-53	1	-
J P Taylor	436.5	105	1337	54	24.75	4-31	-	-
P J Newport	335.1	117	893	36	24.80	4-44	-	-
C C Lewis	266.4	53	972	39	24.92	6-60	2	-
B C Hollioake	275.4	51	908	36	25.22	4-28	-	-
N A M McLean	518.5	105	1575	62	25.40	6-101	2	-
D Gough	340.3	65	1067	42	25.40	6-42	2	-
A J Tudor	184.2	34	737	29	25.41	5-43	1	-
A Dale	249.3	46	794	31	25.61	5-25	1	-
M A Ealham	242.4	83	593	23	25.78	5-23	3	-
I D K Salisbury	387.5	109	958	37	25.89	7-65	2	-
S Elworthy	127	31	415	16	25.93	4-71	-	-
P A J DeFreitas	482.4	114	1363	52	26.21	5-38	3	-
I D Austin	335.4	77	950	36	26.38	4-21	-	-
P J Franks	404.2	87	1375	52	26.44	6-63	4	-
M V Fleming	404.4	115	1008	38	26.52	4-24	-	-
S R Lampitt	416	97	1330	50	26.60	5-33	4	-
M A Robinson	416.1	107	1126	42	26.80	4-72	-	-
G D Rose	480.3	132	1399	52	26.90	5-48	2	-
G R Haynes	227.5	61	705	26	27.11	6-50	2	-
K P Evans	273	73	735	27	27.22	5-92	2	-
M T Brimson	369.5	129	901	33	27.30	4-4	-	-
F A Rose	373.2	59	1367	50	27.34	7-39	3	1
R L Johnson	377.2	77	1369	50	27.38	7-86	1	-
A P van Troost	118	24	415	15	27.66	4-18	-	-
A P Davies	135.5	41	390	14	27.85	2-22	-	-
M J McCague	235.1	45	758	27	28.07	4-40	-	-
M N Bowen	309.1	76	875	31	28.22	7-73	1	-
C M Tolley	324.3	76	960	34	28.23	7-45	3	-
R J Kirtley	490.4	116	1532	54	28.37	7-29	3	1
J E Benjamin	189.1	42	626	22	28.45	6-35	1	-
A F Giles	459.3	154	1025	36	28.47	5-48	1	-
R J Chapman	246.2	44	943	33	28.57	6-105	1	-
D G Cork	545	111	1618	56	28.89	6-119	3	-
G P Butcher	152.4	24	551	19	29.00	4-14	-	-
N Killeen	101.2	25	349	12	29.08	5-49	1	-
M J Rawnsley	172.1	46	497	17	29.23	6-44	2	1
T M Moody	251.1	73	790	27	29.25	5-64	1	-
Mushtaq Ahmed	136	40	411	14	29.35	3-26	-	-
D R Brown	438.2	93	1489	50	29.78	5-40	2	-

Name	Overs	Mdns	Runs	Wkts	Avge	Best	5wI	10wM
C P Schofield	79.4	9	299	10	29.90	4-56	-	-
T F Bloomfield	168.5	34	660	22	30.00	5-67	2	-
G P Swann	199.4	41	666	22	30.27	5-29	1	-
L Klusener	156	38	424	14	30.28	4-66	-	-
S J Harmison	455.5	93	1545	51	30.29	5-70	1	-
M Ntini	184.3	48	578	19	30.42	4-72	-	-
J B Thompson	95.4	20	335	11	30.45	4-52	-	-
G P Wickremasinghe	135.1	26	397	13	30.53	4-69	-	-
J Wood	571.5	113	1910	62	30.80	5-52	2	-
C L Hooper	386.2	104	957	31	30.87	7-93	1	-
M A Butcher	119.4	29	340	11	30.90	4-41	-	-
A R Oram	305.5	75	969	31	31.25	4-37	-	-
G Keedy	182.3	38	563	18	31.27	5-35	1	-
C J Batt	201.5	23	846	27	31.33	6-101	2	-
J P Stephenson	286.4	71	770	24	32.08	4-29	-	-
J D Middlebrook	164.1	45	422	13	32.46	3-20	-	-
D Follett	103	17	325	10	32.50	3-48	-	-
N F Williams	246.5	47	849	26	32.65	4-42	-	-
P A Strang	353.3	105	983	30	32.76	5-166	1	-
M M Patel	418.3	102	1123	34	33.02	5-73	1	-
J H Kallis	226.1	79	529	16	33.06	4-24	-	-
Waqar Younis	100.1	13	397	12	33.08	3-147	-	-
M P Dowman	139	31	397	12	33.08	2-10	-	-
D E Malcolm	334	48	1331	40	33.27	6-54	2	-
A D Mascarenhas	280.5	58	1000	30	33.33	4-31	-	-
D J Eadie	113.5	19	434	13	33.38	2-34	-	-
P J Hartley	353.5	66	1109	33	33.60	4-42	-	-
J P Hewitt	377.3	63	1378	41	33.60	6-71	2	-
M Watkinson	175.4	22	607	18	33.72	5-45	1	-
D P Mather	168.5	32	574	17	33.76	6-74	1	1
K D James	340	70	1083	32	33.84	4-22	-	-
R C Irani	444.3	105	1392	41	33.95	5-47	1	-
M W Alleyne	284.1	82	818	24	34.08	4-63	-	-
S D Udal	191.2	44	549	16	34.31	4-37	-	-
M G Bevan	175.4	27	653	19	34.36	3-36	-	-
M C J Ball	433	108	1173	34	34.50	4-26	-	-
D A Cosker	483.5	127	1265	36	35.13	6-140	1	-
D R Law	247.5	34	1045	29	36.03	5-46	1	-
R D Stemp	409	141	1001	27	37.07	5-191	1	-
I D Blackwell	156.2	32	524	14	37.42	5-115	1	-
M E Trescothick	193.3	45	654	17	38.47	4-82	-	-
A P Grayson	248.2	62	734	19	38.63	3-13	-	-
P M Such	525	128	1475	38	38.81	5-73	2	-
P R Adams	281.2	79	666	17	39.17	4-63	-	-
G Welch	314.3	71	996	25	39.84	4-94	-	-
N M K Smith	329.3	84	957	24	39.87	5-128	1	-
A Sheriyar	286.1	70	962	24	40.08	5-85	1	-
A R K Pierson	258.1	53	842	21	40.09	5-117	1	-
P C R Tufnell	632	162	1602	39	41.07	4-24	-	-

Name	Overs	Mdns	Runs	Wkts	Avge	Best	5wI	10wM
M Hayward	121	21	518	12	43.16	3-34	-	-
N C Phillips	425.4	101	1216	28	43.42	5-56	1	-
P D Collingwood	200.1	53	582	13	44.76	3-89	-	-
A P Cowan	238.3	54	859	19	45.21	3-18	-	-
P Aldred	181.4	38	556	12	46.33	3-30	-	-
G R Loveridge	204	33	655	13	50.38	5-59	1	-
B W Byrne	174.1	31	583	11	53.00	3-103	-	-
P N Weekes	237	37	702	13	54.00	3-113	-	-
B J Phillips	294	55	928	17	54.58	3-66	-	-
R D B Croft	453.5	117	1144	20	57.20	4-76	-	-
M E Cassar	157	29	614	10	61.40	3-26	-	-
R K Illingworth	304	80	853	13	65.61	3-28	-	-

*1998 PCA Awards Dinner,
Lord's Cricket Ground*

1967

Formation of the Professional Cricketers'
Association

1971

The launch of the PCA Player Awards

1975

The creation of a pension scheme

1978

The introduction of the minimum wage

1982

The establishment of The Cricketers'
Association Charity

1985

The standardisation of contracts

1997

The formation of PCA Management Ltd.

The launch of the PCA Business Partnership

First edition PCA Annual Yearbook

The first televised PCA Awards Dinner

1998

The launch for the PCA Hall of Fame

The launch of the PCA Affinity Credit Card

The PCA Cricket in the Community
programme

The launch of the Allrounder newsletter

The formation of FICA

The TakeGuard Insurance project

H.R.H. The Duke of York, presenting the awards

PCA MANAGEMENT LTD

PCA Management Ltd, Hawkstone Park, Weston-Under-Redcastle, Shrewsbury, Shropshire, SY4 5UY. Tel: 01939 200202 Fax: 01939 200699

PCA AWARD WINNERS

HAYTER CUP
PCA PLAYER OF THE YEAR

1970	Mike Procter and Jack Bond
1971	Lance Gibbs
1972	Andy Roberts
1973	Peter Lee
1974	Barry Stead
1975	Zaheer Abbas
1976	Peter Lee
1977	Mike Procter
1978	John Lever
1979	John Lever
1980	Robin Jackman
1981	Richard Hadlee
1982	Malcolm Marshall
1983	Ken McEwan
1984	Richard Hadlee
1985	Neal Radford
1986	Courtney Walsh
1987	Richard Hadlee
1988	Graeme Hick
1989	Jimmy Cook
1990	Graham Gooch
1991	Waqar Younis
1992	Courtney Walsh
1993	Steve Watkin
1994	Brian Lara
1995	Dominic Cork
1996	Phil Simmons
1997	Steve James
1998	Mal Loye

ARLOTT CUP
PCA YOUNG PLAYER OF THE YEAR

1990	Mike Atherton
1991	Dominic Cork
1992	Mark Lathwell
1993	Malachy Loye
1994	John Crawley
1995	Andy Symonds
1996	Chris Silverwood
1997	Ben Hollioake
1998	Andrew Flintoff

HAROLD GOLDBLATT UMPIRES' CUP

1997	Peter Willey
1998	Ray Julian

WATERFORD CRYSTAL
PCA SPECIAL MERIT AWARD

1997	Lord Cowdrey
1998	Dickie Bird

SLAZENGER SHEER INSTINCT
INDIVIDUAL PERFORMANCE AWARD

1997	Alistair Brown
1998	Graeme Hick

THE PRIMARY CLUB

PO Box 12121
London NW1 9WS
Tel: 0171 267 3316
Fax: 0171 485 6808

Derek Underwood, the patron of the Primary Club, qualified for membership in some style in 1965. Playing for Kent against the South Africans he was out first ball twice in the same match.

However, members do not have to be playing Test or county cricket when the ultimate disaster strikes in order to qualify for the club. As long as you are out first ball at ANY level of cricket you are eligible to join The Primary Club.

Why join? The Primary Club is a charity (Registered Charity No. 285285) and all profits from subscriptions, donations and the range of items for sale (ties, sweaters, shirts, mugs, umbrellas, etc.) go to pay for sporting and recreational facilities for the blind and partially sighted. All the club's workers are volunteers.

For many of us sport is an important part of our every day lives; for the blind and partially sighted, sport can mean so much more. The confidence and sense of achievement they get from mastering a physical skill helps them a great deal in tackling the problems of their lives.

MEMBERSHIP APPLICATION

Name	
Address	
Joining subscription:	
To include City tie – £15	
To include Club tie – £15	
To include City & Club tie – £25	
To include Bow tie – £15	
Lady, to include brooch – £10	
DONATION	
TOTAL REMITTANCE TO: 'THE PRIMARY CLUB' £	

Please photocopy this form rather than spoil the book

TIES AND OTHER ITEMS FOR MEMBERS

The City tie has several small reproductions of the club emblem embroidered on navy blue fabric – the Club tie has a single larger one on green A colour leaflet of the full range of clothing and other items will be sent to members.

DEED OF COVENANT

If you wish to consider making a donation under a 4 year (or more) charitable deed or covenant, please tick the box, but do not include this donation in your present remittance. Further details and a form of deed will then be sent to you. Such a deed does not increase the cost to you of your donation but enables the Club to recover income tax. ☐

INDEX OF PLAYERS BY COUNTY

*denotes not registered for the 1999 season. Where a player is known to have moved in the off-season he is listed under his new county.

DERBYSHIRE

ALDRED, P
BLACKWELL, I.D.
CASSAR, M.E.
CLARKE, V.P.
CORK, D.G.
DEAN, K.J.
DEANE, M.J.
DEFREITAS, P.A.J.
GRIFFITHS, S.P.
HARRIS, A.J.
KRIKKEN, K.M.
LACEY, S.J.
MAY, M.R.
ROBERTS, G.M.
ROLLINS, A.S.
SLATER, M.J.
SMITH, T.M.
SPENDLOVE, B.J.
STUBBINGS, S.D.
TWEATS, T.A.
WESTON, R.M.S.
WOOLLEY A.P.

DURHAM

BETTS, M.M.
BOILING J.*
BOON, D.C.
BROWN, S.J.E.
CHAPMAN, S.
COLLINGWOOD, P.D.
DALEY, J.A.
FOSTER, M.J.
GOUGH, M.A.

HARMISON, S.J.
HUTTON, S.*
KILLEEN, N.
LEWIS, J.J.B.
MORRIS, J.E.
MUAZAM ALI
PHILLIPS, N.C.
PRATT, A.
ROBINSON R.
ROSEBERRY, M.A.
SAGGERS, M.J.*
SEARLE, J.P*
SPEAK, N.J.
SPEIGHT, M.P.
SYMINGTON, M.J.
WALKER, A.*
WOOD, J.

ESSEX

BISHOP J.E.
BRINKLEY, J.E.*
COUSINS, D.M.*
COWAN, A.P.
FLANAGAN, I.N.
GRAYSON, A.P.
GROVE, J.O.
HIBBERT, A.J.E.*
HODGSON, T.P.
HUSSAIN, N.
HYAM, B.J.
ILOTT, M.C.
IRANI, R.C.
JEFFERSON W.I.
LAW, D.R.C.
LAW, S.G.

NAPIER, G.R.
PETERS, S.D.
PHILLIPS T.J.
POWELL, J.C.
PRICHARD, P.J.
ROBINSON, D.D.J.
ROLLINS, R.J.
SUCH, P.M.
WILLIAMS, N.F.*
WILSON, D.G.*

GLAMORGAN

CHERRY, D.D.
COSKER, D.A.
CROFT, R.D.B.
DALE, A.
DAVIES, A.P.
DAWOOD I.
EVANS, A.W.
JAMES, S.P.
JONES, S.P.
KALLIS J.H.
LAW, W.L.
MAYNARD, M.P.
NEWELL, K.
PARKIN, O.T.
POWELL, M.J.
SHAW, A.D.
THOMAS, I.J.*
THOMAS, S.D.
TOMLINSON, S.C.B.*
WALLACE, M.A.
WATKIN, S.L.

INDEX OF PLAYERS BY COUNTY

GLOUCESTERSHIRE

ALLEYNE, M.W.
AVERIS, J.M.M.
BALL, M.C.J.
BARNETT, K.J.
CAWDRON, M.J.
CHURCH, M.J.
COOMBES, M.A.
CUNLIFFE, R.J.
DAWSON, R.I.
HANCOCK, T.H.C.
HARVEY, I.J.
HEWSON, D.R.
LAZENBURY, P.S.
LEWIS, J
MACMILLAN, G.I.*
RUSSELL, R.C.
SMITH, A.M.
SNAPE, J.N.
TRAINOR, N.J.
WALSH C.A.*
WILLIAMS, R.C.J.
WINDOWS, M.G.N.
WRIGHT, A.J.*

HAMPSHIRE

AYMES, A.N.
CONNOR, C.A.
FRANCIS, S.R.G.
GARAWAY, M.
HAMBLIN, J.R.C.
HARTLEY, P.J.
JAMES, K.D.
KEECH, M.
KENDALL, W.S.
KENWAY, D.A.

LANEY, J.S.
LUGSDEN, S.
MARU, R.J.*
MASCERANHAS, D.A.
MCLEAN, N.A.M.
MORRIS, A.C.
MORRIS, Z.C.
RENSHAW, S.J.
SAVIDENT, L
SMITH, R.A.
STEPHENSON, J.P.
UDAL, S.D.
WHITAKER, P.R.*
WHITE, G.W.

KENT

BANES, M.J.
BROADHURST, M.
COWDREY, G.R.*
DE LA PENA, J.M.
EALHAM, M.A.
FLEMING, M.V.
FORD, J.A.
FULTON, D.P.
HEADLEY, D.W.
HOCKLEY, J.B.
HOOPER, C.L.*
HOUSE, W.J.
IGGLESDEN, A.P.*
KEY, R.W.T.
LLONG, N.J.
MARSH, S.A.
MASTERS, D.D.
MCCAGUE, M.J.
PATEL, M.M.
PHILLIPS, B.J.
SCOTT, D.A.
SMITH, E.T.

THOMPSON, J.B.
WALKER, M.J.
WALSH, C.D.
WARD, T.R.
WATSON, J.D.
WELLS, A.P.
WILLIS, S.C.

LANCASHIRE

ATHERTON, M.A.
AUSTIN, I.D.
CHAPPLE, G.
CHILTON, M.J.
CRAWLEY, J.P.
FAIRBROTHER, N.H.
FLINTOFF, A.
GREEN, R.J.
HARVEY, M.E.
HAYNES, J.J.
HEGG, W.K.
KEEDY, G.
LLOYD, G.D.
MARTIN, P.J.
MCKEOWN, P.C.
MURALITHARAN, M.
RIDGWAY, P.M.
SCHOFIELD, C.P.
SHADFORD, D.J.
SMETHURST, M.P.
TITCHARD, S.P.*
WASIM AKRAM*
WATKINSON, M.
WOOD, N.T.
YATES, G.

INDEX OF PLAYERS BY COUNTY

LEICESTERSHIRE

BOSWELL, S.A.J.
BRIMSON, M.T.
CROWE, C.D.
DAKIN, J.M.
HABIB, A.
KIRBY, S.P.
KHAN, A. A.
LEWIS, C.C.
MADDY, D.L.
MASON, T.J.
MILLNS, D.J.
MULLALLY, A.D.
NIXON, P.A.
ORMOND, J.
ROBINSON, P.E.
SACHDEVA, A.
SIMMONS, P.V.
SMITH, B.F.
STEVENS, D.I.
SUTCLIFFE, I.J.
WELLS, V.J.
WHITAKER, J.J.
WHITTICASE, P.
WILLIAMSON, D.
WRIGHT, A.S.

MIDDLESEX

ALLEYNE, D.
BATT, C.J.
BLANCHETT, I.N.
BLOOMFIELD, T.F.
BROWN, K.R.*
BROWN, M.J.
BRYAN, R.B.
COOK, S.J.
DUTCH, K.P.

FRASER, A.G.J.
FRASER, A.R.C.
GATTING, M.W.*
GOODCHILD, D.J.
HEWITT, J.P.
HUNT, T.A.
HUTTON, B.L.
JOHNSON, R.L.
KETTLEBOROUGH, R.A.
LANGER, J.L.
LARAMAN, A.W.
LYE, D.F.
MARTIN, N.D.
MAUNDERS, J.K.
NASH, D.C.
POOLEY, J.C.*
RAMPRAKASH, M.R.
SHAH, O.A.
STRAUSS, A.J.
TUFNELL, P.C.R
WEEKES, P.N.

NORTHAMPTONSHIRE

BAILEY, R.J.
BAILEY, T.M.B.
BLAIN, J.A.R.
BROWN, J.F.
CAPEL, D.J.*
CURRAN, K.M.
DAVIES, M.K.
DOBSON, M.C.
FOLLETT, D.
HAYDEN, M.L.
INIFF, D.L.
INNES, K.J.
LOGAN, R.J.
LOYE, M.B.
MALCOLM, D.E.

PENBERTHY, A.L.
POWELL, M.J.
RIPLEY, D.
ROBERTS, D.J.
ROSE, F.A.*
SALES, D.J.
SWANN, A.J.
SWANN, G.P.
TAYLOR, J.P.
WALTON, T.C.*
WARREN, R.J.

NOTTINGHAMSHIRE

AFZAAL, U.
ARCHER, G.F.
BATES, R.T.
BOWEN, M.N.
DOWMAN, M.P.
EVANS, K.P.
FRANKS, P.J.
GALLIAN, J.E.R.
GIE, N.A.
HART, J.P.
JOHNSON, P.
LUCAS, D.
NEWELL, M.
NOON, W.M.
ORAM, A.R.
RANDALL, S.J.
READ, C.M.W.
ROBINSON, R.T.
STEMP, R.D.
STRANG, P.A.
TOLLEY, C.M.
WALKER, L.N.
WELTON, G.E.
WHARF, A.G.
WHILEY, M.J.A.

INDEX OF PLAYERS BY COUNTY

SOMERSET

BOWLER, P.D.
BULBECK, M.P.L.
BURNS, M.
CADDICK, A.R.
COX, J.
ECCLESTONE, S.C.*
HOLLOWAY, P.C.L.
JARVIS, P.W.
JONES, P.S.
KENNIS, G.J.*
KERR, J.I.D.
LATHWELL, M.N.
MUSHTAQ AHMED*
PARSONS, K.A.
PIERSON, A.R.K.
REEVE, D.A.
ROSE, G.D.
SHINE, K.J.
SUTTON, L.D.
TRESCOTHICK, M.E.
TROTT, B.J.
TUCKER, J.
TURNER, R.J.
VAN TROOST, A.P.

SURREY

AMIN, R.M.
BARRETT, K.A.O.
BATTY, G.J.
BATTY, J.N.
BELL, M.A.V.
BENJAMIN, J.E.
BICKNELL, D.J.
BICKNELL, M.P.
BISHOP, I.E.

BROWN, A.D.
BUTCHER, A.R.*
BUTCHER, G.P.
BUTCHER, M.A.
GREENIDGE, C. G.
HOLLIOAKE, A.J.
HOLLIOAKE, B.C.
KNOTT, J.A.
PATTERSON, M.W.
RATCLIFFE, J.D.
SALISBURY, I.D.K.
SAQLAIN MUSHTAQ
SHAHID, N.
STEWART, A.J.
THORPE, G.P.
TUDOR, A.J.
WARD, I.J.

SUSSEX

ADAMS, C.J.
BATES, J.J.
BEVAN, M.G.*
CARPENTER, J.R.
COTTEY, P.A.
DAVIS, R.P.*
DI VENUTO, M.J.
EDWARDS, A.D.
GREENFIELD, K.
HAYWOOD, G.R.
HUMPHRIES, S.
KHAN, W.G.
KIRTLEY, R.J.
LEWRY, J.D.
MARTIN-JENKINS, R.S.C.
MONTGOMERIE, R.R.
MOORES, P.*
NEWELL, M.*
PEIRCE, M.T.E.

RAO, R.K.
RASHID, U.B.A.
ROBINSON, M.A.
STRONG, M.R.
TAYLOR, N.R.*
WILTON, N.J.

WARWICKSHIRE

ALTREE, D.A.
BROWN, D.R.
DAGNALL, C.E.
DONALD, A.A.
EDMOND, M.D.
FROST, T.
GIDDINS, E.S.H.
GILES, A.F.
HEMP, D.L.
KNIGHT, N.V.
LARA, B.C.*
MUNTON, T.A.
OSTLER, D.P.
PENNEY, T.L.
PIPER, K.J.
POWELL, M.J.
RICHARDSON, A.
SHEIKH, M.A.
SINGH, A.
SMALL, G.C.
SMITH, N.M.K.
WAGH, M.
WELCH, G.

INDEX OF PLAYERS BY COUNTY

WORCESTERSHIRE

BATSON, N.E.
CATTERALL, D.N.
CHAPMAN, R.J.
DRIVER, R.C.
ELLIS, S.W.K.*
HAFEEZ, A.
HAYNES, G.R.
HICK, G.A.
ILLINGWORTH, R.K.
LAMPITT, S.R.
LEATHERDALE, D.A.
MIRZA, M.M.
MOODY, T.M.
NEWPORT, P.J.
PATEL, D.
PIPE, D.J.
POLLARD, P.R.
RAWNSLEY, M.J.
RHODES, S.J.
SHERIYAR, A.
SOLANKI, V.S.
SPIRING, K.R.
WESTON, W.P.C.
WILSON, E.J.

GOUGH, D.
HAMILTON, G.M.
HARDEN, R. J.
HOGGARD, M.J.
HUTCHISON, P.M.
INGLIS, J.W.
LEHMANN, D.S.*
MCGRATH, A.
MIDDLEBROOK, J.D.
PARKER, B.
SIDEBOTTOM, R.J.
SILVERWOOD, C.E.W.
VAUGHAN, M.P.
WHITE, C.
WIDDUP, S.
WILKINSON, R.J.
WOOD, M.J.

YORKSHIRE

BLAKEY, R.J.
BLEWETT, G.S.
BYAS, D.
CHAPMAN, C.A.*
CLOUGH, G.D.
DAWSON, R.
ELLISON, C.J.
FELLOWS, G.M.
FISHER, I.D.

PCA MANAGEMENT

WELCOME TO THE ALLROUNDER BUSINESS PARTNERSHIP™

1999 sees the Cricket World Cup played at venues throughout the United Kingdom; it also heralds the introduction of the two-tier cricket system with teams battling it out to the end of the season. This year too sees Channel 4 take over from the BBC TV, breaking a tradition almost as old as the game itself but bringing with it the certainty of greater commercial opportunity and awareness.

Cricket is good business:

51% of all adults have an interest in cricket (22.52 million)
48% of all TV viewers have an interest in cricket (21.15 million)
28%of all newspaper readers have an interest in cricket (12.3 million)

Source: IPSOS-RSI. ITD

The PCA has developed an effective way of combining business with pleasure whilst enjoying a close association with cricket. Companies network successfully with other companies within the Business Partnership enjoying glittering social and celebrity sporting functions.

- The Business Partnership provides an effective innovative vehicle for generating significant business to business opportunities.

- Exclusive hospitality events e.g. 14th September 1999 PCA televised Player of the Year Awards at the Royal Albert Hall.

- Regular Business Partnership seminars.

For a full information pack ring the new membership HOTLINE on 01939 200202 or write to myself Richard Bevan at PCAM Limited, Hawkstone Park, Weston under Redcastle, Shrewsbury, Shropshire, SY4 5UY.

FLEMING
Premier Banking

PCA
PROFESSIONAL CRICKETERS ASSOCIATION

FICA
CRICKET
HALL OF FAME

FICA
FEDERATION OF INTERNATIONAL
CRICKETERS ASSOCIATIONS

QUIZ ANSWERS

1. Mark Waugh
2. England hosted all three
3. Alan Turner
4. Chetan Sharma (for India v New Zealand at Nagpur 1987)
5. Allan Lamb
6. Canada
7. Nathan Astle
8. Gary Kirsten (188* for South Africa v UAE at Rawalpindi 1996)
9. Graeme Fowler (360 runs, av. 72.00)
10. Rodney Hogg (Australia) and Vince Hogg (Zim)
11. John Traicos
12. UAE
13. Dickie Bird (18 matches, 1975-87)
14. Ricky Ponting (102 for Australia v West Indies at Jaipur 1996, aged 21 years 76 days)
15. Asif Iqbal
16. Arjuna Ranatunga (252 runs, av. 84.00)
17. Harris was stumped off a wide
18. Bob Willis
19. India (lost to England) and Pakistan (lost to Australia)
20. Allan Donald (8 wickets, av. 15.75)
21. It is the highest score by a No. 11 in the World Cup
22. Wasim Bari (22 victims, 1975-79)
23. Clive Lloyd
24. Mike Brearley and Geoffrey Boycott
25. Nevill Ground, Tunbridge Wells
26. Ian Botham (30 wickets)
27. East Africa
28. Kevin Wright
29. Martin Crowe (456 runs, av. 114)
30. Roger Twose
31. Mohinder Amarnath
32. Andy Roberts (26 wickets)
33. Javed Miandad
34. Vic Marks
35. Jeff Crowe
36. Zimbabwe's Eddo Brandes. He and Hick both attended Prince Edward School, Harare
37. Kenya
38. Aged 47 in the 1996 tournament, he is the oldest player to have taken part in the World Cup
39. 1987
40. Dayle, Richard and Barry
41. S. Venkataraghavan
42. Dipak Patel
43. Steve Palframan
44. Martin Snedden
45. Viv Richards
46. Sachin Tendulkar (523 runs, av. 87.16 1996)
47. England beat Canada by 8 wickets having bowled them out for 45
48. Bishen Bedi
49. Graeme Fowler and Chris Tavaré
50. Javed Miandad

51. Kepler Wessels (for South Africa)
52. Greg Dyer
53. Joel Garner
54. New Zealand
55. Imran Khan (34 wickets)
56. Wayne Larkins
57. Duncan Fletcher
58. David Boon
59. Aravinda De Silva
60. Graham Gooch (897 runs, av. 44.85)
61. Gary Gilmour
62. It was West Indies' first World Cup defeat
63. Andrew Jones (New Zealand) and Dean Jones (Australia)
64. Dermot Reeve
65. Craig McDermott (27 wickets)
66. Andy Roberts
67. John Bracewell
68. Sachin Tendulkar (806 runs, av. 67.16)
69. Sanath Jayasuriya
70. South Africa (lost to England) and New Zealand (lost to Pakistan)
71. Kevin Curran
72. Sunil Gavaskar
73. David Boon (815 runs, av. 54.33)
74. They became the first side to score 300 in a One-Day International
75. He performed a series of energetic bunny hops intended to mimic the Indian 'keeper
76. Winston Davis
77. Neil Fairbrother (285 runs, av. 57.00)
78. He was the youngest player to make his World Cup debut, when he played v New Zealand at Trent Bridge in 1979 aged 17 years, 237 days
79. It took 60 overs
80. Dennis Amiss (137 v India at Lord's 1975)
81. Trevor Chappell
82. Bernard Julien and Andy Roberts
83. Adrian Kuiper
84. Viv Richards (1013 runs, av. 63.31)
85. Mark Burgess
86. Steve Tikolo
87. Imran Khan (22 matches)
88. Chris Harris
89. Neil Smith
90. Melbourne
91. Ian Gould
92. Steve and Mark Waugh (207 for the 3rd wicket, Australia v Kenya at Vishakhapatnam 1996)
93. Javed Miandad (1083 runs, av. 43.42)
94. Craig Matthews
95. Martin Crowe, 1992
96. Mike Denness
97. Abdul Qadir
98. Arjuna Ranatunga (241 runs, av. 120.50)
99. Sanath Jayasuriya
100. South Africa